Decisions Made Using Assessment Information

	Decision Area	Question to Be Answered
Pre-Referral Classroom Decisions	Provision of Special Help or Enrichment	Should the student be provided with remediation, compensation, or enrichment so that difficulty in learning can be overcome?
	Referral to an Intervention Assistance Team	Should the teacher seek the assistance of an intervention assistance team (composed of other teachers) in planning instructional interventions for an individual student?
	Provision of Intervention Assistance	Should the intervention assistance team provide the student with intensified remediation, compensation, or enrichment?
Entitlement Decisions	Screening	Is more intensive assessment necessary?
	Referral to a Child Study Team	Should the student be referred for formal psycho-educational evaluation, to be conducted by members of a child study team?
	Exceptionality	Does the child meet state criteria for assigning a disability label or a label of gifted and talented?
	Special or Unique Learning Needs	Does the student have special learning needs that require special education assistance so that the outcomes of schooling can be achieved?
	Eligibility	Is the student eligible for special education services?
Post-Entitlement Classroom Decisions	Instructional Planning	What should a teacher teach and how should he or she teach?
	Setting	Where should students be taught?
	Progress Evaluation	To what extent are students making progress toward specific instructional goals?
Accountability Decisions	Program Evaluation	Are specific instructional programs working as school personnel want them to work?
	Accountability	To what extent is education working for students? (Accountability decisions usually are made at the national, state, or school district level.)

ASSESSMENT

SIXTH EDITION

John Salvia
Penn State University

James E. Ysseldyke
University of Minnesota

HOUGHTON MIFFLIN COMPANY

Boston   Toronto   Geneva, Illinois   Palo Alto   Princeton, New Jersey

Senior Sponsoring Editor: Loretta Wolozin
Assistant Editor: Lisa Mafrici
Senior Project Editor: Charline Lake
Senior Production/Design Coordinator: Jill Haber
Senior Manufacturing Coordinator: Marie Barnes
Marketing Manager: Rebecca Dudley

Cover design by Darci Mehall, Aureo Design
Cover image: Susan E. Johnson, *Windows*. Acrylic, 16" x 24"
The photos on pages 2, 78, 196, and 314 are used by permission of the artist,
Susan Johnson.

Printed in the U.S.A.

Library of Congress Catalog Card Number: 94-76551

Student Text ISBN: 0-395-71161-4
Examination Copy ISBN: 0-395-71903-8

1 2 3 4 5 6 7 8 9-DH-98   97   96   95   94

Contents

Part 1   Assessment: An Overview   3

Chapter 1   Assessment of Students   4

Chapter 2   Assessment Processes and Concerns   26

Chapter 3   Legal and Ethical Considerations in Assessment   54

Chapter 8   Validity   162

Chapter 9   Adapting Tests to Accommodate Students with Disabilities   176

Part 3   Assessment in Classrooms   197

Chapter 10   Assessing Behavior Through Observation   198

Chapter 11   Teacher-Made Tests of Achievement   217

List of Tests Reviewed

Tests marked with an asterisk are new to this edition.

Preface

I n the short time since publication of the fifth edition of *Assessment*, much has happened. Clearly, this is a time of extraordinary change and challenge in assessment of students. Consider just a few of the things that are happening.

Goals 2000: The Educate America Act was signed in March, 1994. It specifies eight educational goals—goals that our educational system is to reach by the year 2000. The Goals 2000 legislation calls for development of high national standards and assessments designed to help determine the extent to which students achieve the high standards. Personnel in state departments of education in most states are specifying graduation standards, outcomes, or the goals students are to work toward. And discussions about goals, standards, or outcomes invariably lead to discussions about the ways students will be assessed.

The push to develop high standards is a response to criticism of education and schooling. Since the early 1980s several publications have challenged the status of America's schools and the performance of students. Professionals and the public alike believe that if we set high standards, test students, and hold them responsible, then students will get better.

Nowhere has the call for better accountability been more clear than with respect to students at the margins, and specifically for those who are at risk of poor performance in school. The ways we have educated students with disabilities are being challenged, and the assessment and decision-making process is being rethought. The use of tests to classify and place students is being questioned, and with that questioning comes intensified effort to engage in pre-referral problem solving. Increasingly, assessment has moved into classrooms, and the use of assessments that do not have direct instructional relevance is being re-evaluated.

The debate has brought calls for more assessment, less assessment, and different kinds of assessment. Many educators argue that if we test more, students will show more improvement. Others argue that we should test less and teach more. Most are convinced we need to do a better job of assessing students, either with new tests or new applications of tests. All argue that at this very critical time it is imperative that educators be very knowledgeable about assessment and the ways assessment information is used to make decisions about students.

AUDIENCE FOR THIS BOOK

Assessment, Sixth Edition, is intended for a first course in assessment for those whose careers require understanding and informed use of assessment data. The primary audience comprises those who are or will be teachers in special education at the elementary or secondary level. The secondary audience is the large support system for special educators: school psychologists, child development specialists, counselors, educational administrators, nurses, preschool educators, reading specialists, social workers, speech and language specialists, and specialists in therapeutic recreation. In writing for those who are taking their first course in assessment, we have assumed no prior knowledge of measurement and statistical concepts.

PURPOSE

Students have the right to an appropriate education in the least restrictive educational environment. Decisions regarding the most appropriate environment and the most appropriate program for an individual should be data-based decisions. Assessment is one part of the process of collecting the data necessary for educational decision making, and the administration of tests is one part of assessment. Unfortunately, tests have sometimes been used to restrict educational opportunities; many assessment practices have not been in the best interests of students. Those who assess have a tremendous responsibility; assessment results are used to make decisions that directly and significantly affect students' lives. Those who assess are responsible for knowing the devices they use and for understanding the limitations of those devices and the procedures they require.

Teachers are confronted with the results of tests, checklists, scales, and batteries almost daily. This information is intended to be useful to them in understanding and making educational plans for their students. But the intended use and actual use of assessment information have often differed. However good the intentions of test designers, misuse and misunderstanding of tests may well occur unless teachers are informed consumers and users of tests. To be an informed consumer and user of tests, a teacher must bring to the task certain domains of knowledge, including knowledge of the basic uses of tests, the important attributes of good tests, and the kinds of behaviors sampled by particular tests. This text aims at helping education professionals acquire that knowledge.

THE NEW EDITION

Coverage

Although the sixth edition retains the style, content, and organization of the first five editions, it does embody some major conceptual shifts. It continues to offer evenhanded, documented evaluations of standardized tests in each domain, straightforward and clear coverage of basic assessment concepts, and illustrations of applications to the decision-making process. Major shifts are taking place, however, in assessment practices in the schools. As school personnel strive to move to an ecological approach to assessment, they are engaging in new forms of assessment: portfolio assessment, performance assessment, assessment of instructional environments, and ecobehavioral assessment.

To reflect new assessment approaches, we have added five chapters and have incorporated into the chapters on technical considerations new material specific to these new approaches. The text devoted to reviews of assessment in specific domains is now divided into two parts, one on assessment in classrooms, the other on assessment using formal measures (largely outside of classrooms).

Our description of the kinds of decisions made using assessment information has been extensively revised to reflect current thinking and practice. In previous editions, we described five kinds of decisions made using assessment information. In this new edition, we describe thirteen kinds of decisions, grouped into four areas. We describe the ways assessment information is gathered for purposes of making pre-referral classroom decisions, entitlement decisions, post-entitlement classroom decisions, and accountability/outcomes decisions.

The sixth edition of *Assessment* features five entirely new chapters. Chapter 9 (Adapting Tests to Accommodate Students with Disabilities) covers the extensive work now going on in modification of test stimulus and response requirements to enable students with disabilities to participate in assessment. Chapters 12 (Using Student Portfolios in Assessment) and 13 (Assessing Instructional Ecology) describe new approaches to assessment including portfolio assessment, performance assessment, ecobehavioral assessment, and assessment of instructional environments. Chapter 26 (Assessment of Social-Emotional Behavior), also new to this edition, contains a review and evaluation of the scales most commonly used to rate personal and social behavior. Chapter 30 (Outcomes-Based Accountability Assessment) reviews the emerging practice of collecting data on the extent to which all students, including those with disabilities, are benefiting from their educational experiences.

Three chapters have been extensively revised. The first two chapters of the text now reflect current thinking on the use of assessment information to make decisions about students and many of the new concepts that underlie assessment practices. The chapter on Developmental Appraisal (Chapter 29) has been extensively reworked to include new measures and descriptions of new practices.

Test information has been updated and new reviews have been added. Forty-one new or revised tests are reviewed in this edition of *Assessment*. (A list of all the tests reviewed in this edition follows the Contents.)

Organization

The sixth edition, in four parts, is an introduction to psychoeducational assessment. Part 1, Assessment: An Overview, places testing in the broader context of assessment: Assessment is described as a multifaceted process, the kinds of decisions made using assessment data are delineated, and basic terminology and concepts are introduced. In Chapter 3 (Legal and Ethical Considerations in Assessment), we describe the ways assessment practices are regulated and mandated by legislation and litigation. In Part 2, Basic Concepts of Measurement, we give readers an understanding of the measurement principles needed not only to comprehend the content in Parts 3 and 4 but also to apply and use information obtained from tests they may administer.

In Parts 3 and 4, we review the most commonly used assessment instruments and approaches. In Part 3, Assessment in Classrooms, we address the kinds of assessments that typically take place in classroom settings. The focus of these chapters is on observations, interviews, non–test-based approaches, and those test-based approaches designed specifically to provide information on effective instruction. In Part 4, Assessment Using Formal Measures, we review formal (usually standardized) testing that occurs for the most part outside of classrooms.

Test evaluations follow a similar format. Initially we describe the kinds of behaviors sampled by tests in the domain; then we describe specific tests. For each test, we examine the kinds of behaviors it samples, the adequacy of its norms, the kinds of scores provided, and evidence for technical adequacy (reliability and validity). Consistent with our earlier editions, we evaluate the technical adequacy of tests in light of the standards set by three professional associations (the American Psychological Association, the American Educational Research Association, and the National Council on Measurement in Education) in their document entitled *Standards for Educational and Psychological Testing.*

A summary of chapter content, a list of additional reading, and several study questions appear at the end of each chapter to help readers expand their knowledge and apply the fundamental concepts developed. Appendixes at the end of the text include two tables of statistical data, a list of equations used in the text, a list of test publishers, suggestions for how to review a test, and a description of item-response theory. Complete references for in-text citations follow the appendixes.

Assessment is a controversial topic; we have attempted to be objective and evenhanded in our review and portrayal of current assessment practices.

Acknowledgments

Many people have assisted in our efforts. We wish to express our sincere appreciation to Michael Vanderwood (University of Minnesota) and Nicole Ofiesh (Penn State University), who helped us conduct background research on specific topics. The following individuals provided constructive criticism and helpful suggestions during development of this text:

Judith Finkel, West Chester University

Myra Kraker, Calvin College

David Majsterek, Central Washington University

Donna McNear, Rum River Special Education Cooperative (Cambridge, MN)

Cindi Nixon, East Carolina University

Ellen Nuffer, Keene State College

Hoi Suen, Penn State University (University Park)

Stanley Trent, Michigan State University

Ralph Zalma, Hofstra University

We especially appreciate the contributions of Tom Frank, Penn State University, who revised the section on assessment of hearing difficulties in Chapter 19, Stephen Camarata, Vanderbilt University, who revised Chapter 23 on Assessment of Oral Language, and James Shriner, Clemson University, who co-authored Chapter 26, Assessment of Social-Emotional Behavior.

Loretta Wolozin, Education Editor at Houghton Mifflin, has worked closely with us since the first edition of this text in 1978. Loretta helped us think through the major changes that have taken place in assessment since that time and worked with us to plan how best to reflect those changes in the text. She provided outstanding leadership in obtaining critical reviews of the text, guiding text development, and ensuring that the myriad editorial and production activities were completed on time with high quality. Lisa Mafrici, Assistant Editor at Houghton Mifflin, interacted with us nearly daily to guide the development of the text and provide extensive editorial assistance. Loretta and Lisa have our sincere thanks.

The text represents a collaborative effort, and we believe we have produced an integrated text that speaks for both of us.

John Salvia
Jim Ysseldyke

ASSESSMENT

PART 1

ASSESSMENT: AN OVERVIEW

School personnel regularly use assessment information to make important decisions about students. Part 1 of this text is a description of basic considerations in psychological and educational assessment of students.

Chapter 1 is a description of assessment and includes a delineation of the factors that must be considered in assessment, the various kinds of assessment information school personnel collect, and a description of the steps in the assessment process. In Chapter 2, assessment is more specifically defined, the purposes of assessing students are described, and fundamental assumptions underlying assessment are discussed. Chapter 3 is a description of fundamental legal and ethical considerations in assessment.

The concepts and principles introduced in Part 1 constitute a foundation for informed and critical use of tests and the information they provide.

Chapter 1

Assessment of Students

*A*ll of us have taken tests during our lives. In elementary and secondary school, tests were given to measure our scholastic aptitude or intelligence or to evaluate the extent to which we had profited from instruction. We may have taken personality tests, interest tests, or tests to assist us in vocational selection and career planning. As part of applying for a job, we may have taken civil service examinations or tests of specific skills like typing or manual dexterity. Enlisting in the armed forces means taking a number of tests. Enrolling in college means undergoing entrance examinations. Those of us who decide to go on to graduate school usually have to take an aptitude test; many of those who become teachers have to take a national teacher examination. Physicians, lawyers, psychologists, real estate agents, and many others are required to take tests to demonstrate their competence before being licensed to practice their profession or trade.

We witness today a situation in which school districts increasingly are being held accountable for the performance of their pupils. It is estimated that students attending America's public schools take more than 250 million standardized tests each year. District personnel use tests to document the achievement of a population of students that gets more diverse every year. At the time we prepared this edition, some states (such as Kentucky) were putting procedures into place to base the magnitude of teacher pay increases on (among very few other things) the magnitude of student gains on achievement tests. Performance assessments or portfolio assessments were being used and refined. Educators referred to these new forms of assessment as "alternative assessments," and sometimes as "authentic assessments." Goals 2000, the Educate America Act, was signed into law by President Clinton on March 31, 1994. Goals 2000 contains specific provisions for states to develop high educational standards and tests to measure the extent to which students achieve the standards. Clearly, assessment is "on the front burner" of activities in education.

Throughout their professional careers, teachers, guidance counselors, school social workers, school psychologists, and school administrators will be required to give, score, and interpret a wide variety of tests. Because professional school personnel routinely receive test information from their colleagues within the schools and from community agencies outside the schools, they need a working knowledge of important aspects of testing.

According to the joint committee of the American Psychological Association (APA), the American Educational Research Association (AERA), and the National Council on Measurement in Education (NCME), a test "may be thought of as a set of tasks or questions intended to elicit particular types of behaviors when presented under standardized conditions and to yield scores that have desirable psychometric properties" (1974, p. 2). *Testing,* then, means administering a particular set of questions to an individual or group of individuals in order to obtain a score. That score is the end product of testing.

Testing may be part of a larger process known as *assessment;* however, testing and assessment are not synonymous. Assessment in educational settings is a multifaceted process that involves far more than the administration of a test. When we assess students, we consider the way they perform a variety of tasks in a variety of settings or contexts, the meaning of their performances in terms of the total functioning of the individual, and the likely explanations for those performances. Good assessment procedures take into consideration the fact that anyone's performance on any task is influenced by the demands of the task itself, by the history and characteristics the individual brings to the task, and by the factors inherent in the context in which the assessment is carried out.

Assessment is the process of collecting information. Some of the information that is collected may be test data; much of it will likely be other forms of information. However, assessment is more than just the collection of information; it is collection with a purpose. *Assessment is the process of collecting data for the purposes of making decisions about students.* Historically in special and remedial education, and now increasingly in regular education settings, the focus of assessment is on the adequacy of student progress toward instructional goals or outcomes and on the need for special programs and related services. Specifically, we are concerned with progress or need for services in the three domains in which teachers provide interventions: academic, behavioral, and physical. For example, we may want to know whether Antoine needs special services in order to assist him in developing reading skills (need for service in an academic domain) or the extent to which Felicia is developing physically at a normal rate (progress decision in the physical domain). In Figure 1.1 we show the thirteen kinds of decisions made using assessment information and the three domains (academic, behavioral and physical) in which decisions are made. Throughout this book we try always to be very specific in our discussions of assessment activities and to differentiate assessment practices on the basis of the kind(s) of decisions being made and the area in which decisions are made. We try never to talk about *assessment,* but instead to talk about *assessment for the purpose of . . . .* Note that we have organized the thirteen kinds of decisions into four major types: pre-referral classroom decisions, entitlement decisions, post-entitlement classroom decisions, and accountability/outcomes decisions.

FIGURE 1.1   **The Assessment Decision–Problem Area Matrix**

	Problem Area		
	Academic	Behavioral	Physical
Pre-Referral Classroom Decisions			
Provision of Special Help or Enrichment			
Referral to an Intervention Assistance Team			
Provision of Intervention Assistance			
Entitlement Decisions			
Screening			
Referral			
Exceptionality			
Documentation of Special Learning Needs			
Eligibility			
Post-Entitlement Classroom Decisions			
Instructional Planning			
Setting			
Progress Evaluation			
Accountability/Outcome Decisions			
Program Evaluation			
Accountability			

TYPES OF DECISIONS

The decisions required in special education assessment are varied and complex. They occur in and out of classrooms. Some are decisions about who is eligible for the benefits of special education services, some are about planning instructional interventions for students, and others are about the extent to which students are benefiting from the services they receive. In Table 1.1 (page 8) we list and define briefly the kinds of decisions that are made using assessment information. We describe each of the decisions in the sections that follow. The decisions are grouped into pre-referral classroom decisions, entitlement decisions, post-entitlement classroom decisions, and accountability/outcomes decisions.

Pre-Referral Classroom Decisions

Before students are referred to a child study team, which will consider whether they are entitled to special education services, their classroom teacher typically has carried out a number of interventions. In fact, pre-referral interventions are now required in most states. That is, teachers must try a number of interventions and document their effectiveness prior to referring students.

Decisions to Provide Special Help or Enrichment

Teachers use classroom tests, daily observations, and interviews to decide whether a student is in need of *special assistance*. Generally, when students' rate of progress is 20 to 50 percent of that of other students, teachers have reason to provide special help. When progress is significantly better than that of other students, there is reason to provide enrichment. The process of collecting and using data to decide to provide special help or enrichment is an assessment process. The assessment decision involves a judgment by the teacher that the student is not doing as well as other students (or, is working above the level of other students) and needs special assistance (or enrichment). Provision of special assistance does not involve provision of special education services. Rather, as the first line of defense, most teachers give special help to students who experience difficulty. The help may be in the form of tutoring, Chapter I assistance, assignment of a study buddy, or adaptation of classroom materials and instruction. The help may be designed to remediate a deficiency, compensate for a disability, or provide enrichment. The special assistance might also be provided at home. Parents might give the student assistance with homework or hire a tutor.

Referral to an Intervention Assistance Team

The teacher uses both assessment information obtained as part of routine instruction/assessment, and information derived from monitoring the success of efforts to provide special help. The assessment is a judgment or an observation by the teacher that the student is having difficulty acquiring or retaining behavioral or academic skills. Or, it may be a judgment that the student needs assistance eliminating undesirable behavior.

When the student does not make satisfactory progress even with special help, the teacher may seek assistance from an *intervention assistance team (IAT)*, usually composed of regular education teachers whose role is to help one another come up with ways to teach difficult-to-teach students. The IAT, [sometimes

TABLE 1.1   **Decisions Made Using Assessment Information**

	Decision Area	Question to Be Answered
Pre-Referral Classroom Decisions	Provision of Special Help or Enrichment	Should the student be provided with remediation, compensation, or enrichment so that difficulty in learning can be overcome?
	Referral to an Intervention Assistance Team	Should the teacher seek the assistance of an intervention assistance team (composed of other teachers) in planning instructional interventions for an individual student?
	Provision of Intervention Assistance	Should the intervention assistance team provide the student with intensified remediation, compensation, or enrichment?
Entitlement Decisions	Screening	Is more intensive assessment necessary?
	Referral to a Child Study Team	Should the student be referred for formal psycho-educational evaluation, to be conducted by members of a child study team?
	Exceptionality	Does the child meet state criteria for assigning a disability label or a label of gifted and talented?
	Special or Unique Learning Needs	Does the student have special learning needs that require special education assistance so that the outcomes of schooling can be achieved?
	Eligibility	Is the student eligible for special education services?
Post-Entitlement Classroom Decisions	Instructional Planning	What should a teacher teach and how should he or she teach?
	Setting	Where should students be taught?
	Progress Evaluation	To what extent are students making progress toward specific instructional goals?
Accountability Decisions	Program Evaluation	Are specific instructional programs working as school personnel want them to work?
	Accountability	To what extent is education working for students? (Accountability decisions usually are made at the national, state, or school district level.)

called a pre-referral team, teacher assistance team (TAT), mainstream assistance team (MAT), or school-wide assistance team (SWAT)], works as a problem-solving team. Sometimes the members of the IAT gather data through observation, interview, or testing. When they do so, they are engaging in assessment. The interventions that are developed and put in place by intervention assistance teams are typically called *pre-referral interventions* because they occur prior to formal referral for child study.

Whom do teachers refer to intervention assistance teams? That question can be answered simply: they refer students who bother them. Although the question can be answered simply, it is not easy to predict whether a student will be referred. Different teachers are bothered by different behaviors, although some behaviors and characteristics would probably bother most, if not all, teachers.

Decisions to Provide Intervention Assistance

In 1980 very few states required pre-referral interventions. By 1988 they were required in two-thirds of the states (Carter & Sugai, 1989). Currently about three-fourths of states require pre-referral interventions. The pre-referral intervention (or intervention assistance) process has been put in place in states and local school districts in an effort to reduce referral for testing and over-identification of students for special education services. The process is based on the notion that many of the difficulties for which students are formally referred can be alleviated by adjusting classroom interventions. For example, Connecticut has a special project called the Early Intervention Project: Alternatives to Referral, initiated in 1985, to address the misclassification of students as disabled. The project is described in Figure 1.2. The project is designed to assist teachers in intervening early when students experience difficulty, in an effort to alleviate problems. In projects like the Early Intervention Project, team members receive formal training in assessment. The kinds of interventions that are suggested by intervention assistance teams may involve remediation, compensation, or enrichment.

Entitlement Decisions

Screening Decisions

Screening is the process of collecting data to decide whether more intensive assessment is necessary. Implicit in screening is the notion that students' difficulties may go unnoticed if we do not check for them. It is assumed, for example, that a student might have a hearing difficulty or cognitive deficit that will go unrecognized without screening. Since there is some variability in teachers' tolerances for and awareness of various problems, there may be students in classrooms who are exceptional and who are not having their needs met. School

FIGURE 1.2   **Connecticut's Early Intervention Project: Alternatives to Referral**

Q: What is the Early Intervention Project: Alternatives to Referral?
A: The Early Intervention Project (EIP) is an innovative effort initiated by the Connecticut State Department of Education in 1985 to address the misclassification of students as disabled. Since 1985, five urban districts have participated: Bridgeport, Danbury, Hartford, New Britain, and New London. Nonurban districts have also joined the project over the past several years: Bloomfield, Greenwich, Milford, North Haven, Orange, Oxford, Shelton, Trumbull, and Woodbridge. Ten additional school districts participated beginning with the 1991 to 1992 school year. Since 1988, the EIP has been administered by the Special Education Resource center (SERC). . . . Participation is voluntary based on cooperation between the local district and SERC. The project primarily addresses two emerging issues in special education: (1) the apparent overrepresentation of minority students in certain categories of special education and (2) the increasing numbers of children being inappropriately diagnosed as disabled and placed in special education. The project also represents an initiative to more effectively integrate programs and services between general and special education.

Q: What is the purpose of the Early Intervention Project: Alternatives to Referral?
A: The Early Intervention Project is designed to provide classroom-based services for at-risk students, particularly minority students, experiencing academic or social/behavioral problems. These classroom-based services are provided prior to . . . referral to the Planning and Placement Team for possible placement in special education. It provides early referral and intervention that focus support in the regular education classroom.

Q: What outcomes can districts anticipate from participation in the Project?
A: Through long-term training and ongoing technical assistance provided by SERC, districts involved in the Project will

- Develop a systematic intervention process to be initiated by the regular classroom teacher or others seeking assistance for students experiencing academic or social/behavioral problems;
- Establish a non-special education building team specifically trained to assist classroom teachers in designing alternative strategies within the least restrictive environment of the regular classroom;
- Develop least biased, nonstandardized assessment techniques that provide information about the student's performance in the specific curriculum and within the specific classroom placement.

districts want to find these students and provide special services to them, so screening programs are started. Thus, screening decisions are essentially administrative in nature. All students in particular schools or school districts are given preliminary examinations to ascertain whether any need further, more intensive assessment. Tests may be administered to identify students who differ significantly from their classmates (in either a positive or a negative sense) and who therefore may be eligible for special education services. Just as vision and hearing tests are routinely given to identify pupils with vision or hearing problems, intelligence tests may be administered to identify students who may need special attention, either because of limited intellectual capacity or because of highly superior intellectual ability. Achievement tests, measures of what has been taught to and learned by students, are routinely given to identify students who are experiencing academic difficulty and for whom further assessment may be appropriate.

Screening is an initial stage during which those who may evidence a particular problem, disorder, disability, or disease are sorted out from the general population. Screening has its origins in medicine and uses terminology from medical screening practices. We speak of individuals who perform poorly on screening measures as being "at risk"; we describe individuals as "false positives" when they perform poorly on screening measures but do well on later follow-up assessments, which show that they do not have the condition for which they were screened. Sometimes students show no problems at the time of screening and are screened "normal," but later evidence the very problems for which screening was conducted. These students are said to be "false negatives." Finally, when we talk about the accuracy of screening decisions, we often speak of the "hit rate" (proportion of accurate positive decisions) for screening. In Figure 1.3 we show the relationship between screening decisions and "real" conditions.

Screening takes place at all levels of education. Children are screened before they enter kindergarten or first grade to determine their "readiness" in language, cognitive, and motor development, and in social and emotional functioning. They may also be given vision and hearing screening tests. After they are tested, their performance is compared to standards established by those who make the screening tests. For example, if two-thirds of the children who took the test when it was being developed scored 300 points or better, children who score below 300 could be considered at risk. Test developers usually

FIGURE 1.3   **Hits and Misses in Making Screening Decisions**

	Reality	
Result of Screening	**Student has a certain characteristic**	**Student doesn't have the characteristic**
Student has a certain characteristic	Hit	False Positive
Student doesn't have the characteristic	False Negative	Normal

provide cut-off scores to help educators make decisions. Sometimes students are denied school entrance if they score low on a screening test (parents are asked to delay school entry until the child is "ready" to enter school),[1] sometimes low performance results in the child's being marked for observation and monitoring.

Screening also is used throughout the school years to identify students who need extra attention because their performance is markedly different from "normal" or "average." Here, cut-off scores are based on the average performance of students at various ages or grade levels. The scores of the norm group are used in deciding whether more testing is necessary. Decisions about performance usually are based on single snapshots of student performance or behavior. Decisions about progress usually are made by looking at student performance over time, often using the same test.

At some point educators may come to believe that a student has such different academic or behavioral needs that those needs cannot be met using the current approaches and that the child needs special education if he/she is going to achieve desired outcomes. When students' scores indicate a special need, students may be referred for psychoeducational assessment and given individually administered psychological and educational tests. These tests are used to determine the specific reasons for a student's performance on a screening measure.

Referral Decisions

When a student fails to make satisfactory progress, even with the help of an intervention assistance team, the student may be referred for formal psychoeducational evaluation. *Referral* usually is a formal process involving the completion of a referral form and a request for a team of professionals to decide whether a student's academic, behavioral, or physical development warrants the provision of special education services. The team of professionals is usually called a child study team, though in some states and districts within states these teams go by other names such as IEP team or special education eligibility team. Child study teams make two kinds of decisions: decisions about exceptionality (whether the child is disabled or gifted), and decisions about special learning needs. These teams are composed of regular education teachers, special education teachers, one or more administrators, the student's parent(s), and related services personnel, such as the school psychologist, nurse, social worker, counselor, and so forth, depending on the nature of the case. Recent surveys show that 3 to 5 percent of the students in public schools are referred each year for psychological

---

1. School administrators vary greatly in their views on which skills, abilities, and behaviors students need to enter school. Many view all children as "ready" for school and focus their efforts on getting schools ready for students.

and educational assessment. About 92 percent of those students who are referred are tested, and about 73 percent of those who are tested are declared eligible for special education services (Algozzine, Christenson, & Ysseldyke, 1982).

Exceptionality Decisions

In making exceptionality decisions, the child study team decides whether a student meets the criteria for being a member of a group of students considered *eligible* for special education as specified by the state in which the student lives. If, for example, the student must be shown to have an IQ below 70 and deficits in adaptive behavior in order to be called mentally retarded, one or more team members will administer tests to see if the child scores below the required scores. The team does the official assigning of an exceptionality name, and the criteria used to make the decision are state criteria. For example, teams identify, according to state criteria, categorical conditions such as blind, deaf, mentally retarded, emotionally disturbed, learning disabled, and so forth. They also decide whether youngsters are gifted and talented. Given that some students are multiply disabled, teams must identify the category under which services will be provided. Teams are required to gather assessment information, and it is illegal to base exceptionality decisions on a single test.

Documentation of Special Learning Needs

Child study teams also make decisions about whether students have special learning needs that require provision of special education services. For example, they may document that a student who is blind or visually impaired can be expected to experience academic difficulties without instruction in Braille or the use of large print books. They make a formal statement that the student has special learning needs that require special education assistance, and they link these learning needs to statements about the kinds of assistance required. Increasingly, child study teams rely on the data they receive from those who have conducted pre-referral interventions with individual children. In fact, the purpose of pre-referral intervention is twofold: to try to alleviate difficulties, and to document the kinds of techniques that do and do not improve student outcomes.

Eligibility Decisions

Before the Education for All Handicapped Children Act was passed in 1975, eligibility, labeling, and placement decisions typically were made by administrators or school psychologists. Members of Congress, acting on the belief that individual decision making was capricious and too often wrong, decided that decisions should be made by teams using multiple sources of information.

Before a student may be declared eligible for special education service, the student must be shown to have an exceptionality (a disability or a gift or talent), and the student must be shown to have special learning needs. It is not enough to be disabled. Students can be disabled and not require special education. Students can have special learning needs, but not meet the state criteria for being declared disabled. Students who receive special education are those with disabilities (or special gifts and talents) who *also* have special learning needs and need special education services to achieve educational outcomes.

In addition to the classification system employed by the federal government, every state has an education code that specifies the kinds of students considered handicapped. States have different names for the same handicap. For example, in California some students are called deaf or hard of hearing; in other states, such as Colorado, the same kinds of students are called hearing impaired. Different states have different standards for classification of the same handicap. In Pennsylvania, the maximum IQ for mentally retarded individuals is 80; in Minnesota, the maximum IQ is 70; in California, a black student cannot be classified as mentally retarded on the basis of an individual intelligence test. Some states consider gifted students as exceptional and entitled to special education services; other states do not.

Post-Entitlement Classroom Decisions

Instructional Planning Decisions

Regular education teachers are able to take a standard curriculum and plan instruction around it. Although curricula vary from district to district—largely as a function of the values of community and school—they are appropriate for most students at a given age or grade level. But what about those students who need special help to benefit from a standard curriculum? For these students, school personnel must gather data to plan special programs.

Three kinds of decisions are made in *instructional planning:* what to teach, how to teach it, and what expectations are realistic. Deciding what to teach is a content decision, usually made on the basis of a systematic analysis of the skills that students do and do not have. Scores on tests and other information help teachers decide whether students have specific skills. Test information might be used to decide placement in reading groups or assignment to specific compensatory or remedial programs. Teachers also use information gathered from observations and interviews to decide what to teach. And they obtain information about how to teach by trying different methods of teaching and monitoring students' progress toward instructional goals. Finally, decisions about realistic expectations are always inferences, based largely on observations of performance in school settings and performance on tests.

With the increased attention given to learning disabilities and with federal and state requirements for individualized education programs for exceptional students, we have seen an expansion in the use of curriculum-based assessment procedures in planning instructional efforts. The merits and limitations of tests in planning specific education programs are discussed in several chapters in Parts 3 and 4 of this text. Instructional planning for students with disabilities involves development of an Individualized Educational Plan (IEP). The IEP and the components that are required to be included in it are described in Chapter 14.

Setting Decisions

Setting decisions are often called placement decisions. They involve deciding where to place students for the most appropriate services. School personnel may decide that students should stay in their regular educational setting and that services should be brought to them. They recommend that students be educated in the general education mainstream. The terms *inclusion* or *full inclusion* are increasingly used in place of the term *mainstreaming*. It is common for state education agency personnel to talk about their state's being a full inclusion state or about mandating full inclusion of students with disabilities. The goal of full inclusion is placement and instruction of all students—regardless of the type or severity of their disability—in their neighborhood schools, in the regular classroom.

At the time we were preparing this textbook there was much debate among educators and policy makers regarding the ethics and efficacy of educating students with disabilities in regular school settings along with their peers. Some assert that placement in set-aside structures limits students' cognitive, academic, and social development and that placement in general education settings enhances the development of students with disabilities. Others contend that it is impossible to meet the special learning needs of students with disabilities without providing a full continuum of services. Most educators, however, now believe very strongly that students with disabilities should, to the extent possible, be educated in regular classrooms with their same-age peers. Most believe that extra assistance, necessitated by disabilities, is best provided in regular classes. Most believe that every effort should be made to involve students with disabilities in regular class activities and to encourage their acceptance and social integration. Disagreements come about over defining "to the extent possible," and "every effort." Inclusion is implemented in radically different ways in different schools and school districts. Personnel in one district might believe they have met the intent of full inclusion when they put students with disabilities in general education classes, even without special education supports. Others believe they have met that intent only when students are placed with the necessary supports provided. Still others believe inclusion has occurred only if schools are radically restructured so that all severity levels are included in regular classrooms, there is no separate system called special education, and funds for special education, compensatory education, and general education are pooled.

In school districts today full inclusion is both an action and a state of mind. Some educators talk about having to justify the presence of a student with a disability before the student is included, others about having to justify the student's separation before the student is excluded. Listen carefully as you hear people talk about full inclusion. Listen to the views they express on inclusion, but listen also to how they define inclusion and the kinds of practices they believe give evidence of it. Clearly, throughout all of the discussion and debate on mainstreaming, inclusion, full inclusion, and placement, there is a move to bring services to students rather than students to services.

Setting decisions are made on the basis of a combination of student needs, parent, teacher, or system philosophy about inclusion of students with disabilities in regular education settings, and resources. Most often the decisions are made on the basis of practicality (availability and location of services) and benevolence (what is in the best interests of the child). But the basis can sometimes be more economic, social, and political than pragmatic.

Assessment information is used in making setting decisions, and assessors are charged with deciding the least restrictive environment (LRE) in which the student can be successful. Special education services are delivered in a variety of settings. In 1970 Evelyn Deno described a kind of diagnostic filtering system, called the cascade of educational services. Most students with disabilities are educated in general education settings, fewer in resource settings, and still fewer in special classes or set-aside settings. In 1977 Reynolds and Birch refined the Deno Cascade to illustrate the fact that there is much movement among settings, and they labeled the settings as "diverse mainstream environments," "specialized educational environments," and "limited educational environments." The Reynolds-Birch Cascade is shown in Figure 1.4.

Progress Evaluation Decisions

Parents, teachers, and students themselves have a right and a need to know how students are progressing in school. How do we know if students are learning? One way to know, of course, is to rely on our observations of a student's behavior, and our own feelings and impressions of the student's work. As a parent evaluates a child's development on the basis of general impressions or observations, so teachers evaluate students' progress on the basis of subjective general impressions.

Teachers also collect assessment information to decide whether their students are making progress. They may give unit tests, or they may evaluate portfolios of the students' work (sometimes called portfolio assessment). The data that are

FIGURE 1.4   **Reynolds-Birch Cascade System of Special Education Services**

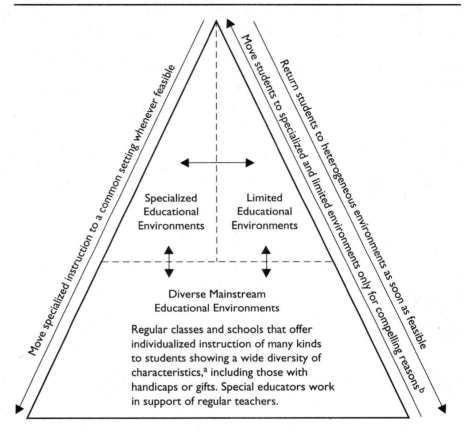

a. It is assumed that no educational "place" is impervious to change and development and that through good efforts many of the specialized and intensive forms of education can be moved into a developing mainstream.

b. It is assumed that students should be removed from the mainstream only for limited periods and compelling reasons; that their progress should be monitored carefully and regularly; and that they should be returned to the mainstream as soon as feasible. All students start their schooling in the mainstream and have a *place* there at all times, even though they may be located in a special setting for some period of time.

SOURCE: From *Teaching Exceptional Children in All America's Schools,* by M.C. Reyonlds and J. Birch. Copyright 1977 by The Council for Exceptional Children. Reprinted with permission.

collected as part of the process of evaluating pupil progress are used to fine-tune education programs or to make changes in teaching strategies. Some of the data collected in progress evaluation tell teachers and parents whether specific instructional objectives have been achieved.

When tests are used to make progress evaluation decisions, it is critical that there be good correspondence between the test and the curriculum. When discussing tests, it is important to distinguish between *attainment* and *achievement*. *Attainment* is what an individual has learned, regardless of where it has been learned. *Achievement* is what has been learned as a result of instruction in the schools. Any test of factual information measures attainment; however, a test of factual information is an achievement test only if it measures what has been directly taught. Only achievement tests can be used to monitor pupil progress. It would be pointless to use a test that did not assess what a teacher had taught.

The best way to collect data for the purpose of evaluating individual students' progress is to sample the skills that are being taught. This method allows teachers to measure the extent to which students have mastered content and to chart their progress toward meeting instructional objectives.

Accountability/Outcomes Decisions

Assessment information is used to make decisions about the extent to which educational programs are working in school systems. It is also used to make decisions about the extent to which education is working for students, including students with disabilities.

Program Evaluation Decisions

Assessment data are collected to evaluate specific programs. Here the emphasis is on gauging the effectiveness of the curriculum in meeting the goals and objectives of the school. School personnel typically use this information for schoolwide curriculum planning. For example, schools can compare two approaches to teaching in a content area by (1) giving tests at the beginning of the year, (2) teaching two comparable groups two different ways, and (3) giving tests at the end of the year. By comparing students' performances before and after, the schools are able to evaluate the effectiveness of the two competing approaches.

The process of assessing educational programs can be complex if a large number of students is involved and if the criteria for making decisions are written in statistical terms. For example, an evaluation of two instructional programs might involve gathering data from hundreds of students and comparing their performances using many statistical tests. Program costs, teacher and student opinions, and the nature of each program's goals and objectives might be compared to determine which program is more effective. This kind of large-scale evaluation probably would be undertaken by a group of administrators working for a school district.

Of course program evaluations can be much less formal. Martha is a friend of ours who is a third-grade teacher. When Martha wants to know the effectiveness of an instructional method that she is using, she does her own evaluation. For example, recently she wanted to know if having students complete activities in their basal readers was as effective as having them use language experience activities. She compared students' written products using both methods and concluded that their language experience activities were better.

Accountability Decisions

America's public schools have come under increasing criticism over the past ten to twelve years. In 1983 a special study panel commissioned by the U.S. Department of Education issued a report, called *A Nation at Risk*, in which it raised concerns about education in America and about the accomplishments of America's students. Increasingly, parents want reports on how students are doing in their schools, legislators want to know how the schools are doing, and policy makers want data on the educational performance of the nation's youth. School personnel regularly administer tests to students, engage in portfolio assessment or performance assessment, and issue reports on the achievement of the students in their schools. Such practices are sometimes called outcomes-based accountability practices. Each year the U.S. Department of Education issues a National Educational Goals Report, which examines the extent to which we are making progress toward the eight national education goals specified in Goals 2000 (see Table 1.2) and includes a variety of assessment information.

MAKING ASSESSMENT DECISIONS

Assessment is the process of collecting data for the purpose of making decisions about students. But, the process of assessment and decision making is seldom straightforward. Students are not referred, tested, declared eligible, placed in special education, and then taught. Rather, the assessment process proceeds differently in different places for different students. Decisions made about students are neither sequential nor mutually exclusive. For example, a teacher may be providing Dominic with special assistance in reading, during which time the Speech-Language pathologist may administer a language screening test to him. Sometimes it takes a long time to go through the sequence of decisions; sometimes the time from screening or referral to provision of services is very short. Some students perform poorly on a screening measure and are referred immedi-

TABLE 1.2   **The Eight National Education Goals**

By the year 2000:

All children will be ready to learn.

The high school graduation rate will increase to at least 90 percent.

Students in grades 4, 8, and 12 will have demonstrated competency over challenging subject matter including English, mathematics, science, foreign languages, civics and government, economics, arts, history, and geography.

The teaching force will have access to programs for the continued improvement of their professional skills.

U S. students will be first in the world in mathematics and science achievement.

Every adult will be literate and will possess the knowledge and skills to compete in a global economy.

Every school will be free of drugs and violence and the unauthorized presence of firearms and alcohol and will offer a disciplined environment conducive to learning.

Every school will promote parternships that will increase parental involvement and participation.

SOURCE: U.S. Congress, Goals 2000: Educate America Act, 1994.

ately to an intervention assistance team or child study team. Others come to the attention of the IAT only after the teacher has provided considerable assistance and the student has not profited to the extent desired.[2] Students who are enrolled in the standard developmental curriculum may demonstrate a potential problem that leads to referral to either an intervention assistance team or child study team. Or, the student may fail to make expected progress, the teacher may provide extra help, and only after the student fails to profit from the extra help is he or she referred to the intervention assistance team. Intervention assistance teams try a number of interventions, and students who fail to perform as expected are referred to the child study team.

Assessment is dynamic and ongoing. Following the declaration of eligibility for services and specification of learning needs for a student, teachers continue

2. Referral may result from a teacher's observations, a parent's request, or the student's own. Context can affect assessment practices. Some students are not referred to an intervention assistance team because their regular class teacher has special expertise in dealing with their disability. Some are more likely to receive assistance in a particular district or state than if they live elsewhere.

to observe how the student performs under differing circumstances and modify instruction accordingly (Algozzine & Ysseldyke, 1992).

When is assessment started? Timing is largely a function of the severity of a disability. The assessment and decision-making process may be shortened in some instances, such as when a parent of a child with severe disabilities initiates a referral. Parents know very early in a child's life that severe disabilities are present. They may contact their family physician, who may spend very little time deciding that a child has a disability; it may be readily apparent. On the other hand, sometimes it is necessary for assessment personnel to engage in extensive assessment to ascertain whether a child has a developmental disorder. In general, it takes longer to decide to declare students with mild disabilities eligible for special education than it does to make the same decision for students with severe disabilities. Some disabilities do not show up until students are in school and experience difficulty with schoolwork. The student may evidence signs of a disability by demonstrating a significant gap between actual and desired performance.

ASSESSMENT DOMAINS

Assessment involves the specification and verification of problems for the purpose of making different kinds of decisions. We just described the kinds of decisions that are made in educational settings. We now describe three kinds of problems with which assessment is usually concerned: academic problems, behavior problems, and physical problems.

Academic Problems

The most common reason students are referred for psychological or educational assessment is that a teacher or parent believes they are not performing as well academically as could be expected. Teachers usually make that decision on the basis of their observations of pupil performance in core content areas: reading, mathematics, written language and communication. When referring students to intervention assistance teams or child study teams for assessment, teachers must specify their concerns. Teachers who refer students for assessment because of "reading problems" provide diagnostic personnel with limited information. To the extent that teachers describe and specify the nature of a student's problems (for example, "Rachel is the poorest reader in the class and consistently has difficulty associating letters with sounds"), they help diagnostic personnel. Some very effective teachers regularly gather information on pupil progress in academic content areas and use those data to make decisions to provide special assistance and/or to refer students.

Academic performance is nearly always assessed in making exceptionality and eligibility decisions. For example, a student referred for reading problems may be given a reading test to provide a comparison of the student's development of reading skills relative to other students in the school or even the nation. The results of the test would be used to verify the existence of a problem.

Academic performance also is usually assessed in making instructional planning decisions. In deciding what to teach a student, the teacher or team must specify those skills that the student does and does not already have.

Behavior Problems

Students are often referred for psychological or educational assessment because they demonstrate behavior problems. Students for whom severe behavior problems can be specified and verified are often declared eligible for special education services. Behavior problems include failure to get along with peers, delinquent activities, and excessive withdrawal, as well as disruptive and noncompliant behavior. For example, Ms. Swanson may be troubled because Larry is so quiet and withdrawn. She might begin to verify that this is actually the problem by counting the frequency of Larry's interactions with his peers. A low count would not, by itself, indicate a problem. Therefore, Ms. Swanson might select another boy whose behavior she judged to be appropriate and count the frequency of his interactions with his peers. She could then verify that Larry interacted much less frequently than a boy who had no problems interacting. Ms. Swanson might plan a social skills training program for Larry to increase the number of positive interactions that he had with his classmates. She could systematically collect data on the effectiveness of this new program and reach some decisions about Larry's progress.

Physical Problems

Physical problems include sensory disabilities (such as in vision or hearing), problems of physical structure (for example, spina bifida or cerebral palsy), and chronic health problems (such as diabetes or asthma). Severe physical problems are often first brought to the attention of parents by physicians before a child enters school. When a child with a severe physical problem enters school, the parents might supply the school with specific information from physicians that confirms and specifies the physical nature of the child's problem.

Milder, but nonetheless important, problems that have not been noticed by the parents are often discovered during routine screening. For example, suppose White Haven Area School district requires that the school nurse (Mr. Slique) regularly conduct hearing tests (for example, a puretone audiometric test for hearing within the specific range). When he screens the first-grade students, Mr. Slique notes that Jane has a 65-decibel loss in her better ear. A hearing loss of such magnitude, if confirmed, would have serious educational implications and would necessitate substantial educational modifications so that Jane could profit from her education. However, the screening assessment was conducted in the nurse's room, which was not soundproofed, and with equipment that had not been checked recently for accuracy. Therefore, Mr. Slique decides that it would be best to have an audiologist see Jane and diagnose her hearing problem. He works with the child study team to refer Jane to the audiologist for more extensive hearing testing.

ASSESSMENT AND SOCIETY

The students we teach in assessment classes often enter the class with questions about the role that testing plays in social decision making. They ask such questions as "Is it fair to place students in special education on the basis of their performance on a test?" "What do tests say about a person?" and "Should an employer decide whether to hire a person on the basis of how that person does on a test?" Our students also question the use of tests in making decisions about college entrance or admission to graduate school. Throughout this text, when appropriate, we address these and other issues on the use of tests in schools. Testing does play a critical role in schools and in society. Many times tests are used to make high-stakes decisions, (which may have a direct and significant effect on individuals' life opportunities or on the continued funding of schools and school systems. The joint committee of three professional associations that developed a set of standards for test construction and use has addressed the kinds of issues our students often raise:

> Educational and psychological testing represents one of the most important contributions of behavioral science to our society. It has provided fundamental and significant improvements over previous practices in industry, government, and education. It has provided a tool for broader and more equitable access to education and employment. Although not all tests are well-developed, nor are all testing practices wise and beneficial, available evidence supports the judgment that the proper use of well-constructed and validated tests provides a better basis for making some important decisions about individuals and programs than would otherwise be available.
>   Educational and psychological testing has also been the target of extensive scrutiny, criticism, and debate both outside and within the professional testing community. The most frequent criticisms are that tests play too great a role in the lives of students and employees and that tests are biased and exclusionary. Individuals and institutions benefit when testing helps them achieve their goals. Society, in turn, benefits when the achievement of individual and institutional goals contributes to the general good. (American Educational Research Association, American Psychological Association, and National Council on Measurement in Education, 1985, p. 1)

SUMMARY

Testing is part of a larger concept: assessment. Assessment data are used to clarify and verify the existence of educational problems in the areas of academic functioning, behavioral and social adaptation, and physical development. Assessment provides data to facilitate decision making. Thirteen kinds of decisions are made using assessment information: decisions about provision of special assistance, referral to an intervention assistance team, provision of intervention assistance, screening, referral to a child study team, exceptionality, documentation of a special learning need, eligibility, instructional planning, setting, progress evaluation, program evaluation, and accountability. Many complex social, political, and ethical issues arise when tests are used to make important decisions about individuals. Assessment is an important activity, and it is critical that it be done right. Throughout the text we address issues in the appropriate and inappropriate use of tests.

STUDY QUESTIONS

1. Differentiate between testing and assessment.
2. Why have most states now instituted pre-referral interventions as a required activity prior to formal referral for assessment?
3. If you were to make an assessment for the purpose of referring a student to a child study team, what kinds of data would you like to have available for the team?
4. All of us have taken achievement tests such as the Iowa Tests of Basic Skills or the Stanford Achievement Tests. Think back to two or three instances in which you took such tests. To what use(s), if any, did you expect the results of these assessments to be put?
5. Why is it important that we have data for purposes of making decisions?
6. What five kinds of decisions are made in deciding whether students are entitled to special education services?

ADDITIONAL READING

Cronbach, L. J. (1990). *Essentials of psychological testing* (5th ed.). New York: Harper & Row. (Chapter 2: Varieties of tests and test interpretations)

Ysseldyke, J. E. (1983). Current practices in making psychoeducational decisions about learning disabled students. *Journal of Learning Disabilities, 16,* 226–233.

Ysseldyke, J. E. (1986). The use of assessment information to make decisions about students. In R. J. Morris & B. Blatt (Eds.), *Special education: Research and trends*. Elmsford, NY: Pergamon Press.

Ysseldyke, J. E., & Algozzine, B. (1995). *Introduction to special education* (3rd ed.). Boston: Houghton Mifflin. (Chapter 6: Assessment practices in special education)

Ysseldyke, J. E., Algozzine, B., & Thurlow, M. L. (1992). *Critical issues in special education*. Boston: Houghton Mifflin. (Chapter 7: Issues in assessment, pp. 169–199)

Chapter 2

Assessment Processes and Concerns

*A*ssessment is the process of collecting data to make decisions. In the context of education, assessment is performed to gain an understanding of an individual's strengths and weaknesses in order to make appropriate educational decisions. Any textbook description of this interactive, individualized, and complex process is necessarily general and linear; thus, to some extent descriptions of data collection and decision making can distort and oversimplify the processes. This chapter begins with a description of the process of collecting data to gain an understanding of a student's strengths and weaknesses. It ends with a description of frequently voiced concerns about assessment and subsequent decision making. Underlying this chapter is the belief that the best educational decisions are based on information; usually, better decisions are based on more information. Although good decisions can be based on a flash of insight, more often they are the result of generating hypotheses, carefully amassing information, and then carefully analyzing that information for consistencies and inconsistencies, support and lack of support for the hypotheses.

THE PROCESS OF ASSESSMENT

When a student is experiencing difficulty in school, two related and complementary types of assessment should be performed. First, the instruction a student has received is assessed to ascertain if the student's difficulties stem from inappropriate instruction (that is, curriculum or teaching). When instruction is found to be inadequate, the student should be afforded appropriate instruction to ascertain if it alleviates the difficulty. When appropriate instruction fails to remediate the difficulty, further assessment of the student is carried out. Each approach is described below.

ASSESSING INSTRUCTION

Until recently, most assessment activities in school settings consisted of efforts to assess the learner. Yet school personnel often have difficulty developing instructional recommendations solely on the basis of information about the characteristics of students. Englemann, Granzin, and Severson (1979) recommended that assessment begin with instructional diagnosis "to determine aspects of instruction that are inadequate, to find out precisely how they are inadequate, and to imply what must be done to correct their inadequacy" (p. 361). In this approach, assessment consists of systematic analysis of instruction in terms of its appropriateness for the learner. Two dimensions are usually considered when instruction is assessed: instructional challenge and instructional environment.

Instructional Challenge

For instruction to be effective, it must be possible for the learner, with a reasonable effort, to master the information (the facts, skills, behavior, or processes) being taught. If the degree to which information challenges a learner is thought of as a continuum, we can think of material as ranging from too easy (unchallenging), to about right in the degree of difficulty (appropriately challenging), to too difficult (too challenging).

Unchallenging Content

Instruction that is too easy for a student teaches information that requires no more practice for either acquisition or retention; the student understands the information and can use it. Usually, unchallenging instruction occurs in two ways. First, a teacher may hold previously mastered goals as the current goals of instruction. Thus, the teacher teaches what is already known. Obviously, if a student already has met the goal, additional instruction or practice wastes time and bores the student. Second, the pace of instruction may be too slow. In this case, a teacher initially provides instruction on new information but fails to recognize when the student has mastered it. Here, too, time is wasted and the student is bored. Levels of mastery that are needed vary by the capabilities of individual students and the design of the curriculum. However, as a rule of thumb, educators frequently use a criterion of a 95 percent correct response rate as the point beyond which students no longer need even independent practice.

Appropriately Challenging Content

Instruction that is appropriately challenging is, of course, neither too easy nor too difficult. Moreover, such instruction is usually motivating because students can see that, with some effort, they will be successful. Depending on the student and the task, challenging material usually produces rates of correct student response between 75 and 95 percent.

Too Challenging Content

Instruction that is too difficult for a student attempts to teach information for which a student lacks significant prerequisites. This problem occurs in two related ways. First, instruction can be too challenging if a student lacks facts, concepts, behavior, or strategies on which the new instruction is based. Two examples are illustrative. (1) If students do not understand addition, they will probably be unsuccessful in learning multiplication beyond some rote memorization. (2) If students do not understand that deciduous trees go dormant in the winter, they may not grasp the difference between dead trees and healthy, but dormant, trees. Second, instruction can be too difficult when its pace is too fast. In this case the student has been exposed to prerequisite information but has not mastered it. For example, a youngster may still be learning to control writing movements when the teacher moves on to writing letters. As a result, the student may still be concentrating on pencil grip instead of learning how specific letters are formed. As is the case with information that is too easy, what is too difficult for a student varies by the capabilities of the student and the design of the curriculum. However, educators generally believe that when average students cannot respond with 70 to 75 percent accuracy, the material is too difficult; for students with severe cognitive handicaps, rates of correct response of less than 80 percent may indicate that the material is too challenging for guided practice. When instruction is too challenging, students do not learn efficiently and often experience frustration; such students are occasionally termed *curriculum casualties*.

Instructional Environment

Instruction involves more than appropriate curriculum. It is a complex activity, the outcomes of which depend on the interaction of many factors. Recognition of this fact has led to efforts to assess the qualitative nature of students' instructional environments (Christenson & Ysseldyke, 1987a, 1987b, and 1993).

Assessment of the instructional environment consists of systematically analyzing the extent to which those factors known to make a difference in pupils' learning are present in the instruction that students receive. In the last twenty five years psychologists and educators have learned much about the attributes of instruction that results in efficient and motivated learning. Yet in many classrooms, instruction is not particularly effective. Too often teachers use a strategy of "cover and pray," in which they talk about the content and pray that the students learn. In these classrooms students are exposed to information, not taught; teachers hope that students somehow learn the information, but they do not assess to make sure that their students have learned. In these classrooms, some students master the curriculum because they are sufficiently capable of learning from exposure or are taught by their parents. Others do not master the curriculum and become teaching disabled. Through no fault of their own, their learning is not commensurate with their abilities. Thus, when students experience difficulty learning, a necessary component of assessment is evaluating the quality of the instruction students have received. Although Chapter 13 deals in greater detail with the ecology of instruction, two dimensions of instruction (classroom management and learning management) are worth describing here.

Classroom Management

Classroom management refers to a collection of organizational goals centered on using time wisely to maximize learning and maintaining a safe classroom environment that is conducive to student learning. In classrooms that are poorly organized, students lose learning opportunities because of disruptions by other students, ineffective grouping, poor transitions between activities, and so forth. In contrast, well-organized classrooms have clearly stated and well understood procedures, consistent consequences for student behavior, and student freedom within a structured environment.

Learning Management

The organization and management of the classroom to ensure learning requires careful attention to detail. Essentially, teachers must oversee the learning situation. Effective teachers demonstrate what is to be learned and provide adequate opportunities for meaningful rehearsal and guided and independent practice with appropriate materials until skills become automatic. Effective teachers give students immediate, specific, and corrective feedback about their performances and provide opportunities to correct mistakes. Effective teachers reinforce desired outcomes. Finally, effective teachers stress understanding, application, and transfer of information.

ASSESSING LEARNERS

When students have received appropriate instruction but are still experiencing academic or behavior problems, school personnel usually begin assembling existing information in order to document the nature of the problem (that is, identify specific strengths and weaknesses) and to generate hypotheses about the problem's likely cause.

Kinds of Information

It is well to remember that a test is only one of several assessment techniques or procedures available for gathering information. During the process of assessment, data from observations, recollections, tests, and judgments all come into play.

Observations

Observations can provide highly accurate, detailed, verifiable information, not only about the person being assessed but also about the contexts in which the observations are being made. For the sake of convenience, observations can be categorized as nonsystematic and systematic.

Nonsystematic Observation   In nonsystematic, or informal, observation, the observer simply watches an individual in his or her environment and takes note of the behaviors, characteristics, and personal interactions that seem significant. Nonsystematic observation tends to be anecdotal and can be subjective and unreplicable. However, nonsystematic observations can provide the basis for determining what to observe systematically.

Systematic Observation   In systematic observation, the observer sets out to observe one or more precisely defined behaviors. The observer specifies observable events that define the behavior and then counts or otherwise measures the frequency, duration, magnitude, or latency of the behaviors. The observer must be careful to observe the important behaviors and characteristics—not just those that are convenient.

Disadvantages of Observations   There are three potential disadvantages in using observations to collect information: imperfect observation, time demands, and observation distortion.

There is a substantial body of research that indicates that humans often both observe and reach decisions based on their observations imperfectly. Two types of imperfect observation are particularly noteworthy: the halo effect and expectancy.

The *halo effect* is the tendency to make subjective judgments on the basis of general attributes. Thus, one subject characteristic, (such as race), may alter the way in which the subject's peer interactions are seen. Salvia and Meisel (1980) have documented the impact on observation of several student characteristics: social class, given names, surnames, race, facial attractiveness, and labels of exceptionality. The halo effect is most likely to influence observations when the behavior or attributes under consideration are not easily observed, are not clearly defined, involve reactions of other people, or are of high moral importance (Guilford, 1936, p. 275). Conversely, providing observers with systematic training in observation, specific procedures, and highly objective situations can substantially reduce or eliminate biased observations. (Salvia & Meisel, 1980).

Expectancy is the tendency to see what one believes. Thus, teachers are more likely to observe better behavior when they believe in the effectiveness of their interventions. The most effective way to prevent expectancies from influencing observations is to keep observers blind, (that is, uninformed about who is receiving intervention or the nature of the intervention. However, this technique is most difficult to implement in schools.

The second disadvantage of observation is that it can be very time-consuming. The more precisely and carefully made, the more time-consuming observations become. Thus, an assessor pays for accurate information by not being able to collect other information. The third disadvantage is that the very presence of an observer may distort or otherwise alter the situation to such a degree that the behavior of the individual being observed also is altered. For example, students may be hesitant to misbehave when an outsider is observing in the classroom.

Recollections

Recalled observations and interpretations of behavior and events are frequently used as an additional source of information. People familiar with the student can be very useful in providing information through interviews and rating scales.

Interviews Interviews can range in structure from casual conversations to highly structured processes in which the interviewer has a predetermined set of questions that are asked in a specified sequence. Generally, the more structured the interview, the more accurate the comparisons of the results of several different interviews.

Rating Scales Rating scales can be considered the most formal type of interview. Rating scales allow questions to be asked in a standardized way and to be accompanied by the same stimulus materials, and they provide a standardized and limited set of response options. The two most commonly used types of response options are Likert-like scaling and frequency estimates. With Likert-like formats, the person responds to a statement by indicating if he or she strongly agrees, agrees somewhat, disagrees somewhat, or strongly disagrees. With frequency estimates, the person responds by indicating how often a behavior or situation occurs (always, frequently, seldom, or never). Some rating scales employ a five-point scale with a neutral midpoint (neither agree nor disagree). Other scales may use six or seven points.

Disadvantages of Recollections In addition to having some of the same disadvantages associated with direct observation, recollections suffer from three other disadvantages. First, the longer the time between observation and recollection, the greater the chance that some memory distortion will occur. For example, important details may be forgotten and some things that are generally consistent with the remembrance may be invented. Second, individuals may not be truthful. People may be unwilling to divulge painful or embarrassing details. They may filter what they tell an interviewer according to what they believe the interviewer hopes to hear. They may provide information selectively or over- or understate problems in order to further their own agendas; for example, parents who do not want their child placed in special education may assert that a child's school avoidance is infrequent even though it is a daily problem. Third, as is true of observations, interviewers may hold a set of expectations that filter what they are told.

Tests

A test is a predetermined set of questions or tasks to which predetermined types of behavioral responses are sought. Tests are particularly useful because they permit tasks and questions to be presented in exactly the same way to each person tested. Because a tester elicits and scores behavior in a predetermined and consistent manner, the performances of several different test takers can be compared no matter who does the testing. Hence, tests tend to make many extrapersonal factors in assessment consistent for all those tested. The price of this consistency is that the predetermined questions, tasks, and responses may not be equally relevant to all students.

Basically, two types of information, quantitative and qualitative, result from the administration of a test. *Quantitative* data are the actual scores achieved on the test. An example of quantitative data is Lee's score of 80 on her math test. *Qualitative* data consist of other observations made while a student is tested and tell us how Lee achieved her score. For example, in earning a score of 80 on her math test, Lee may have solved all of the addition and subtraction problems, with the exception of those that required regrouping. On a language test, Henry may have performed best on measures of his ability to define words while demonstrating a weakness in comprehending verbal statements. When tests are used in assessment, it is not enough simply to know the scores a student earned on a given test; it is important to know how the student earned those scores.

Interpreting Quantitative Test Performance   Once gathered, quantitative data must be interpreted: What do the numbers mean? Interpretation occurs along two dimensions. First, the meaning of a student's performance on a test depends on the standard to which the performance is compared. For example, if Bill got 75 percent correct on his weekly spelling test, his teacher might want to know how other students did on that test, or the teacher might evaluate Bill's performance on an absolute basis (for example, he did not get 90 percent correct, but he bettered the score on his last test). Second, the meaning of a specific performance depends on the other information that has been amassed; in other words, the performance must be contextualized to show how it relates to the other information that has been collected. These two dimensions are often related. Depending on the purpose of assessment and the context, assessors may select test procedures that will provide a particular kind of interpretative information.

All assessments should be objective in the sense that there are predetermined answers or standards for scoring a response. Legally, assessments must be objective in the sense that attitudes, opinions, and idiosyncrasies of the examiner do not affect scoring; any two examiners should score a response in the same way. Objective scoring, per se, does not imply "fair" scoring; it implies only predetermined criteria and standardized scoring procedures. A subjective assessment, by contrast, lacks a predetermined correct answer. Therefore, the examiner's subjective judgments, attitudes, and opinions can affect the scoring. Many people erroneously define an essay test as a subjective test. Such a test can be objective if there are predetermined, explicit criteria for correct responses; the "same" response would be assigned the same score by two or more examiners.

Normative Standards   Most assessments that occur outside of the classroom are norm-referenced. An individual's performance is compared to the performance of peers. In norm-referenced assessment, although the learning of particular content or skills is important, the resulting score is used primarily to ascertain the extent of differential learning, which allows the tester to rank individuals from those who have learned many skills to those who have learned few.

Commercially prepared norm-referenced devices typically are designed primarily to do one thing: to separate the performances of individuals so that there is a distribution of scores. They allow the tester to discriminate among the performances of a number of individuals and to interpret how one person's performance compares to that of other individuals with similar characteristics. Thus a person's performance on a test is measured in reference to the performances of others who are presumably like that person. Commercially prepared norm-referenced tests are standardized on groups of individuals representative of all children, and typical performances for students of certain ages or in certain grades are obtained. The raw score that an individual student earns on a test, which is the number of questions answered correctly, is compared to the scores earned by other students. A transformed score, such as a percentile rank, is used to express the given student's standing in the group of all children of that age or grade. Commercially prepared norm-referenced tests are of two types, point scales and age scales, which differ in how they are constructed.

A *point scale* is constructed by selecting and ordering items of different levels of difficulty. The levels of difficulty are not associated with ages per se. In point scales, the correct responses (that is, points) are summed, and the total raw score is transformed to various derived scales (see Chapter 5).

Age scales are less common today than in the past because of both statistical and conceptual limitations. Age scales are developed by scaling test items in terms of the percentages of children of different ages responding correctly to each test item. For example, an item would be placed at the six-year level if 25 percent of five-year-olds responded to it correctly, 50 percent of six-year-olds responded to it correctly, and 75 percent of seven-year-olds responded to it correctly. When a test question is correctly placed in an age scale, younger children fail the item while older children pass it. The statistical and conceptual limitations of age scales are discussed in Chapter 5 in the sections dealing with developmental scores and quotients. The reader is cautioned that some tests, such as the old Stanford-Binet Test of Intelligence (1972), appear to be age scales but are more correctly considered point scales (compare Salvia, Ysseldyke, & Lee, 1975).

Classroom teachers, counselors, psychologists, speech and language therapists, and others may create their own assessment devices for their own purposes. The primary differences between commercially prepared and custom-made tests are the representativeness of the comparison group (see Chapter 6) and the specificity of the content (see Content Validity in Chapter 8). Teacher-made tests are illustrative of the class of custom-made tests. Teachers usually limit the group to whom an individual's performance is compared. Thus, as one example, a teacher may only compare Bill's performance to that of his classmates—not to that of all students in the same grade. Moreover, what Bill is asked to do (the content of the test) usually reflects the classroom curriculum directly. Thus, Bill's teacher learns how Bill compares to other students in the classroom who receive the same instruction on the same content. As a second example, Bill's special education teacher might want to know if Bill can be integrated for reading instruction in a regular fourth-grade class. The teacher could ask the regular class teacher to nominate two or three other students who are reading at an acceptable level. The special education teacher could assess the reading of these nominated students and Bill's reading to ascertain if Bill is reading as well. If he is, his reading skills are sufficient for integration.

Absolute Standards   In contrast to norm-referenced tests, criterion-referenced tests do not indicate a person's relative standing in skill development; they measure a person's mastery of particular information and skills in terms of absolute standards of mastery. Thus, criterion-referenced tests provide answers to specific questions such as "Does Maureen spell the word *dog* correctly?" "Does Bill read beginning fourth-grade material with 90 percent accuracy?" "Has Harry passed 75 percent of the questions on the driver's test?" In criterion-referenced assessment, the emphasis is on passing one or a series of questions. We are interested in what the particular individual can and cannot do, rather than how that individual's performance compares to those of other people.

When teachers use criterion-referenced tests, the items are often linked directly to specific instructional objectives and therefore facilitate the writing of objectives. Test items frequently sample sequential skills, enabling a teacher not only to know the specific point at which to begin instruction but also to plan those instructional aspects that follow directly in the curricular sequence.

School personnel use different terms to refer to assessment activities that are parts or derivatives of criterion-referenced assessment, including, for example, curriculum-based assessment, objective-referenced assessment, direct assessment, and formative evaluation of student progress. Curriculum-based assessment is defined as "a procedure for determining the instructional needs of a student based on the student's ongoing performance within existing course content" (Tucker, 1985, p. 200). In objective-referenced assessment, tests are referenced to specific instructional objectives rather than to the performance of a peer group or norm group. Pupil performance is evaluated by measuring whether the student has met specific objectives. In direct assessment, a student is required to perform specific skills, rather than the teacher's making inferences about the student's ability to perform the skill. For example, rather than inferring writing skill from tests of writing mechanics and spelling, a teacher would ask a student to write a story. The term *direct* is also used to differentiate such approaches from indirect and inferential approaches such as intelligence testing and personality assessment. Finally, formative evaluation refers to the assessment of progress toward a long-term or major objective (see Bloom, Hastings, and Madaus, 1971).

Comparing Normative and Absolute Standards   Interpretation of a student's performance in both normative and absolute terms is useful in special education. One form of interpretive information is not preferred in all situations.

Obviously when normative comparisons are required, norm-referenced assessments should be made. Norm-referenced interpretations are usually required in screening decisions. For example, if Suzy has 20/100 vision, she sees things at 20 feet that normal individuals see at 100 feet. Suzy's seeing so poorly, as compared to others, warrants further assessment and treatment. Norm-referenced interpretations are usually required for decisions about exceptionality when a cognitive handicap is suspected; tests of intelligence are always norm-referenced.

When tests are administered for the purpose of assisting the classroom teacher in planning and evaluating instructional programs for children, criterion-referenced interpretations are recommended. For example, when planning a program for an individual student, a teacher obviously should be more concerned with identifying the specific skills that the student does or does not have than with knowing how the student compares to others.

Professional Judgments   Assessment requires judgment, and the judgments and assessments made by others can play an important role in assessment. In instances when a diagnostician (the person responsible for performing an assessment) lacks competence to render a judgment, the judgments of those who possess the necessary competence are essential. Diagnosticians seek out other professionals to complement their own skills and background. Thus, referring a student to various specialists (hearing specialists, vision specialists, reading teachers, and so on) is a common and desirable practice in assessment. Judgments by teachers, counselors, psychologists, and practically any other school employee may be useful in particular circumstances. Expertise in making judgments is often a function of familiarity with the student being assessed. Teachers regularly express professional judgments; for example, report-card grades represent the teacher's judgment of a student's academic progress during the marking period; referrals for psychological evaluation represent a different type of judgment based on experience with many students and observations of the particular student. Judgments represent both the best and the worst of assessment data. Judgments made by conscientious, capable, and objective individuals can be an invaluable aid in the assessment process. Inaccurate, biased, subjective judgments can be misleading at best and harmful at worst.

Gathering Information

Information can be categorized as either information that describes how a person is functioning now or information that describes how that person has functioned in the past. Obviously, the distinction between current and historical information blurs, and the point at which current information becomes historical information depends in part on the particular fact or bit of information. For example, if Johnny had his appendix removed three years ago, we know he currently has no appendix.

Using Extant Information

There are three general sources of information available to school personnel: cumulative records, student products, and anecdotal records.

Cumulative Records   State law requires schools to maintain files on each student. Thus, schools maintain extensive records about students, and sometimes their families. Although there is some variability from state to state and district to district, these files are likely to contain basic identifying information (such as name, address, and birth date), current educational status (such as grade and school), and basic educational history. This history may contain previous report cards, results of standardized tests, and attendance records. The cumulative records of exceptional students will also probably contain the results of individually administered tests, reports from other professionals (such as language or occupational therapists), multidisciplinary team evaluations, individualized education plans, assorted state-required paperwork, and perhaps medical information. Thus, a student's cumulative record contains a potential wealth of information about that student's development. This information may be useful in deciding if a problem is chronic or recent, what has been tried with the student, who are the important persons in the student's educational life, and so forth.

Although these records are not public in the sense that anyone can read them, they can be accessed legally in two ways. First, anyone in the school with a legitimate need for the information can obtain access. Thus, for example, a school psychologist, teacher, or counselor may inspect the permanent files of students with whom they are working. Second, parents may authorize professionals working with their children to exchange information with professionals outside the schools. Thus, for example, parents can authorize their family physician to provide information to a school psychologist about their child's medications or health; parents can authorize teachers or school psychologists to provide information to the family physician about the effect of medication on the student's activity level and attention.

Student Products   Students produce volumes of permanent products: essays, drawings, completed worksheets and tests, and so forth. Although some of these products invariably find their way home, a number of products may remain in the teacher's possession. Some teachers assemble portfolios of student work; some teachers keep their own files of student work; some student work may be displayed in the classroom. Teachers also maintain summaries of student work. These summaries can take the form of charts of student progress or evaluations recorded in a grade book. Permanent products and grades are useful sources of information about a student's current level of performance and accomplishment. A student's work can be compared to the permanent products created by other students of similar age and expected outcomes.

Anecdotal Records   Some teachers keep personal notes about unusual occurrences during the school year. These notes may be prepared for several reasons, two of which are especially noteworthy. First, anecdotal records may be useful in documenting the parameters of and conditions under which problem behaviors occur. For example, a teacher might note the antecedents and consequences of a problem behavior in order to form hypotheses about effective interventions. Second, anecdotal records may be useful in providing a fuller record to justify or document a teacher's actions. For example, a teacher might document a parent's concerns mentioned during a telephone conversation in order to establish a record of parent contacts.

Limitations of Extant Information   Extant information has three limitations of which diagnosticians must be aware. First, someone must cull currently important information from other recorded information. Second, a diagnostician cannot control what information was collected in the past; crucial bits of information may never have been collected. Third, the conditions under which the information was collected are unknown or often difficult to evaluate.

Gathering New Data

There are three advantages in having and using current information. The first is the most obvious: current information describes a person's current behavior and characteristics. Information about current status is required for most educational decisions. Second, the diagnostician can select the specific information needed to make the desired decisions. This advantage is particularly relevant because assessment is dynamic. Frequently information leads to more questions that require additional information to answer. Third, current information can be verified.

Putting It Together

As shown in Table 2.1, there are eight general classes of diagnostic information sources. The classification depends on the source of information, the currency of the information (current or historical), and the kinds of information collected (tests, observations, and so forth).

Diagnosticians do not have the time, competence, or opportunity to collect all possible types of information. In cases where specialized information is needed, they must rely on the observations, tests, and judgments of others. If a behavior occurs infrequently or is demonstrated only outside of school, the diagnostician may have to rely on the observations and judgments of others who have more opportunity to collect the information—parents, or perhaps ward attendants in institutional settings. For example, bed-wetting does not occur at school, but few diagnosticians would question the accuracy of parents' reports of bed-wetting. Moreover, if a child is an intermittent bed wetter, a diagnostician might have to spend several nights at the child's home in order to observe the behavior directly. In such cases indirect information is usually adequate.

Finally, it is usually the responsibility of a team to integrate the information

TABLE 2.1   Examples of Different Types of Historical and Current Diagnostic Information

Type of Information	Time at Which Information is Gathered	
	Historical	**Current**
Observations	Previous IEPs prepared by teachers or psychologists Disciplinary notes in permanent file	Anecdotal records placed in personal files by teacher Momentary time sampling of on-task behavior
Recollections	Student's developmental history previously given by parent Rating scale completed last year by parent or teacher	Interviews with former teachers of target student Rating scale completed this year by parent or teacher
Tests	Scores from first-grade screening test Scores from third-grade group achievement tests	Scores on an individual intelligence test Results of criterion-referenced tests given by teacher
Judgments	Physician's diagnosis of attention deficit disorder Grades from previous teachers	Teacher's decision to refer student for evaluation Multidisciplinary team's classification of student as LD

and make decisions. Teams and the types of decisions they make are discussed in Chapters 14 and 15.

Educational Prognosis

Assessment and educational decision making involve predictions, either explicit or implicit ones. A prognosis may be offered for students in their current environment and life circumstances or in some therapeutic or remedial environment. For example, knowing that Harry is mentally retarded and has not profited from instruction leads to the predictions that (1) he will probably not profit from the same types of instruction in the future; (2) he may fall further behind the other children and perhaps even develop problem behaviors; and (3) if he is placed in an environment where he can receive more individual attention and specially designed instruction, he should make more progress academically and socially.

In education, as in most other human service ventures, most predictions are not sufficiently sophisticated to allow mathematical specification. Rather, diagnosticians rely on developmental theory and intervention research to make hypotheses about the variables that should influence outcomes or intensify or attenuate a variable's impact. They then weigh a child's current life circumstances, developmental history, and a variety of extrapersonal factors in reaching decisions and making predictions.

Current Life Circumstances

Any interpretation of an individual's performance and predictions about future success must include an understanding of that individual's current circumstances. Current life circumstances include the student's family, community, and physical abilities and health.

Family   A student's family life contributes enormously to that student's ability to profit educationally. Yet, too frequently students and their families face significant challenges at home: families headed by a single parent, families in which both parents work or neither parent works, families that are homeless. Some families are simply dysfunctional. Whether because of increasing awareness and reporting of problems or increasing family stress, the schools seem to be seeing more students from families with histories of physical, sexual, psychological, and substance abuse. For students who experience difficulties in both school and home, the prognosis frequently is not good. No matter how well intentioned they are, schools seldom can assume the family's nurturing role to overcome the effects of a dysfunctional milieu that affects a student's life for 18 hours each day.

A student's acculturation also is of great importance. Attitudes and values, especially in the early years, are shaped by the family. These attitudes and values have an important relationship to success in school and later life. Beliefs about the worth of schooling, the relationship between effort and outcome, and the ability to overcome adversity and succeed are all important to school success. Culturally determined attitudes about gender roles can have negative effects when they limit a girl's or young woman's educational options, when they restrict the respect of a boy or young man for a woman teacher, and so forth. Willingness to take risks, to trust and cooperate with a relatively unfamiliar adult, and to give substantial effort to tasks similarly influence school performance. Finally, a student's working knowledge of the public culture (societal mores and values, standard American English, and fund of general and specific cultural information) all influence performance on school-related tasks.

Community and Friends   As a child grows older, community and friends play increasingly important roles. To the extent that they are dysfunctional, the student is at risk of failing in school and life. Two concerns are especially noteworthy. First is the safety of the community. For some students, the trip to school is literally a matter of life and death; murder is the leading cause of death in some age groups of children, and the risks are especially great for children of color. For some students, passing by crack houses, roving gangs of thugs ready to steal or extort everything from clothing to lunch money, and metal detectors at the school entrance is a daily occurrence. The second concern relates to the values instilled by community and friends. When a student's community and friends value education, the student has a better prognosis for success in school and life.

Physical Ability and Health   Sensory and physical limitations have serious implications for assessment and schooling. Vision, hearing, and physical handicaps have long-term implications for instruction and assessment; different instructional and assessment procedures may be used with such students. Acute health conditions can produce short-term sensory or physical limitations; for example, otitis media may result in temporary hearing loss.

A student's health and nutritional status can play an important role in the student's performances on a wide variety of tasks and academic development in general. Sick or malnourished children are apt to be lethargic, inattentive, and perhaps irritable. A temporary illness, such as the flu, can result in lost or reduced opportunities for learning. Moreover, children from economically impoverished backgrounds tend to be at greater risk for two reasons: Their physical environments may be more hazardous and their parents may lack the funds to secure medical treatment.

Developmental History

A person's current life circumstances are shaped by the events that make up his or her history of development. Deleterious events may have profound effects on physical and psychological development. Physical and sensory limitations may restrict a student's opportunity to acquire various skills and abilities. A history of poor health or poor nutrition may result in missed opportunities to acquire various skills and abilities. An individual's history of reward and punishment can shape what that person will achieve and how that person will react to others. In short, it is not enough to assess a student's current level of performance; those who assess must also understand what has shaped that current performance.

Extrapersonal Factors

In addition to the skills, characteristics, and abilities a pupil brings to any task, other factors affect the assessment process. How another person interprets or reacts to various behaviors or characteristics can determine whether an individual will even be assessed. For example, some teachers do not understand that a certain amount of physical aggression is typical of young children or that verbal aggression is typical of older students. Such teachers may refer normally aggressive children for assessment because they have interpreted aggression as a symptom of some underlying problem.

The theoretical orientation of the diagnostician also plays an important part in the assessment process. Diagnosticians' backgrounds and training may predispose them to look for certain types of pathologies. Just as Freudians may look for unresolved conflicts and behaviorists may look for antecedents and consequences of particular behaviors, diagnosticians may let their own theoretical orientation color their interpretation of particular information.

Finally, the conditions under which a student is observed or the conditions under which particular behaviors are elicited can influence that student's performance. For example, the level of language used in a question or the presence of competing stimuli in the immediate environment can affect a pupil's responses.

Decision Making

Diagnosticians reach an understanding of a student by integrating information about current performance with information about current life circumstances and developmental history. They try to make sure that their understanding is not tainted by subjectivity or personal values and beliefs. Combined with their knowledge of appropriate practices and legal requirements, their understanding guides decision making and predictions about future performance. For example, a decision to classify a student as exceptional is reached when the assessor makes a judgment that, when all things are considered, the student "fits" a particular category. Obviously, such a decision requires thorough knowledge of the criteria that define a category, in addition to detailed knowledge of the student and that student's current life circumstances.

ASSESSMENT CONCERNS

Decisions in school frequently have important, and occasionally lifelong, consequences. The procedures for gathering data and conducting assessments are matters that are rightfully of great concern to the general public—both individuals directly affected by the assessments (that is, parents, students, and classroom teachers) and individuals indirectly affected (for example, taxpayers and elected officials). These matters are also of great concern to individuals and agencies that license or certify assessors to work in the schools. Finally, these matters are of great concern to the assessment community itself. For convenience, the concerns of these groups are discussed separately; however, the reader should recognize that many of the concerns overlap and are not the exclusive domain of one group or another. Thus, the final portion of this section discusses the social validity of an assessment in relationship to various groups.

Concerns of the General Public

The individuals who are affected by educational decisions are rightly concerned about assessment procedures. They want, and deserve, good decisions. However, any decision can have undesired consequences. Decision making creates "haves" and "have nots." Most people who take a test for a driver's license pass the test; some people fail the test and are denied driving privileges. College entrance tests determine admission for some students and exclusion for others. In the same way, decisions in special and remedial education have consequences. Some consequences are desired, such as extra services for students who are entitled to special education. Other consequences are unwanted, such as denial of special education services or diminished self-esteem resulting from a disability label. Moreover, the desirability of some decisions varies depending on the student; for example, a decision that a child is eligible for special education as a mentally retarded student may be greeted enthusiastically by some parents but roundly rejected by other parents. Concerns of laypeople generally surface when the educational decisions have undesired consequences and are viewed as undemocratic, elitist, or just unfair.

Fairness

Fairness is an imprecise concept psychometrically and legally. It is probably best viewed as a marker for a class of conditions and situations in which the outcomes are thought to be disadvantageous, inaccurate, or wrong. Thus, issues of fairness usually imply dissatisfaction with an outcome. Allegations of unfair procedures might focus on any of the following complaints.

Lack of Opportunity Equal opportunity to learn is a complex and often highly charged issue. The issue is not whether a student lacks skill or the fairness of an assessment to ascertain what skills a student does and does not possess. The issue is the meaning of absent skills and information. When a student lacks information and skill because of restricted or different opportunities to learn, inferences about what that lack of information or skill means must be made with the greatest of care. For example, tests of intelligence assume that test takers have comparable opportunity to acquire the information and concepts elicited. When a student has not had that opportunity, inferences about intelligence are dubious. Lack of opportunity probably has as many causes as any social malady. The following list is not intended to be exhaustive, but illustrative.

- *Indequate District Resources.* In most states, the costs of education are borne largely by local school districts, which rely on property taxes. Because the assessed value of property located within district boundaries varies from district to district, some districts have larger tax bases than others. Thus, the same rate of taxation produces less revenue in poor districts than in richer districts. Moreover, poorer districts usually tax at much higher rates while generating less revenue than richer districts. Limited district resources translate directly into lost opportunities for students: teachers with emergency certificates; curriculum narrowing, resulting in the lack of enrichment or advanced courses; old materials; lack of equipment, such as computers or shops; and so forth.
- *Inadequate Instruction.* Teachers or the district's curriculum may not cover essential content, leading students to be tested on material and concepts never taught or inadequately taught. Or, teachers may not be able to engage their students in meaningful instruction.
- *Student Deficiencies.* Through no fault of their own, students may be unable to take advantage of adequate resources. For example, acute or chronic illness may restrict a student's opportunity to learn material.
- *Inadequate Home Supervision.* Parents may not (1) ensure that children get enough sleep, (2) limit television time, (3) encourage completion of homework, or (4) stress the value of education.

Ethnic and Gender Bias   Related to questions of opportunity are issues of ethnic, racial, and gender fairness. Although we struggle to achieve a society in which the accomplishments of all individuals are valued, not all groups have been treated fairly. The issue of a fair assessment for an individual from a minority group has a long history in the law, philosophy, and education. Three aspects of the issue are particularly relevant to this section of this book. First is the question of representation of individuals from diverse backgrounds in assessment materials. Test materials should present people of color and women in nonstereotypic roles and situations. It is widely believed that failure to do this has a chilling effect on students of color and young women and girls. Second is the issue of experiential opportunities of individuals from diverse backgrounds to acquire the tested skills, information, and values. To the extent that students of color and young women and girls undergo different acculturation, differences in experiential background should be accounted for. For example, tests should have an equal number of questions that are more advantageous for males and questions that are more advantageous for females. Or, test makers could delete questions that elicit pronounced differences in results between males and females or among members of culturally diverse groups. Third, the language and concepts describing students of color and women and girls should be empowering and not racist or sexist.

Subjective Scoring   It is frequently thought to be inappropriate to assess when the criteria for scoring student responses are subjective. Although students who receive the benefit of subjective scoring may not complain, assessors should be prepared to defend an indefensible position when questioned by students who are penalized by subjective scoring procedures. Most people would have trouble accepting scoring criteria that cannot be explicated; for example, a teacher might say to a student that this is a "B" paper without being able to explain how the paper differed from an "A" paper. A subjective criterion of "I know one when I see one" is seldom acceptable to people who have not produced "one." Similarly, when individuals with the same background and qualifications as the assessor reach different judgments about a student's work, that judgment is seldom satisfactory to students who receive lower grades. For example, when every other professor in the department uses one definition of a behavioral objective and Professor Smith uses a different definition, students who produce objectives that meet the wider definition may argue the correctness of their objectives should Professor Smith consider them wrong. Finally, if criteria for scoring are not explicit and objective, marking student answers wrong can lead to accusations of gender, racial, or ethnic discrimination.

Unequal Treatment   Students and parents expect marking standards to be applied consistently. Perhaps no situation is more troubling than when two students receive different scores for essentially the same product. When no cheating is suspected, one would expect student work to be marked uniformly.

Unfair Comparisons   People are frequently sensitive about the people to whom they (or their children) are compared. Thus, comparison groups should be appropriate. It would be inappropriate to compare an eight-year-old's elapsed time in a 100-meter dash to that of a sixteen-year-old. Moreover, comparative evaluations should make logical sense. For example, high school and college students frequently complain when examinations are graded on a curve because this practice requires that some students get lower grades. In the worst case, even students who knew the material well could (possibly) receive a poor grade. Finally, comparisons should take into account issues of diversity. Years ago, test publishers frequently excluded people of color from comparison groups used to establish norms; white people were apparently thought to be all people. Such comparisons failed to take into account the potential impact of cultural differences associated with racial differences. Today, most test authors and publishers have moved beyond such simplistic conceptualizations of comparison groups and included individuals from all of the larger minority groups in the United States. Nonetheless, even these more broadly representative norms may be unsuitable for use with students who are members of smaller minority groups that make up 1 percent of the population or less. When testing students from numerically small minorities that differ substantially in acculturation, there is no simple answer to the question of whether to make normative comparisons. In some cases where no inferences are made about underlying ability (for example, oral reading), normative comparison might be legitimate. In other cases (for example, in the assessment of intelligence or adaptive behavior), such comparisons are probably unwise.

Face Validity

An evaluation procedure should bear a logical relationship to the decision that is to be made. Although there is much more to valid assessment than the mere appearance of the test (see Chapter 8), what is being asked should make intuitive sense to the test taker or parents. For example, an employment test should obviously have something to do with work to be done by the new employee. In the same way, school tests should be authentic in that they should measure outcomes sought by the school.

Concerns of Certification Boards

Certification and licensure boards establish standards to ensure that assessors are appropriately qualified to conduct assessments, and these boards also sanction professionals for practicing beyond their competence. Test administration, scoring, and interpretation require different degrees of training and expertise, depending on the kind of test being administered and the degree of interpretation required to obtain meaning from the test taker's performance. Although most teachers could readily administer or learn to administer group intelligence and achievement tests as well as classroom assessments of achievement, a person must have considerable training to score and interpret most individual intelligence and personality tests. Therefore, all states certify teachers and psychologists who work in the schools on the basis of formal training and sometimes the demonstration of competence.

When pupils are tested, we should be able to assume that the person doing the testing has adequate training to administer the test correctly. We also should be able to assume that the tester can establish rapport with pupils, because students generally perform best in an atmosphere of trust and security. We further assume that the tester knows how to administer the test correctly. Testing consists of standardized presentation of stimuli. To the extent that the person giving the test does not correctly present the questions or materials, the obtained scores lose interpretability. We also assume that the person who administers a test knows how to score the test. Correct scoring is a prerequisite to the attainment of a meaningful picture of a student. Finally, we assume that accurate interpretations can and will be made.

Obviously, professionals should administer only the tests they are qualified to administer. Too often, unfortunately, we hear of people with no training in individual intelligence testing who nonetheless administer individual intelligence tests; or, we see people with no formal training in personality assessment administering or interpreting personality tests. Such tests may look easy enough to give; however, the correct administration, scoring, and interpretation are complex. Because tests are so often used to make decisions that will affect a child's future, this assumption of a skilled observer or tester is especially important.

Concerns of Assessors

Although those responsible for making educational decisions are also concerned with fairness and the appearance of valid testing, their concerns are generally more precise and detailed. There are four generally held areas of concern: accuracy, generalizability, meaning, and utility.

Accuracy

Accuracy is rightly considered a property of the diagnostician. Observations should not distort or incorrectly represent reality—diagnosticians must see what is there. No matter what form assessment takes, the diagnostician must always categorize a student's behavior or products. For example, in classifying behavior, an observer might ask the question "Did Bob hit Harry?" In this case, the diagnostician uses explicit or implicit criteria to make a judgment about Bob's behavior; that is, the diagnostician has a definition of "hit" and decides if Bob's behavior matches that definition. Similarly, when a diagnostician tests Bob, Bob's responses are classified as correct, partially correct, or incorrect; that is, the diagnostician has a definition of "correct" and decides if Bob's response matches that definition.

Inaccuracies occur in assessment because a diagnostician has applied criteria incorrectly or inconsistently and, therefore, has made decisions that are in error. Errors occur when a diagnostician allows a definition to drift or change over time or loses focus or objectivity. The situation in which observations are made has a substantial impact on their accuracy. For example, accuracy can be jeopardized when the behavior is difficult to observe, when there are too many behaviors to observe, when the decision rules are too complex, or when the definition of behavior is unclear or insufficiently detailed. As will be discussed in Chapter 7, it is possible to estimate the accuracy of observations.

Generalizability

Seldom are educators and psychologists interested in a single behavior or response at one specific time, in one context. Usually, diagnosticians want to generalize a student's performance along three dimensions: domain, times, and settings.

Generalization to a Larger Domain   Usually, diagnosticians want to generalize from a student's performance on a few questions to that student's performance on all other similar items. For example, when a student is given a math quiz containing ten multiplication facts, the teacher would like to infer that student's knowledge of all multiplication facts. To allow generalization to other related performances, the sample of behavior must be sufficiently large. Moreover, the behavior sample must be representative of the domain. Thus, a teacher might be willing to generalize answering ten multiplication facts to general knowledge of multiplication facts but should be unwilling to infer skill in all facets of multiplication (such as solving problems with two multiplicands), because the sample is not representative of the entire domain.

Generalization to Other Times   In most cases, a diagnostician would like to assume that behavior observed on one occasion would be observed on similar future occasions because maturation and learning result in stable behavioral and cognitive changes. For example, if Harry knows ten multiplication facts today, we would like to assume that he will know those same facts tomorrow and next week. In this sense, every observation is a prediction. Although assessments are usually stable, they are not invariably stable. Luck is not stable; a student who makes a lot of lucky guesses today will probably not be so lucky tomorrow. Behaviors and skills that are emerging are unlikely to be stable. For example, a student who is learning consonant sounds will not consistently give the correct sound for a consonant until the information is mastered. Unusual conditions in the student being examined often produce unstable results. If Harry has a cold or otitis media, he may not do what he is capable of doing on a test. Similarly, unusual conditions in the assessment setting may produce unstable results. For example, if Harry is distracted during a test, his performance may not be indicative of what he usually can do.

Generalization to Other Settings   Just as assessors are concerned with generalization to larger domains and other times, they are also concerned with generalization to other settings. For example, if Jill reads accurately in school, we would like to assume that she can read materials of similar difficulty at home. When behavior and skills fail to generalize to other settings, teachers and psychologists frequently look for differences between the settings in an attempt to ascertain what conditions or stimuli functionally control the behavior.

Meaning

Implicit in the preceding discussion is the idea that accurately observed and generalizable behavior may have meaning beyond what is directly observed. For example, a child's completion of a human figure drawing may represent artistic ability, intellectual ability, various personality traits, or perceptual-motor skill. None of these constructs are observable but are inferred from behavior and products that are observable, and the inferences to be made vary, depending on the student's opportunity to learn.

Students all come to school with unique background experiences in educational, social, and cultural environments—background experiences that are inextricably intertwined with their school experiences. Diagnosticians often must try to unravel these relationships. One of the most common examples is when psychologists assess a student's intellectual ability. To some extent, all tests of intelligence measure cultural learning in some form (for example, language, general information, and social values). Moreover, the inference drawn from the results of intellectual testing is that students who have learned more than other students from comparable backgrounds have more ability to learn. However, when cultural backgrounds differ, differences in what has been learned cannot be attributed to the ability to learn. A simple example illustrates the problem. A child may be asked to name the four seasons of the year, and the correct (keyed) answer is "summer, fall, winter, and spring." However, in some parts of the country, many boys and girls associate seasons with hunting; thus, they might respond, "buck, doe, rabbit, and turkey." Their response, although not the keyed response, is not wrong; it represents different acculturation. A similar problem occurs when commercially prepared achievement tests are used. When a student's curriculum does not address tested information (or does not address it comprehensively), the student has not had comparable opportunity to learn that information; inferences about the student's ability to profit from instruction are, at best, tenuous. Finally, acculturation is a matter of experiential background rather than of gender, skin color, race, or ethnic background (although one's acculturation may be associated with any of these). When we say that a child's acculturation differs from that of the majority, we are saying the child's *experiential background* differs. It is that different experience, and not the child's ethnic origin, for example, that leads the child to respond differently from the children on whom the test was standardized.

Another way in which opportunity affects the meaning of a student's performance is when that student is disabled. Not only do students with disabilities frequently undergo different acculturation, but their sensory and physical limitations can have significant impact on tested performance. A test or an individual test item invariably measures an individual's ability to receive a stimulus and then express a response. Skill in the content area measured by a test cannot be measured accurately if it is beyond the capabilities of the student to meet the stimulus and response demands of a question. Common sense tells us that if a student cannot read directions or write responses, a test requiring these abilities is inappropriate. In such cases, the test measures inability in reading directions or writing answers rather than skill or ability in the content being assessed. A student with a severe visual disability may know the content of a written test but earn a low score because of visual impairment. A student without arms may know the content of the test but may not answer any questions correctly because of an inability to write. Similarly, students with communication disorders may know the answers to the questions a tester asks but may be unable (or unwilling) to respond to even the most sensitively administered individual test that requires oral answers. Children with physical or sensory handicaps may also perform more slowly than nonhandicapped children; a test that awards points for the speed as well as the accuracy of response would not be a valid test of such a child's mastery of content.

A major clue to the meaningfulness of a test is the presence of individuals of different backgrounds and abilities in the standardization sample. When students from diverse backgrounds are included, test authors have the possibility of discovering if their test materials are meaningful (as well as unbiased) for children from a variety of backgrounds. When students from diverse backgrounds are included in the norms in the same proportions they are found in the general population, the derived scores are potentially meaningful.

Utility

Finally, diagnosticians are concerned about the usefulness of their assessment procedures. Several topics could be considered in a discussion of utility, but two—efficiency and sensitivity—are particularly relevant for our purposes.

Efficiency   Efficiency refers to the speed and economy of data collection. Diagnosticians try to gather a wide variety of general information, sacrificing some accuracy to delineate the problem, and then focus their efforts with more accurate and sensitive, but time-consuming, assessments. Usually highly accurate and specific information takes longer to accumulate than less accurate and less specific information. For example, group-administered tests are far more efficient than individually administered tests. However, a group test often provides substantially less information than an individual test does. Most group tests survey content rather than provide detailed information about a student's abilities and weaknesses. In addition, valuable qualitative information cannot be collected because of the format of group tests. The examiner may provide oral directions for younger children, but, for children beyond the fourth grade, the directions usually are written; the examiner typically cannot rephrase, probe, clarify, or prompt to elicit a student's best performance; the examiner cannot control the tempo and pace of the testing, or interrupt or terminate the test when a student becomes fatigued. The scoring of group-administered tests is also more efficient because students usually write or mark answers rather than make extended responses that take more time to score; indeed, because most group tests are machine scored, examiners seldom see a student's responses to individual questions. Similarly, teacher judgments or ratings of behavior are more efficient to collect than systematic behavioral observations; however, behavioral observations tend to be more accurate and are usually less subject to various biases.

Sensitivity   Sensitivity refers to the ability of an assessment procedure to detect small differences in students. Sensitivity is especially important when assessments are made to ascertain if students have made relatively small changes as a result of instruction or when diagnosticians want to make fine discriminations among test takers. For instruction to be both sensitive and efficient, the narrow range of development in which the student is functioning is assessed with sufficient items to discriminate. Thus, the teacher or psychologist must have an accurate idea of where a student currently functions.

Social Validity of Assessment

Social validity refers to consumers' access to and satisfaction with the assessment procedures. Three classes of consumers are relevant in this discussion: parents and students, diagnosticians, and school administrators.

Parents and Students

For parents and students, social validity generally translates into issues of access and disposition. *Access* is a general term that refers to the availability of the assessment. For example, can parents and students get to the physical location in which the assessment is to be conducted? Is the assessment scheduled at a convenient time? Because of the large number of families with a single parent or in which both parents work, finding a convenient time and location often means that teachers and psychologists must work outside of normal school hours. *Disposition* is a general term that refers to the willingness of students or parents to complete the assessment. For students this means giving their best efforts during assessment; for parents this means cooperating during interviews, completing questionnaires, and participating in decision making.

Diagnosticians

For diagnosticians, social validity translates into issues of ease of administration and utility. If diagnosticians find a particular test or approach undesirable, it is less likely that they will use that approach. Many relatively worthwhile tests stay on the shelf because they are very difficult to administer or score. Others are not used because school personnel do not like the test items, format, or some other aspect of the test. Still others are not used because school personnel believe the measures provide meaningless or useless information.

School Administrators

For administrators, the acceptability of an assessment procedure often becomes an issue of money and risk management. A key responsibility of administrators is to manage money. Thus, when two assessment procedures produce comparable information, the less expensive one (in terms of time and cost) is preferred. Thus, procedures that result in fewer completed assessments or assessments that require overtime pay for diagnosticians are typically not used if there are comparable procedures that do not make such demands on resources. Similarly, if an assessment procedure increases the risk of litigation or due process proceedings, it is less likely to be used than procedures with minimal risk.

SUMMARY

When a student is experiencing difficulty in school, the instruction that student has received is assessed to ascertain the probable cause of that student's difficulties. A curriculum is inappropriate when it is too easy or too hard; instruction can be ineffective because of poor classroom management (lack of organization, disruptive behavior, poor transitioning, and so forth) or poor learning management (lack of opportunity for student practice, lack of feedback, failure to teach for higher-level thinking skills, and so forth). Students who experience difficulties and have had inadequate instruction should be given appropriate instruction before it is assumed that they themselves are the root of the problem.

When instruction is deemed appropriate, the learners themselves are assessed. A variety of information from multiple sources is usually collected or pulled together from existing data. This information may take the form of systematic or nonsystematic observations, interviews, rating scales, judgments of other professionals, and tests. Student performances may be evaluated by comparing them to the performances of other students or to an absolute standard (such as a criterion of 90 percent correct). This information is used to make predictions about students either in their current situation or in some alternative (therapeutic) situation. A variety of factors are considered in reaching a prognosis: family situation, community ties and friendships, the student's physical ability and health, and developmental history.

Because the process of assessment is quite complex and educational decisions frequently have lifelong consequences, people are rightfully concerned about the entire process. Parents and the general public are frequently concerned about fairness, equal opportunity, ethnic and gender bias, and the appearance of proper assessment procedures. Individuals charged with overseeing the qualifications of those conducting assessments are rightfully concerned about diagnostician qualifications and training. And diagnosticians themselves are concerned about the accuracy, generalizability, and meaning of the information they collect to facilitate decision making.

STUDY QUESTIONS

1. It is assumed that people who give tests to students are adequately trained to do so. What broad skills should a qualified assessor have? What happens when people who do not have these competencies assess students?

2. How might you evaluate the extent to which the students you assess have acculturation comparable to that of those in a test's norm group?
3. Differentiate between an observation and an inference and give two examples of each.
4. Prior to testing, from what sources might an examiner wish to gather information to begin understanding the nature and context of a student's problem?
5. Differentiate between norm-referenced and criterion-referenced tests and give an advantage of each.
6. Lupe's parents are migrant workers who have just moved into the area. Lupe is enrolled in second grade a few weeks before the annual standardized achievement tests are administered. The decision is made to let her take the tests in Mr. Peno's room, although he is not her teacher, since he speaks Spanish (the language that Lupe speaks at home). Is this sufficient to ensure test validity for Lupe? Defend your answer.

ADDITIONAL READING

Boehm, A., & Weinberg, R. A. (1987). *The classroom observer: A guide for developing observation skills.* New York: Teachers College Press.

Christenson, S. L., & Ysseldyke, J. E. (1989). Assessing student performance: An important change is needed. *Journal of School Psychology, 27,* 409–426.

Deno, S. L. (1985). Curriculum-based measurement: The emerging alternative. *Exceptional Children, 15(3),* 219–232.

Deno, S. L. (1986). Formative evaluation of individual school programs: A new role for school psychologists. *School Psychology Review, 15(3),* 358–374.

Fuchs, L. S., & Fuchs, D. (1986). Linking assessment to instructional interventions: An overview. *School Psychology Review, 15(3),* 318–323.

Germann, G., & Tindal, G. (1985). An application of curriculum-based assessment: The use of direct and repeated measurement. *Exceptional Children, 52(3),* 244–265.

Howell, K. W. (1986). Direct assessment of academic performance. *School Psychology Review, 15(3),* 324–335.

Lentz, F. E., & Shapiro, E. S. (1986). Functional assessment of the academic environment. *School Psychology Review, 15(3),* 346–357.

Marston, D., & Magnusson, D. (1985). Implementing curriculum-based measurement in special and regular education settings. *Exceptional Children, 52(3),* 266–276.

Newland, T. E. (1973). Assumptions underlying psychological testing. *Journal of School Psychology, 11*, 316–322.

Newland, T. E. (1980). Psychological assessment of exceptional children and youth. In W. Cruickshank (Ed.), *Psychology of exceptional children and youth.* Englewood Cliffs, NJ: Prentice-Hall.

Semmell, M. I., & Thiagarajan, S. (1973). Observation systems and the special education teacher. *Focus on Exceptional Children, 5*, 1–12.

Shapiro, E. S. (1987). *Behavioral assessment in school psychology.* Hillsdale, NJ: Erlbaum.

Shapiro, E. S. (1989). *Academic skills problems: Direct assessment and intervention.* New York: Guilford Press.

Shapiro, E. S., & Kratochwill, T. R. (Eds.) (1988). *Behavioral assessment in schools: Conceptual foundations and practical applications.* New York: Guilford Press.

Ysseldyke, J. E., & Christenson, S. L. (1987). Evaluating students' instructional environments. *Remedial and Special Education, 8*, 17–24.

Ysseldyke, J. E., & Shinn, M. (1981). Psychoeducational evaluation: Procedures, considerations, and limitations. In D. Hallahan & J. Kauffman (Eds.), *The handbook of special education.* Englewood Cliffs, NJ: Prentice-Hall.

Chapter 3

Legal and Ethical Considerations in Assessment

*M*uch of the practice of assessing students is the direct result of legislation, guidelines, and court cases. If you were to interview directors of special education in your area and ask them why students are assessed, they might initially tell you that students are assessed to provide information on how best to teach them. Pressed harder, these directors would probably tell you that students are assessed because assessment is required by law. They might also tell you that specific kinds of students (for example, minority students) are *not* assessed because in some instances such assessments have been forbidden by the courts. Federal laws mandate that students must be assessed before they are entitled to special education services. Such laws also mandate that there must be an individualized education plan for every student with a disability and that instructional objectives for each of these students must be derived from a comprehensive individualized assessment.

In this chapter we first examine legislation that has affected assessment. We then describe major court cases in which specific kinds of assessment activities have been prescribed and talk about some of the ethical standards on assessment that have been developed by professional associations. We close the chapter by reviewing guidelines for the collection, maintenance, and dissemination of pupil records.

Laws

Five laws have had important effects on assessment practices: Section 504 of the Rehabilitation Act of 1973 (Public Law 93-112); the Education for All Handicapped Children Act of 1975 (Public Law 94-142); the 1986 Amendments to the Education for All Handicapped Children Act (Public Law 99-457); the Individuals with Disabilities Education Act of 1990 (Public Law 101-476); and the Americans with Disabilities Act of 1992 (Public Law 101-336). In Table 3.1 we list the major provisions of these five laws.

Section 504 of the Rehabilitation Act of 1973

Section 504 of the Rehabilitation Act of 1973 (Public Law 93-112), which was finally adopted in 1977, prohibits discrimination against people with disabilities. The Act states:

> No otherwise qualified handicapped individual shall, solely by reason of his handicap, be excluded from the participation in, be denied the benefits of, or be subjected to discrimination in any program or activity receiving federal financial assistance.

Since states and school districts depend, at least in part, on receiving federal money in order to educate students with disabilities, most choose to comply with this mandate.

Most of the provisions of Section 504 were incorporated into and expanded in the Education for All Handicapped Children Act of 1975 and the Americans with Disabilities Act of 1992. Section 504 and the Americans with Disabilities Act are broader than the Education for All Handicapped Children Act because their provisions are not restricted to a specific age group or to education. Section 504 is the law most often cited in court cases involving employment of people with disabilities or appropriate education in colleges and universities for students with disabilities. Section 504 has been used to secure services for students with conditions not formally listed in the disabilities education legislation. For example, over the past five or six years Section 504 has been used to get services for students who have attention deficit disorders (ADD/ADHD), which are not classified as disabilities within the Individuals with Disabilities Education Act.

The Education for All Handicapped Children Act of 1975

Education is a responsibility of state rather than federal government. No provision of the U.S. Constitution mandates education. Yet every state has compulsory education laws, which require students to attend school. In 1975, the U.S. Congress passed a compulsory special education law, the Education for All Handicapped Children Act (often known by its congressional number, Public Law 94-142). Ballard and Zettel (1977) described that law as designed to meet four major purposes:

TABLE 3.1   **Major Federal Laws and Their Key Provisions**

Act	Provisions
Section 504 of the Rehabilitation Act of 1973 (Public Law 93-112)	It is illegal to deny participation in activities, benefits of programs, or to in any way discriminate against a person with a disability solely because of the disability.
	Individuals with disabilities must have equal access to programs and services.
	Auxiliary aids must be provided to individuals with impaired speaking, manual, or sensory skills.
Education for All Handicapped Children Act of 1975 (Public Law 94-142)	Students with disabilities have the right to a free, appropriate public education.
	Schools must have on file an individualized education plan for each studet with a disability.
	Parents have the right to inspect school records on their child. When changes are made in a student's educational placement or program, parents must be informed. Parents have the right to challenge what is in records or to challenge changes in placement.
	Students with disabilities have the right to be educated in the least restrictive educational environment.
	Students with disabilities must be assessed in ways that are considered fair and nondiscriminatory. They have specific protections.
1986 Amendments to the Education for All Handicapped Children Act (Public Law 99-457)	All rights of the Education for All Handicapped Children Act are extended to preschoolers with disabilities.
	Each school district must conduct a multidisciplinary assessment and develop for each preschool child with a disability an individualized family service plan (IFSP).
Individuals with Disabilities Education Act of 1992 (Public Law 101-476)	This act reauthorizes the Education for All Handicapped Children Act.
	Two new disability categories (traumatic brain injury and autism) are added to the definition of students with disabilities.
	A comprehensive definition of transition services is added.
Americans with Disabilities Act of 1992 (Public Law 101-336)	Discrimination on the basis of disability is prohibited in employment, services rendered by state and local governments, places of public accommodation, transportation, and telecommunication services.

1. To guarantee that special education services are available to children who need them
2. To ensure that decisions about providing services to students with disabilities are made in fair and appropriate ways
3. To set clear management and auditing requirements and procedures for special education at all levels of government
4. To provide federal funds to help states educate students with disabilities

Much of what happens in assessment is directly mandated by one of the four provisions of Public Law 94-142. These provisions are described in the following sections.

Individualized Education Plan (IEP) Provisions

Public Law 94-142 specifies that all students with disabilities have the right to a free, appropriate public education and that schools must have an individualized education plan (IEP) for each student with a disability. In the IEP, school personnel must specify the long-term and short-term goals of the instructional program. IEPs must be based on a comprehensive assessment by a multidisciplinary team. We stress here the fact that assessment data are collected for the purpose of helping team members specify the components of the IEP. The team must specify not only goals and objectives but also plans for implementing the instructional program. They must specify how and when progress toward accomplishment of objectives will be evaluated. Figure 3.1 (pages 58 and 59) is an example of an IEP for a student in a Minnesota school district. Note that specific assessment activities that form the basis for the plan are listed, as are specific instructional goals or objectives.

IEPs are to be formulated by a multidisciplinary team (child study team) meeting with the parents. Parents have the right to agree (or disagree) with the contents of the plan.

Protection in Evaluation Procedures (PEP) Provisions

Congress included a number of specific requirements in Public Law 94-142. These requirements were designed to protect students and help ensure that assessment procedures and activities would be fair, equitable, and nondiscriminatory. Specifically, Congress mandated eight provisions.

1. Tests are to be selected and administered so as to be racially and culturally nondiscriminatory.
2. To the extent feasible, students are to be assessed in their native language or primary mode of communication.

FIGURE 3.1   **An Individualized Education Program**

INDIVIDUALIZED EDUCATION PROGRAM

11/11/95
Date

Thompson   *J.*
STUDENT: Last Name   First   Middle
                                                                          5.3   8/4/85

School of Attendance   Home School   Grade Level   Birthdate/Age

School Address   School Telephone Number

Child Study Team Members

LD Teacher
Case Manager

Homeroom   *Parents*
Name   Title   Name   Title

Facilitator
Name   Title   Name   Title

Speech
Name   Title   Name   Title

Summary of Assessment Results

IDENTIFIED STUDENT NEEDS: *Reading from last half of*
DISTAR II – present performance level

LONG-TERM GOALS: *To improve reading achievement level by at*
least one year's gain. To improve math achievement to grade level.
To improve language skills by one year's gain.

SHORT-TERM GOALS: *Master Level 4 vocabulary and reading*
skills. Master math skills in basic curriculum. Master
spelling words from Level 3 list. Complete units 1-9 from
Level 3 curriculum.

MAINSTREAM MODIFICATIONS: _____

(continued)

Description of Services to Be Provided

Type of service	Teacher	Starting date	Amt. of time per day	OBJECTIVES AND CRITERIA FOR ATTAINMENT
SLD Level III	LD Teacher	11/11/95	2½ hrs	*Reading:* Will know all vocabulary through the "Honeycomb" level. Will master skills as presented through DISTAR II. Will know 123 sound-symbols presented in "Sound Way to Reading." *Math:* Will pass all tests at basic 4 level. *Spelling:* 5 words each week from Level 3 list. *Language:* Will complete units 1-9 of the grade 4 language program. Will also complete supplemental units from "Language Step by Step."

Mainstream classes	Teacher	Amt. of time per day	OBJECTIVES AND CRITERIA FOR ATTAINMENT
		3½ hrs	*Out-of-seat behavior:* Sit attentively and listen during mainstream class discussions. A simple management plan will be implemented if he does not meet this expectation. *Mainstream modifications of social studies:* Will keep a folder in which he expresses through drawing the topics his class will cover. Modified district social studies curriculum. No formal testing will be done. An oral reader will read text to him, and oral questions will be asked.

The following equipment, and other changes in personnel, transportation, curriculum, methods, and educational services will be made:

DISTAR II reading program spelling Level 3; "Sound Way to Reading" program; vocabulary tapes

Substantiation of least restrictive alternatives: *The planning team has determined the student's academic needs are best met with direct SLD support in reading, math, language, and spelling.*

Anticipated Length of Plan: __1 yr__ The next periodic review will be held: __May 1996__

☐ I do approve this program placement and the above IEP

☐ I do not approve this placement and/or the IEP

☐ I request a conciliation conference

_____
PARENT/GUARDIAN

_____
PRINCIPAL or Designee

3. Tests must have been validated for the specific purpose for which they are used.
4. Tests must be administered by trained personnel in conformance with the instructions provided by the test producer.
5. Tests used with students must include those designed to provide information about specific educational needs, and not just a general intelligence quotient.
6. Decisions about students are to be based on more than performance on a single test.
7. Evaluations are to be made by a multidisciplinary team that includes at least one teacher or other specialist with knowledge in the area of suspected disability.
8. Children must be assessed in all areas related to a specific disability, including—where appropriate—health, vision, hearing, social and emotional status, general intelligence, academic performance, communicative skills, and motor skills.

Least Restrictive Environment (LRE) Provisions

In writing the Education for All Handicapped Children Act, Congress wanted to ensure that, to the greatest extent appropriate, handicapped students would be placed in settings that would maximize their opportunities to interact with nonhandicapped students. Section 612(S)(B) states,

> To the maximum extent appropriate, handicapped children . . . are educated with children who are not handicapped, and that special classes, separate schooling, or other removal of handicapped children from the regular educational environment occurs only when the nature or the severity of the handicap is such that education in regular classes with the use of supplementary aids and services cannot be achieved satisfactorily.

The least restrictive environment provisions arose out of court cases in which state and federal courts had ruled that when two equally appropriate placements were available for a student with a disability, the most normal placement was preferred.

Due Process Provisions

In Section 615 of Public Law 94-142, Congress specified the procedures that schools and school personnel would have to follow to ensure due process in decision making. Specifically, when a decision affecting a student's educational environment is to be made, the student's parents or guardians must be given the opportunity to be heard and the right to have an impartial due process hearing to resolve conflicting opinions.

Schools must provide opportunities for parents to inspect the records that are kept on their children and to challenge material that they believe should not be included in those records. Parents have the right to have their child evaluated by an independent party and to have the results of that evaluation considered when psychoeducational decisions are made. In addition, parents must receive written notification before any education agency can begin an evaluation that might result in changes in the placement of students.

The 1986 Amendments to the Education for All Handicapped Children Act

In 1986 Congress passed a major set of amendments to the Education for All Handicapped Children Act, extending all rights and protections of the law to preschoolers with disabilities. The provisions of this set of amendments, called Public Law 99-457, require states to provide a free appropriate public education to children with disabilities ages 3 through 5 by school year 1990–1991. In addition, these amendments provide grants to states so that they can offer interdisciplinary educational services to infants and toddlers with disabilities and their families. Thus, states now have a significant incentive to serve children with disabilities from birth through age 2. This bill also expands Public Law 94-142 by requiring that noneducational federal, state, and local resources and services be made available to all children with disabilities. Federal or state-funded agencies other than schools can no longer argue that they cannot provide services to children if the services can be provided by schools.

Public Law 99-457 specifies that each school district must use a multidisciplinary assessment to develop an individualized family service plan (IFSP) for each child. The IFSP must include

- A statement of the child's present level of cognitive, social, speech and language, and self-help development
- A statement of the family's strengths and needs related to enhancing the child's development
- A statement of the major outcomes expected for the child and family
- Criteria, procedures, and timelines for measuring progress
- A statement of the specific early intervention services necessary to meet the unique needs of the child and family, including methods, frequency, and intensity of service
- Projected dates for initiation and expected duration of services
- The name of the person who will manage the case
- Procedures for transition from early intervention into a preschool program

The Individuals with Disabilities Education Act (IDEA)

The Individuals with Disabilities Education Act of 1992 (IDEA) (Public Law 101-476) is a reauthorization of Public Law 94-142. Congress renamed the Education for All Handicapped Children Act and reaffirmed a national intent to support alternative education for students with special learning needs. To reflect contemporary practices, Congress replaced references to "handicapped children" with "children with disabilities." Two new disability categories (autism and traumatic brain injury) were added to the definition of "children with disabilities" and a comprehensive definition of "transition services" (services to ensure smooth movement from school to post-school activities) was added. The law also specified that schools must develop individual transition plans for students who are 16 years of age or older.

The Americans with Disabilities Act (ADA)

The purpose of the Americans with Disabilities Act of 1992 (ADA) (Public Law 101-336) is to extend to people with disabilities civil rights equal to those guaranteed without regard to race, color, national origin, gender, and religion through the Civil Rights Act of 1964. ADA prohibits discrimination on the basis of disability in employment, in the provision of services by state and local governments, in places of public accommodation, in the provision of transportation, and in the provision of telecommunication services, such as phones. The ADA says that employers cannot discriminate against individuals with disabilities. Employers must use employment application procedures (including assessments) that enable individuals with disabilities to apply for jobs. In making decisions about whom to hire, promote, or discharge, employers are not allowed to take into account a person's disability. Individuals with disabilities should not be paid differently than others, they have the same rights to job training, and they are to have the same privileges of employment as others.

COURT CASES

Several major court cases preceded passage of Public Law 94-142, and it has been argued that the court cases led Congress to pass that law (Bersoff, 1979). Many issues were contested. In the mid-1960s, a suit was brought against the Washington, D.C. schools on behalf of black students, who were assigned in disproportionate numbers to lower-ability groups or tracks. The chief issue was the fairness of using ability and achievement tests to assign students to groups or tracks. Judge Skelly Wright ruled against tests:

> The evidence shows that the method by which track assignments are made depends essentially on standardized aptitude tests which, although given on a system-wide basis, are completely inappropriate for use with a large segment of the student body. Because these tests are standardized primarily on and are relevant to a white middle-class group of students, they produce inaccurate and misleading test scores when given to lower-class and Negro students. (*Hansen v. Hobson*, 1967, p. 514)

After the ruling in *Hansen v. Hobson,* both ability grouping and standardized testing came under intense judicial scrutiny. Repeatedly, plaintiffs have argued that the use of standardized ability and achievement tests results in disproportionate placement of poor and minority students both in lower educational tracks and in special education. Judges have most often, although not always, ruled in favor of plaintiffs.

Another important court case, *Tinker v. Des Moines Independent Community School District,* set the stage for legislation and later litigation. Although this case had nothing to do with assessment, it furthered the notion of civil rights for all students that underlies laws that do address assessment. The issue it addressed was whether students had the right to wear black armbands to protest U.S. involvement in the Vietnam War. The court ruled that children are persons under the Constitution, have civil rights independent of their parents, and do not lose those civil rights when they attend school.

In 1972, in *Mills v. Board of Education,* the court asserted the rights of students to a due process hearing prior to exclusion from school, the right of handicapped students to an appropriate education, and the unconstitutionality of the exclusion of handicapped students from said education. Three points are important:

1. Exclusion of students labeled as behavior problems, mentally retarded, emotionally disturbed, or hyperactive is unconstitutional.
2. Any student with a disability has the right to a "constructive education" including appropriate specialized instruction.
3. Due process of law requires a hearing prior to exclusion, termination, or classification into a special program.

Two major court cases addressed misclassification of students as disabled. In both cases a consent agreement was reached: The cases were settled out of court when schools agreed to a number of actions. In *Diana v. the Board of Education* (1970), the California Department of Education agreed (1) to test all children whose primary language was not English in both their primary language and English, (2) to eliminate unfair verbal items from tests, (3) to reevaluate all Mexican-American and Chinese students enrolled in classes for the educable mentally retarded, using only nonverbal items and testing them in their native language, and (4) to develop IQ tests that reflect Mexican-American culture and are standardized only on Mexican-Americans. In *Covarrubias v. San Diego Unified School District* (1971), plaintiffs won the right to monetary damages as a result of being misclassified as disabled.

In 1971, the Pennsylvania Association for Retarded Children sued the Commonwealth of Pennsylvania for excluding mentally retarded students from public school programs. The state agreed to engage in extensive efforts to locate and assess all mentally retarded students in the state; all students placed in public school classes for the mentally retarded were also reevaluated.

The best known court decision after passage of Public Law 94-142 was a 1979 decision in response to a case that began in 1971, *Larry P. v. Riles*. The result of that case was threefold:

1. The state of California was forced to stop using, permitting the use of, or approving the use of any standardized intelligence test for identification of black educable mentally retarded children, or to stop placing them in special classes for the educable mentally retarded.
2. Defendants were ordered to monitor or eliminate disproportionate placement of black students in such classes in California.
3. Defendants were ordered to reevaluate every black child currently identified as an educable mentally retarded pupil without using standardized intelligence tests.

The issue of bias in assessment was not settled in the *Larry P.* case; it continues to be debated in the nation's courtrooms. *PASE v. Hannon* (1980) was a class action suit brought by Parents in Action on Special Education on behalf of "all black children who have been or will be placed in special classes for the educable mentally handicapped in the Chicago school system" (p. 2). Plaintiffs observed that whereas 62 percent of the enrollment of the Chicago public schools was black, black students comprised 82 percent of the enrollment in classes for the educable mentally handicapped.

The judge ruled in favor of the defendants, stating that he could find little evidence that the tests used to determine the children's placements were, in fact, biased. The ruling was clearly contrary to *Larry P.* Judge Grady addressed this fact:

> As is now obvious, the witnesses and the arguments which persuaded Judge Peckham [the judge in the *Larry P.* case] have not persuaded me. Moreover, I believe the issue in the case cannot properly be analyzed without a detailed examination of the items on the tests. It is clear that this was not undertaken in the *Larry P.* case. (p. 108)

Judge Grady found only eight items on the WISC-R and one item on the Stanford-Binet to be biased against black children. He further stated that poor performance on these items alone was not sufficient to result in the misclassification of black students as educable mentally handicapped.

In 1993 the *Larry P.* case was again revisited. This time parents of African-American students expressed the concern that forbidding school personnel from giving intelligence tests to African-American students had a discriminatory effect in that the students could not be considered eligible for services offered to students with learning disabilities. In California, identification of a student as learning disabled requires meeting specified criteria, one of which is a significant discrepancy between ability and achievement. Ability is to be measured with an intelligence test. The judge in this instance ruled in favor of the argument raised by the parents, and declared that it was once again permissible to administer intelligence tests to African-American students.

One other court case, in Mississippi, also addressed assessment practices with minority students. In February 1979, U.S. District Judge Orma Smith approved a consent decree settling the four-year-old case *Mattie T. v. Holladay* (Civil Action No. DC-75-31-S, N.D. Miss.). The case was filed on behalf of all school-aged children classified as disabled in Mississippi and charged the Mississippi Department of Education with failure to meet the requirements of Public Law 94-142. Under this decree the following agreements were reached:

1. Specific criteria were established for determining when a school district can place handicapped children in classes and buildings separate from regular education programs.
2. The state had to hire outside experts to evaluate and revamp the entire state procedure for classifying and placing students with disabilities.
3. A timetable was set for the assessment process.
4. Each school district had to identify children misclassified as mentally retarded and give them an opportunity to enroll in a compensatory education program.
5. School districts were prohibited from removing students from school for more than three days.
6. The Mississippi Department of Education was required to monitor local school districts' compliance with the law.

The most far-reaching requirement in this case was the one mandating a reworking of assessment procedures and timelines.

Clearly, courts can keep school personnel from testing students, or at least from giving specific kinds of tests to specific kinds of students. Moreover, the inverse is true: Courts can require school systems to administer tests. This was one of the outcomes of the *Pennsylvania Association for Retarded Children (PARC) v. Commonwealth of Pennsylvania* case, as school personnel were required to engage in massive efforts to locate mentally retarded students. It also was an outcome of *Frederick L. v. Thomas* (1976, 1977). In that action, the Philadelphia public schools were charged with failure to provide an appropriate education to students with learning disabilities and with serving too few learning disabled students. The Philadelphia schools were required to engage in massive screening and follow up with individual psychoeducational evaluations to identify all learning disabled students in the system.

In a recent court case in Louisiana (*Luke S. & Han S. v. Nix et al.*, 1981),[1] attorneys sued the Louisiana Department of Education for failure to evaluate re-

1. The names Luke S. and Han S. represent Luke Skywalker and Han Solo, characters from Star Wars. The attorneys for the plaintiffs selected these names because they felt they were taking on the Empire (the Louisiana Department of Education).

ferred children in a timely fashion. In a consent decree, the state agreed to increase the number of assessment personnel statewide and to assess larger percentages of students in accord with state assessment criteria and in a timely manner. In July 1983 a supplemental agreement was reached. It found that students were being assessed in a timely manner, but state criteria for appropriate assessment were not being followed. The state agreed to implement statewide training of all assessment personnel.

ETHICAL CONSIDERATIONS

Professionals who assess students have the responsibility to engage in ethical behavior. Many professional associations have put together sets of ethical standards to guide the practice of their members; many of these standards relate directly to assessment practices. Here we cite a number of important ethical considerations, borrowing heavily from the American Psychological Association's *Ethical Principles of Psychologists* (APA, 1981) and the National Association of School Psychologists' *Principles for Professional Ethics* (NASP, undated). We have not cited the standards explicitly, but we have distilled from them a number of specific ethical considerations.

Responsibility for the Consequences of One's Work

The assessment of students is a social act that has specific social and educational consequences. Those who assess students use assessment data to make decisions about the students, and the decisions can significantly affect an individual's life opportunities. Those who assess students must accept responsibility for the consequences of their work, and they must make every effort to be certain that their services are used appropriately. In short, they are committed to the application of professional expertise to promote improvement in the quality of life available to the student, family, school, and community. For the individual who assesses students, this ethical standard may mean refusing to engage in assessment activities that are desired by a school system but that are clearly inappropriate.

Recognizing the Boundaries of One's Competence

Those who are entrusted with the responsibility for assessing and making decisions about students have differing degrees of competence. Not only must professionals regularly engage in self-assessment to be aware of their limitations, they should also recognize the limitations of the techniques they use. For the individual this sometimes means refusing to engage in activities in areas in which one is not competent. It also means using techniques that meet recognized standards. And, it means engaging in the necessary continuing education to maintain high standards of competence.

As schools become increasingly diverse, it is necessary for professionals to demonstrate sensitivity in working with people from different cultural and linguistic backgrounds and with children who have different types of disabling conditions. Assessors should have experience working with students of diverse backgrounds and demonstrate competence in doing so, or they should refrain from assessing and making decisions about such students.

Confidentiality of Information

Those who assess students regularly obtain a considerable amount of very personal information about those students. It is expected that such information will be held in strict confidence. A general ethical principle held by most professional organizations is that confidentiality may be broken only when there is clear and imminent danger to an individual or society. Results of pupil performance on tests must not be discussed informally with school staff. Formal reports of pupil performance on tests must be released only with the permission of the persons tested or their parents or guardians.

Those who assess students are to make provisions for maintaining confidentiality in the storage and disposal of records. When working with minors or other persons who are unable to give voluntary informed consent, assessors are to take special care to protect these persons' best interests.

Adherence to Professional Standards on Assessment

A joint committee of the American Educational Research Association, the American Psychological Association, and the National Council on Measurement in Education publishes a document entitled *Standards for Educational and Psychological Testing*. These standards specify a set of requirements for test development and use. It is imperative that those who develop tests behave in accord with the standards and that those who assess students use instruments and techniques that meet the standards. In Parts 3 and 4 of this text we review commonly used tests and talk about the extent to which those tests meet the standards. We provide information to help test users make informed judgments about the technical adequacy of specific tests. There is no federal or state agency that acts to limit the publication or use of technically inadequate tests. Only by refusing to use technically inadequate tests will users force developers to improve them. Think about this: If you were a test developer, would you continue to publish a test that few people purchased and used? Would you make changes in a technically inadequate test that yielded a large annual profit to you or your firm if people continued to buy and use it the way it was?

Test Security

Those who assess students are expected to maintain test security. It is expected that assessors will not reveal to others the content of specific tests or test items. At the same time assessors must be willing and able to back up decisions that may adversely affect individuals with the test data on which those decisions are based.

PUPIL RECORDS: COLLECTION, MAINTENANCE, AND DISSEMINATION

Policies and standards for the collection, maintenance, and dissemination of information about children must balance two sometimes conflicting needs. Parents and children have a basic right to privacy; schools need to collect and use information about children (and sometimes parents) in order to plan appropriate educational programs. Schools and parents have a common goal: to promote the welfare of children. In theory schools and parents should agree on what constitutes and promotes a child's welfare, and in practice schools and parents generally do work cooperatively.

On the other hand, there have been situations in which there has been no cooperation or in which schools have operated against the best interests and basic rights of children and parents. School personnel have often flagrantly disregarded the rights to privacy of parents and children. Educationally irrelevant information about the personal lives of parents as well as subjective, impressionistic, unverified information about parents and children has been amassed by the schools. Parents and children have been denied access to pupil records, and therefore they have effectively been denied the opportunity to challenge, correct, or supplement those records. At the same time, schools have on occasion irresponsibly released pupil information to public and private agencies that had no legitimate need for or right to the information. Worse yet, parents and children were often not even informed that the information had been accumulated or released.

Abuses in the collection, maintenance, and dissemination of pupil information were of sufficient magnitude that the Russell Sage Foundation convened a conference in 1969 to deal with the problem. Professors of education, school administrators, sociologists, psychologists, professors of law, and a juvenile court judge participated in the conference to develop voluntary guidelines for the proper collection, maintenance, and dissemination of pupil data. Since then, the guidelines that were developed at the Russell Sage Foundation conference (Goslin, 1969) have been widely accepted and implemented.

In 1974, many of the recommended guidelines became federal law when the Family Educational Rights and Privacy Act (Public Law 93-380, commonly called the Buckley amendment) was enacted. The basic provisions of the act are quite simple. Any educational agency that accepts federal money (preschools, elementary and secondary schools, community colleges, and colleges and universities) must give parents the opportunity to inspect, challenge, and correct their children's records. (Students aged 18 or older are given the same rights in regard to their own records.) Also, educational agencies must not release identifiable data without the parents' written consent. Violators of the provisions of the Family Educational Rights and Privacy Act are subject to punishment; no federal funds are given to agencies found to be in violation of the law.

The remainder of this chapter deals with specific issues and principles in the collection, maintenance, and dissemination of pupil information. Our discussion draws on the issues raised by and the recommendations of the Russell Sage Foundation Conference Guidelines (hereafter referred to as RSFCG). The Buckley amendment is considered as it applies, as are specific provisions of the Education for All Handicapped Children Act and the Individuals with Disabilities Education Act.

Collection of Pupil Information

Schools collect massive amounts of information about individual pupils and their parents. As we said in Chapter 1, information can be used for a number of legitimate educational decisions: special assistance, referral, screening, exceptionality, eligibility, instructional planning, pupil evaluation, setting, and program evaluation decisions. A considerable amount of data must be collected if a school system is to function effectively in delivering educational services to children and in reporting the results of its educational programs to the various community, state, and federal agencies to which it may be responsible.

Classes of Information

The RSFCG delineated three classes of information that schools typically collect. The first class of information (category A) includes the basic, minimum information schools need to collect in order to operate an educational program. Category A data include identifying information (the child's and parents' names and address, the student's age, and so forth) as well as the student's educational progress (grades completed, achievement evaluations, attendance).

Category B data are test results and other verified information useful to the school in planning a student's educational program or maintaining a student "safely" in school. Some of the data that pertain to maintaining a student safely in school can be considered absolutely necessary. For example, having available medical and pharmacological information about severe allergic reactions such as a sensitivity to bee stings, special diets for children with certain chronic diseases such as diabetes, and unusual medical conditions such as hemophilia may mean the difference between life and death. Other category B data may not be absolutely necessary, but they are nonetheless clearly important in providing an appropriate educational program for a student. Intelligence test data are clearly relevant if the school places a student in a special program for the mentally retarded. Certain types of aptitude or ability data may be necessary if the school district attempts to differentiate instruction on the basis of differences in abilities. Systematic observations, counselor ratings, and various standardized test scores may be used in cases where a student has problems that are thought to interfere with school progress. Certain types of information about a family's background may be important in selecting and interpreting tests used for guidance and placement or in individualizing instruction.

Category C data include information that may be *potentially* useful. When we are gathering information, we often do not know whether a particular bit of information is important or should be followed up. Category C can be considered as the repository for unevaluated but potentially useful information until it can be considered category B information or until it is removed from the student's records.

Consent

According to the RSFCG, no data should be collected without the consent of parents or their agents. The RSFCG accept the notion of representational consent for the collection of category A information and certain types of category B data (for example, intelligence or aptitude tests). *Representational consent* means that consent to collect data is given by appropriately elected officials, such as the state legislature.

The RSFCG recommend that individual informed consent be obtained for the collection of information not directly relevant and essential to the education of particular children. Individual informed consent should be obtained in writing prior to the collection of category C data. The assumption underlying the notion of informed consent is that the parent (or pupil) is "reasonably competent to understand the nature and consequences of his decision" (Goslin, 1969, p. 17). Individual consent usually should be required for the collection of family information (religion, income, occupation, and so on), personality data, and other noneducational information.

In its section on procedural safeguards, the Education for All Handicapped Children Act (Public Law 94-142) mandates that written prior notice be given to the parents or guardians of a child whenever an educational agency proposes to initiate or change (or refuses to initiate or change) the identification, evaluation, or educational placement of the child or the provision of a free and appropriate education to the child. It further requires that the notice fully inform the parent, in the parent's native language, of all appeal procedures available. Thus, schools must inform parents of their right to present any and all complaints regarding the identification, evaluation, or placement of their child, their right to an impartial due process hearing, and their right to appeal decisions reached at a due process hearing, if necessary, by bringing civil action against a school district.

The collection of research data requires individual informed consent of parents. Various professional groups, such as the American Psychological Association and the National Association of School Psychologists, consider the collection of data without informed consent to be unethical; according to the Buckley amendment, it is *illegal* to experiment with children without prior informed consent. Typically, informed consent for research-related data collection requires that the pupil or parents understand (1) the purpose of and procedures involved in the investigations, (2) any risks involved in participation in the research, (3) the fact that all participants will remain anonymous, and (4) their option to withdraw from the research at any time.

Verification

Some distinctions must be made in terms of the quality of the information being collected. Verification is a key concept. *Verifying information* means ascertaining or confirming the information's truth, accuracy, or correctness. Depending on the type of information, verification may take several forms. For observations or ratings, verification means confirmation by another individual. For standardized test data, verification means conducting a reliable and valid assessment.[2]

Information that is not verified cannot be considered category A or B data. Unverified information can be collected, but every attempt should be made to verify such information before it is retained. For example, serious misconduct or extremely withdrawn behavior is of direct concern to the schools. Initial reports of such behavior by a teacher or counselor are typically based on unverified observations. The unverified information provides hints, hypotheses, and starting points for diagnosis. However, if the data are not confirmable, they should not be collected and must not be retained. Similarly, data from unreliable tests should, we believe, be considered unverified information unless other data are presented to confirm the results.

Maintenance of Pupil Information

The decision to keep test results and other information should be governed by three principles. First, the information should be retained only as long as there is a continuing need for it. In any event, only category A and category B data that are verified data of clear educational value should be retained. A pupil's school records should be periodically examined, and information that is no longer educationally relevant or no longer accurate should be removed. Natural transition points (for example, promotion from elementary school to junior high) should always be used to remove material from students' files.

The second major principle in the maintenance of pupil information is that parents have the right to inspect, challenge, and supplement student records.

---

2. The concepts of reliability and validity are defined and discussed in detail in Chapters 7 and 8.

The Russell Sage Foundation Conference Guidelines recommended that formal procedures should be established whereby a student or his or her parents might challenge the validity of any information contained in categories A or B (Goslin, 1969, p. 23). This recommendation presupposes that parents have access to the data.

Parents of children with disabilities and special gifts and talents have had the right to inspect, challenge, and supplement their children's school records for some time. The landmark right-to-education case (*Pennsylvania Association for Retarded Children v. Commonwealth of Pennsylvania*) not only won the guarantee of a free, public, appropriate educational program for all retarded children in Pennsylvania but also guaranteed parents the right to inspect and challenge the contents of their children's school records. The consent agreement that terminated this suit specified the right of parents to a due process hearing:

> The notice of the due process hearing shall inform the parent or guardian of his right . . . to examine before the hearing his child's school records including any tests or reports upon which the proposed action may be based, of his right to present evidence of his own. (71-42, Sec. 2f)

In Pennsylvania, the right to education and the right to a due process hearing before changes are made in educational placement have been extended to all exceptional individuals, including the gifted. After 1972, several other right-to-education suits were brought against other state departments of education.

Parents of all children won the right to inspect, challenge, and supplement their children's school records in 1974. The Buckley amendment brought the force of federal law to the RSFCG recommendations and the various right-to-education cases. No educational agencies receiving federal support may prevent parents (or persons 18 years of age or older) from (1) inspecting all official files and data related to their children or themselves, (2) challenging the content of such files, and (3) correcting or deleting inaccurate, misleading, or inappropriate information contained in the records.

In Public Law 94-142 the provisions of the Buckley amendment are again reiterated. Parents or guardians must be given the opportunity to examine all relevant records with respect to the identification, evaluation, and educational placement of the child and the free and appropriate public education of the child and the opportunity to obtain an independent evaluation of the child. Again, if parents have complaints, they may request an impartial due process hearing to challenge either the records or the school's decision regarding their child. The law specifies further that parents have the right to (1) be accompanied and advised by counsel and by individuals with special knowledge or training with respect to the problems of children with disabilities, (2) present evidence and confront, cross-examine, and compel the attendance of witnesses, (3) have a written or electronic verbatim record of such hearing, and (4) have written findings of facts and decisions.

The third major principle in the maintenance of pupil records is that the records should be protected from snoopers, both inside and outside the school system. In the past, secretaries, custodians, and even other students have had access, at least potentially, to pupil records. "Curious" teachers and administrators who had no legitimate educational interest had access. Individuals outside the schools, such as credit bureaus, have often found it easy to obtain information about former or current students. To make sure that only individuals with a legitimate need have access to the information contained in a pupil's records, the RSFCG recommend that pupil records be kept under lock and key. Adequate security mechanisms are necessary to ensure that the information in a pupil's records is not available to unauthorized personnel.

Dissemination of Pupil Information

Both access to information by officials and dissemination of information to individuals and agencies outside the school need to be considered. In both cases, the guiding principles are (1) the protection of pupils' and parents' rights of privacy and (2) the legitimate need to know of the person or agency to whom the information is disseminated.

Access Within the Schools

The Russell Sage Foundation conference recommended that category A and category B data may be released within the school district to school officials with a legitimate educational interest. Those desiring access to pupil records should sign a form stating why they need to inspect the records; a list of people who have had access to their child's files and the reasons why access was sought should be available to parents (Goslin, 1969). The provisions of the Buckley amendment correspond to the Russell Sage Foundation Conference Guidelines (Goslin, 1969):

> All persons, agencies, or organizations desiring access to the records of a student shall be required to sign a written form which shall be kept permanently with the file of the student, but only for inspection by the parents or student, indicating specifically the legitimate educational or other interest that each person, agency, or organization has in seeking this information. (Sec. 438, 4A)

When a pupil transfers from one school district to another, that pupil's records are also transferred. The Buckley amendment is very specific as to the conditions of transfer. When a pupil's file is transferred to another school or school system in which the pupil plans to enroll, the school must (1) notify the pupil's parents that the records have been transferred, (2) send the parents a copy of the transferred records if the parents so desire, and (3) provide the parents with an opportunity to challenge the content of the transferred data.

Access to Individuals and Agencies Outside the Schools

School personnel collect information about pupils enrolled in the school system for educationally relevant purposes. There is an implicit agreement between the schools and parents that the *only* justification for collecting and keeping any pupil data is educational relevance. However, because the schools have so much information about pupils, they are often asked for pupil data by potential employers, credit agencies, insurance companies, police, the armed services, the courts, and various social agencies. To divulge information to any of these sources is a violation of this implicit trust, unless the pupil (if over 18) or the parents request that the information be released. Note that the courts and various administrative agencies have the power to subpoena pupil records from schools. In such cases, the Buckley amendment requires that the parents be notified that the records will be turned over in compliance with the subpoena.

Except in the case of the subpoena of records or their transfer to another school district, the RSFCG recommend that no school personnel release *any* pupil information without the written consent of the parents. The Buckley amendment takes a similar position when it states that no educational agency may release pupil information unless "there is written consent from the student's parents specifying records to be released, the reasons for such release, and to whom, and with a copy of the records to be released to the student's parents and the student if desired by the parents" (Sec. 438, b2A). Although the Buckley amendment lists exceptions, such as applications for financial aid, the thrust of the law and of the Russell Sage Foundation Conference Guidelines is to control the dissemination of personal pupil information.

Communicating in Language the General Public Can Understand

Those who assess students have a responsibility to make certain that the information they disseminate is put in the hands of authorized persons and is used to help the individual assessed. Assessment findings are to be communicated in language readily understood by the school staff. In communicating written information, those who assess students must be certain that their interpretations of test results are clear and in a language easily understood so that the information may be used to the betterment of the student assessed.

SUMMARY

The practice of assessing students takes place in a social, political, and legal context. Much of assessment takes place because it is mandated by law. School personnel are required to assess students before declaring them eligible for special education services. The major piece of legislation that currently serves as a guide for assessment activities is the Individuals with Disabilities Education Act (Public Law 101-476). The law reauthorized the Education for All Handicapped Children Act of 1975 (Public Law 94-142), an act which included provisions specifying that schools must have individualized education plans for students, that students must be educated in least restrictive environments, and that students who are assessed have due process rights. The law also specified a number of ways in which students who are evaluated are to be protected.

Public Law 99-457, a set of amendments to the Education for All Handicapped Children Act, was enacted in 1986 to extend the right to an education to preschoolers with disabilities and to extend the right to noneducational federal, state, and local resources and services to all children with disabilities.

The practice of assessing students changes as courts define and set limits on that practice. We showed how assessment practices have changed as a function of specific court cases.

Those who assess students have certain ethical responsibilities. They are responsible for the consequences of their actions and for recognizing the limits of their competence. There are specific requirements for confidentiality of information obtained in assessment and for keeping the content of tests secure. Those who assess students should adhere to the professional standards outlined in *Standards for Educational and Psychological Testing*.

Schools are entrusted with the lives of children. Each day, decisions are made that are intended to be in the children's best interests. These decisions are based on both objective information and professional interpretation of that information. The schools must exercise their power over the lives of children very carefully. When school personnel collect data, they must make sure that the data are educationally relevant; their authority does not include the power to snoop and pry needlessly. The schools need latitude in deciding what information is educationally relevant, but the parents must have the right to check and halt the school's attempts to collect some types of information. Parents' informed consent to the collection of information about their children is basic to the family's right to privacy.

The schools should periodically examine all pupil records and destroy all information that is not of immediate or long-term utility or that has not been verified. The information that is retained must be guarded. Parents and students over 18 must be given the opportunity to examine records, to correct or delete information, and to supplement the data contained in files. Sometimes the release of information that has been gathered could be damaging or embarrassing to children and their families. Schools must not release data to outside agencies except under subpoena or with the written consent of parents or a pupil who is over 18. As in all areas of testing and data maintenance, common sense and common decency are required.

STUDY QUESTIONS

1. What were the major purposes of Public Law 94-142, the Education for All Handicapped Children Act of 1975?
2. What four things must be specified in an individualized education plan (IEP)?
3. How did the Individuals with Disabilities Education Act of 1992 update Public Law 94-142? What new provisions were added?
4. How might you go about deciding the extent to which a test was fair for use in making decisions about a specific student?
5. Identify two major court cases and describe the effect they have had on the practice of assessing students.
6. Under what circumstances is it ethically appropriate to divulge the scores that a client earned on a test?
7. What kinds of information on a student can one school send to another school? For which of these must the permission of the student or the student's parent or guardian first be obtained?

ADDITIONAL READING

American Educational Research Association, American Psychological Association, and National Council on Measurement in Education. (1985). *Standards for educational and psychological testing*. Washington, DC: American Psychological Association.

Bersoff, D. (1979). Regarding psychologists testily: Legal regulation of psychological assessment in the public schools. *Maryland Law Review, 39,* 27–120.

Clearinghouse on the Handicapped, Office of Special Education and Rehabilitative Services, U.S. Department of Education. (1988). *Summary of existing legislation affecting persons with disabilities*. Washington, DC: U.S. Government Printing Office.

Litigation and special education. (1986). *Exceptional Children, 52(4)*. (This special issue describes ten court cases in the field of special education, several of which are significant tests of policy and practice in the assessment of handicapped and potentially handicapped students.)

Rothstein, L. F. (1990). *Special education law*. White Plains, NY: Longman.

Sage, D. D., & Burrello, L. C. (1988). *Public policy and management in special education*. Englewood Cliffs, NJ: Prentice-Hall.

Smith, B. (Ed.) (1988). *Mapping the future for children with special needs: PL 99–457*. Iowa City: University of Iowa.

Ysseldyke, J. E., & Algozzine, B. (1995). *Introduction to special education.* Boston: Houghton Mifflin. (Chapter 3: Legal considerations in special education)

Ysseldyke, J. E., Algozzine, B., & Thurlow, M. L. (1992). *Critical issues in special education.* Boston: Houghton Mifflin. (Chapter 8: Legal issues in special education)

Zerkel, P., & Richardson, S. N. (1988). *A digest of Supreme Court decisions affecting education* (2nd ed.) Bloomington, IN: Phi Delta Kappa Educational Foundation.

PART 2

BASIC CONCEPTS OF MEASUREMENT

*P*art 2 deals with basic statistical and measurement concepts. Chapter 4 is intended for the person with little or no background in descriptive statistics; it contains a discussion of the major concepts necessary for understanding most of the remaining chapters in this part and later parts of the book. In Chapter 5 we discuss the scores typically used in norm-referenced and criterion-referenced assessment. The most frequently used scores in norm-referenced assessment compare a student to other students who make up the test norms. Of criterion-referenced scores (which are most often used in classrooms), the two types of scores that are most useful are percent correct (accuracy) and rate of correct responses (fluency). Chapter 6 discusses how normative samples are usually obtained and the important characteristics of individuals in these samples. Chapter 7 provides an introduction to reliability and is often the most difficult chapter for students. This chapter deals with the important concept that scores are fallible and with the amount of error associated with scores. In Chapter 8, the last chapter in this part of the text, we introduce the concept of test validity. Validity, the extent to which a test or other procedure produces results that assess what is intended by an examiner, is *the* most important and inclusive aspect of a test's technical adequacy.

Basic statistics and psychometric theory are the foundation of test development and use. Neither subject is easy to master, but both are important. The development and use of tests by people who lack understanding of either statistics or theory have resulted in many abuses in educational evaluation and decision making. This is the rationale for including Part 2. We realize that numbers and formulas often scare both beginning students and seasoned veterans. Yet, they lie at the heart of testing. Everyone who uses tests and test results must understand both in order to evaluate students fairly and intelligently.

The reader should bear in mind that many nuances and subtleties of basic statistics and measurement are not discussed, and no derivations or proofs are presented. We explain psychometric theory from a classical perspective and provide equations and computational examples to show how particular numbers are obtained as well as to provide material for a logical understanding of critical measurement concepts. Finally, we alert the reader that this text has many audiences, some of whom may have advanced understanding of other theories and statistical procedures that are clearly beyond the scope of this book. For example, some widely used tests are constructed using item-response (or latent trait) theory; we review these tests but provide no discussion of the underlying theory. Similarly, test authors and researchers frequently use advanced multivariate statistical procedures to validate tests; we occasionally mention these procedures, but we provide no statistical explanations. Thus, our emphasis in Part 2 and the remaining sections of this book is on the basic technical information that a consumer needs to understand in order to interpret most tests.

Chapter 4

Descriptive Statistics

W e use descriptive statistics to describe or summarize data. In testing, the data are scores: several scores on one individual, one score on several individuals, or several scores on several individuals. Descriptive statistics are calculated with the basic mathematical operations of addition, subtraction, multiplication, and division, as well as simple exponential operations (squares and square roots). Advanced knowledge of mathematics is not required, although many calculations are repetitive and tedious. Calculators and computers facilitate these calculations, and for many applications test authors provide tables of all of the pertinent descriptive statistics. This chapter deals with the basic concepts needed for an understanding of descriptive statistics. Specifically, it discusses scales of measurement, distributions, measures of central tendency, measures of dispersion, and measures of relationship (correlation).

SCALES OF MEASUREMENT

The ways in which data can be summarized depend on some characteristics of the scores that are to be described. With some types of scores, we can use all of the basic mathematical operations; with other types of scores, none of the basic mathematical operations can be used. The scale on which performances are measured determines how we can describe those performances. There are four scales of measurement: nominal, ordinal, ratio, and equal interval.[1]

Ordinal and equal-interval scales are the most frequently used scales in norm-referenced measurement. Nominal and ratio scales are seldom used. The four scales are distinguished primarily on the basis of the relationship between adjacent, or consecutive, values on the measurement continuum. An *adjacent value* in this case means a potential or possible value rather than an obtained or measured value. In Figure 4.1, which depicts a portion of a yardstick, the possi-

1. For a more complete discussion, see S. S. Stevens, "Mathematics, Measurement, and Psychophysics" in *Handbook of Experimental Psychology,* ed. S. S. Stevens, p. 23, (New York: Wiley, 1951).

ble values are any points between 2 inches and 6 inches, measured in intervals of eighths of an inch. Any two consecutive points (for instance, 3⅛ inches and 3¼ inches) are adjacent values. Any two points on the scale that have values intervening between them (for instance, 3⅛ inches and 4¼ inches) are *not* adjacent points. We could, of course, think of adjacent intervals larger than ⅛ of an inch. For example, adjacent 1-inch intervals could be considered, and the adjacent points would then be 1 inch, 2 inches, and so on.

Nominal Scales

On *nominal scales*, adjacent values have no inherent relationship. Nominal scales name values on the scale. For example, at the local ice cream shop, ice cream flavor is a variable. The specific values that this variable can take are names: chocolate, strawberry, tutti-frutti, mocha almond fudge, and others. The first flavor listed is not better than the second flavor listed. Banana sherbet is not better than orange sherbet (although many may prefer one or the other). In education and psychology, we occasionally use nominal scales to describe attributes (for example, sex or eye color), geographic region in which a person resides (for example, the Pacific Northwest), educational classification (for example, learning disabled or emotionally disturbed), and so forth. However, few, if any, test scores are nominal.

Because values on a nominal scale represent names, the various mathematical operations cannot be performed with these values. For example, we cannot average banana and orange sherbet. Mathematically all we can do with nominal scales is determine the frequency of each value (for example, how many times orange sherbet is chosen).

An occasionally confusing aspect of nominal scales is that numbers may be used as names. For example, numbers on athletic shirts identify players, in the

FIGURE 4.1   **Adjacent and Nonadjacent Values**

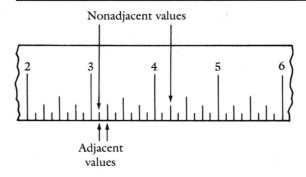

same way that social security numbers identify people. When numbers are used to name people or objects and when these numbers have no inherent relationship to one another in terms of their adjacent values, the scale of measurement is a nominal scale. An obvious illustration of a nominal scale is the assignment of numbers to football players. A number is used simply to refer to an individual player. The player who wears number 80 is not necessarily a better player than 70 or 77; 80 is just a different player. Numbers 68 and 69, which are typically thought of as adjacent values, have no relationship to each other on a nominal scale; there is no implied rank ordering in the numbers worn on the shirts. It would not make any sense to add up shirt numbers or to compute the players' average social security number to determine which athletic team is the best.

Ordinal Scales

Ordinal scales order things from better to worse or from worse to better. A scale may be ordinal whether or not numbers are used to designate locations on the scale. For example, locations on ordinal scales are sometimes designated by names. All adjectival comparisons are ordinal: good, better, best; tall, taller, tallest; poor, worse, worst, and so forth. Classroom teachers may use other adjectives (for example, novice, intermediate, and expert) to name the values of a variable. Thus, an ordinal scale may have as few as two or three adjectives as values, one of which is assigned to each individual being ranked. Such names always imply the quantitative relationship of better or worse. More frequently, ordinal scales use numbers to designate locations of the variable. Ordinal numbers (that is, first, second, third, and so on) designate locations; for example, ordinal numbers are used to indicate standing in the graduating class, the top twenty football or basketball teams, the winner and finalists in the Miss America Contest, and so forth. Thus, ordinal values can be assigned all along the continuum (for example, class standing) or only in some parts of the continuum (for example, the top twenty teams); in the latter case, there is an implicit last rank (loser, not top twenty, and so forth).

Ordinal scales order or rank information or scores on some kind of continuum. Adjacent numbers on an ordinal scale indicate higher or lower value. A simple example of an ordinal scale is a ranking of persons from first to last for some trait or characteristic, such as weight or test scores. Suppose Ms. Smith administers a test to her arithmetic class, in which twenty-five students are enrolled. The test results are reported in Table 4.1. Column 1 gives the name of each student, and column 2 contains each child's raw score. Column 3 contains the ranking of the twenty-five students; the children are listed in decreasing rank order from the student with the "best" performance to the student with the "worst" performance. It is important to note that the difference in each student's raw score and the raw score of the immediately preceding student is not the same as the difference in rank for the two. Differences in adjacent *ranks* do

TABLE 4.1   **Ranking of Students in Ms. Smith's Arithmetic Class**

Student	Raw-Score Total	Rank	Difference Between Score and Next Higher Score
Bob	27	1	0
Lucy	26	2	1
Sam	22	3	4
Mary	20	4	2
Luis	18	5	2
Barbara	17	6	1
Carmen	16		
Jane	16	8	1
Charles J.	16		
Hector	14		
Virginia	14		
Manuel	14		
Sean	14	13	2
Joanne	14		
Jim	14		
John	14		
Charles B	12		
Jing-Jen	12	18	2
Ron	12		
Carole	11	20	1
Bernice	10	21	1
Hugh	8	22	2
Lance	6	23	2
Ludwig	2	24	4
Harpo	1	25	1

not reflect the magnitude of differences in raw scores. The difficult concept to keep in mind is that although the difference between *rank scores* (first, second, third, and so on) is 1 everywhere on the scale, the differences between the raw scores that correspond to the ranks are not equal.

In education we often use ordinal scales. As we shall see in Chapter 5, many test scores are ordinal: age equivalents, grade equivalents, and percentages. Thus, ordinal scales have some interpretative value; however, they are not suitable for more complex interpretations that require some mathematical comparison (for example, calculating averages or differences between achievement in mathematics and reading).

Ratio Scales

Ratio scales have all the characteristics of ordinal scales, and two additional ones. First, the magnitude of the difference between any two adjacent points on the scale is the same. For example, weight in pounds is measured on a ratio scale; the difference between 15 and 16 pounds is the same as the difference between 124 and 125 pounds. In Table 4.1, if we assume that each raw-score point that makes up the student's total score is of the same value, then the total test score is a ratio scale. This assumption requires that we accept the notion that the difference between 18 and 17 correct is the same as the difference between 11 and 10 correct (or between any other pair of adjacent scores).

The second additional characteristic is that ratio scales have an absolute and logical zero. For instance, temperature on the Kelvin scale is a ratio scale. Absolute zero on that scale indicates the complete cessation of molecular action, or the absence of heat. The absolute zero of a ratio scale, allows one to construct ratios with scores. For example, if John weighs 200 pounds and Shawn weighs 100 pounds, John weighs twice as much as Shawn. Few, if any, educational or psychological tests give this type of score.

When ratio scales are used, all mathematical operations can be performed. We can add scores, square scores, create ratios of and differences between scores, and so forth. Thus, ratio scales are potentially very useful. In education and psychology, ratio scales are associated almost exclusively with the measurement of physical characteristics (for example, height and weight) and some time-based measures (for example, times in a 100-meter dash).

Equal-Interval Scales

Equal-interval scales are ratio scales without an absolute and logical zero. Fahrenheit and Celsius temperature scales are equal-interval, not ratio, scales—neither zero Fahrenheit nor zero Celsius indicate an absolute absence of heat. Because equal-interval scales lack an absolute zero, we cannot construct ratios with data measured on this scale.

Consider the information in Figure 4.2 (page 86). The differences among lines A, B, C, and D are readily measured. We can start measuring from any point, such as from the point where line S intersects lines A, B, C, and D. The portion of line A to the right of S is ½ inch long; line B to the right of S is 1 inch long; line C to the right of S is 1¼ inches long; and line D to the right of S is 1¾ inches long. The lines are measured on an equal-interval scale, and the differences among the lines would be the same no matter where the starting point, S, was located. However, because S is not a logical and absolute zero, we cannot make ratio comparisons among the lines. Although we began measuring from S and found line A to measure ½ inch from S and line B to measure 1 inch from S,

FIGURE 4.2   **The Measurement of Lines as a Function of the Starting Point**

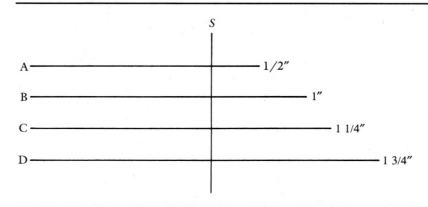

the whole of line B is obviously not twice as long as the whole of line A. In the same way that line B is not twice as long as line A, an IQ of 100 is not twice as large as an IQ of 50; IQ is not measured on a ratio scale.

In education and psychology, we often use equal-interval scales. As we shall see in Chapter 5, all standard scores are equal interval. Because we can add, subtract, multiply, and divide data measured on an equal-interval scale, these scales can be very useful when complex interpretations of test scores are made.

DISTRIBUTIONS

Distributions of scores may be graphed to demonstrate visually the relations among the scores in the group or set. In such graphs, the horizontal axis *(abscissa)* is the continuum on which the individuals are measured; the vertical axis *(ordinate)* is the frequency (or the number) of individuals earning any given score shown on the abscissa. Three types of graphs of distributions are common in education and psychology: *histograms, polygrams,* and *curves.* To illustrate these, let us graph the examination scores already presented in Table 4.1. The scores earned on Ms. Smith's arithmetic examination can be grouped in three-point intervals (that is, 1 to 3, 4 to 6, . . . , 25 to 27). The grouped scores are presented as a histogram in the upper part of Figure 4.3. In the middle part of that figure, the same data are presented as a polygram; note that the midpoints of the intervals used in the histogram are connected in constructing the polygram. The lower part of Figure 4.3 shows a smoothed curve.

Distributions are defined by four characteristics: mean, variance, skew, and kurtosis. The *mean* is the arithmetic average of the scores and is the balance point of the distribution. The *variance* describes the "spread," or clustering, of

FIGURE 4.3   **Distribution of Ms. Smith's Pupils on a Histogram, Polygram, and Curve**

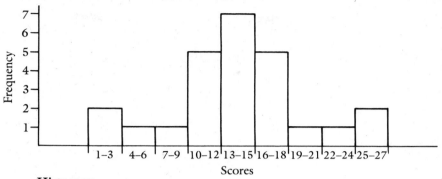

Histogram

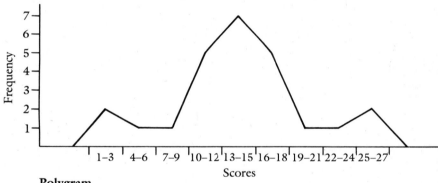

Polygram

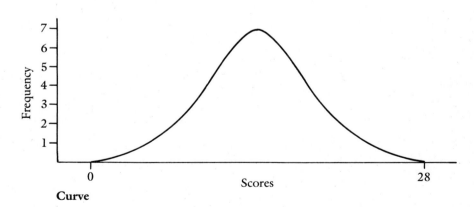

Curve

scores in a distribution. Both of these characteristics are discussed in greater detail in later sections.

Skew refers to the symmetry of a distribution. The distribution of scores from Ms. Smith's exam is not skewed; the distribution is *symmetrical*. However, if Ms. Smith had given a very easy test on which many students earned very high scores while only a few students earned low scores, the distribution would have been skewed. In such a case, the distribution would have "tailed off" to the low end and would be called a *negatively skewed* distribution. On the other hand, if she had given a very hard test on which most of her students earned low scores and relatively few earned high scores, the distribution of scores would have tailed off to the higher end of the continuum. Such a distribution is called a *positively skewed* distribution. Figure 4.4 shows an example of a positively skewed curve and a negatively skewed curve. The label assigned to a skewed distribution is determined by the direction of the tail of the distribu-

FIGURE 4.4   **Positive and Negative Skews**

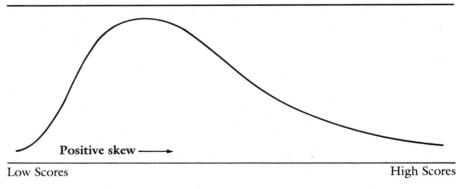

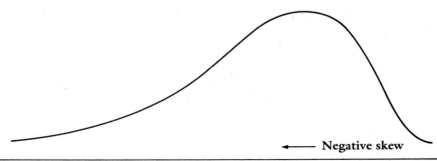

tion. Skewed distributions in which the tail is in the upper (higher-score) end are positively skewed, whereas those in which the tail slopes toward the lower end are negatively skewed.

Kurtosis, the fourth characteristic of curves, describes the peakedness of a curve, or the rate at which a curve rises. Distributions that are flat and rise slowly, such as the distribution formed by the scores on Ms. Smith's test, are called *platykurtic curves.* (*Platy*kurtic curves are flat, just as a plate or a plateau is flat.) Fast-rising curves are called *leptokurtic curves.* Tests that do not "spread out" (or discriminate among) those taking the test are typically leptokurtic. Figure 4.5 illustrates a platykurtic and a leptokurtic curve.

The *normal curve* is a particular symmetrical curve. Many variables are distributed normally in nature; many are not. The *only* value of the normal curve lies in the fact that it is known exactly how many cases fall between any two points on the horizontal axis of the curve.

FIGURE 4.5   **A Platykurtic and a Leptokurtic Curve**

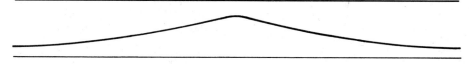

Platykurtic curve

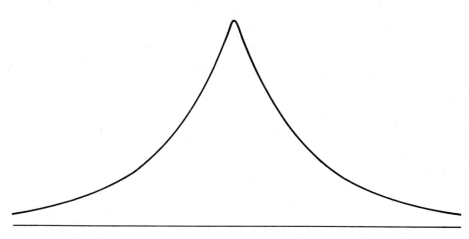

Leptokurtic curve

BASIC NOTATION

A number of symbols are used in statistics, and different authors use different symbols. The symbols that we will use in this book are given in Table 4.2. The summation Sign Σ means "add the following"; X denotes any score. The number of scores in a distribution is symbolized by N; f is used to denote the frequency of occurrence of a particular score. The arithmetic average (mean) of a distribution is denoted by $\overline{X}$. The variance of a distribution is symbolized by S^2 and the standard deviation by S.

MEASURES OF CENTRAL TENDENCY

A set of scores can be described by their average (for example, the average score on this week's spelling test was 92 percent correct). This information gives us a general description of how the group as a whole performed. Actually three different averages are used: mode, median, and mean. The *mode* is defined as the score most frequently obtained. A mode (if there is one) can be found for data on a nominal, ordinal, ratio, or equal-interval scale. Distributions may have two modes (if they do, they are called bimodal distributions), or they may have more than two. The mode of the distribution of raw scores obtained by Ms. Smith's class on the arithmetic test is readily apparent from an inspection of the data in Table 4.1 and the graphs in Figure 4.3 (page 87). The mode of this distribution is 14; seven children earned this score.

A *median* is the score that divides the top 50 percent of test takers from the bottom 50 percent. It is that point on a scale above which 50 percent of the cases (people, *not* scores) occur and below which 50 percent of the cases occur. Medians can be found for data that are ordinal, equal-interval, and ratio; they should not be used with nominal scales. The median score may or may not actually be earned by a student. For the set of scores 4, 5, 7, and 8, the median is 6,

TABLE 4.2   **Commonly Used Statistical Symbols**

Symbol	Meaning
Σ	Summation sign
X	Any score
N	Number of cases
f	Frequency
$\overline{X}$	Mean
S^2	Variance
S	Standard deviation

although no one earned a score of 6. For the set of scores 4, 5, 6, 7, and 8, the median is 6, and someone earned that score.

The *mean* is the arithmetic average of the scores in a distribution. It is the sum of the scores divided by the number of scores. Means should be computed only on ratio and equal-interval scales. The formula for computing the mean, using statistical notation, is given in equation 4.1.

$$\overline{X} = \frac{\sum X}{N}$$

$$(4.1)$$

Using the scores obtained from Ms. Smith's arithmetic examination (Table 4.1), we find that the sum of the scores is 350 and that the number of scores is 25. The mean (arithmetic average), then, is 14. The mean was earned by seven children in the class. The mean, like the median, may or may not be earned by a child in the distribution.

The mode, median, and mean have particular relationships depending on the symmetry (skew) of a distribution. As Figure 4.6 shows, in symmetrical uni-modal distributions, the mode, median, and mean are at the same point. In positively skewed distributions, the median and mean are displaced toward the positive tail of the curve; the mode is a lower value than the median, and the median is a lower value than the mean. In negatively skewed distributions, the median and mean are displaced toward the negative tail of the curve; the mode is a higher value than the median, and the median is a higher value than the mean.

MEASURES OF DISPERSION

Although a mean tells us about a group's average performance, it does not tell us how close to the average people scored. For example, did everyone earn 92 percent correct on the weekly spelling test, or were the scores spread out from 0 to 100 percent? To describe how scores spread out, we use three indexes of dispersion: range, variance, and standard deviation. All three measures can be computed when the scale of measurement is ratio or equal interval, and none of the three can be computed when the scale of measurement is nominal. Range can be calculated with ordinal data.

The *range* is the distance between the extremes of a distribution, including those extremes; it is the highest score less the lowest score plus 1. On Ms. Smith's test (Table 4.1), it is 27 (27 = 27 − 1 + 1). The range is a relatively crude measure of dispersion, since it is based on only two bits of information.

The variance and the standard deviation are the most important indexes of dispersion. The *variance* is a numerical index describing the dispersion of a set of scores around the mean of the distribution. Specifically, the *variance* (S^2) is the average squared-distance of the scores from the mean. Since the variance is an average, it is not affected by the number of cases in the set or distribution. Large sets of scores may have large or small variances; small sets of scores may

FIGURE 4.6   **Relationships Among Mode, Median, and Mean for Symmetrical and Asymmetrical Distributions**

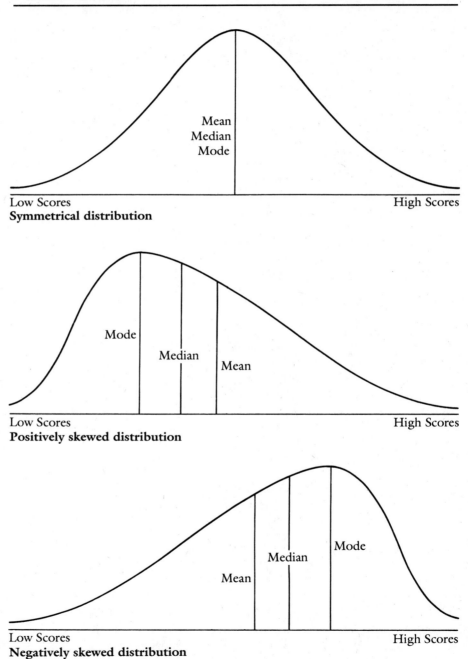

Symmetrical distribution

Positively skewed distribution

Negatively skewed distribution

have large or small variances. Also, since the variance is measured in terms of distance from the mean, it is not related to the actual value of the mean. Distributions with large means may have large or small variances; distributions with small means may have large or small variances. The variance of a distribution may be computed with equation 4.2. The variance (S^2) equals the sum (Σ) of the square of each score less the mean $[(X - \overline{X})^2]$ divided by the number of scores (N).

$$S^2 = \frac{\Sigma \ (X - \overline{X})^2}{N}$$

(4.2)

Let us use the scores from Ms. Smith's arithmetic test again to compute variance (see Table 4.3). Column 2 in Table 4.3 contains the score earned by each student. The first step in computing the variance is to find the mean. Therefore, the scores are added and the sum (350) is divided by the number of scores (25). The mean in this example is 14. The next step is to subtract the mean from each score; this is done in column 3 of Table 4.3, which is labeled $X - \overline{X}$. Note that

TABLE 4.3   **Computation of the Variance of Ms. Smith's Arithmetic Test**

Student	Test Score	$X - \overline{X}$	$(X - \overline{X})^2$
Bob	27	13	169
Lucy	26	12	144
Sam	22	8	64
Mary	20	6	36
Luis	18	4	16
Barbara	17	3	9
Carmen	16	2	4
Jane	16	2	4
Charles J.	16	2	4
Hector	14	0	0
Virginia	14	0	0
Manuel	14	0	0
Sean	14	0	0
Joanne	14	0	0
Jim	14	0	0
John	14	0	0
Charles B	12	−2	4
Jing-Jen	12	−2	4
Ron	12	−2	4
Carole	11	−3	9
Bernice	10	−4	16
Hugh	8	−6	36
Lance	6	−8	64
Ludwig	2	−12	144
Harpo	1	−13	169
SUM	350	0	900

scores above the mean are positive, scores at the mean are zero, and scores below the mean are negative. The differences (column 3) are then squared (multiplied by themselves); the squared differences are in column 4, labeled $(X - \bar{X})^2$. Note that all numbers in this column are positive. The squared differences are then summed; in this example, the sum of all the squared distances of scores from the mean of the distribution is 900. The variance equals the sum of all the squared distances of scores from the mean divided by the number of scores; in this case, the variance equals 900/25, or 36.

The variance is very important in psychometric theory but has very limited application in score interpretation. However, its calculation is necessary for the computation of the standard deviation (S), which is very important in the interpretation of test scores. The standard deviation is the positive square root $(\sqrt{})$ of the variance.[2] Thus, in our example, since the variance is 36, the standard deviation is 6. In later chapters, the standard deviation will be used in other computations such as standard scores and the standard error of measurement.

The standard deviation is used as a *unit of measurement* in much the same way an inch or a ton is used as a unit of measurement. When scores are equal interval, they can be measured in terms of standard deviation units from the mean. The advantage of measuring in standard deviations is that when the distribution is normal, we know exactly how many cases occur between the mean and the particular standard deviation. As shown in Figure 4.7, approximately 34 percent of the cases in a normal distribution always occur between the mean and one standard deviation (S) either above or below the mean. Thus, approximately 68 percent of all cases occur between one standard deviation below and one standard deviation above the mean (34% + 34% = 68%). Approximately 14 percent of the cases occur between one and two standard deviations below the mean or between one and two standard deviations above the mean. Thus, about 48 percent of all cases occur between the mean and two standard deviations either above or below the mean (34% + 14% = 48%). About 96 percent of all cases occur between two standard deviations above and two standard deviations below the mean. Appendix 2 lists the proportion of cases in a normal distribution occurring between the mean and any standard deviation above or below the mean. As an example, if we enter Appendix 2 at .44 (that is, .4 and .04), we find the number .1700. This number means that 1,700/10,000 (17 percent) of the cases in the normal curve occur between the mean and .44 standard deviation from the mean, either below or above the mean. Thirty-three percent of the cases fall below .44 standard deviation below the mean. (Half of the cases, 50 percent, fall below the mean; 17 percent fall between −0.44 S and the mean; 50 percent less 17 percent equals 33 percent.)

As shown by the positions and values for scales A, B, and C in Figure 4.7, it does not matter what the values of the mean and standard deviation are. The relationship holds for various obtained values of the mean and the standard devia-

2. The square root of a particular number is the number that when multiplied by itself produces the particular number. For example: $\sqrt{144} = 12$, $\sqrt{25} = 5$, $\sqrt{4} = 2$.

FIGURE 4.7   **Scores on Three Scales, Expressed in Standard Deviation Units**

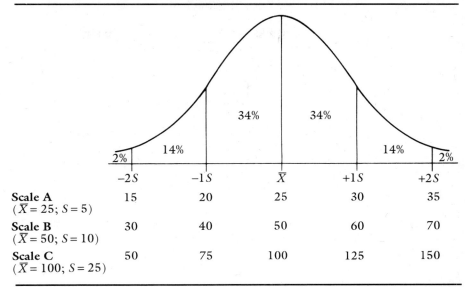

	$-2S$	$-1S$	$\overline{X}$	$+1S$	$+2S$
Scale A ($\overline{X} = 25$; $S = 5$)	15	20	25	30	35
Scale B ($\overline{X} = 50$; $S = 10$)	30	40	50	60	70
Scale C ($\overline{X} = 100$; $S = 25$)	50	75	100	125	150

tion. For scale A, where the mean is 25 and the standard deviation is 5, 34 percent of the scores occur between the mean (25) and one standard deviation below the mean (20) *or* between the mean and one standard deviation above the mean (30). Similarly, for scale B, where the mean is 50 and the standard deviation is 10, 34 percent of the cases occur between the mean (50) and one standard deviation below the mean (40) *or* between the mean and one standard deviation above the mean (60).

It is extremely important that those who use tests to make decisions about students be aware of the means and standard deviations of the tests they use. Some intelligence tests, for example, have a mean of 100 and a standard deviation of 16. If scores on those tests are normally distributed, we would expect approximately 68 percent of the school population to have IQs between 84 and 116. Another intelligence test may have a mean of 100 and a standard deviation of 24. We would expect approximately 68 percent of the school population to have IQs between 76 and 124 if scores on that test are normally distributed. The meaning of a score in a distribution depends on the mean, the standard deviation, and the shape of that distribution. This is an obvious point, yet it is often overlooked. For example, some states use an absolute score in the school code for the placement and retention of mentally retarded children in special education programs; Pennsylvania uses a score of 79 for maintaining eligibility for placement. On the Stanford-Binet Intelligence Scale (fourth edition) or the third edition of the Wechsler Intelligence Scale for Children (WISC III), which have a standard deviation of 15, a score of 79 is 1.4 standard deviations below the mean [(79–100)/15]. On some older tests, with a standard deviation of 16 (such as the McCarthy Scales of Children's Abilities), an IQ of 79 is 1.3 standard deviations below the mean [(79–100)/16]. If a single absolute score is specified, *different* levels of eligibility for special education classes may be inadvertently written into the school code unintentionally.

CORRELATION

Correlations quantify relationships between variables. *Correlation coefficients* are numerical indexes of these relationships. They tell us the extent to which any two variables go together, the extent to which changes in one variable are reflected by changes in the second variable. These coefficients are used in measurement to estimate both the reliability and the validity of a test. Correlation coefficients can range in value from .00 to *either* +1.00 or –1.00. The sign (+ or –) indicates the direction of the relationship; the number indicates the magnitude of the relationship. A correlation coefficient of .00 between two variables means that there is no relationship between the variables. The variables are independent; changes in one variable are not related to changes in the second variable. A correlation coefficient of either +1.00 or –1.00 indicates a perfect relationship between two variables. Thus, if you know a person's score on one variable, you can predict that person's score on the second variable exactly. Correlation coefficients between .00 and 1.00 allow some prediction, and the greater the coefficient, the greater its predictive power.

Correlation coefficients are very important in assessment. As we shall see in Chapter 7, they are used to estimate the amount of error associated with measurement. In Chapter 8, we shall show that correlation coefficients are also used to estimate a test's validity.

The Pearson Product-Moment Correlation Coefficient

The most commonly used correlation coefficient is the Pearson product-moment correlation coefficient (r). This is an index of the straight-line (linear) relationship between two variables measured on an equal-interval scale. Suppose Ms. Smith administered a second exam to her arithmetic class. The results of the first exam (the data from Table 4.1) are reproduced in column 2 of Table 4.4; the results of the second exam are presented in column 3. (For the sake of simplicity, the example has been constructed so that the second test has the same mean and the same standard deviation as the first test—that is, 14 and 6, respectively). The two scores for each student are plotted on a graph (called a *scattergram*, or *scatterplot*) in Figure 4.8 (page 98). The scatterplot contains twenty-five points, one for each child. The figure indicates that there is a pronounced

TABLE 4.4   **Scores Earned on Two Tests Administered by Ms. Smith to Her Arithmetic Class**

Student	Raw Score, Test 1	Raw Score, Test 2
Bob	27	26
Lucy	26	22
Sam	22	20
Mary	20	27
Luis	18	14
Barbara	17	18
Carmen	16	16
Jane	16	17
Charles J.	16	16
Hector	14	14
Virginia	14	14
Manuel	14	16
Sean	14	14
Joanne	14	12
Jim	14	14
John	14	12
Charles B	12	14
Jing-Jen	12	11
Ron	12	12
Carole	11	10
Bernice	10	14
Hugh	8	6
Lance	6	1
Ludwig	2	2
Harpo	1	8

tendency for high scores on the first test to be associated with high scores on the second test. There is a *positive* relationship (correlation) between the first and second tests. The line drawn through the scatterplot in Figure 4.8 is called a *regression line*. When the points corresponding to each pair of scores cluster closely around the regression line, there is a high degree of relationship. The points from Table 4.4 do cluster closely around the regression line; there is a high correlation (specifically, .89) between the first and second tests.[3] If all the points fell on the regression line, there would be a perfect correlation (1.00).

Figure 4.9 (page 99) shows six scatterplots of different degrees of relationship. In parts a and b, all points fall on the regression line so that the correlation

3. The correlation coefficient can be computed with the following formula:

$$r = \frac{N\Sigma\,XY-(\Sigma\,X)(\Sigma\,Y)}{\sqrt{N\Sigma X^2-(\Sigma\,X)^2}\,\sqrt{N\Sigma Y^2-(\Sigma Y)^2}}$$

FIGURE 4.8   **Scatterplot of the Two Tests Administered by Ms. Smith**

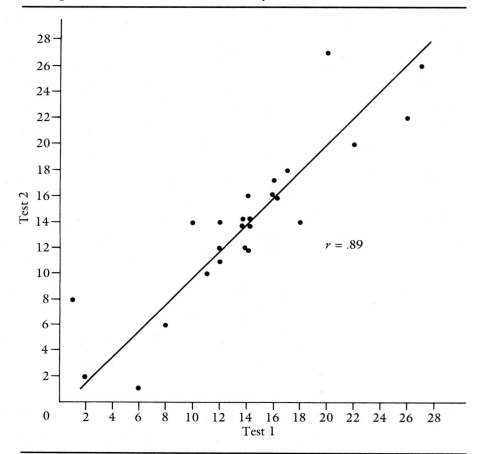

between the variables is perfect. Part a has a correlation coefficient of +1.00; high scores on one test are associated with high scores on the other test. Part b has a correlation of −1.00; high scores on one test are associated with low scores on the other test (this negative correlation is called an *inverse* relationship). Parts c and d show a high degree of positive and negative relationship, respectively. Note that the departures from the regression lines are associated with lower degrees of relationship. Parts e and f show scatterplots with a low degree of relationship. Note the wide departures from the regression lines.

Zero correlation can occur in three ways, as shown in Figure 4.10 (page 100). First, if the scatterplot is essentially circular (part a), the correlation is .00. In such a case, there is no relationship between the two variables; each value of the first variable can be associated with any (and perhaps all) values of the second

FIGURE 4.9   **Six Scatterplots of Different Degrees and Directions of Relationship**

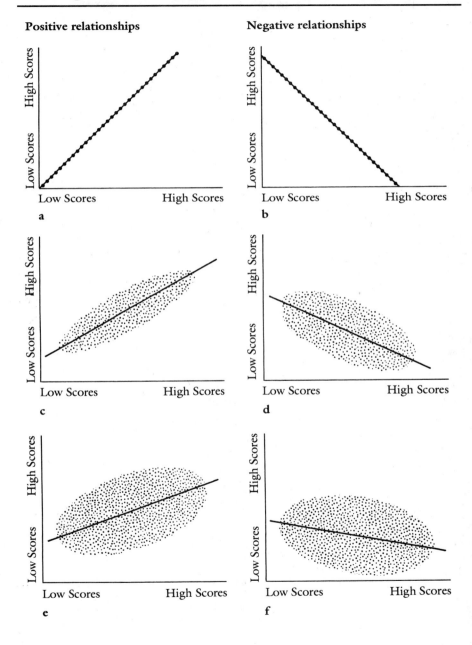

FIGURE 4.10   **Three Zero-Order, Linear Correlations**

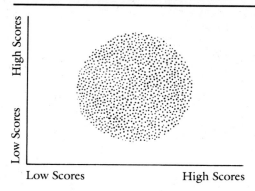

a. No relationship

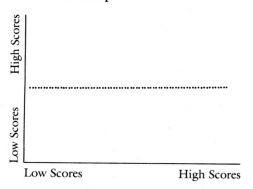

b. No relationship; one variable is constant

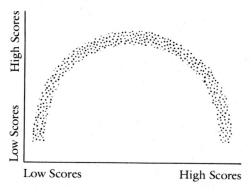

c. No linear relationship; relationship is curvilinear

variable. Second, if either variable is constant (part b), the correlation is .00. For example, if a researcher tried to correlate sex and reading achievement with a sample made up entirely of boys, the correlation would be zero because sex would have only one value (male); sex would be a constant, not a variable. Third, two variables can be related in a nonlinear way (part c). For example, willingness to take risks is related to age. Younger children and adults are less willing to take risks than teenagers. Although there is a strong curvilinear relationship, the *linear* regression line would parallel one of the axes. Thus, there is a curvilinear relationship, but the coefficient of linear correlation is approximately .00.

Variant Correlation Coefficients

Six variations of linear correlation are commonly found in test manuals and research literature dealing with reliability and validity. Four are members of the Pearson family of correlation coefficients, which means that they are computed by the same (or by a computationally equivalent) formula (see footnote 3). Two variations are not members of the Pearson family of coefficients and are calculated differently. These six coefficients are used in different situations.

Pearson-Family Coefficients

Different names are typically given to the Pearson product-moment correlation coefficient depending on the scale of measurement used. The first member of the family of correlation coefficients is called the *Pearson product-moment* correlation coefficient and is symbolized by the letter r. This name or symbol is used when the variables to be correlated are measured on an equal-interval (or ratio) scale. The second member of the Pearson family is called the *Spearman rho* (ρ). This coefficient is used when both variables are measured on an ordinal scale. The third and fourth members of the Pearson family are used when either or both of the variables to be correlated are naturally occurring dichotomous variables (for example, male/female). When a naturally occurring dichotomous variable such as sex is correlated with a continuous, equal-interval variable (height measured in inches, for example), the correlation coefficient is called a *point biserial* correlation coefficient ($r_{pt.bis}$). When two sets of naturally occurring dichotomous variables (for example, male/female and dead/alive) are correlated, the correlation coefficient is called a *phi* coefficient ($\emptyset$).

Non–Pearson-Family Coefficients

A continuous variable can be forced into a dichotomy. For example, the entire range of intelligence can be dichotomized into "smart" and "dull" at some arbitrary point on the continuum. If a variable that has been forced into an arbitrary dichotomy (for example, smart/dull) is correlated with a continuous equal-interval variable (for example, grade-point average), the resulting coefficient is called a *biserial* correlation coefficient (r_{bis}). If two arbitrarily dichotomized variables (for example, tall/short, smart/dull) are correlated, the coefficient is called a *tetrachoric* correlation coefficient (r_{tet}). These two correlation coefficients are computed differently from the way the Pearson-family coefficients are computed.

Relationship Among Correlation Coefficients

Table 4.5 lists the different correlation coefficients commonly used in measurement that we have discussed.

In test manuals you will often see correlations between individual test items or between each test item and the total test score. Test authors typically report phi and point biserial correlation coefficients rather than tetrachoric and biserial coefficients in such cases. In selecting particular coefficients, an author makes an assumption about the nature of correct or incorrect responses. An author who selects phi and point biserial correlations assumes that each response is either correct or incorrect; there are no "in betweens." The author who reports tetrachoric and biserial correlations assumes that the answer to each test item falls on a continuum ranging from totally correct to totally incorrect, even though the

TABLE 4.5   **Correlation Coefficients**

Characteristics of Variable 2	Characteristics of Variable 1			
	Pearson Family			Non-Pearson Family
	Ordinal	Equal interval	Natural dichotomy	Forced dichotomy
Ordinal	Spearman's rho (ρ)			
Equal interval		Pearson product-moment (r)	Point biserial ($r_{pt.\ bis}$)	Biserial (r_{bis})
Natural dichotomy			Phi ($\emptyset$)	
Forced dichotomy				Tetrachoric (r_{tet})

individual items are scored only as right or wrong. The differences between Pearson-family and non–Pearson-family coefficients should not cause a test administrator any difficulty. Modern tests rely almost exclusively on Pearson-family coefficients. But occasionally one sees r_{tet} or r_{bis}.

Causality

No discussion of correlation is complete without a mention of causality. Correlation is a necessary but not a sufficient condition for determining causality. Two variables cannot be causally related unless they are correlated. However, the mere presence of a correlation does not imply causality. For any correlation between two variables (A and B), three causal interpretations are possible: A causes B; B causes A; or a third variable, C, causes both A and B. For example, fire-fighters (A) are often present at fires (B). Firefighters do not cause fires (A does not cause B).[4] Fires cause firefighters to be present (B causes A). As a second example, in a sample of children ranging from 6 months to 8 years of age, we might find a positive relationship between shoe size and mental age. Clearly, however, big feet do not cause intelligence (A does not cause B). Moreover, intelligence does not cause big feet (B does not cause A). More likely, as children grow older (C) they tend to increase in both shoe size and mental age; C causes both A and B.

Although the above examples illustrate fairly obvious instances of inappropriate reasoning, in testing situations the errors or potential errors are not so clear. For example, scores on intelligence tests and scores on achievement tests are correlated. Some argue that intelligence causes achievement; others argue that achievement causes intelligence. Since there are at least three possible interpretations of correlational data—and since correlational data do not tell us which interpretation is true—we must never draw causal conclusions from such data.

SUMMARY

Descriptive statistics provide summary information about groups of individuals. Data can be obtained on one of four scales of measurement: *nominal, ordinal, ratio,* and *equal-interval* scales. Collections of scores are called *distributions.* Distributions are defined by four characteristics: *mean, variance, skew,* and *kurtosis.* Depending on the scale of measurement, three indexes may be used to indicate a distribution's central tendency: the *mode,* (the most frequent score), the *median* (the score that separates the top 50 percent from the bottom 50 percent), and the *mean* (the arithmetic average). Depending on the scale of measurement, the dispersion of a distribution can be described by three indexes: the

4. Exceptions have been reported by Bradbury (1953).

range of scores, the *variance*, and the *standard deviation*. The quantification of the relationship between two variables is called *correlation*. When there is no relationship between variables, the correlation is zero. When there is a perfect relationship between variables, the correlation is 1. A plus or a minus sign indicates the type of relationship, not the magnitude of the relationship. A positive correlation indicates that high scores on one variable are associated with high scores on the second variable. A negative correlation indicates an inverse relationship: High scores on one variable are associated with low scores on the other variable. There are several types of correlations that are often used in tests.

Study Questions

1. All third-grade pupils in a particular state took an achievement test. The superintendent of public instruction reviewed the test results and in a news conference reported concern for the quality of education in the state. The superintendent reported, "Half the third-grade children in this state performed below the state average." What is foolish about that statement?
2. What is the relationship among the mode, median, and mean in a normal distribution?
3. The following statements about test A and test B are known to be true: Tests A and B measure the same behavior; tests A and B have means of 100; test A has a standard deviation of 15; and test B has a standard deviation of 5.
   a. Following classroom instruction, the pupils in Mr. Radley's room earn an average score of 130 on test A. Pupils in Ms. Purple's room earn an average score on test B of 110. On this basis, the local principal concludes that Mr. Radley is a better teacher than Ms. Purple. Why is this conclusion inappropriate?
   b. Assuming the pupils were equal prior to instruction, what conclusions could the principal legitimately make?
4. On the Stanford-Binet Intelligence Scale, Harry earns an IQ of 52 and Ralph earns an IQ of 104. Their teacher concludes that Ralph is twice as smart as Harry. To what extent is this conclusion warranted?

Problems

1. Ms. Robbins administers a test to ten children in her class. The children earn the following scores: 14, 28, 49, 49, 49, 77, 84, 84, 91, and 105. For this distribution of scores, find the following:
   a. Mode
   b. Mean
   c. Range
   d. Variance and standard deviation

2. Mr. Garcia administers the same test to six children in his class. The children earn the following scores: 21, 27, 30, 54, 39, and 63. For these scores, find the following:
   a. Mean
   b. Range
   c. Variance and standard deviation
3. Ms. Shumway administers a test to six children in her nursery school program. The children earn the following scores: 23, 33, 38, 53, 78, and 93. Find the mean and standard deviation of these six scores.
4. Using Appendix 2, find the proportion of cases that occur
   a. Between the mean and the following standard deviation units: −1.5, +.37, +.08, +2.75.
   b. Between + and −1.7S, between + and −.55S, and between + and −2.1S.
   c. Above −.7S, +1.3S, and +1.9S.
   d. Below −.7S, +1.3S, and +1.9S.

Answers

1. (a) 49; (b) 63; (c) 92; (d) 784 and 28
2. (a) 39; (b) 43; (c) 225 and 15
3. Mean = 53; standard deviation = 25
4. (a) .4332, .1443, .0319, .4970; (b) .9108, .4176, .9642; (c) .7580, .0968, .0287; (d) .2420, .9032, .9713.

ADDITIONAL READING

Psychological Corporation (1966). *Test Service Bulletin No. 148: The Normal Curve*. New York: Psychological Corporation.

Chapter 5

Quantification of Test Performance

Most behaviors occur without being systematically observed, quantified, and evaluated, and the vast majority occur in situations not specifically structured to quantify and evaluate them. Assessment is an exception. Tests and systematic observations occur in structured, standardized situations. Tests require the presentation of standardized materials to an individual in a predetermined manner in order to evaluate that individual's responses using predetermined criteria. Systematic observations require the use of predetermined definitions of behavior to be observed at predetermined times.

How the individual's responses are quantified depends on the materials used, the intent of the test author, and the diagnostician's intent in choosing the procedure. If we were interested only in determining if a student had learned a specific fact or concept (for example, What is 3 + 5?), we would make explicit the criteria for what constitutes a correct response and would classify the student's response as right or wrong, without quantifying the result. Keeping track of each student's mastery of all specific facts and concepts, however, would be a record-keeping nightmare, even with a computer in every classroom. Therefore, this approach is generally restricted to the most essential information that each student must master. If we were interested in determining whether a student had learned a finite set of facts (for example, the sums of all combinations of single-digit numbers), we could readily quantify a student's performance as the number of facts known or the percentage of facts known.

More often, though, the information that we wish to assess is not finite, and it is impractical or impossible to assess all the facts and relationships that might be tested. For example, it seems unlikely that anyone could make up a test to assess a student's knowledge of every aspect of all Shakespeare's plays; however, even if it were possible, it would be virtually impossible to administer all the possible questions to a student in one or even several settings. Even when we cannot test much of the information on a topic, we still may want to estimate how much of the information students have learned. To do so, testers are forced to ask a few questions and base their inferences about all the information (called the *domain*) on student responses to the sample of questions. When we sample knowledge of a domain with a smaller number of items, we assume that a student's performance on all the items in the domain can be accurately inferred from the performance on the sample of items. Particular items are only important as representatives of the domain and have little individual importance. Moreover, we generally cannot infer the percent correct on the entire domain directly from a test unless the items are representative, a condition that is never known on an *a priori* basis.

SCORES USED IN NORM-REFERENCED ASSESSMENT

When a large domain is assessed, a student's performance is typically interpreted by comparing it to the performances of a group of subjects of known demographic characteristics (age, sex, grade in school, and so on). This group is called a *normative sample* or *norm group*. The comparison scores are called *derived scores* and are of two types: developmental scores and scores of relative standing.

Developmental Scores

Developmental Levels

Developmental scores are one type of derived (or transformed) score. The most common types of developmental scores are age equivalents (mental ages, for example) and grade equivalents. Suppose the average performance of ten-year-old children on an intelligence test was twenty-seven correct answers. Further, suppose that Horace answered twenty-seven questions correctly. Horace answered as many questions correctly as the average of ten-year-old children. He earns a mental age of 10 years. An *age equivalent* means that a child's raw score is the average (the median or mean) performance for that age group. Age equivalents are expressed in years and months; a hyphen is used in age scores (for example, 7-1 for 7 years, 1 month old). A *grade equivalent* means that a child's raw score is the average (the median or mean) performance for a particular grade. Grade equivalents are expressed in grades and tenths of grades; a decimal point is used in grade scores (for example, 7.1). Age-equivalent and grade-equivalent scores are interpreted as a performance equal to the average of *X*-year-olds and the average of *X*th graders' performance, respectively.

Suppose we gave a test to 1,000 children, one hundred of each age (within two weeks of their birthday) from 5 to 14 years. For each one hundred children at each age, there is a distribution with a mean. These hypothetical means are shown in Figure 5.1, connected by a curved line. As the figure shows, a raw score of 16 corresponds exactly to the average score earned by children in the

FIGURE 5.1   **Mean Number Correct for Ten Age Groups: An Example of Arriving at Age-Equivalent Scores**

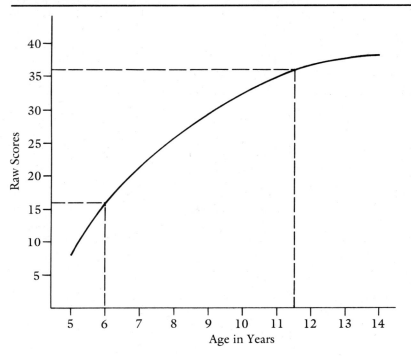

six-year-old distribution. Thus, the child who earns a score of 16 has an age equivalent of 6 years, 0 months, or 6-0. A score of 36, by contrast, falls between the average of the eleven-year-old distribution and the average of the twelve-year-old distribution. A raw score of 36 would be estimated (*interpolated*) as an age score of 11-6; it would be awarded a score between 11 and 12, despite the fact that no children between 11 and 12 years of age were tested. A score of 4 would fall below the average of the lowest age group, the five-year-olds. If a child earned a raw score of 4, that child's age equivalent would be estimated (*extrapolated*) by continuing the curve in Figure 5.1. A raw score of 4 could be extrapolated to be the equivalent of an age score of 3-6 although no children that young are included in the sample. Similarly, a score greater than the average performance of the oldest children could also be extrapolated.

The interpretation of age and grade equivalents requires great care. Five problems occur in the use of developmental scores. The first problem is systematic misinterpretation. Students who earn an age equivalent of 12-0 have merely answered correctly as many questions as the average of children 12 years of age. They have not necessarily "performed as" a twelve-year-old child would; they may well have attacked the problems in a different way or demonstrated a different performance pattern from many twelve-year-old students. Similarly, a second grader and a ninth grader may both earn grade equivalents of 4.0. They probably have not performed identically. Thorndike and Hagen (1978) have suggested that it is more likely that the younger child has performed lower-level work with greater accuracy (for instance, successfully answered thirty-eight of the forty-five problems attempted), whereas the older child has attempted more problems with less accuracy (for instance, successfully answered thirty-eight of the seventy-eight problems attempted).

The second problem inherent in the use of developmental scores is the need for interpolation and extrapolation. Average age and grade scores are estimated for groups of children who are never tested. Consequently, a child can earn a grade equivalent of 3.2 when only children in the first and middle of third grade have ever been tested; or a child can earn a grade equivalent of 8.0 even though no children above the sixth grade have been tested.

The third problem is that the use of developmental scores promotes typological thinking. The average 12-0 pupil is a statistical abstraction surrounded by a family with 1.2 other children, 0.8 of a dog, and 2.3 automobiles; in other words, the average child does not exist. Average 12-0 children more accurately represent a range of performances, typically the middle 50 percent.

The fourth problem is that equivalent scores imply a false standard of performance. One expects a third grader to perform at a third-grade level or a nine-year-old to perform at a nine-year-old level. However, the way equivalent scores are constructed ensures that 50 percent of any age or grade group will perform below age or grade level because half of the test takers earn scores below the median.

The fifth problem with developmental scores is that such scales tend to be ordinal, not equal interval. The line relating the number correct to the various ages is typically curved, with a flattening of the curve at higher ages or grades. Figure 5.1 is a typical developmental curve. Because the scales are ordinal and not based on equal-interval units, scores on these scales should not be added or multiplied in any computation.

Developmental Quotients

Before we try to interpret a developmental score (for example, a mental age), we must know the age of the person whose score is being calculated. Knowing developmental age as well as chronological age (CA) allows us to judge an individual's relative performance. Suppose Horace earns a mental age (MA) of 120 months. If Horace is 8 years (96 months) old, his performance is above average. If he is 35 years old, however, it's below average. The relationship between developmental age and chronological age is often quantified as a developmental quotient. For example, a *ratio IQ* is

$$IQ = \frac{MA \text{ (in months)}}{CA \text{ (in months)}} \times 100$$

The developmental age is often interpreted as the level of functioning, whereas the quotient is interpreted as the rate of development. In any such scheme, a third variable, chronological age, is always involved. Of the three variables, only chronological age and the developmental quotient are independent of each other (that is, uncorrelated). The developmental age is related to both of the other two variables. In the case of intelligence, the developmental age is far more closely associated with chronological age than it is with the quotient (Kappauf, 1973). Developmental levels do not provide independent information. They only summarize data for age (or grade) and relative standing.

All the problems that apply to developmental levels also apply to developmental quotients. There is one additional problem that is particularly bothersome. The variance of developmental scores within different chronological age or grade groups may not be the same. This can cause two related problems. First, the same quotient may mean different things at different ages. For example, a developmental quotient of 120 at age 5 may mean that Billy performs better than 55 percent of five-year-olds. However, a developmental quotient of 120 at age 11 may mean that Billy performs better than 53 or 58 percent (or some other percent) of the eleven-year-olds. Second, different quotients at different ages can mean the same thing. For example, whereas a developmental quotient of 120 may mean that Sally performs better than 55 percent of five-year-olds, a developmental quotient of 110 at age 10 could mean that Sally performs better than 55 percent of ten-year-olds. Thus, different variances at different ages and grades render score interpretation impossible without knowing what the variance is.

Scores of Relative Standing

Unlike developmental scores, scores of relative standing use more information than the mean or median to interpret a person's test score. Moreover, when the same type of relative-standing score is used, the units of measurement are exactly the same. Thus, we can compare the performances of different people even when they differ in age, and we can compare one person's scores on several different tests. This specificity of meaning is very useful. For example, it is not particularly helpful to know that George is 70 inches tall, Bill is 6 feet 3 inches tall, Bruce is 1.93 meters tall, and Alan is 177.8 centimeters tall. To compare their heights, it is necessary to transform the heights into comparable units. In feet and inches, the men's heights are as follows: George, 5 feet 10 inches; Bill, 6 feet 3 inches; Bruce, 6 feet 4 inches; and Alan, 5 feet 10 inches. Scores of relative standing put raw scores into comparable units.

Percentile Family

Percentile ranks (percentiles) can be used when the scale of measurement is ordinal or equal interval. They are derived scores that indicate the percentage of people or scores that occur *at or below* a given raw score. The percentage correct is *not* the same as the percentage of people scoring below a given score. Percentiles corresponding to particular scores can be computed by a four-step sequence.

1. Arrange the scores from the highest to the lowest (that is, best to worst).
2. Compute the percentage of cases occurring *below* the score to which you wish to assign a percentile rank.
3. Compute the percentage of cases occurring *at* the score to which you wish to assign a percentile rank.
4. Add the percentage of cases occurring below the score to one-half the percentage of cases occurring at the score to obtain the percentile rank.

Table 5.1 gives a numerical example. Mr. Greenberg gave a test to his developmental reading class, which has an enrollment of twenty-five children. The scores are presented in column 1, and the number of children obtaining each score (the *frequency*) is shown in column 2. Column 3 gives the percentage of all twenty-five scores that each obtained score represents. Column 4 contains the percentage of all twenty-five scores that occurred below that particular score. In the last group of columns, the percentile rank is computed. Only one child

TABLE 5.1   **Computing Percentile Ranks for a Hypothetical Class of Twenty-Five**

				Percentile Rank				
Score	Frequency	Percent at the Score	Percent Below the Score	Percent Below the Score	+	Half of Percent at the Score	=	Percentile
50	2	8	92	92	+	(1/2)(8)	=	96
49	0							
48	4	16	76	76	+	(1/2)(16)	=	84
47	0							
46	5	20	56	56	+	(1/2)(20)	=	66
45	5	20	36	36	+	(1/2)(20)	=	46
44	3	12	24	24	+	(1/2)(12)	=	30
43	2	8	16	16	+	(1/2)(8)	=	20
42	0	—	—					
41	0	—	—					
40	2	8	8	8	+	(1/2)(8)	=	12
39	0	—	—					
38	1	4	4	4	+	(1/2)(4)	=	6
.								
.								
.								
24	1	4	0	0	+	(1/2)(4)	=	2

scored 24; the one score is 1/25 of the class, or 4 percent. No one scored lower than 24; so 0 percent (0/25) of the scores is below 24. The child who scored 24 received a percentile rank of 2—that is, 0 plus one-half of 4. The next score obtained is 38, and again only one child received this score. Four percent of the total (1/25) scored at 38, and 4 percent of the total scored below 38. Therefore, the percentile rank corresponding to a score of 38 is 6—that is, 4 + (1/2)(4). Two children earned a score of 40, and two children scored below 40. Therefore, the percentile rank for a score of 40 is 12—that is, 8 + (1/2)(8). The same procedure is followed for every score obtained. The best score in the class, 50, was obtained by two students. The percentile rank corresponding to the highest score in the class is 96.

The interpretation of percentile ranks is based on the percent of *people*. The data from Table 5.1 provide a specific example. All students who score 48 on the test have a percentile rank of 84. These four students have *scored as well as or better than* 84 percent of their classmates on the test. Similarly, an individual who obtains a percentile rank of 21 on an intelligence test has scored as well as or better than 21 percent of the people in the norm sample.

Because the percentile rank is computed using one-half of the percentage of those obtaining a particular score, it is not possible to have percentile ranks of either 0 or 100. Generally, percentile ranks contain decimals, so it's possible for a score to receive a percentile rank of 99.9 or 0.1. The fiftieth percentile rank is the median.

Deciles are bands of percentiles that are ten percentile ranks in width; each decile contains 10 percent of the norm group. The first decile contains percentile ranks from .1 to 9.9; the second decile contains percentile ranks from 10 to 19.9; the tenth decile contains percentile ranks from 90 to 99.9.

Quartiles are bands of percentiles that are twenty-five percentile ranks in width; each quartile contains 25 percent of the norm group. The first quartile contains percentile ranks from .1 to 24.9; the fourth quartile contains the ranks 75 to 99.9.

Standard Scores

A standardized distribution is a set of scores that have been transformed so that the mean and standard deviation of the set take predetermined (standard) values. The most basic standardized distribution is the z distribution. A z distribution has a predetermined mean of zero and a predetermined standard deviation of 1. To transform raw scores (for example, the number correct on a test) to z-scores, the mean of the distribution is subtracted from each raw score; this operation sets the mean at zero. Next, the difference between the raw score and the mean is divided by the standard deviation; this operation sets the standard deviation at 1.

Standard score is the general name for any derived score that has been standardized. Although a distribution of scores can be standardized to produce any predetermined mean and standard deviation, there are five commonly used standard-score distributions.

z-Scores   As just indicated, *z-scores* are standard scores, the distribution of which has a mean of zero and a standard deviation of 1. Any raw score can be converted to a z-score by using equation 5.1.

$$z = \frac{X - \overline{X}}{S}$$

(5.1)

A z-score equals the raw score less the mean of the distribution, divided by the standard deviation of the distribution. The z-scores are interpreted as standard deviation units. Thus, a z-score of +1.5 means that the score is 1.5 standard deviations *above* the mean of the group. A z-score of −.6 means that the score is .6 standard deviation *below* the mean. A z-score of 0 is the mean performance.

Because + and − signs have a tendency to "get lost" and decimals may be awkward in practical situations, z-scores often are transformed to other standard scores. The general formula for changing a z-score into a different standard score is given by equation 5.2. In the equation, *SS* stands for any standard score, as does the subscript *ss*. Thus, any standard score equals the mean of the distribution of standard scores ($\overline{X}_{ss}$) plus the product of the standard deviation of the distribution of standard scores (S_{ss}) multiplied by the z-score.

$$SS = \overline{X}_{ss} + (S_{ss})(z)$$

(5.2)

T-Scores   A *T-score* is a standard score with a mean of 50 and a standard deviation of 10. In Table 5.2, five z-scores are converted to T-scores. A T-score of 60 is 10 points above the mean (50). Since the standard deviation is 10, a T-score of 60 is one standard deviation above the mean.

Deviation IQs   When first introduced, the IQ was defined as the ratio of mental age (MA) to chronological age (CA) multiplied by 100. Soon statisticians found that MA has different variances and standard deviations at different chronological ages. Consequently, the same IQ has different meanings at different ages; the same IQ corresponds to different z-scores at different ages. To remedy that situation, MAs are converted to z-scores for each age group, and z-scores are converted to deviation IQs. *Deviation IQs* are standard scores with a mean of 100 and a standard deviation usually of 15 but occasionally of 16. A z-score can be converted to a deviation IQ by equation 5.2. In Table 5.3, five z-

TABLE 5.2   **Converting z-Scores to T-Scores**

z-Score	T-Score = 50+ (10)(z)
z = +1.0	60 = 50 + (10)(+1.0)
z = −1.5	35 = 50 + (10)(−1.5)
z = −2.1	29 = 50 + (10)(−2.1)
z = +3.6	86 = 50 + (10)(+3.6)
z = .0	50 = 50 + (10)(.0)

TABLE 5.3   **Converting z-Scores to Deviation IQs ($\overline{X}$ = 100)**

z-Score	IQ (S = 15)	IQ (S = 16)
−2.00	70	68
−1.00	85	84
.00	100	100
+1.00	115	116
+2.00	130	132

scores are converted to deviation IQs with standard deviations of 15 (column 2) and 16 (column 3).

Normal-Curve Equivalents   *Normal-curve equivalents* are standard scores with a mean equal to 50 and a standard deviation equal to 21.06. Although the standard deviation may at first appear a bit strange, this scale divides the normal curve into 100 equal intervals.

Stanines   *Stanines* (short for *stan*dard *nines*) are standard-score bands that divide a distribution into nine parts. The first stanine includes all scores that are 1.75 standard deviations or more below the mean, and the ninth stanine includes all scores 1.75 or more standard deviations above the mean. The second through eighth stanines are each .5 standard deviation in width, with the fifth stanine ranging from .25 standard deviation below the mean to .25 standard deviation above the mean.

Advantages and Disadvantages of Standard Scores   Standard scores are frequently more difficult to interpret than percentile scores because the concepts of means and standard deviations are not widely understood by people without some statistical knowledge. Thus, standard scores may be more difficult for students and their parents to understand. Aside from this disadvantage, standard scores offer all the advantages of percentiles. Moreover, standard scores have an additional advantage. Because standard scores are equal interval, they can be combined (for example, added or averaged).[1]

1. Standard scores also solve another subtle problem. When scores are combined in a total or composite, the elements of that composite (for example, eighteen scores from weekly spelling tests that are averaged to obtain a semester average) do not count the same (that is, they do not carry the same weight) *unless they have equal variances.* Tests that have larger variances contribute more to the composite than tests with smaller variances. When each of the elements have been standardized into the same scores (for example, when each of the weekly spelling tests have been standardized as z-scores), the elements will carry exactly the same weight when they are combined. Moreover, the only way that a teacher can weight tests differentially is to standardize all the tests and then multiply by the weight. For example, if a teacher wished to count the second test as three times the first test, the scores on both tests would have to be standardized and the second test scores then multiplied by three before the scores were combined.

Concluding Comments on Derived Scores

Test authors provide tables to convert raw scores into derived scores. Thus, test users do not have to calculate derived scores. However, test users may wish to convert raw scores to other standard scores for which no conversion tables are provided. Because all standard scores are based on z-scores, standard scores have the same relationship to each other regardless of a distribution's shape. Therefore, standard scores can be transformed into other standard scores readily with the formulas provided earlier in this chapter. Standard scores can be converted to percentiles without conversion tables only when the distribution of scores is normal. In normal distributions, the relationship between percentiles and standard scores is known. Figure 5.2 compares various standard scores and percentiles for normal distributions. When the distribution of scores is not normal, conversion tables are necessary to convert percentiles to standard scores (or vice versa). These conversion tables are test specific so that they can only be provided by a test author. Moreover, conversion tables are always required to convert developmental scores to scores of relative standing, even when the distribution of test scores is normal. If the only derived score available on a test is an age equivalent, then there is no way for a test user to convert raw scores to percentiles or standard scores.

The selection of the particular type of score to use and to report depends on the purpose of testing and the sophistication of the consumer. In our opinion,

FIGURE 5.2   **Relationship Among Selected Standard Scores, Percentiles, and One Age Score and the Normal Curve**

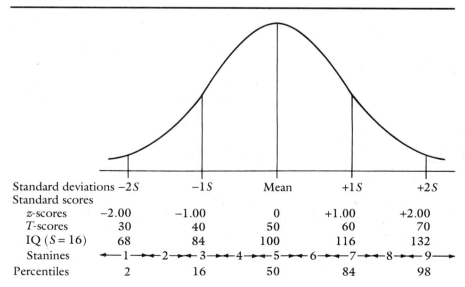

Standard deviations	−2S	−1S	Mean	+1S	+2S
Standard scores					
z-scores	−2.00	−1.00	0	+1.00	+2.00
T-scores	30	40	50	60	70
IQ (S = 16)	68	84	100	116	132
Stanines	← 1 → ← 2 →	← 3 → ← 4 →	← 5 → ← 6 →	← 7 → ← 8 →	← 9 →
Percentiles	2	16	50	84	98

developmental scores should never be used. These scores are readily misinterpreted by both lay and professional people. In order to understand the precise meaning of developmental scores, one must generally know both the mean and standard deviation and then *convert* the developmental score to a more meaningful score, a score of relative standing. Various professional organizations (for example, the International Reading Association, the American Psychological Association, the National Council on Measurement in Education, and the Council for Exceptional Children) also hold very negative official opinions about developmental scores and quotients.

Standard scores are convenient for test authors. Their use allows an author to give equal weight to various test components or subtests. Their utility for the consumer is twofold. First, *if* the score distribution is normal, the consumer can readily convert standard scores to percentile ranks. Second, because standard scores are equal-interval scores, they are useful in analyzing strengths and weaknesses of individual students and in research.

We favor the use of percentiles. These unpretentious scores require the fewest assumptions for accurate interpretation. The scale of measurement need only be ordinal, although it is very appropriate to compute percentiles on equal-interval or ratio data. The distribution of scores need not be normal; percentiles can be computed for any shape of distribution. They are readily understood by professionals, parents, and students. Most important, however, is the fact that percentiles tell us nothing more than what any norm-referenced derived score can tell us—namely, an individual's relative standing in a group. Reporting scores in percentiles may remove some of the aura surrounding test scores, but it permits test results to be presented in terms users can understand.

CRITERION-REFERENCED SCORES

Unlike norm-referenced scores that compare a student's performance to the performances of other students, criterion-referenced scores compare a student's performance to an objective and absolute standard (criterion) of performance. Criterion-referenced measures are of two types: scores on single skills and scores on multiple skills.

Single-Skill Scores

The most basic score used in criterion-referenced assessment is pass-fail, right-wrong, or some variation on this theme. Usually, one option in this dichotomous scoring scheme is defined precisely, and the other option is scored by default. For example, a right response to "1 + 2 = ?" might be defined as "3, written intelligibly and in the correct orientation"; a wrong response would be one that fails to meet one or more of the criteria for a correct response.

Single-skill scores may also be scored along a dimension that ranges from completely correct to completely incorrect. For example, a teacher might give partial credit for a response because the student used the correct algorithm to solve a mathematics problem even though the student's answer was incorrect. Frequently, continuum scoring of single skills is used to show progress toward mastery of a skill. For example, in a daily living or life skills curriculum, a teacher might scale drinking from a cup without assistance in several ways. The teacher might observe frequency of proper drinking and scale it as usually, frequently, seldom, or never drinks from a cup without assistance. Or, that teacher might scale drinking on the basis of assistance needed by a student (drinks from a cup without assistance, drinks from a cup with verbal prompts, drinks from a cup with physical guidance, or does not drink from a cup). Of course, each point on the continuum requires careful definition. However, multiple points along a continuum can be useful when trying to document slow progress toward a goal.

Some newer types of assessment (for example, portfolio assessment and authentic assessment) appear similar to single-dimension, criterion-referenced assessment. These newer forms of assessment frequently scale performance from "novice" to "expert" on some dimension. However, the points along the continuum are frequently so subjective that they are virtually impossible to define or assess consistently. We view these types of "assessment" as scaled opinions about student performance rather than meaningful assessments of student performance; therefore, we are reluctant to consider them within the category of criterion-referenced assessment.

Multiple-Skill Scores

When multiple skills (for example, addition facts), complex skills (for example, oral reading), or multiple observations of single skills are assessed, it is common to express the number of correct or incorrect responses as a function of the total number of responses (for example, percent correct) or as a function of time (for example, the number of correct responses per minute). Below, we refer to these two types of scores as percentages and rates. We realize that percentages are, indeed, rates, but the professional literature frequently refers to scores expressed in time units as rates and distinguishes these scores from percentages based on the number of opportunities. We use the common jargon with the understanding that it is at odds with the usual meanings.

Percentage

Percentages are widely used in a variety of assessment contexts. For example, percent correct is probably the score most frequently used by teachers in the assessment of academic skills; prevalence (the percentage of time a behavior occurs) is frequently used in systematic observation. Percentages are often the basis of other criterion-referenced scores. Three of the most commonly used derivative scores are accuracy, retention, and instructional level.

Accuracy   Accuracy refers to one of two different scores that define percent correct. The first is based on the number of *possible* correct responses and is calculated by multiplying 100 times the ratio of the number of correct responses to the number of possible responses. For example, if Billy gets 25 correct answers on a fifty-item test, he earns a score of 50 percent correct.

The second type of percentage score is based on the number of *attempted* responses and is calculated by multiplying 100 times the ratio of the number of correct responses to the number of *attempted* responses. This form of percent correct is most commonly used when a teacher intentionally uses an assessment procedure that precludes a student from responding to all items.[2] For example, a teacher may ask a student to read orally for two minutes, but it may not be possible for the student (or the teacher) to read the passage in the time allotted. Thus, Billy may attempt 175 words in a 350-word passage in two minutes; if he reads 150 words correctly, his percentage correct would be about 86 percent, that is, $100 \cdot (150/175)$.

Retention   Retention refers to the percentage of learned information that is recalled. Retention may also be termed recall, maintenance, or memory of what has been learned. Regardless of label, it is calculated in the same way: divide the number recalled by the number originally learned and multiply that ratio by 100. For example, if Helen learned 40 sight vocabulary words and recalled 30 of them two weeks later, her retention would be 75 percent; that is, $100 \cdot (30/40)$. Because forgetting becomes more likely as the interval between the learning and the retention assessment increases, retention is usually qualified by the period of time between attainment of mastery and assessment of precall. Thus, Helen's retention would be stated as 75 percent over a two-week period.

Verbal Labels for Percentages   Frequently, percentages are given verbal labels that are intended to facilitate instruction. The two most commonly used labels are "mastery" and "instructional level." *Mastery* divides the percentage continuum in two: mastery is generally set at 90 percent correct and nonmastery is less than 90 percent. The criterion of 90 percent for mastery is arbitrary, and sometimes in real life we set the skill level for mastery considerably higher. For example, we would probably want to define mastery of looking both ways before crossing a street as close to 100 percent correct.

Instructional level divides the percentage range into three segments: frustration, instructional, and independent levels. By convention, frustration level is

2. A situation in which there are more opportunities to respond than time to respond is termed a *free operant*. Free operant situations arise in assessments that are timed to allow the opportunity for unlimited increase in rate. They are also used frequently in precision teaching.

usually defined as less than 85 percent correct, instructional level is defined as between 85 and 95 percent correct, and independent level is defined as above 95 percent correct. For example, in reading, students who decode more than 95 percent of the words should be able to use context cues and word attack skills to read a passage without assistance;[3] students who decode between 85 and 95 percent of the words in a passage should be able to read and comprehend that passage with assistance; students who cannot decode 85 percent of the words in a passage will probably have difficulty comprehending the material even with assistance.

Rate

Teachers often want their students to have a supply of information "at their fingertips," so that they can respond fluently (or automatically) without thinking. For example, teachers may want their students to recognize sight words without having to sound them out, recall addition facts without having to think about them, or supply Spanish words for their English equivalents. When fluency or automaticity is the desired level of performance, teachers may calculate the rate of correct response. *Rate* is defined as the number of correct responses in a specific time frame (for example, the number of words read correctly per minute). Criterion rates for successful performance are usually determined empirically. For example, readers with satisfactory comprehension usually read connected prose at rates of 100 or more words per minute (Mercer and Mercer, 1985). Readers interested in desired rates for a variety of academic skills are referred to Salvia and Hughes (1990).

SUMMARY

One method of interpreting student scores is to compare them to the scores of a group of students of known characteristics called a norm group. Scores interpreted this way are called norm-referenced scores. Two types of norm-referenced comparisons can be made—across ages and within ages. Developmental scores (that is, age and grade equivalents) compare students' performances across age or grade groups. Within a group, comparisons can be made using several different types of scores that have different characteristics. A *developmental quotient* (an age or grade equivalent divided by chronological age or actual grade placement, respectively) is the least desirable within-age comparison. Of greater value are standard scores (for example, z-scores, T-scores, and deviation IQs). Such scores have a predetermined mean and standard deviation that define them. The best derived scores for general use are percentile ranks.

---

3. Students should not be given homework (independent practice) unless they are at the independent level.

A second method of interpreting student scores is to compare scores to an absolute standard of performance. Two types of criterion-referenced scores are commonly used: single-skill scores and multiple-skill scores. Single-skill scores are usually scored dichotomously (for example, pass-fail), but may be scaled on a continuum (for example, usually, frequently, never). Whether scored dichotomously or along a continuum, the scoring criteria always should be expressed in precise and observable terms. Multiple skills (for example, writing weekly spelling words) are scored as the percent correct or as the number of correct responses in a specific period of time (for example, number of words read correctly per minute).

STUDY QUESTIONS

1. Eleanore and Audrey take an intelligence test. Eleanore obtains an MA of 3-5 and Audrey obtains an MA of 12-2. The test had been standardized on fifty boys and girls at each of the following ages: 3-0 to 3-1, 4-0 to 4-1, 5-0 to 5-1, 6-0 to 6-1, and 7-0 to 7-1. The psychologist reports that Eleanore functions like a child aged 3 years and 5 months, whereas Audrey has the mental age of a twelve-year-old child. Identify five problems inherent in these interpretations.
2. Differentiate between a *ratio IQ* (developmental quotient) and a *deviation IQ*. Why is a deviation IQ preferable?
3. Sam earned a percentile rank of 83 on a kindergarten admission test. What is the statistical meaning of his score? To what *decile* does the score correspond? To what *quartile* does the score correspond?
4. Marietta takes a battery of standardized tests. The results are as follows:
   Test A: Mental age = 8-6
   Test B: Reading grade equivalent = 3.1
   Test C: Developmental age = 8-4
   Test D: Developmental quotient = 103
   Test E: Percentile rank 56.
   What must the teacher do in order to interpret Marietta's performances on these five scales and compare the performances to each other?
5. Andrew earns a stanine of 1 on an intelligence test. To what *z*-scores, percentile ranks, and *T*-scores does his stanine score correspond?
6. Distinguish between frustration level, instructional level, and independent level. Why are these distinctions important?

PROBLEMS

Turn back to Table 4.4 (page 97), which shows the results of the two tests Ms. Smith gave to her arithmetic class. For test 1, make the following computations.

1. Compute the percentile rank for each student.
2. Compute each student's z-score.
3. Convert Bob's, Sam's, Sean's, and Carole's z-scores to T-scores.
4. Convert Lucy's, Carmen's, John's, and Ludwig's z-scores to deviation IQs with a mean of 100 and a standard deviation of 15.

Answers

1. 98, 94, 90, 86, 82, 78, 70, 70, 70, 50, 50, 50, 50, 50, 50, 50, 30, 30, 30, 22, 18, 14, 10, 6, 2
2. 2.17, 2.00, 1.33, 1.00, .67, .5, .33, .33, .33, 0, 0, 0, 0, 0, 0, 0, −.33, −.33, −.33, −.5, −.67, −1 .00, −1.33, −2.00, −2.17
3. 72, 63, 50, 45
4. 130, 105, 100, 70

Chapter 6

Norms

*I*t is seldom possible to test everyone in a particular population, because the membership of the population is constantly changing. Some children who are in the six-year-old population today will be 7 years old tomorrow. Grade populations change at least once a year. Moreover, testing an entire population is not only virtually impossible but also unnecessary. The characteristics of a population can be accurately estimated from the characteristics of a representative subset of the population (called a *sample*); inferences based on what one has learned from a sample can be extended to a population at large. Thus, the normative samples used in norm-referenced assessment are intended to allow inferences to be made about a population.

In norm-referenced assessment, norms are important for two reasons. First, the normative sample is often used to obtain the various statistics on which the final selection of test items is based. Consequently, the adequacy of the standardization sample can affect measures of internal consistency, item-total correlations, and indexes of item difficulty (the proportion of individuals passing a specific test item, or *p-value*), as well as item selection and item-scoring procedures.

The second reason that norms are important is more obvious. In norm-referenced assessment, an individual's performance is evaluated in terms of other people's performances.[1] All the derived, norm-referenced scores that were described in Chapter 5—percentiles, standard scores, and the rest—are based on the performance of the individuals in the normative sample. When we use norm-referenced tests, we compare the performances of the individuals we test to the performances of the individuals in the norm group. Even if a test is otherwise satisfactory, test scores may be misleading if the norms are inadequate. The adequacy of a test's norms depends on three factors: the representativeness of the norm sample, the number of cases in the norm sample, and the relevance of the norms to the purpose of testing.

---

1. Although the emphasis in this chapter is on individuals, the reader should understand that norms can also be used to interpret the performance of groups of individuals.

REPRESENTATIVENESS

In evaluating representativeness, particular attention must be paid to demographic variables because of their relationship (either theoretical or empirical) to what the test is intended to measure. Which demographic variables are significant for a particular test depends on the content of the test and/or the construct being measured.

Representativeness hinges on two questions. The first is, Does the norm sample contain the same kinds of people as the population that the norms are intended to represent? *Kinds* of people usually refers to relative levels of maturation, levels of skill development, and degrees of acculturation. The second question of representativeness is, Are the various kinds of people present in the sample in the same proportion as they are in the population of reference?

When we compare a student's performance to a norm sample in order to predict future behavior, we assume that the student has had an opportunity to acquire skills, concepts, or experiences comparable to the opportunities of the students in the norm sample. When we compare a student's performance to a norm sample in order to understand better that student's current level of functioning, we need assume only that the norm sample is representative of the population. The distinction between understanding current level of functioning and predicting future behavior is part of the controversy over culture-free (or culture-fair) testing. If a ten-year-old student has had no opportunity to learn to read (and consequently has not acquired the skills), the tester who notes that the student *currently* lacks this skill is not being unfair or biased. But if the student being tested and the students in the normative sample have not had comparable opportunities to acquire the behaviors sampled in the test, it may be misleading to use the student's test score to predict future behavior. When we predict future behavior, we assume that students have learned what they can learn. Students who have had no chance to learn have not been able to demonstrate what they can learn. Not knowing how well such students will learn given the opportunity, we cannot use their test scores to make predictions.

Kinds of People

Several factors are usually considered in the development of norms for psychoeducational tests. Following is a brief discussion of the most commonly considered factors, together with a rationale for the importance of each.

Age

A student's age is an excellent general indicator of several important factors. Physiological maturation is an important variable in motor and perceptual-motor tests, and age is directly related to maturation. It would be foolish to say that a six-year-old child lacks physical stamina because that child can run only as long as 2 percent of all ten-year-olds. Six-year-old children are not as big and strong as ten-year-old children. Consequently, we would not want to compare children of different ages on tests involving physical, developmental effects.

A student's amount of experience with practically everything is a function of age. Indeed, age is an excellent indicator of the opportunity to acquire skills, information, and concepts. Mental growth (as measured by mental ages) and chronological ages are very highly correlated; Kappauf (1973) has empirically estimated the correlation to be in excess of .90. Again, it would usually be inappropriate to compare a six-year-old's fund of general information with that of a twelve-year-old. The six-year-old simply has not been around as long and therefore has not had the opportunity to acquire as much information.

The relationship of a particular skill or ability to age is an empirical issue. Different abilities may be expected to have different growth curves (see Guilford, 1967, pp. 417–426). Thus, test authors should demonstrate the relationship of age and the ability being assessed prior to establishing age norms.

Grade

All achievement tests and some intelligence tests measure the results of systematic academic instruction. Students of different ages are present in most grades, and grade in school bears a more direct relationship to what is taught in school than does age. Some seven-year-old children may not be enrolled in school; some may be in kindergarten, some in first grade, some in second grade, and some even in third grade. Thus, the academic proficiency of seven-year-olds can be expected to be more closely related to what they have been taught than to their age. Consequently, grade norms are more appropriate than age norms for achievement tests that are used with students of school age.

Gender

Gender also plays an important role in a child's development. There are pronounced differences between girls and boys in typical patterns of physical development around puberty (Tanner, 1970). Personality differences have long been reported; for example, boys have tended to be more aggressive than girls (Mischel, 1970). Small gender differences have also been reported in intellectual development. For example, Roberts (1971) reported that boys scored higher than girls on the Vocabulary and Block Design subtests of the Wechsler Intelligence Scale for Children. But the magnitude of sex differences on ability, achievement, and aptitude measures is nearly always very small; the male and female distributions overlap a great deal.

Although gender-role expectations seem to be changing, gender still may systematically limit the types of activities in which a child engages. This may result from such influences as modeling, peer pressure, or responsiveness to the attitudes of significant adults. For whatever reasons, males and females differ systematically on tests, and students of both genders should be represented in the norm sample. Appropriate representation is especially important for behaviors on which there are known gender differences.

Acculturation of Parents

The level of acculturation of a child's parents or guardians has a direct impact on a student's performance on intellectual and academic tests. One can consider the academic or occupational attainment (socioeconomic status) of the parents as an indication of the child's acculturation as well as the level of acculturation in the home. There is a consistent relationship between these indexes of acculturation and the performance of the child on various psychoeducational measures. Parental occupation and income have been consistently reported to be related to school achievement (for example, Schaie & Roberts, 1971) and intelligence (for example, Burt, 1959; Roberts, 1971). The causes of these consistent social-class differences have been debated for years (see Gottesman, 1968), with some scholars favoring genetic interpretations of differences, others favoring environmental interpretations, and still others favoring interpretations based on the interaction of genetics and environment. Although the causes of class differences are beyond the scope of this text, the fact of social-class differences is undeniable. For this reason, test standardizations should include children of all social classes.

Geographic Factors

Different geographic regions of the United States differ in values and mores, and various psychoeducational tests reflect these regional differences. Historically, regional differences in intelligence and achievement have been well documented (for example, Ginzberg & Bray, 1953 and Schaie & Roberts, 1971). Community size and density have also been related to academic and intellectual development (Schaie & Roberts, 1971). Potential explanations for these relationships are numerous—for example, differential funding of education and selective migration. Regardless of the reasons for geographical differences, test norms should include individuals from all geographic regions as well as from urban, suburban, and rural residences.

Race and Ethnic Cultural Differences

Race is a particularly sensitive issue, especially since the scientific community has often been insensitive to the issue and has even on occasion been blatantly racist (for example, Down, 1866/1969). Indeed, until fairly recently, test authors excluded nonwhite individuals from standardization samples; for example, as recently as 1972, the Stanford Binet Intelligence Scale excluded minorities.

Although differences in achievement and tested intelligence appear to be narrowing from previously reported discrepancies (for example, Roberts, 1971; Coleman et al., 1966), many differences persist. And, as is the case of differences in acculturation, gender, and geographic area, most explanations for racial and ethnic differences are beyond the scope of this text. However, the fact of racial and cultural differences must be kept in mind for two reasons. First, to the extent that individuals of different races undergo cultural experiences that differ even within social class and geographic region, norm samples that exclude (or underrepresent) them are unrepresentative of the total population. The second reason involves item selection. If individuals from different cultures are excluded from field tests of test items, item difficulty estimates (p-values) and point biserial (item-total) correlations may be inaccurate. Hence, the test scaling may be in error. We believe that both these arguments have merit. It is important to include individuals of all racial and ethnic groups both in field tests of items and in the standardization of a test.

Intelligence

A representative sample of individuals, in terms of their level of intellectual functioning, is essential for standardizing an intelligence test—or any other kind of test. Intelligence is related to a number of variables that are considered in psychoeducational assessment. It is certainly related to achievement, since most intelligence tests were actually developed to predict school success. Correlations of achievement and intelligence ranging between .60 and .80 are typical (for example, Hieronymus, Hoover, & Lindquist, 1986). Since language development and facility are often considered an indication of intellectual development, intelligence tests are often verbally oriented. Consequently, one would also expect to find substantial correlations between scores on tests of intelligence and scores on tests of linguistic or psycholinguistic ability. Items thought to reflect perceptual ability appear on intelligence tests, and Thurstone (1944) found various perceptual tasks to be a factor in intelligence. Koppitz (1975) reports substantial correlations between scores on the Bender Visual Motor Gestalt Test and scores on intelligence tests. Thus, intelligence should be considered in the development of norms for perceptual and perceptual-motor tests.

In the development of norms for intelligence tests per se, it is essential to test the full range of intellectual ability. Limiting the sample to students enrolled in and attending school (usually regular classes) restricts the norms. Failure to consider the individuals classified as mentally retarded in standardization procedures introduces systematic bias into test norms. It has been estimated that 3 percent of the school-age population may be mentally retarded (Robinson & Robinson, 1976; Farber, 1968, pp. 46, 58). Dingman and Tarjan (1960) estimated that there is an excess frequency at the lower end of the intelligence distribution, probably as a result of pathological genetic conditions. They estimated that the mean IQ of this group was approximately 32, with a standard deviation approximately the same as that in the intellectually normal population.

Exclusion of such a large portion of the school-age population seriously biases the estimate of the population mean and standard deviation. For example, let us assume that a test is standardized excluding individuals with mental retardation and that the scores of the students in the normative sample are converted to deviation IQs with a mean of 100 and a standard deviation of 16. Increasing the sample by including 3 percent more subjects whose scores have a mean IQ of 32 and a standard deviation of 16 would have the same effect as including the individuals with mental retardation who were excluded. The mean would be lowered from 100 to 98.[2] The standard deviation would be increased from 16 to 19.7.[3]

A score that fell two standard deviations below the mean would be 68 without the individuals with retardation; it would be 59 if they were included. Representative sampling would substantially reduce the ranks of students labeled mentally retarded because test means and standard deviations would more accurately reflect the performance of the entire population. (However, it would not reduce the number of students having problems in school.)

Similar arguments can be made for the exclusion of students with any disability. Their exclusion biases the norms and possibly the scoring procedures.[4]

Age of Norms

An often overlooked consideration in representativeness is when the norms were developed. We live in an age of rapidly expanding knowledge and rapidly expanding communication of knowledge. Students of today know more than did the students of the 1930s or the 1940s. Students of today probably know less than will the students of tomorrow. For a norm sample to be representative, it must be current. Moreover, during the late 1960s and 1970s, the social fabric of the United States changed substantially. The civil rights and right-to-education movements brought much-needed reform to the U.S. education system. Thus, comparing a present-day nine-year-old student's performance with the performance of 1970 nine-year-olds appears unwise. The point at which norms become outdated is more judgmental than empirical and will depend in part on the ability or skill being assessed. With these cautions, it seems to us that fifteen

2. If the number of subjects in the norm group is 1,000 and the mean is 100, the sum of all scores is 100,000. If 30 children (3 percent of 1,000) whose mean is 32 are added to the 1,000 children, the sum of all scores is increased by 960(that is, 30 x 32). The mean of the 1,030 children is 98(that is, 100,960/1,030).

3. The variance is computationally equal to $\Sigma X^2/N - (\Sigma X/N)^2$. If the number of subjects (N) is 1,000 and the mean is 100, the sum of all scores is 100,000; if the standard deviation is 16, the variance is 256. By substituting these figures into the preceding formula, we obtain the sum of the squared scores, which is 10,256,000. If we increase the sample by 30 children whose scores have a mean of 32 and standard deviation of 16, we increase the sum of the squared scores by 38,400. The variance of the 1,030 children is 386.76; the standard deviation (the square root of the variance) is 19.67.

4. In Chapter 30 we discuss the inclusion of students with disabilities in the assessment of educational outcomes.

years is about the maximum useful life for norm samples. Some states (for example, Texas) are recommending much shorter norm life.

Special Population Characteristics

Some characteristics of the sample and of the population are important only for particular types of tests. For example, test authors often caution test users to make sure the content of achievement tests reflects the content of the test user's classroom curriculum. However, the test author must also make sure that the content is appropriate for the norm sample. Thus, for reading diagnostic tests, which often measure specific skills such as syllabication and sound blending, the author should specify the curriculum followed by the students in the norm sample. If a visual, sight-vocabulary orientation is used by students in the norm sample, the derived scores of students taught by a phonics method may be inflated; that is, the students taught by the phonics method may earn relatively high scores when compared to the less skilled students in the norm group.

Tests used to identify students with particular problems should include such children in their standardization sample. For example, the Illinois Test of Psycholinguistic Abilities was often used to identify individuals with psycholinguistic dysfunctions that presumably underlie academic difficulties. Yet the norm sample included "only those children demonstrating average intellectual functioning, average school achievement, average characteristics of personal-social adjustment, sensory-motor integrity, and coming from predominantly English-speaking families" (Paraskevopoulos & Kirk, 1969, pp. 51–52). How can a test be used to identify individuals whose academic difficulties are caused by psycholinguistic dysfunction when such individuals are excluded from the normative sample? A student who earns the same score as any student in the norm sample has earned a score associated with school success.

Proportion of the Kinds of People

Implicit in the preceding discussion of characteristics of the representative normative sample was the notion that the various kinds of people should be included in the same proportion in the sample as they occur in the general population. The development of systematic norms requires systematic data collection, which is both time-consuming and expensive. It is incumbent on the author of a test to demonstrate that its norms are in fact representative. Samples that are convenient, such as samples consisting of volunteers, are not necessarily representative; in fact, they are probably unrepresentative. Large numbers of subjects do not guarantee a representative sample. Roosevelt was reelected president of the United States, even though predictions based on a large sample had proclaimed that Alf Landon would be the next president. The problem was that the sample was unrepresentative of the voting population.

Because representative samples require careful selection, test authors or publishers usually develop sampling plans to try to obtain subjects in the correct proportions. Sampling plans usually involve the selection of communities of specific sizes within geographic regions. Cluster sampling and selection of representative communities (or some combination of the two) are two common methods of choosing these communities. In cluster sampling, urban areas and the surrounding suburban and rural communities are selected. Such sampling plans have the advantage of requiring fewer testers and less travel. When a sampling plan calls for the selection of representative communities, a "representative" community is usually defined as one in which the mean demographic characteristics (such as educational level and income) of residents are approximately the same as the national or regional average. For example, in the 1990 U.S. Census, about 52 percent of the population was female; 19 percent had attended college for at least four years; about 30 percent had not completed high school; and so forth. A representative community would thus be one in which about 52 percent of the population was female, about 19 percent had attended college for four years, and so forth.

Neither cluster sampling nor selection of representative communities guarantees that the subjects within the norms are, as a group, representative of the population: The sample selected may not be representative of the representative community. Consequently, test authors often tinker with norms to make them representative on important characteristics. One method of adjusting norms is to systematically oversample subjects (that is, to select many more subjects than are needed) and then drop subjects until a representative sample has been achieved. Another method is to weight subjects within the normative sample differentially. Subjects with underrepresented characteristics may be counted as more than one subject and subjects with overrepresented characteristics may be counted as fractions of persons. In such ways, norm samples can be manipulated to conform with population characteristics.

Test authors should demonstrate that their norms are representative by presenting data that show the correspondence of their sample to the population. Preferably this correspondence should be shown for each age or grade group. Because of the constraint of limited space in a technical manual, however, one generally sees these data only for the total sample.

SMOOTHING NORMS

After the norm sample has been finalized, norm tables are prepared. Because of minor sampling errors, even well-selected norm groups will show minor fluctuations in distribution shape. Minor smoothing is believed to result in better estimates of derived scores, means, and standard deviations. For example, there might be a few outliers—scores at the extremes of a distribution that are not contiguous to the distribution scores but several points beyond what would be considered the highest or lowest score in a distribution. A test author might drop outliers. Similarly, the progression of group means from age to age may not be consistent, or group variances might differ slightly from age to age for no apparent reason. As a result, test developers will often smooth these values to conform to a theoretical or empirically generated model of performance (for example, using predicted means rather than obtained means).

Smoothing is also done to remove unwanted fluctuations in the shapes of age or grade distributions by adjusting the relationship between standard scores and percentiles. Even when normal test distributions are expected on the basis of theory, the obtained distributions of scores are never completely normal. For example, several models of intelligence posit a normal distribution of scores; in practice, the distribution–test scores are skewed because of an excess of low-scoring individuals. Thus, standard scores do not correspond to the percentile ranks that are expected in a normal distribution. In such cases, a test author may force standard scores into a normal distribution by assigning them to percentile ranks on the basis of the relationship between standard scores and percentiles found in normal distributions. For example, a raw score corresponding to the 84th percentile will be assigned a T-score of 60, regardless of the calculated value. The process, called area transformation, or *normalizing a distribution*, is discussed in detail in advanced measurement texts (for example, Ghiselli, 1964). When normal distributions are not expected, a test developer may remove minor inconsistencies in distribution shapes from age to age or grade to grade. To smooth out minor inconsistencies, test authors may average the percentile ranks associated with specific standard scores. For example, a T-score of 60 might be associated with percentile ranks of 72, 74, 73, and 73 in six-, seven-, eight-, and nine-year-old groups. These percentiles could be averaged, and T-scores of 60 in each age group would be assigned a percentile rank of 73.

NUMBER OF SUBJECTS

The number of subjects in a norm sample is important for several reasons. First, the number of subjects should be large enough to guarantee stability. "If the number of cases is small we cannot put much dependence on the norms, since another group consisting of the same number of persons might give quite different results. The larger the number of cases the more stable will be the norms" (Ghiselli, 1964, p. 49). Next, the number of cases should be large enough so that infrequent elements in the population can be represented. Finally, there should be enough subjects that the sizes of interpolations and extrapolations are relatively small. In a normally distributed array of scores, one hundred subjects is the minimum number for which a full range of percentiles can be computed and for which standard scores between ± 2.3 standard deviations can be computed without extrapolation. Consequently, we believe that one hundred should be the minimum number of persons in any norm sample. If the test spans a number of ages or grades, the norm sample should contain at least one hundred subjects per age or grade.

RELEVANCE OF THE NORMS

The major question regarding relevance of norms concerns the extent to which people in the norm sample provide comparisons that are relevant in terms of the purpose for which the test was administered. For some purposes, national norms are the most appropriate. If we are interested in knowing how a particular student is developing intellectually, perceptually, linguistically, or physically, national norms would be the most appropriate.

In other circumstances, norms developed on a particular portion of the population may be meaningful. For example, if we wished to ascertain the degree to which a student had profited from his twelve years of schooling, norms developed for the particular school district he had been served by might be appropriate. Suppose the school district is providing such poor educational services that, as a district, it falls well below the national average. If this is the case, our twelfth grader could earn a percentile rank of 75 based on district norms and a percentile rank of only 35 based on representative national norms. Still, despite the fact that his score is low in comparison to scores made nationwide, it's clear that our student has made comparatively good use of the inadequate services he has been getting. The same relationship between scores based on national norms and scores based on local norms might also be obtained if the school district were teaching materials not covered by the achievement test.

Local norms may be more useful in retrospective interpretations of a student's performance than in predictive interpretations. Thus, in the preceding example, if the content of the local achievement test was appropriate in terms of what the schools were actually attempting to teach, we could conclude that the student had profited from instruction but nonetheless would probably be at a disadvantage if he entered college.

In some cases, norms based on particular groups may be more relevant than those based on the population as a whole. Some devices are standardized on special populations: The Nebraska Test of Learning Aptitude is standardized on individuals with deafness; the AAMD Adaptive Behavior Scale is standardized on individuals with mental retardation; and the Blind Learning Aptitude Test is standardized on individuals who are blind. Aptitude tests are often standardized on individuals in specific trades or professions. The utility of special population norms is similar to the utility of local norms: They are likely to be more useful in retrospective comparisons than in future predictions. Without knowing how the special population corresponds to the general population, inferences may not be appropriate. Suppose a student with a severe hearing impairment earns a learning quotient of 115 derived from norms based on individuals with hearing impairments. One knows only that the person scored better than the average person with a severe disability. The basic question that must be addressed is, Does the score based on special population norms lead to correct interpretations? Thus, the test user must know how the change in norms affects prediction.

There are specific instances in which special population norms have been misused. When a person's performance is similar to that of a special population, it does not mean the person belongs to or should belong to that population. Because Mary earns the same score as a typical lawyer on a test of legal aptitude does not mean Mary is or should become a lawyer. The argument that she should contains a logical fallacy, an undistributed middle term. (Clearly, if dogs eat meat and university professors eat meat, dogs are not university professors.)

Reasoning of this sort is often inferred when criterion groups are used in test standardization. Such inferences are valid if it can be demonstrated that *only* members of a particular group score in a particular manner. If some people who are not members of the particular group earn the same scores as members of that group, the relationship between group membership and scores should be quantified. For example, let us assume that 90 percent of youngsters with brain damage make unusual (perhaps rotated, distorted, or simplified) reproductions of geometric designs. Let us also assume that 3 percent of the population is brain injured. If only individuals without brain damage made normal drawings, we could say with certainty that anyone who makes normal drawings is not brain injured. However, since 10 percent of individuals with brain-injuries make normal reproductions, we cannot be so sure: .31 percent of the individuals who make normal drawings are brain injured.

Moreover, in some instances, the "normal" population makes deviant responses. Assume that 20 percent of the normal population and all brain-injured children make unusual drawings. If 3 percent of the population is brain injured, 22.4 percent of the population will perform as brain injured (100% of 3% + 20% of 97% = 22.4%). A deviant performance on the test would mean only a 13 percent (.03/.224) chance that the person was brain injured.

USING NORMS CORRECTLY

The manuals accompanying commercially prepared tests usually contain a table that allows a tester to convert raw scores to various derived scores, such as percentile ranks, without laborious calculations. Occasionally, the tester is even confronted with several tables for converting raw scores. For example, it is not uncommon for the same manual to contain one set of tables for converting raw scores to percentile ranks on the basis of the age of the person tested and another set of tables for converting raw scores to percentile ranks on the basis of the school grade of the person tested. The tester must select tables based either on age or on grade. To select the appropriate table, the tester must determine the population to which the performance of the sample is inferred. This can be learned by examining how the norm group was selected. If the test author sampled by grades in school, then the population of reference is students in a particular grade; consequently, the grade tables should be used for converting raw scores to derived scores. Conversely, if the test author sampled by age, the age tables should be used, since the population of reference is a particular age group.

Tests often lose their power to discriminate near the extremes of the distribution. For example, an intelligence test might be constructed in such a way that even if a person failed every item, it might be impossible for that person to earn an IQ of less than 50. Since complete failure on a test provides little or no information about what a person can do, testers often administer tests based on a norm sample of people younger than the test taker. Although such a procedure may provide useful qualitative information, it cannot provide norm-referenced interpretations because the ages of the individuals in the norm group and the age of the person being tested are not the same. Another serious error is committed when the tester uses a person's mental age to obtain derived scores from conversion tables set up on the basis of chronological age. The reasoning behind such practices, we suppose, is that if the person functions as an eight-year-old child intellectually, the use of conversion tables based on the performances of eight-year-old children is appropriate. Such practices are incorrect, since the norms were not established by sampling persons of a particular mental age. When assessing the reading skill of an adolescent or adult who performs below the first percentile, a tester has little need for further or more precise norm-referenced comparisons. The tester already knows the person is not a good reader. If the examiner wants to ascertain which reading skills a person has or lacks, a criterion-referenced (norm-free) device would be more suitable. Sometimes the most appropriate use of norms is no use at all.

To use norms effectively, the tester must be sure that the norm sample is appropriate both for the purpose of testing and for the person being tested.

Concluding Comment: *Caveat Emptor*

If the test author recognizes that the test norms are inadequate, the test user should be explicitly cautioned (AERA et al., 1985). The inadequacies do not, however, disappear on the inclusion of a cautionary note; the test is still inadequate. It is occasionally argued that inadequate norms are better than no norms at all. This argument is analogous to the argument that even a broken clock is correct twice a day. With 86,400 seconds in a day, remarking that a clock is right twice a day is an overly optimistic way of saying that the clock is wrong 99.99 percent of the time. Inadequate norms do not allow meaningful and accurate inferences about the population. If poor norms are used, misinterpretations follow. The test user seldom knows whether a particular test has an inflated or deflated mean or variance.

A joint committee of the American Educational Research Association (AERA), the American Psychological Association, and the National Council on Measurement in Education (1985) prepared a pamphlet, *Standards for Educa-*

tional and Psychological Testing, which outlines the standards to which test authors should adhere: "Norms that are presented should refer to clearly described groups. These groups should be the ones with whom users of the test will ordinarily wish to compare the people who are tested" (p. 33). The pamphlet states that the test author should report how the sample was selected and whether any bias was present in the sample. The author should also describe the sampling techniques and the resultant sample in sufficient detail for the test user to judge the utility of the norms. "Reports of norming studies should include the year in which normative data were collected, provide descriptive statistics, and describe the sampling design and participation rates in sufficient detail so that the study can be evaluated for appropriateness" (p. 33).

In the marketplace of testing, let the buyer beware.

SUMMARY

The normative sample is important because it is the group of individuals with whom a tested person is compared. Norms should be representative of the population to which comparisons are made. A number of variables are typically considered important: age, grade, sex, acculturation of the persons tested and of their parents, geographic factors, race, intelligence, the date the norms were established, and special population characteristics. The norm sample should contain the same types of people in the same proportion as are found in the population of reference. The norm sample should be large enough to be stable and to provide a full range of derived scores. The norms should be relevant in terms of the purposes of testing, and they should be used correctly.

STUDY QUESTIONS

1. Identify two fundamental reasons that norms are important.
2. Willy Smith has only one leg. His teacher concludes that he cannot be tested in reading because no test demonstrates inclusion of one-legged children in its normative group. To what extent is the teacher's conclusion warranted?
3. Test X is standardized on fifty boys and fifty girls at each grade level from kindergarten through sixth grade. The children who made up the norm group were white, middle-class children living in Mount Pleasant, Michigan. Separate norm tables are provided for boys and girls in each grade. Danny, a third-grade black child residing in Oakland, California, is tested with test X, and the norm tables are used to interpret his score.
   a. To how many children is Danny being compared?
   b. To whose performance is Danny's performance being compared?
   c. What assumptions are being made about the relationship between Danny's acculturation and the acculturation of the normative sample?

4. Many tests were initially developed to discriminate between brain-injured and non-brain-injured adults. These same tests are now used to identify brain-injured children. Why is such a use inappropriate?
5. Under what conditions are local norms useful?
6. How might the author of a test demonstrate that its normative sample is representative of the population of children attending school in the United States?
7. Read the manual of any achievement test. How were the individuals in the normative sample selected? Is the normative sample representative of a particular population in terms of gender, ethnicity, and parental educational attainment? Were students with disabilities included in the norms? If so, how did the test authors assure that they would be included in the correct proportions?

ADDITIONAL READING

American Educational Research Association, American Psychological Association, & National Council on Measurement in Education (1985). *Standards for educational and psychological testing.* Washington, DC: American Psychological Association, pp. 31–34.

Chapter 7

Reliability

When we assess, we are interested in *generalizing* what we see today under one set of conditions to other occasions. For example, if we cannot generalize Billy's reading skills that are observed during testing to the classroom situation, then the test data are of little or no value. To the extent that we can generalize from a particular set of observations (a test, for example), those observations are reliable.

Reliability is a major consideration in evaluating an assessment procedure. For example, when we give a person an individually administered test, we would like to be able to generalize the results in three different ways. We would like to assume that if another tester were to score the exam, the results would be the same; we would not usually be confident about a student's test score if different examiners evaluated the same response differently. We would also like to assume that the behavior we see today would be seen tomorrow (or next week) if we were to test again; behaviors that are stable are generally of interest in educational settings. Finally, we would like to assume that similar but different test questions would give us similar results; we would like to be able to generalize to other similar test items. Thus, there are three kinds of reliability. Reliability for generalizing to different scorers is called *interrater*, or *interscorer*, *reliability*. Reliability for generalizing to different times is called *stability*, or *test-retest*, *reliability*. Reliability for generalizing to other test items is called *alternate form*, or *internal-consistency*, *reliability*.

It is useful to describe specifically what we mean by generalization. Suppose that Ms. Amig wanted to assess her kindergartners' recognition of upper- and lowercase letters of the English alphabet. She could assess the *domain*—all fifty-two upper- and lowercase letters—or she could sample from the domain. For example, she could ask each of her students to name the following letters: A, h, j, L, q, r, R, u, V, w. She would like to assume that another sample of letters (say, b, E, k, m, s, T, U, v, w, z) would lead to the same scores by her students. Moreover, she would like to assume that each student would earn the same derived score on any sample from the domain or on all the items in the domain. Thus, she wants to *generalize* from a sample of items to all the other items in the domain from which the sample was drawn. However, Ms. Amig wants more than that. Suppose that she tests her pupils on Monday morning at 9:30 A.M. She would like to assume that the students would earn the same scores if they were tested Tuesday at 1:45 P.M. There is a domain of times as well as a domain of items. A test on any one occasion is a sample from the domain of all times. Ms. Amig would like to generalize the results found on one sample of time to the domain. Her pupils' knowledge of the alphabet would not be very useful if they knew the letters only on Monday at 9:30 A.M. Finally, suppose Ms. Amig listened to her students say the letters of the alphabet. She would like to assume that any other teacher would score her students' responses in just the same way. It would not be very useful if she assigned Barney a score of 70 percent correct, but another teacher scored Barney's performance as 50 percent or 90 percent correct. There is a domain of scorers, and any one scorer is a sample from the domain of scorers. Ms. Amig would like to generalize her scoring to the scoring of any other comparably trained scorer. Her evaluation of her pupils' skills would not be very useful if other teachers would make different evaluations of the same behavior.

An easy way to think of reliability is to think of any obtained score as consisting of two parts: *true score* and *error*. By definition, error is uncorrelated with true score and is essentially random. Error is best thought of as lack of generalizability that results from the failure to get a representative sample from the domain. For example, a sample of alphabet letters that consisted of A, B, C, D, and E would probably provide a much easier test than other samples of letters. A systematically easier sample would inflate the scores earned by Ms. Amig's students. Similarly, a sample made up of the most difficult letters would probably deflate the scores earned by her students. Thus, error—failure to select a representative sample of items—can raise or lower scores. The average (mean) of error in the long run is equal to zero. In the long run, the samples that raise scores are balanced by samples that lower scores. If Ms. Amig made up and administered all the possible four-letter tests, a student's mean performance would be that student's true score. There would be no error associated with that score. However, there would be a distribution of test scores around that mean; it would be a distribution of obtained test scores centered on the true score.

Another way to think of a true score is to view it as the score that a student would earn if the entire domain of items were assessed. On achievement tests dealing with beginning material and with certain types of behavioral observations, it is occasionally possible to assess an entire domain (for example, reading and writing the letters of the alphabet or knowing all the addition, subtraction, multiplication, and division facts). In such cases, the obtained score is a student's true score, and there is no need to estimate the test's item reliability. Opportunities to assess an entire domain are very limited, even in the primary grades. It is often impossible to assess an entire achievement domain in more advanced curricula. Moreover, it is never possible to assess the entire domain when a hypothetical construct (such as intelligence or visual perception) is being assessed. Therefore, in these cases item reliability should always be estimated. The same argument can be made for reliability (generalization) over times and scores. If one time makes up the entire domain, then the student's performance at that time is the student's true score, although such a situation is difficult to imagine. Similarly, if evaluation by only one person makes up the entire domain, then the performance as assessed by that one person consititutes the entire domain, and the student's scores are true scores. Although such a situation is also difficult to imagine in the schools, outside of school personal evaluations are frequently all that matters. For example, your evaluation of the food at a restaurant is the only evaluation that is probably important in determining if the food was good.

As you may recall from the discussion in Chapter 2, people should always be concerned about error during assessment. Although there is always some degree of error, the important question is, How much error is attached to a particular score? Unfortunately, a direct answer to this question is not readily available. To estimate both the amount of error attached to a score and the amount of error in general, two statistics are needed: (1) a reliability coefficient for the particular generalization and (2) the standard error of measurement.

THE RELIABILITY COEFFICIENT

The symbol used to denote a reliability coefficient is r with two identical subscripts (for example, r_{xx} or r_{aa}). The *reliability coefficient* is generally defined as the square of the correlation between obtained scores and true scores on a measure (r_{xt}^2). This quantity is identical to the ratio of the variance of true scores to the variance of obtained scores for a distribution. (The variance of obtained scores equals the variance of true scores plus the variance of error.) Accordingly, a reliability coefficient indicates the *proportion* of variability in a set of scores that reflects true differences among individuals. In the special case where two equivalent forms of a test exist, the Pearson product-moment correlation coefficient between scores from the two forms is equal to the reliability coefficient for either form. These relationships are summarized in equation 7.1, where x and x' are parallel measures, and S^2 is, of course, the variance.

$$r_{xx'} = r_{xt}^2 = \frac{S^2 \text{ true scores}}{S^2 \text{ obtained scores}} = r_{xx'} \tag{7.1}$$

If there is relatively little error, the ratio of true-score variance to obtained-score variance approaches a reliability index of 1.00 (*perfect reliability*); if there is a relatively large amount of error, the ratio of true-score variance to obtained-score variance approaches .00 (*total unreliability*).[1] Thus, a test with a reliability coefficient of .90 has relatively less error of measurement and is more reliable than a test with a reliability coefficient of .50.

1. Although it is mathematically possible to obtain a negative reliability estimate, such an obtained coefficient is theoretically meaningless.

Different methods of estimating a reliability coefficient are used, depending on what generalization one wishes to make. Test authors should always report the extent to which one can generalize to different times and the degree to which one can generalize to different samples of questions or items. If a test is difficult to score, the test author should also report the extent to which one can generalize to different scorers.

Generalizing to Different Times

Test-retest reliability is an index of *stability*. Educators are interested in many human traits and characteristics that, theoretically, change very little over time. For example, children diagnosed as colorblind at age 5 are expected to be diagnosed as colorblind at any time in their lives. Colorblindness is an inherited trait that cannot be corrected. Consequently, the trait should be perfectly stable. When an assessment identifies a student as colorblind on one occasion and not colorblind on a later occasion, the assessment is unreliable.

Other traits are less stable than color vision over a long period of time; they are developmental. For example, people's heights will increase from birth through adulthood. The increases are relatively slow and predictable. Consequently, measurement with a reliable ruler should indicate few changes in height over a one-month period. Radical changes in people's heights (especially decreases) over short periods of time would cause us to question the reliability of the measurement device. Most educational and psychological characteristics are conceptualized much as height is. For example, we expect reading achievement to increase with length of schooling but to be relatively stable over short periods of time, such as two weeks. Devices used to assess traits and characteristics must produce sufficiently consistent and stable results if those results are to have practical meaning for making educational decisions.

The procedure for obtaining a stability coefficient is fairly simple. A large number of students are tested. A short time later (preferably two weeks, but in practice the time interval can vary from one day to several months), they are retested with the same device. The students' scores from the two administrations are then correlated. The obtained correlation coefficient is the *stability coefficient*.

Estimates of the amount of error derived from stability coefficients tend to be inflated. Any change in a student's true score attributable to maturation or learning is added to the error variance unless every student in the sample changes in the same way. Thus, if there is a "maturational spurt" between the two test administrations for only a few students, the change in the true score is incorporated into the error term. Similarly, if some of the students cannot answer some of the questions on the first administration of the test but learn the answers by the second administration, the learning (change in true score) is interpreted as error. The experience of taking the test once may also make answering the same questions the second time easier; the first test may sensitize the student to the second administration of the test. Generally, however, the closer together in time the test and retest are, the higher the reliability is, since within a shorter time span there is less chance of true scores changing.

Generalizing to Different Item Samples

There are two main approaches for estimating the extent to which we can generalize to different samples of items. The first approach requires that test authors develop two (or more) similar tests, called alternate forms; the second approach does not.

Alternate forms of a test are defined as two tests that measure the same trait or skill to the same extent and are standardized on the same population. Alternate forms offer essentially equivalent tests; sometimes, in fact, they're called *equivalent forms*. Let's look at a nonpsychometric example. All 12-inch rulers sold at a local variety store are thought to be the equivalent (or alternate form) of any other ruler. If one purchased a red ruler and a green ruler and measured several objects with both, one would expect a high correlation between the green measurements and the red measurements. This example is analogous to alternate-form reliability. There is one important difference, however. Alternate forms of tests do not contain the same items. Still, though the items are different, the means and variances for the two tests are assumed to be (or should be) the same. In the absence of error of measurement, any subject would be expected to earn the same score on both forms.

To estimate the reliability coefficient for two alternate forms (A and B) of a test, a large sample of students is tested with both forms. Half the subjects receive form A, then form B; the other half receive form B, then form A. Scores from the two forms are correlated. The correlation coefficient is a reliability coefficient.

Estimates of reliability based on alternate forms are subject to one of the same constraints as stability coefficients: The more time that passes between the administration of the two (or more) forms, the greater the likelihood of change in true scores. Unlike stability coefficients, alternate-form reliability estimates are less subject to a sensitization effect because the subjects are not tested with the same items twice.

The second approach to estimating the extent to which we can generalize to different test items does not require that the authors develop more than one form of the test. This method of estimating a test's reliability, called *internal consistency*, is a little different.

Suppose we wanted to use this second method to estimate the reliability of a ten-item test. After the test was constructed, we would administer it to a sample of students (for example, twenty students). The results of this hypothetical test are presented in Table 7.1. If the ten individual test items all measure the same

TABLE 7.1   **Hypothetical Performance of Twenty Children on a Ten-Item Test**

	Items										Totals		
Child	1	2	3	4	5	6	7	8	9	10	Total Test	Evens Correct	Odds Correct
1	+	+	+	−	+	−	−	−	+	−	5	1	4
2	+	+	+	+	−	+	+	+	−	+	8	5	3
3	+	+	−	+	+	+	+	−	+	+	8	4	4
4	+	+	+	+	+	+	+	+	−	+	9	5	4
5	+	+	+	+	+	+	+	+	+	−	9	4	5
6	+	+	−	+	−	+	+	+	+	+	8	5	3
7	+	+	+	+	+	−	+	−	+	+	8	3	5
8	+	+	+	−	+	+	+	+	+	+	9	4	5
9	+	+	+	+	+	+	−	+	+	+	9	5	4
10	+	+	+	+	+	−	+	+	+	+	9	4	5
11	+	+	+	+	+	−	+	−	−	−	6	2	4
12	+	+	−	+	+	+	+	+	+	+	9	5	4
13	+	+	+	−	−	+	−	+	−	−	5	3	2
14	+	+	+	+	+	+	+	−	+	+	9	4	5
15	+	+	−	+	+	−	−	−	−	−	4	2	2
16	+	+	+	+	+	+	+	+	+	+	10	5	5
17	+	−	+	−	−	−	−	−	−	−	2	0	2
18	+	−	+	+	+	+	+	+	+	+	9	4	5
19	+	+	+	+	−	+	+	+	+	+	9	5	4
20	+	−	−	−	−	+	−	+	−	−	3	2	1

skill or ability, we can divide the test into two five-item tests, each measuring that same skill or ability. Thus, after the test is administered, we can create two alternate forms of the test, each containing one-half of the total number of test items, or five items. We can then correlate the two sets of scores and obtain an estimate of the reliability of each of the two halves in the same way we would estimate the reliability of two alternate forms of a test. This procedure for estimating a test's reliability is called a *split-half reliability estimate.*

It should be apparent that there are many ways to divide a test into two equal-length tests. The ten-item test described above can be divided into over 100 different pairs of five-item tests. If the ten items in our full test are arranged in order of increasing difficulty, both halves should contain items from the beginning of the test (that is, easier items) and items from the end of the test (harder items). There are many ways of dividing such a test (for example, grouping items 1, 4, 5, 8, 9, and items 2, 3, 6, 7, 10). The most common way to divide a test is by odd-numbered and even-numbered items (see the columns labeled "Evens Correct" and "Odds Correct" in Table 7.1).

Odd-even division and the subsequent correlation of the two halves of a test is a common method for estimating a test's internal-consistency reliability, but it is not necessarily the best method. A more generalizable method of estimating internal consistency has been developed by Cronbach (1951) and is called *coefficient alpha*. Coefficient alpha is the average split-half correlation based on all possible divisions of a test into two parts. In practice there is no need to compute all possible correlation coefficients; coefficient alpha can be computed from the variances of individual test items and the variance of the total test score as shown in equation 7.2, where *k* is the number of items in the test.

$$r_{aa} = \frac{k}{k-1} \left(1 - \frac{\Sigma S^2_{items}}{S^2_{test}} \right)$$

(7.2)

Coefficient alpha can be used when test items are scored pass-fail or when more than one point is awarded for a correct response. An earlier, more restricted method of estimating a test's reliability, based on the average correlation between all possible split halves, was developed by Kuder and Richardson. This procedure, called *KR-20*, is coefficient alpha for dichotomously scored test items (that is, items that can be scored only right or wrong). Equation 7.2 can be used with dichotomous data; however, in this case the resulting estimate of reliability is usually called a KR-20 estimate rather than coefficient alpha.[2]

There are two major considerations in the use of internal-consistency estimates. First, this method should not be used for timed tests or tests that are not completed by all those being tested. Second, it provides no estimate of stability over time.

Generalizing to Different Scorers

There are two very different approaches to estimating the extent to which we can generalize to different scorers. The first way is similar to the ways of estimating generalizability that we have just discussed. Two testers score a set of tests independently. Scores obtained by each tester for the set are then correlated. The resulting correlation coefficient is a reliability coefficient for scorers. For example, suppose that a psychologist (Ms. Hawthorne) was interested in the distortion of body image in emotionally disturbed school children. Further, suppose she decided to assess distortion by evaluating the human-figure drawings of such children. Even with explicit criteria for what constitutes a distorted image, scoring of human-figure drawings is difficult. Would another, equally trained, tester—Mr. Torrance—arrive at the same conclusions as Ms. Hawthorne? Can Ms. Hawthorne's judgments be generalized to other testers and scorers? To quantify the extent to which this type of generalization is possible, the two testers could evaluate the human-figure drawings made by a class of emotionally disturbed pupils. As shown in Table 7.2, there would be two ratings

2. Sometimes a test author will estimate KR-20 with a formula called KR-21.

TABLE 7.2   **Judgment of Distorted Body Image in a Class of Emotionally Disturbed Children**

Child Number	Ms. Hawthorne	Mr. Torrance
1	normal	normal
2	distorted	distorted
3	distorted	normal
4	normal	normal
5	normal	normal
6	distorted	distorted
7	distorted	distorted
8	distorted	normal
9	normal	normal
10	normal	distorted
11	distorted	distorted
12	normal	normal
13	normal	normal
14	normal	normal
15	distorted	distorted
16	normal	distorted
17	normal	normal
18	distorted	distorted
19	normal	distorted
20	normal	distorted

of distortion of body image for each drawing, and these two scores could be correlated. The resulting correlation coefficient (phi = .41) would be an estimate of interscorer reliability or agreement.

The second approach to estimating generalizability to different scorers is prevalent in applied behavioral analysis. Instead of correlating the two scorers' ratings, percentage of agreement between raters is computed. Four indexes of percent agreement are used. *Simple agreement* is calculated by dividing the smaller number of occurrences by the larger number of occurrences and multiplying the quotient by 100. As Table 7.2 shows, Ms. Hawthorne observed eight distorted drawings and Mr. Torrance observed ten distorted drawings. Their simple agreement is 80 percent; that is, (8/10)(100). This index may be quite misleading, however, because agreement for each observation is not considered. Thus, it is possible (although not very likely) for two scorers to observe the same number of distorted drawings but disagree with each other on which drawings are distorted. Therefore, the use of simple agreement should be restricted to those circumstances in which it is the only index that can be computed (for example, in assessing the latency of a response or the frequency of behavior under

TABLE 7.3   **Summary of Agreements and Disagreements from Table 7.2**

	Ms. Hawthorne Distorted Drawings	Ms. Hawthorne Normal Drawings	
Mr. Torrance Normal Drawings	2	8	$\Sigma = 10$
Mr. Torrance Distorted Drawings	6 $\Sigma = 8$	4 $\Sigma = 12$	$\Sigma = 10$ $N = 20$

continuous observation). A more precise way of computing percentage of agreement is to consider agreement for each data point. The computation of *point-to-point agreement* takes each data point into consideration (see equation 7.3).

percent point-to-point agreement =
$$\frac{(100)\text{Number of agreements on occurrence and nonoccurrence}}{\text{Number of observations}} \quad (7.3)$$

The data from Table 7.2 are summarized in Table 7.3. The point-to-point agreement is computed by adding the frequency of agreement for occurrence (in this example, the occurrence of distorted drawings, $n = 6$) and frequency of agreement for nonoccurrence (in this example, nonoccurence is represented by normal drawings, $n = 8$), dividing this sum by the total number of observations, and multiplying the quotient by 100. Point-to-point agreement for the data in Table 7.3 is .70 [that is, $(14/20)(100)$]. When the occurrences and nonoccurrences of a behavior differ substantially, point-to-point agreement overestimates the accuracy of the set of observations. In such cases, a more precise way of computing the percentage of agreement is to compute the percentage of *agreement for the occurrence of the target behavior* (see equation 7.4).

percent agreement on occurrence =
$$\frac{(100)\text{ Number of agreements on occurrence}}{\text{Number of observations – number of agreements on nonoccurrence}} \quad (7.4)$$

In this example, since Ms. Hawthorne is interested in the occurrences of distorted body image, it might make better sense to only look at how well the two raters agree on the occurrence. The eight nonoccurrences (normal drawings) on which Ms. Hawthorne and Mr. Torrance agree are not of interest and are ignored. Using the data in Table 7.3, the percentage of agreement for occurrence is 50 percent; that is, $(100)(6)/(20 - 8)$.

Both point-to-point agreement and agreement of occurrence indexes can be affected systematically by chance agreement. Thus, both indexes tend to overestimate agreement. Cohen (1960) developed a coefficient of agreement, called *kappa*, that adjusts the proportion of agreement by removing the proportion of agreement that one would find by chance. Kappa values range from -1.00 (total disagreement) to $+1.00$ (total agreement); a value of zero indicates chance agreement. Thus, a positive index of agreement indicates agreement above what one would expect to find by chance. The computation of kappa is more complicated than other agreement indexes (see equation 7.5, where P equals proportion).

$$\text{Kappa} = \frac{P_{\text{occurrence}} - P_{\text{expected}}}{1 - P_{\text{expected}}} \tag{7.5}$$

Because kappa is more readily calculated using proportions rather than frequencies, the frequencies from Table 7.3 are displayed in Table 7.4 as proportions (that is, the frequency divided by the 20 total observations); the marginal frequencies (that is, Ms. Hawthorne's and Mr. Torrance's proportions of normal and distorted drawings) are in parentheses.

The expected proportion of occurrence (that is, of distorted drawings) equals the product of the proportions of occurrence for each observer (in this example, .50 and .40); the expected proportion of nonoccurrence (that is, of normal drawing) equals the product of the proportions of nonoccurrence for each observer (in this example, .50 and .60). The expected proportion of agree-

TABLE 7.4   **Proportions of Agreements and Disagreements from Table 7.2**

	Ms. Hawthorne Distorted Drawings	Ms. Hawthorne Normal Drawings	Row Proportions
Mr. Torrance Normal Drawings	.10 (i.e., 2/10)	.40 (i.e., 8/20)	(.50)
Mr. Torrance Distorted Drawings	.30 (i.e., 6/20)	.20 (i.e., 4/20)	(.50)
Column Proportions	(.40)	(.60)	

ment equals the sum of the expected proportion of agreement for occurrence and the expected proportion of agreement for nonoccurrence; in this example, .50 = (.50 • .40) + .(.50 • .60). Substituting these values into equation 7.5, we find that kappa equals .40; that is, (.40 + .30 − .20 − .30) / (1 − .20 − .30). Thus, the ratings of drawings by Ms. Hawthorne and Mr. Torrance demonstrate some agreement beyond what one would expect by chance; however, we should not have great confidence in their scoring.

Given the increased interest in subjective forms of assessment such as portfolio assessment (see Chapter 12), holistic scoring, and holistic observation, interscorer agreement takes on added importance. Unfortunately, we find that subjective assessments usually lack interscorer agreement.

FACTORS AFFECTING RELIABILITY

Several factors affect a test's reliability and can inflate or deflate reliability estimates.

Test Length

As a general rule, the more items in a test, the more reliable the test. Thus, long tests tend to be more reliable than short tests. This fact is especially important in an internal-consistency estimate of reliability, because in this kind of estimate the number of test items is reduced by 50 percent. Split-half estimates of reliability actually estimate the reliability of half the test. Therefore, such estimates are appropriately corrected by a formula developed by Spearman and Brown. As shown in equation 7.6, the reliability of the total test is equal to twice the reliability as estimated by internal consistency divided by the sum of 1 plus the reliability estimate.

$$r_{xx} = \frac{2r_{(1/2)(1/2)}}{1 + r_{(1/2)(1/2)}} \tag{7.6}$$

For example, if a split-half estimate of internal consistency were computed on a test and found to be .80, the corrected estimated reliability would be .89:

$$.89 = \frac{(2)(.80)}{1 + .80} = \frac{1.60}{1.80}$$

A related issue is the number of effective items for each test taker. Tests are generally more reliable in the middle ranges of scores (for example, $\pm 1.5S$). For a test to be effective at the extremes of a distribution, there must be a sufficient number of difficult items for very superior pupils as well as a sufficient number of easy items for deficient pupils. Often there are not enough very easy and very hard items on a test. Therefore, extremely high or extremely low scores tend to be less reliable than scores in the middle of a distribution.

Test-Retest Interval

As previously noted, a person's true abilities can and do change between two administrations of a test. The greater the amount of time between the two administrations, the more likely the possibility that true scores will change. Thus, when employing stability or alternate-form estimates of reliability, one must pay close attention to the interval between tests. Generally, the shorter the interval, the higher the estimated reliability.

Constriction of Range

Constriction of range refers to the range of ability of the people whose performances are used to estimate a test's reliability. When the range of ability of these people is less than the range of ability in the population, a test's reliability will be underestimated. The more constricted the range of ability, the more biased (underestimated) the reliability coefficient will be.

As Figure 7.1 shows, alternative forms of a test produce a strong positive correlation when the entire range of the test is used. However, within any restricted range of the test, as illustrated by the dark rectangular outline, the correlation may be very low. (Although it is possible to correct a correlation coefficient for restriction in range, it is generally unwise to do so.)

FIGURE 7.1   **Constricting the Range of Test Scores Reduces the Estimate of a Test's Reliability**

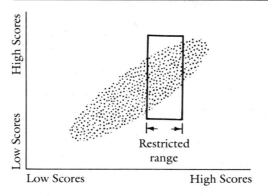

SOURCE: From *Psychological Testing* (p. 115) by A. Anastasi, 1954 (New York: Macmillan). Copyright 1954 by The Macmillan Company. Copyright renewed 1982 by Anne Anastasi. Adapted by permission of the publisher.

A related problem is that *extension* of range *overestimates* a test's reliability. Figure 7.2 illustrates correlations of scores on alternate-form tests given to students in first, third, and fifth grades. The scatterplot for each grade, considered separately, indicates poor reliability. However, spelling-test scores increase as a function of schooling; students in higher grades earn higher scores. When test authors combine the scores for several grades (or from several ages), poor correlations may be combined to produce a spuriously high correlation.

Guessing

Guessing is responding randomly to items. Even if a guess results in a correct response, it introduces error into a test score and into our interpretation of that score.

Variation Within the Testing Situation

The amount of error that the testing situation introduces into the results of testing can vary considerably. Children can misread or misunderstand the directions for a test, get a headache halfway through testing, lose their place on the answer sheet, break the point on their pencil, or choose to watch a squirrel eat nuts on the windowsill of the classroom rather than take the test. All such situational variations introduce an indeterminate amount of error in testing and, in doing so, lower reliability.

FIGURE 7.2   **Extending the Range of Test Scores May Spuriously Increase the Estimate of a Test's Reliability**

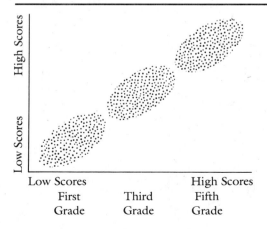

WHAT RELIABILITY METHOD SHOULD BE USED?

The first consideration in choosing a method of determining a test's reliability is the type of generalization one wishes to make. One must select the method that goes with the generalization. For example, if one were interested in generalizing about the stability of a score or observation, the appropriate method would be test-retest correlations. It would be inappropriate to use interscorer agreement as an estimate of the extent to which one can generalize to different times. Additional considerations in selecting the reliability method to be used include the following:

1. When estimating stability, the convention is to retest after two weeks. There is nothing special about the two-week period, but if all test authors used the same interval, it would be easier to compare the relative stability of tests.
2. When estimating the extent to which we can generalize to similar test items, we subscribe to Nunnally's (1967, p. 217) hierarchy for estimating reliability. The first choice is to use alternate-form reliability with a two-week interval. (Again, there is nothing special about two weeks; it is just a convention.) If alternate forms are not available, divide the test into equivalent halves and administer the halves in a two-week interval, correcting the correlation by the Spearman-Brown formula given in equation 7.6. When alternate forms are not available and subjects cannot be tested more than once, use coefficient alpha.
3. When estimating the extent to which we can generalize among different scorers, we prefer computing correlation coefficients rather than percentages of agreement. Correlation coefficients bear a direct relationship to other indicators of reliability and other uses of reliability coefficients; percentages of agreement do not. We also realize that current practice is to report percentages of agreement and not to bother with the other uses of the reliability coefficient. If one uses percent agreement to estimate interscorer reliability, kappa should be used when possible.

STANDARD ERROR OF MEASUREMENT

The standard error of measurement (SEM) is another index of test error. The SEM allows one to *estimate* the amount of each type of error associated with true scores. One can compute standard errors of measurement for scorers, times, and item samples. However, SEMs are usually computed only on stability and item samples.

Earlier we discussed the generalization of performance on one sample of items to the domain. This process provides a convenient example for the interpretation of the standard error of measurement. Consider the alphabet recognition task again. There are many samples of ten-letter tests that could be developed. If we constructed one hundred of these tests and tested one kindergartner, we would probably find that the distribution of scores for that kindergartner was approximately normal. The mean of that distribution would be the student's true score. The distribution around the true score would be the result of imperfect samples of letters; some letter samples would overestimate the pupil's ability, and others would underestimate it. Thus, the distribution would be the result of error. The standard deviation of that distribution is the standard deviation of errors attributable to sampling and is called the *standard error of measurement* (SEM).

When students are assessed with norm-referenced tests, they are typically tested only once. Therefore, we cannot generate a distribution similar to the one shown in Figure 7.3. Consequently, we do not know the test taker's true score or the variance of the measurement error that forms the distribution around that person's true score. By using what we know about the test's standard deviation and its reliability for items, we can estimate what that error distribution would be. However, when estimating the error distribution for one student, test users should understand that the standard error of measurement is an average; some standard errors will be greater than that average and some will be less.

Equation 7.7 is the general formula for finding the standard error of measurement. The standard error of measurement (SEM) equals the standard deviation of the obtained scores (S) multiplied by the square root of 1 minus the reliability coefficient ($\sqrt{1 - r_{xx}}$). The type of unit (IQ, raw score, and so forth) in which the standard deviation is expressed is the unit in which the SEM is expressed. Thus, if the test scores have been converted to T-scores, the standard

FIGURE 7.3   **The Standard Error of Measurement Is the Standard Deviation of the Error Distribution Around a True Score for One Subject**

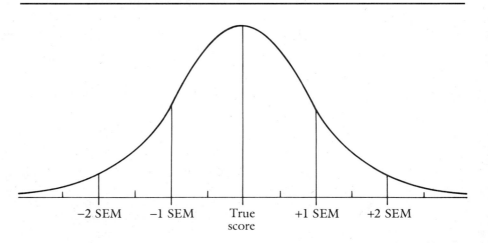

TABLE 7.5   **Relationship Between Reliability Coefficient (r_{xx}) and SEM (Part A) and Between Standard Deviation (S) and SEM (Part B)**

Part A			Part B		
S	r_{xx}	SEM	S	r_{xx}	SEM
10	.96	2	5	.91	1.5
10	.84	4	10	.91	3.0
10	.75	5	15	.91	4.5
10	.64	6	20	.91	6.0
10	.36	8	25	.91	7.5

deviation is in T-score units and is 10; the SEM is also in T-score units. Similarly, if the reliability coefficient is based on stability, then the SEM is for times of testing. If the reliability coefficient is based on different scorers, then the SEM is for testers/observers.

$$SEM = S \sqrt{1 - r_{xx}} \qquad (7.7)$$

From equation 7.7 it is apparent that as the standard deviation increases, the SEM increases; and as the reliability coefficient decreases, the SEM increases. In Part A of Table 7.5 the same standard deviation (10) is used with different reliability coefficients. As reliability coefficients decrease, SEMs increase. When the reliability coefficient is .96, the SEM is 2; when the reliability is .64, the SEM is 6. In Part B of Table 7.5, different standard deviations are used with the same reliability coefficient (r_{xx} = .91). As the standard deviation increases, the SEM increases.

Because measurement error is unavoidable, there is always some uncertainty about an individual's true score. The standard error of measurement provides information about the certainty or confidence with which a test score can be interpreted. When the SEM is relatively large, the uncertainty is large; we cannot be very sure of the individual's score. When the SEM is relatively small, the uncertainty is small; we can be more certain of the score.

ESTIMATED TRUE SCORES

Unfortunately, we never know a subject's true score. Moreover, the obtained score on a test is not the best estimate of the true score. As mentioned in the previous discussion, true scores and errors are uncorrelated. However, obtained scores and errors *are* correlated. Scores above the test mean have more "lucky" error (error that raises the obtained score above the true score), whereas scores below the mean have more "unlucky" error (error that lowers the obtained score below the true score). An easy way to understand this effect is to think of a test on which a student guesses on half the test items. If all the guesses are correct, the student has been very lucky and earns a high grade. However, if all the guesses are incorrect, the student has been unlucky and earns a low grade. Thus, obtained scores above or below the mean are often more discrepant from the true scores than obtained scores closer to the mean. As Figure 7.4 illustrates, the less reliable the test, the greater the discrepancy between obtained scores and true scores. Nunnally (1967, p. 220) has provided an equation (equation 7.8) for determining the estimated true score (X'). The estimated true score equals

FIGURE 7.4   **Relationship Between True-Score Distribution and Obtained-Score Distribution for Reliable and Unreliable Tests**

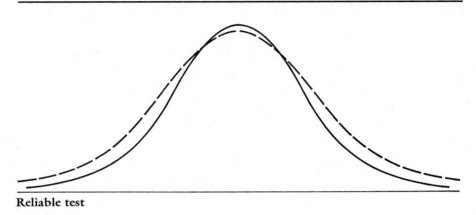

Reliable test

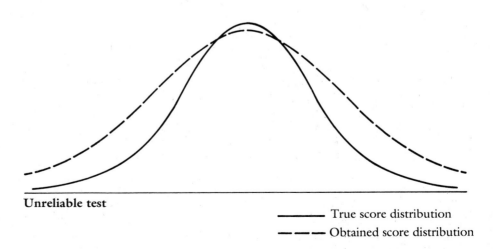

Unreliable test

————— True score distribution

— — — Obtained score distribution

the test mean plus the product of the reliability coefficient and the difference between the obtained score and the group mean.

$$X' = \overline{X} + (r_{xx})(X - \overline{X}) \qquad (7.8)$$

The particular mean that one uses is the subject of some controversy. We believe the preferred mean is the mean of the demographic group that best represents the particular child. Thus, if the student is Asian and resides in a middle-class urban area, the most appropriate mean would be the mean of same-age Asian students from middle socioeconomic backgrounds who live in urban areas. In the absence of means for particular students of particular backgrounds, one is forced to use the overall mean for the student's age. As mentioned earlier in this chapter, the choice of reliability coefficient depends on the type of generalization one wishes to make.

The discrepancy between obtained scores and estimated true scores is a function of both the reliability of the obtained scores and the difference between the obtained score and the mean. Table 7.6 illustrates a general case in which the mean in each example is 100 and the obtained scores are 90, 75, and 50. The reliability coefficients are .90, .70, and .50.

When the reliability coefficient is constant, the further an obtained score is from the mean, the greater the discrepancy between the obtained score and the estimated true score. For example, when the obtained score is 90 and the estimated reliability is .90, the estimated true score is 91 [that is, 91 = 100 + (.90)(90 − 100)]. Thus, the difference between the estimated true score and the obtained score is 1. However, when the obtained score is 50 and the reliability coefficient is .90, the estimated true score is 55 [that is, 100 + (.90)(50 − 100)].

TABLE 7.6   **Estimated True Scores for Different Obtained Scores on Tests with Different Reliability Coefficients**

Test Mean ($\overline{X}$)	Realiability Coefficient (r_{xx})	Obtained Score (X)	Estimated True Score (X')	Difference Between Obtained Score and Estimated True Score
100	.90	90	91.0	1.0
100	.90	75	77.5	2.5
100	.90	50	55.0	5.0
100	.70	90	93.0	3.0
100	.70	75	82.5	7.5
100	.70	50	65.0	15.0
100	.50	90	95.0	5.0
100	.50	75	87.5	12.5
100	.50	50	75.0	25.0

Thus, the difference between the estimated true score and the obtained score is 5.

When the reliability coefficient changes, less reliable measures produce larger differences between obtained and estimated true scores. For example, when the obtained score is 75 and the reliability coefficient is .90, the estimated true score is 77.5 [that is, 100 + (.90)(75 − 100)]. Thus, the difference between the estimated true score and the obtained score is 2.5. However, when the reliability coefficient is .50, the estimated true score rises to 87.5 [that is, 100 + (.50)(75 − 100)]. Thus, the difference between the estimated true score and the obtained score is 12.5.

When the obtained score is below the test mean and the reliability coefficient is less than 1.00, the estimated true score is *always* higher than the obtained score. Conversely, when the obtained score is above the test mean and the reliability coefficient is less than 1.00, the estimated true score is *always* lower than the obtained score. Note that equation 7.8 does not give the *true score,* only the *estimated true score.*

CONFIDENCE INTERVALS

Although we can never know a person's true score, we can *estimate* the likelihood that a person's true score might be found within a specified range of scores. This range is called a *confidence interval.* A 50-percent confidence interval is a range of values within which the true score will be found about 50 percent of the time. Of course, about 50 percent of the time the true score will be outside the interval. A larger range—a wider confidence interval—could make us feel more certain that we have included the true score within the range. For example, 90-percent, 95-percent, and 99-percent confidence intervals can be constructed; with confidence intervals as certain as these, chances of the true score falling outside of the confidence interval are about 10 percent, 5 percent, and 1 percent, respectively.

There is some disagreement over how to construct confidence intervals (see Kubiszyn & Borich, 1984) or even whether to construct confidence intervals at all (see Sabers, Feldt, & Reschly, 1988). In the following sections, we use the statistics recommended by Nunnally (1978): estimated true score and standard error of measurement. Others (for example, Kubiszyn & Borich, 1984) prefer to use the estimated true score and the standard error of estimation[3] (which is the average standard deviation of true scores around an obtained score) rather than the standard error of measurement. When test reliability is high, the difference in the two procedures is negligible.

---

3. The standard error of estimation equals the product of the standard deviation and square root of the product of the reliability coefficient multiplied by 1 minus the reliability coefficient:

$$S \sqrt{r_{xx}(1 - r_{xx})}.$$

Establishing Confidence Intervals for True Scores

The characteristics of a normal curve have already been discussed. We can apply the relationship between z-scores and areas under the normal curve to the normal distribution of error around a true score. We can use equation 7.8 to estimate the mean of the distribution (the true score) and equation 7.7 to estimate the standard deviation of the distribution (the standard error of measurement). With these two estimates, we can construct a confidence interval for the true score. Since 68 percent of all elements in a normal distribution fall within one standard deviation of the mean, there is about a 68 percent chance that the true score is within one SEM of the estimated true score. We can construct an interval with almost any degree of confidence except 100 percent confidence. Table 7.7 shows the extreme area for the z-scores most commonly used in constructing confidence intervals. The extreme area is the proportion of cases in the tail of the curve, that is, the area from plus or minus two standard deviations to and the asymptote of the curve. The general formula for a confidence interval (c.i.) is given in equation 7.9. The lower limit of the confidence interval equals the estimated true score less the product of the z-score associated with that level of confidence and the standard error of measurement. The upper limit of the confidence interval is the estimated true score plus the product of the z-score and the SEM.

$$\text{Lower limit of c.i.} = X' - (z\text{-score})(\text{SEM})$$
$$\text{Upper limit of c.i.} = X' + (z\text{-score})(\text{SEM}) \tag{7.9}$$

To construct a symmetrical confidence interval for a true score, follow this simple procedure:

1. Select the degree of confidence; for example, 95 percent.
2. Find the z-score associated with that degree of confidence (for example, a 95-percent confidence interval is between z-scores of -1.96 and $+1.96$).
3. Multiply each z-score associated with the confidence interval (for example, 1.96 for 95-percent confidence) by the SEM.

TABLE 7.7   **Commonly Used z-Scores, Extreme Areas, and Area Included Between + and − z-Score Values**

z-Score	Extreme Area	Area Between + and −
.67	25.0%	50%
1.00	16.0%	68%
1.64	5.0%	90%
1.96	2.5%	95%
2.33	1.0%	98%
2.57	.5%	99%

4. Find the estimated true score.
5. Take the product of the z-score and the SEM, and both add it to and subtract it from the estimated true score.

For example, assume that a person's estimated true score is 75 and that the SEM is 5. Further assume that you wish to be about 68-percent sure of constructing an interval that will contain the true score. Table 7.7 shows that a 68-percent degree of confidence is associated with a z-score of 1. Thus, about 68 percent of the time, the true score will be contained in the interval of 70 to 80 [that is, $75 - (1)(5)$ to $75 + (1)(5)$]; there is about a 16-percent chance that the true score is less than 70 and about a 16-percent chance that the true score is greater than 80. If you are unwilling to be wrong about 32 percent of the time, you must increase the width of the confidence interval. Thus, with the same true score (75) and SEM (5), if you wish 95-percent confidence, the size of the interval must be increased; it would have to range from 65 to 85 [that is, $75 - (1.96)(5)$ to $75 + (1.96)(5)$]. About 95 percent of the time the true score will be contained within that interval; there is about a 2.5-percent chance that the true score is less than 65, and there is about a 2.5-percent chance that it is greater than 85.

DIFFERENCE SCORES

In many applied settings, we are interested in differences between two scores. For example, we might wish to know if a student's reading achievement is commensurate to her intellectual ability, or we might want to know if the achievement score obtained after instruction (that is, a post-test) is greater than the achievement score obtained prior to instruction (that is, a pre-test). In many definitions of educational disorders (for example, learning disabilities), a "significant" discrepancy is a defining characteristic of the disorder. In other disorders (for example, mental retardation), significant discrepancies are not expected.

Because significant differences are used so frequently in special and remedial education, it is important for users of test information to understand the meaning of a "significant discrepancy." Salvia and Good (1982) have discussed three different meanings of the term *significant difference*. The first meaning, a *reliable* difference, is the most pertinent to our discussion of reliability, although it is not the most important consideration in general. A difference is considered reliable when it is unlikely to have occurred by chance. Because every test score has some error associated with it, two test scores could appear discrepant by chance or because of the measurement error associated with each test score. However, Salvia and Good point out that the fact that a difference is real does not mean that it is rare. A large proportion of students may show reliable discrepancies. Moreover, even if a difference is reliable and rare, it may not have educational implications. Educators and psychologists are interested in meaningful differences. One can be sure that unreliable differences are not meaningful. (These differences are the result of chance.) Probably because only reliable differences can be meaningful and too little emphasis has been placed on rarity and meaningfulness of a difference, diagnosticians have relied heavily on a difference's reliability for interpretation.

Difference scores are usually less reliable than the scores on which the differences are based. The reliability of a difference between two scores (A and B) is a function of three things: (1) the reliability of test A, (2) the reliability of test B, and (3) the correlation between tests A and B. In addition, differences in norm groups can produce differences in obtained scores. For example, suppose that June was absolutely average in reading and intellectual ability. Further suppose that she was tested with an intelligence test normed on a sample of students somewhat lower in ability than the general population. June would earn an IQ that was above the mean. Suppose that the test to measure reading was normed on a sample of students whose achievement was somewhat higher than the general population. June would earn a reading score somewhat lower than the mean. If the disparity in norms were sufficiently large, June might appear to have a significant discrepancy between her intellectual ability and her reading achievement. However, that discrepancy would be an artifact of inaccurate norms.

There are several approaches to evaluating the reliability of a difference. The following two methods are particularly useful but rest on different assumptions and combine the data in different ways (that is, use different formulas).

One method uses a regression model and was originally described by Thorndike (1963). Within this model, one score is presumed to cause the second score. For example, intelligence is believed to determine achievement. Therefore, intelligence is identified as an independent (or predictor) variable, and achievement is identified as the dependent (or predicted) variable. When the predicted score (for example, the predicted achievement score) differs from the achievement score that is actually obtained, a deficit exists. The reliability of a predicted difference is given by equation 7.10.

$$\hat{D} = \frac{r_{bb} + (r_{aa})(r^2_{ab}) - 2r^2_{ab}}{1 - r^2_{ab}} \tag{7.10}$$

The reliability of a predicted difference ($\hat{D}$) is equal to the reliability of the dependent variable (r_{bb}) plus the product of the reliability of the independent variable (r_{aa}) and the square of the correlation between the independent variable and the dependent variable ($r_{aa}\, r^2_{ab}$) less twice the squared correlation of the independent and dependent variable ($2r^2_{ab}$). This value is divided by 1 minus the squared correlation between independent and dependent variables ($1 - r^2_{ab}$). The standard deviation of predicted differences (S), also called the standard error of estimate, is given in equation 7.11. The standard deviation of predicted differences is equal to the standard deviation of the dependent variable (S_b) multiplied by the square root of 1 minus the squared correlation between independent and dependent variables $(\sqrt{1 - r_{ab}^2})$.

$$S_{\text{dif}} = S_b \sqrt{1 - r_{ab}^2} \qquad (7.11)$$

The second method of evaluating the reliability of a difference was proposed by Stake and Wardrop (1971). In this method, one variable is not assumed to be the cause of the other; neither variable is identified as the independent variable. However, this method does require that both measures be in the same unit of measurement (for example, T-scores or IQs). The reliability of a difference in obtained scores is given in equation 7.12. The reliability of an obtained difference equals the average reliability of the two tests $[1/2 \ (r_{aa} + r_{bb})]$ less the correlation between the two tests (r_{ab}); this difference is divided by 1 minus the correlation between the two tests $(1 - r_{ab})$.

$$r_{\text{dif}} = \frac{\frac{1}{2}(r_{aa} + r_{bb}) - r_{ab}}{1 - r_{ab}} \qquad (7.12)$$

The standard deviation for obtained differences is given in equation 7.13.

$$S_{\text{dif}} = \sqrt{S_a^2 + S_b^2 - 2r_{ab}S_aS_b} \qquad (7.13)$$

The standard deviation of an obtained difference is equal to the square root of the sum of the variances of tests A and B $(S_a^2 + S_b^2)$ less twice the product of the correlation of A and B multiplied by the standard deviations of A and B $(2r_{ab}S_aS_b)$.

The reliability and standard deviation of an obtained difference can be combined to estimate the standard error of measurement of the obtained difference using equation 7.7. The standard deviation of the difference is substituted for the test's standard deviation (S) in that equation; the reliability of the difference is substituted for the test's reliability (r_{xx}) in the equation. These substitutions generate equation 7.14.

$$\text{SEM}_{\text{dif}} = \sqrt{S_a^2 + S_b^2 - 2r_{ab}S_aS_b} \ \sqrt{1 - \frac{\frac{1}{2}(r_{aa} + r_{bb}) - r_{ab}}{1 - r_{ab}}} \qquad (7.14)$$

The standard error of measurement of a difference describes the distribution of differences between obtained scores. To evaluate difference scores, the simplest method is to establish a level of confidence (for example, 95 percent) and find the z-score associated with that level of confidence (1.96). We then divide the obtained difference by the SEM of the difference. If the quotient exceeds the z-score associated with the level of confidence selected (1.96), the obtained difference is reliable. We can also estimate the true difference in the same manner as we estimate a true score on one test. In general, we assume that the group mean difference is .00. Thus, the formula for estimating the true difference for a particular student simplifies to equation 7.15.

$$\text{Estimated true difference} = (\text{obtained difference})(r_{xx(\text{dif})}) \qquad (7.15)$$

Desirable Standards

It is important for test authors to present sufficient information in test manuals for the test user to interpret test results accurately. For a test to be valid (to measure what its authors claim it measures), it must be reliable. Although it is not the only condition that must be met, reliability is a necessary condition for validity. No test can measure what it purports to measure unless it's reliable. No score is interpretable unless it's reliable.

Therefore, test authors and publishers must present sufficient reliability data to allow the user to evaluate the reliability of the test scores that are to be interpreted. Thus, reliability estimates should be presented for intermediate (for example, subtest) scores when they are to be interpreted. Moreover, reliability estimates should be reported for each age and grade. Furthermore, these indexes should be presented clearly in tabular form in one place. Test authors should not play hide and seek with reliability data. Test authors who recommend computing difference scores should provide, whenever possible, the reliability of the difference and the SEM of the difference. Once test users have access to reliability data, they must judge the adequacy of the test.

How high must a test's reliability be before it can be used in applied settings? The answer depends on the use to which test data are put. A simple answer is to use the most reliable test available. However, such a response may be misleading, for the "best" test may be too unreliable for any application (for example, its reliability may only be .45). We recommend that the following two standards of reliability be used in applied settings.

1. *Group Data*. If test scores are to be used for administrative purposes and are reported for groups of individuals, a reliability of .60 should probably be the minimum.
2. *Individual Data*. If a test score is used to make a decision for an individual student, a much higher standard of reliability is demanded. When important educational decisions are to be made for a student, such as decisions about tracking and placement in a special class, the minimum standard should be .90. When the decision being made is a screening decision, such as a recommendation that a child receive further assessment, there is still need for high reliability. For screening devices, we recommend an .80 standard.

Finally, we strongly recommend that confidence intervals be used when reporting test performance.

Summary

The term *reliability* refers to the ability to generalize from a sample to a domain. The domains to which we usually want to generalize are other times (stability or test-retest reliability), other scorers (interrater or interscorer reliability), and other items (alternate-form or internal-consistency reliability). Reliability coefficients may range from .00 (total lack of reliability) to 1.00 (total reliability); .90 is recommended as the minimum standard for tests used to make important educational decisions for students. There are several factors that affect reliability: the method used to calculate the reliability coefficient, test length, the test-retest interval, constriction of range, guessing, and variation within the testing situation.

In diagnostic work, the reliability coefficient has four major uses: It allows the user to (1) estimate the test's relative freedom from measurement error, (2) estimate an individual subject's true score, (3) find the standard error of measurement, and (4) estimate confidence intervals for a subject's true score. The discussion of estimated true scores, standard error of measurement, and confidence intervals can be extended to difference or discrepancy scores. The reliability of a difference score is affected by the reliability of the tests and by the correlation between the tests on which the difference is based. Differences in norm samples also affect difference scores, but this effect cannot be evaluated. Provided the two tests are correlated, difference scores are less reliable than the average of the reliabilities of the tests on which the difference is based.

Although we have devoted an entire chapter to reliability, one must bear in mind that reliability is important only insofar as it affects the validity of an assessment.

STUDY QUESTIONS

1. Why is it necessary for a test to be reliable?
2. Test A and test B have identical means and standard deviations. Test A has a standard error of measurement of 4.8; test B has a standard error of measurement of 16.3. Which test is more reliable, and why?
3. What is the greatest limitation of reliability estimates based on test-retest correlation?
4. List and explain five factors that affect the estimated reliability of a test.
5. The standard error of measurement is the standard deviation of what? Illustrate your answer with a drawing.

PROBLEMS

1. Mr. Treacher administers an intelligence test to his class. For this test, $\overline{X} = 100$, $S = 16$, and $r_{rx} = .75$. Five children earn the following scores: 68, 124, 84, 100, and 148. What are the estimated true scores for these children?
2. What is the standard error of measurement for the intelligence test in problem 1?

3. What are the upper and lower boundaries of a symmetrical confidence interval of 95 percent for the first child in problem 1?
4. What are the upper and lower boundaries of a symmetrical confidence interval of 50 percent for the child in problem 1 who earns a score of 100?
5. Test A and test B have reliabilities of .90 and .80; the correlation between tests A and B is .50. What is the reliability of a difference between scores on test A and test B?

Answers

1. 76, 118, 88, 100, 136
2. 8
3. 92, 60
4. 105, 95
5. .70

ADDITIONAL READING

American Educational Research Association, American Psychological Association, & National Council on Measurement in Education (1985). *Standards for educational and psychological tests.* Washington, DC: American Psychological Association.

Coates, T., & Thoresen, C. (1978). Using generalization theory in behavioral observation. *Behavior Therapy, 9,* 605–613.

Cronbach, L., Gleser, G., Nanda, H., & Rajaratnam, N. (1972). *The dependability of behavioral measurement: Theory of generalizability of scores and profiles.* New York: Wiley.

Ghiselli, E. E. (1964). *Theory of psychological measurement.* New York: McGraw-Hill. (Chapter 8, pp. 207–253)

Kazdin, A. (1982). *Single-case research designs.* New York: Oxford University Press. (Chapter 3: Interobserver agreement)

Salvia, J., & Good, R. (1982). Significant discrepancies in the classification of pupils: Differentiating the concept. In J. T. Neisworth (Ed.), *Assessment in special education.* Rockville, MD: Aspen Systems.

Chapter 8

Validity

*V*alidity is the extent to which an assessment procedure measures what its authors or users claim it measures.[1] Validity refers to "the appropriateness, meaningfulness, and usefulness of the specific inferences" (AERA et al., 1985, p. 9) that can be made on the basis of observations or test results. Some inferences may be valid; others may be invalid.

Validity is a property of test-based inferences and not a property of the test itself.[2] However, the characteristics of a test and the inferences that can be appropriately drawn are closely related. Thus, one commonly speaks of a test's validity. Although a variety of inferences can be drawn from a student's test performance, the validity of each inference should be considered separately. That is, a particular inference has (or lacks) some degree of validity. The validity of a collection of inferences is based on the totality of information that accumulates over time. However, test authors are expected to provide some evidence of a test's validity for specific inferences at the time the test is offered for use.

METHODS OF TEST VALIDATION

The process of gathering information about the appropriateness of inferences is called *validation*. The evidence that can be brought to bear on an inference's validity can be categorized to facilitate explanation. Yet, the reader should keep in mind that categorization is an artificial device to explain the possibilities; there are not separate validities.

Some evidence of a test's validity have already been discussed in preceding chapters (that is, the meaning of test scores, reliability, the adequacy of the test's standardization and, when applicable, the test's norms). In this chapter, three additional sources of evidence are considered: content validity, criterion-related validity, and construct validity.

1. Some [for example, Messick (1989, p. 19)] take the position that validity also refers to the social consequences of testing.
2. Validity can be a property of any type of assessment procedure (not just tests), although systematic validation is the most highly developed for commercially available tests and rating scales.

Content Validity

To judge a test's validity, those who assess students must have a clear understanding of the traits, abilities, or skills that are to be measured. One must define what is to be measured before deciding how the measuring is to be done. The specific definition will depend on a test author's own definition of and assumptions about the domain to be measured as well as scientific consensus.

Content validity is the extent to which a test's items actually represent the domain to be measured. It is a major source of evidence in the validation process for any educational or psychological test and many other forms of assessment (such as observations and ratings). Evidence of valid content is especially important in the measurement of achievement and adaptive behavior and is most easily understood in this context. A careful examination of a test's content is necessary; frequently, test developers rely on panels of experts for judgments about the appropriateness of test content. Whether test content is examined by experts or those who use the tests, the examination is judgmental in nature and requires a clear definition of the domain or universe represented. The relevance of the test universe to the proposed test use and the procedures followed in generating test content to represent that universe should be described (AERA et al., 1985, p. 14). Thus, in developing a test, it is important that a test developer consider the purposes for which a test is going to be used and then specify adequately the universe of content that a test is intended to represent. For instructional decisions, it is important to demonstrate agreement between the test and the specific instructional or curricular areas it is meant to cover. It is also necessary to make sure that the format and response properties of the items or tasks that make up a test are representative of the universe of possible item and response types for the particular area being assessed.

Evidence of content validity is associated with three factors: the appropriateness of the types of items included in a test, the completeness of the item sample, and the way in which the items assess the content.

Appropriateness of Included Items

In examining the appropriateness of the items included in a test we must ask, Is this an appropriate test question? and Does this test item really measure the domain or construct? Consider the four test items from a hypothetical primary (kindergarten through grade 2) arithmetic achievement test presented in Figure 8.1. The first item requires the student to read and add two single-digit numbers whose sum is less than 10. This seems to be an appropriate item for an elementary arithmetic achievement test. The second item requires the student to complete a geometric progression. Although this item is mathematical, the skills and knowledge required to complete the question correctly are not taught in any elementary school curriculum by the second grade. Therefore, the question should be rejected as an invalid item for an arithmetic achievement test to be used with children in kindergarten through the second grade. The third item

FIGURE 8.1   **Sample Multiple-Choice Questions for an Elementary-level (K–2) Arithmetic Achievement Test**

1. Three and six are _____ .
   a. 4
   b. 7
   c. 8
   d. 9
2. What number follows in this series? 1, 2.5, 6.25, _____
   a. 10
   b. 12.5
   c. 15.625
   d. 18.50
3. Cuánto son tres y dos?
   a. 3
   b. 4
   c. 5
   d. 6
4. Ille puer puellas _____ .
   a. amo
   b. amat
   c. amamus
   d. amant

also requires the student to read and add two single-digit numbers whose sum is less than 10. However, the question is written in Spanish. Although the content of the question is suitable (this is an elementary addition problem), the methods of presentation require other skills. Failure to complete the item correctly could be attributed to the fact that the child does not know Spanish and/or to the fact that the child does not know 3 + 2 = 5. One should conclude that the item is not valid for an arithmetic test for children who do not read Spanish. The fourth item requires that the student select the correct form of the Latin verb amare ("to love"). Clearly, this is an inappropriate item for an elementary arithmetic test and should be rejected as invalid.

In addition to making judgments about how appropriately an item fits within a domain, test developers often rely on point biserial correlations between individual test items and the total score to make decisions about item appropriateness. Items that do not correlate positively and at least moderately (that is, .25 or .30 or more) with the total score are dropped. Retaining only items that have positive correlations with the total score ensures homogeneous test items and internally consistent (reliable) tests. Moreover, when test items are homogenous, they are likely to be measuring the same skill or trait. Therefore, to obtain reliable tests, test developers are likely to drop items that do not statistically fit the domain.

When domains are not homogeneous, selecting items on the basis of point biserial correlations to produce an internally consistent test can jeopardize validity. Therefore, it is generally a good idea to analyze the structure of a domain, either logically or statistically.[3] When a domain is composed of two or more homogeneous classes of test items, homogenous subtests (representing each factor) can be developed using point biserial correlations. In this way, the validity of the test can be heightened.

Completeness of Content

Test content must be examined to ascertain the completeness of the item sample. The validity of any elementary arithmetic test would be questioned if it included only problems requiring the addition of single-digit numbers whose sum was less than 10. One would reasonably expect an arithmetic test to include a far broader sample of tasks (for example, addition of two- and three-digit numbers, subtraction, understanding the process of addition, and so forth). Incomplete assessment of a domain usually results in an invalid appraisal.

How Content Is Measured

Content must be examined to ascertain how the test items assess content. The *how* of measurement is multifaceted. In one question in Figure 8.1, the student was expected to add two single-digit numbers whose sum was less than 10. However, one could evaluate a child's arithmetic skills in a variety of ways. The child might be required to recognize the correct answer in a multiple-choice array, supply the correct answer, demonstrate the addition process with manipulatives, apply the proper addition facts in a word problem, or analyze the condition under which the mathematical relationship obtains. The method of measurement may affect the outcome.[4]

Ensuring Content Validity

One way to ensure content validity of a test is to construct a test that measures the desired content in the desired way. Bloom, Hastings, and Madaus (1971) devoted several hundred pages to this topic in their classic text *Handbook of For-*

---

3. Advanced statistical techniques such as factor analysis are appropriately used in this sort of analysis. These statistical procedures are well beyond the discussion of descriptive statistics provided in Chapter 4. The interested reader should consult a text on multivariate statistical analysis.

4. This aspect of validity is currently being hotly debated by those favoring constructed responses such as extended responses, performances, or demonstrations. Current theory and research methods as they apply to trait or ability congruence under different methods of measurement are still emerging. Much of the current methodology is an outgrowth of Campbell and Fiske's (1959) early work and is a topic too advanced for this text. There is, however, an emerging consensus that the methods used to assess student knowledge or ability should closely parallel those used in instruction.

mative and Summative Evaluation of Student Learning. They recommended that authors of achievement tests develop a table of specifications for the content to be tested. Such a table can be readily generalized to other types of tests. A table of specifications formally enumerates the particular contents of a test and the processes (or behaviors) it assesses. *Content* refers to the particular domains or subdomains the test author wishes to assess. The task of test authors is to specify the content as precisely as possible in order to convey clearly to both themselves and the test user what is being measured. The next step is to specify how the particular content objectives will be measured (the process by which the measurement will occur). Several types of measurement are possible; they range from knowledge objectives to evaluation objectives. The definitions used by Bloom (1956) and Bloom, Hastings, and Madaus (1971) follow.

1. *Knowledge* is the "recall or recognition of specific elements in a subject area" (Bloom et al., 1971, p. 41).
2. *Comprehension* is evaluated with three types of measurement: translation, interpretation, and extrapolation. Translation refers to rewording information or putting it into one's own words. Interpretation is evidenced "when a student can go beyond recognizing the separate parts of a communication and can see the interrelationships among the parts" (Bloom et al., 1971, p. 149). Interpretation also is evidenced when a student can differentiate the essentials of a message from unimportant elements. Extrapolation refers to the student's ability to go beyond literal comprehension and to make inferences about what the anticipated outcome of an action is or what will happen next.
3. *Application* is "the use of abstractions in particular and concrete situations. The abstractions may be in the form of general ideas, rules or procedures, or generalized methods. The abstractions may also be technical principles, ideas, and theories which must be remembered and applied" (Bloom, 1956, p. 205).
4. *Analysis* is "the breakdown of a communication into its constituent elements or parts such that the relative hierarchy of ideas is made clear and/or the relations between ideas expressed are made explicit. Such analyses are intended to clarify the communication, to indicate how the communication is organized, and the way in which it manages to convey its effects, as well as its basis and arrangements" (Bloom, 1956, p. 205).
5. *Synthesis* refers to "the putting together of elements and parts so as to form a whole. This involves the process of working with pieces, parts, elements, etc., and arranging and combining them in such a way as to constitute a pattern or structure not clearly there before" (Bloom, 1956, p. 206).
6. *Evaluation* means "the making of judgments about the value, for some purpose, of ideas, works, solutions, methods, material, etc. It involves the use of criteria as well as standards for appraising the extent to which particulars are accurate, effective, economical, or satisfying. The judgments may be quantitative or qualitative, and the criteria may be either those determined by the student or those which are given to him" (Bloom, 1956, p. 185).

TABLE 8.1   Table of Specifications for a Hypothetical Reliability Test

Processes	Contents				
	Reliability Coefficient	Standard Error of Measurement	Estimated True Scores	Confidence Intervals	Difference Scores
Knowledge	3 questions	2 questions	1 question	1 question	1 question
Comprehension	5 questions	2 questions	1 question	3 questions	1 question
Application	Not tested	2 questions	1 question	5 questions	Not tested
Analysis	Not tested	Not tested	Not tested	Not tested	Not tested
Synthesis	Not tested	Not tested	Not tested	Not tested	Not tested
Evaluation	Not tested	Not tested	Not tested	Not tested	Not tested

To illustrate how a table of specifications can be used, let us assume that we wish to develop a test to assess the understanding of reliability demonstrated by beginning students. The first step is to enumerate the *content areas* of the domain. Using Chapter 7 as a guide, we could assess the following areas: the reliability coefficient (its meaning, methods of estimating it, and factors affecting it), standard error of measurement (its meaning and computation), estimated true scores, confidence intervals (their meaning and computation), and difference scores. One might reasonably expect a test user to have a better understanding of the meaning of the reliability coefficient and the construction and interpretation of confidence intervals. Therefore, these content areas could be stressed. The next step is to specify the *processes* by which the content areas are to be measured. One might expect beginning students to demonstrate understanding at the *knowledge, comprehension,* and *application* levels only. Therefore, the test might not contain items assessing analysis, synthesis, or evaluation. A table of specifications for this hypothetical test would resemble Table 8.1.

The number of questions used to assess each cell also is given in the table. The table of specifications shows that, of the twenty-eight questions in the test, eight deal with the reliability coefficient and nine deal with confidence intervals; eight questions assess knowledge, twelve questions assess comprehension, and eight assess application. Thus, the hypothetical test assesses a student's understanding of reliability by emphasizing comprehension of the reliability coefficient and applications of confidence intervals.

Extension to Other Forms of Assessment

The preceding discussion of content validity also applies to other forms of assessment. In systematic observation, the content of the observation protocol takes two forms. First, the contexts in which observation takes place can be considered an issue of content validity. For example, a behavior can occur in several contexts; thus, a teacher might observe Harry to see the frequency of his hitting in class, at recess, during lunch, and so forth. Second, when states or traits are observed (for example, cooperation), the specific behaviors chosen to represent the state or trait are clearly issues of content validity. For example, turn-taking, sharing toys, using polite language (for example, "please") could be considered as exemplars of cooperation.

In unstandardized assessment procedures such as portfolio assessment, content validity is an especially critical issue. The contents of the portfolio—what is included and what is excluded—should portray the student's work in the domain accurately. The student's work should be representative of all important dimensions within the domain, and work not pertinent to the domain should be excluded from the assessment process (although such work may be kept in the student's portfolio).

Criterion-Related Validity

Criterion-related validity refers to the extent to which a person's performance on a criterion measure can be estimated from that person's performance on the assessment procedure being validated. This prediction is usually expressed as a correlation between the assessment procedure (for example, a test) and the criterion. The correlation coefficient is called a *validity coefficient.*

Two types of criterion-related validity are commonly described: concurrent validity and predictive validity. These terms denote the time when a person's performance on the criterion measure is obtained. *Concurrent* criterion-related validity refers to how accurately a person's current performance (for example, test score) estimates that person's performance on the criterion measure *at the same time.* *Predictive* criterion-related validity refers to how accurately a person's current performance (for example, test score) estimates that person's performance on the criterion measure *at a later time.* Thus, concurrent and predictive criterion-related validity refer to the temporal sequence by which a person's performance on some criterion measure is estimated on the basis of that person's current assessment; concurrent and predictive validity differ in the time at which scores on the criterion measure are obtained.

The nature of the criterion measure is extremely important. The criterion itself must be valid if it is to be used to establish the validity of another measure. Let's investigate this point by looking briefly at two examples of criterion-related validation, the first concurrent and the second predictive.

An Example of Concurrent Criterion-Related Validity

A basic concurrent criterion-related validity question is, Does a person's performance measured with a new or experimental test allow the accurate estimation of that person's performance on a criterion measure that has been widely accepted as valid? For example, if the Acme Ruler Company manufactures yardsticks, how do we know that a person's height as measured by an Acme yardstick is that person's true height? How do we know that the "Acme foot" is really a foot? The first step is to find a valid criterion measure.

The National Bureau of Standards maintains "the" foot (.3048 meter), and "the" foot is the logical choice for a criterion measure. We can take several things to the Bureau and measure them with both the Acme foot and the standard foot. If the two sets of measurements correspond closely (that is, are highly correlated and have very similar means and standard deviations), we can conclude that the Acme foot is a valid measure of length.

Similarly, if we are developing a test of achievement, we can ask, How does knowledge of a person's score on our achievement test allow the estimation of that person's score on a criterion measure? How do we know that our new test really measures achievement? Again, the first step is to find a valid criterion measure. However, there is no National Bureau of Standards for educational tests. Therefore, we must turn to a less-than-perfect criterion. There are two basic choices: other achievement tests that are presumed to be valid and judgments of achievement by teachers, parents, and the students themselves. We can, of course, use both tests and judgments. If our new test presents evidence of content validity and elicits test scores corresponding closely (correlating significantly) to judgments and scores from other achievement tests presumed to be valid, we can conclude that there is evidence for our new test's validity.

An Example of Predictive Criterion-Related Validity

The basic predictive criterion-related validity question is, Does knowledge of a person's score allow an accurate estimation of that person's score on a criterion measure administered some time in the future? For example, if Acme Ruler Company decides to diversify and manufacture tests of color vision, how do we know that a diagnosis of colorblindness made on the basis of the Acme test is accurate? How do we know that an Acme-based diagnosis will correspond to next month's diagnosis made by an ophthalmologist? We can test several children with the Acme test, schedule an appointment with an ophthalmologist, and compare the Acme-based diagnoses with the ophthalmologist's diagnoses. If the Acme test accurately predicts the ophthalmologist's diagnoses, we can conclude that the Acme test is a valid measure of color vision.

Similarly, if we are developing a test to assess reading readiness, we can ask, "Does knowledge of a student's score on our reading readiness test allow an accurate estimation of the student's actual readiness for subsequent instruction?" How do we know that our test really assesses reading readiness? Again, the first step is to find a valid criterion measure. In this case, the student's initial progress in reading can be used. Reading progress can be assessed by a reading achievement test (presumed to be valid) or by teacher judgments of reading ability or reading readiness at the time reading instruction is actually begun. If our reading readiness test has content validity and corresponds closely with either later teacher judgments of readiness or validly assessed reading skill, we can conclude that ours is a valid test of reading readiness.

Three aspects of criterion-related validity are extremely important. First, "All criterion measures should be described accurately, and the rationale for choosing them as relevant criteria should be made explicit" (AERA et al., 1985, p. 16). Obviously, because the validity of the assessment procedure (for example, a test) is established by its relationship to a criterion, the criterion itself must be valid. Thus, test authors need to present sufficient information to allow test users to judge the adequacy of the criterion. Second, "A report of a criterion-related validity study should provide a description of the sample and the statistical analysis used to determine the degree of predictive accuracy. Basic statistics should include numbers of cases (and the reasons for eliminating any cases), measures of central tendency and variability, relationships, and a description of any marked tendency toward non-normality of distribution" (AERA et al., 1985, p. 16). You will see in later sections of this book that many of the validity studies for tests we review are based on small samples, samples of convenience, or very restrictive samples (taken, for example, from one location or one private school). It is important that test authors show that their test is valid not only for the recommended purposes of the test but also for the kinds of people who will be tested. Third, test authors must provide information on the limits of generalizability of validity information.

Extension to Other Forms of Assessment

The preceding discussion of criterion-related validity also applies to other forms of assessment. For example, in systematic observation some form of time sampling is often used. An observer might use momentary time sampling (see Chapter 10) and record what a target pupil is doing every 10 seconds. An appropriate question is, Does the sampling procedure affect the record of the student's performance? To investigate this question, one usually compares the data obtained by observing target students both when continuous observation is used and when momentary time sampling is used. Similarly, if one wished to evaluate criterion validity of portfolio assessment, an appropriate criterion would have to be selected (for example, all of a student's work—tests, work not included in the portfolio, and so forth). The score or scores assigned to the portfolio could then be compared to the score or scores based on the totality of student work during the marking period.

Construct Validity

Construct validity refers to the extent to which a procedure or test measures a theoretical trait or characteristic. Construct validity is especially important for measures of process, such as intelligence or scientific inquiry. To provide evidence of construct validity, a test author must rely on indirect evidence and inference. The definition of the construct and the theory from which the construct is derived allow us to make certain predictions that can be confirmed or disconfirmed. In a real sense, one does not validate inferences from tests or other assessment procedures; one conducts experiments to demonstrate that the inferences are *not* valid. Continued inability to disconfirm the inferences, in effect, validates the inferences. For example, intellectual ability is generally believed to be developmental. We could hypothesize that if we were to conduct an investigation, a test of intelligence would be correlated with chronological age. If we found that a test of intelligence did not correlate with chronological age, this finding would cast serious doubt on the test as a measure of intelligence. (The experiment would disconfirm the test as a measure of intelligence.) However, the presence of a substantial correlation between chronological age and scores on the test does not confirm that the test is a measure of intelligence.[5] Gradually, one accumulates evidence that the test continues to act in the way that it would if it were a valid measure of the construct. As the research evidence accumulates, some claim to construct validity can be made.

Several types of evidence are generally brought to bear in research on construct validity. For example, we often expect differences in the behavior of individuals with different levels of a trait or characteristic. Thus, a test to assess learning ability should be able to differentiate between fast and slow learners. One can predict, therefore, that the individuals who learn more in a given amount of time have more learning ability; that is, they would have higher scores on a measure of learning ability. If children with IQs of 125 on test X learn more material in one week than do children with IQs of 100 on test X, there would be a failure to disconfirm the test as a valid measure of learning ability. In that sense, there would be some evidence for inference that the test measures intelligence. Other examples of this type of research are numerous. We would expect tests of intelligence to predict school achievement, readiness tests to predict school achievement, and so forth.

FACTORS AFFECTING VALIDITY

Whenever an assessment procedure fails to measure what it purports to measure, validity is threatened. Consequently, any factor that results in measuring "something else" affects validity. Unsystematic error (unreliability) and systematic error (bias) threaten validity.

Reliability

Reliability sets the upper limit of a test's validity. Thus, reliability is a necessary but not a sufficient condition for valid measurement. Thus, all valid tests are re-

---

5. Many test authors systematically ensure that their tests will be correlated with age. Authors may use a positive correlation between age or grade and passing an item as a criterion for item inclusion. Some psychometricians advocate even more sophisticated methods—for example, item-characteristic curves (Thorndike, 1982)—to ensure that test scores are correlated with chronological age. Many other abilities besides intelligence correlate with chronological age, for example, achievement, perceptual abilities, and language skills.

liable; unreliable tests are not valid; and reliable tests may or may not be valid. The validity of a particular procedure can never exceed the reliability of that procedure because unreliable procedures measure error; valid procedures measure the traits they are designed to measure. The relationship between the reliability and validity of any procedure is expressed in equation 8.1. The empirically determined validity coefficient (r_{xy}) equals the correlation between true scores on the two variables ($r_{x(t)y(t)}$) multiplied by the square root of the product of the reliability coefficients of test X and test Y ($r_{xx}r_{yy}$).

$$r_{xy} = r_{x(t)y(t)} \sqrt{r_{xx}\, r_{yy}} \qquad (8.1)$$

Systematic Bias

Method of Measurement

The method used to measure a skill or trait is often believed to affect what score a child will receive. A true score can be considered a composite of trait variance and method-of-measurement variance (Campbell & Fiske, 1959). To take a classic example, Werner and Strauss (1941) conducted a series of experiments to ascertain the effect of brain injury on figure-background perception; all of their subjects were individuals with mental retardation. They presented stimulus items tachistoscopically for a fraction of a second and asked their subjects to name what they saw. They found that individuals with brain injury responded more often to the background stimuli than did the individuals without brain injury. They concluded that brain injury results in a dysfunction in figure-ground perception. However, the method of testing (tachistoscopic presentation) and the trait to be tested (figure-ground perception) were confounded by the testing procedure. Rubin (1969) later demonstrated that under different testing procedures there were no differences between individuals with and without brain injury in figure-background responses. The differences between the findings of Strauss and Rubin are attributable to *how* figure-background perception was measured. It seems likely that Strauss was measuring perceptual speed because of his method of measurement. To the extent that trait or skill scores include variance attributable to method of measurement, these scores may lack validity.

Enabling Behaviors

Enabling behaviors and knowledge are skills and facts that a person must rely on to demonstrate a target behavior or knowledge. For example, to demonstrate knowledge of causes of the American Civil War on an essay examination, a student must additionally be able to write. The student cannot produce the targeted behavior (that is, the written answer) without the enabling behavior (i.e., writing).

Several behaviors are assumed in any testing situation. We must assume that the subject is fluent in the language in which the test is prepared and administered if there are any verbal components to the test directions or test responses. Yet in many states with substantial Spanish-speaking populations, students whose primary language is not English are tested in English. Intelligence testing in English of non–English-speaking children was sufficiently commonplace that a group of parents brought suit against a school district *(Diana v. State Board of Education,* 1970). Deaf students are routinely given the Performance subtests of the Wechsler Adult Intelligence Scales (Baumgartner, 1993) even though they cannot hear the directions. Children with communication disorders often are required to respond orally to test questions. Such obvious limitations in or absences of enabling behaviors are frequently overlooked in testing situations, even though they invalidate the test's inferences for these students.

Item Selection

Test items often presume that the subjects taking the test have had exposure to concepts and skills measured by the test. For example, standardized achievement tests presume that the students who are taking the tests have been exposed to similar curricula. If a teacher has not taught the content being tested, inferences about a student's ability to master the curriculum are invalid.

Administration Errors

Unless a test is administered according to the standardized procedures, the inferences based on the test are invalid. Suppose Ms. Williams wished to demonstrate how effective her teaching was by administering an intelligence test and an achievement test to her class. She allows the students five minutes less than the standardized time limits on the intelligence test and five minutes more on the standardized achievement test. The result is that the students earn higher achievement scores (because they had too much time) and lower intelligence test scores (because they did not have enough time). The inference that slow students had learned more than anticipated would not be valid.

Norms

Scores based on the performance of unrepresentative norms lead to incorrect estimates of relative standing in the general population. To the extent that the normative sample is systematically unrepresentative of the general population in either central tendency or variability, the differences based on such scores are incorrect and invalid.

RESPONSIBILITY FOR VALID ASSESSMENT

The valid use of assessment procedures is the responsibility of both the author and the user of the assessment procedure.

Evidence of validity should be presented for the major types of inferences for which the use of a test is recommended. A rationale should be provided to support the particular mix of evidence presented for the intended uses. . . . If validity for some common interpretation has not been investigated, that fact should be made clear, and potential users should be cautioned about making such interpretations. (AERA et al., 1985, p. 13)

SUMMARY

Validity is the *only* technical characteristic of an assessment procedure in which we are interested. All other technical considerations, such as reliability, are subsumed under the concept of validity and are analyzed separately to simplify the discussion of validity. We must know if inferences derived from an assessment are accurate. Adequate norms, reliability, and lack of bias are all necessary conditions for validity. None—separately or in total—is sufficient to guarantee validity.

Systematic evaluation of validity is based on several types of information. The content may be inspected to see if each item is valid and to ensure that all aspects of the domain are represented. If a standard or criterion of known validity is available, the test should be compared to that standard. The construct validity of all tests should be examined.

Several factors affect the validity of inferences derived from tests: reliability, systematic bias, enabling behaviors, item selection, administration errors, and test norms. Problems with these factors can invalidate test inferences.

STUDY QUESTIONS

1. Why must test authors demonstrate validity for inferences based on their tests?
2. What is the relationship between reliability and validity?
3. Identify three factors that must be considered in the establishment of content validity.
4. Ms. Wilson uses a new math curriculum to teach her class of third graders. She uses a traditional math test to assess pupil progress. All pupils score in the bottom quartile according to the test norms. What can Ms. Wilson legitimately conclude?
5. There are many tests whose manuals include absolutely no evidence as to validity. These tests are used in schools to make important educational decisions about children. Under what circumstances could such tests be used?
6. Kim Ngo, a recent arrival from a Vietnamese orphanage, speaks no English. When she enrolls in a U.S. school, her intelligence is assessed by means of a verbal test that has English directions and requires English responses. Kim performs poorly on the test, earning an IQ of 37. The tester concludes that Kim is a student with severe mental retardation and recommends placement

in a special class. Identify two major errors in the interpretation of the test results.

7. Professor Johnson develops a test that he claims can be used to identify children with learning disabilities who will profit from perceptual-motor training. What must he do to demonstrate that his test is valid?

ADDITIONAL READING

American Educational Research Association, American Psychological Association, & National Council on Measurement in Education (1985). *Standards for educational and psychological tests*. Washington, DC: American Psychological Association.

Bagnato, S. (1982). Developmental scales and developmental curricula: Forging a linkage for early intervention. In J. T. Neisworth (Ed.), *Assessment in special education*. Rockville, MD: Aspen Systems.

Fuchs, L., Fuchs, D., & Maxwell, L. (1988). The validity of informal reading comprehension measures. *Remedial and special education, 9*(2), 20–28.

Kazdin, A. (1982). *Single-case research designs*. New York: Oxford University Press. (Chapter 2: Behavioral assessment)

Messick, S. (1989). Validity. In R. L. Linn (Ed.), *Educational measurement* (3rd ed., pp. 13–103). New York: ACE/Macmillan.

Snow, R. (1993). Construct validity and constructed response tests. In R. Bennett and W. Ward (Eds.), *Constructive versus choice in cognitive measurement: Issues in constructed response, performance testing, and portfolio assessment*. Hillsdale, NJ: Lawrence Erlbaum.

Chapter 9

Adapting Tests to Accommodate Students with Disabilities

*T*his is the sixth edition of *Assessment*; the first edition was published in 1978. None of the five previous editions of this text had a separate chapter on testing accommodations, modifications, or adaptations. Rather, we talked about adapting measures for students with disabilities and about such matters as out-of-level testing as part of the discussions of domain-specific testing. So, for example, when we described intelligence tests, we devoted a portion of the chapter to tests that included modified stimulus or response properties, or that were normed on separate groups of students with disabilities, and that thus were designed for use with special populations of students. Why, then, is there now a separate chapter devoted to this topic?

WHY BE CONCERNED ABOUT TESTING ADAPTATIONS?

Changes in Student Population

Since the mid-1970s considerable attention has been paid to including students considered to be "at the margins" in neighborhood schools, general education settings, and regular instructional programs. Tyler (1987) attributes much of this change in focus to changes in the U.S. employment picture. He points out that as late as 1900, 61 percent of the U.S. labor force was employed in unskilled jobs, and that in 1910 more than half of the children in school dropped out before completing sixth grade. Today, less than 5 percent of the labor force is engaged in unskilled work. Students need higher level skills and considerably more formal schooling than in the past. Reynolds (1993) points out that these days there is a steep price to be paid—socially and economically—when one's education is neglected, even for students at the margins. At the same time, he points out that "Educating all children and youth, including those most inconvenient and difficult to serve, means facing up to truly complex problems" (p. 47).

As legislators and educational bureaucrats make educational policies, they are now compelled to make them for *all* children and youth, including those with severe disabilities. The clear focus in recent education legislation is on excellence *with* equity. And, as policy makers attempt to develop practices that will result in improved educational outcomes, they rely on data on children's educational performance. Most of the data they use come from district-administered and state-administered tests. Some come from national tests like the National Assessment of Educational Progress, a national test given periodically to a sample of America's school children. But relying on assessment data presents problems. One set of problems involves deciding whom to include in assessments and the kinds of modifications that can be made in order to include students with disabilities. Another set of problems arises as states and school districts try to move to new forms of assessment such as performance tests or portfolio assessments, and try to have all students participate in those assessments.

There are major issues to confront when deciding to use assessment information to make local, state, and national policy decisions. If students with disabilities are excluded from assessments, then the data on which policy decisions are made are data on only part of the school population—the top 85 percent. If students with disabilities are excluded from assessment (the "accountability" track), then they may also be removed from the "curriculum track." Policy decisions should be made on the basis of information reflecting all students. If data are going to be gathered on all students, then major decisions must be made on the kinds of data to be collected and how tests are to be modified or adapted to include students with disabilities.

Changes in Educational Standards

Over the past fifteen years major efforts have been made to reform or restructure schools. As part of that effort, there has been a push to specify high standards for student acquisition of subject matter content, and an accompanying push for measurement of the extent to which students meet the high standards. The United States has a developing and rich tradition of assessing students' progress as a measure of the overall quality of its educational system. Scores on cumulative tests administered at selected school transitions (such as upon promotion from one grade to another or at graduation) serve as data for decision making and documentation of the need for improvements and programs.

National data collection programs such as the National Assessment of Educational Progress (NAEP) and the National Education Longitudinal Study (NELS) are a few examples of recent and continuing efforts to provide periodic data on the educational status of America's school children. Policy makers, parents, and the general public increasingly want to know how schools are doing in educating students, including students with disabilities. But historically, and continuing today, there has been widespread exclusion of students with disabilities from state and national testing (McGrew, Thurlow, Shriner, & Spiegel, 1992). Now, with increasing inclusion of students with disabilities in regular education environments, there is considerable push for participation of these students in testing. Reynolds (1993) notes that "Assessment practices—like bowling balls—are often directed mainly 'down the middle'." Low achieving students and those with disabilities often are excluded.

The school reform bill Goals 2000: The Educate America Act is a major impetus for including students with disabilities in assessments, especially assessments completed for accountability purposes. Goals 2000 states that the eight national goals are for *all* students, including students with disabilities. Goals 2000 specifies that high content standards are to be developed in specific academic areas and that states should develop standards and assessments. The act calls for establishment of a National Educational Standards and Improvement Council (NESIC) that will approve the voluntary standards and assessments developed by states. Goals 2000 specifies that NESIC will not approve standards and assessments unless they specify how students with disabilities will meet the standards and participate in the assessments.

State education agencies in nearly every state are engaging in critical analysis of the standards, objectives, outcomes, skills, or behaviors (the terms differ from location to location) that they want students to demonstrate upon completion of school. Content area professional agencies, such as the National Council of Teachers of Mathematics and the National Science Foundation, are developing sets of standards in specific content areas, such as math, geography, and science. As they do so, they must decide the extent to which standards should be the same for students with and without disabilities. And, of course, groups that develop standards must come up with ways of assessing the extent to which students are meeting the standards. They then must decide which kinds of assessments to use and the extent to which assessments ought to be the same for students with and without disabilities.

The Need for Accurate Measurement

Tests are used to make important decisions that can have a significant effect on individuals' life opportunities. It is critical that the assessment practices used to gather information on individual students provide accurate information. In

Chapter 1 we described the kinds of decisions that are made using assessment information, and in Chapter 2 we described the kinds of concerns people have about using test information to make decisions: They are concerned about fairness, acceptability, and consequences. Unless modifications are made in testing, testing practices run the risk of being unfair for students with disabilities. Especially when school personnel rely on test information to make decisions about exceptionality, special needs and need for special services, or instructional planning, we want the person's performance to reflect actual skill or ability rather than sensory or physical limitations.

Many disagree about the extent to which modifying measures makes testing fair and acceptable. For example, parents may hold conflicting opinions on the issues involved. On one hand, they want their children with disabilities to participate in testing, because they want decision makers to have data on the performance of all children. On the other hand, they do not want their children to go through the hardship of taking tests that are difficult for them to complete.

There are major issues in the use of assessment information to make decisions about *individuals*. Students with disabilities have difficulty taking tests if the item format is such that, because of their disability, it is harder or impossible for them to understand what they are supposed to do or what the response requirements are. They also experience difficulty if they attempt to take a test but their disability makes it impossible for them to respond in a way that can be evaluated accurately. According to the Education for All Handicapped Children Act (Public Law 94-142), section 300.532, "State and local education agencies are to ensure that when a test is administered to a child with impaired sensory, manual, or speaking skills, the test results accurately reflect the child's aptitude or achievement level or whatever other factors the test purports to measure, rather than reflecting the child's impaired sensory, manual, or speaking skills (except where those skills are the factors which the test purports to measure)."

In this chapter we first review the two major issues of participation in assessment and accommodation of measures. In doing so we focus more on group measurement activities than on individual appraisal. We then describe some major legal considerations in participation and accommodation. We describe things that impede getting an accurate picture of students. In the remainder of the chapter we describe current practice and best practice in making decisions about who ought to participate in assessments, and then describe current practice and best practice in making accommodation decisions. Our descriptions are of what is considered best practice at this time. There are many opinions, often conflicting, about accommodation and inclusion. Our recommendations should be viewed as tentative, since further research and practice will, in all likelihood, produce additional information that suggests further or different modifications.

As you read this chapter, remember that the major objective of assessment is to benefit students. It can do so either by enabling us to develop interventions that help a child achieve the objectives of schooling or by informing local, state, and national policy decisions that benefit all students, including individuals with disabilities.

THE TWIN ISSUES OF PARTICIPATION AND ACCOMMODATION IN TESTING

Although there are many issues surrounding the assessment of students with disabilities, most of the issues can be grouped into two areas: participation and accommodation. In this section we describe these two issues. In later sections we provide considerably more detail on them.

Participation

Educators use assessment information for many purposes. When screening, program evaluation, or accountability decisions are made, then inclusion in testing is an issue. Too often assumptions are made prior to testing that certain students should be excluded because "we already know how they would perform" or because "the student should not be subjected to the pain of participation" or because "they could not possibly respond correctly to the test items."

When data are collected for large-scale (district, state, or national) assessments, the outcomes have major implications for funding, real estate values, and reputations of teachers and administrators. Because it is widely believed that including students with disabilities would lower scores, these students are often excluded from participation. Indeed, some would argue that including scores earned by students with disabilities actually biases the results of large-scale assessments.

Current legislation explictly states that national educational goals and standards are to apply to all students. If students with disabilities are not included in assessment, then a biased picture of local, state, or national performance is presented. As demonstrated in Chapter 6, exclusion of low scoring students does inflate the mean and reduce the variance of scores. This bias has substantial effect when cut-off scores are used to identify individual students, although the effect on mean performance is not particularly large.

Accommodation

Accommodation involves adapting or modifying measures to enable students with disabilities to participate in assessment. What legitimate modifications can be made in assessment materials and/or procedures that still allow valid assessment results to be obtained? Reschly (1993) put the issue well when he stated:

> My experience as a member of the state of Georgia Assessment Advisory Board (where state-wide educational assessment programs in Georgia and other states are reviewed) and the American Psychological Association Committee on Psychological Tests and Assessments (where various proposals for national literacy tests or assessment have been reviewed) indicates that assessment mechanics (e.g., item types), test content, and scaling typically dominate discussions at the expense of consideration of why the assessment is done, what will be assessed, what interpretation will result, how the results will be used, and what consequences will be established for good and poor performance. (p. 37)

Concern about accommodations applies to individual and large-scale group assessments. The concerns are both legal (Do individuals have a right to take modified tests?) and technical (To what extent can we modify measures and still have technically adequate tests?)

FACTORS AFFECTING ACCURATE ASSESSMENT

Five factors impede getting an accurate picture of students' abilities and skills: the students' ability to understand assessment stimuli, the students' ability to respond to assessment stimuli, the nature of the norm group, the appropriateness of the level of the items (sufficient basal and ceiling), and the students' lack of exposure to the curriculum being tested. These factors are reviewed in this section.

Ability to Understand Assessment Stimuli

Assessments are considered unfair if the test stimuli are in a format that is not understood by the student. For example, tests in print are considered unfair for students with severe visual impairments and blindness. Tests with oral directions are considered unfair for students with hearing impairments. In fact, since the law requires that students be assessed in their primary language, and since the primary language of many students who are deaf is not English, written assessments in English are considered unfair and invalid for many deaf students. When students cannot understand test stimuli because of a sensory or physical limitation, then performance on the test is more reflective of the sensory or physical limitation than of actual skill or ability. Such a test is invalid and illegal.

Ability to Respond

All assessment measures require that students produce a response. For example, intelligence tests require verbal or written (multiple-choice) responses, and perceptual-motor measures require a motor response. To the extent that physical or sensory limitations inhibit accurate responding, test results are more indicative of physical or sensory disabilities than of actual skill or ability. Again, such tests are invalid and illegal.

The Nature of the Norm Group

Norm-referenced tests are standardized on groups of individuals, and the performance of the person assessed is compared to the performance of the norm group. To the extent that the test was administered to the student differently than it was to the norm group, the comparison is considered unfair and invalid. Modification of measures involves changing either stimulus presentation or response requirements. The modification may make the test items easier or harder. Although qualitative or criterion-referenced interpretations of such test performance are acceptable, norm-referenced comparisons are flawed. The *Standards for Educational and Psychological Testing*, a joint publication of three professional associations, specifies that when tests are modified, they must be renormed or be considered invalid.

Appropriateness of the Level of the Items

In earlier chapters we pointed out that tests are developed for use with specific age ranges of students or with those who have a particular range of skills. One issue to be decided in making participation and accommodation decisions is the extent to which a student can and should be given an out-of-level test (one intended for use with older or younger students). Assessors are tempted to give out-of-level tests when an age-appropriate test contains either an insufficient number of easy items or not enough hard items for the student being assessed. Of course, when out-of-level tests are given, and norm-referenced interpretations are made, the student is being compared to a group of students who differ from him or her. We have no idea how same-age or same-grade students would perform in the level.

Exposure to the Curriculum Being Tested

One of the issues of fairness raised by the general public is the administration of tests that contain content that students have not had an opportunity to learn.

This same issue applies to the business of making adaptation and accommodation decisions. Students with motor disabilities have not had an opportunity to learn the content of a test requiring motor responses. Students with sensory impairments have not had an opportunity to learn the content of test items that use verbal or auditory stimuli. This issue is especially challenging to address when students have been raised and educated in cultures that differ quite markedly from the culture of the test. To the extent that students have not had an opportunity to learn the content of the test (they were absent when the content was taught, the content is not taught in the schools in which they were present, or the content was taught in ways that were not effective for the student), they likely will not perform well on the test. Their performance will reflect more a lack of opportunity to learn than limited skill and ability.

LEGAL CONSIDERATIONS

By law, students with disabilities have a right to be included in assessments, and accommodations in testing should be made in order to enable them to participate. This legal argument is derived largely from the Fourteenth amendment to the constitution (which guarantees the right to equal protection and to due process). Public Law 94-142 includes provisions that guarantee the right to education and due process. Also, section 504 of the Rehabilitation Act of 1973 indicates that it is illegal to exclude people from participation solely because of a disability.

The Americans with Disabilities Act of 1992 (ADA) applies to making testing inclusion and accommodation decisions in that all individuals must have access to exams used to provide credentials or licenses. Agencies administering tests must provide auxiliary aids and/or modifications to enable individuals with disabilities to participate in assessment; and they may not charge the individual for costs incurred in making special provisions. Modifications that may be provided include an architecturally accessible testing site, a distraction-free space, an alternative location, test schedule variation, extended time, the use of a scribe, sign language interpreter, reader, or adaptive equipment, and modifications of the test presentation and/or response format.

CURRENT PRACTICE IN PARTICIPATION DECISIONS

We noted earlier that issues of participation in testing arise largely in connection with making screening decisions and with making large-scale assessments for the purpose of program evaluation or accountability decisions. Typical practice in screening is to exclude students with severe disabilities from screening, assume that they would fail the screening measure, and then count them as failing the measure. When it comes to large-scale assessments for the purpose of making accountability decisions, there is considerable variability in practice.

Some methods that have been used to decide whether to include or exclude students with disabilities in national, state, or local testing programs follow:

- Exclude from testing any student who is disabled and is on an IEP.
- Include in testing any student who has an IEP if the student spends more than 50 percent of the time in mainstream classes.
- Let an IEP team decide whether each individual student with a disability should participate in assessments.
- Permit the meeting of IEP goals to substitute for performance on a test (that is, exclude students with IEPs from testing, and count as evidence of accomplishment whether students met IEP objectives).
- Require that all but a predetermined percentage of students with disabilities participate in state and national testing, but require that those who are excluded be assessed using alternative assessments and that results be reported on all students.
- Allow teachers to decide who participates and who does not.
- Allow parents to decide whether their exceptional child participates.
- Allow students to decide whether they participate.
- Exclude those whom school personnel decide cannot participate meaningfully.
- Make decisions on the basis of category of disability (for example, students with learning disabilities will participate, but those who are blind will not).
- Include only those for whom assessors believe the test will yield a reliable and valid measure of the student's performance.
- Include only students who have been exposed to the content of the curriculum that is assessed by the test.

Thurlow, Ysseldyke, & Silverstein (1993) gathered data from twenty-eight states on the criteria they use to make decisions about which students to include in state testing. In Table 9.1 we show the kinds of variables that are used by these states in making inclusion/exclusion decisions.

In 1993, Ysseldyke and Thurlow asked a number of measurement experts to make recommendations about how best to make decisions about inclusion of students with disabilities in large-scale testing. A number of conflicting opinions were expressed. Some experts felt that exclusion of all students with disabilities was acceptable, because their small number would not change scores much. Others felt that all students with disabilities should participate in testing. We think that the position that currently makes most sense is somewhere between these two extremes.

Along with conflicting opinions on who should participate in assessment are many conflicting opinions on who should make the decision whether students

TABLE 9.1   Variables Included in Testing Eligibility Criteria Used by States

State	Appropriate Accommodations	Course/Percentage Mainstreamed	Curricular Validity	Grade Level	IEP	Parent/Guardian	Receiving Special Ed Services/Percentage Time	Specific Handicap/Severity of Disability	Student Unable to Participate Meaningfully in Testing	Test Situations Adversely Affect Student	Test Will Yield a Valid and Reliable Measure of Student's Performance
AK					X						
AL	X				X						X
AR		X									
AZ		X				X	X	X			
CT			X							X	X
DE		X		X	X					X	
FL					X		X	X			
GA								X			
HI							X	X			
ID		X				X					
IN		X									
LA				X							
MA						X					
MD			X								
ME	X						X				X
MI		X			X	X	X				
MO					X						
MT							X				
NC					X	X		X			
NJ			X		X					X	
NM	X										X
SC					X						
SD									X		
UT		X							X		
VA			X			X					
WA									X		X
WI	X	X	X								
WV					X						

with disabilities should participate. The following are alternative perspectives on when to have students with disabilities participate in assessment.

Include All Students with Disabilities

Those who espouse the view that everyone ought to participate in assessments usually go on to indicate how alternative measures should be administered in order to get data on some students or to explain how tests might be adapted so that everyone can participate in the data collection process. The point is that we ought to be gathering and reporting data on all students. Algozzine (1993) contends that the simple solution is to include all students in assessments, and states that "As is often the case in education, the simple solution is set aside and the practice wants to be complex." He goes on to say that

> If all students are included, differences in performance across comparison groups are due to naturally occurring differences in characteristics of comparison groups. If some students are excluded, differences in performance across comparison groups are not due to naturally occurring differences in characteristics of performance groups. For example, if one state excludes all and another excludes some students with learning disabilities, reporting and comparing outcomes across states become meaningless. (p. 8)

The view that all students should be included in assessment (or that we should gather data on all students) goes hand in glove with the view that all students should be included in general education settings, classrooms, and in communities. Koehler (1993), the Director of Assessment in Arizona, contends,

> What can be said with some certainty at this point is that by the very act of including all special needs students in the Arizona State Assessment Program and providing means for them to access the curriculum goals and assessments, a strong message has been delivered to the schools in Arizona, that for once educational practice is consistent with the educational rhetoric regarding the inclusion of all students within the community of learners. (p. 18)

Permit Some Kinds of Students with Disabilities to Participate

Students with disabilities demonstrate different kinds of disabilities and differing severities within kinds. Reschly (1993) differentiated two kinds of students with disabilities in school-age populations: those for whom there are, and those for whom there are not, identifiable biological anomalies that are functionally related to behavioral limitations. The vast majority of students with disabilities do not have identifiable biological anomalies that would interfere with participating in state and national assessment programs.

Those who believe that only some students with disabilities should participate in large-scale assessments hold that the appropriateness of participation or exclusion depends on the level of severity and type of disability. If disability severity and type are not taken into account, they contend, assessment results for as many as half of all students with disability may reflect their disability rather than the competency being assessed. From this viewpoint, students with severe (usually biologically based) disabilities would be excluded from participation in state and national assessment programs. Data on these students could still be collected by means of alternative assessments.

Include Students with Disabilities in Assessments of Cultural Imperatives

Reynolds (1993) differentiates schooling on the basis of what he calls cultural imperatives. These include:

Language, in all receptive and expressive forms, including speaking, listening, comprehending, reading, and writing

Mathematics, including counting, measuring, computing, and problem solving

Social Skills, including abilities involved in cooperation, group life, and good citizenship in a democratic society; also avoidance of destructive behavior

Self-dependence, including knowledge of the basics of self-help, health and safety; also including eventual employment and satisfying life in open community

Reynolds contends that "the point of importance here is to identify those aspects of learning that are so basic and universally important that we ought to know how everyone is progressing and how effective our school programs are in teaching them. Assessment processes here are not addressed to how well pupils play the piccolo, use the cross-cut saw, or write poetry; such abilities are electives as are literally hundreds of other domains of learning, many of them reflected in school curricula" (p. 49-50).

Those who espouse this view hold that students with disabilities should participate in assessments in areas of cultural electives only if they have participated in instruction in those areas—essentially, only if it can be demonstrated that they have had an opportunity to learn the content being assessed. Others contend that such a view will keep students out of curricula to which they could, should, or need to be exposed.

Include Students with Disabilities When Certain Data Collection Procedures Are Used

In Chapter 2 we described the kinds of procedures that are used to gather data on students: tests, observations, interviews, and record review. One view on participation in assessment holds that all students should participate when the mode of data collection is observation or record review. Further, this view holds that students with disabilities ought to participate when data are collected by interviewing others (for example, teachers or parents), and, to the extent possible, when interviewing the student. Observation and/or interviewing are methods of data collection that typically do not put unfair requirements (understanding stimuli or being able to give a response) on the student.

Do Not Encourage Unwarranted Exclusion

At this time there are major incentives for exclusion of students with disabilities from assessments. Oftentimes the results of large-scale assessments are published, sometimes in community newspapers. This creates an incentive for school personnel to exclude from such reports the performance of individuals with disabilities; on the average this makes the school personnel look better. Poor performance might result in a decrease in community support for the schools, no new taxes or reduced taxes, lower real estate values, or decreased job security for teachers and administrators. If comparisons are made among states, or among school districts within states, there is an incentive to exclude students with disabilities. Finally, the latest school reforms increasingly include performance incentives for teachers and administrators. In Kentucky, for example, merit increases and sanctions for teachers are tied to student achievement. In many of our nation's large school districts, administrator salaries and continued employment are dependent on gains in student achievement. Both practices create incentives for controlling the kinds of students one has to include in instruction and the kinds of students for whose outcomes one has to be held responsible. Reschly (1993) defines unwarranted exclusion as "directed or arranged non-participation in state or national assessment programs involving students for whom the assessment content is appropriate to curriculum goals pursued in their educational programs and the receptive or expressive language demands of the assessment tasks are within the students' behavioral repertoire" (p. 41). He and others argue that such unwarranted exclusion ought to be prohibited.

Allow Exclusion of up to Two Percent of Students

One approach to making participation decisions that is gaining increasing support is to allow schools to exclude up to 2 percent of their student population from large-scale assessments. School personnel would still have to report how this 2 percent of the population is doing in school, but might do so using alternative tests, performance measures, portfolios, or other forms of assessment. It is thought that enabling school personnel to make this decision will enable them to exclude students for whom participation would not be meaningful, either because of their inability to meet stimulus and response demands or because they have not been exposed to the curriculum being tested.

RECOMMENDATIONS FOR MAKING PARTICIPATION DECISIONS

Students with disabilities routinely are included in testing for the purpose of making screening and eligibility decisions. Our discussion of participation in testing is specific to participation in large-scale assessments. The following are our current recommendations about how such participation decisions ought to be made. At the time we prepared this text, personnel at the National Center on Educational Outcomes, the National Center on Educational Statistics, and the Office of Special Education Programs were drawing up guidelines on how to make these decisions. Recommendations had been published about national assessments (Ysseldyke, Thurlow, McGrew, & Vanderwood, 1994) and state assessments (Ysseldyke, Thurlow, McGrew, & Shriner 1994). Watch publications of the National Center on Educational Outcomes for any changes in the proposed guidelines. We offer the following as reasonable guidelines for making decisions about inclusion in large-scale assessments.

- Include students with disabilities when trying out items in order to identify problematic item formats and the need for more items at lower levels, for example. In this way, instruments can be modified during the development phase (items can be dropped, modified, or added) to allow greater numbers of students with disabilities to participate meaningfully.
- Include all students with disabilities in taking some form of an assessment. When a sampling procedure is used, the sample must be representative of all students. Accommodations and alternative measures (as specified later in this chapter) will be necessary to achieve this.
- Include students with disabilities in the reporting of assessment results. Data on the performance of all students are needed; therefore scores must be reported for all students. Reports of results from students taking alternative assessments and from information provided by informed respondents should be included in reports.
- Provide incentives for school districts to include students with disabilities in their large-scale assessment activities.

CURRENT PRACTICE IN TESTING ACCOMMODATIONS

Practice in making test accommodations runs the gamut from permitting no modifications and requiring that any students who are included in local, state, and national assessments take standard versions of tests being used to allowing extensive alternative assessment procedures. Thurlow, Ysseldyke, and Silverstein (1993) investigated the kinds of testing accommodations, adaptations, and modifications allowed in state and national assessments. The kinds of adaptations allowed are listed in Table 9.2. Note that some of the modifications involve changes in the way the test is presented, some involve modifications in response format, others are setting adaptations, while others involve relaxing time constraints. The American College Testing Program is the organization responsible for organizing and administering the American College

TABLE 9.2   **Common Testing Accommodations, Modifications, and Adaptations**

Aspect to Be Modified	Type of Modification
Presentation Format	Braille edition of test Use of magnifying equipment Large-print edition of test Oral reading of directions Signing of directions Interpretation of directions
Response Format	Mark response in test book Use template for responding Point to response Give response orally Give response in sign language Use typewriter for responding Use computer for responding Receive assistance and interpretation with responses
Setting of Test	Alone, in test carrel With small group At home In special education class
Timing of Test	Extended time More breaks during testing Extending testing sessions over several days.

Test (ACT). The following accommodations for students with disabilities are allowed on the ACT: extended time, large type, Braille, audio cassette editions of the test, the use of a reader, assistance in filling out the answer folder, and signing of instructions. Individuals with disabilities may bring to the exam assistive devices such as a Brailler, template and stylus, magnifying glass, or tape recorder.

Educational Testing Service (ETS) is the organization responsible for administering the Scholastic Aptitude Test (SAT) and the Graduate Record Exam (GRE). It offers alternative test formats (Braille, cassette, large type), alternative ways to record answers (large-type answer sheets, typewriter), assistive personnel such as a reader or an amanuensis (a person who writes down the response for the student being tested), assistive devices such as an abacus or opticon, separate testing locations, and extra time. Neither ETS nor ACT will allow students who contend that they have dyscalculia to use calculators. This is an issue in current court cases (Phillips, 1992). In Table 9.3 (page 192) we show the kinds of accommodations that are permitted in twenty-one states.

RECOMMENDATIONS ON MAKING ACCOMMODATION DECISIONS

As with participation decisions, there are major debates about the kinds of accommodations that ought to be permitted in testing. And, there are major arguments about the extent to which making accommodations in testing destroys the technical adequacy of tests.

Making Decisions About Individuals

The issues involved in making accommodation decisions extend to more than screening and accountability. In fact, they play a major role in decisions about exceptionality, special need, eligibility, and instructional planning. We think there are some reasonable guidelines for best practice in making decisions about individuals.

- Conduct all assessments in the student's native language or mode of communication. In a recent ruling on this issue, Davilla (1989), then Assistant Secretary of Education, wrote "If a person is deaf or blind, or has no written language, the mode of communication would be that normally used by the person (such as sign language, Braille, or oral communication)" and "under the Education of the Handicapped act, testing or evaluation materials must be administered in a child's native language or other mode of communication

TABLE 9.3 **Accommodations Allowed by States**

State	Alternative Presentation					Alternative Response						Alternative Setting			Alternative Scheduling/Time			Other		
	Oral reading or signing directions	Braille	Large print	Interpret directions	Computer/typewriter	Oral response	Sign language	Point to response	Mark answer book	Assistance interpretation	Small group	Individually or in carrel	At home	In special education class	More time	More breaks	More breaks within one day	Accommodation based on approval of appointed committee	Accommodation based on classroom activities	Accommodation based on IEP
AL		X	X		X	X			X		X	X	X	X	X	X	X	X		
AR	X	X	X		X	X			X		X	X	X		X	X		X		X
CT		X	X	X	X			X		X		X						X		
DE															O	X				
FL		X	X		X				X	X	X	X				X				
GA		X	X	O	X						X	X							X	
HI		X	X																	
IN															X					
LA	X	X	X		X					X	X	X		X	X				X	X
MA	X	X	X		X			X	X		X	X		X					X	X
MD	X							X								O	X			X
ME		X	X		X	X		X	X	X	X	X	X	X			X	X	X	X
MO																X				X
NC		X																		
NJ	X	X	X	X	X	X	X	X	X		X	X		X	X	X				X
NY	X	X	X	X	X	X					X				X	X				X
OH		X	X							X	X				X	X	X			
TN	X	X	X	X						X	X	X			O	X				
TX	X	X	X	X	X	X						X								
VA		X				X					X	X		X		X				X
WI	X	X			X	X				X	X	X		X	X	X	X			X

X = Allowed by a written document

O = Directly prohibited by a written document

appropriate to the child." Loeding & Crittenden (1993) point out that for students who are deaf, the primary communication mode is either a visual-spatial, natural sign language used by members of the American Deaf Community called American Sign Language (ASL) or a manually coded form of English, such as Signed English, Pidgin Sign English (PSE), Seeing Essential English (SEE 1), Signing Exact English (SEE 2), or Sign-Supported Speech/English. Therefore, they argue, "traditional paper-and-pencil tests are inaccessible, invalid and inappropriate to the deaf student because the tests are written in English only." (p. 19)

- Format accommodations should be made when the purpose of testing is not substantially impaired. It should be demonstrated that the accommodations assist the individual in responding but do not provide content assistance (for example, a scribe should record the response of the person being tested—not interpret what the person says, include his or her additional knowledge, and then record a response).
- Permit adaptations in assessment only for individuals with a disability documented by a licensed professional.
- With students who are deaf, use multimedia-based assessments that use videodisk, CD-ROM, CD-1, or digital video interactive technology. A videodisk-based assessment designed for individuals with hearing impairments is currently at the prototype stage and has been developed for a portion of the Scholastic Aptitude Test. The prototype makes both ASL and English-order signs available.
- Make normative comparisons only to groups whose membership includes students whose background set of experiences and opportunities are like those of students being tested.

Making Decisions About Groups

There are a number of recommendations that can be implemented when collecting assessment data for purposes of making decisions about groups of students. Among these are the following:

- Allow partial participation in an assessment by students with disabilities. Some assessments have multiple components, some of which can be completed by a student with a disability. Students should be allowed to participate in parts of assessments.
- Use an alternative assessment for some students. Those students whose curriculum differs significantly from the content of the assessment should be assessed using an alternative assessment.
- Use modifications that make a student more comfortable and secure in the test setting (for example, using carrels or separate rooms for administration).

- Permit the use of modifications that do not destroy the validity of measures (for example, amplification, magnification, large print, Braille, augmentative communication, sign language, or word processor).
- Conduct research on presentation alternatives, response alternatives, setting alternatives, and timing/scheduling alternatives. As new technologies and procedures are developed, subject them to validation research with an eye to including them in the array of permitted adaptations.

SUMMARY

Recent education legislation mandates high standards for all students. It also mandates that all students, including those with disabilities, participate in assessments to ascertain the extent to which those high standards are being met. Although the system of standards and assessments is voluntary, states cannot have them approved without specifying how students with disabilities will participate. In this chapter we outlined recommendations for making decisions about who should participate in assessments. We recommended that students with disabilities should be included in test development and should take tests and that any reports of results of pupil performance should include reports on how students with disabilities performed.

To enable students with disabilities to participate in assessments, certain accommodations will be necessary. We outlined a set of recommendations for making accommodations in assessments.

STUDY QUESTIONS

1. What are the major factors serving as an impetus for increased participation of students with disabilities in large-scale state and national assessments?
2. Why should students with disabilities participate in large-scale assessments?
3. What factors impede getting an accurate picture of student performance on tests?
4. We have recommended a set of practices for including students with disabilities in assessments. What things can teachers and other school personnel do to ensure that participation happens?

ADDITIONAL READING

Thurlow, M. L., Ysseldyke, J. E., & Silverstein, B. (1993). *Testing accommodations for students with disabilities: A review of the literature.* Synthesis Report 4. Minneapolis, MN: National Center on Educational Outcomes.

Willingham, W. W., Ragosta, M., Bennett, R. E., Braun, H., Rock, D. A., & Powers, D. E. (1988). *Testing handicapped people.* Boston: Allyn and Bacon.

Educational Testing Service. (1990). *Testing persons with disabilities: A report for ETS programs and their constituents.* Princeton, NJ: Author.

PART 3

ASSESSMENT IN CLASSROOMS

The development of assessment has never been static, and its improvement has seldom been merely incremental. Scientific positivism was embraced by the mental testing movement, and objective (scientific) tests gained widespread acceptance during the first half of this century. However, by the 1960s experience with the use of norm-referenced, objectively scored tests suggested that they had a variety of technical shortcomings. A subsequent flurry of activity produced norm-referenced tests with greater reliability and substantially better norms. However, educators frequently used these tests in inappropriate ways (for example, to plan and evaluate instruction). As educators learned that these tests could not be used effectively to facilitate classroom decisions, other procedures were developed. Thus, systematic observation procedures, so successful in experimental psychology, were adopted for classroom use. Similarly, there was renewed interest in the development of teacher-made tests. Although systematic observation and teacher-made tests were widely accepted and effectively used, many educators were still dissatisfied with the perceived limitations of these assessment techniques. During the late 1980s and early 1990s, interest grew in more subjective and qualitative approaches to assessment.

Educational assessment may appear to have come full circle, but educators have gotten off at different points. Thus, today there is no shortage of opinions about how classroom assessments ought to be conducted. Some educators still rely on norm-referenced achievement tests to plan and evaluate instruction; some rely on systematic observation; some rely on teacher-made tests and curriculum-based assessment; some rely on subjective and qualitative judgments to assess classroom learning; and some rely on a combination of approaches.

In Part 3 of this text, Assessment in Classrooms, we discuss those approaches most likely to be used by classroom teachers. We do not consider these approaches to be informal or unstandardized. They are frequently formal: Students know that they are being assessed and that the assessments count for something. They are frequently standardized: Students receive the same directions and tasks, and their responses are frequently scored using the same criteria. These approaches to assessment are used most frequently by classroom teachers, but we also recognize that some specialists (such as school psychologists and speech and language therapists) may use these approaches.

Part 3 begins with a chapter on observation that provides a general overview of basic considerations and good practice. The next chapter, Teacher-Made Tests of Achievement, provides an overview of objective and performance measures constructed by teachers. The third chapter in this section, Using Student Portfolios in Assessment, provides an overview of an emerging, but controversial, approach to classroom assessment. The next chapter deals with assessing the instructional ecology of classrooms. The last chapter in this part discusses the decisions made by regular and special teachers.

Chapter 10

Assessing Behavior Through Observation

*I*n the general sense, the term *observation* refers to the process of gaining information through one's senses—visual, auditory, and so forth. Observation can be used to assess behavior, states, physical characteristics, and permanent products of behavior (such as a child's poem). In this chapter, we use the term *behavioral observation* to refer to observation of behavior *other* than behavior that has been elicited by a predetermined and standardized set of stimuli—that is, test behavior.

There are two basic approaches to observation—qualitative and quantitative. Qualitative observation is essentially descriptive. The observer begins without preconceived ideas about what will be observed and describes behavior that seems important. There are also two basic approaches to qualitative observation—ethnographic and participant-observer (see Suen & Ary, 1989). The difference between the two approaches lies in the behavior of the observer. In ethnographic observation, the observer only watches what is occurring. In the participant-observer approach, the observer joins the target social group and participates in its activities. In either case, observation occurs over prolonged periods, and the observer tries to note all the activities and contexts. Although qualitative approaches may have intuitive appeal, they suffer from four limitations: (1) sophisticated and highly trained observers are required; (2) data collection requires a burdensome investment of time (sometimes years); (3) the observer's notes can be difficult to interpret and summarize; and (4) it is often difficult to maintain scientific objectivity (Suen & Ary, 1989).

Often some qualitative observation precedes quantitative observation. For example, an observer might watch students in specific situations to get a general feel for what is going on. Then that observer might set out to measure specific behaviors that are thought to be particularly important. This form of qualitative observation is sometimes referred to as *nonsystematic observation* or *monitoring* (that is, paying attention and noting important events). Probably the most common way of conducting nonsystematic observations is to keep anecdotal records of behaviors that seem important to the observer. These records should, at the minimum, contain a complete description of the behavior and the context in which it occurred.

In this chapter, we stress quantitative approaches to observation. (Chapter 13 offers more coverage of qualitative approaches.) Quantitative observation is distinguished by five characteristics. First, the goal of observation is to measure (for example, count) specific behaviors. Second, the behaviors being observed have been defined previously and precisely. Third, before observation, procedures are developed for gathering objective and replicable information about the behavior. Fourth, the times and places for observation are carefully selected and specified. Fifth, the ways in which behavior will be quantified are specified prior to observation.

The major criticism of quantitative approaches is that they may oversimplify the meaning and interpretation of behavior. Despite this criticism, quantitative analysis of behavior has proven to be very useful in developing theory and practice related to the modification of human behavior. Assessment based on quantitative behavioral observation is a topic suitable for an entire text, and only a general overview of good practices for those who develop and use behavioral observations can be provided in this chapter; interested readers are referred to texts by Boehm and Weinberg (1988), Alberto and Troutman (1990), or Salvia and Hughes (1990), among others. Readers interested in the statistical bases of measurement procedures used in systematic observation may consult the text by Suen and Ary (1989). Finally, the procedures and concepts discussed in detail in preceding chapters are not reexplained here.

WHY DO TEACHERS OBSERVE BEHAVIOR?

Humans are always monitoring external events, and the behavior of others is a primary target for our attention. Teachers are constantly monitoring themselves and their students. Sometimes they are just keeping an eye on things to make sure that their classrooms are safe and orderly, to anticipate disruptive or dangerous situations, or just to keep track of how things are going in a general sense. Often they notice behavior or situations that seem important and require their attention: the fire alarm has sounded, Harvey has a knife, Betty is asleep, Jo is wandering around the classroom, and so forth. In other situations, often as a result of their general monitoring, teachers look for very specific behavior to observe: social behavior that should be reinforced, attention to task, performance of particular skills, and so forth. Information gained from observation can be used to make academic and social instructional decisions—for example, planning or evaluating instructional programs for individuals or groups of students.

GENERAL CONSIDERATIONS

Behavior that is to be analyzed quantitatively can be observed as it occurs (in real time), or at times after it has occurred, by using devices such as video or audio recorders that can replay, slow down, or speed up records of behavior displays. Observation can be enhanced with equipment (for example, a telescope), or it can occur with only one's unaided senses. Observational systems can be classified along two dimensions: (1) obtrusive versus unobtrusive and (2) contrived versus naturalistic.

Obtrusive Versus Unobtrusive Observation

When antisocial, offensive, or highly personal or undesirable behaviors are targeted for assessment, observation often is conducted surreptitiously. Behaviors of these types tend not to occur if they are overtly monitored. For example, parents who hit their children privately may be very hesitant to do so publicly. To make observations of such behavior, observers can use hidden cameras that require minimum light or use extrasensitive recorders; or a human observer can become a trusted person around whom the target individual will act naturally.

Behavior that is not antisocial, immoral, or highly personal may also nonetheless be distorted by observation. For example, when a principal sits in the back of a probationary teacher's classroom for a periodic evaluation, both the teacher's and the students' behaviors may be affected by the principal's presence. Often students are better behaved or respond more enthusiastically, in the mistaken belief that the principal is there to watch them. The teacher may write more frequently on the chalkboard, repeat directions more often, ask more questions of particular students, or give more positive reinforcement than usual, in the belief that the principal values those techniques. Moreover, a video camera, audio microphone, unusually bright light, or one-way mirrors can signal that someone is watching and, thus, become stimuli that set the occasion for atypical behavior.

Unobtrusive observations do not affect the way people behave. It is fortunate that most people quickly become desensitized to observers or observation equipment when the observers or equipment are part of their daily environment. A number of things can be done to hasten desensitization. Observers can sit behind or to the side of a classroom, and they can avoid eye contact and verbal interactions with students. Recording equipment that cannot be hidden can be left in operating position at all times. Moreover, any indication that the equipment is operating can be avoided. For example, if a red light comes on when a video camera is recording, students are likely to pay attention to the camera when the light is on; the red light should be disabled or hidden. Observation and recording can become part of the everyday classroom routine. In any event, assessment should not begin until the persons to be observed are desensitized and are acting in their usual ways.

Contrived Versus Naturalistic Observation

Contrived observations occur when a situation is set up before a student is introduced into it. For example, a playroom may be set up with toys that allow aggressive play (such as guns or punching-bag dolls) or with many desirable toys. The child may be given a book and told to go into the room and read or may simply be told to wait in the room. Other adults or children in the situation may be confederates of the observer and be instructed to behave in particular ways. For example, an older child might be told not to share toys with the child who is the target of the observation, or an adult might be told to initiate a conversation on a specific topic with the target child.

In contrast, naturalistic settings are not contrived. For example, specific toys are not added to or removed from a playroom; the furniture is arranged as it always is arranged.

DEFINING BEHAVIOR

It is worth repeating that behavior is observable. Moreover, behavior is always defined in terms of its observable attributes. Depending on the particular behavior and the reasons for observation, behavior can be described in several ways. Often the function that a behavior serves in the environment is described (for example, uses a pencil to write) and assessed. Sometimes, the topography of a behavior is assessed (for example, holds pencil at a 45-degree angle to the paper, grasping pencil between thumb and index finger with support from the middle finger).

The measurement of behavior, whether an individual behavior or a category of behavior, is based on four characteristics: duration, latency, frequency, and amplitude. These characteristics can be measured directly.

Duration

Behaviors that have discrete beginnings and endings may be assessed in terms of their *duration,* that is, the length of time a behavior lasts. The duration of a behavior is usually standardized two ways. First, the average duration of each occurrence may be computed. For example, Billy is out of his seat four times during a 30-minute activity, and the duration of the episodes are 1 minute, 3 minutes, 7 minutes, and 5 minutes; then the average duration is 4 minutes [that is, $(1 + 3 + 7 + 5)/4$]. Second, the total duration may be computed. For example, Billy was out of his seat a total of 16 minutes. Often total duration is expressed as a rate by dividing the total occurrence by the length of an observation. This proportion of duration is often called the *prevalence* of the behavior. In the preceding example, Billy's prevalence is .53 (that is, 16/30).

Latency

The term *latency* refers to the length of time between a signal to perform and the beginning of the behavior. For example, a teacher might request students to take out their books. Sam's latency for that task is the length of time between the teacher's request and Sam's placing his book on his desk. When latency is assessed, the behavior must have a discrete beginning.

Frequency

Behaviors that have discrete beginnings and endings may have their *frequency* of occurrence counted. When the time periods in which the behavior is counted vary, frequencies are usually converted to rates. Using rate of behavior allows one to compare the occurrence of behavior across settings. For example, three episodes of out-of-seat behavior in 15 minutes may be converted to a rate of 12 per hour. However, Alberto and Troutman (1990) suggest that frequency should not be used under two conditions: (1) when the behavior occurs at such a high rate that it cannot be counted accurately (for example, many stereotypic behaviors, such as foot tapping, can occur almost constantly), and (2) when a behavior occurs over a prolonged period of time (for example, cooperative play during a game of monopoly).

Amplitude

The term *amplitude* refers to the intensity of the behavior. In many settings, amplitude can be measured precisely (for example, with noise meters). However, in the classroom it is usually measured with less precision. Often, amplitude is estimated by rating the behavior on a scale that crudely calibrates amplitude in terms of the behavior itself (for example, crying might be scaled as "whimpering," "sobbing," "crying," and "screaming"). Amplitude may also be calibrated in terms of its objective or subjective impact on others. For example, the objective impact of hitting might be scaled as "without apparent physical damage," "resulting in bruising," and "causing bleeding." More subjective behavior ratings estimate the internal impact on others; for example, a student's humming could be scaled as "does not disturb others," "disturbs students seated nearby," or "disturbs students in the adjoining classroom."

The characteristic of behavior to be assessed should make sense; we should assess the most relevant aspect of behavior in a particular situation. For example, if Billy is wandering around the classroom during the reading period, observing the duration of that behavior makes more sense than observing the frequency, latency, or amplitude of the behavior. If Minerva is always slow to follow directions, observing her latency makes more sense than assessing the frequency or amplitude of her behavior. For most behaviors, frequency and duration are the characteristics measured.

SAMPLING BEHAVIOR

As is the case for any assessment procedure, one can either try to assess the entire domain of behavior or sample from it. And the sampling procedures assess the same aspects that were discussed in Chapters 7 and 8—contexts, items (in this case behaviors), and times.

Contexts

When specific behaviors become the targets of intervention, it is useful to measure the behavior in a variety of contexts. Usually the sampling of contexts is purposeful rather than random. We might want to know, for example, how Jesse's behavior in the resource room differs from his behavior in the regular classroom. Consistent or inconsistent performance across settings and contexts can provide useful information about what events might set the occasion for the behavior. Differences between the settings in which a behavior occurs and does not occur can provide potentially useful hypotheses about setting events (that is, environmental events that set the occasion for the performance of an action) and discriminative stimuli (that is, stimuli that are consistently present when a behavior is reinforced and come to bring out behavior even in the absence of the original reinforcer).[1] Bringing behavior under the control of a discriminative stimulus is often an effective way of modifying it. For example, students might be taught to talk quietly (use their "inside voice") when they are in the classroom or hallway.

Similarly, consistent or inconsistent performance across settings and contexts can provide useful information about how the consequences of a behavior are affecting that behavior. (The consequences of a behavior maintain, increase, or decrease behavior.) Manipulating the consequences of a behavior can increase or decrease its occurrence. For example, if Joey's friends usually laugh and congrat-

---

1. Discriminative stimuli are not conditioned stimuli in the Pavlovian sense that they elicit reflexive behavior. Discriminative stimuli provide a signal to the individual to engage in a particular behavior because that behavior has been reinforced in the presence of that signal.

ulate him when he makes a sexist remark, their reactions may be reinforcing his behavior. If his friends could be made to stop laughing and congratulating him, Joey's behavior might change.

Behaviors

Teachers and psychologists may be interested in measurement of and intervention on a particular behavior or a constellation of behaviors (for example, cooperation). When one views a target behavior as important in and of itself, other behaviors are not sampled, and only other contexts and times must be considered. For example, does Marc fail to take turns at the slide before school, during recess, and after school? Does the behavior manifest itself at home and at his neighborhood playground as well as at school? When a specific behavior is of concern and when it can be modified across times and contexts, the problem is solved.

However, when one views a target behavior as part of a constellation of behavior, behavior sampling will be required in addition to sampling contexts and times. In such cases, the specific behaviors are aggregated into a total score, much as subtests are aggregated into total scores (although the statistical methods would be different). For example, Marc's failure to take turns using the slide on the playground may be viewed as representative of a whole class of behavior (that is, cooperation). Treating a single behavior as an element within a category of behavior requires that the content validity of the category be established. A variety of behaviors representative of cooperation would have to be sampled (for example, taking turns on other equipment, following the rules of games, working with others to attain a common goal, and so forth). If the problem was found in other areas of cooperation, successful intervention on the class of behavior (with generalization to other times and contexts) would correct the behavior problem. In yet other instances, failure to take turns on the slide might be viewed as a symptom of a dysfunction in a hypothetical and internal process. For example, some might even argue that failure to take turns might indicate immaturity or even fixation at the anal stage of psychosocial development. With this orientation to the behavior, intervention would be aimed at the hypothesized internal cause rather than at the surface behavior (failure to take turns on the slide). The success of the intervention would be judged by the same criteria used when a behavior is believed to be one of many included in a syndrome—modification across behaviors, times, and contexts.

Times

With the exception of some criminal acts, few behaviors are noteworthy unless they happen more than once. Behavioral recurrence over time is termed *stability* or *maintenance*. There are almost an infinite number of times in a person's lifetime to exhibit a particular behavior. Moreover, it is probably impossible and certainly unnecessary to observe a person continuously during his or her entire life. Thus, temporal sampling is always performed, and any single observation is merely a sample from the domain.

Time sampling always requires the establishment of blocks of times (called *observation sessions*) in which observations will be made. A session might consist of a continuous period of time (for example, one school day). More often, sessions are discontinuous blocks of time (for example, every Monday for a semester). Moreover, observers can record behavior continuously within sessions or they can sample within a session (that is, record discontinuously). Continuous observation requires the expenditure of more resources than discontinuous observation. When the observation session is long (for example, when it spans several days), continuous sampling can be very expensive and is often intrusive.

Two options are commonly used to estimate behavior in very long observation sessions. In the first option, rating scales can be used to obtain approximate estimates of the four characteristics of behavior. Following are some examples of such ratings.

- *Frequency.* A parent might be asked to rate the frequency of a behavior. How often does Patsy usually pick up her toys—always, frequently, seldom, never?
- *Duration.* A parent might be asked to rate how long Patsy typically watches TV each night—more than 3 hours, 2–3, 1–2, or less than 1 hour?
- *Latency.* A parent might be asked to rate how quickly Patsy usually responds to requests—immediately, quickly, slowly; or not at all (ignores requests)?
- *Amplitude.* A parent might be asked to rate how much of a fuss Patsy usually makes at bedtime—screams, cries, begs to stay up, or goes to bed without fuss?

In the second option, duration and frequency are sampled systematically during prolonged observation intervals. Three different sampling plans have been advocated: whole-interval recording, partial-interval recording, and momentary time sampling.

Whole-Interval Recording

In this sampling procedure, an observation session is subdivided into intervals. Usually observation intervals of equal length are spaced equally through the session, although recording and observation intervals need not be the same length. In whole-interval recording, a behavior is scored as having occurred only when it occurs throughout the entire interval. Thus, it is scored only if it is occurring when the interval begins and continues through the end of the interval.

Partial-Interval Recording

This sampling procedure is quite similar to whole-interval recording. An observation session is subdivided into intervals, and the intervals in which the behavior occurs are noted. The difference between the whole-interval and partial-interval procedures is that in partial-interval recording, an occurrence is scored if it occurs during any part of the interval. Thus, if a behavior begins before the interval begins and ends within the interval, an occurrence is scored; if a behavior starts after the beginning of the interval, an occurrence is scored; if two or more episodes of behavior begin and end within the interval, an occurrence is scored.

Momentary Time Sampling

This is the most efficient sampling procedure. An observation session is subdivided into intervals. If a behavior is occurring at the last moment of the interval, an occurrence is recorded; if the behavior is not occurring at the last moment of the interval, a nonoccurrence is recorded.

Salvia and Hughes (1990) have summarized a number of studies investigating the accuracy of these time-sampling procedures. Both whole-interval and partial-interval sampling procedures provide inaccurate estimates of duration and frequency.[2] Momentary time sampling provides an unbiased estimate of the proportion of time the behavior occurs but can underestimate the frequency of a behavior. The simplest way to estimate frequency seems to be continuous recording with shorter observation sessions.

TARGETING BEHAVIOR FOR OBSERVATION

Observations are usually conducted on behavior that may require modification or behavior that may indicate a disabling condition. These behaviors are harmful, stereotypic, infrequent, or inappropriate at the times exhibited.

Harmful Behavior

Behavior that is self-injurious or physically dangerous to others is almost always targeted for intervention. Self-injurious behavior includes such actions as head banging, eye gouging, self-biting or self-hitting, smoking, drug abuse, and so forth. Potentially harmful behavior can include leaning back in a desk or being careless with reagents in the chemistry experiment. Behaviors harmful to others are those that directly inflict injury (for example, hitting or stabbing) or are likely to injure others (for example, pushing other students on stairs or subway platforms, bullying, or verbally instigating physical altercations). Unusually aggressive behavior may also be targeted for intervention. Although most students will display aggressive behavior, some children go far beyond what can be con-

---

2. Suen and Ary (1989) have provided procedures whereby the sampled frequencies can be adjusted to provide accurate frequency estimates, and the error associated with estimates of prevalence can be readily determined for each sampling plan.

sidered typical or acceptable. These students may be described as hot-tempered, quick-tempered, or volatile. Overly aggressive behavior may be physical or verbal. In addition to the possibility of causing physical harm, high rates of aggressive behavior may isolate the aggressor socially.

Stereotypic Behavior

Stereotypes (for example, hand flapping, rocking, and certain verbalizations such as inappropriate shrieks) are outside the realm of culturally normative behavior. Such behavior calls attention to students and marks them as abnormal to trained psychologists, or unusual to untrained observers. Stereotypic behaviors are often targeted for intervention.

Infrequent or Absent Desirable Behavior

Incompletely developed behavior, especially that related to physiological development (for example, walking), is often targeted for intervention. Intervention usually occurs when these behaviors enable desirable functional skills or social acceptance. Shaping is usually used to develop absent behavior, whereas reinforcement is used to increase the frequency of behavior that is within a student's repertoire but exhibited at rates that are too low.

Normal Behavior Exhibited in Inappropriate Contexts

Many behaviors are appropriate in very specific contexts but are considered inappropriate or even abnormal when exhibited in other contexts. Usually, the problems caused by behavior in inappropriate contexts is attributed to lack of stimulus control. Behavior that is commonly termed *private* falls into this category; elimination and sexual activity are two examples. The goal of intervention should not be to eliminate these behaviors but should be to confine them to socially appropriate conditions. Behavior that is often called *disruptive* also falls into this category. For example, running and yelling are very acceptable and normal when exhibited on the playground; they are disruptive in a classroom.

A teacher may decide on the basis of logic and experience that a particular behavior should be modified. For example, harmful behavior should not be tolerated in a classroom or school; behavior that is a prerequisite for learning academic material must be developed. In other cases, a teacher may seek the advice of a colleague, supervisor, or parent about the desirability of intervention. For example, a teacher might not know if certain behavior is typical of a culturally different student. How much flexibility does a teacher have in altering the goals in an academic area? Yet in other cases, a teacher might rely on the judgments of students or adults to see if a particular behavior is troublesome or distracting for them. For example, does Bob's reading of problems aloud during arithmetic tests bother others? To ascertain if particular behavior bothers others, teachers can ask students directly, have them rate disturbing or distracting behavior, or perhaps use sociometric techniques to learn if a student is being rejected or isolated by his or her behavior.[3]

For infrequent prosocial behavior or frequent disturbing behavior, a teacher may well wish to get a better idea of the magnitude and pervasiveness of the problem before initiating a comprehensive observational analysis. Casual observation can provide information about the frequency and amplitude of the behavior; carefully noting the antecedents, consequences, and contexts may provide useful information about possible interventions, if an intervention is warranted. If casual observations are made, anecdotal records of these casual observations should be maintained.

CONDUCTING SYSTEMATIC OBSERVATIONS

Preparation

Careful preparation is essential in order for accurate and valid observational data to be obtained. Five steps should guide the preparation for systematic observation.

1. Define target behaviors.

Target behaviors should be defined precisely in observable terms. Reference to internal processes (for example, understanding or appreciating) are avoided. It is also useful to include examples of instances and noninstances of the behavior. It is helpful to anticipate potentially difficult discriminations. Therefore, instances should include subtle exhibitions of the target behavior, and noninstances should include related behaviors and behavior with similar topographies. The definition of the target behavior should include the characteristic of the behavior that will be measured (for example, frequency or latency).

2. Select contexts.

The target behavior should be observed systematically in at least three contexts: the context in which the behavior was noted as troublesome (for example, in

3. The sociometric technique is a method for evaluating the social acceptance of individual pupils and the social structure of a group. Students complete a form indicating their choice of seating companions, work companions, and play companions. Teachers look at the number of times an individual student is chosen by others. They also look at who chooses whom.

reading instruction), a similar context (for example, in math instruction), and a dissimilar context (for example, in physical education or recess).

3. Select observation schedule.

Two choices must be made, and these choices are related to the contexts for observation. The first choice is the session length. In the schools, session length cannot exceed the period of time spanning a student's arrival and departure (including getting on and off the school bus, if appropriate). More often session length is related to instructional periods or blocks of time within an instructional period (for example, 15 minutes in the middle of small-group reading instruction). The second choice to be made is for continuous versus discontinuous observation, and this choice will depend on the resources available and the specific behaviors that will be observed. When very-low-frequency behavior or behavior that must be stopped (for example, physical assaults) is observed, continuous recording is convenient and efficient. For other behavior, discontinuous observation is usually preferred, and momentary time sampling usually is the easiest and most accurate for teachers and psychologists to use. However, any discontinuous observation schedule requires some equipment to signal exactly when observation is to occur. The most common equipment is a portable audio cassette player and a tape with pure tones recorded at the desired intervals. One student or several students in sequence may be observed. For example, three students can be observed in a series of 5-second intervals. An audio tape would signal every 5 seconds. On the first signal, Henry would be observed; on the second signal, Joyce would be observed; on the third signal, Bruce would be observed; on the fourth signal, Henry would be observed again; and so forth.

4. Develop recording procedures.

The recording of observations must also be planned. When a few students are observed for the occurrence of relatively infrequent behaviors, simple procedures can be used. Their behavior can be observed continuously and counted using a tally sheet or a wrist counter. When time sampling is used, observations must be recorded for each time interval; thus, some type of recording form is required. In the simplest form, the recording sheet contains identifying information (for example, name of target student, name of observer, date and time of observation session, observation-interval length, and so forth) and two columns. The first column shows the time interval, and the second column contains places for the observer to indicate whether the behavior occurred during each interval. More complicated recording forms may be used for multiple behaviors and students. When multiple behaviors are observed, they are often given code numbers. For example, "out of seat" might be coded as 1; "in seat but off task" might be coded as 2; "in seat and on task" might be coded 3; and "no opportunity to observe" might be coded 4. Such codes should be included on the observation record form. Figure 10.1 shows a simple form on which to record multiple behaviors of students.

Complex observational systems tend to be less accurate than simple ones. Complexity increases as a function of the number of different behaviors that are assessed and the number of individuals who are observed. Moreover, both the proportion of target individuals to total individuals and the proportion of target behaviors that occur to the number of target behaviors to be recorded also have an impact on accuracy. The surest way to reduce inaccuracies in observations attributable to complexity is to keep things relatively simple.

5. Select means of observation.

The choice of human observers or electronic recorders will depend on the availability of resources. If electronic recorders are available and can be used in the

FIGURE 10.1   **A Simple Recording Form for Three Students and Two Behaviors**

Observer: *Mr. Jackson*

Date: *2/15/95*

Times of observation: *10:15 to 11:00*

Observation interval: *10 sec*

Instructional activity: *Oral reading*

Students observed:

S1 = *Henry J.*

S2 = *Bruce H.*

S3 = *Joyce W.*

Codes:

1 = out of seat
2 = in seat but off task
3 = in seat, on task
4 = no opportunity to observe

	S1	S2	S3
1	____	____	____
2	____	____	____
3	____	____	____
4	____	____	____
5	____	____	____
.			
.			
.			
179	____	____	____
180	____	____	____

desired environments and contexts, they can be used when continuous observation is warranted. If other personnel are available, they can be trained to observe and record the target behaviors accurately. Training should include didactic instruction in defining behavior, the use of time sampling (if it is to be used), how to record behavior, and practice using the observation system. Training is always continued until the desired level of accuracy is reached. Observers' accuracy is evaluated by comparing their responses to each other's or to a criterion rating (usually a previously scored videotape). Generally, very high agreement is required before one can assume that observers are ready to conduct observations independently. Ultimately, the decision of how to collect the data should also be based on efficiency. For example, if it takes longer to desensitize students to an obtrusive video recorder than it takes to train observers, human observers are preferred.

Data Gathering

As with any type of assessment information, two general sources of error can reduce the accuracy of observation. First, random error can result in over- or underestimates of behavior. Second, systematic error biases the data in a consistent direction; for example, behavior is systematically overcounted or undercounted. Careful preparation and systematic monitoring of the observation process can head off trouble. Before observation begins, human observers should make sure that they have an extra supply of recording forms, spare pens or pencils, and something to write on (for example, a clipboard or table top). When electronic recording used, equipment should be checked before every observation session to make sure it is in good working condition. When portable equipment is employed, the observer should have extra batteries, signal tapes, or recording tapes available. Before observation, a checklist of equipment and materials that will be used during the observation can be prepared, and everything that is needed for the observation session can be assembled. Also, before the observation session, the observer should check out the setting to locate appropriate vantage points for equipment or furniture.

Random Error

Random errors in observation and recording usually affect observer agreement. Observers may change the criteria for the occurrence of a behavior, they may forget behavior codes, or they may use the recording forms incorrectly. Because changes in agreement can signal something is wrong, the accuracy of observational data should be checked periodically. The usual procedure is to have two observers who observe and record on the same schedule in the same session. The two records are then compared, and an index of agreement (for example, kappa—see Chapter 7) is computed. Poor agreement suggests the need for retraining or revision of the observation procedures. Periodic retraining and allowing observers to keep the definitions and codes for target behaviors with them can alleviate some of the problems. Finally, when observers know that their accuracy is being systematically checked, they are usually more accurate. Thus, observers might be led to believe that their observations are always being checked.

One of the most vexing factors affecting the accuracy of observations is the incorrect recording of correctly observed behavior. Even when observers have applied the criterion for the occurrence of a behavior correctly, they may record their decision incorrectly. For example, if 1 is used to indicate occurrence and zero (0) is used to indicate nonoccurrence, the observer might accidentally record 0 for a behavior that has occurred. Inaccuracy can be attributed to three related factors.

1. *Lack of familiarity with the recording system.* Practice using a recording system is absolutely necessary when several behaviors or several students are observed. Practice is also called for when the target behaviors are difficult to define or when they are difficult to observe.
2. *Insufficient time to record.* Sufficient time must be allowed to record the occurrence of behavior. Problems can arise when using momentary time sampling if the observation intervals are spaced too closely (for example, 1- or 5-second intervals). Observers who are counting several different high-frequency behaviors may record inaccurately. Generally, inadequate opportunities for observers to record can be circumvented by electronic recording of the observation session; replaying and stopping gives observers unlimited time to observe and record.
3. *Lack of concentration.* It may be hard for observers to remain alert for long periods of time (for example, one hour), especially if the target behavior occurs infrequently and is difficult to detect. Using several observers who take turns or recording sessions for later evaluation can reduce the time that an observer must maintain vigilance. Similarly, when it is difficult to maintain vigilance because the observational context is noisy, busy, or otherwise distracting, electronic recording may be useful in focusing on target subjects and eliminating ambient noise.

Unusual events and departures from the observation plan (for example, a missed observation interval) can be noted directly on the observation form. Finally, observation should begin and end at the planned times.

Systematic Error

Systematic errors are difficult to detect. To minimize error, four steps can be taken:

1. Guard against unintended changes in the observation process.[4]

When assessment is carried out over extended periods of time, observers may talk to each other about the definitions that they are using or how they cope with difficult discriminations. Consequently, one observer's departure from standardized procedures may spread to other observers. When the observers change together, modifications of the standard procedures and definitions will not be detected by examining interobserver agreement. Techniques for reducing changes in observers over time include keeping the scoring criteria available to observers, meeting with the observers on a regular basis to discuss difficulties encountered during observation, and providing periodic retraining.

Like human observers, equipment can change over time. Audio signal tapes (used to indicate the moment a student should be observed) may stretch after repeated uses; a 10-second interval may become an 11-second interval. Similarly, the batteries in playback units can lose power, and signal tapes may play slower. Therefore, equipment should be cleaned periodically, and signal tapes should be checked for accuracy.

2. Desensitize students.

The introduction of equipment or new adults into a classroom as well as changes in teacher routines can signal to students that observations are going on. Overt measurement can alter the target's behavior or the topography of the behavior. Usually the pupil change is temporary. For example, when Janey knows that she is being observed, she may be more accurate, deliberate, or compliant. However, as observation becomes a part of the daily routine, students' behavior usually returns to what is typical for them. This return to typical patterns of behavior defines desensitization functionally. The data generated from systematic observation should not be used until the students who are observed are no longer affected by the observation procedures and equipment or personnel. However, sometimes the change in behavior is permanent. For example, if a teacher were watching for the extortion of lunch money, Billy might wait until no observers were present or demand the money in more subtle ways. In such cases, valid data would not be obtained through overt observation, and different procedures would have to be developed, or the observation would have to be abandoned.

3. Minimize observer expectancies.

Sometimes what an observer believes will happen affects what is seen and recorded. For example, if an observer expects an intervention to increase a behavior, that observer might unconsciously alter the criteria for evaluating that

---

4. Technically, general changes in the observation process over time are called *instrumentation problems*.

behavior or evaluate approximations of the target behavior as having occurred. The more subtle or complex the target behavior is, the more susceptible it may be to expectation. The easiest way to avoid expectations during observations is for the observer to be blind to the purpose of the assessment. When video or audio tapes are used to record behavior, the order in which they are evaluated can be randomized so that observers do not know what portion of an observation is being scored. When it is impossible or impractical to keep observers blind to the purpose, the importance of accurate observation should be stressed and rewarded.

4. Motivate observers.

Inaccurate observation is sometimes attributed to lack of motivation on the part of an observer. Motivation can be increased by providing rewards and feedback, stressing the importance of the observations, reducing the length of observation sessions, and not allowing observation sessions to become routine.

Data Summarization

Depending on the particular characteristic of behavior being measured, observational data may be summarized in different ways. When duration or frequency is the characteristic of interest, observations are usually summarized as rates (that is, the prevalence or the number of occurrences per minute or hour). Latency and amplitude should be summarized statistically by the mean and standard deviation or median and range. All counts and calculations should be checked for accuracy.

CRITERIA FOR EVALUATING OBSERVED PERFORMANCES

Once accurate observational data are collected and summarized, they must be interpreted. Some behavior can be judged on *a priori* bases, for example, unsafe and harmful behavior. Most behavior is not evaluated simply by its presence. For example, knowing that the prevalence of Billy's out-of-seat behavior is 10 percent during instruction in content areas does not provide much information about whether that behavior should be decreased.

Behavior rates can be evaluated in several ways. Normative data may be available for some behavior, or in some cases data from behavior rating scales and tests can provide general guidelines. In the absence of such data, social comparisons can be made. In social comparison, a peer whose behavior is considered appropriate is observed. The peer's rate of behavior is then used as the standard against which to evaluate the target student's rate of behavior. The social tolerance for a behavior can also be used as a criterion. For example, the degree to which different rates of out-of-seat behavior disturb a teacher or peers can be assessed. Teachers and peers could be asked to rate how disturbing is the out-of-seat behavior of students who exhibit different rates of behavior. In a somewhat different vein, the contagion of the behavior to others can be a crucial consideration in teacher judgments of unacceptable behavior. Thus, the effects of different rates of behavior can be assessed to see if there is a threshold above which other students initiate undesirable behavior.

SUMMARY

Behavioral observation is the process of gaining information visually, aurally, or through other senses. It can be used to assess any behavior or product of behavior; it cannot be used to assess events that are not observable (for example, thinking, feeling, or believing). Although behavior may be defined functionally or topographically, it is measured in terms of its duration, latency, frequency, and amplitude. Moreover, one can assess the entire domain of behavior or sample from the domain along three dimensions: contexts, behaviors, and times. Each dimension can provide important and useful information about the behavior and how it is maintained in the environment. Three different sampling plans have been advocated for measuring the duration and frequency of behavior: whole-interval recording, partial-interval recording, and momentary time sampling. Of these three methods, momentary time sampling is the most useful and in general is the most accurate.

Observations are usually conducted on behavior that may require modification or behavior that may indicate a disability condition: harmful behavior, stereotypic behavior, infrequent or absent desirable behavior, or normal behavior shown in inappropriate contexts.

Conducting systematic observations requires as much care and precision as testing during preparation, data gathering, and data summarization. When an observer is preparing to conduct systematic observations, (1) target behaviors must be carefully defined; (2) the contexts in which observations will be conducted and the observation schedule itself must be carefully selected; (3) the recording procedures must be thoughtfully developed; and (4) the means by which data will be collected must be decided (for example, using human observers).

When gathering data, the observer should minimize both random and systematic error. Random error is usually attributed to lack of familiarity with the recording system, to insufficient time to record, or to lack of concentration. Systematic error is usually attributed to unintended changes in the observation process, to failure to desensitize target students, to observer expectancies, or to unmotivated observers. Finally, like all other assessment procedures, observations of student performances must be evaluated. Some behavior can be judged on *a priori* bases—for example, unsafe and harmful behavior. Other behavior is evaluated on the basis of normative data, social comparison, or social tolerance.

STUDY QUESTIONS

1. Explain each of the four types of behavior that are frequently targeted for intervention.
2. What things should an observer consider when preparing to conduct systematic observations?
3. Name four types of systematic errors that can occur during observation. What can an observer do to minimize these types of errors?
4. Name three types of random errors that can occur during observation. What can an observer do to minimize these types of errors?

ADDITIONAL READING

Alberto, P., & Troutman, A. (1990). *Applied behavior analysis for teachers* (3rd ed.). Columbus, OH: Merrill.

Boehm, A. E., & Weinberg, R. A. (1988). *The classroom observer: A guide for developing observation skills* (2nd ed.). New York: Teachers College Press.

Greenwood, C. R. (in press). Conceptual, methodological, and technological advances in classroom observational assessment. *Diagnostique.*

Lentz, F. E. (1988). Direct observation and measurement of academic skills: A conceptual review. In E. S. Shapiro & T. R. Kratochwill (Eds.), *Behavioral assessment in schools: Conceptual foundations and practical applications* (pp. 76–120). New York: Guilford.

Salvia, J., & Hughes, C. (1990). *Curriculum-based assessment: Testing what is taught.* New York: Macmillan. (Chapter 9, Assessment of adaptive and social behavior)

Suen, H., & Ary, D. (1989). *Analyzing quantitative behavioral observation data.* Hillsdale, NJ: Lawrence Erlbaum.

Chapter 11

Teacher-Made Tests of Achievement

*M*ost evaluations of student achievement are conducted by teachers with materials that they have developed themselves, and the assessment practices that are actually used by teachers in classrooms are not well documented. This chapter provides a general overview of good practices for teachers who develop their own tests for classroom assessment in the core areas of reading, mathematics, spelling, and written language. Classroom assessment is a topic suitable for an entire text, and only a general overview of the formats used to test and the criteria by which pupil performance is evaluated can be treated here. For more specific information on test construction, educational decision making, and managing assessment within the classroom, interested readers are referred to texts by Gronlund (1985) and Salvia and Hughes (1990), among others. Finally, procedures that we discuss in detail in other chapters are not reexplained here.

WHY DO TEACHERS ASSESS ACHIEVEMENT?

Teachers regularly set aside time to assess their pupils for a variety of purposes. Most commonly, teachers make up tests to ascertain the extent to which their students have learned or are learning what has been taught or assigned. Knowledge about the extent to which students have mastered curricula allows teachers to make decisions on a variety of fronts—selection of current and future instructional objectives, placement of students in instructional groups, evaluation of the teachers' own instructional performances, and the necessity of referring students to other educational specialists for additional instructional services. Each of these decisions should be based on student achievement of instructional objectives. When students have met their instructional objectives, it is time to move on to new or related objectives. Students who meet objectives so rapidly that they are being held back by slower peers can be grouped for enrichment activities or faster-paced instruction; slower students can be grouped so that necessary concepts can be learned to mastery without impeding the progress of their faster-learning peers. When many students in a classroom fail to learn material, teachers should suspect that something is wrong with their materials, techniques, or some other aspect of instruction. For example, the students may lack prerequisite concepts or skills, or the instruction may be too fast-paced or poorly sequenced. Finally, when students lag far behind their peers in crucial curricular areas, teachers may seek outside help. For example, a student may receive Chapter I assistance (special remedial or compensatory instruction for students with difficulties who attend schools with large numbers of poor students), be tutored, be placed in a slower educational track, or be referred to a child study team to determine entitlement to receive other special educational services.

ADVANTAGES OF TEACHER-MADE TESTS

Often teacher-made tests are not held in high regard. For example, some measurement specialists (such as Thorndike & Hagen, 1978) list carefully prepared test items as an advantage of norm-referenced achievement tests. By implication, careful preparation of questions may not be a characteristic of teacher-made tests. In addition, terms such as "informal" or "unstandardized" may be used to describe teacher-made tests. As a group, however, teacher-made tests cannot be considered informal, because they are not given haphazardly or casually. They also cannot be considered unstandardized, because students usually receive the same materials and directions, and the same criteria usually are used in correcting student answers. Perhaps a better characterization of teacher-made tests is that they are not usually subject to public scrutiny and may be more variable than commercial tests in terms of their technical adequacy (that is, reliability and validity). However, these characterizations are, themselves, speculative.

Teacher-made tests can be better suited to evaluation of student achievement than commercially prepared, norm-referenced achievement tests. The disadvantages of commercially prepared tests readily illustrate the two potential advantages of teacher-made tests: curriculum match and sensitivity.

First, commercially prepared tests are rarely designed to assess achievement within specific curricula. Rather, these tests are intentionally constructed to have general applicability so that they can be used with students in almost any curriculum. This intentional generality is in sharp contrast to the development of distinctive curricula. It has become increasingly clear that various curriculum series differ from one another in the particular educational objectives covered, the performance level expected of students, and the sequence of objectives; for example, DISTAR mathematics differs from Scott, Foresman mathematics (Shriner & Salvia, 1988). Even within the same curriculum series, teachers modify instruction to provide enrichment or remedial instruction. Thus, two teachers using the same curriculum series may offer different instruction. Although teachers may not construct tests that match curriculum, they are in the best position to know precisely what has been taught and what level of performance is expected from students. Consequently, they are the only ones who could match testing to instruction.

The second disadvantage of commercially prepared, norm-referenced tests is that the overwhelming majority are intended, first and foremost, to discriminate among test takers efficiently. Developers of norm-referenced tests try to strike a balance between including the minimum number of test items to allow reliable discrimination and including enough items to ensure content validity. This practice results in relatively insensitive tests that are unable to discriminate small changes in pupil performance. For example, to produce a reliable, norm-referenced test it may be unnecessary to discriminate students who know the single-digit addition facts with 2s, 4s, and 6s from those who also know them with 3s, 5s, and 7s. However, when instruction is provided in all single-digit addends, teachers likely would want to know, for example, which students have not yet mastered the 4s (and which of the 4s) so that they can provide further instruction. Moreover, once students have mastered the 4s, the change in their skill level should be observable from changed test performance.

In short, teachers need tests that are sensitive to small changes in knowledge. Norm-referenced tests are not well suited to this purpose, not only because they contain relatively few relevant items but also because they seldom are published in multiple forms. Teachers who are concerned with pupil mastery of specific concepts and skills are in a position to test a narrow range of objectives directly and frequently.

TESTING FORMATS USED BY TEACHERS

When a teacher wants to compare the performance of several students on a skill or set of skills or wants to assess pupil performance over time, the assessment must be standardized. Otherwise, observed differences could be reasonably attributed to differences in testing procedures. To be standardized, tests must use consistent directions, criteria for scoring, and procedures (for example, time allowed students to complete a test). Almost any test can be standardized if it results in observable behavior or a permanent product (for example, a student's written response).

When a teacher wants to use a test to assess the extent to which an individual pupil has mastered a skill or set or skills, then it is important that the competencies to be demonstrated are specified clearly. Teachers will need to know the objectives, standards, or outcomes that they expect students to work toward mastering, and they will need to specify the level of performance that is acceptable.

Test formats can be classified along two dimensions. The first dimension is the modality through which the item is presented. Test items usually require a student to look at or to listen to the question, although other modalities may be substituted depending on the particulars of a situation or on characteristics of students. The second dimension is the modality through which a student responds. Test items usually require an oral or written response, although pointing responses are frequently used with nonverbal students. Teachers may use the terms "see-write," "see-say," "hear-write," and "hear-say" to specify the testing dimensions.

In addition, "write" formats can be of two types. Select formats require students to indicate their choice from an array of the possible answers (usually called *response options*). True-false, multiple-choice, and matching are the three common select formats. However, these are not the only possible formats; for example, students may be required to circle incorrectly spelled words or words that should be capitalized in text. Formats requiring students to select the correct answer can be used to assess much more than the recognition of information, although they are certainly useful for that purpose. Select formats can also be used to assess understanding, the ability to draw inferences, and the correct application of principles. Select questions are not usually well suited for assessing achievement at the levels of analysis, synthesis, and evaluation. (See Chapter 8 for a discussion of Bloom's levels of measurement.)

Supply formats require a student to produce a written or oral response. This response can be as restricted as the answer to a computation problem or a one-word response to a question such as "When did the potato famine begin in Ireland?" Often the response to supply questions is more involved and can require a student to produce a sentence, a paragraph, or several pages to answer the question satisfactorily.

As a general rule, supply questions can be prepared fairly quickly, but scoring them may be very time-consuming. Even when one-word responses or numbers are requested, teachers may have difficulty finding the response on a student's test paper, deciphering the handwriting, or correctly applying criteria for awarding points. In contrast, select formats usually require a considerable amount of time to prepare but, once prepared, they can be scored quickly and by almost anyone.

The particular formats teachers select are influenced by their purposes for testing and the characteristics of the test takers. Testing formats are essentially bottom-up or top-down. Bottom-up formats assess the mastery of specific objectives to allow generalizations about student competence in a particular domain. Top-down formats survey general competence in a domain and assess in greater depth those topics in which mastery is incomplete. For day-to-day monitoring of instruction and selecting short-term instructional objectives, we favor bottom-up assessment. With this type of assessment, teachers can be relatively sure that specific objectives have been mastered and that they are not spending needless instructional time teaching students what they already know. For determining starting places for instruction with new students and for assessing maintenance and generalization of previously learned material, we favor top-down assessment. Generally, this approach should be more efficient in terms of teachers' and students' time, because broader survey tests can cover a lot of material in a short period of time.

With students who are able to read and write independently, see-write formats are generally more efficient for both individual students and groups. When testing individual students, teachers or teacher aides can give the testing materials to the students and can proceed with other activities while the students are completing the test. Moreover, having students write their responses allows a teacher to defer correcting examinations until a convenient time.

See-say formats are also useful. Teacher aides or other students can listen to the test takers' responses and correct them on the spot or record them for later evaluation. Moreover, many teachers have access to electronic equipment that can greatly facilitate the use of see-say formats (for example, tape recorders or videotape camcorders).

The hear-write format is especially useful with select formats for younger students and students who cannot read independently. This format can also be used for testing groups of students and is routinely used in the assessment of spelling when students are required to write words from dictation. With other content, teachers can give directions and read the test questions aloud, and students can mark their responses. The primary difficulty with a hear-write format with groups of students is the pacing of test items; teachers must allot sufficient time between items for slower responding students to make their selections.

Hear-say formats are most suitable for assessing individual students who do not write independently or who write at such slow speeds that their written responses are unrepresentative of what they know. Even with this format, teachers need not preside over the assessment; other students or a teacher aide can administer, record, and perhaps evaluate the student's responses.

CONSIDERATIONS IN PREPARING TESTS

Teachers need to build skills in developing tests that are fair, reliable, and valid. The following kinds of considerations are important in developing or preparing tests.

Selecting Specific Areas of the Curriculum

Tests are samples of behavior. When narrow skills are being assessed (for example, spelling words from dictation), either all the components of the domain should be tested (in this case, all the assigned spelling words) or a representative sample should be selected and assessed. The qualifier "representative" implies that an appropriate number of easy and difficult words, as well as words from the beginning, middle, and end of the assignment, will be selected. When more complex domains are assessed, teachers should concentrate on the more important facts or relationships and avoid the trivial.

Writing Relevant Questions

Teachers must select and use a sufficient number of questions to allow valid inferences about students' mastery of all the material taught in class. Nothing offends test takers quite as much as a test's failure to cover material they have studied and know, except perhaps their own failure to guess what content a teacher believes to be important enough to test. In addition, "fair" implies that the way in which the question is asked is familiar and expected by the student. For example, if students were to take a test on the addition of single-digit integers, it would be a bad idea to test them using a missing addend format (for example, "4 + __ = 7") unless that format had been specifically taught and was expected by the students.

Organizing and Sequencing Items

The organization of a test is a function of many factors. When a teacher wants a student to complete all of the items and indicate mastery of content (a power test), then it is best to intersperse easy and difficult items. When the desire is to measure automaticity or the number of items that can be completed within a specific time period (time test), it is best to organize items from easy to difficult. Pages of test questions or problems to be solved should not be cluttered.

Developing Formats for Presentation and Response Modes

Different formats can be used within the same test, although it is generally a good idea to group questions in the same format together. Regardless of the format used, the primary consideration is that the test questions are a fair sample of the material being assessed.

Writing Directions for Administration

Regardless of question format, the directions should indicate clearly what a student is to do—for example, "Circle the correct option," "Choose the best answer," "Match each item in column b to one item in column a," and so forth. Also, teachers should explain what, if any, materials may be used by students, time limits, any unusual scoring procedures (for example, penalties for guessing), and point value when the students are mature enough to be given questions that have different point values.

Developing Systematic Procedures for Observing Behavior and Scoring Responses

Teachers must have predetermined and planned ways to record observed behavior or to keep portfolios of students' responses. They must also have systematic ways of scoring responses, and predetermined scoring criteria.

Establishing Criteria for the Interpretation of Student Performance

Teachers must specify in advance the criteria they will use for assigning grades or weighting assignments. For example, they may want to specify that students who earn a certain number of points on a test earn a specific grade, or they may want to assign grades on the basis of the class distribution of performance. In either case, they must specify what it takes to earn certain grades or how assignments will be evaluated and weighted.

SELECT FORMATS

Three types of select formats are commonly used: multiple-choice, matching, and true-false. Of the three, multiple-choice questions are clearly the most useful.

Multiple-Choice Questions

Multiple-choice questions are the most difficult to prepare. These questions have two parts: a stem that contains the question and a response set that contains the correct answer, called the *keyed* response, and incorrect options, called *distracters*. In preparing multiple-choice questions, teachers should generally follow these guidelines.

- Keep the response options short and of approximately equal length. Students learn quickly that longer options tend to be correct.
- Keep material that is common to all options in the stem. For example, if the first word in each option is "the," it should be put into the stem and removed from the options.

- Avoid grammatical tip-offs. Students can discard grammatically incorrect options. For example, when the correct answer must be plural, alert students will disregard singular options; when the correct answer must be a noun, students will disregard options that are verbs.
- Avoid implausible options. In the best questions, even distracters should be attractive to students who do not know the answer. Common errors and misconceptions are often good distracters.
- Make sure that one and only one option is correct. Students should not have to read their teachers' minds to guess which wrong answer is the *least* wrong or which right answer is the *most* correct.
- Avoid interdependent questions. Generally it is bad practice to make the selection of the correct option dependent on getting a prior question correct.
- Vary the position of the correct response in the options. Students will recognize patterns of correct options (for example, when the correct answers to a sequence of questions are a, b, c, d, a, b, c, d) or a teacher's preference for a specific position (for example, c).
- Avoid options that indicate multiple correct options (for example, "all of the above" or "both a and b are correct"). These options often simplify the question.
- Avoid similar incorrect options. Students who can eliminate one of the two similar options can readily dismiss the other one.
- Avoid using the same words and examples that were used in the students' texts or in class presentations.
- Make sure that one question does not provide information that can be used to answer another question. For example, teachers should not introduce one question with "In 1492 Columbus landed in the Western _____ " and then ask another question requesting the year in which Columbus arrived in the Western hemisphere.

When appropriate, teachers can make multiple-choice questions more challenging by asking students to recognize an instance of a rule or concept, by requiring students to recall and use material that is not present in the question, or by increasing the number of options.[1] In no case should teachers deliberately mislead or trick students.

Matching Questions

Matching questions are a variant of multiple-choice questions in which a set of stems is associated with a set of options simultaneously. Generally the content of

---

1. For younger children, three options are generally difficult enough. Older students can be expected to answer questions with four or five options.

matching questions is limited to simple factual associations (Gronlund, 1985). Usually teachers prepare matching questions so that there are as many options as stems and an option can be associated only once with a stem in the set. Although we do not recommend their use, there are other possibilities: more options than stems, selection of all correct options for one stem, and using an option more than once.[2] The latter possibilities increase the difficulty of the question set considerably.

In general we prefer multiple-choice questions over matching questions. Almost any matching question can be written as a series of multiple-choice questions in which the same or similar options are used. Of course, the correct response will change. However, teachers wishing to use matching questions should consider the following guidelines.

- Each set of matching items should have some dimension in common (e.g., explorers, dates of discovery). This makes preparation easier for the teacher and provides the student with some insight into the relationship required to select the correct option.
- Keep the length of stems approximately the same, and keep the length and grammar used in the options equivalent. At best, mixing grammatical forms will eliminate some options for some questions; at worst, it will provide the correct answer to a question.
- Make sure that one and only one option is correct for each stem.
- Vary the sequence of correct responses when more than one matching question is asked.
- Avoid using the same words and examples that were used in the students' texts or in class presentations.

It is easier for a student when questions and options are presented in two columns. When there is a difference in the length of the items in each column, the longer item should be used as the stem. Stems should be placed on the left and options on the right, rather than stems above with options below them. Moreover, all the elements of the question should be kept on one page. Finally, teachers often allow students to draw lines to connect questions and options. Although this has the obvious advantage of helping students keep track of where their answers should be placed, erasures or scratch-outs can be a headache to the person who corrects the test. There is a commercially available product (Learning Wrap Ups) that has cards printed with stems and answers and a shoelace with which to "lace" stems to correct answers. The correct lacing pattern is printed on the back, so it is self-correcting. Teachers could make such cards fairly easily, as an alternative to trying to correct tests with lots of erasures.

---

2. Scoring for these options is complicated. Generally, separate errors are counted for selecting an incorrect option and failing to select a correct option. Thus, the number of errors can be very large.

True-False Statements

In most cases, true-false statements should simply not be used. Their utility lies primarily in assessing knowledge of factual information, which can be better assessed with other formats. Effective true-false items are difficult to prepare. Because guessing the correct answer is so likely—50 percent—the reliability of true-false tests is generally low. As a result, they may well have limited validity. Nonetheless, if a teacher chooses to use this format, a few suggestions should be followed.

- Avoid specific determiners such as "all," "never," "always," and so on.
- Avoid sweeping generalizations. Such statements tend to be true, but students can often think of minor exceptions. Thus, there is a problem in the criterion for evaluating the truthfulness of the question. Attempts to avoid the problem by adding restrictive conditions (for example, "with minor exceptions") either render the question obviously true or leave a student trying to guess what the restrictive condition means.
- Avoid convoluted sentences. Tests should assess knowledge of content, not a student's ability to comprehend difficult prose.
- Keep true and false statements approximately the same length. As is the case with longer options on multiple-choice questions, longer true-false statements tend to be true.
- Balance the number of true and false statements. If a student recognizes that there are more of one type of statement than the other, the odds of guessing the correct answer will exceed 50 percent.

Special Considerations for Students with Disabilities

In developing and using items that employ a select format, teachers must pay attention to individual differences among students, and particularly to disabilities that might interfere with performance. For example, students with skill deficits in remembering things for short periods of time, or who do not attend well to verbally or visually presented information, may have difficulty with multiple-choice items. Students who have difficulty figuring out organization of visually presented material will have difficulty with matching items.

SUPPLY FORMATS

It is useful to distinguish between items requiring a student to write one- or two-word responses (fill-in questions) and those requiring more extended responses (essay questions). Both types of items require careful delineation of what constitutes a correct response (that is, criteria for scoring). It is generally best for teachers to prepare criteria for a correct response at the time they prepare the question. In that way they can ensure that the question is written in such a way as to elicit the correct type of answers—or at least not mislead students—and perhaps save time when correcting exams. (If teachers change criteria for a correct response after they have scored a few questions, they should rescore all previously scored questions with the revised criteria.)

Fill-In Questions

Aside from mathematics problems that require students to calculate an answer and writing spelling words from dictation, fill-in questions require a student to complete a statement by adding a concept or fact. For example, "_____ arrived in America in 1492." Fill-ins are useful in assessing objectives at the knowledge and comprehension levels; they are not useful in assessing objectives at the levels of application, analysis, synthesis, and evaluation. Teachers preparing fill-in questions should follow these guidelines.

- Keep each sentence short. Generally, the less superfluous information in an item, the clearer the question will be to the student and the less likely it will be for one question to cue another.
- If a two-word answer is required, teachers should use two blanks to indicate this in the sentence.
- Avoid sentences with multiple blanks. For example, the item, "In the year _____ , _____ discovered _____" is so vague that practically any date, name, and event can be inserted correctly, even ones that are irrelevant to the content; for example, "In 1994, Henry discovered girls."
- Keep the size of all blanks consistent and large enough to accommodate the longest answer readily. The size of the blank should not provide a clue about the length of the correct word.

The most problematic aspect of fill-in questions is the necessity of developing an appropriate response bank of acceptable answers. Often some student errors may consist of a partially correct response; teachers must decide which answers will receive partial credit, full credit, and no credit. For example, a question may anticipate "Columbus" as the correct response, but a student might write "that Italian dude who was looking for the short-cut to India for the Spanish king and queen." In deciding how far afield to go in crediting unanticipated responses, teachers should carefully look over test questions to see if the student's answer comes from information presented in another question (for example, "The Spanish monarch employed an Italian sailor to find a shorter route to _____).

Extended Responses

Essay questions are most useful in assessing instructional objectives prepared at a comprehension level or higher. Two major problems are associated with extended response questions. First, teachers are generally able to sample only a limited amount of information because answers may take a long time for students to write. Second, extended essay responses are the most difficult type of answer to score. To avoid subjectivity and inconsistency, teachers should use a scoring key that assigns specific point values for each element in the ideal or criterion answer. In most cases, spelling and grammatical errors should not be deducted from the point total. Moreover, bonus points should not be awarded for particularly detailed responses; many good students will provide a complete answer to one question and spend any extra time working on questions that are more difficult for them. Finally, teachers should be prepared to deal with responses in which a student tries to bluff a correct answer. Rather than leave a question unanswered, some students may answer a related question that was not asked, or they may structure their response so that they can omit important information that they cannot remember or never knew. Sometimes they will even write a poem or a treatise on why the question asked is unimportant or irrelevant. Therefore, teachers must be very specific about how they will award points, stick to their criteria unless they discover something is wrong with them, and not give credit to creative bluffs.

Teachers should also be very precise in the directions that they give so that students will not have to guess what responses their teachers will credit. Below are a number of verbs (and their meanings) that are commonly used in essay questions. It is often worthwhile to explain these terms in the test directions to make sure that students know what kind of answer is desired.

- *Describe*, *define*, and *identify* mean to give the meaning, essential characteristics, and/or place within a taxonomy.
- *List* means to enumerate and implies that complete sentences and paragraphs are not required unless specifically requested.
- *Discuss* requires more than a description, definition, or identification; a student is expected to draw implications and elucidate relationships.
- *Explain* means to analyze and make clear or comprehensible a concept, event, principle, relationship, or so forth; thus, *explain* requires going beyond a definition to describe the hows or whys.
- *Compare* means to identify and explain similarities among two or more things.
- *Contrast* means to identify and explain differences among two or more things.
- *Evaluate* means to give the value of something and implies an enumeration and explanation of assets and liabilities, pros and cons.

Finally, unless students know the questions in advance, teachers should allow students sufficient time for planning and rereading answers. For example, if teachers believe 10 minutes are necessary to write an extended essay to answer a question that requires original thinking, they might allow 20 minutes for the question. The less fluent the students, the greater the proportion of time that should be allotted.

Special Considerations in Assessing Students with Disabilities

In developing items that employ a supply format, teachers must pay attention to individual differences among learners and particularly to disabilities that may interfere with performance. For example, students who write very slowly can be expected to have difficulty with fill-in or essay questions. Students who have considerable difficulty expressing themselves in writing will likely have difficulty completing or performing well on essay examinations. Remember, it is important to assess the skills that students have, not the effects of disability conditions.

ASSESSMENT IN CORE ACHIEVEMENT AREAS

The assessment procedures used by teachers are a function of the content being taught, the criterion to which content is to be learned (e.g., 80-percent mastery), and the characteristics of their students. With primary-level curricula in core areas, teachers usually want more than knowledge from their students; they want the material learned so well that correct responses are automatic. For example, teachers do not want their students to think about forming the letter *a*, sounding out the word *the*, or using number lines to solve simple addition problems such as "3 + 5 = ____"; they want their students to respond immediately and correctly. Even in intermediate-level materials, teachers seek highly proficient responding from their students, whether that performance involves two-digit multiplication, reading short stories, writing short stories, or writing spelling words from dictation. However, teachers in all grades, but especially in secondary schools, are also interested in their students' understanding of vast amounts of information about their social, cultural, and physical worlds as well as their acquisition and application of critical thinking skills. The assessment of skills taught to high degrees of proficiency is quite different from the assessment of understanding and critical thinking skills.

In the sections that follow, core achievement areas are discussed in terms of three important attributes: the skills and information to be learned within the major strands of most curricula, the assessment of skills to be learned to proficiency, and the assessment of understanding of information and concepts. Critical thinking skills are usually embedded within content areas and are assessed in the same ways as understanding of information is assessed—with written multiple-choice and extended-essay questions.

Reading

Reading is usually divided into decoding skills and comprehension. The specific behaviors included in each of these subdomains will depend on the particular curriculum and its sequencing.

Beginning Skills

Beginning decoding can include letter recognition, letter-sound correspondences, sight vocabulary, phonics, and in some curricula, morphology. Automaticity is the end goal for the skills to be learned. See-say (for example, "What letter is this?") and hear-say (for example, "What sound does the letter ____ make?") formats are regularly used for both instruction and assessment. During students' acquisition of specific skills, teachers should first stress the accuracy of student responses. Generally this concern translates into allowing a moment or two for students to think about their responses. A generally accepted criterion for the completion for early learning is 90 percent correct. As soon as accuracy has been attained (and sometimes before complete attainment), teachers change their criteria from accurate responses to fast and accurate responses. For see-say formats, fluent students will need no thinking time for simple material; for example, they should be able to respond as rapidly as teachers can change stimuli to questions such as "What is this letter?" For the most difficult content (for example, recognition of long or visually difficult words such as *through*), no more than a second or two should be needed by a student to verify the stimulus. However, when students have visual or articulation difficulties, these standards are unlikely to be appropriate.

For beginners, reading comprehension is usually assessed in one of three ways. The most direct method is to have students retell what they have read without access to the reading passage. Retold passages may be scored on the basis of the number of words recalled. Fuchs, Fuchs, and Maxwell (1988) have offered two relatively simple scoring procedures that appear to offer valid indications of comprehension. Retelling may be conducted orally or in writing. With students who have relatively undeveloped writing skills, retelling should be oral when it is used to assess comprehension, but may be in writing as a practice or drill activity. Teachers can listen to students retell, or students can retell using tape recorders so that their efforts can be evaluated later.

A second common method of assessing comprehension is to ask students questions about what they have read. Questions should address main ideas, important relationships, and relevant details. Questions may be supply or select, and either hear-say or see-write formats can be used conveniently. As is the case with retelling, teachers should concentrate their efforts on the gist of the passage.

A third convenient, although indirect, method of assessing reading comprehension is to assess the rate of oral reading. Although this procedure may initially seem a bit strange, the rate of oral reading does appear to be empirically related to comprehension (Deno, 1985; Fuchs et al., 1988). Moreover, the relationship between rate and comprehension is logical: Slow oral readers must expend their energy decoding words (for example, attending to letters, remembering letter-sound associations, blending sounds, or searching for context cues) rather than concentrating on the meaning of what is written. Therefore, teachers probably should concentrate on the rate of oral reading regularly with beginning readers. To assess reading rate, teachers should have students read for 2 minutes from appropriate materials. The reading passage should include familiar vocabulary, syntax, and content; the passage must be longer than the amount any student can read in the 2-minute period. Teachers have their own copy of the passage on which to note errors. The number of words read correctly and the number of errors made in 2 minutes are each divided by 2 to calculate the rate per minute. Mercer and Mercer (1985) suggest a rate of 80 words per minute (with two or fewer errors) as a desirable goal for reading words from lists and a rate of 100 words per minute (with two or fewer errors) for words in text. See Chapter 21 for a fuller discussion of errors in oral reading.

Advanced Skills

Students who have already mastered basic sight vocabulary and decoding skills generally read silently. Emphasis for these students shifts, and new demands are made. Decoding moves from oral reading to silent reading with subvocalization (that is, saying the words and phrases to oneself) to visual scanning without subvocalization; thus, the reading rates of some students may exceed 1,000 words per minute. Scanning for main ideas and information may also be taught systematically. The demands for reading comprehension may go well beyond the literal comprehension of a passage; summarization, drawing inferences, recognizing and understanding symbolism, sarcasm, irony, and so forth may be systematically taught. For these advanced students, the gist of a passage is usually more important than the details. Teachers of more advanced students may wish to score retold passages on the basis of main ideas, important relationships, and details recalled correctly and the number of errors (that is, ideas, relationships, and details omitted plus the insertion of material not included in the passage). In such cases, the different types of information can be weighted differently or the use of comprehension strategies (for example, summarization) can be encouraged. However, it appears that read-write assessment formats using multiple-choice and extended-essay questions are more commonly used.

Informal Reading Inventories

When making decisions about referral or initial placement in a reading curriculum, teachers often develop informal reading inventories (IRIs). These inventories primarily assess decoding and reading comprehension over a wide range of skill levels within the specific reading curricula used in a classroom.[3] Thus, they are top-down assessments that span several levels of difficulty.

IRIs are given to locate the reading levels at which a student reads independently, requires instruction, and is frustrated. Techniques for developing IRIs and the criteria used to define independent, instructional, and frustration reading levels vary. Teachers should use a series of graded reading passages that range from below a student's actual placement to a year or two years above the actual placement. If a reading series prepared for several grade levels is used, passages can be selected from the beginning, middle, and end of each grade. Students begin reading the easiest material and continue reading until they can decode less than 85 percent of words. Salvia and Hughes (1990) recommend an accuracy rate of 95 percent for independent reading and consider 85- to 95-percent accuracy as the level at which a student requires instruction.

Mathematics

Eight major components are usually considered in comprehensive mathematics curricula: readiness skills, vocabulary and concepts, numeration, whole-number operations, fractions and decimals, ratios and percents, measurement, and geometry (Salvia & Hughes, 1990). At any grade level, the specific skills and concepts included in each of these subdomains will depend on the particular curriculum and its sequencing. Mathematics curricula usually contain (1) problem sets in which only computations are performed and (2) word problems that require selection and application of the correct algorithm and computation. The difficulty of application problems goes well beyond the difficulty of the computation involved and is related to three factors: the number of steps involved in the solution [for example, a student might have to add and then multiply (Caldwell & Goldin, 1979)]; the amount of extraneous information (Englert, Culatta, & Horn, 1987); and whether the mathematical operation is directly implied by the vocabulary used in the problem [for example, words such as *and* or *more* imply addition whereas words such as *each* may imply division (see Bachor, Stacy, & Freeze, 1986)]. Although reading level is popularly believed to affect the difficulty of word problems, its effect is not clearly established (see Bachor, 1990; Paul, Nibbelink, & Hoover, 1986).

Beginning Skills

The whole-number operations of addition, subtraction, multiplication, and division are the core of the elementary mathematics curriculum. Readiness for beginning students includes such basics as classification, one-to-one correspondence, and counting. Vocabulary and concepts are generally restricted to

---

3. Some authors may include reading interest as a subdomain.

quantitative words (for example, *same, equal, larger*) and spatial concepts (for example, *left, above, next to*). Numeration deals with writing and identifying numbers, counting, ordering, and so forth.

See-write is probably the most frequently used format in the assessment of mathematical skills, although see-say formats are not uncommon. For content associated with readiness, vocabulary and concepts, numeration, and applications, matching formats are commonly used. Accuracy is stressed, and 90 to 95 percent correct is commonly used as the criterion. For computation, accuracy and fluency are stressed in beginning mathematics; teachers do not stop their instruction when students respond accurately, but they continue instruction to build automaticity. Consequently, a teacher may accept somewhat lower rates of accuracy (that is, 80 percent). When working toward fluency, teachers usually use probes.[4] Perhaps the most useful criterion for math probes assessing computation is the number of correct digits (in an answer) written per minute and not the number of correct answers per minute. The actual criterion rate will depend on the operation, the type of material (for example, addition facts versus addition of two-digit numbers with regrouping), and the characteristics of the particular students. Students with motor difficulties may be held to a lower criterion or assessed with see-say formats. For see-write formats, students may be expected to write answers to addition and subtraction problems at rates between 50 and 80 digits per minute and answers to simple multiplication and division problems at rates between 40 and 50 digits per minute (Salvia & Hughes, 1990).

Advanced Skills

The more advanced mathematical skills (that is, fractions, decimals, ratios, percents, and geometry) build on whole-number operations. These skills are taught to levels of comprehension and application. Unlike beginning skills, assessment formats are almost exclusively see-write, and accuracy is stressed over fluency except for a few facts such as "½ equals .5 equals 50 percent." Teachers must take into account the extent to which specific student disabilities will interfere with performance of advanced skills. For example, difficulties in sequencing information and in comprehension may interfere with students' performance on items that require problem solving and comprehension of mathematical concepts.

Spelling

Although spelling is considered by many as a component of written language, in elementary school it is generally taught as a separate subject. Therefore, it is treated separately in this chapter. Spelling is the production of letters in correct

---

4. Probes are small samples of behavior. For example, in assessing skill in addition of single-digit numbers, the student might be given only two single-digit addition problems.

sequence to form a word. The specific words that are assigned as spelling words may come from several sources: spelling curricula, word lists, content areas, or a student's own written work. In high school and college, students are expected to use dictionaries and to spell correctly any word they use. Between that point and fourth grade or so, spelling words are typically assigned, and students are left to their own devices to learn them. In the first three grades, spelling is usually taught systematically using phonics, morphology, rote memorization, or some combination of the three approaches.

Teachers may assess mastery of the prespelling rules associated with the particular approach they are teaching. For example, when a phonics approach is used, students may have to demonstrate mastery of writing the letters associated with specific vowels, consonants, consonant blends, diphthongs, and digraphs. Teachers assess mastery of spelling in at least four ways:

- *Recognition Response.* The teacher provides students with lists of alternative spellings of words (usually three or four alternatives) and reads a word to the student. The student must select the correct spelling of the dictated word from the alternatives. Emphasis is on accuracy.
- *Spelling Dictated Single Words.* Teachers dictate words and students write them down. Although teachers often give a spelling word and then use it in a sentence, students find the task easier if just the spelling word is given (Horn, 1967). Moreover, the findings from recent research suggest that a seven-second interval between words is sufficient (Shinn, Tindall, & Stein, 1988).
- *Spelling Words in Context.* Students write paragraphs using words given by the teacher. This approach is as much a measure of written expression as of spelling. The teacher can also use this approach in instruction of written language by asking students to write paragraphs and counting the number of words spelled correctly.
- *Student's Ability to Monitor Errors.* Some teachers teach students to monitor their own performance by finding and correcting spelling errors in the daily assignments they complete.

Written Language

Written language is no doubt the most complex and difficult domain for teachers to assess. Assessment differs widely for beginners and advanced students. Once the preliminary skills of letter formation and rudimentary spelling have been mastered, written-language curricula usually stress content and style (that is, grammar, mechanics, and diction).

Beginning Skills

The most basic instruction in written language is penmanship, in which the formation and spacing among uppercase (capital) and lowercase printed and cursive letters are taught. Early instruction stresses accuracy, and criteria are generally qualitative. After accuracy has been attained, teachers may provide extended practice to move students toward automaticity. If this is done, teachers will evaluate performance on the basis of students' rates of writing letters. Target rates are usually in the range of 80 to 100 letters per minute for students without motor handicaps.

Content generation for beginners is often reduced to generation of words in meaningful sequence. Teachers may use story starters (that is, pictures or a few words that act as stimuli) to prompt student writing. When the allotted time for writing is over, teachers count the number of words or divide the number of words by the time to obtain a measure of rate. Although this sounds relatively easy, decisions for what constitutes a word must be made. For example, one-letter words are seldom counted. Teachers also use the percentage of correct words to assess content production. To be considered correct, the word must be spelled correctly, be capitalized if appropriate, be grammatically correct, and be followed by the correct punctuation (Isaacson, 1988). Criteria for an acceptable percentage of correct words are still the subject of discussion. For now, social comparison, by which one student's writing output is compared to the output of students whose writing is judged acceptable, can provide teachers with rough approximations. Teaching usually boils down to focusing on capitalization, simple punctuation, and basic grammar (for example, subject-verb agreement). Teachers may use multiple-choice or fill-in tests to assess comprehension of grammatical conventions or rules.

Advanced Skills

Comprehension and application of advanced grammar and mechanics can be tested readily with multiple-choice or fill-in questions. Thus, this aspect of written language can be assessed systematically and objectively. The evaluation of content generation by advanced students is far more difficult than counting correct words. Teachers may consider the quality of ideas, the sequencing of ideas, the coherence of ideas, and consideration of the reading audience. In practice, teachers use holistic judgments of content (Cooper, 1977). In addition, they may point out errors in style or indicate topics that might benefit from greater elaboration or clarification. Objectively scoring any of these attributes is very difficult, and extended scoring keys and practice are necessary to obtain reliable judgments, if they are ever attained. More objective scoring systems for content require computer analysis and at this time are beyond the resources of most classroom teachers.

POTENTIAL SOURCES OF DIFFICULTY IN THE USE OF TEACHER-MADE TESTS

In order to be useful, teacher-made tests must avoid three pitfalls. The first two are easily avoided; the third is more difficult.

First, teachers should not rely solely on a single summative assessment to evaluate student achievement after a course of instruction. Such assessments do not provide teachers with information to plan and modify sequences of instruction. Moreover, minor technical inadequacies can be magnified when a single summative measure is used. Rather, teachers should test progress toward educational objectives at least two or three times a week. Frequent testing is most important when instruction is aimed at developing automatic or fluent responses in students. Although fluency is most commonly associated with primary curricula, it is not restricted to reading, writing, and arithmetic. For example, instruction in foreign language, sports, and music often is aimed at automaticity. Second, teachers should not use unstandardized testing procedures. In order to conduct frequent assessments that are meaningful, the tests that are used to assess the same objectives must be equivalent. Therefore, the content must be equivalent from test to test; moreover, test directions, kinds of cues or hints, testing formats, criteria for correct responses, and type of score (for example, rates or percentage correct) must be the same.

Third, teachers should develop technically adequate assessment procedures. Two aspects of this adequacy are especially important. First, the tests must have content validity. Seldom should there be problems with content validity when direct performances are used. For example, the materials used in finding a student's rate of oral reading should have content validity when they come from that student's reading materials; tests used to assess mastery of addition facts will have content validity because they assess the facts that have been taught. A problem with content validity is more likely when teachers use tests to assess achievement outside of the tool subjects (reading, math, language arts). Although only teachers can develop tests that truly mirror instruction, teachers must not only know what has been taught but also prepare devices that test what has been taught. About the only way to guarantee that an assessment covers the content is to develop tables of specifications for the content of instruction and testing. However, test items geared to specific content may still be ineffective (see Chapter 8). Careful preparation in and of itself cannot guarantee the validity of one question or set of questions. The only way a teacher can know that the questions are good is to field-test the questions, and make revisions based on the results. Realistically speaking, teachers do not have the time for field-testing and revision prior to giving a test. Therefore, teachers must usually give a test and then delete or discount poor items. The poor items can be edited, and the revised questions used the next time the examination is needed. In this way, the responses from one group of students become a field test for a subsequent group of students. When teachers use this approach, they should not return tests to students because students may pass questions down from year to year.

The second aspect of technical adequacy is reliability. Interscorer agreement is a major concern for any test using a supply format but is especially important when extended responses are evaluated. Agreement can be increased by developing precise scoring guides for all questions of this type and by sticking with the criteria. Interscorer agreement should not be a problem for tests using select or restricted fill-in formats. For select and fill-in tests, internal consistency is of primary concern. Unfortunately, very few people can prepare a set of homogeneous test questions the first time. However, at the same time that they revise poor items, teachers can delete or revise items to increase a test's homogeneity (that is, delete or revise items that have correlations with the total score of .25 or less). Additional items can also be prepared for the next test.

SUMMARY

Teachers assess during instruction in order to monitor pupil progress. Careful monitoring is necessary if instruction is to be modified, errors are to be corrected early, and appropriate instructional pacing is to be maintained. Teachers also assess at the end of an instructional sequence to evaluate what their students have learned, assign grades, and select future instructional objectives. Because teacher-made tests are seldom subject to public scrutiny, many test theorists have doubts about their technical adequacy. However, teacher-made tests have several advantages over professionally prepared tests. Most important are (1) the capability of teachers to tailor their tests' content to the content of their teaching and (2) the potential to include many more pertinent test items, thereby allowing teachers to make finer discriminations. Tests require students to select or supply responses to stimuli. The stimuli are usually auditory or visual, and student responses are usually vocal or written. For testing in core academic areas (that is, reading, mathematics, spelling, and written language), testing formats will vary, depending on the criteria that teachers use to evaluate learning and the level at which objectives are prepared. When fluent responses are sought by teachers, student performances in reading, math, and spelling are directly evaluated by supply formats. Select formats (that is, multiple-choice and matching) are useful in assessing instructional objectives prepared at the levels of knowledge, comprehension, and application. They are not well suited to higher-level objectives. Supply formats (that is, fill-in or extended essay) have varying utility. Fill-in questions can be used in much the same way as questions prepared in select formats. Extended essays can be used to assess objectives prepared at levels higher than knowledge, although they are probably best reserved for objectives stressing analysis, synthesis, and evaluation. Teacher-made tests are most useful when they are administered during and after instruction, are carefully standardized, have content validity, and are reliable.

STUDY QUESTIONS

1. Explain the advantages and disadvantages of multiple-choice, matching, and true-false questions.

2. Explain how teachers can use student-performance data gathered during instruction.
3. Explain the advantages of teacher-made tests.

ADDITIONAL READING

Gronlund, N. (1985). *Measurement and evaluation in teaching* (5th ed.). New York: Macmillan. (Part 2, Constructing classroom tests)

Salvia, J., & Hughes, C. (1990). *Curriculum-based assessment: Testing what is taught*. New York: Macmillan. (Chapter 4, Development of appropriate assessment procedures: Collection and summarization of results)

Chapter 12

Using Student Portfolios in Assessment

Standardized, norm-referenced achievement tests and teacher-made multiple-choice and short-answer tests have come under increased scrutiny, and assessment practices in the schools have evolved rapidly in response to this scrutiny. Journals directed at educators have devoted entire issues to alternative assessment, and more than five hundred papers and numerous books addressing alternative assessment have been published. Among the approaches proposed to supplement or replace standardized, norm-referenced achievement tests and teacher-made multiple-choice and short-answer tests are curriculum-based assessment (Fuchs & Fuchs, 1986; Salvia & Hughes, 1990), judgment-based assessment (Bagnato & Neisworth, 1990), dynamic assessment (Lidz, 1991), and authentic assessment (Meyer, 1992; Archbald & Newman, 1988; Maeroff, 1991).

Many of the recommendations that derive from these alternative approaches to assessment are quite different from those derived from more traditional approaches. However, the alternatives share two common goals. First, they emphasize a more direct examination of student performance. For example, in the area of reading, advocates of both curriculum-based assessment and the whole language approach stress reading and understanding. Second, they seek to improve the validity of assessment by basing assessment on student performance and products that relate more directly to the curriculum and society at large. For example, advocates of curriculum-based assessment tie assessment directly to the curriculum, advocates of the whole language approach emphasize reading authentic literature rather than doing phonic worksheets.

The use of portfolios in the schools is one attempt to provide more relevant assessment to enhance instructional decision making and the evaluation of pupil progress. A number of different models of portfolio assessment have been advocated, and the profession is far from reaching consensus about what constitutes a portfolio or how one should be used in assessment. For example, the content of student portfolios for science will be different from those used for basic literacy education. Moreover, even within one academic discipline (for example, literacy education), there are a variety of approaches. Given the heterogeneity of positions and beliefs about how to assemble and use portfolios, characterizations of portfolio assessment are necessarily general.

CONCERNS ABOUT CURRENT ASSESSMENT PRACTICES

The impetus for portfolio assessment comes, in part, from concerns about current assessment practices, many of which are, indeed, imperfect. We discuss three concerns that seem to us most important and widespread.

Over-Reliance on Norm-Referenced Achievement Tests

Norm-referenced tests provide a snapshot of general student achievement and can provide a point of departure for more intensive and extensive assessment of an individual student. When these tests are misused or misapplied, those responsible for assessment are fairly criticized. Two misuses of norm-referenced achievement tests are especially noteworthy.

Assessing a Student's Ability to Profit from Instruction

We have argued in this and previous editions that when norm-referenced (or any other type of) achievement tests do not correspond to a student's curriculum, one cannot infer that low scores indicate that student's failure to profit from instruction. When students have not been exposed to the content of a test, low scores obviously do not warrant such an inference because (1) norm-referenced achievement tests frequently do not correspond well to specific curricula, especially in mathematics and reading (see, for example, Chapters 20 and 21); and (2) scores that students earn on these tests are related to the degree of curricular match (Good & Salvia, 1989).

Guiding Instruction

For a variety of reasons, norm-referenced achievement tests are not suitable for guiding day-to-day instruction. First, these tests are specifically designed to produce stable scores. In practice the stability of scores makes tests insensitive to small but important changes in student learning. Thus, students who are developing slowly may show no gains in tested performance. For these students, standardized, norm-referenced tests may not be valid measures of progress.

Second, the results of group-administered, machine-scored tests are frequently unavailable to teachers until weeks after administration. Thus, scores may not be pertinent to a student's current level of functioning. Moreover, when only test scores are reported, teachers have no opportunity to analyze errors or ascertain patterns of strength and weakness within an academic area (for example, decoding in reading); scores are aggregations of strengths and weaknesses.

Third, even when a teacher administers and scores a norm-referenced achievement test, there are problems. Most norm-referenced tests do not contain enough test items to allow judgments about a student's understanding or mastery of specific elements of the curriculum that guide instructional decision making.

Thus, group-administered achievement tests are unlikely to be useful to teachers in making day-to-day instructional decisions—and few professional educators or test authors would claim that these tests are suitable for this purpose.

Confusing What Can Be and What Should Be Assessed

Some critics of current testing practices believe that tests determine curricula. These critics contend that the contents of tests are incorrectly viewed as valuable educational outcomes that determine what should be taught. Thus, instead of achievement tests reflecting valued educational outcomes, curricula reflect the content of achievement tests, which may not be valuable. This phenomenon is readily illustrated. Suppose Bobby does not know the location of Nigeria. If his instruction has not been directed to teaching the location of countries in Africa and if this information is valued in his school, then Bobby's and other students' failure to locate Nigeria as part of an achievement test might suggest curricular revision. However, locating Nigeria on a world map may be viewed as a trivial outcome when compared to understanding how European imperialism resulted in the creation of African nations composed of traditional enemies.

Multiple-choice and short-answer (that is, objective) test formats are criticized for determining not only what is learned, but how learning occurs. Thus, constructivists believe objective testing formats lead curricula away from contextualized information upon which students reflect critically; according to this view, tests, and multiple-choice tests in particular, restrict instruction in higher-order thinking skills (see, for example, Camp, 1993). Some even blame the poor achievement of American students (when compared to students from Europe and Asia) on multiple-choice tests, noting that European and Asian systems rely more heavily on written essays, oral presentations, and exhibits of student work that put knowledge in context and require higher-order thinking skills (Hacker & Hathaway, 1991).[1]

1. Obviously, there are other important differences between U.S. educational systems and those in Europe and Asia. For example, the responsibility for education tends to be more decentralized in the United States.

For many, education reform goes hand-in-hand with reforms in assessment. Without reforms in assessment, reforms in curriculum and instruction may be impeded. For example, the National Council of Teachers of Mathematics (NCTM) has noted that

> Objective tests, first developed in the 1910s, were once considered an example of the application of "modern" scientific techniques. Today, we are both technologically and intellectually equipped to improve on outdated methods and instruments—*the continued use of which would be counterproductive to the needed reforms in school mathematics* [stress added]. (1993, p. 13)

Certainly, if current assessment procedures do not reflect curricula, students may earn lower test scores. Thus,

> Unless corresponding changes are made in assessment practices, promising new programs developed by teachers and schools will certainly crash as they come into contact with outdated, but often-used and revered, tests. (NCTM, 1993, p. 14)

Not only might objective testing formats impede educational reform, but alternative assessment formats are believed to promote educational reform. For example, Fredricksen and Collins have written that a "systemically valid test is one that induces in the education system curricular and instructional changes that foster the development of cognitive skills that the test is designed to measure" (1989, p. 27).

Over-Reliance on Objective and Quantifiable Measures

Some proponents of alternative assessment believe that more subjective and qualitative approaches are better for assessing many important educational outcomes (for example, writing for specific audiences or using the scientific method). Many teachers already use such methods to assess student performance in music, art, photography, drafting, writing, wood shop, and so forth. Teachers also draw inferences and make judgments in more concrete domains. For example, teachers examine student computations to judge whether pupils have used correct mathematical algorithms. Thus, subjective and qualitative judgments can provide valuable additional information for use in educational decision making.

However, today the role of qualitative and subjective appraisals has broadened and, in some circles, is replacing more objective and quantitative assessment procedures. Dwyer (1993) noted an increased tolerance for subjectivity and a valuing of human judgment and intuition over precise decision rules and logical operations. Some advocate that student work should be assessed more within the context of who students are. For example, Gitomer (1993) has noted the belief that the more assessors know about students, the more accurate are their judgments.

Yet, subjective appraisals present some serious problems for those charged with conducting educational and psychological evaluations. For good reason, examiners and teachers historically have aspired to be objective, impartial, and disinterested appraisers. As Bennett points out, human judgment "seems to be distrusted because it has so often been a historical companion to bias" (1993, p. 17). Bennett's observation is particularly apropos in special education, where disability labels can bias and distort subjective evaluations (see for example, Salvia and Meisel, 1980). This inherent weakness in subjective evaluation in part explains the emphasis that interscorer reliability (see Chapter 7) has received in the professional literature as well as the legal mandates for objective criteria for evaluating the progress of students with disabilities.[2]

The remainder of this chapter addresses one alternative to standardized, norm-referenced assessment: portfolio assessment. In subsequent sections, we describe portfolio assessment as currently advocated, discuss weaknesses in current practice, and recommend modifications in portfolio assessment practices to overcome some shortcomings.

PORTFOLIO ASSESSMENT

Portfolios go beyond simple display of sample products. Portfolios are intended to facilitate judgments about student performance. They are collections of products used to demonstrate what a person has done and, by inference, what a person is capable of doing. Collecting a variety of products into a portfolio has allowed artists and craftspeople to show the range and depth of creative accomplishment. For a long time, portfolios have played an integral part of the evaluation process in fields such as art, music, photography, journalism, commercial arts, and modeling (Winograd & Gaskins, 1992). In these contexts, where judgments of quality are personal and subjective, a portfolio allows potential employers or customers to decide for themselves if they like an artisan's work.

The use of work samples is neither new nor innovative in U.S. classrooms. We are all familiar with student work displayed in classrooms. Teachers frequently show parents samples of their children's work on back-to-school nights. These samples are tangible proof for students, parents, and building visitors of what pupils create—stories, poems, drawings, mechanical devices.

As indicated in the preceding section, in the past the use of portfolios was largely restricted to school subjects where creative activities were taught and evaluated. Now, portfolios are being applied to more traditional academic areas (that is, writing, reading, mathematics, and sciences) to serve several purposes:

2. As one example, federal regulations require IEPs to contain "appropriate objective criteria . . . for determining whether the short-term instructional objectives are being achieved." (34 CFR § 300.46(a)(5))

- To document student effort
- To document student growth and achievement
- To augment information from other assessment methods
- To provide a public accounting of the quality of educational programs

Portfolio assessment projects have been initiated at state-wide levels (for example, in Vermont, Kentucky, and California). Other states (for example, Pennsylvania) recognize portfolios as one of several assessment options. In addition, several school districts have initiated portfolio projects.

Portfolio Assessment Defined

Although different authors stress different components of portfolio assessment (for example, Adams, 1991; Arter & Spandel, 1992; Camp, 1993; Dwyer, 1993; Grace & Shores, 1992; Meisels & Steele, 1991; Valencia, McGinley, & Pearson, 1990), six elements are generally highlighted in the literature advocating this form of assessment.

- *Targeting valued outcomes for assessment.* Generally, valued outcomes include those that require higher levels of understanding (that is, analysis, synthesis, and evaluation), those that require applying specific processes or strategies to reach answers, and those that are complex and challenging.
- *Using tasks that mirror work in the real world.* Authentic assessments require students to solve the types of problems found in the "real" world. These problems may be ill-structured (open-ended), require significant amounts of student time to solve, or require students to integrate knowledge and skills rather than treat them as discrete entities.
- *Encouraging cooperation among learners and between teacher and student.* Outcomes to be assessed should include products or performances created by groups of students as well as by individual students.
- *Using multiple dimensions to evaluate student work.* In portfolio assessment, teachers should evaluate more than content knowledge. They should also consider content-specific strategies, methods of inquiry, and work processes that are essential components of student learning.
- *Encouraging student reflection.* Students should think critically about what they and their peers have created or accomplished, and they should strive to improve their products. Thus, teachers should encourage students to revise and polish their work rather than turning in a one-shot test, essay, or project.
- *Integrating assessment and instruction.* Assessment must serve instructional purposes from which it is inseparable. Thus, assessment should do more than provide accurate information about student performance on a continuous basis, it should also motivate students and facilitate teaching.

Portfolio Content

Portfolios should be tailored for a specific purpose. Without a predetermined purpose, a portfolio is just a pile of papers or projects placed in a folder. Thus, portfolio contents should be consistent with the purposes for collecting work and bear logically on the decision that is to be reached. Depending on its purpose, a portfolio might include classroom assignments, rough drafts, work developed especially for the portfolio, audio tapes, a list of books that have been read, tests, checklists, journal entries, videotapes, completed projects, art work, computer projects, response logs, and reading logs (Polin, 1991).

Collaboration of students and teachers is integral to the creation of portfolios. Thus, decisions about what to include in a portfolio are made in consultations between students and their teachers, frequently during regularly scheduled conferences. (Notes from these conferences may also be included in portfolios.) The guidelines for student participation that have been suggested in the professional literature, however, tend to be conflicting. For example, some advocate having students select a product that they think is particularly good or of which they are particularly proud; others advocate having students select a product they do not like. Some educators believe that what students select and the rationales for their selections are as important as the pieces themselves (Arter & Spandel, 1992; Frazier & Paulson, 1992; Hebert, 1992; Mills, 1989; Paulson, Paulson, & Meyer, 1991; Wolf, 1989).[3]

Portfolios often include the students' self-evaluations and reflections. Advocates of portfolio assessment encourage the inclusion of reflective statements in which students express their feelings about the specific contents and topics in their portfolios. Teachers can ask students why they have chosen to include certain products, why a product was important, and how they went about completing their work. In addition, students can comment on what they have learned, whether they have met their goals, and what future goals they would like to accomplish.[4]

Using Portfolios to Evaluate Student Work

Advocates of the use of portfolios as assessment tools frequently discuss four aspects of assessment: responsibility for developing performance standards, dimensions to be evaluated, dimension scaling, and responsibility for actual evaluation of portfolios.

---

3. This belief suggests portfolio assessment requires sophisticated understanding of students' motivation and ability to think critically.
4. Although this type of information can be collected easily, its use is not clearly explained in the literature on portfolio assessment.

Responsibility for Developing Performance Standards

Conflicting advice is offered in the literature on who should set performance standards. Dwyer (1993) notes that teachers should not let politicians or other external groups set standards. Others (such as Tierney, Carter, & Desai, 1991; Winograd & Gaskins, 1992) have urged teachers to let students develop their own personal criteria. Gitomer (1993) reports that others have advocated that teachers and students share responsibility for setting standards. It is interesting that parents are seldom mentioned as stakeholders in decisions about performance standards—though when students have disabilities, their parents must be included in the decision-making process for establishing goals and performance criteria. Finally, despite the competing proposals for who should set standards, everyone seems to agree that the standards should be public.

Dimensions to Be Evaluated

A decision must be made about the specific dimensions to rate. The specific dimensions are generally intended to assess a student's effort (sometimes termed commitment or purposefulness), use of specific strategies or problems (for example, scientific method), problem solving, and overall quality of the product (usually evaluated holistically). Some (see Tierney et al., 1991) advocate having the entire class select the dimensions; others advocate evaluating dimensions developed outside the classroom (LeMahieu et al., 1992). The specific dimensions to be evaluated are, of course, a function of the subject matter and the purpose of the assessment.

Dimension Scaling

All scoring systems of which we are aware use ordinal scaling. First, the number of points on the scale must be determined; typically, from three to nine are used. Next, the end points of the scale are *anchored*—given a verbal description of student performance. These anchors may be generic (for example, *master performance* through *novice performance* or *strong performance* through *weak performance*) or they may be more focused (for example, *there is evidence of serious effort and personal commitment within the portfolio*). Intervening points on the scale may or may not have verbal descriptors.

Responsibility for Portfolio Evaluation

Obviously, teachers have a responsibility to score portfolios, but they are frequently urged to allow students to evaluate their own work using both established and personal criteria and to monitor their own progress (Adams, 1991; Arter & Spandel, 1992; Hansen, 1992; Polin, 1991; Tierney, Carter, & Desai, 1991; Winograd & Gaskins, 1992). Seldom is instruction in scoring recommended or demonstrated. Thus, teachers and students are usually left to their own devices when it comes to scoring.

Because the evaluation of portfolios is frequently subjective, moderation is sometimes used in grading students. *Moderation* is the practice of using several scorers for the same performance—not unlike the procedure used for judging Olympic ice skating. The scores awarded to an individual performance may be tempered by discarding scores at the extreme (that is, the highest and lowest scores) or by averaging (or summing) the raters' scores. In this way, idiosyncratic scores have less of a distorting effect, and the average rating should more closely approximate the performer's true score. However, moderation requires several raters or judges.

Examples of Scoring Systems Used in Writing

Scoring systems for portfolios in written language are among the most extensively described and probably the most extensively used. Below, we describe three examples of scoring systems in current use. These systems have been selected not because they are particularly good but because they are representative.

Portfolio Analysis Guide   Tierney, Carter, and Desai (1991) suggest one scoring scheme, a "Continua of Descriptors." The dimensions to be evaluated in each portfolio are decided upon by the entire class and a holistic guide is developed. Within dimensions are performance continua that may include versatility, process, response, problem solving, and purposefulness. Teachers and students use the continua as a basis for rating a student's work on each dimension. Ratings range from *strong performance* to *needs improvement*. The authors provide examples of the types of performance at each end of the continua; these are quite qualitative and lack operational explanations. Portfolios are then analyzed by comparing each portfolio with the descriptors in the guide. This guide is intended to identify areas where individual students can benefit from additional instruction.

Upper Arlington (Ohio) School District Scale   A holistic scoring scheme from the Upper Arlington School District in Ohio allows ratings on an eight-point scale (ranging from two to nine). The overall appearance and the general quality of individual pieces are considered in rating the whole portfolio. Teachers use eight-point rating scales to evaluate portfolios on four dimensions:

- Diversity in types of writing (outstanding through lacking)
- Use of the writing process (clear indication through little or no indication)
- Effort and personal commitment (evidence of serious effort through sloppy, incomplete, and disorganized)
- General quality (High quality pieces have strong voice, demonstrate sophisticated ideas, stay on topic, are well organized, have well developed paragraphs that include specific and pertinent details, have well developed sentences, and have few or no punctuation, usage, and/or spelling errors; poor quality pieces lack sophisticated ideas, have more than one or no main idea, have little or no

organization, have several mechanical errors, and have no variety of sentence types or interesting diction.)

Pittsburgh Portfolio Project   The Pittsburgh Public Schools use a writing assessment scheme organized around three major dimensions, each having a number of characteristics (LeMahieu, Eresh, & Wallace, 1992). The dimensions and characteristics follow.

Accomplishment as a Writer includes:

- Meeting worthwhile challenges
- Establishing and maintaining purpose
- Using technique and traces of genre
- Controlling conventions, vocabulary, and sentence structure
- Being aware of the needs of the audience
- Using language, sound, images, tone, voice, humor, metaphor, and playfulness

Use of Processes and Strategies for Writing includes:

- Using pre-writing strategies effectively
- Using drafts to discover and shape ideas
- Using conferencing opportunities to refine writing
- Using revision (reshaping, refocusing, refining) effectively

Development as a Writer includes:

- Making an investment in writing tasks
- Increasing engagement in writing
- Developing sense of self as a writer
- Evolving personal criteria and standards for writing
- Being able to see strengths and needs in one's writing
- Demonstrating risk taking and innovation in interpreting writing tasks
- Using writing for various purposes, genres, and writing audiences, progressing from early to late pieces

A six-point Likert scale is used to score student work with respect to each characteristic along a continuum ranging from inadequate performance to outstanding performance.

Scoring Systems Used in Mathematics and Science

Scoring systems used for written language are better developed than those used in other academic areas. Scoring systems in mathematics education frequently assess *process* (solving problems, making valid arguments, explaining reasoning used to arrive at solutions, using technology appropriately) and *content* (the type of arithmetic used in the problem, such as addition or quadratic equations) (compare National Council of Teachers of Mathematics, 1993, p. 114; Pandey & Smith, 1991).

In science, a scoring system may use both technical and substantive criteria. When written records of experiments (or *doing science*) are kept, Collins (1993)[5] has described some technical criteria that could be used:

(1) Is there a goal statement? (2) Is there a rationale for the goal statement? (3) Is there a guide that helps the assessor find his/her way through the evidence? (4) Does each piece of evidence have a caption that states what the document is and why it is evidence? (5) Is there a final reflection? (6) Are all prescribed pieces of evidence present? (7) Is there variety among the evidence? And (8) has all redundant evidence been removed? (p. 126)

Substantive criteria address two issues:

(1) Is the assessor convinced by this collection of evidence that the person who has developed the portfolio has achieved or made progress toward the goal? And, (2) if not, what additional evidence would be needed to convince me? (p. 126)

Shavelson, Baxter, and Pine (1991) also give examples of scoring rubrics for some specific science projects.

An Example of the Use of Portfolios in Special Education

The Kentucky Systems Change Project for Students with Severe Disabilities has developed the Kentucky Alternative Portfolio Project (undated) to evaluate the twenty-eight outcomes listed in Table 12.1. Evidence relating to these outcomes is evaluated holistically on a four-point scale: novice, apprentice, proficient, and distinguished. Verbal descriptions are provided for each level of performance. Using the outcome *interpersonal relationships* as an example, a *novice* performance is indicated when the student "responds to interactions with teacher, family, and/or only disabled peers"; an *apprentice* performance is indicated when the student "initiates interactions with non-disabled peers"; a *proficient* performance is indicated when the student "initiates and sustains interactions with non-disabled peers over time"; and a *distinguished* performance is indicated when the student "has clearly established mutual friendships with non-disabled peers" (p. 16).

ISSUES AND CONCERNS TO BE RESOLVED

The use of portfolios, either as an addition to other assessment procedures or as a replacement for other forms of assessment done by teachers, has considerable intuitive appeal. However, portfolio assessment is a new approach, and assessment specialists still need to resolve issues related to the assembling and scoring of portfolios, veracity of items included, bias, instructional utility, efficiency, and use in actual practice.

---

5. Although Collins' paper focuses on teaching science to undergraduate college students, the descriptions are applicable, with modification, to general education.

TABLE 12.1   **Outcomes Assessed in the Kentucky Alternative Portfolio Project**

Outcome	Description
Accessing Information	Using research tools to locate information.
Reading	Constructing meaning from printed materials.
Quantifying	Communicating ideas by quantifying numbers.
Classifying	Using a classification system to organize information.
Writing	Communicating ideas and information to a variety of audiences.
Speaking	Communicating ideas through speaking.
Using Electronic Technology	Using computers, etc., to gather, organize, and disseminate ideas.
Nature of Scientific Activity	Using scientific skills to solve real-life problems.
Patterns	Understanding past and present events and predicting future events.
Constancy	Understanding the tendency for things in nature to move toward a steady state.
Number	Understanding numbers
Democratic Principles	Recognizing and applying principles of justice, equality, etc., to real-life situations
Structure and Function of Political Systems	Recognizing the forms of government and addressing issues such as authority, power, civil action, and rights and responsibilities.
Structure and Function of Social Systems	Recognizing social groupings and institutions and issues important to them.
Cultural Diversity	Interacting effectively and cooperatively with individuals from diverse backgrounds.
Structure and Function of Economic Systems	Making decisions about producing and consuming goods and services.
Interpersonal Relationships	Acquiring an understanding of self and others through observation, analysis, and interpretation of human behavior.
Production	Creating products and making presentations to express ideas and feelings.
Family Life and Parenting	Demonstrating positive individual and family life skills.
Consumerism	Making effective decisions as a consumer.
Physical Wellness	Demonstrating skills and responsibility in understanding physical health.
Mental and Emotional Wellness	Demonstrating positive strategies for achieving and maintaining mental and emotional health.
Community Health Systems	Assessing and accessing community resources.
Psychomotor Skills	Performing psychomotor skills in a variety of settings.
Lifetime Physical Activities	Demonstrating knowledge, skills, and values having lifetime implications for involvement in physical activities.
Career Path	Having strategies for selecting career options.
Employability Attributes	Demonstrating school-to-work or post-secondary transition skills.
Post-Secondary Opportunities Search	Accessing employment.

Assembling Portfolios

General Issues

What goes into a portfolio is of fundamental concern because educational decisions will be based, at least in part, on these student products. Teachers have been urged to structure portfolios according to the type of decision that they will make. Yet, the literature on portfolio assessment offers little practical guidance about (1) the types of decision teachers should be making, (2) the characteristics (for example, amount) of the content used for specific decisions, or (3) criteria to guide decision making about any of the following:

- Grading
- Identification and remediation of a student's academic weaknesses
- Instructional improvement and staff development
- Eligibility for entitlement programs (such as special education)
- Assessing educational outcomes
- Educational reform

This absence of theory and empirical research to guide practice in portfolio assessment stands in stark contrast to other approaches to classroom assessment (for example, curriculum-based assessment).

Portfolio assessment has developed largely outside the field of special and remedial education. A consequence, perhaps, is that many of the decisions made on behalf of students in special education do not appear to have been considered. Similarly, advocates of portfolio assessment do not appear to have considered the processes and criteria upon which these decisions are based. Many decisions in special and remedial education rely, at least in part, on inter-student comparisons. For example, a student may be referred for pre-referral intervention on the bases of both failing to meet standards of performance *and* being substantially behind other students in class; a boy with a learning disability might be mainstreamed in a regular classroom when his achievement is commensurate with that of a nondisabled student in the classroom. Because the content of portfolios is not standardized from student to student, inter-student comparisons based on portfolio assessment are extremely difficult. Thus, portfolios, in the form advocated by most supporters, are unlikely to gain widespread acceptance in special education.[6]

If portfolios replace tests, educators will need to address some issues of record maintenance. Portfolios can be maintained for a specific marking period, a semester, a year, or a career. When portfolios are used to make long-term decisions (such as determining eligibility, documenting attainment of outcomes required for graduation, documenting the provision of quality education, and so forth), some guidelines for maintenance of records will have to be established. (See Chapter 3.) Storage and retrieval of portfolios may present problems even with digital technology. Although it is possible to maintain electronic copies of portfolios on CD (compact disk), currently the costs are staggering.

---

6. We note that many advocates of portfolio assessment (as well as advocates of other alternative forms of assessment) oppose interstudent comparisons on philosophical grounds. (See, for example, The National Council of Teachers of Mathematics, 1993.)

Specific Issues

Content Selection   Will a student's portfolio include everything a student has done in an area or just a sample of products? For example, should the portfolio contain all or some of the notes, outlines, drafts, corrected copies, and rewrites of every product a student has created for a semester or year? When portfolios contain everything students have created during a year, their contents become more variable, but teachers do not have to decide what to include. However, teachers will spend more time in evaluation if they score all products in their students' portfolios.

Quality of Student Work   Conflicting advice is offered in the literature about what student work to include. In the absence of research, we can only speculate about the usefulness of different criteria for including student work in portfolios. Some advocate including the student's best work. "Best work" portfolios show what a student is capable of producing; they are likely to be the most useful in assessing a student's attainment of specific educational goals or outcomes. However, these portfolios fail to provide information about the variability of student work and the quality of typical work. Others advocate including a student's typical work in the portfolio. Although "typical work" portfolios may be the most useful in making decisions, they do not provide information about the variability of student work or about the best and worst of a student's work. Finally, some recommend including a range of quality in a student's portfolio. Such portfolios provide the most information, but they may not be pertinent to some decisions.

Student Participation in Selection   Student participation in content selection is frequently recommended in the professional literature. As mentioned earlier, students may be asked to select pieces that they think are particularly good or pieces that they do not like. The diagnostic and instructional implications for including products chosen for such reasons are unclear. For example, it is not established that products a student likes lead to the same instructional and diagnostic decisions as products the student dislikes; we do not know if there are interactions between student criteria for selection and the quality of various decisions that are made in schools. Finally, we can locate no evidence to suggest that students, let alone students with cognitive disabilities, can determine what content is pertinent to the multitude of decisions that teachers must make.

Sufficient Information for Decision Making   It is axiomatic that accurate and valid information is the basis for good educational decision making. The psychometric theories on which achievement tests are based allow users to estimate a student's true score on the domain of interest. When these tests do not contain enough items to draw reliable inferences about a student's true score, test authors can estimate (with the Spearman-Brown formula) the number of additional items needed to make their tests reliable. Psychometricians have yet to develop the necessary theories to allow similar estimation of true scores from portfolios. Most would agree that portfolios should contain enough products to allow reliable appraisal, but at this time it is unclear how one would know what the minimum number of pieces should be.[7] What does seem to be clear is that many who write about portfolios urge teachers to base their assessments on untimed, extended projects (see, for example, Camp, 1993). Such projects require multiple constellations of skills that vary considerably across tasks; successful products depend on context-situated skills, as well as knowledge of the context itself (Bennett, 1993, p. 9). Thus, generalizations from one constructed response or performance to other constructed responses are problematic. Teachers cannot assume that because a child performed poorly (or well) on one project, other performances will be similarly poor (or good). It is important that educational decisions be based on more than one pertinent product in a student's portfolio, but when individual products in a portfolio require extended time to create, it is unlikely that multiple products will be available.

Scoring Portfolios

The majority of articles on portfolio assessment elaborate on the importance of scoring and evaluation systems and the philosophical bases for establishing criteria for judging a portfolio's merit; little attention is devoted to the specifics of scoring student work. Evaluation processes are loosely defined, if explained at all (Arter & Spandel, 1992; Polin, 1991), and educators are offered few specifics to guide their evaluations of portfolios. Yet, scoring projects and constructed responses is neither simple nor straightforward.

Score Interpretation

Meaning of Evaluative Descriptions   Whether products are evaluated for the presence or absence of specific attributes or on some dimension, interpretation of the resulting scores is likely to present some problems. Consider a science project described by Shavelson, Baxter, and Pine (1991). A teacher asks students to determine which of three paper towels holds the most water. If the students saturate and weigh the towels, the care with which they weigh the towels can be evaluated on a three-point scale (that is, *yes, no,* or *a little sloppy*). However, the meanings of *yes, no,* or *a little sloppy* are undefined. Or consider the evaluation of a student's written language project in which various elements are scored as *novice, apprentice, proficient,* and *distinguished*. These terms are likely to lack meaning to anyone unfamiliar with the context-specific meanings developed by

---

7. The bromide "the more, the better" is no doubt correct, but it fails to address the issue of threshold of adequacy. Additionally, the more pieces included in a portfolio, the more time is required for assessment. Therefore, when efficiency is a consideration, portfolios should not contain more products than are needed to make reliable decisions.

a teacher in the classroom. Indeed, we find no evidence to suggest that teacher (or student) ratings of portfolio products are meaningful to anyone outside of the classroom or school. Thus, parents and policy makers may find them less useful than other types of descriptions or scores.[8]

Generalizability of Scores   Generalizability of scores presents two problems. First, we know very little about the number of products necessary to estimate a student's ability accurately. For example, Shavelson, Gao, and Baxter (1991) found that from eight to twenty performances were needed to estimate a student's problem-solving ability in mathematics and science accurately. Yet such estimates will likely vary by the content area (that is, physics, general science, algebra, and so forth), specific curriculum, and the grade level at which the material is taught. Second, there is some evidence that evaluation context affects student performance (for example, Gearhart, et al., 1992). What students are asked to do and the circumstances under which they are asked to perform will affect outcome and, necessarily, inferences about what students have learned and what they are capable of doing.[9]

Lack of Inter-Student Comparisons   Although advocates of portfolio assessment often eschew inter-student comparisons, these comparisons are invariably part of the information needed to qualify students for special or remedial services. In schools where inter-individual comparisons are based on portfolios with variable contents, making valid comparisons will be a formidable undertaking. In schools where inter-individual comparisons are avoided, portfolio assessment is unlikely to provide useful information for a variety of decisions.

Student Reflections   The role of student reflections, often suggested for inclusion in portfolio assessment, is unclear. Although student reflections and self-evaluations may be motivational or otherwise useful instructionally, it remains to be demonstrated how these reflections facilitate or contribute to assessments of academic or behavioral development. Since student ratings are influenced by a desire to please the teacher, these ratings may not be independent (or particularly meaningful).

Score Aggregation

Portfolio ratings are aggregated both within individual pieces and across pieces in a portfolio. When one piece of student work is evaluated on several dimensions and then given a summary rating, the summary rating represents an aggregate of the ratings of the component dimensions. For example, suppose a

8. We have heard of advocates of portfolio assessment suggesting that teachers give parents their child's portfolio and allow the parents to judge for themselves how their child is doing. This is not a satisfactory response to a legitimate concern.
9. Some writers use the term *context* to refer to a specific domain (for example, history or mathematics).

teacher was evaluating a student's *Accomplishment as a Writer*—one dimension used in the Pittsburgh Portfolio Project discussed earlier. Further suppose that the student's performance varied on the six subdimensions. Each subdimension is rated on a six-point Likert scale along a continuum ranging from inadequate performance to outstanding performance. Having rated each subdimension, how does the teacher determine the overall rating? If the rating scale is ordinal, scores from the subdimensions should not be added or averaged. If the scores are assumed to be equal interval, should they be weighted equally? Unless the scores from the subdimensions are converted to z-scores before weighing, they will be weighted by their variance.

When the summary scores from several pieces are aggregated to arrive at a portfolio score, there are additional problems. Portfolios are intended to include a variety of work. For example, a writing portfolio may consist of poetry, reactions to short stories or news items, journal entries, drafts of extended pieces of prose, and so forth. Insofar as different scoring rubrics are used for different types of writing, summary ratings will be based on different considerations. Thus, the summary ratings will compare apples and oranges, and interpretation of these aggregates will be very challenging.

To illustrate, consider the following scenario. A teacher wishes to make a decision about a student's literacy progress over the course of a semester using the student's portfolio as the basis of the decision. The portfolio contains seventeen items produced during the semester:

- A videotape of the student's classroom presentation on Harriet Tubman (a project prepared during the first nine weeks of the semester)
- One group paper about dinosaurs and some drawings (a project prepared during the last nine weeks of the semester)
- Six biweekly journal entries, completed at home, giving personal reactions to poems read during the first six weeks of the semester
- Three weekly journal entries, completed in school, giving personal reactions to short stories read in class during the middle six weeks of the semester
- Six weekly journal entries, completed at home and in school, giving personal reactions to articles appearing in a student newspaper (completed during the last six weeks of the semester)

Further assume that the teacher uses Pittsburgh's scoring rubric to judge twenty subdimensions associated with the three dimensions. Each of the scores ranges ordinally from 1 to 6. How does the teacher combine the scores? Does the teacher aggregate scores from journal entries with group projects? Does the teacher combine scores across different reading materials (that is, poetry, short stories, and articles from the student newspaper)? How would a teacher incorporate judgments on progress over time, since the materials and tasks vary systematically over the semester? One thing is certain: Different aggregation procedures will yield different summary evaluations.

Guidelines for aggregating ratings are seldom provided to teachers, and there is no evidence that teachers (or students) who invent their own guidelines apply them consistently. Thus, the meanings of summary ratings of individual pieces and the portfolio as a whole are likely to be idiosyncratic and inconsistently applied.

Score Reliability

Without clear and objective scoring rubrics to guide the evaluation of multiple skills and complex attributes, portfolio assessment is prone to unreliable scoring. Moreover, the products that students construct or create and that are put into portfolios are, by their very nature, difficult to score consistently, whether individual pieces in a portfolio are evaluated separately or aggregated. Part of the difficulty lies in subjective scoring. As Dwyer noted, efforts at educational reform, and particularly reform of assessment, have celebrated subjectivity: There are "clear indications that their [reformers'] orientation includes increasing tolerance for subjectivity, and a valuing of human judgment—and even intuition—over precise decision rules and logical operations" (1993, p. 269). However, precise decision rules and logical operations bring consistency to scoring.

What happens without precise scoring rules is well documented. The research literature in evaluating written language is the most extensive, although written language is difficult to score under any system. In several studies dealing with holistic scoring of writing samples, Breland and colleagues found interscorer agreement ranging from .52 to .65 (Breland, et al., 1987; Breland, 1983). In the National Assessment of Educational Progress's portfolio study (Educational Testing Service, 1990), interscorer agreement was computed for ratings of three types of writing (narratives, informatives, and persuasives) on a six-point scale. Interscorer reliabilities ranged from .76 to .89, probably because the scorers had received intensive training just before evaluating the portfolios.

Consistent scoring of student writing is even more difficult when students can select topics and genres. As Dorans and Schmitt have noted, "to the extent that a constructed-response item is unconstrained and examinees are free to produce any response they wish, the test scorer has a difficult and challenging task of extracting information from examinee responses. To date the psychometrics for dealing with this unconstrained response type have lagged behind the development and administration of these items" (1993, p. 135). As Breland and colleagues (Breland et al., 1987; Breland, 1983) have found, interscorer agreement drops from the range of .52 to .65 to a range of .36 to .46 when the writing tasks vary. Early experience in evaluating writing portfolios in Vermont also reflects this tendency. Camp noted that writing teachers received considerable training before scoring portfolios.

The criteria for evaluating the portfolios were developed by a statewide committee of writing teachers and applied to sample portfolios by fourth- and eighth-grade teachers in regional meetings throughout the state. They were refined as a result of these experiences. The five portfolio criteria focus on characteristics of writing that are sufficiently generic to be observable in pieces written for different purposes and audiences: clarity of purpose; organization of ideas or information; use of specific detail; personal expression or voice; and appropriate usage, mechanics, and grammar. In the process of applying the portfolio criteria and examining them in relation to the design for the portfolio, the teachers begin to internalize the criteria and to refine their understanding of the portfolio's purpose. (1993, pp. 201–202)

These portfolios were assessed using four-point scales. "Depending on the grade and subject, the average correlation between raters (across the five or seven scales) ranged from .33 to .43" (Koretz, 1993, p. 2).

Similar findings have been reported in other content areas. For example in a study dealing with scoring science notebooks, Baxter, et al., (1992) found similarly low interscorer agreement (.66) although direct observations were more reliable. Consistent problems have also been noted in the scoring of mathematics portfolios (Koretz, et al., 1993). Thus, the evidence to date suggests that level of agreement when teachers score portfolios, especially when the portfolios contain constructed responses, is likely to be below the generally accepted criteria for reliable assessment (.90).

Although research dealing with consistent scoring of portfolios by students is lacking, some indirect evidence is available. Gordon (1990) found that teachers' criteria for judging good stories were often quite different from the criteria used by students. Thus, to the extent that students' evaluations are included in assessment, systematic variation will be introduced. Also, because the literature on portfolio assessment fails to address special training for students who self-evaluate, it is likely that students' criteria and scoring will produce more error than that produced by teachers specifically trained in scoring performances and constructed performances.

Finally, research on behavioral observation, in which definitions of target behaviors are considerably more precise and objective, strongly suggests that as the complexity of observation increases, interscorer agreement decreases (Salvia & Hunt, 1984). Consistent monitoring of and feedback about accuracy can reduce or prevent drifting of criteria, which contributes to lack of reliability (Salvia & Hunt, 1984). These issues remain unaddressed by advocates of portfolio assessment.

In summary, the very nature of portfolio assessment makes reliable scoring extremely difficult. Thus, one should expect different teachers to award different scores to the same piece of work or portfolio. As Bennett has noted, "[constructed responses] by their very nature will produce less reliable scores. Lower reliability will make the measurement of new constructs relatively inaccurate, limiting the ability to generalize performance beyond the administered tasks and the specific raters grading them" (1993, p. 9). Although advocates of portfolio assessment have downplayed or ignored these problems, the problems have not gone away and will not go away until scoring procedures, as well as procedures for training scorers, are improved.

Veracity of Products

Teachers must determine that their students actually created the products in their portfolios (Gearhart, et al., 1993). For example, how does a teacher know whether students completed the work or handed in someone else's work under their names? Did a parent, sibling, or friend do the homework? Similarly, if a student revises a paper based on the teacher's formal review of a draft, is the revision considered the student's work or the teacher's? Teachers will need some way to authenticate or weigh the student's contribution to each product. The easiest solution is to use only work completed in class, but this criterion severely restricts a teacher's options.

The uncritical emphasis on cooperative learning espoused by advocates of portfolio assessment further complicates assessment. There are multiple models of cooperative learning: *student team learning* (for example, Slavin, 1983), in which there are always group goals and individual responsibility; *learning together* (for example, Johnson & Johnson, 1986), in which there are always group goals and sometimes individual accountability; *group investigation* (Sharan & Sharan, 1976) and *jigsaw* (Aronson, et al., 1978), in which each team member has a specialized task; and *groups of four* (Burns, 1981), with little or no structure. Only when there is individual responsibility can there be individual assessment.[10] Moreover, there are no widely accepted (or compelling) methods for separating the work of an individual from that of the group (Baker, O'Neil, Jr., & Linn, 1993).

Bias

Many advocates of portfolio assessment seem to believe that, if subjective appraisal replaced objective assessment in the schools, prejudice and bias would be somehow reduced.[11] Assertions that subjectively scored portfolios are less biased appear to be based on ignorance of or cavalier disregard of a substantial research literature. As noted in Chapter 2, researchers have repeatedly shown the susceptibility of subjective decision making to stereotypes associated with race, ethnicity, social class, and gender. Especially pertinent to those working with students with disabilities is the substantial research literature demonstrating that subjective teacher evaluations are quite susceptible to the biasing effects of disability labels (such as mental retardation). Thus, all the relevant research seems to argue against subjective methods of appraisal when more objective methods are available.

10. There is a considerable body of research suggesting that "cooperative learning methods can be an effective means of increasing student achievement, but only if they incorporate group goals and individual accountability" (Slavin, 1990, p. 32).
11. Problems with biased scoring standards are tacitly recognized when moderation is used to overcome different internal criteria and biases in subjective ratings. However, moderation assumes that most of the judges are free of bias.

Although objective tests have been used for prejudicial purposes, it is also true that slavery, segregation, disenfranchisement of women, and unfair employment practices (among other biased practices) long preceded the use of objective tests. Indeed, one of the driving forces in the mental testing movement was the desire to use objective evaluations to eliminate bias. Moreover, legal and societal redress of biased practices has been based primarily on objective evidence. Finally, Snow (1993) has pointed out that bias can be determined objectively and eliminated from objectively scored tests. At this juncture, we cannot say the same of portfolio assessment.

Of course, assessment procedures may be biased in ways other than their scoring. In addition to content considerations, test format may produce systematic advantage (or disadvantage) for some groups. For example, students of different ethnicity vary in their willingness to attempt open-ended types of questions (Koretz, et al., 1992). Snow (1993) has summarized other relevant findings.

- Extended responses (for example, essay questions) produce greater anxiety in students; objective formats seem to help more anxious students.
- The less structured the instruction (a condition associated with portfolio assessment), the greater is the effect of a student's intelligence. Structure facilitates learning for students with lower ability.
- Women do better on tests requiring constructed responses.

Instructional Utility

Portfolios supposedly have two instructional advantages. First, portfolios are favored because they are believed to promote higher-order thinking skills. This belief has yet to be supported empirically. Baker and associates (1993, p. 1211) have summarized the current state of affairs in assessing extended student performances (the preferred form of material to be included in portfolios).

> Advocates of performance-based assessment have been remarkably remiss in providing clear-cut conceptual frameworks for their efforts. Many rather loosely link their exemplars to measurement of higher order thinking without documenting the cognitive processes that students use. Neither explicit frameworks for generating assessments nor detailed descriptions of student learning are offered. Most of the arguments in favor of performance-based assessment, therefore, are based on single instances, essentially hand-crafted exercises whose virtues are assumed because they have been developed by teachers or because they are thought to model good instructional practice.

Later in the same article, they also point out that

> . . . students' instructional experiences (and the nature of practice on the task) can subvert intentions to measure higher order thinking. With repeated instructional

> exposure, nominally higher order tasks, such as constructing analyses of a drama or a geometric proof, can be transformed into rote tasks, a fact that may go undetected without collateral information about instructional processes (Baker, et al., 1993, p. 1211)

Similarly, Snow (1993) has noted that when students expect essay examinations, they try to learn how text authors have structured the material as well as the content. Thus, students do not tend to construct their own structure; instead, they try to memorize someone else's.

Second, portfolios are favored because they are believed to facilitate instructional decision making. Clearly, student products accumulated in portfolios are instructionally relevant. Unlike the empirical validity associated with other forms of alternative assessment (for example, curriculum-based assessment), however, the evidence supporting the role of portfolios, apart from bold and unsupported assertions or testimonials from teachers, remains largely intuitive or unreported. The difficulty is that tying student performance to instructional decision making is neither a simple nor straightforward matter. Because portfolio assessment has developed largely outside special and remedial education, it may not be well suited for some of the decisions that must be made in these contexts. These decisions are discussed in detail in Chapters 14 and 30, but a few examples are illustrative in this context.

- How are portfolio contents related to the criterion used to decide if a student is making satisfactory progress?
- How are portfolio contents related to the criterion used to decide if a student should be referred to ascertain eligibility for special education?
- How are portfolio contents related to decisions to alter instruction when a student is not making satisfactory progress?
- How can a student's portfolio be used to make decisions about mainstreaming and inclusion?
- How can a student's portfolio be used to determine current instructional levels?
- How can a student's portfolio be used to determine rates of acquisition and retention?

Besides the issues of scoring and bias, which clearly impinge on classroom decision making, there are two additional indications that portfolios may lack instructional utility. One potentially serious issue is sensitivity to change. For any classroom assessment to be useful, it must be sufficiently sensitive to small but important student changes. We find no empirical evidence for the ability of portfolio scoring systems to detect important changes in student development, (Unlike the empirical validity associated with other forms of alternative assessment). If portfolio scoring systems do not detect important changes, then teachers cannot gauge the effectiveness of their instruction over relatively short periods of time. Indeed, as Linn and Baker (1992, p. 8) have noted, global scores "would not help teachers to improve teaching and learning. They would function like a qualitative stanine." A second potentially serious issue is the frequency with which assessments can be conducted. Unlike other forms of assessment that rely on one- or two-minute probes to assess student progress, portfolios frequently contain extended projects. Teachers may find it difficult to use extended projects to adjust instruction on a daily or weekly basis. Thus, students who are not progressing satisfactorily may experience prolonged periods of failure before their difficulties become apparent to their teachers.

Efficiency

Efficiency is always an issue in assessment. Two issues are especially pertinent when considering portfolio assessment.

Time and Money

The first issue is the actual time devoted to assessment activities. In those models of portfolio assessment in which assessment is the shared responsibility of both teacher and student and in which assessment occurs during conferences, the instructional value of the evaluation may be worth the added time that must be invested. However, this remains an empirical question.

The evaluation of an extended project is, by its very nature, labor intensive. Yet to produce generalizable estimates of student ability and learning, teachers must have several projects. Using the estimates offered by Shavelson, Gao, and Baxter, (1991), teachers will need from eight to twenty projects to evaluate each student's ability in mathematics and science. Clearly, this is a substantial investment of teacher time; the impact of this time investment on instruction remains unclear. However, one should expect some reasonable trade-off between depth of coverage and breadth of coverage. Thus, in those classrooms where portfolios are used to collect extended projects, there is likely to be narrowed curricular content.

In those models of portfolio assessment using moderation, inordinate amounts of time could be diverted from teaching. Consider the use of portfolio assessment to assign semester grades in English at the secondary level, where teachers have five classes of twenty-five or thirty students each. If three teachers score each portfolio, each teacher would be required to evaluate between 375 and 450 portfolios, instead of 125 to 150 without moderation. Even highly dedicated teachers might find this prospect burdensome.

An issue related to time is cost. Because portfolio assessment is labor intensive and requires considerable teacher time, cost can be a factor. Moreover, when high-stakes scores are moderated, the costs can soar (Nuttall, 1992).

Additional Training

The second issue is training. Even when given considerable training in methods of subjective appraisal, raters typically produce unreliable ratings. Yet, even assuming for the sake of argument that the current amounts of training were adequate, additional training to maintain high levels of agreement in portfolio assessment will be necessary. Retraining requires a considerable investment of time and resources. To date, advocates of portfolio assessment have infrequently considered the costs of training, retraining, and maintenance of scoring standards.

Use of Portfolios in Practice

In practice, portfolio assessment falls far short of even the modest standards recommended by portfolio advocates. Calfee and Perfumo (1993) conducted a national survey seeking information about portfolio practices and visited several schools and classrooms where portfolios were used. Their findings suggest a state of anarchy in which inconsistent practice was the rule. They found:

- No clear indication of how achievement was measured
- No guidelines to help teachers analyze, score, or grade portfolios
- Use of normative rather than developmental procedures
- An absence of procedures to establish reliability
- An absence of procedures to establish validity

In their surveys and site visits, they found that the popularity of portfolios appeared to be a local reaction to external control—the perception seemed to be, the *rebels* do portfolios (p. 536).

Concluding Comments

The rhetoric used by many advocates of portfolio assessment suggests that portfolio assessment is widely accepted, is sweeping the country, and is the wave of the future. This is hardly the case. Moreover, as educators and parents gain experience with portfolio assessment, many difficulties are being recognized (see, for example, Madaus, 1993). Especially in special and remedial education (with its roots firmly established in federal law, empirical research, and psychometric theory), portfolio assessment will require more than slogans and rhetoric to win converts. Satisfactory solutions must be found for problems associated with content selection, scoring, validity, and efficiency.

IMPROVING PORTFOLIO ASSESSMENT PRACTICES

Those who wish to use portfolios for assessment purposes should give serious consideration to the assembly and evaluation of portfolios. Greater objectivity, less complexity, more scorer training, and greater comparability of portfolio contents are the keys to better practice.

Collecting Student Products

The content of a portfolio should be tailored to the purpose of assessment, but teachers seldom know all the decisions they will have to make at the beginning of the year. For example, they may not know that Mary will be referred to the school assistance team late in the first semester. Because retrieval of papers and projects can be difficult (and live performances are unretrievable if not recorded), it is probably a good idea to collect all potentially useful student work into their portfolios. Teachers can then assemble decision-specific portfolios.

Teachers *can* be sure that certain types of decisions (for example, grading) will be made during a semester or year. In these cases, teachers should carefully plan the semester's activities to ensure that there will be a sufficient number of products at appropriate times in the term to make anticipated decisions. If teachers intend to assess progress, they should plan to include in portfolios comparable products from throughout the term. Teachers should also include the criteria for scoring each type of product in the portfolio so that these criteria remain consistent over time.

Using portfolios to make high-stakes decisions requires considerably more structure. For meaningful comparisons of a student's progress over time or comparisons of students, portfolios must have comparable content. For example, it is very difficult for a teacher to judge student progress in writing from diverse products such as a poem, observations from a science walk, a letter, and a story; it is similarly difficult for teachers to compare the progress of two students when one student's portfolio contains persuasive prose and the other student's portfolio contains haiku. The products themselves are not comparable. Generally, the more comparable the products, the less prone to error are the assessments.

Finally, in practice some compromise between total student selection and total teacher selection is possible. For example, licensure and certification boards use highly structured portfolios as part of their evaluation.

Objective Scoring of Portfolios

In the last fifty years a substantial research literature on consistent rating and scoring has developed. Scoring portfolios requires essentially the same processes as conducting systematic observations. Specifically, careful preparation is necessary for the scoring of portfolios to be reliable and valid. Criteria should be specified clearly to allow different scorers to agree on whether specific target outcomes have occurred; references to internal process should be minimized. (See

Chapter 10.) Finally, consistent scoring requires instances and noninstances of what meets criteria.

Unfortunately, current practices in portfolio assessment contradict most of what we have learned from research. To be minimally acceptable, portfolio scoring schemes must be sufficiently objective to withstand parent and student disagreement with scores (and grades) and potential court challenges about fairness (Davis & Felknor, 1994). Historically, subjective scoring systems have failed to meet minimum standards. The obvious alternative is more objective scoring systems. One place to start objectifying scoring is to anchor scales in observable and objective characteristics of a performance or product. Without observable anchors, scale values such as *novice performance*, *strong performance*, and *evidence of serious effort* have no objective referents and are likely to defy consistent judging. A second way in which consistency can be increased is to simplify scoring rubrics. Indeed, Koretz (1993) mentioned scoring rubrics that were too complex or unclear as a possible cause of the unreliable evaluations found in the initial Vermont portfolio studies.

Training and Retraining of Scorers

Even when clear scoring standards have been developed, one should not assume that teachers will apply the scoring standards consistently without training. Scoring constructed responses (for example, essays) is *very* difficult. Therefore, teachers should be provided with direct and systematic instruction until they are able to score portfolios consistently.[12]

Training should not end once teachers have mastered the scoring system. There is a strong tendency for scorers to lose their accuracy over time. For example, with experience a teacher may develop idiosyncratic scoring rules or may stop using some scoring criteria. Thus, scoring criteria drift. To maintain consistency over time, scorers require periodic retraining.

CONCLUDING COMMENTS

Currently, there appears to be more conviction than empirical support for the use of portfolios. The lack of empirical support can be partly attributed to a rejection of quantitative methods and an empirical orientation; many advocates of portfolio assessment staunchly believe in the superiority of qualitative approaches to assessment. Thus, the published literature created by these advocates consists essentially of testimonials about what is wrong with tests of all

---

12. In addition to helping scorers achieve consistency, training has the added benefit of uncovering scoring criteria that are unclear. Inconsistent scoring following training strongly suggests that the scoring criteria should be revised. Thus, training acts as a field test for scoring criteria and procedures.

kinds (but especially objectively scored tests), rejection of quantitative methods of assessing students, and advice about constructing portfolios. Even given the most optimistic interpretation of the validity of portfolio assessment, we believe that the current literature provides an insufficient basis for acceptance of portfolio assessment on any basis other than experimental. More pessimistically, we concur with Siegler's (1989, p. 15) observation that ". . . if cognitive assessment techniques contain biases that jeopardize the validity of their outcomes, the time does not seem ripe to advocate their use in classrooms." At this time, portfolios offer great research opportunities. Yet, educators must also remember the requirements of the Buckley Amendment (see Chapter 3), which mandates informed consent before students can participate in research. We conclude with Dwyer's (1993) observation about assessment:

> It is the unfortunate tendency, in education as well as in other complex systems, for bad practice to drive out good. This tendency means that for innovative as well as traditional assessment systems, we must anticipate ways in which the system is likely to be debased. Safeguards against bad practice, to the extent that such practices can be reasonably anticipated, must be designed into the assessment system. Also implied is an obligation, as part of on-going validation, to ensure the integrity of the system. (p. 287)

SUMMARY

Interest in portfolio assessment stems from general concern about the validity and utility of norm-referenced achievement tests, the potential negative effects that standardized tests may have on learning, dissatisfaction in some circles with objective appraisal, and the belief that reform in the area of assessment can drive or support broader efforts in educational reform. Six elements define portfolio assessment: targeting valued outcomes for assessment, using tasks that mirror the work in the real world, encouraging cooperation among learners and between teacher and student, using multiple dimensions to evaluate student work, encouraging student reflection, and integrating assessment and instruction. Depending on its purpose, the contents of a portfolio can vary considerably. Despite an initial surge in interest in the use of portfolios, several concerns and limitations have not been systematically addressed: criteria for including work in a student's portfolio, the nature of student participation in content selection, ensuring a sufficient amount of content generated by a student to reach valid decisions, and how portfolio assessment can be made more reliable with consistency of scoring and breadth of sampling of student performances. In addition, there are concerns about biased scoring, instructional utility, and efficiency. Portfolio assessment will remain difficult and expensive for schools, and those who wish to pursue this alternative should give serious attention to how portfolios are assembled and evaluated. Objectivity, less complexity, and comparability are the keys to better practice.

STUDY QUESTIONS

1. Why is interscorer agreement important in portfolio assessment?
2. How might a scoring rubric be developed to increase objective scoring of portfolios?
3. How might portfolios be used with students with disabilities to determine eligibility for special educational services?

ADDITIONAL READING

Madaus, G. (1993). A national testing system: Manna from above? A historical/technological perspective. *Educational Assessment, 1,* 9–26.

Nuttall, D. (1992). Performance assessment: The message from England. *Educational Leadership, 49* (8), 54–57.

Wiggins, G. (1989). A true test: Toward more authentic and equitable assessment. *Phi Delta Kappan*, May, 703–713.

Chapter 13

Assessing Instructional Ecology

S tudent assessment cannot be considered complete without an assessment of the student's instructional needs in the context of the classroom. This observation seems so obvious that few would disagree with it. Yet, in practice, most psychoeducational decisions for a student are made without careful, systematic analysis of the instructional ecology. In this chapter, we review systematic assessment of instructional environments. It is important to assess instructional environments because the quickest, most direct way to change student performance and outcomes is to modify or adapt the environment in which students are taught. As early as 1963, Ogden Lindsley introduced the concept of *prosthetic environments*—environments for maximizing the behavioral efficiency of children with disabilities who show deficits when forced to behave in average environments. He described procedures for modifying the environment to improve student performance. Before teachers or assessors can modify instructional environments, however, they need to know a lot about the nature of the environments in which students are being taught.

In this chapter, we first consider instructional ecology and the kinds of factors that are related to instructional outcomes and then describe ways to gather data on (assess the presence or absence of) those factors.

WHAT IS THE INSTRUCTIONAL ECOLOGY?

Ecology is the term we use to refer to mutual relations between organisms and their environments. When we talk about *instructional ecology,* we are referring to the relationships between students and their instructional environments. Students' behavior and academic performance are influenced by the environment in which they are taught. Each student brings to instructional settings a set of individual characteristics and a learning history. And each student responds differently to teachers' instructional efforts. There is a reciprocal relationship between students and instructional environments, and those who assess the instructional ecology are interested in that relationship.

The product of schooling (what students learn, or *outcomes*) is a function of (1) the content goals of the school, as expressed in scheduling and implementation of instruction, and (2) the instructional procedures employed by teachers, as expressed in terms of their success in managing students' responses to academic tasks (Greenwood, Carta, Kamps & Arreaga-Mayer, 1990). Those who engage in assessments of instructional environments evaluate, among other things, classroom structures; the amont of time allocated to instruction; the amount of time students are actively engaged in responding to instruction; the ways in which instructions are given for school tasks; the pacing of instruction; and the ways in which teachers use information on student performance to change or adapt instruction.

The Importance of Home Support for Learning

Instructional outcomes are a function of an interaction between individuals and instructional ecologies. But the nature of this interaction is, in part, determined by the extent to which there is home support for the learning that occurs in school. Home and family factors contribute to effective instructional environments. Outcomes are better when there is a strong collaborative relationship between homes and schools. When parents support teachers (and teachers support parents), supplement instruction in classrooms, and provide their children with an educative environment, outcomes improve. Those who assess instructional ecologies have devised procedures for systematic assessment of home support for learning.

FACTORS THAT CONTRIBUTE TO ACADEMIC AND BEHAVIORAL PROBLEMS IN SCHOOL

When educators are asked to indicate why students experience difficulty and fail in school, they give four categories of causes. (Of course, educators also attribute success in school to these same four factors.) Most often, educators argue that school difficulties are caused by deficits, disorders, dysfunctions, or disabilities suffered by the student—for example the child is brain-injured, mentally retarded, blind, emotionally disturbed, or has a learning disability. The second factor to which school learning problems are attributed is home and family problems. Educators contend that students who experience difficulty in school come from dysfunctional families, families in which there is little or no discipline, and home settings in which there is not an educative environment. The third factor to which school problems are attributed is lack of effective instruction. Those who espouse this view argue that we know a great deal about the kinds of instructional practices that enhance student outcomes. When these factors are not present, or are not present in ways that they should be, students experience academic and behavioral problems. Finally, it is contended that some of the difficulties that students experience in school are due to the ways schools are organized, ways that just do not make sense for some students. In this chapter, our focus is on the third and fourth factors for success or failure. We consider ways in which effective instruction and school organizational factors contribute to school outcomes.

In the first part of this chapter, we review factors that are related to instructional results for students, and in the sections that follow, we review current practice in ecobehavioral assessment and assessment of instructional environments.

Carroll's Model of School Learning

More than thirty years ago, John Carroll (1963) proposed a model of school learning that is the basis for most models of learning applied in schools today. Carroll's model is shown in Figure 13.1. According to Carroll, the amount a student learns is a function of the amount of time the student actually spends learning divided by the amount of time the student needs to learn what is being taught. The amount of time spent learning is influenced by *opportunity*, which represents the time officially scheduled for learning and the time allocated by teachers and instructional programs, and *perseverance*, which represents the amount of time the student is willing to engage actively in learning, particularly when the task becomes more difficult and the student may be facing failure. Carroll posited that time needed to learn is dependent upon the student's aptitude and ability to understand instruction and on the quality of instruction.

FIGURE 13.1   **Carroll's Model of School Learning**

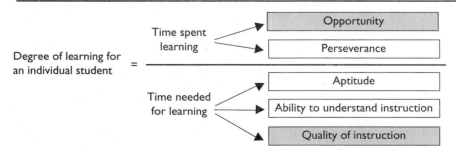

Aptitude is defined by Carroll as the amount of time needed to learn a task under optimal conditions. Carroll talks about aptitude as being task-specific and speaks of students' "aptitude for learning this task"(Carroll, 1985, 63). *Ability to understand instruction* is seen as a function of the student's general intelligence and how adequately tasks are explained. *Quality of instruction* within Carroll's model is a function of the nature, objectives, content, and hierarchical structure of teacher-provided instruction and instructional materials. Quality of instruction varies as a function of the clarity of the task requirements, adequacy of task presentation and of sequencing and pacing, and the degree to which the learner's unique needs have been considered during the instructional presentation. In Figure 13.1 we have shaded "opportunity" and "quality of instruction," as these are the factors we consider in detail in this chapter.

Walberg's Meta-Analytic Research

Walberg (1984) reported the results of a quantitative synthesis of the results of more than 3,000 studies of factors that influence student educational outcomes. He identified three causal influences:

- Aptitude (ability, development, and motivation to learn)
- Instruction (quality of the instructional experience and amount of student engagement in it)
- Environment (home, classroom peers, and television)

Note that the factors that Walberg concluded are important to student learning outcomes parallel those that Carroll argued were important, with one exception. Walberg concluded that it is important that there be home support for learning in school.

Ysseldyke and Christenson Literature Review

Ysseldyke and Christenson (1987a) conducted a review of the literature on effective instruction. They identified student characteristics that were said or shown to be related to student outcomes. They also identified environmental factors (school district conditions, within-school conditions, and general family characteristics) and instructional factors related to instructional outcomes. The Ysseldyke and Christenson review served as the foundation for the development of the Algozzine-Ysseldyke Model of Effective Instruction. Algozzine and Ysseldyke (1992) identified four components of effective instruction (planning, managing, delivering, and evaluating), the major principles of effective instruction for each component, and several strategies for putting principles into practice in classrooms. The Algozzine-Ysseldyke Model of Effective Instruction is shown in Figure 13.2. Whether teachers instruct students who are gifted, nondisabled, mildly disabled, or severely disabled, teachers must plan, manage, deliver, and evaluate instruction.

Planning Instruction

Effective instruction does not occur by chance. It must be planned. Instructional outcomes are enhanced by effective *instructional planning* for individual students. If all students in a class were at the same instructional level and if the goals and objectives of schooling were clearly defined and the same for all students, then instruction would consist of doing the same things with all students, being certain to do them in the right order and at the right time. But all students are not alike, and the goals and objectives of instruction are not the same for all students. Schools are becoming increasingly diverse environments each year. This is why instructional planning is such an important part of teaching and assessment.

Outcomes are enhanced when teaching goals and teacher expectations for student performance and success are stated clearly and are understood by the student. Those who plan instruction must decide what to teach and how to teach, and they must communicate realistic expectations to individual learners.

Deciding What to Teach   We know from the literature on effective instruction that learning outcomes are better when instruction is matched appropriately to the level of skill development of the learner. We can check on a school's performance in this area by looking at the extent to which school personnel have accurately diagnosed learner strengths and weaknesses, carefully considered the kinds of skills taught in the curriculum, and matched the student to the content of instruction at the right level. You probably have experienced situations in which instruction was too easy or too difficult for you. Outcomes are diminished when this is the case.

Deciding How to Teach   Decisions must also be made about how to teach. It is difficult to know ahead of time the kinds of instructional practices that will be effective with individual students. Rather, teachers experiment with alternative teaching approaches until they identify the combination of approaches that works best in moving students toward instructional goals. Educators can assess the extent to which there are clear instructional goals for individual students.

Communicating Realistic Expectations   The third principle of effective instructional planning is that results are enhanced when realistic expectations are communicated to students. Effective teachers identify gaps between a student's actual and expected levels of performance. They use the information they obtain to set instructional goals and objectives that are realistic—neither too low nor too high. And the goals and expectations must be communicated clearly to the

FIGURE 13.2   **The Algozzine-Ysseldyke Model of Effective Instruction**

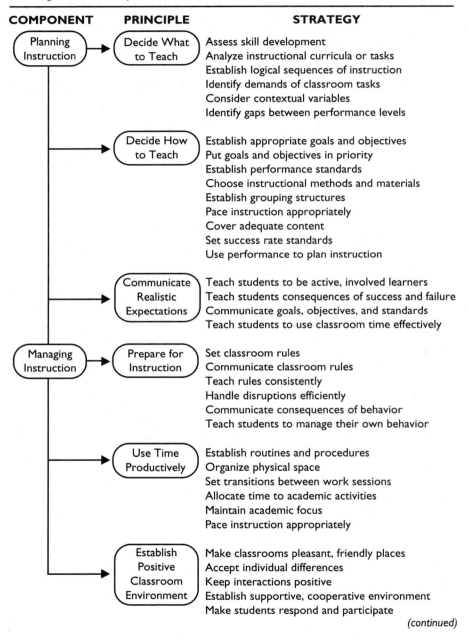

COMPONENT	PRINCIPLE	STRATEGY
Planning Instruction	Decide What to Teach	Assess skill development Analyze instructional curricula or tasks Establish logical sequences of instruction Identify demands of classroom tasks Consider contextual variables Identify gaps between performance levels
	Decide How to Teach	Establish appropriate goals and objectives Put goals and objectives in priority Establish performance standards Choose instructional methods and materials Establish grouping structures Pace instruction appropriately Cover adequate content Set success rate standards Use performance to plan instruction
	Communicate Realistic Expectations	Teach students to be active, involved learners Teach students consequences of success and failure Communicate goals, objectives, and standards Teach students to use classroom time effectively
Managing Instruction	Prepare for Instruction	Set classroom rules Communicate classroom rules Teach rules consistently Handle disruptions efficiently Communicate consequences of behavior Teach students to manage their own behavior
	Use Time Productively	Establish routines and procedures Organize physical space Set transitions between work sessions Allocate time to academic activities Maintain academic focus Pace instruction appropriately
	Establish Positive Classroom Environment	Make classrooms pleasant, friendly places Accept individual differences Keep interactions positive Establish supportive, cooperative environment Make students respond and participate

(continued)

FIGURE 13.2   **(continued)**

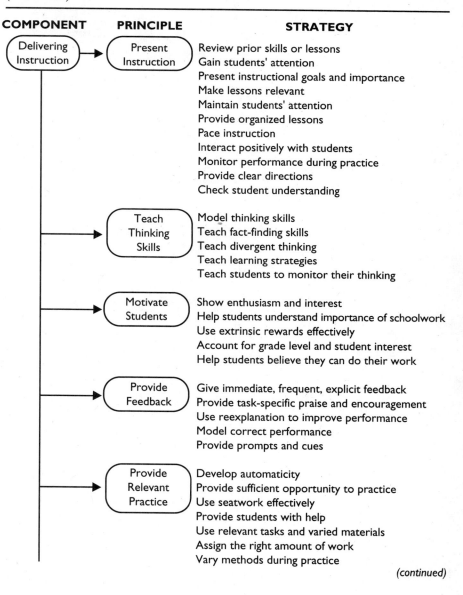

COMPONENT	**PRINCIPLE**	**STRATEGY**
Delivering Instruction	Present Instruction	Review prior skills or lessons Gain students' attention Present instructional goals and importance Make lessons relevant Maintain students' attention Provide organized lessons Pace instruction Interact positively with students Monitor performance during practice Provide clear directions Check student understanding
	Teach Thinking Skills	Model thinking skills Teach fact-finding skills Teach divergent thinking Teach learning strategies Teach students to monitor their thinking
	Motivate Students	Show enthusiasm and interest Help students understand importance of schoolwork Use extrinsic rewards effectively Account for grade level and student interest Help students believe they can do their work
	Provide Feedback	Give immediate, frequent, explicit feedback Provide task-specific praise and encouragement Use reexplanation to improve performance Model correct performance Provide prompts and cues
	Provide Relevant Practice	Develop automaticity Provide sufficient opportunity to practice Use seatwork effectively Provide students with help Use relevant tasks and varied materials Assign the right amount of work Vary methods during practice

(continued)

FIGURE 13.2   **The Algozzine-Ysseldyke Model of Effective Instruction (continued)**

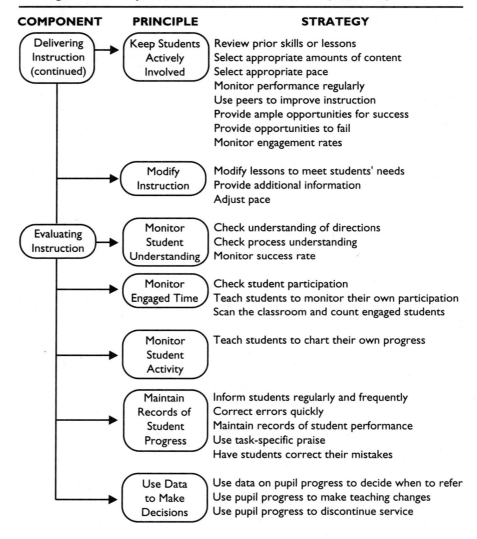

student. Outcomes are enhanced when students understand what they are expected to do. Note that failure to communicate goals and expectations can occur either because the teacher fails to communicate clearly or because the child does not understand what is communicated.

It is essential that those who assess students also engage in assessment of the extent to which instruction is planned appropriately for the student and matched to the student's level of skill development.

Managing Instruction

Discipline is consistently identified as a concern on public and professional opinion polls about education. There are two things that are necessary for effectively managed instruction: efficiency and warmth. Instructional outcomes for students are enhanced when classrooms are managed efficiently and when there is a sense of positiveness in the school environment. When we evaluate the extent to which effective instruction is occurring for individual students, we assess classroom management. Principles of effective classroom management include preparing for effective instruction, using time effectively, and establishing a positive classroom environment. Appropriate discipline practices emerge when these principles are put into practice.

Preparing for Effective Instruction   Effective teachers establish classroom rules and communicate them early in the school year. They teach individual students the consequences of following and not following their rules, and they handle rule infractions and other disruptions as quickly as possible after they occur. When this does not happen for individual students, then outcomes are diminished. In evaluating the instructional ecology, assessors take into account the extent to which rules have been communicated to the individual student, whether the student knows and understands the rules, and whether rule infractions by the student are handled immediately.

Using Time Effectively   Students achieve better instructional outcomes when they make effective use of their time. Teachers can modify the instructional environment to help students make good use of their time by establishing routines (e.g., students know what to do when they are finished with their work), organizing physical space so that students are placed in settings that limit distractions, keeping students focused on academic work, pacing instruction appropriately, and making sure that students understand task directions.

Establishing a Positive Classroom Environment   Students are more motivated to learn in environments in which they feel accepted. Assessors should take into account whether the classrooms in which students find themselves accept individual differences and are supportive. They should also look at the extent to which the student's teachers interact positively with him or her.

Delivering Instruction

Teaching is systematic presentation of content necessary for mastery of the subject matter being taught. Good teaching involves carefully planned delivery of instruction focused on specific academic tasks and content areas. Instructional delivery is a complex process involving appropriate instructional matches, the clear presentation of lessons while following specific instructional procedures, the allocation of sufficient time to instruction of individual learners, and sufficient opportunity for students to respond.

Matching Instruction to the Level of the Learner   The diversity of students in today's classrooms presents special challenges for teachers. The range of skill development in specific content areas between the students in a classroom can be as great as three years for second-grade students and six years for seventh-grade students. Assessors need to take into account the extent to which the instruction that individual students receive is matched appropriately to their level of skill development. If instruction is pitched too high or too low, then steps can be taken to fine-tune it to the level of the learner.

Presenting Lessons Clearly and Using Specific Instructional Procedures   Instructional outcomes for individual students are enhanced when the lessons are made relevant to their backgrounds and teachers include a review of previously learned material. Assessors should consider the extent to which the procedures used to present information are effective with the individual student, whether the student understands what he or she is to do, and whether the student spends sufficient time in relevant practice. They should also consider the extent to which the student attends to instruction, receives specific feedback on performance, and is taught until mastery of content.

Giving Students Opportunity to Respond   Outcomes are better for individual students when they get ample opportunity to respond to appropriate content and materials. Assessors must consider the extent to which students are actively involved in instruction and whether they are responding to instruction often enough to be expected to profit from it.

Evaluating Instruction

Evaluation is an important part of teaching. It is the means by which teachers decide whether the approach they are using is effective with individual students. Assessors must take into account the extent to which evaluation data are collected on students and used to make changes in instructional programs. They do so by considering the extent to which teachers monitor pupil performance and do so directly and frequently. Knowing how students are doing enables teachers (or assessors) to make changes in the ways that the students are being taught or in the content of instruction.

Monitoring Student Performance   Outcomes are better for individual students when their performance is monitored and used to make changes in instruction. Assessors need to look at how student understanding, academic engaged time, and progress are monitored. They also need to look at how the data are used to make instructional decisions or decisions to refer students for further assessment.

Direct and Frequent Measurement   It is also important to monitor student performance directly and frequently. Assessors need to consider the directness and frequency with which pupil progress and performance are monitored, as well as the directness and frequency with which the data are used to make instructional decisions.

In this chapter, we consider two approaches to gathering data on students' instructional environments or ecologies: ecobehavioral assessment and the Instructional Environment System–II. Ecobehavioral assessment is used to gather data on how students spend their time in school, looking specifically at opportunity to learn and academic engaged time. The Instructional Environment System–II, a methodology developed by Ysseldyke and Christenson (1993), is used to systematically analyze the qualitative nature of instruction that students receive in classroom and home environments.

ECOBEHAVIORAL ASSESSMENT

The term *ecobehavioral assessment* is used in educational assessment to describe observations of functional relationships (or interactions) between student behavior and its ecological contexts. The approach is used to identify interactions among student behavior, teacher behavior, time allocated to instruction, physical grouping structures, types of tasks being used, and instructional content. Ecobehavioral assessment thus enables educators to identify natural instructional conditions that are associated with academic success, behavioral competence, or challenging behaviors. Increasingly, ecobehavioral assessment is being used to develop and validate specific instructional procedures, develop a number of approaches to the reduction of challenging behaviors, improve understanding of the components of effective instruction including the identification of instructional risk factors, and provide a better understanding of how the quality of implementation affects student outcomes (Greenwood, Carta & Atwater, 1991). Ecobehavioral assessment is one way to gather data on the opportunity to learn, an important component of Carroll's Model of School Learning and of the Algozzine-Ysseldyke Model of Effective Instruction.

Ecobehavioral assessment approaches have been developed by Charles Greenwood, Judith Carta, Joe Delquadri, and their colleagues at the Juniper Gardens Children's Project in Kansas City, Kansas. The first version of the system was developed by Greenwood, Delquadri, and Hall (1978) and was called the Code for Instructional Structure and Student Academic Response (abbreviated as CISSAR). In the original system, nineteen student codes that could be combined into three composite variables were defined. The current CISSAR taxonomy is shown in Figure 13.3. Assessors can categorize ecobehavioral events into student behaviors, teacher behaviors, and ecology. CISSAR uses momentary time sampling (10-second intervals) over the entire school day. Observers record the ecology (specific activity, task used to control instruction, and

FIGURE 13.3   **CISSAR Taxonomy**

BEHAVIOR

STUDENT BEHAVIORS   TEACHER BEHAVIORS

Academic Responses	Task Management	Competing Responses	Teacher Position	Teacher Behavior
1. Writing	1. AttndTask	1. Disrupt	1. InFront	1. NoResp
2. PlayAca	2. RaiseHnd	2. PlayInapp	2. AtDesk	2. Teaching
3. ReadAloud	3. LookMtrls	3. TaskInapp	3. AmongStud	3. OtherTalk
4. RdSilent	4. Moves	4. TalkInapp	4. Side	4. Approval
5. TalkAca	5. PlayApp	5. LocInapp	5. Back	5. Disapprov
6. AnsAcaQst		6. LookArnd	6. Out	
7. AskAcaQst		7. Self-Stim		

ECOLOGY

Activity	Task	Structure
1. Reading	1. Readers	1. EntirGrp
2. Math	2. Workbooks	2. SmallGrp
3. Spelling	3. Worksheet	3. Indiv
4. Hndwrtng	4. Paper&Pen	
5. Language	5. LstnLect	
6. Science	6. OthMedia	
7. SocStud	7. Tch/StDis	
8. Arts/Crft	8. Fetch/Put	
9. FreeTime		
10. BusMgmnt		
11. Transit		
12. Cn'tTell		

class structure), teacher behavior (teacher position and behavior), and student behavior (academic responses, competing responses, and task management responses). After observational data have been recorded, the assessor can determine the frequency of occurrence of specific behaviors and the interactions among behaviors and environmental stimuli.

Two derivatives of CISSAR have been developed over the past ten to twelve years. One of these, Ecobehavioral System for Complex Assessments of Preschool Environments (ESCAPE), was developed for use with preschool children. The other, the mainstream version of CISSAR (MS-CISSAR), was designed to be used in observations of students with disabilities in regular classes. The MS-CISSAR taxonomy is shown in Figure 13.4. The three derivative systems (CISSAR, ESCAPE, and MS-CISSAR) have been combined in a new software program, EcoBehavioral Assessment System Software (EBASS).

FIGURE 13.4   **MS-CISSAR Taxonomy**

BEHAVIOR

STUDENT BEHAVIORS

Academic Responses	Task Management	Competing Responses
1. Writing	1. RaiseHnd	1. Agression
2. TskPartic	2. PlayAppro	2. Disrupt
3. ReadAloud	3. ManipMtl	3. TalkInapp
4. RdSilent	4. Move	4. LookArnd
5. TalkAca	5. TalkMgmnt	5. NonComply
6. NoAcaRsp	6. Attention	6. Self-Stim
	7. NoMgmnt	7. SelfAbuse
		8. NoInappro

TEACHER BEHAVIORS

Teacher Definition	Teacher Behavior	Teacher Approval	Teacher Focus	Teacher Position
1. Regular	1. QuestAca	1. Approval	1. Target	1. InFront
2. SpecialEd	2. QuestMgmt	2. DisApprov	2. Targt+Oth	2. AtDesk
3. Aide/Para	3. QstDscpln	3. Neither	3. NoOne	3. OutOfRoom
4. StudntTch	4. CmndAca		4. Other	4. Side
5. Volunteer	5. CmndMgmnt			5. Back
6. RelatdSrv	6. CmdDscpln			
7. Substitut	7. TalkAca			
8. PeerTutor	8. TalkMgmnt			
9. NoStaff	9. TalkDscpln			
	10. TlkNonAca			
	11. NonVbPrmt			
	12. Attention			
	13. ReadAloud			
	14. Sing			
	15. NoRespons			

ECOLOGY

Setting	Activity	Task	Physical Arrangement	Instructional Grouping
1. ReglarCls	1. Reading	1. Readers	1. EntirGrp	1. WholeClss
2. SpecialEd	2. Math	2. Workbooks	2. DivideGrp	2. SmallGrp
3. ResrceRm	3. Spelling	3. Worksheet	3. Individual	3. OneOnOne
4. Chapt1Lab	4. Hndwrtng	4. Paper&Pen		4. Indepndnt
5. Library	5. Language	5. LstnLect		5. NoInstrct
6. MusicRm	6. Science	6. OthMedia		
7. ArtRoom	7. SocStud	7. Discussn		
8. TherapyRm	8. PreVocat	8. Fetch/Put		
9. Hall	9. GrssMotor	9. NoTask		
10. Auditori	10. DailyLiv			
11. Other	11. Self-Care			
	12. Arts/Crft			
	13. FreeTime			
	14. BusMgmnt			
	15. Transit			
	16. Music			
	17. TimeOut			
	18. NoActvty			
	19. Cn'tTell			
	20. Other			

Ecobehavioral Assessment System Software (EBASS)

EBASS (Greenwood & Carta, 1994) is an MS-DOS software system that enables school personnel to conduct systematic classroom observational assessments using laptop, notebook, or hand-held computers with at least one 720K floppy drive. The EBASS package contains an assessment manual, technical guide, computer software, and videotapes (to illustrate use of the system).

EBASS was designed specifically for school psychologists, but it may be used by other professionals responsible for assessment, teacher training, and program evaluation activities, including instructional staff in regular and special education. Typical applications include assessments of individual students for the purpose of planning instructional interventions, evaluation of individual pupil progress, or evaluation of educational programs. Computerization allows computer-assisted training in instrument use, calibration of reliability checks, instrument modification (each of the three measures can be downsized into shorter measures), simple and complex data analyses, caseload management, and data base capabilities.

Methodology

The classroom observer chooses whichever observational instrument is appropriate (ESCAPE, CISSAR, or MS-CISSAR) and uses a laptop or notebook computer to go into classrooms and gather data in 10-second intervals. The training package available with EBASS is used to teach observers what to look for and how to code behaviors. The training system is self-instructional and includes short lessons, classroom video examples, computer exercises with feedback, and observational practice. It takes about 8 to 10 hours to learn any of the three instruments, and additional time is needed for data collection practice.

Reports

Reports from an observation may be in one of two basic forms: percentage occurrence for all events or probabilities of student behavior given specific arrangements of the classroom ecology. These latter probabilities are called conditional probabilities. The computer can print reports based on a single observation, on observations sequenced by time of observation, and on observations pooled over time. The professional who uses EBASS is able to give the teacher information on academic engaged time, the occurrence of inappropriate behavior, and the occurrence of task management responses. The strength of EBASS is that it provides very precise information on the frequency of occurrence of specific kinds of behaviors (e.g., writing, playing inappropriately, waiting, and disruptive behavior) *and* on the kinds of contextual factors associated with the occurrence of each of the behaviors. Examples of EBASS reports are shown in Figures 13.5 and 13.6. Figure 13.5 illustrates the academic-response profile for an individual student. The student was observed for an entire day. He spent

FIGURE 13.5   **EBASS Academic Response Profile**

```
----------------------------------------------------------------
CODES            FREQ        PERCENTAGE OCCURRENCE
-----------------------------------------0--20--40--60--80--100
Writing            37        11.94%    |X
TskPartic          11         3.55%    |
ReadAloud          12         3.87%    |
RdSilent           64        20.65%    |XXX
TalkAca            29         9.35%    |X
----------------------------------------------------------------
AcaRspComp        154        53.65%    |XXXXXXXX
NoAcaRsp          153        49.35%    |XXXXXXXX
Missing             4         1.29%    |
----------------------------------------------------------------
TOTAL             310       100.00%
----------------------------------------------------------------
Press ENTER to continue.
```

11.94 percent of the day writing, 20.65 percent of the day reading silently, and so forth. The profile also shows that this student was responding to academic content 53.65 percent of the school day and making no academic response 49.35 percent of the day. Figure 13.6 (page 282) shows a probability analysis for writing behavior and illustrates that there are important relationships between students' writing behavior and environmental conditions. The probability of writing was .01 when readers were used versus .27 when paper-and-pencil tasks were used versus .04 during discussion; this is in comparison to an unconditional probability of .15. The assessor would be able to tell the teacher that the probability of writing behavior decreases significantly when readers are used and increases significantly when paper-and-pencil tasks are used during reading. Discussion also reduces the probability of a writing response. The probability of outcome behaviors (writing) given context variables is shown in the bottom half of Figure 13.6.

EBASS may also be used in making normative peer comparisons—comparisons of the behaviors of an individual student to the average of a peer group. Figure 13.7 (page 283) illustrates a normative peer comparison. It shows that the target student was looking around during twelve intervals (3.88 percent of the day) and talking inappropriately during eight intervals (2.59 percent of the day). The student's peers look around 3.29 percent of the time and talk inappropriately only .33 percent of the time. The difference in competing student and peer responses is also shown, and the magnitude of the differences has been computed. When D-STAT = 0, the student's performance is exactly like that of his or her peers. The larger D-STAT, the more different the student is in comparison to the peer group. Normative peer comparison data are very useful in making eligibility or exceptionality decisions.

FIGURE 13.6   **EBASS Probability Analysis of Ecobehavioral Relations**

```
--------<ECOLOGICAL MODEL>----------|----<OUTCOME Behavior>---

        ACTIVITY AND TASK                ACADEMIC RESPONDING

                                      OUTCOME BEHAVIORS:Writing
------------------------------------|-------------------------
--<ECOLOGICAL MODEL>---|---<VALUES>          COND         SIGNIFI-
(at least 10% of data)  FREQ PCT   FREQ PROB Z-SCORE CANCE
---------------------- ---- ---    ---- ---- -------- ------
Writing+Readers          75   30     1  0.01 -2.664    .01
Writing+Paper/Pen        71   29    19  0.27  2.295    .05
Writing+Discussn         56   22     2  0.04 -1.980    .05
Spelling+Paper/Pen       47   19    15  0.32  2.782    .01
------------------------------------|-------------------------
                                      UNCONDITIONAL
                                      PROBABILITY
                                    |-------------------------
TOTAL SEQUENCES USED    249   80    37  0.15
TOTAL SEQUENCES RECORDED 310
------------------------------------|-------------------------
Press ENTER to continue.
```

```
                    Probability of Outcome Behaviors
ECOLOGICAL MODEL     0       0.1      0.2      0.3      0.4
     Values         |--------|--------|--------|--------|-

Writing+Readers    0.01XXXXXXXXXXXXX|
Writing+Paper/Pen                   |XXXXXXXXXXXXX0.27
Writing+Discussn   0.04XXXXXXXXXX|
Spelling+Paper/Pen                  |XXXXXXXXXXXXXXXXX0.32
                                    |
                                  0.15
                    (base probability level)
Press ENTER to continue.
```

FIGURE 13.7   **EBASS Normative Peer Comparison**

```
COMPETING RESPONSE: (Descriptive Comparison)
------------------------------------------------------------------
CODES      TARGET PROFILE   INDEX PROFILE  DISCREPANCY PROFILE
--------|---------------|---------------|--------------------
           Freq  Percent   Freq  Percent    Diff  DiffSq
           ----  -------   ----  -------     ----  ------
Agression   0     0.00      0     0.00       0.00  0.00
Disrupt     0     0.00      0     0.00       0.00  0.00
TalkInapp   8     2.59      1     0.33       2.26  5.11
LookArnd   12     3.88     10     3.29       0.59  0.35
NonComply   0     0.00      0     0.00       0.00  0.00
Self-Stim   0     0.00      7     2.30      -2.30  5.30
SelfAbuse   1     0.32      1     0.33      -0.01  0.00
NoInappro 285    92.23    274    90.13       2.10  4.42
Missing     3     0.97     11     3.62      -2.65  7.01
--------|---------------|---------------|--------------------
TOTAL     309            304                 9.9  22.188 SUM
                                                   4.71  D-STAT
------------------------------------------------------------------
Press ENTER to continue.
```

```
COMPETING RESPONSE:(Graphic Display)
------------------------------------------------------------------
CODES      TARGET PROFILE   INDEX PROFILE  DISCREPANCY PROFILE
-----------|--------------|---------------|--------------------
Agression        |              |                   |
Disrupt          |              |                   |
TalkInapp   2.6%|_          0.3%|_          2.3%    |_
LookArnd    3.9%|_          3.3%|_          0.6%    |_
NonComply        |              |                   |
Self-Stim        |          2.3%|_         -2.3%    |
SelfAbuse   0.3%|_          0.3%|_         -0.0%    _|
NoInappro  92.2%|____      90.1%|_____     2.1%    |_
Missing     1.0%|_          3.6%|_         -2.6%    _|
-----------|--------------|---------------|--------------------
TOTAL      100.0% (n=309) 100.0% (n=304)
------------------------------------------------------------------
Press ENTER to continue.
```

ASSESSMENT OF INSTRUCTIONAL ENVIRONMENTS

The Instructional Environment System–II

According to Carroll, the degree of learning achieved by an individual student is a function of time spent learning divided by time needed to learn. An important aspect of time needed to learn is the quality of instruction. We noted earlier that quality of instruction varies according to several factors, including the clarity of task demands, adequacy of task presentation, adequacy of pacing, and the like. The Algozzine-Ysseldyke model of effective instruction includes a number of principles and strategies that, if present, would enhance the likelihood that students would achieve desired outcomes. The Instructional Environment System–II is designed to be used to gather data on the extent to which components of effective instruction are present in a student's instructional environment (home, school, or a combination of both).

In 1987, Ysseldyke and Christenson published TIES (Ysseldyke & Christenson, 1987b), the first comprehensive methodology enabling education professionals to systematically gather data on the extent to which components of effective instruction were present in students' instructional environments at school. In 1993, TIES was updated and expanded as TIES-II. The focus of TIES-II is on the referred student, and the question for the important adults in the referred student's life is "How can the classroom and home environments be manipulated to elicit more appropriate responses from the student?"

Based on the belief that student performance in school is a function of an interaction between the student and the learning (instructional) environment, TIES-II provides a set of observational and interview forms, administration procedures, and an organizational structure that allows educators to both identify and address the instructional needs of individual students. The system is used to help professionals gather essential information on twelve instructional environment components and five home-support-for-learning components. The instructional and home components on which data are collected are listed and defined briefly in Table 13.1 (pages 285–286).

TIES-II is a flexible system that allows professionals to select the data collection tools they will use. Among the tools available for use are an instructional needs form, which is a checklist, and a free-response form to be completed by the teacher, indicating the kinds of things that have been found effective and ineffective with the referred student. The assessor uses an observation form to gather data in the classroom. The student is observed, and the observation form is completed; the student is interviewed, and the student interview form is completed. Similarly, when the teacher is interviewed, the teacher interview form is completed. The observer then uses the instructional environment form to rate the extent to which each of the twelve classroom components is (1) present and (2) im-

TABLE 13.1   Components of the TIES-II

	Component	Definition
Instructional Environment Components	Instructional Match	The student's needs are assessed accurately, and instruction is matched appropriately to the results of the instructional diagnosis.
	Teacher Expectations	There are realistic, yet high expectations for both the amount and the accuracy of work to be completed by the student, and these are communicated clearly to the student.
	Classroom Environment	The classroom management techniques used are effective for this student; there is a positive, supportive classroom atmosphere, and time is used productively.
	Instructional Presentation	Instruction is presented in a clear and effective manner; directions contain sufficient information for this student to understand what kinds of behaviors or skills are to be demonstrated, and the student's understanding is checked.
	Cognitive Emphasis	Thinking skills and learning strategies for completing assignments are communicated explicitly to the student.
	Motivational Strategies	Effective strategies for heightening student interest and student effort are used.
	Relevant Practice	The student is given adequate opportunity to practice with appropriate materials and to achieve a high success rate. Classroom tasks are clearly important to achieving instructional goals.
	Informed Feedback	The student receives relatively immediate and specific information on his or her performance or behavior; when the student makes mistakes, correction is provided.
	Academic Engaged Time	The student is actively engaged in responding to academic content; the teacher monitors the extent to which the student is actively engaged and redirects the student when the student is unengaged.
	Adaptive Instruction	The curriculum is modified within reason to accommodate the student's unique and specific instructional needs.
	Progress Evaluation	There is direct, frequent measurement of the student's progress toward completion of instructional objectives; data on the student's performance and progress are used to plan future instruction.
	Student Understanding	The student demonstrates an accurate understanding of what is to be done in the classroom.

(table continues)

TABLE 13.1 (continued)

Component		Definition
Home-Support-for-Learning Components	Expectations and Attributions	High, realistic expectations about school work are communicated to the child; the value of working hard in school is emphasized.
	Discipline Orientation	There is an authoritative, not permissive or authoritarian, approach to discipline; the child is monitored and supervised by adults.
	Effective Home Environment	The parent-child relationship is generally positive and supportive.
	Parent Participation	There is an educative home environment, and others participate in the child's schooling at home and/or at school.
	Structure for Learning	Organization and daily routines facilitate the completion of school work, and the child's academic learning is supported.

SOURCE: From "Identifying students' instructional needs in the context of classroom and home environments" by J. E. Ysseldyke, S. L. Christenson, and J. F. Kovaleski, *Teaching Exceptional Children, 26,* (1994), 37–41. Copyright 1994 by The Council for Exceptional Children. Reprinted with permission.

portant in the student's instructional environment. A parent interview form is used to gather data on the extent to which each of the five home learning components is present in the student's home environment. After the assessor interviews the parents or receives the completed form from them, he or she completes the home-support-for-learning form. All ratings are qualitative judgments—judgments by a professional of the extent to which the factors are present.

The assessor meets with a team of professionals, including the teacher, to plan an instructional intervention for the student. TIES-II outlines a detailed intervention planning process. The TIES-II manual includes a very extensive review of the literature on effective instruction that served as a basis for identification of the components of effective instruction and the home-support-for-learning components.

SUMMARY

Learning happens when the learning environment is modified to facilitate an appropriate response from the student. Education and psychology have rich traditions of assessing students in order to identify causes of academic and behavioral difficulties and to develop interventions. More recently, the focus has shifted to the belief that the quickest way to close the gap between actual and desired student performance is to apply principles of effective instruction. Doing so requires identification of the extent to which the learner is getting an opportunity to learn and is willing to engage actively in learning, particularly when tasks become very difficult. It also requires identification of the extent to which components of effective instruction are present in a student's instructional environment and components of effective home support for learning are present in the home environment. In this chapter, we reviewed two systems—the EcoBehavioral Assessment System Software (EBASS) and the Instructional Environment System–II (TIES-II).

EBASS is a computerized observational system that is designed to be used to gather very specific information on student behavior in class. TIES-II is a qualitative observation-and-interview system designed to provide more global judgments of the extent to which a student is exposed to effective instruction. Both systems are new ways of taking into account the interactions between students, tasks, and instructional methodologies that determine the extent to which a student achieves desired outcomes. They provide a new way to look at complex interactions among individuals and contextual factors and enable us to identify naturally occurring effective procedures in classrooms.

STUDY QUESTIONS

1. Define "instructional ecology," and describe why it is important to take this into account in assessment.

2. What are the four components of effective instruction? Define each.
3. How might ecobehavioral assessment be used? What kinds of data might be collected, and what kinds of decisions might be made using the data?
4. How might TIES-II be used? What kinds of data might be collected, and what kinds of decisions might be made using the data?

ADDITIONAL READING

Greenwood, C. R. (1992). *Conceptual, methodological and technological advances in classroom observational assessment.* Kansas City, KS: unpublished manuscript.

Greeenwood, C. R., Carta, J. J., & Atwater, J. (1991). Ecobehavioral analysis in the classroom: Review and implications. *Journal of Behavioral Education, 1,* 59–77.

Greenwood, C. R., Carta, J. J., Kamps, D., & Arreaga-Mayer, C. (1990). Ecobehavioral analysis of classroom instruction. In S. R. Schroeder (Ed.), *Ecobehavioral analysis and developmental disabilities: The twenty-first century* (pp. 33–63). New York: Springer-Verlag.

Kamps, D. M., Leonard, B. R., Dugan, E. P., Boland, B., & Greenwood, C. R. (1991). The use of ecobehavioral assessment to identify naturally occurring effective procedures in classrooms serving students with autism and other developmental disabilities. *Journal of Behavioral Education, 1,* 367–397.

Ysseldyke, J. E. & Christenson, S. L. (1993). *The Instructional Environment System–II.* Longmont, CO: Sopris West.

Ysseldyke, J. E., Christenson, S. L. & Kovaleski, J. F. (1994). Identifying students' instructional needs in the context of classroom and home environments. *Teaching Exceptional Children, 26* (3), 37–41.

Chapter 14

Teacher Decision Making

*E*ach regular and special education teacher makes literally hundreds of professional decisions every day. Some decisions affect classroom management whereas others affect instructional management. Some types of decisions occur infrequently, whereas others occur several times each day. In this chapter, we are concerned with the decisions that teachers make about the adequacy and appropriateness of instruction for students who need special assistance, students who are at risk, and students who are exceptional.

The lines of responsibility for students who are exceptional are fluid, and regular teachers are taking increased responsibility for the education of students with disabilities. For example, students with a variety of disabilities are fully included in regular classrooms in some school districts. Nonetheless, we have divided this chapter into three sections that reflect the primary responsibilities of regular and special teachers; collaborative decision making is also discussed. Regular teachers are largely responsible for identifying students with sufficiently severe learning or behavior difficulties to be considered for special education. Special education teachers are largely responsible for providing education for students with disabilities. In mainstream and inclusive settings, regular and special educators share responsibility for both students who are gifted and talented and students who have disabilities.

DECISIONS PRIOR TO REFERRAL

The vast majority of students are presumed to be normal when they begin school; most complete their schooling under the same presumption. However, approximately 40 percent of all students will experience difficulty during their school careers, and approximately 10 to 12 percent of all students who actually enter school will experience sufficient difficulty to be identified as handicapped during their school careers. Most of the students identified as disabled will receive special education services because they need special instruction. Some students with disabilities (e.g., students with certain chronic health impairments) will not need special education but will require special related services that must be provided under Section 504 of the Rehabilitation Act of 1973.

In this portion of the chapter, we deal with those decisions that precede entitlement to special education. Before referring students for possible identification as exceptional, regular educators take several steps, some of which are mandated by state regulations. The first step is to recognize that a problem exists; the remaining steps may vary in sequence by state or district.

Recognition of a Problem

At some point in a student's schooling, regular educators may come to believe that the student has such different academic or behavioral needs that he or she will require special assistance to achieve desired educational outcomes. The threshold of recognition varies from teacher to teacher and may be a function of several factors: teacher skill and experience, class size, availability of alternative materials and curriculum, ability and behavior of other students in the class, and the teacher's tolerance for atypical progress or behavior. Generally, when a student is performing at a rate that is 20 percent to 50 percent of that of other students, a teacher has reason to be concerned.

Academic Needs

A teacher's recognition of academic need is usually triggered in one of two ways. First, the teacher may recognize a student has special academic needs when that student cannot be maintained in the lowest instructional groups in a class—that is, the student becomes an instructional isolate. For example, Mr. Santos may see that Alex is not acquiring skills, information, or processes at a fast enough rate to keep up with even the slowest students in the class. Second, the teacher may recognize that a student has special academic needs when that student performs adequately in most academic areas but has extreme difficulty in one or two important core skills, such as reading. For example, Sammy may be good student in every subject but reading and writing. *Why* a student is having difficulty is seldom clear at this point in the decision-making process. Obviously, not all achievement problems require special education. There are multiple reasons for school failure, and these reasons may often interact with each other.

Ineffective Instruction   Some students make progress under almost any instructional conditions. When students enter a learning situation with emerging skills and a wealth of information, such students merely need the opportunity to continue learning and developing skills. These students will learn in spite of ineffective instructional methodology.

However, many students enter a learning situation with far less developed skills, and much better instruction is required. Without effective instruction, these students are in danger of becoming casualties of the educational system because most students make progress only when they have sufficient opportunity to learn and when the approaches used to teach them are effective. Some of these students may fail to learn because they are given only limited opportunity to learn. This situation can occur in several ways:

- Some students may lack the prerequisites for learning specific content. In such cases, the content to be learned may be too difficult because the student must learn the prerequisites and the new content simultaneously. For example, Mr. Santos may give Alex a reader in which he knows only 70 percent of the words. Alex will be forced to learn the sight vocabulary that he lacks while at the same time trying to comprehend what he is reading. The chances are that he will not comprehend the material because there are too many unknown words (Salvia & Hughes, 1990).
- The school curriculum may be so cluttered with special events and extras that insufficient time can be devoted to core content areas. Students who need more extensive and intensive instruction in order to learn may suffer from the discrepancy between the amount of instruction (or time) they need and the time allocated to teaching them.
- The teacher may lack the skills to teach specific subject matter. For example, in some rural areas it may not be possible to attract physics teachers, so the biology teacher may have to teach the course and stay one or two lectures ahead of the students.
- A teacher may lack sufficient pedagogical knowledge to teach students who are not independent learners. Although there is a wealth of information about teaching methods that promote student learning (see Stevens & Rosenshine, 1981), this information is not as widely known to teachers and supervisors as one would hope. Thus, some educators may not know how to present new material, structure learning opportunities, provide opportunities for guided and independent practice, or give effective feedback. And, given the number of families in which all adults work, there is less opportunity for parents to provide supplementary instruction at home to overcome faulty instruction in school.
- A teacher may be committed to ineffective instructional methods. A considerable amount of effort has gone into the empirical evaluation of various instructional approaches. Yet much of this research fails to find its way into the classroom. For example, a number of school districts have enthusiastically adopted a whole-language approach to reading because of its philosophical appeal. Yet the empirical research comparing whole-language with other approaches to reading instruction suggests no overwhelming benefit. Indeed, basal approaches to reading appear to have a better effect on reading comprehension than whole-language approaches; basal approaches also appear more effective than whole-language approaches with disadvantaged students (Stahl & Miller, 1989).

Before investing in expensive and extensive assessment of the student, it is almost always preferable to examine the effectiveness of the curriculum and instruction. It is impossible to be certain whether a student's difficulties are the result of ineffective instruction without modifying teaching methods or curriculum and then observing the effects of the modifications. If a student begins to make better progress with modified instruction, the chances are that ineffective instruction was the source of the difficulty. A few students make little progress in spite of systematic application of sound instructional principles shown to be generally effective. These are the students who require special instruction.

Individual Differences   Even the best general teaching methods and curricula do not work well with every student. Although the research on how different individual characteristics interact with learning is far from clear, there is some reason to believe that students have different learning styles that cause teaching methods to be differentially effective (Cronbach & Snow, 1977). For example, students with relatively high IQs tend to learn mathematics somewhat better when discovery approaches are used, although more direct methods are equally effective with students with lower IQs (see Maynard & Strickland, 1969). As another example, some students appear to learn rote material easily but have difficulty with more conceptual material (see Jensen, 1974). Similarly, whereas some students may find particular content interesting and therefore are likely to be intrinsically motivated to learn, other students may find the same content boring.

Cultural differences also affect academic learning. For example, reading is an interactive process in which an author's writing is interpreted on the basis of a reader's experience and knowledge. To the extent that students from different cultures have different experiences, their comprehension of some written materials may differ. Thus, students from different cultural groups may have different understandings of, for example, "all men are created equal." Similarly, cultural norms for instructional dialogues between teacher and student may vary, especially when the teacher and student are of different sexes. Boys and girls may be raised differently, with different expectations, in some cultures. Thus, it may be culturally appropriate for women and girls to be reticent in their responses to male teachers. Similarly, teachers may feel ill-equipped to teach students from different cultures. For example, teachers might be hesitant to discipline students from another culture, or teachers may not have culturally relevant examples to illustrate concepts and ideas.

Thus, generally effective instruction may be ill-suited to a particular student. It is impossible to be certain whether a student's difficulties are the result of different learning styles, inadequate motivation, or cultural differences without modifying instruction and observing the effect of the modifications. If a student begins to make better progress with modified instruction, the reasons for the initial difficulties are not particularly important. Because antecedents cannot always be inferred from consequences, we cannot assume that the teacher has isolated the source of the difficulty.

Behavioral Needs

Regular educators may also come to believe that a student has such different behavioral needs that the student will require special assistance to achieve desired educational outcomes. As discussed in Chapter 10, any behavior that falls outside the range typically expected—too much or too little compliance, too much or too little assertiveness, too much or too little activity, and so forth—could be problematic in and of itself. In other cases, a behavior may be problematic because it interferes with learning. For example, failure to pay attention, sleeping in class, or being unable to work cooperatively could all impede learning. As is true with academic learning problems, *why* a student is having difficulty may be unclear. The problem may lie in the teacher's inability to manage classroom behavior, the student's behavior or a combination of both.

Ineffective Classroom Management   A teacher may lack sufficient knowledge, skill, or willingness to structure and manage a classroom effectively. Many students come to school with well-developed interpersonal and intrapersonal skills, and such students are well-behaved and easily directed or coached in almost any setting. Other students enter the classroom with far less developed skills. For these students, teachers need much better management skills. In classrooms in which teachers lack these skills, the behavior of such students may interfere with their own learning and the learning of their peers. Thus, teachers must know how to manage classroom behavior and be willing to do so. Classroom management is one of the more emotional topics in education, and often teachers' personal values and beliefs affect their willingness to control their classrooms. Although there has been extensive empirical support demonstrating the effectiveness of various management techniques for some time (see Alberto & Troutman, 1990; Bleckman, 1985; O'Leary & O'Leary, 1972), these techniques may be rejected by some teachers on philosophical grounds. Occasionally, teachers may know how to manage behavior and be willing to do so generally but unwilling to deal with specific students for some reason. For example, some Anglo teachers may be hesitant to discipline minority students.

Individual Differences   Even when teachers use generally effective management strategies, they may be unable to control some students effectively. For example, some students may be difficult to manage because they have never had to control their behavior before, because they reject women as authority figures, or because they seek any kind of attention, positive or negative. Other students may not get enough sleep or nutritious food to be alert and ready to participate and learn in school.

Thus, generally effective management strategies may be ill-suited to a particular student. Because there is seldom a perfect relationship between undesirable behavior and its cause, it is impossible to know *a priori* if a student's difficulties are the result of different values, lack of learning, or flawed management techniques without modifying management strategies and observing the effect of the modifications. If a student begins to behave better with the modifications, the reasons for the initial difficulties are not particularly important (and one cannot assume that the teacher has found the cause of the difficulty).

PRE-REFERRAL DECISIONS

Early on, special educators adopted the term *referral* to designate a request to evaluate a student for special education eligibility and entitlement. Subsequently, an additional step was added to the process. Because the term *referral* had already gained widespread acceptance, the new step was called pre-referral, although this step clearly involves referral too. We use the term *pre-referral* to describe assessment and intervention activities that occur prior to formal referral to determine eligibility for special education.

Decision 1: Provide Special Assistance

Because so many academic and behavioral problems can be remediated or eliminated by classroom teachers, the first decision that a teacher should make is to provide students who are experiencing difficulties with a little extra help. Frequently, this special assistance will take the form of more of the same instruction, attempts to obtain parental help, and occasionally informal consultation with other teachers or building specialists. The special assistance can also take the form of Title I services. If the student responds to the special assistance and the problems are solved, no further action (with the exception of perhaps more careful monitoring) is required.

Decision 2: Refer to Intervention Assistance Team

When teachers are unable to address a student's academic or behavioral problems effectively, they often seek formal help from a specialist or staff support team. Staff support teams are known by different names in different states; for example, in Pennsylvania they are called instructional support teams. Often they are called *teacher assistance teams* (Chalfant, Pysh, & Moultrie, 1979), although they may also be known as *mainstream assistance teams, building-based teams, intervention assistance teams,* or *school-wide assistance teams.* Stokes (1982) defined a staff support team as

. . . a school-based problem-solving group whose purpose is to provide a vehicle for discussion of issues related to specific needs of teachers or students and to offer consultation and follow-up assistance to staff. The team can respond to staff needs in a variety of ways. It can provide immediate crisis intervention, short-term consultation, continuous support, or the securing of information, resources, or training for those who request its services. By providing problem-specific support and assistance to individuals and groups, the team can help teachers and other professionals to become more skillful, gain confidence, and feel more efficacious in their work with students. (p. 3)

The makeup of the teams vary by state. In Pennsylvania, for example, instructional support teams are composed of specially trained regular educators who are responsible for pre-referral activities whenever learning problems are suspected. Although job titles of team members may vary considerably from state to state or within states, team members should be skilled in areas of learning, assessment, classroom management, curriculum modification, and interpersonal communication, among others.

Obviously, students should not receive special education simply because they are casualties of a certain teaching style or curriculum. Nor should students receive special education when better teaching or management would allow them to make satisfactory progress in regular education. Thus, when a teacher seeks help in addressing the special needs of a student, the first form of help offered should be providing the regular classroom teacher with additional strategies and materials. The goals of pre-referral assessment and intervention are (1) to remediate, if possible, student difficulties before they become disabling; (2) to provide remediation in the least restrictive environment; and (3) if the problems cannot be dealt with effectively, to verify that they are not caused by the school (i.e., to establish that they reside within the child and/or the family). Typically, there are five stages of pre-referral activities (Graden, Casey, & Bonstrom, 1983). They include (1) making a formal request for services, (2) clarifying the problem, (3) designing interventions, (4) implementing the intervention, and (5) evaluating the intervention's effect.

Making the Request

Because pre-referral intervention is a formalized process, a formal request for services may be required. This formal request may require a form similar to that shown in Figure 14.1. If a pre-referral form is used, it should contain identifying information (such as teacher and student names), the specific problems for which the teacher is seeking consultation, the interventions that have already been attempted in the classroom, the effectiveness of those interventions, and current academic instructional levels. This information allows those responsible for providing consultation to decide if the problem warrants their further attention.

FIGURE 14.1   **Request for Pre-Referral Consultation**

Request for Pre-Referral Consultation

Student _____ Sex _____ Date of Birth _____

Referring Teacher _____ Grade _____ School _____

Specific Educational/Behavioral Problems:

_____

_____

_____

_____

Current Level or Materials in Deficit Areas:

_____

_____

_____

Specific Interventions to Improve Performance in Deficit Areas and Their Effectiveness:

_____

_____

_____

_____

What Special Services Does the Student Receive (e.g., Title I Reading, Speech Therapy)?

_____

_____

Most Convenient Days and Times for Consultation:

_____

_____

Clarifying the Problem

In the initial consultation, the team works with the classroom teacher to specify the nature of a problem or the specific areas of difficulty. These difficulties should be stated in terms of observable behavior, not hypothesized causes of the problem. For example, the teacher may specify a problem by saying that

"Heather does not recognize the letters of the alphabet" or that "Matthew does not complete homework assignments." The focus is on the discrepancy between actual and desired performance.

The team may seek additional information; the referring teacher may be asked to describe in some detail the contexts in which problems occur. For example, the classroom teacher maybe asked to provide a more detailed description of the student's curriculum, the way in which the teacher interacts with or responds to the student, the student's interactions with the teacher as well as with classmates, instructional groupings and seating arrangements, and antecedents and consequences of the student's behaviors. The referring teacher may also be asked to specify the ways in which the student's behavior affects the teacher or other students and the extent to which the behavior is incongruent with the teacher's expectations. When multiple problems are identified, they may be ranked in order of importance for action.

Finally, as part of the consultation, a member of the staff support team may observe the pupil in the classroom to verify the nature and extent of the problem. In relevant school settings, a designated member of the team observes the student, notes the frequency and duration of behaviors of concern, and ascertains the extent to which the student's behavior differs from that of classmates. At this point (or later in the process), the perceptions of the student and the student's parents may also be sought.

Designing Interventions

Next, the team and the referring teacher design interventions to remediate the most pressing problems. The team may need to coach the referring teacher on how to implement the interventions. Initially, the interventions should be based on empirically validated procedures that are known to be generally effective. In addition, parents, other school personnel, and the student may be involved in the intervention.

A major factor determining whether an intervention will be tried or implemented by teachers is feasibility. Those who conduct assessments and make recommendations about teaching must consider the extent to which the interventions they recommend are feasible. (Unfortunately, too often feasibility is determined on the basis of how much of a "hassle" the intervention planning will be—how much work it will take to implement a given program.) Phillips (1990) identified eight major considerations in making decisions about feasibility. Using the dimensions she identified, we list below a number of specific points assessors might address:

- *Degree of Disruption.* How much will the intervention I recommend disrupt school procedures or teacher routines?
- *Side Effects.* To what extent are there undesirable side effects for the student (for example, social ostracism), peers, home and family, and faculty?

- *Support Services Required.* How readily available are the support services required, and are the costs reasonable?
- *Prerequisite Competencies.* Does the teacher have the necessary knowledge, motivation, and experience to be able to implement the intervention? Does the teacher have a philosophical bias against the recommended intervention?
- *Control.* Does the teacher have control of the necessary variables to ensure the success of the intervention?
- *Immediacy of Results.* Will the student's behavioral change be quick enough for the teacher to be reinforced for implementing the intervention?
- *Consequence of Nonintervention.* What are the short- and long-term prognoses for the student if the behaviors are left uncorrected?
- *Potential for Transition.* Is it reasonable to expect that the intervention will lead to student self-regulation and generalize to other settings, curriculum areas, or even to other students who are experiencing similar difficulty?

The intervention plan should include a clear specification of the skills to be developed or the behavior to be changed, the methods to be used to effect the change, the criterion performance to be attained, the duration of the intervention or the criterion for termination, the location of the intervention, and the names of the individuals responsible for each aspect of the intervention. Moreover, it is generally a good idea to maintain a written record of these details. This record might be as informal as a set of notes from the team meeting, or it might be a formal document such as the one shown in Figure 14.2.

Teachers should have a clearly established criterion for a successful intervention. At minimum, the interventions should bring the student's performance to an acceptable or tolerable level. For academic difficulties, this usually means accelerating the rate of acquisition. For an instructional isolate, achievement must improve sufficiently to allow placement in an instructional group. For example, if Bernie currently cannot read the material used in the lowest reading group, the team would need to know the level of the materials used by the lowest instructional group. In addition, the team would need to know the probable level of materials that group will be using when Bernie's intervention is completed. For students with more variable patterns of achievement, intervention is directed toward improving performance in areas of weakness to a level that approximates performance in areas of strength.

Setting criteria for modifying behavioral problems is much the same process as setting targets for academic problems. When the goal is to change behavior, the teacher should select two or three students who are behaving appropriately. These students should not be the best behaved students but students in the middle of the range of acceptable behavior. The frequency, duration, latency, or amplitude of their behavior should be used as the criteria. Usually the behavior of the appropriate students is stable, so the team does not have to predict where they will be at the end of the intervention.

FIGURE 14.2   **An Intervention Plan**

Pre-Referral Intervention Plan

Complete one form for each targeted problem.

Student _____ Sex _____ Date of Birth _____

Referring Teacher _____ Grade ___ School _____

Intervention Objectives:

Behavior to be changed:

Criterion for success/termination of intervention:

Duration of intervention:

Location of intervention:

Person responsible for implementing the intervention:

Strategies:

Instructional methods:

Instructional materials:

Special equipment:

Signatures:

_____   _____
            (Referring Teacher)   (Date)

_____   _____
     (Member, Teacher Assistance Team)   (Date)

Implicit in this discussion is the idea that the interventions will reach the criterion for success within the time allotted. Thus, the team not only desires progress toward the criterion, but it also wants that progress to occur at specific rate—or faster.

Implementing the Interventions

The interventions should then be conducted as planned. Occasionally, a member of the team will observe the teacher using the planned strategy or special materials to ensure that the intervention is being carried out faithfully.

Evaluating the Effect of the Interventions

The effect of the interventions should be evaluated frequently enough to allow fine-tuning of the teaching methods and materials. Frequently, student performance is graphed to create learning pictures (Salvia & Hughes, 1990). Effective programs designed to increase desired behavior produce results like those shown in Figure 14.3: The student usually shows an increase in the desired behavior and a decrease in the number of errors. It is also possible for successful programs to produce *only* increasingly correct responses or *only* a decrease in errors. Ineffective programs show no increase in correct responses or no decrease in errors, or both.

To assess a student's rate of behavior change, we graph the acceleration of a desired behavior (or the deceleration of an undesired behavior) as a separate line called an *aimline*, as shown in Figure 14.4. The aimline connects the student's current level of performance with the point that represents both the desired

FIGURE 14.3   **A Graph of a Successful Learning Intervention**

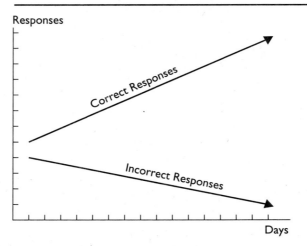

FIGURE 14.4   **A Graph of Student Progress with an Aimline**

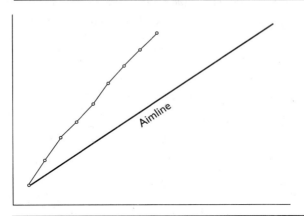

level of behavior and the time at which the behavior is to be attained. The student's progress is compared to the aimline. When behavior is targeted for increase, we expect the student's progress to be above the aimline; when behavior is targeted for decrease, we expect the student's progress to be below the aimline. Thus, a teacher, the intervention assistance team, or the student can look at the graph and make a decision about the adequacy of progress.

Decision 3: When Adequate Progress Is Made

When adequate progress is being made, the intervention should obviously be continued until the criterion is reached. When better-than-anticipated progress is being made, the teacher or team can decide to set a more ambitious goal (e.g., raise the level of desired performance) without changing the aim date, or they can set an earlier target for achieving the criterion without changing the level of performance.

Decision 4: When Inadequate Progress Is Made

Salvia and Hughes (1990, pp. 121–122) offer various suggestions for instructional modification depending on the pattern of student performance in relation to the aimline. Although a discussion of instructional methods is beyond the scope of this text, some examples can illustrate the kinds of things a teacher might do when faced with inadequate progress. When a student demonstrates no correct responses, (or too few), the goal may be too difficult; the team should consider changing the goal to include attainment of a prerequisite skill.

When a student demonstrates correct responses but too many errors, the teacher should consider modeling or prompting and more closely monitoring practice. When a student demonstrates accurate but slow responding, the teacher can encourage faster performance by providing incentives or additional practice. When performance is consistently below the aimline (three days is generally considered a significant amount of time), the teacher might consider varying the instructional methods or incentives. Finally, when a student's performance worsens, the teacher should question the motivational value of the task, vary any drill or practice activities, or discuss the performance directly with the student.

Decision 5: Refer the Student for Psychoeducational Evaluation

When several interventions have been tried without sufficient success, the student is likely to be referred for psychoeducational evaluation to ascertain eligibility for special education. Determination of eligibility requires further assessment by specialists, such as school psychologists, who use commercially prepared instruments. These instruments are discussed in Chapters 16 through 28. Eligibility and related decision making are discussed in Chapters 29 and 30.

DECISIONS MADE IN SPECIAL EDUCATION

The decisions made on behalf of students who are eligible for special education deal primarily with the design and implementation of their individual educational programs (IEPs). The IEP is a blueprint for instruction and specifies the goals, procedures, and related services for an individual eligible student. Assessment data are important for such planning. Numerous books and hundreds of articles in professional and scientific journals discuss the importance of using assessment data to plan instructional programs for students. Public Law 94-142 and the Individuals with Disabilities Education Act require a thorough assessment that results in an individualized education plan (IEP). Pupils are treated differentially on the basis of their individualized education programs. Moreover, most educators would agree that it is desirable to individualize programs for students in special and remedial education since the regular education programs have not proved beneficial to them.

The IEP

IEP decisions are always made collaboratively. At the very least, special education teachers, a representative of the school administration, and parents participate in the development of an IEP; other specialists, child advocates, and the students themselves may also participate in the decision making.

The minimum content of IEPs is specified in federal regulations. Here, we discuss what we believe are the four most important components: goals, methods, least restrictive environment, and related services.

Component 1: Goals

IEPs must contain statements about long-term (annual) goals and short-term objectives. Thus, parents and teachers must agree on where a student's instruction is headed and what the important steps are on the way to reaching the goals. Selection of long-term goals must take into consideration both parent and student aspirations and prognosis for the student's attainment of various important educational outcomes. Unfortunately, formal discussion about educational outcomes *per se* is not legally required during the creation of IEPs and is frequently avoided by parents and teachers. Nonetheless, the long-range outcomes (whether tacitly or publicly acknowledged) determine the annual goals, which in turn determine shorter-term objectives. We also must recognize that some parents may have unrealistic aspirations for their children, whereas others may not have sufficiently ambitious hopes; nor are school personnel immune to unrealistic prognoses. Thus, there is always the potential for conflict between schools and parents about what is hoped for and what is probable for a student.

Educational Outcomes   Other than those students identified as gifted, any student receiving special education will lag significantly behind his or her nondisabled peers in one or more areas.[1] Parents and teachers have two fundamental choices in dealing with these areas of significant deficit. First, they can intensify instruction in hopes of remediating the deficit; however, because the school day is finite, they will have to give less attention to some other area of the curriculum. Second, they can give up on the deficit and invest their efforts in compensatory strategies or intensified efforts in other curricular areas. Either option alters the educational outcomes for a student, and this is a fundamental distinction between regular and special education. We hold different outcomes for students completing special education programs. For some students, the differences are pervasive. For example, anticipated educational outcomes for a student with profound cognitive disabilities may be related to employment in a sheltered environment or perhaps simply worthwhile use of leisure time (without employment). For a student with mild disabilities, the anticipated educational outcomes might be the development of skills and knowledge necessary for enrollment in college after graduation from high school. Moreover, some outcomes are not exclusively emphasized in either special or regular education. Depending on the needs and abilities of the individual stu-

1. Some gifted students have learning disabilities. Thus, these gifted students will also have significant deficits.

dent, the anticipated outcomes are likely to be a combination of special and more general outcomes. For example, we would not expect all deaf students to be fluent oral communicators, although we would expect them to attain other generally prescribed educational outcomes; we would not expect quadriplegics to pass a swimming test, although we might well expect them to meet other educational outcomes.

Not only do educational outcomes vary, the levels of goal attainment within the same general outcome may differ. Therefore, even when the outcomes sound similar, they may differ because we may not expect that the goals will be attained at the same level of proficiency. For example, all students might be required to complete three years of high school mathematics in order to graduate. However, what is actually taught in the special education mathematics courses and in the lowest track of the regular mathematics courses may not be comparable. In social studies, we might require all students to learn about taxes. However, mentally retarded students may learn where and how to get help with paying their taxes, whereas nondisabled students might learn how a constitutional amendment was necessary before an individual income tax could be levied by the federal government.

The selection of educational outcomes requires a thorough understanding of a student's abilities and disabilities. The more schools and parents know about a student, the clearer their understanding becomes of what outcomes might be reasonably expected. The more time schools have to work with a student, the greater the outcomes that might be accomplished. A different set of educational outcomes may be selected early in a student's career when it becomes apparent that the student has profound and pervasive disabilities. For students with milder disabilities, different outcomes are often selected by default. Special educators and parents first try to remediate the disability or provide compensatory mechanisms so that the student can attain more generally desired educational outcomes. Only when these efforts fail are alternative outcomes embraced.

Goals and Objectives: Curriculum Choice and Instructional Design   Long-term goals are derived from our beliefs about a student's prognosis and the educational outcomes we hope the student attains. Curricula to produce these outcomes are selected or developed on the basis of these beliefs. Within the curricula are the longer-term goals and short-term objectives.

Assessment plays an important role in determining goals and objectives. Curriculum-based assessment is used to place pupils within the sequence of instruction and thereby, facilitate decisions about what to teach. These procedures assess a student's ongoing performance with respect to the curriculum that the student is being taught. As such, they provide the assessor with a detailed analysis of the skills the student has and has not mastered. By learning what goals the student has already attained and by knowing what goals have yet to be attained, teachers and parents can select the next goal or objective in the sequence.

Decisions about goals and objectives also include decisions about instructional algorithms (the ways we teach or try to achieve instructional goals). Often, teachers have a choice of algorithms for reaching the same goal. The most obvious examples come from the education of sensorily handicapped students, whose sensory loss precludes certain types of instruction. However, we often change algorithms for pupils who are not sensorily handicapped. For example, we may wish educable mentally retarded and learning disabled students to compute long-division problems correctly. However, we might not use the typical "goes into" paradigm. We may instruct them in the correct use of a pocket calculator rather than teaching them the usual algorithm of long division. We might even use a cumulative subtraction algorithm. Thus, although the goal might be the same, the means by which we achieve the goal may differ considerably.

Finally, specific objectives may vary, although the goals and algorithms do not differ. For example, in teaching language arts to adolescents with learning disabilities, we might have objectives that require the students to "tell" rather than to "write." We might also lower the level of mastery of the objective. For example, we may require students in a regular U.S. history class to analyze the causes of the Civil War, whereas special education students may only be required to demonstrate their comprehension of the causes by explaining "in their own words" how slavery was a cause of the war.

Component 2: Instructional Methods

Historically, psychologists and educators have been interested in how a student's abilities affect instructional methods in the belief that, if instruction could be matched to specific abilities, better student learning would occur. In special education, this approach led to a search for test-identified strengths and weaknesses and, subsequently, to the development of instructional procedures that capitalized on areas of strength or avoided weaker abilities. For example, test scores from the first edition of the Developmental Test of Visual Perception (Frostig, Maslow, Lefever, & Whittlesey, 1964), the Illinois Test of Psycholinguistic Abilities (Kirk, McCarthy, & Kirk, 1968), and the Purdue Perceptual-Motor Survey (Roach & Kephart, 1966) were at one time believed to have instructional meaning. In part because test-identified abilities were frequently unreliable and in part because special instructional methods did not result in better learning, this approach to instruction gradually lost favor, although some educators today still cling to a belief in this approach.

Currently, a less well-defined approach to tailoring instruction to individual needs is gaining popularity—an approach based on *cognitive development* (see Resnick, 1987). Like previous attempts, this approach tries to match instruction to student attributes. This time, however, the attributes are hypothetical cognitive structures and learning processes. Although this approach offers promise, it is far from validated. As one advocate of the approach notes, "Widespread adoption and application will require much more work and is likely more than a few years away" (Bruer, 1993, p. 263). We concur.

At present, the best way to teach handicapped learners is to rely on generally effective procedures. Teachers can do several things to make it easier for their pupils to learn the material, skill, or behavior. They can model the desired behavior. They can break down the terminal goal into its component parts and teach each of the steps and its integration. They can teach the objective in a variety of contexts with a variety of materials to facilitate generalization. They can provide time for practice, and they can choose the schedule on which practice is done (in other words, distributed versus massed practice). Several techniques that are under the direct control of the teacher can be employed to instruct any learner effectively. To help pupils recall information that has been taught, teachers may organize the material that a pupil is to learn, provide rehearsal strategies, or employ overlearning or distributed practice. There are also a number of things that teachers can do to elicit responses that have already been acquired. Various reinforcers and punishers have been shown to be effective in the control of behavior.

Assessment personnel can help teachers identify specific areas in which instructional difficulties exist, and they can help teachers plan interventions in light of information gained from assessments. Recently developed procedures (Ysseldyke & Christenson, 1987b; Ysseldyke, Christenson, & Kovaleski, 1994) can aid assessment personnel in determining the nature of students' instructional environments. Procedures such as The Instructional Environment System–II (Ysseldyke & Christenson, 1993) may be used to pinpoint the extent to which a student's academic or behavioral problems are a function of factors in the instructional environment and to identify starting points for designing appropriate interventions for individual students. Yet, there is just no way to decide ahead of time how best to teach a specific student. At present, we recommend that teachers first rely on general principles that are known and demonstrated to be effective in facilitating learning for handicapped students. However, we can seldom find validated translations of these principles into actual classroom activities and procedures. Moreover, even if we did find studies that demonstrated that a particular application of a learning principle worked for a research sample, we still could not be certain that it would work for specific students in a specific classroom. The odds are that it will, but we cannot be sure. Consequently, we must treat our translation of these principles, known to be effective, as tentative. In a real sense, we hypothesize that our treatment will work, but we need to verify that it has worked. Deno and Mirkin (1977) make this point cogently:

> At the present time we are unable to prescribe specific and effective changes in instruction for individual pupils with certainty. Therefore, changes in instructional programs which are arranged for an individual child can be treated only as hypotheses which must be empirically tested before a decision can be made whether they are effective for that child. (p. 11)

Teaching is experimental in nature. Generally, there is no data base to guide our selection of specific tasks or materials. Decisions are made about particular strategies, methods, and materials to use in instruction, but these decisions must be tentative. The decision maker makes some good guesses about what will work and then implements an instructional program. We do not know whether the decisions are correct until we gather data on the extent to which the instructional programs actually work; we never know the program will work until it has worked.

Tests do provide some very limited information about how to teach. Tests of intelligence, for example, yield information that gives a teacher some hints about teaching. Generally, the lower a pupil's intelligence, the more practice the student will require for mastery—but a score of 55 on the WISC-III does not tell the teacher whether a pupil needs 25 percent or 250 percent more practice. It does alert the teacher to the likelihood that the pupil will need more practice than the average student will. Other tenuous hints can be derived, but we feel that it is better to rely on direct observation of how a student learns in order to make adjustments in the learning program. Thus, to see if we had provided enough practice, we would observe Sally's recall of information rather than looking at Sally's IQ. We cannot do anything about Sally's IQ, but we can do something about the amount of practice she gets.

Component 3: Least Restrictive Appropriate Environment

Federal law and regulations express a clear preference for educating students with disabilities as close as possible to their homes and to the maximum extent appropriate with their nondisabled peers. "The removal of children with disabilities from the regular educational environment should occur only when the nature or severity of the disability is such that education in regular classes with the use of supplementary aids and services cannot be achieved satisfactorily" (*Federal Register*, 1992, §300.5, 300.550, 44823). The selection of the appropriate option should be based on the educational needs of the student, although other factors may also come into play.

Placement Options   There is a hierarchy of placements that ranges from the least restrictive (i.e., educating students with disabilities in a regular education classroom with a regular teacher who receives consultative services from a special education teacher) to the most restrictive (i.e., educating students with disabilities in segregated residential facilities that provide services only to students with disabilities). Between these two extremes are at least five other options.

- *Instructional support from a special education teacher in the regular classroom.* In this arrangement, eligible students remain in the regular classroom in their neighborhood schools, and the special education teacher comes to the student to provide whatever specialized instruction is necessary.

- *Instructional support from a special education teacher in a resource room.* In this arrangement, eligible students remain in a regular classroom for most of the day. When they need specialized instruction, they go to a special education resource room to receive services from a special education teacher. Because districts may not have a sufficient number of students with disabilities in each school to warrant establishing a resource room program at each school, a student may be assigned to a regular education classroom that is not in the student's neighborhood school.
- *Part-time instruction in a special education classroom.* In this arrangement, eligible students have some classes or subject matter taught by the special education teacher and the rest taught in the regular classroom. As is the case with resource rooms, the regular education classroom may not be in the student's neighborhood school.
- *Full-time instruction in a special education classroom with limited integration.* In this arrangement, eligible students receive all academic instruction from a special education teacher in a special classroom. Eligible students may be integrated with nondisabled peers for specials (e.g., lunch, recess, and assemblies) and nonacademic classes (e.g., art and music).
- *Full-time instruction in a special education classroom without integration.* In this arrangement, eligible students have no interaction with their nondisabled peers, and their classrooms may be in a special day school that serves only students with disabilities.

Factors Affecting the Placement Choice   The selection of a particular option should be based on the intensity of education needed by the eligible student: The less intensive the intervention needed by the student, the less restrictive the environment; the more intensive the intervention needed by the student, the more restrictive the environment. Determining the intensity of an intervention is a procedure that is less than scientific. Frequently, there is some correspondence between the severity of disability and the intensity of service needed, but that correspondence is not perfect. Therefore, special education teachers and parents should consider the frequency and duration of the needed interventions. The more frequent an intervention is (e.g., every morning) and the longer its duration (e.g., 20 minutes per morning), the more likely it is that the intervention will be provided in more, rather than less, restrictive settings. When frequent and long interventions are needed, the student will have less opportunity to participate with nondisabled peers, no matter what setting that student is placed in. Obviously, if students require round-the-clock intervention, they cannot get what they need from a resource room program.

In addition to the nature of needed interventions, parents and teachers may also reasonably consider the following factors when deciding on the type of placement:

- *Disruption.* Bringing a special education teacher into a regular classroom or pulling a student out of a regular classroom may be disruptive. For example, some students with disabilities cannot handle transitions: They get lost between classrooms, or they forget to go to their resource room. When eligible students have a lot of difficulty with changing schedules or making transitions between events, then less restrictive options may not be currently appropriate.

- *Well-Being of Nondisabled Individuals.* Eligible students will seldom be integrated when they present a clear danger to the welfare of nondisabled peers or teachers. For example, assaultive and disruptive students are likely to be placed in more restrictive environments.
- *Well-Being of the Disabled Student.* Many students with disabilities require some degree of protection—in some cases, from nondisabled peers who may tease or physically abuse a student who is different; in other cases, from other students with disabilities. For example, the parents of a seriously withdrawn student may decide not to place their child in a classroom for emotionally disturbed students when those students are assaultive.
- *Labeling.* Many parents, especially those of students with milder handicaps, reject disability labels. They desire special education services, but they want these services without having their child be labeled. Such parents often prefer consultative or itinerant services for their children.
- *Inclusion.* Some parents are willing to forgo the instruction benefits of special education for the potential social benefits of having their children educated exclusively with nondisabled peers. For such parents, full inclusion is the only option.

There are also pragmatic considerations in selecting the educational setting. One very real consideration is that a school district may not be able to provide a full range of options for economic reasons. In such districts, parents are offered a choice among existing options unless they are willing to go through a due process hearing or court hearing. A second consideration is instructional efficiency. When several students require the same intervention, the special education teacher can often form an instructional group. Thus, it will probably cost less to provide the special education services. A third consideration is the specific teachers. Some teachers are better than others, and parents may well opt for a more highly regarded teacher who works in a more restrictive setting.

Parents and special education teachers must realize that selecting a placement option is an imprecise endeavor. The criteria for picking one option over another are unclear, and choices should be regarded as best guesses. However, assessment data can facilitate this decision. One helpful type of information concerns the performance of nondisabled peers. Deno (1985) has described a process he called *peer referencing*. In addition to gathering data on the eligible student, teachers gather information on the performance of potential classmates. An examiner might, for example, frequently and repeatedly assess the number of words per minute that the student reads aloud from the basal text used in the student's classroom. In order to have a basis for comparison, the examiner would also ask all students in the regular class to read aloud passages from the same basal text and would record the number of words each read correctly per minute. Figure 14.5 is an illustration of how such information might be recorded graphically. The graph shows the growth in reading performance of a sixth-grade student named Rodney over a fourteen-week time interval. Also illustrated on the graph is the average performance of Rodney's peers. The average peer read about 120 words per minute. Over time, Rodney's performance improved from about 30 words per minute read correctly to about 90 words per minute read correctly. Note that this comparison is expressed at the top of the graph as a normative peer comparison. Rodney's performance im-

FIGURE 14.5   Rodney's Performance in Reading Aloud from a Basal Reader

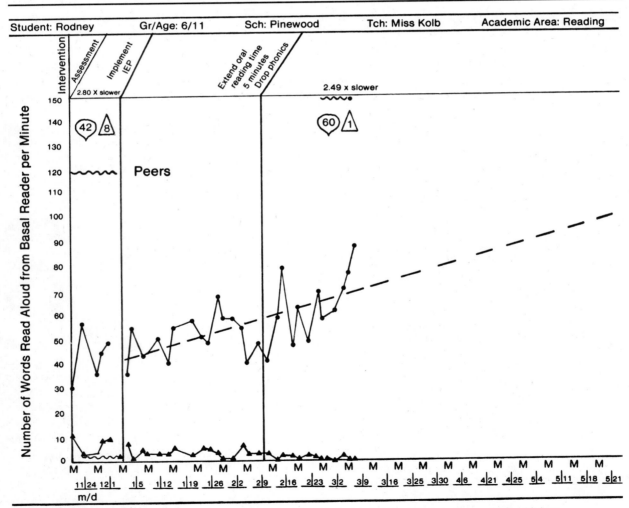

proved from reading 2.80 times slower than his peers to reading 2.49 times slower than his peers.

Component 4: Related Services

In addition to special instruction, eligible students are entitled to developmental, corrective, and other supportive services if such services are needed for the students to benefit from special education; federal legislation uses the term *related services*, which has been widely adopted by states and school districts. Related services include both those not typically provided by schools and those typically provided (*Federal Register*, 1992, §300.16, 44803).

Types of Services   Schools must provide students with disabilities a variety of services to which nondisabled students are seldom entitled. Services include, but are not limited to, the following types:

- *Audiology.* Allowable services include evaluation of hearing, habilitation (e.g., programs in auditory training, speech reading, and speech conservation), amplification (including the fitting of hearing aids), and hearing conservation programs.
- *Psychological Services.* Psychological services allowed include testing, observation, and consultation.
- *Physical and Occupational Therapy.* These therapies can be used to (1) improve, develop, or restore functional impairments caused by illness, injury, or deprivation and (2) improve independent functioning. These therapies may also be used with preschool populations to prevent impairment or further loss of function.
- *Recreational Therapy.* Allowable programs include those located in the schools and community agencies that provide general recreation programs, therapeutic recreation, and assessment of leisure functioning.
- *Counseling Services.* Either group or individual counseling may be provided for students and their parents. Student counseling includes rehabilitation counseling that focuses on career development, employment preparation, achievement of independence, and integration in the workplace and community; it also includes psychological counseling. Parental counseling includes therapies addressing problems in the student's living situation (i.e., home, school, and community) that affect the student's schooling. Parental counseling also includes assistance to help parents understand their child's special needs as well as information about child development.
- *Medical Services.* Diagnostic and evaluative services required to determine medically related disabilities are allowed.

The schools must also provide students with disabilities the services they typically provide to all children. Thus, schools must provide speech and language services to students with impairments; however, they must also provide habilitative and preventative programs and counseling about speech and language impairments to parents, children, and teachers. Schools must also provide school health and school social work services. Finally, schools must provide transportation for eligible students to and from school, between schools, and among school buildings, and must supply any required special equipment, such as ramps.

Although these related services are mandatory for students who need them to profit from their special education, there is nothing to prohibit a school from offering other services. Thus, schools may offer additional services free of charge to eligible students.

Establishing Need for Related Services Although federal law is very clear about the need to provide related services to students with disabilities, it remains unclear how that need should be established. In practice, most schools or parents seek an evaluation by a specialist. The specialist notes a problem and expresses a belief that a specific therapy could be successful and benefit the student. Thus, need is frequently based on professional opinion.

We must also note that related services can be very costly, and some school districts try to avoid their provision. We have heard of districts that maintain that they do not offer a service even though that service is mandated by law for students who need it.

SUMMARY

Both regular and special educators have responsibilities for students with disabilities. These responsibilities vary as a function of the severity of a student's disability and the way in which individual states and school districts provide educational services. However, both regular and special education personnel will necessarily be involved in decision making with regard to students with exceptional needs. First, educators may be involved in identifying students with severe learning or behavioral problems who are believed to be in need of special education services. Second, educators may be involved in providing special assistance to students who are experiencing difficulties in the classroom. When the special assistance is insufficient to meet the students' needs, educators are involved in referrals for psychoeducational evaluation. When this evaluation indicates that a student is entitled to special education and/or related services, a number of other decisions must be made. All students receiving special education must have IEPs. As part of the process of developing an IEP, educators and parents (as well as other individuals) participate on decision-making teams to select appropriate educational or habilitative goals, instructional methods, related services, and the setting in which the student will receive special education. The decisions made by educators should be based on accurate and meaningful data.

STUDY QUESTIONS

1. Give five examples of why classroom instruction may be ineffective for a specific student.
2. Give examples of three different related services that might be necessary for a hypothetical student with a disability. Why are these services required for the student to benefit from special education?
3. Explain the concept of least restrictive environment. What are the most important components of this concept, and on what types of information would educators base their decision to place a student in a least restrictive environment?
4. Provide a rationale for pre-referral intervention (e.g., special assistance).
5. Upon what information should parents and teachers base decisions about educational goals and instructional methods?

ADDITIONAL READING

Salvia, J., & Hughes, C. (1990). *Curriculum Based Assessment: Testing What Is Taught.* New York: Macmillan. (Chapter 2: Specify Reasons for Assessment, pp. 25–39)

Stahl, S., & Miller, P. (1989). Whole language and language experience approaches for beginning reading: A quantitative research synthesis. *Review of Educational Research, 59 (1)*, 87–116.

Stevens, R., & Rosenshine, B. (1981). Advances in research on teaching. *Exceptional Education Quarterly, 2 (1)*, 1–9.

PART 4

ASSESSMENT USING FORMAL MEASURES

*P*art 4 deals with tests and scales used to make decisions entitling students to special educational services. The first chapter in this section (Making Entitlement Decisions) deals specifically with criteria for providing special education and related services to students with disabilities. The remaining chapters describe the most common domains in which assessment of processes (or abilities) and products are conducted. With the exception of Chapter 16 (an overview of intelligence), each chapter in this part focuses on a different process or skill domain. Each chapter opens with an explanation of why the domain is assessed. We next provide a general overview of the components of the domain (that is, the behaviors that are usually assessed) and then discuss the more commonly used tests within the domain. Each chapter concludes with some suggestions for coping with problems in assessing the domain and a general summary of chapter content.

The criteria we used in selecting and reviewing specific tests warrant some discussion. First, in selecting tests, we could not, and did not, include all the available measures for each domain. Rather, we tried to select representative and commonly used devices in each area. Readers interested in tests not reviewed in this section may want to consult books devoted entirely to test reviews, such as *Tests: A Comprehen-*

sive Reference for Assessments in Psychology, Education, and Business (Sweetland & Keyser, 1991) or *Buros' Mental Measurements Yearbooks.* Second, in evaluating the technical adequacy of each test, we restricted our evaluation to information in the test manuals. There were two reasons for this decision: (1) As stated in the *Standards for Educational and Psychological Tests* (APA, 1985), test authors are responsible for providing all necessary technical information in their test manuals. The test authors must have some basis for claiming that their tests are valid. Therefore, we searched the manuals for technical information that supports the test authors' contentions. (2) An attempt to include the vast body of research literature on commonly used tests would have resulted in a multivolume opus that would be impossible to publish as a current work. Entire books have been written on the subject of using and interpreting single tests.

In reviewing each test, we always use the same format. We describe the general format of the test and the specific behaviors that the test is designed to sample; these descriptions allow the reader to evaluate the extent to which specific tests sample the domain. Next, we describe the kinds of scores that the test provides for the practitioner; this gives information about the meaning and interpretation of those scores. Next, we examine the standardization sample for each test; this enables the reader to judge—recalling the discussion in Chapter 6—the adequacy of the norm group and to evaluate the appropriateness of each test for use with specific populations of students. Next, we evaluate the evidence of reliability for each test, using the standards set forth in Chapter 7. Next, for each device we examine evidence of its validity and evaluate the adequacy of the evidence in light of the standards set forth in Chapter 8. Finally, we give a summary of each test.

We urge our readers to examine the research on tests in which they might be interested. Test users are ultimately responsible for test selection and interpretation. Thus, if you are considering using a particular test that has incomplete or inadequate technical characteristics, it is your responsibility to demonstrate its validity. Current research may provide the support you need to demonstrate the validity of your assessment. Therefore, we urge our readers to go beyond our reviews.

Chapter 15

Making Entitlement Decisions

*A*ll of us are classified within several types of systems. Sociologists may assign us to particular social classes according to our education, occupation, and income. Government classifies individuals in several ways: as adult or minor, citizen or noncitizen, voter or nonvoter, felon, adjudicated delinquent, and so forth. When we are ill, a physician classifies our sickness: cold, strep throat, or herpes simplex. Psychiatrists may classify clients according to the *Diagnostic and Statistical Manual of Mental Disorders—Revised*. (DSM-III-R)

The term *entitlement* has come to be associated with benefits derived from classification; individuals who meet various criteria are entitled to the benefits specified in the law. Thus, for individuals who meet legal criteria for eligibility, classification systems can bring benefits: Social Security benefits, food stamps, veterans' benefits, Aid to Families with Dependent Children benefits, and so forth. Indeed, these benefits are a substantial portion of the federal and state budgets. Of importance for us in special and remedial education is entitlement to special education services. Individuals who meet the legal criteria are classified as eligible for special and remedial services, and this is one of the primary reasons for classifying students in the public schools.

RATIONALE FOR ENTITLEMENT

Think about all the students in preschool, elementary, and secondary educational systems. Except in the Lake Wobegon School District,[1] most students have one problem or another at some time during their school careers: Some students are unhappy to be in school; some students are defiant; some students drop out of school; some students persist but do not achieve desired educational outcomes; some students do not learn as much as is predicted by their in-

---

1. Lake Wobegon is a mythical community in which all the children are above average.

tellectual ability; some students have recurrent "bad hair" days. Most problems do not entitle a student to special assistance. The bases for policies to provide special help for some students but not others are seldom made explicit. However, at least three appear to operate.

Lack of Academic Success

The first basis for providing special help is that a student must experience a lack of academic success. This criterion is either implicit or explicit in every federal definition of disability in educational regulations.

- Children with disabilities "need special education."
- Autism "adversely affects a child's educational performance."
- Deaf-blindness "causes . . . severe educational problems."
- Hearing impairment "adversely affects a child's educational performance."
- Mental retardation "adversely affects a child's educational performance."
- Multiple disabilities "cause . . . severe educational problems."
- Orthopedic impairment "adversely affects a child's educational performance."
- Other health impairment "adversely affects a child's educational performance."
- Serious emotional disturbance "adversely affects a child's educational performance."
- Specific learning disability "results in an imperfect ability to listen, think, speak, read, write, spell, or do mathematical calculations."
- Speech or language impairment "adversely affects a child's educational performance."
- Traumatic brain injury "adversely affects a child's educational performance."
- Visual impairment "adversely affects a child's educational performance." (34 CFR §300.7)

Moreover, no other problem appears in every definition of disability. Thus, poor educational performance is a criterion for entitlement.

No-Fault Failure

Poor educational performance is a necessary, but insufficient, condition for entitlement to special education. The poor educational performance must be caused by one or more official disabilities.[2] Not all causes of poor educational performance qualify as a disability. Two sets of circumstances appear to exclude some problems: the problems are not sufficiently severe, or the problems are of the student's (or family's) own doing. For example, there is a considerable amount

2. Both federal and state legislation provide for educational entitlements not based on exceptionality, but these entitlements are not part of special education.

of research showing that unattractive people are at a disadvantage in American society: They receive lower grades (Salvia, Algozzine, & Sheare, 1977), have lower self-concepts and peer acceptance (Salvia, Sheare, & Algozzine, 1975), and so forth. Yet, there are no special educational services for students with cosmetic disabilities. Similarly, there is no question of the role played in learning by motivation. Yet, there are no special educational services for students with motivational deficits—perhaps because motivation is widely believed to be volitional. Finally, there are no special educational services for students who fail to make academic progress because of poor instruction or faulty curriculum—perhaps because society is unwilling to acknowledge officially that students may be harmed by the educational system.

Federal legislation catalogues the problems required for entitlement. These problems share two characteristics. They are all believed severe enough to preclude school success without substantial intervention or accommodation, and they are all beyond the control of students and their families. Thus, this criterion relieves students, their families, and schools of any culpability for academic failure.

Political Action

The first two bases are insufficient to entitle students to special educational services. Federal and most state legislation does not include all severe conditions that affect learning (for example, attention deficit disorder). Moreover, various disabilities have been added to the list of entitling conditions over the years (for example, learning disabilities and autism).

The basis for adding disabilities to the approved list of exceptionalities is political. Frequently, coalitions of parents and professionals lobby Congress, the courts, and their state legislatures to include specific exceptionalities. For example, students with more severe forms of mental retardation were excluded from public schools in Pennsylvania until 1972, when parents and professions brought suit against the Commonwealth in order to gain access to the public educational system for these individuals. Finally, we note that in some states, advocates have succeeded in mandating programs for students who are gifted, whereas in other states programs for gifted students are permissive (not mandatory). To our knowledge, once a group has been entitled to special education services, entitlement has never been removed.

Problems Associated with the Criteria

Four problems with the criteria used to determine eligibility for special services are especially noteworthy. First, we find the prevalent (but mistaken) belief that special educational services are for students who could benefit from them. Thus, in many circles educational need is believed to be sufficient for entitlement. Clearly, this belief is contradicted by pertinent law, regulations, and litigation. Nonetheless, educators usually have strong humanitarian beliefs, so when they see students with problems, they want to get those students the services they believe are required. Too often, the regulations may be bent so that students fit entitlement criteria.

Second, the definitions that appear in state and federal regulations frequently are very imprecise. The imprecision of federal regulations creates variability in standards among states; the imprecision of state regulations creates variability in standards among districts within states. Thus, students who are eligible in one state or district may not be eligible in other states or districts. Nowhere is this lack of precision more notable than in the definition of learning disability. How does one assess an "imperfect ability to listen, think, speak, read, write, spell, or to do mathematical calculations"? In practice, this imperfect ability is defined as a severe discrepancy between intellectual ability and achievement. However, there is no consensus about the meaning of severe discrepancy; certainly there is no widely accepted mathematical formula to ascertain severe discrepancy. Finally, to some extent, discrepancies between achievement and intelligence are determined by the specific tests used. Thus, one test battery might produce a significant discrepancy whereas another battery would not produce a discrepancy for the same student.

Third, the definitions treat disabilities as though they were discrete categories. However, most diagnosticians are hard pressed to distinguish between primary and secondary mental retardation or primary or secondary emotional disturbance. Distinctions between individuals with severe mental retardation with autistic-like behaviors and autistic individuals are practically impossible to make with any certainty.

Fourth, parents may often prefer the label associated with one disability (for example, autism or learning disabled) over the label associated with another (for example, mentally retarded). Because of the procedural safeguards afforded students with special needs and their parents, school districts may become embroiled in lengthy and unnecessarily adversarial hearings in which each side has an expert testifying that contradictory and often mutually exclusive labels are correct. School personnel find themselves in a no-win situation because the definitions and their operationalizations are so imprecise. As a result, school districts frequently give parents the label and program they want, rather than what educators in the district, in their best professional judgments, believe the student needs. Districts are reluctant to risk litigation because parents can frequently find an expert to contradict the district staff.

ENTITLEMENTS

Once society has decided that government should come to the aid of individuals whose achievement is seriously impeded by a few select disabilities, those individuals become entitled to special treatment. Special education has four components: the special services provided, different outcomes, procedural safeguards, and special fiscal arrangements.

Special Services

The federal and state governments extend special benefits to each student entitled to special education. Especially pertinent is the guarantee of a free and appropriate public education that includes specially designed instruction (as detailed in each student's Individualized Education Plan), special materials, special equipment and technology, and the provision of a variety of related services believed necessary for the student to profit from special education. Other benefits include (1) formal education continuing until the student graduates or reaches 21 years of age, (2) instruction by teachers who have had special coursework and practicum experiences and may have special certification, (3) instruction in smaller classes, and (4) testing accommodations (see Chapter 9).

Different Outcomes

Students receiving special education are frequently exempted from various curricular requirements that are established for students in general education. For example, students who complete their individual transition plan are eligible for a high school diploma, regardless of whether they have completed the general graduation requirements mandated for all other students. Not only are students who receive special education exempted from some general educational outcomes mandated for all other graduating students, these students may also be held to much different outcomes. For example, students with more severe disabilities may be taught skills associated with daily living, using public transportation, building and maintaining interpersonal relationships, and using social services.

Procedural Safeguards

Students who are eligible for special education (or are believed to be eligible) are afforded several procedural safeguards beyond those offered to all students. These safeguards are discussed in detail in Chapter 3. Here, we only reiterate the safeguards usually associated with special education entitlement:

- Prior notice and parental consent prior to identification, evaluation, or educational placement
- Parental participation in multidisciplinary teams to determine exceptionality

- Parental participation in IEP meetings to ascertain eligibility and to plan educational programs
- Protection from unfair, biased, and inappropriate evaluation
- Right to an independent evaluation
- Recourse to administrative due process proceedings to redress conditions specifically guaranteed

Special Fiscal Arrangements

Special educational services generally cost more than the educational services provided for most students in regular education. Part or all of the additional costs are borne by state and federal government. Determining that Joey is not succeeding in school because of mental retardation determines, in essence, that part of his special education will be paid for under special provisions of federal and state law. Thus, in the schools, eligibility decisions are also decisions about whether a child is entitled to additional help paid for by special funds earmarked for children with specific disabilities.

DETERMINING ELIGIBILITY FOR SPECIAL SERVICES

The determination of eligibility for special educational services is based on a multidisciplinary evaluation (MDE) conducted by a multidisciplinary team (MDT). The team assembles and evaluates information (that is, conducts an MDE) to determine if a student meets two criteria. First, the student must be in need of special education;[3] second, the student must be exceptional.

Establishing Educational Need

Students with milder academic and behavioral disabilities and without obvious sensory or motor disabilities usually are presumed to be normal when they enter school. However, during their education it becomes clear to school personnel that these students have significant problems. They demonstrate marked discrepancies from mainstream expectations or from the achievement and behavior of typical peers. These discrepancies are usually verified by normative compar-

---

3. Under the requirements of Section 504 of the 1973 Rehabilitation Act, students with disabilities are entitled to related services even when they do not need special education. For example, a student in the early stages of muscular dystrophy may require physical therapy, but the disease may not have progressed so far that the student requires special education. In such cases, a school district is required to provide the needed services, but the funding for these services does not come from special education budgets.

isons (that is, use of norm-referenced assessment devices) or peer referencing.[4] The magnitude of a problem necessary to consider a student for special education is not codified, and there are many opinions on this issue. Whereas some say a student should be performing at half the level of his or her peers, others believe only a 20 percent discrepancy is necessary. Marston and Magnusson (1985) recommend that students receive special education services when they are two years behind their peers.

The presence of a discrepancy alone does not establish need, because there are many causes for a discrepancy. Thus, school personnel usually engage in a number of remedial and compensatory activities designed to reduce or eliminate the discrepancy. As discussed in Chapter 14, interventions initially may be designed and implemented by the classroom teacher. When the teacher's interventions are unsuccessful, then the student is referred to a teacher assistance team that designs and may help implement further interventions. Need for special educational services for students with mild disabilities is established when one of two conditions is met. First, if the interventions of the student assistance team have not reduced (or eliminated) the discrepancy in achievement or behavior, there is a strong possibility that the student needs special education. Obviously, if the interventions are poorly conceptualized or haphazardly implemented, the case for special education is not made. Thus, failures of interventions only suggest need. However, when well conceived and carefully implemented interventions fail, the possibility of special need is strong. Second, interventions by the special assistance team might remediate the student's academic or behavioral deficits but be so intrusive, labor intensive, or specialized that a regular classroom teacher cannot continue to intervene without seriously detracting from the education of other students in the classroom. Thus, successful interventions may be too intensive or extensive for use in regular education.

For students with severe disabilities, the process of demonstrating need for special education is easier. From accumulated research and professional experience, educators know that students with certain disabilities (for example, blindness, deafness, severe mental retardation, autism, and so on) will not succeed in school without special education. Thus, educators (and relevant legislation) assume that the presence of a severe disability is sufficient to demonstrate the need for special educational services.

Establishing Exceptionality

When educational need is established, the student is referred to a multidisciplinary team (MDT). The multidisciplinary team determines if a student is exceptional.

---

4. *Peer referencing* is a term used by Deno (1985) to describe a procedure for comparing a target student's performance to that of satisfactorily performing peers; see Chapter 14.

Composition of the Multidisciplinary Team

The team must include a "teacher or other specialist with knowledge in the areas of suspected disability" (34 CFR §300.532) and individuals knowledgeable about the student and the meaning of evaluation data (34 CFR §300.533). When a student is suspected of having a learning disability, the team must also include "a person qualified to conduct individual diagnostic evaluations of children" (34 CFR §300.540). In practice, diagnosticians and parents are usually members of MDTs.

Responsibilities of the Multidisciplinary Team

The team is responsible for gathering information and making a decision about a student's exceptionality. In theory, the decision-making process is straightforward. The MDT compares the student's performance to see if it meets the criteria for a specific exceptionality. Thus, it must collect, at minimum, information required by the definition of exceptionality. Federal regulations (34 CFR §300.532) require that a student be "assessed in all areas related to the suspected disability, including, if appropriate, health, vision, hearing, social and emotional status, general intelligence, academic performance, communicative status, and motor abilities" Regulations (34 CFR §300.533) also require the team to:

- Draw upon information from a variety of sources, including aptitude and achievement tests, teacher recommendations, physical condition, social or cultural background, and adaptive behavior
- Ensure that information obtained from all of these sources is documented and carefully considered.

Official Exceptionalities

Several classification systems are used in the United States schools today. Different terms are used in different states to specify the handicapping conditions that entitle a student to special education services. The most frequently used terms and criteria are those required for reporting under the regulations of the Individuals with Disabilities Education Act (IDEA). The definitions used in regulations for IDEA (34 CFR §300.7) are given below in italics.

Autism Autistic students are those who demonstrate *developmental disability significantly affecting verbal and nonverbal communication and social interactions generally evident before age 3, that adversely affects a child's educational performance. Other characteristics often associated with autism are engagement in repetitive activities and stereotyped movements, resistance to environmental change or change in daily routines, and unusual responses to sensory experiences. The term [autism] does not apply if a child's educational performance is adversely affected primarily because the child has a serious emotional disturbance. . . .* Students with suspected autism are usually evaluated by speech and language specialists and psychologists. When the student has limited intellectual ability, it is often very difficult to distinguish autism from severe forms of mental retardation.

Mental Retardation   Mentally retarded pupils are those who demonstrate *significantly subaverage intellectual functioning existing concurrently with deficits in adaptive behavior, and manifested during the developmental period, that adversely affects a child's educational performance.* Students who are eventually labeled mentally retarded are often referred because of generalized slowness: they lag behind their age mates in most areas of academic achievement, social and emotional development, language ability, and perhaps physical development. This slowness must be demonstrated on an individually administered test of intelligence that is appropriate for the student being assessed. Thus, the test must be appropriate not only for the age of the student but also for the pupil's acculturation and physical and sensory abilities. However, a test of intelligence is not enough. The pupil must also demonstrate slowness in adaptive behavior. An assessment for mental retardation should always contain an assessment of achievement, intelligence, and adaptive behavior.

Learning Disability   Learning-disabled pupils are those who demonstrate *a disorder in one or more of the basic psychological processes involved in understanding or in using language, spoken or written, that may manifest itself in the imperfect ability to listen, think, read, write, spell, or do mathematical calculations. The term [learning disabilities] includes such conditions as perceptual handicaps, brain injury, minimal brain dysfunction, dyslexia, and developmental aphasia. The term does not apply to children who have learning problems that are primarily the result of visual, hearing, or motor disabilities, of mental retardation, emotional disturbance, or environmental, cultural or economic disadvantage.* Students who are eventually labeled learning disabled are often referred because of inconsistent performance; they are likely to have pronounced patterns of academic and cognitive strengths and weaknesses. For example, Harry may grasp mathematics and social concepts quite well, but he may not learn to read no matter what his teacher tries; Joyce may be reading at grade level, be a good speller, have highly developed language skills, but not be able to master addition and subtraction facts. Criteria for eligibility for services for the learning disabled vary considerably from state to state. Generally, a pupil must demonstrate normal (or at least nonretarded) general intellectual development on an individually administered test of intelligence. The student must also demonstrate, on an individually administered test of achievement, some areas that are within the normal range while demonstrating significantly delayed development in other areas of achievement, and demonstrate (corrected) hearing and vision within normal limits. Eligible pupils would not have significant emotional problems or cultural disadvantage. Finally, the basic process disorder that causes the learning disability may or may not have to be tested, depending on the particular state's education code. If it is assessed, measures of visual and auditory perception as well as measures of linguistic and psycholinguistic abilities would be administered.

Emotional Disturbance   Emotionally disturbed pupils exhibit *one or more of the following characteristics over a long period of time and to a marked degree that adversely affects educational performance: (a) an inability to learn which cannot be explained by intellectual, sensory, or health factors; (b) an inability to build or maintain satisfactory interpersonal relationships with peers and teachers; (c) inappropriate types of behavior or feelings under normal circumstances; (d) a general pervasive mood of unhappiness or depression; or (e) a tendency to develop physical symptoms or fears associated with personal or school problems.* Students who are eventually labeled emotionally disturbed are often referred for problems in interpersonal relations (for example, fighting or extreme noncompliance) and/or unusual behavior (for example, unexplained episodes of crying or extreme mood swings). Requirements for establishing a pupil's eligibility for special education services for the emotionally disturbed vary markedly among the states. Some or all of the following sources of information may be used in determining eligibility: observational data, behavior rating scales, psychological evaluations, and examination by a board-certified psychiatrist or psychologist.

Traumatic Brain Injury   Students with traumatic brain injury have *an acquired injury to the brain caused by an external physical force, resulting in total or partial functional disability or psychological impairment, or both, that adversely affects a child's educational performance. The term applies to open or closed head injuries resulting in impairments in one or more areas, such as cognition; language; memory; attention; reasoning; abstract thinking; judgment; problem-solving; sensory, perceptual and motor abilities; psychosocial behavior; physical functions; information processing; and speech. The term does not apply to brain injuries that are congenital or degenerative, or brain injuries induced by birth trauma.* Students with traumatic brain injury have normal development until they sustain a severe head injury. As a result of this injury they are disabled. Most head injuries are the result of an accident (frequently automobile accidents) but may also occur as a result of physical abuse or intentional harm (for example, being shot). Traumatic brain injury will be diagnosed by a physician who is usually a specialist (a neurologist), and educators identify the school-based deficits.

Speech or Language Impairment   A student with a speech or language impairment has *a communication disorder such as stuttering, impaired articulation, a language impairment, or a voice impairment that adversely affects a child's educational performance.* Many children will experience some developmental problems in their speech and language. For example, children frequently have difficulty with the *r* sound and say *wabbit* instead of *rabbit*. Similarly, many children will use incorrect grammar, especially with internal plurals; for example, children may say, "My dog has four foots." Such difficulties are so common as to be considered a part of normal speech development. However, when such speech and language errors continue to occur beyond the age when most children have developed correct speech or language, there is cause for concern. School personnel identify the educational disability, while speech and language specialists use a variety of assessment procedures (norm-referenced tests, systematic observation, and criterion-referenced tests) to identify the speech and language disability.

Visual Impairment   A student with a visual impairment has *an impairment in vision that, even with correction, adversely affects a child's educational development. [Visual impairment] includes both partial sight and blindness.* Students with severe visual impairments are usually identified before entering school, although some partially sighted students may not be identified until school age, when visual demands increase. Assessments of previously undiagnosed visually impaired students may indicate gross and fine motor problems or variable visual performance (that is, performance that varies with the size of print, amount of light, and fatigue, for example). Visual acuity and visual field are usually assessed by an ophthalmologist. A specialist usually assesses functional vision through systematic observation of a student's responses to various types of paper, print sizes, lighting conditions, and so forth.

Deafness and Hearing Impairment   Deafness is *an impairment in hearing that is so severe that the child is impaired in processing linguistic information through hearing, with or without amplification, [and] that adversely affects the child's educational performance.* A student with a hearing impairment has *an impairment in hearing, whether permanent or fluctuating, that adversely affects a child's educational performance but this is not included under the definition of deafness.* Even severe hearing impairments may be difficult to identify in the first years of life, and students with milder hearing impairments may not be identified until school age. Referrals for undiagnosed hearing-impaired students may indicate both expressive and receptive language problems, variable hearing performance, problems in attending to aural tasks, and perhaps problems in peer relationships. Diagnosis of hearing impairment is usually made by audiologists, who identify the auditory disability, in conjunction with school personnel, who identify the educational disability.

Orthopedic Impairments   An orthopedic impairment *adversely affects a child's educational performance. The term includes impairments caused by congenital anomaly (e.g., clubfoot, absence of some member, etc.), impairments caused by disease (e.g., poliomyelitis, bone tuberculosis, etc.), and impairments from other causes (e.g., cerebral palsy, amputations, and fractures or burns that cause contractures).* Pupils with physical disabilities are generally identified prior to entering school. However, accidents and disease may impair a previously normal student. Medical diagnosis establishes the presence of the condition. The severity of the condition may be established in part by medical opinion and in part by systematic observation of the particular student.

Other Health Impairment   *Other health impairments are conditions that limit strength, vitality or alertness, [or] chronic or acute health problems, such as a heart condition, tuberculosis, rheumatic fever, nephritis, asthma, sickle cell anemia, hemophilia, epilepsy, lead poisoning, leukemia, or diabetes that adversely affect a child's educational performance.* Diagnosis of health impairments is usually made by physicians, who identify the health problems, and school personnel, who identify the educational disability.

The Process of Determining Exceptionality

In practice, deciding whether a student is exceptional can be complex. MDT evaluations frequently (and correctly) go beyond the information required by the entitlement criteria. MDTs collect information to rule out other possible disabling conditions. Sometimes the condition that initiates the referral is *not* the disabling condition. Those who are responsible for classification of pupils must adopt a point of view that is, in part, disconfirmatory—a point of view that looks to disprove the working hypothesis. Assessors must collect information that would allow them to reject the classification if a pupil proves to be not disabled or to suffer from a different disability. For example, if Harvey were referred for possible classification as a mentally retarded student, we would try to select tests of intelligence and adaptive behavior on which he would do well, to disconfirm the working hypothesis. As another example, if Tom were referred for inconsistent performance in expressive language even though his other skills—especially math and science—were average, we might infer that he could have a learning disability. What would it take to reject the hypothesis that he is learning disabled? If we could show that his problem was caused by a sensorineural hearing loss, he would not be learning disabled; if his problem arose because his primary language is a dialect of English, he would not be learning disabled; if he suffered from recurrent bouts of otitis media (middle-ear infections), he would not be learning disabled. Therefore, the MDT must consider other possible causes of his behavior and collect data that would allow them to evaluate these other explanations.

Finally, in attempting to establish that a student should be classified as disabled, we often must choose among competing procedures and tests. There are different tests to *operationalize* the eligibility requirements. For example, to be mentally retarded in Pennsylvania, a pupil must earn a score of less than 80 on an individually administered test of intelligence. However, as we show in Chapter 17, individual tests of intelligence are not interchangeable. They differ significantly in the behaviors they sample and in the adequacy of their norms and reliability and slightly in their standard deviations. A dull, but normal, person may earn an IQ of less than 80 on one or two tests of intelligence but earn scores greater than 80 on two others. Thus, if we had to assess such a student, we could be caught in a terrible dilemma of conflicting information. The routes around and through the dilemma are easier to state than to accomplish. First, we should choose (and put the most faith in) objective, technically adequate (reliable and well-normed) procedures that have demonstrated validity for the particular purpose of classification. Second, we must consider the *specific* validity. For example, we must consider the culture in which the student grew up and how that culture interacts with the content of the test. A test's technical manuals may contain information about the wisdom of using the test with individuals of various cultures; or the research literature may have information for the particular cultural group to which a student belongs. Often theory can guide us in the absence of research. Sometimes it is just not possible to test validly, and we must also recognize that fact. Finally, when we find ourselves in a swamp of conflicting data, we must remember *why* we gathered the data. In this example, we would have gathered the data to learn whether a student met the eligibility requirement, an IQ equal to or less than 79. (Note that the reason for giving an intelligence test was *not* to see if the student needed help; we already knew that.)

SUMMARY

Assessment data are collected to make decisions about a student's need for special educational services and exceptionality. When students are exceptional *and* have such intense or special instructional needs that these needs cannot be met in regular education, they are classified as entitled to special education. Entitlement is an administrative act. Federal and most state special education laws contain provisions specifying that students must be classified before they can be declared eligible for services. Criteria for establishing the existence of handicapping conditions are specified in rules or guidelines, and assessment data are used to ascertain the extent to which the criteria are met.

STUDY QUESTIONS

1. Why is it necessary for government to set standards for providing services to certain types of handicapped students?
2. List and explain three benefits of classification of handicapped students.
3. How would you conduct an assessment to see if a boy (age 8) is eligible for special education classes?

ADDITIONAL READING

Cromwell, R. L., Blashfield, R. K., & Strauss, J. S. (1975). Criteria for classification systems. In N. Hobbs (Ed.), *Issues in the classification of children* (Vol. 1). San Francisco: Jossey-Bass.

Keogh, B. (1987). Learning disabilities: In defense of a construct. *Learning Disabilities Research, 3*(1), 4–9.

Reschly, D. J. (1987). Learning characteristics of mildly handicapped students: Implications for classification, placement, and programming. In M. C. Wang, M. C. Reynolds, & H. J. Walberg (Eds.), *The handbook of special education: Research and practice.* Oxford, England: Pergamon Press.

Reynolds, M. C., & Lakin, K. C. (1987). Noncategorical special education: Models for research and practice. In M. C. Wang, M. C. Reynolds, & H. J. Walberg (Eds.), *The handbook of special education: Research and practice.* Oxford, England: Pergamon Press.

Shinn, M. R. (Ed.) (1989). *Curriculum-based measurement: Assessing special children.* New York: Guilford.

Ysseldyke, J. E. (1987). Classification. In M. C. Wang, M. C. Reynolds, & H. J. Walberg (Eds.), *The handbook of special education: Research and practice.* Oxford, England: Pergamon Press.

Ysseldyke, J. E., Algozzine, B., & Epps, S. (1983). A logical and empirical analysis of current practice in classifying students as handicapped. *Exceptional Children, 50,* 160–166.

Chapter 16

Assessment of Intelligence: An Overview

N o other area of assessment has generated as much attention, controversy, and debate as "intelligence" testing. For centuries philosophers, psychologists, educators, and laypeople have debated the meaning of intelligence. Numerous definitions of the term *intelligence* have been proposed, each definition serving as a stimulus for counterdefinitions and counterproposals. Several theories have been advanced to describe and explain intelligence and its development. The extent to which intelligence is genetically or environmentally determined has been of special concern. Genetic determinists, environmental determinists, and interactionists have all observed differences in the intelligence test performances of different populations of children. The interpretation of group differences in intelligence measurements and the practice of testing the intelligence of schoolchildren have been topics of recurrent controversy and debate, aired in professional journals, the popular press, and on television. In some instances the courts have acted to curtail or halt intelligence assessment in the public schools; in others the courts have defined what comprises intelligence assessment. Debate and controversy have flourished about whether intelligence tests should be given, what intelligence tests measure, and how different levels of performance attained by different populations are to be explained.

No one, however, has seen a thing called intelligence. Rather, we observe differences in the ways people behave—either differences in everyday behavior in a variety of situations or differences in responses to standard stimuli or sets of stimuli; then we attribute those differences to a construct called *intelligence*. In this sense, intelligence is an inferred entity, a term or construct we use to explain differences in present behavior and to predict differences in future behavior.

We have repeatedly stressed the fact that any test assesses a sample of behavior. So, too, intelligence tests evaluate samples of behavior. Regardless of how an individual's performance is viewed and interpreted, intelligence tests and items on those tests simply sample behaviors. A variety of different kinds of behavior samplings are used to assess intelligence; in most cases, the kinds of behaviors sampled reflect a test author's conception of intelligence. In this chapter we review the kinds of behaviors sampled by intelligence tests, with particular emphasis on the psychological demands of different test items as a function of pupil characteristics.

INTELLIGENCE TESTS AS SAMPLES OF BEHAVIOR

There is a hypothetical domain of items that could be used to assess intelligence. In practice, it is impossible to administer every item in the domain to a student whose intelligence we want to assess. The dots in Figure 16.1 represent different items in the domain of behaviors that could be used to assess intelligence. No two tests evaluate identical samples of behavior; some tests overlap in the kinds of behaviors they sample, and others do not. No test samples all possible behaviors in the domain. In Figure 16.1 we see that tests A and D sample different behaviors. Both tests assess some behaviors sampled by test E. None of the tests sample all the possible behaviors in the domain.

The characterization of behaviors sampled by intelligence tests is complex. Some persons have argued, for example, that intelligence tests assess a student's capacity to profit from instruction, whereas others argue that such tests assess merely what has been learned; some have characterized intelligence tests as either verbal or nonverbal; some characterize intelligence tests as either culturally biased or culture fair. In actuality, nearly any contention regarding what intelligence tests measure can be supported. The relative merit of competing opin-

FIGURE 16.1   **Intelligence Tests as Samples of Behavior from a Larger Domain of Behaviors**

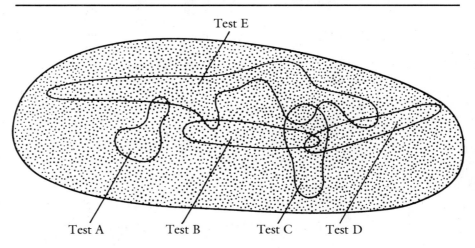

ions, theories, and contentions is primarily a function of the interaction between the characteristics of an individual and the psychological demands of items in an intelligence test. It is also a function of the stimulus and response requirements of the items.

There are many kinds of nonverbal behavior samples. A test might require children to point to objects in response to directions read by the examiner, to build block towers, to manipulate colored blocks in order to reproduce a design, or to copy symbols or designs on paper. Similarly, there are many kinds of verbal behavior samples. We could, for example, ask students factual questions, like "Who wrote *Huckleberry Finn?*" We could ask them to define words or to identify similarities and differences in words or objects. We could ask them to state actions they would take in specific social situations or to repeat sequences of digits. Test items may be presented orally, or the test takers may have to read the items themselves.

Similar behaviors may be assessed in different ways. In assessing vocabulary, for example, the examiner may ask pupils to define words, to name pictures, to select a synonym of a stimulus word, or to point to pictures depicting words read by the examiner. All four kinds of assessments are called *vocabulary tests,* yet they sample different behaviors. The psychological demands of the items change with the ways the behavior is assessed.

In evaluating the performance of individuals on intelligence tests, teachers, administrators, counselors, and diagnostic specialists must go beyond test names and scores to look at the kinds of behaviors sampled on the test. They must be willing to question the ways test stimuli are presented, to question the response requirements, and to evaluate the psychological demands placed on the individual.

THE EFFECT OF PUPIL CHARACTERISTICS ON ASSESSMENT OF INTELLIGENCE

Acculturation is the most important characteristic to consider in evaluating performance on intelligence tests. Acculturation refers to an individual's particular set of background experiences and opportunities to learn in both formal and informal educational settings. This, in turn, depends on the experiences available in the person's environment (that is, culture) and the length of time the person has had to assimilate those experiences. The culture in which an individual lives and the length of time that the person has lived in that culture effectively determine the psychological demands presented by a test item. Simply knowing the kind of behavior sampled by a test is not enough, for the same test item may create different psychological demands for different people.

Suppose, for example, that we assess intelligence by asking children to tell how hail and sleet are alike. Children may fail the item for very different reasons.

A child who does not know what hail and sleet are stands little chance of telling how hail and sleet are alike. He will fail the item simply because he does not know the meanings of the words. Another child may know what hail is and what sleet is but fail the item because she is unable to integrate these two words into a conceptual category (precipitation). The psychological demand of the item changes as a function of the children's acculturation. For the child who has not learned the meanings of the words, the item assesses vocabulary. For the child who knows the meanings of the words, the item is a generalization task.

In considering individuals' performance on intelligence tests, we need to know how acculturation affects test performance. Items on intelligence tests range along a continuum, from items that sample fundamental psychological behaviors relatively unaffected by learning history to items that sample primarily learned behavior. To determine exactly what is being assessed, we need to know the essential background of the student. Consider for a moment the following item:

> Jeff went walking in the forest. He saw a porcupine that he tried to take home for a pet. It got away from him, but when he got home his father took him to the doctor. Why?

For a student who knows what a porcupine is, that a porcupine has quills, and that quills are sharp, the item can assess comprehension, abstract reasoning, and problem-solving skill. The student who does not know any of that information may very well fail the item. In this case, failure is due not to an inability to comprehend or solve the problem but to a deficiency in background experience.

Similarly, we could ask a child to identify the seasons of the year. The experiences available in children's environments are reflected in the way they respond to this item. Children from central Illinois, who experience four discernibly different climatic conditions, may well respond, "Summer, fall, winter, and spring." Children from central Pennsylvania, who also experience four discernibly different climatic conditions but who live in an environment where hunting is prevalent, might respond, "Buck season, doe season, rabbit season, and squirrel season." Within specific cultures, both responses are logical and appropriate; only one is scored as correct.

Items on intelligence tests also sample different behaviors as a function of the age of the child assessed. Age and acculturation are positively related; older children in general have had more opportunities to acquire the skills assessed by intelligence tests. The performances of five-year-old children on an item requiring them to tell how a cardinal, a bluejay, and a swallow are alike are almost entirely a function of their knowledge of the word meanings. Most college students know the meanings of the three words; for them, the item assesses primarily their ability to identify similarities and integrate words or objects into a conceptual category. As children get older, they have increasing opportunity to acquire the elements of the collective intelligence of a culture.

The interaction between acculturation and the behavior sampled determines the psychological demands of an intelligence test item. For this reason, it is impossible to define exactly what intelligence tests assess. *Identical test items place different psychological demands on different children.* Thirteen kinds of behaviors sampled by intelligence tests are described in the next section of this chapter. For the sake of illustration, let us assume that there are only three discrete sets of background experiences, which we identify as *m*. (This is a very conservative estimate; there are probably many times this number in the United States alone.) To further simplify our example, let us consider only the thirteen kinds of behaviors sampled by intelligence tests, identified as *n*, rather than the millions of items that could be used to sample each of the thirteen kinds. Even with these very restrictive conditions, there are still $(mn)!/m!n!$ possible interactions between behavior samples and types of acculturation, or $(3 \cdot 13)!/3!13!$. This very restrictive estimate produces more than 1.35×10^{32} interactions. No wonder there is controversy about what intelligence tests measure! They measure more things than we can conceive of; they measure different things for different children.

Used appropriately, intelligence tests can provide information that can lead to the enhancement of individual opportunity and protection of the rights of students. Used inappropriately, they can restrict opportunity and rights.

The next two chapters review commonly used group-administered and individually administered intelligence tests, with particular reference to the kinds of behaviors sampled by those tests and their technical adequacy.

BEHAVIORS SAMPLED BY INTELLIGENCE TESTS

Regardless of the interpretation of measured intelligence, it is a fact that intelligence tests simply sample behaviors. This section describes the kinds of behaviors sampled.

Discrimination

Intelligence test items that sample skill in discrimination usually present a variety of stimuli and ask the student to find the one that is different from all the others. Figural, symbolic, or semantic discrimination may be assessed. Figure 16.2 illustrates items assessing discrimination: items a and b assess discrimination of figures; items c and d assess symbolic discrimination; items e and f assess semantic discrimination. In each case, the student must identify the item that is different from the others. The psychological demand of the items, however, differs depending on the student's age and particular set of background experiences.

FIGURE 16.2   **Items that Assess Figural, Symbolic, and Semantic Discrimination**

Figural discrimination

a.   ●   ●   ▲   ●

b.

Symbolic discrimination

c.   4   A   Q   W

d.

Semantic discrimination

e.   elephant   horse   monkey   truck

f.   Hispanic   French   Arabian   Germanic

Generalization

Items assessing generalization present a stimulus and ask the student to identify which of several response possibilities goes with the stimulus. Again, the content of the items may be figural, symbolic, or semantic; the difficulty may range from simple matching to a more difficult type of classification. Figure 16.3 illustrates several items assessing generalization. In each case, the student is given a stimulus element and required to identify the one that is like it or that goes with it.

Motor Behavior

Many items on intelligence tests require a motor response. The intellectual level of very young children, for example, is often assessed by items requiring them to throw objects, walk, follow moving objects with their eyes, demonstrate a pincer grasp in picking up objects, build block towers, and place geometric forms in a recessed-form board. Most motor items at higher age levels are actually visual-motor items. The student may be required to copy geometric designs, trace paths through a maze, or reconstruct designs from memory. Obviously, since motor responses can be required for items assessing understanding and concep-

FIGURE 16.3   **Items that Assess Figural, Symbolic, and Semantic Generalization**

Figural generalization

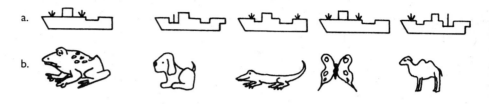

Symbolic generalization

c.	J	H	8	6	9
d.	81	21	23	26	25

Semantic generalization

e.	tree	car	man	house	walk
f.	salvia	flashlight	frog	tulip	banana

tualization, many items assess motor behavior at the same time that they assess other behaviors.

General Information

Items on intelligence tests sometimes require a student to answer specific factual questions, such as "In what direction would you travel if you were to go from Poland to Argentina?" and "What is the cube root of 8?" Essentially, such items are like the kinds of items in achievement tests; they assess primarily what has been learned.

Vocabulary

Many different kinds of test items are used to assess vocabulary. The student must in some cases name pictures and in others point to objects in response to words read by the examiner. Some vocabulary items require the student to produce oral definitions of words, whereas others call for reading a definition and selecting one of several words to match the definition. Some tests score a student's definitions of words as simply pass or fail; others use a weighted scoring system to reflect the degree of abstraction used in defining words. The Wechsler Intelligence Scale for Children–III, for example, assigns 0 points to incorrect definitions, 1 point to definitions that are descriptive (an orange is round) or functional (an orange is to eat), and 2 points to more abstract definitions (an orange is a citrus fruit).

Induction

Induction items present a series of examples and require the student to induce a governing principle. For example, the student is given a magnet and several different cloth, wooden, and metal objects and is asked to try to pick up the objects with the magnet. After several trials, the student is asked to state a rule or principle about the kinds of objects that magnets can pick up.

Comprehension

There are three kinds of items used to assess comprehension: items related to directions, printed material, or societal customs and mores. In some instances, the examiner presents a specific situation and asks what actions the student would take (for example, "What would you do if you saw a train approaching a washed-out bridge?"). In other cases, the examiner reads paragraphs to a student and then asks specific questions about the content of the paragraphs. In still other instances, the student is asked questions about social mores, like "Why should we keep promises?"

Sequencing

Items assessing sequencing consist of a series of stimuli that have a progressive relationship among them. The student must identify a response that continues the relationship. Four sequencing items are illustrated in Figure 16.4.

Detail Recognition

In general, not many tests or test items assess detail recognition. Those that do evaluate the completeness and detail with which a student solves problems. For example, certain drawing tests, such as the Goodenough-Harris, evaluate a stu-

FIGURE 16.4   **Items that Assess Sequencing Skill**

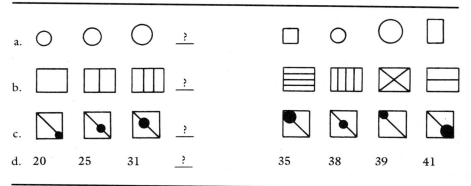

dent's drawing of a person on the basis of inclusion of detail. The more details in a student's drawing, the more credit the student earns. In other instances, items require a student to count the blocks in pictured piles of blocks in which some of the blocks are not directly visible, to copy geometric designs, or to identify missing parts in pictures. To do so correctly, the student must attend to detail in the stimulus drawings and reflect this attention to detail in making responses.

Analogies

"A is to B as C is to ____" is the usual form for analogies. Element A is related to element B. The student must identify the response that has the same relationship to C as B has to A. Figure 16.5 illustrates several different analogy items.

FIGURE 16.5   **Analogy Items**

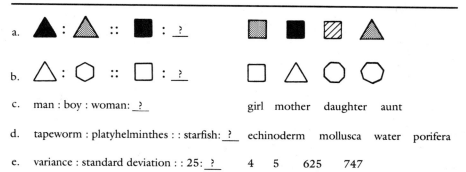

Pattern Completion

Some tests and test items require a student to select from several possibilities the missing part of a pattern or matrix. Figures 16.6 and 16.7 illustrate two different completion items. The item in Figure 16.6 requires identification of a missing part in a pattern. The item in Figure 16.7 calls for identification of the response that completes the matrix by continuing the horizontal, vertical, and diagonal sequences.

Abstract Reasoning

A variety of items on intelligence tests sample abstract reasoning ability. The Stanford-Binet Intelligence Scale, for example, presents absurd verbal statements and pictures and asks the student to identify the absurdity. It also includes

FIGURE 16.6   **A Pattern-Completion Item**

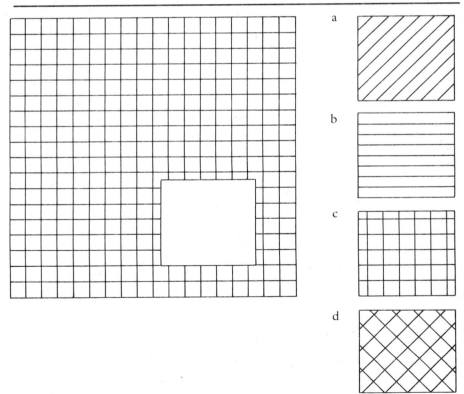

FIGURE 16.7   **A Matrix-Completion Item**

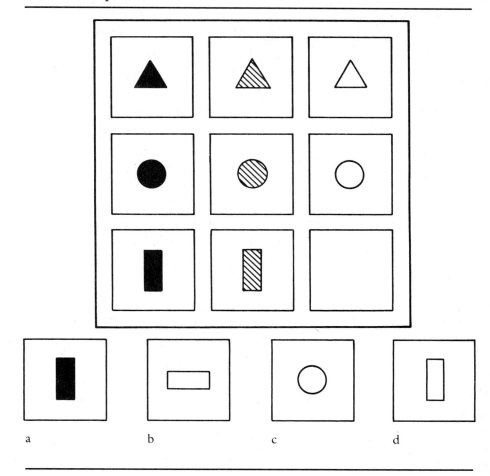

a series of proverbs whose essential meanings the student must state. In the Stanford-Binet and other scales, arithmetic-reasoning problems are often thought to assess abstract reasoning.

Memory

Several different kinds of tasks assess memory: repetition of sequences of digits presented orally, reproduction of geometric designs from memory, verbatim repetition of sentences, and reconstruction of the essential meaning of paragraphs or stories. Simply saying that an item assesses memory is too simplistic.

We need to ask, Memory for what? The psychological demand of a memory task changes in relation to both the method of assessment and the meaningfulness of the material to be recalled.

SUMMARY

The practice of intellectual assessment of children is currently marked by controversy. However, much of that controversy could be set aside if intelligence tests were viewed appropriately. Intelligence tests simply assess samples of behavior. And different intelligence tests sample different behaviors. For that reason, it is wrong to speak of a person's IQ. Instead, we can refer only to a person's IQ on a specific test. An IQ on the Stanford-Binet IV Intelligence Scale is not derived from the same samples of behaviors as an IQ on any other intelligence test. Because the behavior samples are different for different tests, one must always ask, "IQ *on what test?*"

The same test may make different psychological demands on test takers, depending on their ages and acculturation. Test results mean different things for different students. It is imperative that we be especially aware of the relationship between a person's acculturation and the acculturation of the norm group to which that person is compared.

Although many different kinds of behaviors are sampled by intelligence tests, we have described thirteen kinds: discrimination, generalization, motor behavior, general information, vocabulary, induction, comprehension, sequencing, detail recognition, analogies, abstract reasoning, memory, and pattern completion.

STUDY QUESTIONS

1. How would you demonstrate that a particular test item measured intelligence?
2. Describe at least three kinds of behaviors sampled by intelligence tests.
3. Bill Jones fails an item requiring him to state the difference between an optimist and a pessimist. Give two explanations for Bill's failure.
4. The school psychologist tells you that Emily Andrews has an IQ of 89. What additional information do you need before you are able to know the meaning of the score?
5. Using the categorization of behavior samplings described in this chapter, identify the kind or kinds of behaviors sampled by the following test items.
   a. How many legs does an octopus have?
   b. In what way are first and last alike?
   c. Find the one that is different: (1) table (2) bed (3) pillow (4) chair.
   d. Who wrote *Macbeth?*

e. Window is to sill as door is to _____ . (1) knob (2) entrance (3) threshold (4) pane

f. Define *hieroglyphic*.

g. Identify the one that comes next: 3, 6, 9, _____. (1) 12 (2) 11 (3) 18 (4) 15

6. Public Law 94-142 requires nondiscriminatory assessment of handicapped children. How can you demonstrate that a test is nondiscriminatory?

ADDITIONAL READING

Cancro, R. (Ed.) (1980). *Intelligence: Genetic and environmental contributions.* New York: Grune & Stratton.

Cronbach, L. J. (1975). Five decades of public controversy over mental testing. *American Psychologist, 30,* 1–14.

Siegel, L. S. (1989). IQ is irrelevant to the definition of learning disabilities. *Journal of Learning Disabilities, 22,* 469–479.

Torgeson, J. K. (1989). Why IQ is relevant to the definition of learning disabilities. *Journal of Learning Disabilities, 22,* 484–486.

Chapter 17

Assessment of Intelligence: Individual Tests

*I*n Chapter 16 we discussed the various kinds of behaviors sampled by intelligence tests and indicated that different tests sample different behaviors. In this chapter we will review the most commonly used individually administered intelligence tests, with special reference to the kinds of behaviors they sample and to their technical adequacy.

Few individual intelligence tests can or should be administered by classroom teachers. Yet, over the last few years, test developers have developed intelligence tests that teachers or other nonpsychologists should be able to administer. For example, the Test of Nonverbal Intelligence–2 is specifically designed to be given by teachers. The Slosson Intelligence Test–Revised is described as equivalent to the Stanford Binet Intelligence Scale, yet it can be given by people with no formal training in assessment. You will recall that one of the basic assumptions underlying psychoeducational assessment is that the person who uses a test should be adequately trained to administer, score, and interpret it. The correct administration, scoring, and interpretation of individual intelligence tests is complex. Despite the claims of test developers, we believe such tests should be used only by licensed or certified psychologists, who have received specific training in their use.

Three kinds of individually administered intelligence tests are reviewed in this chapter. First, we review the most commonly used global measures of intelligence—the Stanford-Binet Intelligence Scale IV, the three Wechsler scales, the Slosson Intelligence Test–Revised, and the Detroit Tests of Learning Aptitude–3. In general, these tests sample the thirteen different kinds of behavior described in Chapter 16. In the fifth edition of this text, we reviewed one other measure, the McCarthy Scales of Children's Abilities. The norms for that scale are so dated that use of it has declined and is discouraged.

In the second section of this chapter we review the most commonly used picture vocabulary test: the Peabody Picture Vocabulary Test–Revised. In the 1991 edition of *Assessment* we reviewed two other picture vocabulary tests (the

Quick Test and the Full-Range Picture Vocabulary Test). Their norms are simply too dated to allow continued use of the tests.

Many children have disabilities (for example blindness, deafness, and physical disabilities) that interfere with their capability to respond to traditional general intelligence tests. This fact has led several test authors to develop individually administered tests designed to assess the intelligence of blind, deaf, or physically disabled students and students with multiple handicaps. In the third section of this chapter, we review individually administered tests designed for use with special populations of children. Some measures (the Pictorial Test of Intelligence, the Leiter International Performance Scale, the Blind Learning Aptitude Test) have fallen out of favor because their norms are so dated. Although we reviewed those measures in earlier editions of this textbook, we do not include them here, and we discourage their continued use for norm-referenced purposes. Two commonly used individually administered tests of intelligence (the Woodcock-Johnson–Revised and the Kaufman Assessment Battery for Children) are parts of diagnostic systems and are discussed in Chapter 28.

WHY DO WE GIVE INDIVIDUAL INTELLIGENCE TESTS?

Individually administered intelligence tests are most frequently used for making exceptionality, eligibility, and educational placement decisions. State special education eligibility guidelines and criteria typically specify that the collection of data about intellectual functioning must be included in the decision-making process for eligibility and placement decisions and that these data must come from individual intellectual evaluation by a certified school psychologist.

GENERAL INTELLIGENCE TESTS

Stanford-Binet Intelligence Scale: Fourth Edition

*T*he fourth edition of the Stanford-Binet (SB) (Thorndike, Hagen, & Sattler, 1985) is the latest version of the scale originally developed by Alfred Binet in 1905 and revised for American children by Terman and Merrill (1916, 1937). The 1960 version of the scale combined the best items from earlier forms into one form (L-M) and provided new norms with deviation IQs. Although the scale was re-normed for the 1972 normative edition (Terman & Merrill, 1973), this edition was not a revision because the 1960 items were used.

The fourth edition maintains some continuity with the past, but also brings the SB up to date. It eliminates age scores because—even though the concept of mental age played an important role in earlier editions of the scale—age scales have several drawbacks. Like its predecessors, the new SB is an individually administered, norm-referenced measure of general intelligence that can be given to persons between the ages of 2 and 23.

Fifteen subtests are grouped into four areas: verbal reasoning, quantitative reasoning, abstract/visual reasoning, and short-term memory. The authors retained as many types of items from the 1960 version as could be fit into one of these four areas. Because of the extended range of ages, not all test takers are given all subtests; a complete battery requires from eight to thirteen subtests. Nevertheless, under certain circumstances (for screening, the identification of gifted students, or the assessment of students with school-learning difficulties), various abbreviated test batteries may be used. These batteries are listed below according to the behavior sampled.

VERBAL REASONING

Vocabulary   There are forty-six vocabulary items. The first fourteen use a picture vocabulary format. The remainder are presented orally and visually (on a printed form) and answered orally.

Comprehension   The forty-two comprehension items require a test taker to explain why something is done or what should be done (for example, the sample items are "Why do buildings have fire escapes?" and "Why should lawyers be licensed?").

Absurdities   This thirty-two-item subtest requires a test taker to explain why the pictures presented are absurd (for example, one of a fish being walked).

Verbal Relations   The test taker is presented with four objects and must explain in what way three of them are alike and the fourth is different. (For example, in response to the sample item "Jim, Bob, Kate, not John," the test taker is expected to answer that the first three names are nicknames, or informal names, and the last is not.)

QUANTITATIVE REASONING

Quantitative   This subtest assesses computation skills using forty-eight problems in two formats. The first twelve questions, designed for youngsters, require the test taker to use a counting tray and blocks to answer mathematical questions (for example, questions about counting). Questions geared to older individuals take the form of pictures or written questions.

Number Series   The test taker is presented with a series of numbers and expected to induce the rule that governs the series. (For example, a student presented with the sample sequence 4, 9, 16, 25, 36, _____ is expected to complete the series with 49, because $4 = 2^2$, $9 = 3^2$, $16 = 4^2$, $25 = 5^2$, $36 = 6^2$, and $49 = 7^2$.) There are twenty-six problems in this subtest.

Equation Building   The test taker is presented with a sequence of numbers and mathematical symbols and instructed to arrange them in a way that forms a valid equation. (For example, a student given the sample series 2, 2, 8, 4, x, +, = is expected to reformulate the sequence as $2 \times 2 + 4 = 8$.) There are eighteen equations.

ABSTRACT/VISUAL REASONING

Pattern Analysis   Because the SB covers a wide range of ages, two sets of materials are used in this subtest. A three-hole form board is used with very young children, who must place geometric forms in the correct holes or combine parts to make the geometric forms and then place them in the correct holes. Older individuals are given up to nine cubes with various geometric patterns; they are then shown a stimulus design and asked to reproduce it with the cubes. Credit is awarded on the basis of accuracy and completion within the time limits.

Copying   The twenty-eight items on this subtest consist of designs of increasing complexity to be copied by the test taker. The type of copying required depends on the level of the test. At the lower levels, the designs are copied with blocks. At the higher levels, the designs are drawn with a pencil.

Matrices Two types of problems are given in this subtest. The first twenty-two problems, designed for younger children, are multiple-choice matrix-completion problems. The first twelve involve 2 x 2 matrices; the next ten involve 3 x 3 matrices. The last four problems, for older children, require the test taker to complete the matrices by writing the correct responses. The format of each of these problems is the same: a 3 x 3 matrix in which each of the nine stimuli is actually a smaller 3 x 3 matrix.

Paper Folding and Cutting This eighteen-item, multiple-choice subtest consists of pictures. Each item has two parts: The item stem shows how a rectangular sheet of paper is folded and cut; the response options include one that correctly shows what the paper would look like after it had been cut and unfolded. The most difficult item has three folds and one area cut out.

SHORT-TERM MEMORY

Bead Memory Beads of different colors (red, white, blue) and shapes (flat, round, spherical, conical, cylindrical) are used in this subtest. The type of items used depends on the level at which testing occurs. On lower-level items, the subject is required to look at one bead for 2 seconds (or two beads for 3 seconds) and then correctly identify the bead (beads) on a card containing assorted pictures of beads. At higher levels, the subject looks for 5 seconds at a picture of colored beads of different shapes strung on a stick and then must reproduce the design with his or her own beads and stick.

Memory for Sentences The examiner reads a sentence and the test taker must repeat that sentence verbatim. The forty-two sentences range from simple (of the type: "Marv walked the cat") to complex (of the type "Books and reading were now a very important part of Rosemary's everyday plans, opening new worlds and bringing new adventures her way").

Memory for Digits After listening to a sequence of digits, the test taker must repeat it. Half of the sequences are to be repeated backward.

Memory for Objects This subtest assesses visual sequential memory with fourteen items. After showing a picture of a common object for one second and then another picture of a different object for one second, the examiner shows a picture containing several objects, including the two that were shown previously. The test taker must select the previously shown pictures in the order in which they were shown. At the highest level, a subject may be shown eight objects and asked to recall them in order.

SCORES

Raw scores for each subtest are converted to Standard Age Scores (SAS). These scores have a mean of 50 and a standard deviation of 8. Subtest scores are combined into area scores and an overall composite score, each with a mean of 100 and a standard deviation of 16. Extensive tables are provided for these conversions. The procedures for extrapolating scores at the extremes are carefully reported and appear appropriate.

NORMS

The normative sample was selected on the basis of five variables: age, sex, ethnicity (white, black, Hispanic, and Asian/Pacific Islander), geographic region, and community size. Extensive tables provided in the technical manual indicate reasonably good correspondence on each of these variables. When an appropriate number of subjects with particular characteristics could not be located, those who were tested were weighted so as to count for more than one; similarly, when there were too many subjects with a particular characteristic, each was weighted so as to count for less than one.

RELIABILITY

Internal-consistency (KR-20), SEMs, and stability co-efficients are reported for each subtest, for each area, and for the composite at each age level. As would be expected, subtest reliabilities are lower than compos-ite reliabilities. The test authors recommend that the composite score "be used as the primary source of in-formation for making decisions" (Thorndike, Hagen, & Sattler, 1986, p. 38). All KR-20s for these SAS composites are excellent; they range from a low of .95 to a high of .99. Test-retest data were available for two groups of children, five-year-olds (n = 57) and eight-year-olds (n = 55). Stability coefficients for these two groups were .91 and .90.

KR-20s for the areas are based on different num-bers of subtests. The more subtests, the higher the reliability. For abstract reasoning, all reliabilities ex-ceed .90, except when two subtests are used at ages 2 and 3. For quantitative reasoning, internal consisten-cies based on one subtest are all lower than .90; those based on two or more subtests are all higher than .90, with the exception of those for seven-year-olds when a two-test composite is used. For short-term memory, all area scores have reliabilities ex-ceeding .90 when three or four subtests are used. When only two subtests are used, nine of the seven-teen age groups have reliabilities for the short-term memory area in the high .80s; the rest are in the low .90s. Stabilities for areas ranged from a low of .51 (quantitative reasoning at age 5) to a high of .88 (verbal reasoning, also at age 5).

VALIDITY

The authors explain the SB within the context of current theoretical formulations about intelligence, justifying the development of a scale that assesses g, a general factor. The primary validity of interest for an intelligence scale is its construct validity. For the new SB, construct validity was established by conducting factor analyses to confirm a g factor and factors for each of the areas. Although g held up across ages, the factor structure varied for different age groups. For example, the quantitative factor did not emerge until after age 11.

Several concurrent validity studies were also con-ducted with the new SB. In one study, using a sam-ple of children between about 2 and 10 years of age, the old SB (form L-M) correlated with the new com-posite IQ (r = .81). In another study, using a sample of children between about 6 and 13 years of age, the Wechsler Intelligence Scale for Children–Revised Full Scale IQ was highly correlated with the SB com-posite IQ (r = .83). The correlation of the new SB was .80 with the Wechsler Preschool and Primary Scale of Intelligence and .91 with the Wechsler Adult Intelligence Scale–Revised. For a sample of children (mean age = 7-0, standard deviation = 2-5), the cor-relation of the SB with the Mental Processing Com-posite of the Kaufman Assessment Battery for Chil-dren was .89.

Finally, eight studies examined the performance of previously identified gifted, learning disabled, and mentally retarded students on the SB. These studies are difficult to interpret because criteria vary dramat-ically from state to state. No data are presented to in-dicate the degree of correspondence between deci-sions based on the new SB and the original decisions based on other devices. As would be expected, stu-dents classified as gifted received higher than average composite IQs (mean composite IQ 123.3, S = 11.2); students classified as learning disabled re-ceived lower than average composite IQs (mean composite IQ = 85.1, S = 14.6); and students classi-fied as mentally retarded received the lowest com-posite IQs (mean composite IQ = 54.9, S = 16.2).

SUMMARY

The fourth edition of the Stanford-Binet Intelli-gence Scale is a marked improvement over previous editions. The behavior sample is psychologically interesting and the materials are appealing. Not only does the SB provide the technical data needed to evaluate the adequacy of its reliability and norms, but the data indicate a well-normed and highly reliable device. There is also ample evidence of content and concurrent validity and some evidence of construct validity. It is unclear how effective the new SB will be in identifying students who are exceptional. It is becoming clear, however, that the SB requires significantly more time to administer than do other individually administered tests of intelligence.

The Wechsler Scales

*T*hree different measures of intelligence have been constructed by David Wechsler. Wechsler summarized his views on the concept of intelligence by stating that "intelligence is the overall capacity of an individual to understand and cope with the world around him" (Wechsler, 1974, p. 5). The definition is consistent with his original one in which he stated that intelligence is "the capacity of the individual to act purposefully, to think rationally, and to deal effectively with his or her environment" (1974, p. 3). Wechsler states that his definition of intelligence differs from the conceptions of others in two important respects:

> 1. It conceives of intelligence as an overall or global entity; that is, a multidetermined and multifaceted entity rather than an independent, uniquely defined trait.
> 2. It avoids singling out any ability (e.g., abstract reasoning), however esteemed as crucial or overwhelmingly important. In particular, it avoids equating general intelligence with intellectual ability. (Wechsler, 1974, p. 5)

The original Wechsler scale, the Wechsler-Bellevue Intelligence Scale (1939), designed to assess the intelligence of adults, was revised in 1955 and called the Wechsler Adult Intelligence Scale (WAIS). Its present form is called the Wechsler Adult Intelligence Scale–Revised (WAIS-R). In 1949, Wechsler developed the Wechsler Intelligence Scale for Children (WISC). This scale was revised and restandardized in 1974 and again in 1991. Its present form was developed by personnel at the Psychological Corporation and is called the Wechsler Intelligence Scale for Children–III (WISC-III). In 1967, Wechsler developed a downward extension of the WISC, the Wechsler Preschool and Primary Scale of Intelligence (WPPSI). The WPPSI was revised and restandardized in 1989 and is now called the WPPSI-R. Although the three scales are similar in form and content, they are distinct scales designed for use with persons at different age levels. The WAIS-R is designed for use with individuals over 16 years of age; the WISC-III is designed to assess the intelligence of persons 6 through 16 years of age; the WPPSI-R is used with children ages 3 through 7. All three scales are point scales; all three include both verbal and performance subtests. Subtests of the three Wechsler scales are summarized in Table 17.1.

Although the Wechsler scales differ in terms of age-level appropriateness, they sample similar behaviors. Descriptions of the behaviors sampled by each of the verbal and performance subtests follow; differences in format among the three scales are noted where appropriate.

Information   The Information subtest assesses ability to answer specific factual questions. The content is learned; it consists of information that a person is expected to have acquired in both formal and informal educational settings. The examinee is asked questions such as "Which fast food franchise is represented by the symbol of a colonel?"

Comprehension   The Comprehension subtest assesses ability to comprehend verbal directions or to understand specific customs and mores. The exami-

TABLE 17.1   **Subtests of the Three Wechsler scales**

	WAIS-R	WISC-III	WPPSI-R
Verbal subtests			
Information	X	X	X
Comprehension	X	X	X
Similarities	X	X	X
Arithmetic	X	X	X
Vocabulary	X	X	X
Digit Span	X	S[b]	—
Sentences	—	—	S
Performance subtests			
Picture Completion	S	X	X
Picture Arrangement	X	X	—
Block Design	X	X	X
Object Assembly	X	X	X
Coding[a]	X	X	X
Symbol Search	—	S[c]	—
Mazes	—	S	X
Geometric Design	—	—	X

[a] Called Digit Symbol on the WAIS-R and Animal Pegs on the WPPSI-R
[b] S indicates that although the subtest is included in the scale, it is considered a supplementary subtest and was not used in establishing IQ tables.
[c] Symbol search can be substituted only for Coding.

nee is asked questions such as "Why is it important to wear boots after a large snowfall?"

Similarities   This subtest requires identification of similarities or commonalities in superficially unrelated verbal stimuli.

Arithmetic   This subtest assesses ability to solve problems requiring the application of arithmetic operations. Individual items range from relatively simple counting tasks on the WPPSI to conceptually and computationally more difficult problems on the WISC-III and the WAIS.

Vocabulary   Items on the Vocabulary subtest assess ability to define words. For the WPPSI-R, the Vocabulary subtest is a two-part test. At the lower age

levels, children are required to name pictured objects. At higher age levels, the child defines words.

Digit Span   This subtest assesses immediate recall of orally presented digits. There is no Digit Span subtest for the WPPSI-R.

Sentences   This subtest is included only in the WPPSI-R. It assesses ability to repeat sentences verbatim.

Picture Completion   This subtest assesses the ability to identify missing parts in pictures.

Picture Arrangement   The Picture Arrangement subtest assesses comprehension, sequencing, and identification of relationships by requiring a person to place pictures in sequence to produce a logically correct story.

Block Design   This subtest assesses ability to manipulate blocks in order to reproduce a stimulus design that is presented visually.

Object Assembly   This subtest assesses ability to place disjointed puzzle pieces together to form complete objects. The WPPSI-R now includes an Object Assembly subtest; the subtest was not included in the WPPSI.

Coding   This subtest assesses the ability to associate certain symbols with others and to copy them on paper. The WAIS-R calls this subtest Digit Symbol; the WPPSI-R uses the Animal Pegs subtest in place of the Coding subtest. Instead of copying symbols on paper, the child must associate certain colored cubes with specific animals and match them.

Symbol Search   This supplementary subtest appears only on the WISC-III and it can be used only to substitute for the Coding subtest. The test consists of a series of paired groups of symbols, each pair including a target group and a search group. The child scans the two groups and indicates whether the target symbol appears in the search group.

Mazes   The Mazes subtest assesses ability to trace a path through progressively more difficult mazes.

Geometric Design   This subtest appears on only the WPPSI-R. Two distinct types of tasks are included. The first section is a visual recognition task. The child looks at a simple design and, with the stimulus in full view, picks one like it from a response array. The remaining items require the child to copy a geometric design by drawing.

SCORES

Raw scores obtained on the three Wechsler scales are transformed to scaled scores with a mean of 10 and a standard deviation of 3. The scaled scores for verbal subtests, performance subtests, and all subtests combined are added and then transformed to obtain verbal, performance, and full-scale IQs. IQs for the Wechsler scales are deviation IQs with a mean of 100 and a standard deviation of 15. For the WPPSI-R and the WISC-III, but not for the WAIS-R, raw scores may be transformed to test ages. Test ages represent the average performance on each of the subtests by individuals of specific ages. Four factor scores may be obtained for the WISC-III: Verbal Comprehension, Perceptual Organization, Freedom from Distractibility, and Processing Speed.

The Wechsler intelligence scales employ a differential scoring system for some of the subtests. Responses for the Information, Digit Span, Sentences, Picture Completion, and Geometric Designs subtests are scored pass-fail. A weighted scoring system is used for the Comprehension, Similarities, and Vocabulary subtests. Incorrect responses receive a score of 0, lower-level or lower-quality responses are assigned a score of 1, and more abstract responses are assigned a score of 2. The remainder of the subtests are timed. Individuals who complete the tasks in relatively short periods of time receive more credit. These differential weightings of responses must be given special consideration, especially when the timed tests are used with children who demonstrate motor impairments that interfere with the speed of response.

NORMS

All three Wechsler intelligence scales were standardized by selecting stratified samples and having individual examiners around the country administer the tests to specified kinds of individuals.

The WAIS-R was standardized "based on groups considered representative of the United States adult population" (Wechsler, 1981, p. 16). A stratified sampling plan based on age, sex, race, geographic region, occupation, education, and urban-rural residence was used. Proportions of specific kinds of individuals were included commensurate with their representation in the 1950 census. The WAIS-R was standardized on 1,880 adults, and extensive tables in the manual compare the percentage of the U.S. population to the percentage of specific kinds of individuals in the norms.

The WISC-III was standardized on 2,200 children ages 6½ to 16½. The standardization group was stratified on the basis of age, race/ethnicity, geographic region, and parent education (used as a measure of socioeconomic status), according to 1988 U.S. Census information. Extensive tables in the manual are used to compare sample data with census data. Although the sample looks representative overall, there are some matters of concern. The sample is stratified, but sufficient attention was not paid to cross-tabulations. For example, although 51 percent of the white group had some college education, 27.9 percent of the black group and 19.9 percent of the Hispanic group had some college education. The majority of the black and white samples came from the Northcentral and South regions of the country, whereas the majority of the Hispanic and Other groups came from the South and West.

The WPPSI-R was administered to over 2,100 children, including 1,700 children used for norming and an oversample of 400 minority children used to investigate item bias. The sample was stratified by age, and within age on the basis of sex, geographic region, ethnicity, and parental education and occupation. The standardization sample is made up of a hundred boys and a hundred girls at each age in half-year age intervals. Tables in the manual show the match of proportions in the standardization sample to proportions in 1986 census data. The sample is representative of the U.S. population of children ages 3 to 7.

RELIABILITY

Internal-consistency reliability is reported for the WAIS-R, WISC-III, and WPPSI-R in the form of split-half reliability coefficients. The reliabilities differ for the specific subtests and the age levels on which the coefficients are based. Ranges of reliability for the three scales are listed in Table 17.2. Reliabili-

ties for the separate subtests are reliabilities of scaled scores, whereas reliabilities for verbal, performance, and full-scale IQs are reliabilities for the IQs. Reliabilities for the Coding (Digit Symbol) subtest on the WAIS-R, the Symbol Search and Coding subtests of the WISC-III, and the Coding (Animal Pegs) subtest of the WPPSI-R are test-retest reliabilities. There are a number of age levels for which reliability data are not reported for the Coding and Symbol Search subtests of the WISC-III. Test-retest reliabilities are reported at three age levels for all subtests of the WISC-III in the test manual and range from .54 to .89. Internal-consistency reliability coefficients for most subtests are lower than .80 on the WISC-III, so the subtests should not be used in making important decisions for individuals. Reliabilities for the WPPSI-R subtests are low. All reliabilities are below .90 with three exceptions: Information at ages 3 and 4-5 and picture completion at age 4-5. Reliabilities of the WPPSI-R subtests are especially low at age 7. Reliabilities of composite scores are considerably higher than those for subtests. We recommend that interpretations of the WPPSI-R be at the composite score level, rather than at the subtest level.

VALIDITY

No evidence for the validity of the WAIS-R is included in the manual. Instead, the authors argue that (1) the WAIS-R and WAIS overlap considerably in content, (2) there are many studies of the validity of the WAIS, and (3) the WAIS-R will no doubt correlate with other measures of global intelligence as well as the WAIS did. In fact, 20 percent of the items on the WAIS-R are new items. It cannot be asserted that the WAIS-R is valid because the Wechsler-Bellevue and WAIS were valid.

Most of the information presented in the WISC-III manual in support of the validity of the test consists of information on the validity of the WISC-R. The two measures are not the same. The authors do present evidence for convergent and discriminant validity: They show that the verbal subtests correlate more highly with one another than with the performance subtests, and that the performance subtests

TABLE 17.2   **Split-Half Reliabilities for Subtests of the Three Wechsler Scales**

	WAIS-R	WISC-III	WPPSI-R
Verbal subtests			
Information	.87–.91	.73–.88	.62–.90
Comprehension	.77–.90	.72–.85	.59–.88
Similarities	.78–.87	.74–.84	.54–.89
Arithmetic	.73–.87	.71–.82	.66–.81
Vocabulary	.94–.96	.79–.91	.74–.87
Digit Span	.70–.89[a]	.79–.91	—
Sentences	—	—	.73–.88
Verbal IQ	.95–.97	.92–.96	.86–.96
Performance subtests			
Picture Completion	.71–.89	.72–.84	.72–.89
Picture Arrangement	.66–.82	.70–.84	—
Block Design	.83–.89	.77–.92	.79–.88
Object Assembly	.52–.73	.65–.76	.54–.70
Coding[b]	.73–.86[a]	.70–.90	.58[a]
Mazes	—	.61–.80	.65–.85
Geometric Design	—	—	.68–.86
Performance IQ	.86–.94	.80–.94	.85–.93
Full-scale IQ	.96–.98	.94–.97	.90–.97

[a] Test-retest reliability
[b] Animal Pegs for WPPSI-R and Digit Symbol for the WAIS-R. On the WISC-III the Symbol Search subtest is used instead of the Coding subtest.

correlate more highly with each other than with the verbal subtests. Evidence that the WISC-III correlates highly with the WISC-R is used as evidence in support of the contention that the two tests are measuring the same constructs. Finally, the WISC-III was correlated with the Otis-Lennon School Ability Test. Correlation of the full-scale WISC-III IQ and the Otis Lennon IQ was .73. A study of correlation of the WISC-III and the Differential Ability Scales (Elliott, 1990) is reported. The sample consisted only of twenty-seven children ages 7 to 17. Moderate to high correlations (.70s to .80s) are reported.

Evidence for the validity of the WPPSI-R is presented in the manual. Much of the evidence is evidence for the validity of the WPPSI. Since 50 percent of the items on the WPPSI-R are new and it has been restandardized, evidence for validity of the WPPSI is irrelevant to validity of the WPPSI-R.

The WPPSI-R is shown to correlate very highly with the WISC-R for fifty students ages 72–86 months living in Jacksonville, Florida. Correlations with the Stanford-Binet IV were shown to be moderate. Performance on the WPPSI-R is more closely related to performance on the McCarthy Scales than to performance on the Stanford-Binet IV. Correlations between performance on the WPPSI-R and the Kaufman Assessment Battery for Children are low.

Scores earned by children on the WPPSI-R are generally lower than scores they earn on other measures. The manual reports that student scores on the WPPSI-R Full Scale IQ are 8 points lower than their scores on the WPPSI, 7 points lower than their scores on the WISC-R, 2 points lower than their scores on the Stanford-Binet IV, and 6 points lower than their scores on the Kaufman Assessment Battery for Children.

SUMMARY

The three Wechsler intelligence scales (WAIS-R, WISC-III, WPPSI-R) are widely used individually administered intelligence tests. Although they are designed for different age levels, the three scales are similar in content and format. Evidence for the reliability of the three scales is good. Reliabilities are much lower for subtests, and subtest scores should not be used in making placement decisions. Evidence for validity, as presented in the manuals, is either nonexistent (WAIS-R) or very limited (WISC-III and WPPSI-R).

Slosson Intelligence Test–Revised

T he Slosson Intelligence Test–Revised (SIT-R) (Nicholson & Hibpshman, 1990) is a quickly administered and scored screening test designed to provide information about an individual's cognitive ability and help determine if a more thorough evaluation is needed. Whereas other individually administered measures of intelligence are designed to give an examiner both a quantitative and a qualitative picture of intellectual functioning, the SIT-R is designed merely to yield a score—a quantitative index of verbal intellectual functioning.

SIT-R items were designed to measure verbal intelligence in the following six domains:

Vocabulary: An assessment of the student's ability to use, understand and define words orally

Similarities and Differences: An assessment of an individual's skills in identifying similarities in superficially unrelated objects or concepts, or dissimilar attributes of objects or concepts that have most things in common

Comprehension: An assessment of knowledge of proper social behavior and ability to interpret sayings and proverbs

Quantitative: An assessment of the student's skill in completing mental calculations, remembering essential numbers, and identifying and using the mathematical processes required to calculate correct answers

Auditory Memory: An assessment of the individual's skills in repeating sequences of digits and sentences presented orally. Repetitions are both forward and backward.

The SIT-R is designed to be administered by "teachers, principals, guidance counselors, special education and learning disability teachers, psychologists, psychometrists, social workers, and other responsible persons who, in their professional work, often need to evaluate an individual's mental ability" (Nicholson & Hibpshman, 1990, p. 1). The authors do not report an age range of individuals who may be tested with the SIT-R. And, the authors do not specify an age range of those who participated in the norming sample. Norms tables are reported for individuals ages 4 to 18. The authors include a number of specific suggestions for assessing individuals with disabilities. They suggest test adaptations when such people are assessed. Yet, they provide no data on the effects of the adaptations, and no data on how individuals with disabilities perform on the measure.

SCORES

Raw scores for the SIT-R may be transformed to Total Standard Scores (TSS) with a mean of 100 and a standard deviation of 16. TSSs may also be expressed as percentile ranks, normal curve equivalents, *T*-scores, or stanines. We caution users to be very careful in using the scores for the SIT-R. The scores described in the manual do not match those in the tables. For example, in the manual the authors state that "Those in the standardization group whose chronological age is eleven years 4 months (11.3 years) had a raw score mean between 102–104." Yet the norms table lists a raw score range of 93–95 for those with a mean age of 11.3. Rather than expressing age scores in the conventional manner (years and months; e.g., 11-4) the authors express them as decimals.

NORMS

The SIT-R was standardized by having individuals who had been users of the original SIT, as well as other professionals, give the test to subjects "in given age ranges without regard to gender, ethnicity, educational or occupational level" (Nicholson & Hibpshman, p. 15). Then, the authors selected the protocols of 1,854 individuals to match the U.S. population, using data from the 1990 World Almanac. No effort was made to match subjects on the basis of geographic region. Based on census data, the Slosson sample over-represented individuals from professional, service, and farming occupations, individuals from families in which the parents had completed post-secondary schooling, and white people. It under-represented individuals from Northcentral states, individuals whose parents' occupation is described as "production, craft, repair, operators, and fabricators," individuals whose parents did not complete high school, and individuals who are "Native, Hispanic, Pacific Island Americans, and other similar groups." There is also a significant disparity between the size of the population centers from which the SIT-R sample was drawn and the size of population centers in the United States. Most SIT-R standardization subjects came from population centers of fewer than 50,000. No cross-tabulations are shown for normative data. Thus, we do not know how many of the males were black, how many of the students whose parents had completed college came from the South, and so forth. Those who use the SIT-R norms are comparing those they test to an unknown group.

RELIABILITY

Studies of the reliability of the SIT-R are inadequately described. The authors report split-half reliabilities by age for different numbers of students at each age. The students are not described in the manual. The size of the reliability sample was 1,793 individuals, and this number doesn't match the norm group. Reliabilities in excess of .88 are reported, but we do not know on whom the data are based.

One study of test-retest reliability is reported. A coefficient of .96 was obtained based on the performance of forty-one individuals on two administrations of the test one week apart. The group is not described.

VALIDITY

Data on validity of the SIT-R are weak. The authors argue that the test has construct validity because it measures aspects of what others say is intelligence. They argue content validity by asserting that their items measure content in six domains. They argue criterion-related validity by reporting correlations between SIT-R performance and WAIS-R performance for ten subjects of unknown characteristics. They also report correlations of the SIT-R with the WISC-III for thirty-one subjects of unknown characteristics.

SUMMARY

The Slosson Intelligence Test–Revised is a screening instrument designed to give estimates of verbal intelligence. The norm sample for this test is inadequately described. Evidence for reliability and validity are inadequate. We advise those who assess children to use more comprehensive measures than the SIT-R, such as the Stanford-Binet IV, the WISC-III, or the Woodcock-Johnson–Revised.

Detroit Tests of Learning Aptitude–3

*T*he Detroit Tests of Learning Aptitude–3 (DTLA-3) (Hammill, 1991) is a revision of the Detroit Tests of Learning Aptitude originally published in 1935 and revised in 1967 by Baker and Leland. The tests were revised by Hammill in 1985 and then again in 1991. The test is described as a measure of developed abilities, a concept first used by Anastasi (1980). She argued that the considerable confusion created by using the terms *aptitude*, *intelligence*, and *achievement* could be reduced by substituting for each the word *abilities*. Hammill (1991) adopts Anastasi's notion of developed abilities and a fundamental assumption that goes along with the term. Anastasi (1988) stated that:

> All ability tests—whether they be designed as general intelligence tests, multiple aptitude batteries, special aptitude tests, or achievement tests—measure the level of development attained by the individual in one or more abilities. No test reveals how or why the individual reached that level. (p. 413)

Hammill (1991) says that depending on the orientation or needs of the user of the DTLA-3, the test "can be used as a measure of intelligence, aptitude, or achievement."

There are four principal uses for the test: "(a) to determine strengths and weaknesses among developed mental abilities, (b) to identify children and youths who are significantly below their peers in important abilities, (c) to make predictions about future performance, and (d) to serve as a measurement device in research studies investigating aptitude, intelligence, and cognitive behavior" (Hammill, 1991, p. 14). The DTLA-3 consists of eleven subtests that measure different but interrelated developed mental abilities in students ages 6-0 through 17-11; the test takes between 50 minutes and 2 hours to administer. See the next section for a description of a version of the scale, the Detroit Tests of Learning Aptitude–Primary (DTLA-P2), used with children ages 3-0 through 9-0. The eleven subtests that make up the DTLA-3 are as follows.

Word Opposites   A stimulus word is read aloud, and the student is asked to state a word that means the opposite of the stimulus word.

Design Sequences   The student is shown a card for 5 seconds that contains a sequence of designs. The student must then manipulate cubes to reproduce the design from memory.

Sentence Imitation   The examiner reads a sentence and the student must repeat the sentence precisely.

Reversed Letters   The examiner says a series of letter names at the rate of one letter per second, and the subject writes each letter in the series in reversed order.

Story Construction   The student is shown pictures and asked to make up stories in response to the pictures.

Design Reproduction   Geometric forms are presented for specified time intervals and then removed. The student must draw the forms from memory.

Basic Information   The student must answer specific factual questions that assess knowledge of everyday situations, rather than knowledge acquired in school.

Symbolic Relations   The student is shown a design and then must select from among six possible responses the pattern that completes the design. The items are from the Test of Nonverbal Intelligence–2 (Brown, Sherbenou, & Johnsen, 1990).

Word Sequences   The student is required to repeat a series of unrelated and isolated words read by the examiner.

Story Sequences   The examinee is shown a series of cartoon-like pictures and must put these into sequence in order to depict a story. The student indicates the order by putting numbered chips under the pictures.

Picture Fragments The student must say the names of pictured items that have missing parts.

The DTLA-3 provides sixteen composite scores in addition to the eleven subtest scores. By using composite scores the examiner can make numerous interpretations of the performance of the student assessed. The grouping and re-grouping of standard scores for subtests enables users to fit the test within any one of several theoretical frameworks. The General Mental Ability Composite is obtained by combining the standard scores on all eleven subtests. The second composite, the Optimal Level Composite, is obtained by combining the four highest standard scores earned by the student. The test author believes that this composite controls for deficiencies or disabilities in specific areas and that it is the best measure of the potential of the individual. There are six composites that are labeled Domain Composites and eight composites that are called Theoretical Composites. Subtest scores that are combined to make up the Domain Composites and Theoretical Composites are listed in Table 17.3. The theoretical composites are indications of how the DTLA-3 subtests map domains described in major theories of intelligence.

An examiner administers all items of the Design Sequences, Reversed Letters, Story Construction, and Story Sequences subtests. On the remaining subtests, examiners start testing at a specified point and continue until a ceiling is reached. On all tests with ceilings except Design Reproduction, the ceiling is that point at which the student has failed five consecutive items. On Design Reproduction the ceiling is reached when the student has received a score of zero on three consecutive drawings.

Hammill (1991) provides a conceptualization of the DTLA-3 according to the framework of sampled behaviors outlined in Chapter 16. In Table 17.4 (page 359) we have reproduced his matching of the DTLA-3 subtests to our conceptual framework.

SCORES

A raw score, percentile, standard score, and age equivalent are obtained for each of the subtests. The standard scores have a mean of 10 and a standard deviation of 3. In addition, the examiner can obtain a quotient and percentile score for each of the sixteen composites. Each of the quotients has a mean of 100 and a standard deviation of 15. A software scoring and reporting system for the DTLA-3 is available for use with the test.

NORMS

The DTLA-3 was standardized on 2,587 individuals living in thirty-six states. The author indicates that since six subtests were retained from the DTLA-2, these were not restandardized. Rather, data from the 1984 norms were used. The retained subtests are Word Opposites, Sentence Imitation, Story Construction, Design Reproduction, Symbolic Relations, and Word Sequences. The remainder of the test was standardized during 1989 and 1990 using two procedures. First, a major site was selected from each of the U.S. census regions. The sites were in Florida, Michigan, New York, and Colorado. The site coordinators at these sites hired people to conduct the standardization testing. The author says that schools were selected so that the demographic characteristics of the sample would match those of the region as a whole, and that students were selected from "intact classrooms," but it is not clear how many schools or cities were involved in testing. A second approach was also used. The author purchased a mailing list of diagnostic personnel from a commercial mail order company and sent letters asking these personnel to participate in the standardization. Those who agreed were asked to give tests to ten to thirty students. Use of these procedures provided 1,055 students in the 1989–1990 standardization, in addition to the 1,532 used from the 1984 standardization. The author provides tables in the manual comparing the percentage of the sample to the percentage of the nation for each of the sample

TABLE 17.3   **Domains and Theoretical Composites of the DTLA-3**

	DTLA-3 Subtests										
	WO	**DS**	**SI**	**RL**	**SC**	**DR**	**BI**	**SR**	**WS**	**SS**	**PF**
Linguistic Domain											
Verbal Composite	X		X	X	X		X		X		X
Non-Verbal Composite		X				X		X		X	
Attentional Domain											
Attention-Enhanced Composite		X	X	X		X			X	X	
Attention-Reduced Composite	X				X	X	X				X
Motoric Domain											
Motor-Enhanced Composite		X		X		X			X		
Motor-Reduced Composite	X		X		X		X	X	X		X
Theoretical Composites											
Fluid Intelligence		X				X		X			
Crystallized Intelligence (The above two composites are based on Cattell & Horn's model.)	X		X	X	X		X		X	X	X
Associative Level		X	X	X		X			X		X
Cognitive Level (The above two composites are based on Jensen's model.)	X				X		X	X		X	
Simultaneous Processing	X		X		X	X	X	X			X
Successive Processing (The above two composites are based on Das's model.)		X		X					X	X	
Verbal Scale	X		X	X	X		X		X		X
Performance Scale (The above two composites are based on Wechsler's model.)		X				X		X	X		

WO = Word Opposites; DS = Design Sequences; SI = Sentence Imitation; RL = Reversed Letters; SC = Story Construction; DR = Design Reproduction; BI = Basic Information; SR = Symbolic Relations; WS = Word Sequences; SS = Story Sequences; PF = Picture Fragments.

TABLE 17.4 DTLA-3 Subtests Organized According to Salvia and Ysseldyke's Classification System

Classification System	DTLA-3 Subtests										
	WO	DS	SI	RL	SC	DR	BI	SR	WS	SS	PF
Discrimination						X					
Generalization											
Motor		X		X		X				X	
General Information							X				
Vocabulary	X				X						
Induction											
Comprehension					X					X	
Sequencing		X	X	X	X				X	X	
Detail Recognition						X					
Analogies								X			
Abstract Reasoning								X			
Memory		X	X	X		X			X		
Pattern Completion											X

WO = Word Opposites; DS = Design Sequences; SI = Sentence Imitation; RL = Reversed Letters; SC = Story Construction; DR = Design Reproduction; BI = Basic Information; SR = Symbolic Relations; WS = Word Sequences; SS = Story Sequences; PF = Picture Fragments.

SOURCE: Hammill, D.D. (1991). *Detroit Tests of Learning Aptitude-3.* Austin, TX: Pro Ed, p. 78.

characteristics (race, ethnicity, gender, location of residence, and geographic area).

The procedures used to standardize the DTLA-3 are confusing to us. First, the Preface to the DTLA-3 contains this statement:

> As one can imagine with a test as popular as the DTLA, we receive numerous constructive comments about our subtests. We used these suggestions to alter the formats of Object Sequences, Letter Sequences, and Story Construction. Object Sequences and Letter Sequences were reformulated and retitled Design Sequences and Reversed Letters, respectively. Story Construction pictures were drawn to include more action and more realistic depictions of events. (p. ix)

However, in the description of norming procedures the author indicates that some standardization data are from 1984 and some are from 1989–1990. He states that normative data for six subtests (those retained from the DTLA-2) were drawn in 1984. It is not clear whether the entire DTLA-3 was given to the 1989–1990 sample. It looks like only the new subtests were given. Yet, some of the subtests retained were reformatted, combined, reformulated, and redrawn. The author has not conducted comparative studies of the DTLA-2 and DTLA-3 to show the extent to which the two normative samples perform in a similar way.

After reading and re-reading the descriptions in the manual, we were left with the following questions:

- Are norms for the six retained subtests based on the 1984 standardization only, or were these subtests given during the 1989–1990 standardization?
- How can scores from the various subtests be combined into the sixteen composite scores when the individual subtests were standardized on different populations? On whom, then, are the composite scores standardized?

- Tables comparing the standardization sample to the national census breakdown are shown in the manual. Yet, we only know the numbers of individuals for main variables and cross-tabulations for age. Other important cross-tabulations (showing, for example, how many students of each racial group were from each geographic region) are not provided. Did most of the males come from the Northeast? Were most of the African-American students from the West?

RELIABILITY

Data on internal-consistency and test-retest reliability are presented in the manual. The internal consistency coefficients are based on the performance of 600 students (50 at each age level) whose protocols were selected randomly from the norm sample (which norm sample is not specified). Reliability coefficients for the subtests ranged from .70 to .95; reliability coefficients for the composites all exceeded .68. Test-retest reliability was established by giving the test twice to a group of thirty-four students who resided in Austin, Texas. The students ranged in age from 6 to 17, and the test was given at two-week intervals. The obtained reliabilities were .77 to .96 for subtest scores and .82 to .96 for the composite scores.

VALIDITY

Considerable information related to the validity of the DTLA-3 is presented in the test manual. There are sections on content validity, criterion-related validity, and construct validity.

Most of the evidence for the validity of the test is based on an analysis of the rationale for the formats and items included in each subtest. The author demonstrates in detail how and why the items were selected. As additional evidence for content validity, the author shows how the DTLA-3 measures each of the thirteen types of behaviors sampled by intelligence test items, which we described in Chapter 16 of this text.

A third form of evidence for the content validity of the DTLA-3 is the author's demonstration of how the subtests assess aspects of intelligence within the Cattell-Horn, Wechsler, Jensen, and Das models.

Evidence for the criterion-related validity of the scale is based in part on the DTLA-2 and in part on the DTLA-3. Since six subtests on the two measures are the same, data on validity of those six subtests is based on how some of the students in the 1984 standardization sample performed on other tests. Data were obtained from the records of seventy-six students who had been given the WISC-R, and twenty-five students who had been given the Peabody Picture Vocabulary Test–Revised. Times of test administration are not specified; all of the students were either enrolled in special education classes or being screened for special education placement. Correlations of the subtest scores ranged from .42 to .76 with the WISC-R and from .40 to .72 with the PPVT-R.

As further evidence for the construct validity of the DTLA-3, fifty students attending school in Austin, Texas took the DTLA-3, DTLA-Primary 2, Kaufman Assessment Battery for Children, and the Scholastic Aptitude Scale. Of the 891 correlation coefficients reported, only 38 were nonsignificant. The author uses this as evidence that the tests measure the same constructs. McGhee (1991) tested fifty children from a rural Georgia community with the DTLA-3 and the Cognitive Battery of the Woodcock-Johnson Psychoeducational Battery–Revised. The obtained average correlation coefficient of .64 is high.

Good evidence for the construct validity of this test is provided. The author demonstrates that scores on the measure increase with age, that the abilities measured by the DTLA-3 are related to each other because they all measure general developed abilities, that the scores on the measure correlate highly with measures of academic achievement, and that one factor underlies the scores earned on the test.

SUMMARY

The Detroit Tests of Learning Aptitude–3 is used to provide a measure of developed abilities in eleven subtests and sixteen composite areas. There are questions about the extent to which the test was normed on a stratified sample of the U.S. population. There is good evidence for the internal-consistency and test-retest reliability of the scale, and extensive information on the validity of the test.

Detroit Tests of Learning Aptitude–Primary 2

*T*he Detroit Tests of Learning Aptitude–Primary 2 (DTLA-P2) (Hammill & Bryant, 1991) is a special level of the Detroit Tests of Learning Aptitude designed to measure developed mental abilities of children ages 3-0 to 9-0. The test consists of one hundred items (thirty fewer than on the DTLA-P published in 1985), arranged in developmental order from the easiest to the most difficult. Examiners start testing at different points depending on the age of the child being assessed, and it takes between 15 and 45 minutes to give the test. They test until the child fails eight consecutive items. Items in the DTLA-P2 sample fifteen kinds of behaviors: articulation of speech sounds, matching semantic concepts, copying designs, repeating digits, drawing a figure of a person, sequencing letters, following directions that involve manual dexterity, sequencing pictured objects, following oral directions, identifying fragmented pictures, repeating sentences, solving visual abstract reasoning problems, using visual discrimination skills, producing antonyms, repeating a series of unrelated words, and identifying pictured objects.

Items are scored pass-fail, and item responses are clustered in a variety of ways to produce a General Mental Ability score and six subtest scores. Subtests are clustered in three domains. The Verbal subtest assesses knowledge of words and their use; the Nonverbal subtest is a measure of the student's skill in identifying perceptual relationships, reasoning without words, recalling objects and letters, and drawing figures from memory. The Attention-Enhanced subtest is a measure of concentration and short-term memory; the Attention-Reduced subtest measures long-term memory. Items in the Motor-Enhanced subtest are used to assess complex manual dexterity; those in the Motor-Free subtest are relatively motor-free. Each item is assigned to one of the two subtests in each domain. The basis for deciding which items belonged in specific domains is not described.

The authors of the DTLA-P2 identify the same four purposes for using the test as for the DTLA-3. The authors also encourage users to compute differences between subtest scores within domains. They state that "A significant difference between two subtest scores within a domain has clinical relevance and should be probed further through additional testing or clinical observation to determine the cause of the discrepancy"(Hammill & Bryant, 1991, p. 9).

In selecting items for the DTLA-P2, the authors cut thirty items from the DTLA-P to reduce the amount of time it took to administer the test. They also re-set the basal and ceiling criteria from ten failures in a row to eight in a row. The format of the picture book used in this edition was changed for some of the subtests. The verbal instructions were on the pictures for the DTLA-P; now they are in the manual.

SCORES

A raw score, percentile, and quotient (standard score) are obtained for each subtest. Standard scores for subtests have a mean of 100 and a standard deviation of 15.

NORMS

The DTLA-P2 norms are based on two standardization samples, one from 1985 and one from 1989–1990. In 1985 the DTLA-P was standardized on 1,676 children from thirty-six states. The sample was selected by asking users of the DTLA-2 to test twenty to thirty students in their area by administering the DTLA-P. Individuals who had assisted in the development of other tests put out by the same publisher also gave the DTLA-P. Finally, teams of examiners trained by the authors went to the various geographic regions and administered the test. According to the authors, "the sites were selected particularly because their demographic characteristics were similar to those of the nation as a whole" (Hammill & Bryant, 1986, p. 33). Scores were retained for 1,476 of the original 1,676 children in the 1985 standardization (those for whom item performance data were available).

In 1989–1990 the authors administered the DTLA-P2 to another 619 children selected using the same procedures as those used for the DTLA-3. Examiners were selected from the mailing list of a commercial publisher, and those who agreed to administer the test did so. Data in the manual indicate a close correspondence to 1988 census data. Like the DTLA-3, the DTLA-P2 only provides cross-tabulations for age and each of the other stratification variables. None are shown for the other variables (gender, race, geographic region, location of residence). Thus, we do not know whether most of the females came from the South, or Hispanic children from the Northeast, and so forth.

Item difficulties were re-computed, item order was changed, minor changes were made in test materials, and changes were made in basal and ceiling rules between the first and second editions of this test. The standardization sample is twofold: Children in the 1985 sample took the DTLA-P and those in the 1989–1990 sample took the DTLA-P2. We think those who use the scale are comparing children to an unknown norm group.

RELIABILITY

Data on internal-consistency and test-retest reliability are provided. Internal-consistency reliability coefficients were computed on a subset of children from the standardization sample (fifty children at each of seven age levels). All coefficients exceeded .80.

The authors report the results of two investigations of test-retest reliability. In the first, sixty-seven students from a parochial school in Cedar Park, Texas took the test twice at one-week intervals. In the second, children enrolled in a Head Start program in Austin, Texas took the test twice at one-week intervals. All reliability coefficients exceeded .80, and all but sixteen of the reliability coefficients exceeded .90.

The studies reported in support of the reliability of the DTLA-P2 contain exactly the same numbers of children, have the same test-retest interval, and were conducted at the same schools as two studies conducted for the DTLA-P and reported in the 1986 manual. In the 1991 manual, though, the data are reported for the DTLA-P2. For the DTLA-P all but two of the reliabilities exceeded .80. Now all but sixteen exceed .80. In 1986 reliabilities were reported for subtests. Now the subtests are a bit reconfigured. We assume data from the 1986 study were used to calibrate test-retest reliability for the 1991 edition of the test. The authors do not indicate the time of the study but do indicate that the data are for the DTLA-P2 and that "The results of both studies provide ample evidence of the stability reliability of the DTLA-P2 with different groups of children." At best, data on the reliability of the DTLA-P2 are very limited.

VALIDITY

Most of the validity evidence is based on studies with the DTLA-P. The authors did take a sample of 300 students from the 1985 standardization and re-score their tests using the 1991 version. Correlations were in excess of .88. The authors conclude that the DTLA-P and DTLA-P2 are essentially equivalent tests, and that data on validity of the DTLA-P apply to the DTLA-P2. Three criterion-related validity studies are reported for the DTLA-P2. Three studies are reported showing the relationship between performance on the DTLA-P2 and measures of achievement. The evidence for validity of the measure is good.

SUMMARY

The DTLA-P2 is designed to measure developed mental abilities in children between 3 and 9 years of age. Users of the test obtain scores for each of six subtests and also obtain a general mental ability index. The norms for the test are based on separate standardizations conducted in 1985 and 1989–1990. Information on how the norm sample for the test was stratified is incomplete. There is good evidence for internal-consistency reliability of the scale, but data on test-retest reliability seem to be limited to the earlier edition of the test. There is good evidence for the criterion-related and predictive validity of the scale.

PICTURE VOCABULARY TESTS

A number of picture vocabulary tests are among the most widely used tests for assessment of intelligence. Before describing an individual picture vocabulary test, we believe it is important to state what these devices measure. The tests are not measures of intelligence per se; rather, they measure only one aspect of intelligence, receptive vocabulary. Picture vocabulary tests present pictures to the test taker, who is asked to identify those pictures that correspond to words read by the examiner. Some authors of picture vocabulary measures state that the tests measure receptive vocabulary; others equate receptive vocabulary with intelligence and claim that their tests assess intelligence. Because the tests measure only one aspect of intelligence, they should not be used to make eligibility decisions. Some commonly used picture vocabulary tests were reviewed in earlier editions of this textbook. They have not been updated for so long that they are no longer useful. We review only one picture vocabulary test in this section of the chapter. Other measures used to assess receptive vocabulary are reviewed in Chapter 23, Assessment of Oral Language.

Peabody Picture Vocabulary Test–Revised

The Peabody Picture Vocabulary Test–Revised (PPVT-R) (Dunn & Dunn, 1981) is an individually administered, norm-referenced measure of receptive (hearing) vocabulary designed to provide an index of achievement and/or scholastic aptitude. The authors of the test state that

> The PPVT-R is designed primarily to measure a subject's receptive (hearing) vocabulary for Standard American English. In this sense, it is an achievement test, since it shows the extent of English vocabulary acquisition.

> Another function is to provide a quick estimate of one major aspect of verbal ability for subjects who have grown up in a standard English-speaking environment. In this sense, it is a scholastic aptitude test. It is not, however, a comprehensive test of general intelligence. Instead, it measures only one important facet of general intelligence: vocabulary. (Dunn & Dunn, 1981, p. 6)

On the PPVT-R, a revision of the Peabody Picture Vocabulary Test that originally appeared in 1959 and later in 1965, two-thirds of the items are new. There are two parallel forms of the test (forms L and M), and the test may be administered to persons between 2½ and 40 years of age.

The PPVT-R is administered in easel format, with the examiner showing the test taker a series of plates on which four pictures are drawn. The examiner reads a stimulus word for each plate, and the person being tested points to the picture that best represents the stimulus word. The PPVT-R is an untimed power test, and it usually takes from 10 to 15 minutes to administer. The test is accompanied by both a manual and a technical manual, the latter providing extensive data on the development and technical characteristics of the test.

SCORES

The student's raw score is the number of pictures correctly identified between basal and ceiling items. The test employs a multiple-choice format. The basal is the highest level at which a person makes eight consecutive correct responses; the ceiling is defined as that point at which a person makes six errors in consecutive items. Raw scores may be transformed to age equivalents, standard scores ($X = 100$, $S = 15$), percentile ranks, and stanines. True score confidence bands are provided for obtained scores, and the authors use asymmetrical confidence intervals (see Chapter 7) for extreme scores.

NORMS

The development of the PPVT-R began with a four-stage item tryout program between 1976 and 1978. A total of 9,099 persons were tested using 684 experimental items. This initial item tryout was followed by administration of 504 items (252 per form) to 5,717 persons as part of an item-calibration study. Subjects for this phase of test development were selected from a sample drawn on the basis of geographic region, rural-urban residence, socioeconomic status, and race (in preschool and first grade only). Both traditional item analysis and Rasch-

Wright latent trait methods were used to select final items for the two forms of the test.[1]

The PPVT-R was standardized on a representative national sample of 4,200 students, ages 2½ through 18, and on 828 adults. The 2½ to 18 sample was selected on the basis of geographic region, parental occupation, sex, race, and community size. Data in the technical manual illustrate close agreement between sample proportions and 1970 U.S. Census proportions. The adult sample was selected in proportion to the 1970 U.S. Census occupational data, and according to geographic region and sex. Again, the composition of the adult sample closely approximates census data.

RELIABILITY

Extensive reliability data are provided in the technical manual for the PPVT-R. The section on reliability begins with a description of the relationship between performance on the 1965 and 1981 editions of the test. These data are of heuristic interest only, owing to extensive revision of the test.

Three kinds of reliability data are reported for the PPVT-R: split-half indexes of internal consistency; immediate test-retest reliability using alternate forms; and delayed test-retest reliability (nine to thirty-one days delay) using alternate forms. Split-half reliability coefficients ranged from .67 to .88 with a median of .80 on form L, and from .61 to .88 with a median of .81 on form M for the younger (ages 2½ to 18) population, and from .80 to .85 with a median of .82 on form L for the adult population. Immediate test-retest data were collected on 642 children and adolescents. Reliabilities for raw scores for single-age groups ranged from .73 to .91, with a median reliability of .82. Reliabilities for standard scores for single-age groups ranged from .71 to .89, with a median of .79.

Delayed test-retest data were obtained by administering the test to 962 children and adolescents. Re-

1. See Appendix 6 for a general description of Rasch scaling and item response theory.

liabilities for raw scores for single-age groups ranged from .52 to .90 (median = .78), and reliabilities for standard scores for single-age groups ranged from .54 to .90 (median = .77). The PPVT-R has satisfactory reliability for screening purposes, the intended use of the test.

VALIDITY

There are no data in the PPVT-R manual on the validity of the test.

SUMMARY

The PPVT-R is an individually administered, norm-referenced measure of receptive vocabulary. The test is well developed and adequately standardized. Data in the technical manual indicate adequate reliability for screening purposes, but there are no data on validity of the measure. Overall, the technical characteristics of this scale far surpass those of other picture vocabulary tests. If used properly and with the awareness that it samples *only* receptive vocabulary, the PPVT-R can serve as a useful screening device.

SCALES FOR SPECIAL POPULATIONS

As noted in the introduction to this chapter, a variety of devices have been developed to assess the intellectual capability of people who have difficulty responding to traditional devices. Assessment of special populations is usually carried out by one of the three following practices.

1. *Adapting Test Items.* In some cases, examiners change the procedures for administering an item to compensate for the disabilities of the person they are testing. Items normally timed are presented without time limits; verbal items are presented in pantomime; and so on. In such efforts, examiners often forget to consider the fact that the test is standardized using standard administration procedures. If, as is usually the case, examiners use the published norms for the test, they may make inappropriate comparisons. The individuals on whom the test was standardized will have been tested using procedures *different* from those adapted procedures an examiner chooses to use.

2. *Using Response-Fair Tests.* In other cases, examiners select tests to which the person can respond with minimal difficulty. Some tests, for example, employ no verbal instructions and require no verbalized responses. Deaf persons can respond and items can be given to deaf persons. However, many of the tests that can be given are standardized on people who do not have disabilities. The acculturation of individuals with disabilities differs from that of nondisabled people. In this instance the normative comparisons are unfair because the acculturation of those tested differs from the acculturation of those on whom the test is standardized.

3. *Using Tests Designed for and Standardized on Populations of Individuals with Disabilities.* In still other cases, when examiners are required to test persons who demonstrate specific disabilities, they choose to use tests developed for use with and standardized on specific groups of individuals with disabilities. A limited number of such devices are available, but they have the distinct ad-

vantages of appropriateness in both response requirements and normative comparisons. Unfortunately, nearly all of the tests designed for use with special populations have very outdated norms. These originally fine tests (for example, the Blind Learning Aptitude Test, the Leiter International Performance Scale, the Nebraska Test of Learning Aptitude, and the Pictorial Test of Intelligence) have not been re-normed and updated at appropriate times.

In assessing special populations, examiners must be concerned with two restrictions. They must be sure that response requirements are fair and reasonable—that is, that the person being tested can reasonably be expected to be able to respond—and they must be cautious in the use of norms and be reasonably certain that those they test have had comparable acculturation to those in the normative sample. The remainder of this chapter describes devices most often used with special populations.

The Nebraska Test of Learning Aptitude

The Nebraska Test of Learning Aptitude (NTLA) (Hiskey, 1966) is an individually administered test designed to assess the learning aptitude of deaf and hearing individuals between 3 and 16 years of age. The NTLA has twelve subtests with instructions for pantomime administration of the test to deaf persons and verbal directions for use with hearing children. To use the NTLA, the examiner must have considerable experience in individual intellectual assessment. To assess deaf children, the examiner should have specialized preparation and considerable experience working with the deaf. The manual for the NTLA includes suggestions about specific procedures to use in establishing rapport with deaf children, including suggested ways of correcting mistakes and of giving the child nonverbal reinforcement.

The NTLA was standardized using pantomime directions with deaf children and verbal directions with hearing children. For that reason, if pantomime directions are used, the scoring must be based on the norms for deaf children. If verbal directions are used, scoring must be based on the norms for hearing children.

Each of the twelve subtests is a power test, beginning with very simple items designed to give the child practice in the kind of behavior being sampled. Response requirements in all subtests are nonverbal; the test taker chooses one of several alternatives by pointing or makes a motor response such as stringing beads or drawing parts of pictures. Some subtests are administered only to three- to ten-year-olds; some are administered to all ages; others are given only to those 11 years old or older. A description of the twelve subtests follows.

Bead Patterns (ages 3 to 10)   This subtest assesses ability to string beads, copy bead patterns, and reproduce bead patterns from memory.

Memory for Color (ages 3 to 10)   This subtest assesses ability to remember a visually presented series of colors after a short delay.

Picture Identification (ages 3 to 10)   This subtest assesses ability to match identical pictures of increasing complexity.

Picture Association (ages 3 to 10)   This subtest assesses the ability to match pictures to other picture pairs on the basis of perceptual and conceptual relationships.

Paper Folding (ages 3 to 10) This subtest assesses ability to fold pieces of paper to reproduce a sequence of folds previously made by the examiner.

Visual Attention Span (all ages) This subtest assesses ability to remember sequences of pictures after a short delay.

Block Patterns (all ages) This subtest assesses ability to build block patterns from pictorial representations including three-dimensional arrays. The test taker is allowed 2 minutes to build each pattern and receives bonus points for faster solutions.

Completion of Drawings (all ages) This subtest assesses ability to isolate missing parts in line drawings and to draw in missing parts with a pencil.

Memory for Digit (ages 11 and above) This subtest assesses ability to reproduce sequences of visually presented digits. A sequence on a card is shown, the card is removed, and the test taker must reproduce the sequence using plastic digits. (This subtest is omitted if mental retardation is suspected.)

Puzzle Blocks (ages 11 and above) This subtest assesses ability to assemble disjointed cubes into a whole. It employs varying time limits, and bonus points are given for rapid solutions.

Picture Analogies (ages 11 and above) This subtest assesses ability to solve visually presented analogies. Three pictures are shown and there is a relationship between the first two. The third picture bears the same relationship to a fourth picture, which must be chosen from a response bank.

Spatial Reasoning (ages 11 and above) This subtest presents a whole figure and several samples of disjointed parts. It requires identification of the sample that could be put together to form the whole object.

The NTLA is a point scale; that is, the child earns points on the specific subtests that are administered.

Different subtests employ different ceiling rules. Criteria for stopping each of the subtests are adequately described in the test manual.

SCORES

The kinds of scores obtained for the NTLA depend on how the test is administered. As noted earlier, the NTLA may be administered either in pantomime or verbally. When the test is administered in pantomime, the norms for deaf children are used to obtain a learning age (LA) and a learning quotient (LQ). When the test is administered verbally, the norms for hearing children are used to obtain a mental age (MA) and an intelligence quotient (IQ). Both scores and quotients are based on the median subtest learning ages and mental ages. The author recommends that in interpreting the test performance of hearing children, teachers and diagnostic specialists rely primarily on the MA. He advises that the learning age and learning quotient obtained for deaf children are not equivalent or comparable to MAs and IQs. He recommends that the learning age should be the only score used to interpret the performance of deaf children.

NORMS

The NTLA was originally developed in 1941. Norms for hearing children were first published in 1957, and the revised edition of the test with norms for both deaf and hearing children was published in 1966 (Hiskey, 1966). The standardization sample for the 1941 edition included 466 children enrolled in state schools for the deaf in seven midwestern states and in one day school for the deaf in Lincoln, Nebraska.

In the revision and restandardization of the NTLA, Hiskey added one subtest (Spatial Reasoning) and many more difficult items. The revised NTLA was administered to 1,107 deaf children and 1,101 hearing children between the ages of 2-6 and 17-5 in ten "widely separate states." The deaf children were primarily from state schools for the deaf; no other data on the nature of the normative sample are reported. The hearing children were selected on the basis of their parents' occupational levels, with reference to the percentages found in the 1960 census. Hiskey states that "the samples included representatives from minority groups, although no effort was made to obtain a specified percentage of such children" (p. 10).

For the purpose of establishing age norms, the children from both samples were divided into fifteen age groups (all children between 2-6 and 3-5 were placed in the 3-year-old group, and so on). The number of children at each year level varied more for the deaf (25 to 106) than for the hearing (47 to 85). The samples of three- and four-year-old deaf children and the samples of older hearing children were limited in size. The final item placement was based on the performance of deaf children, and there are no comparisons reported in the manual between the performances of deaf children and hearing children. Thus, although evidence is reported on the increasing difficulty of items within subtests for deaf children, comparable data for hearing children are not reported. The published norms are based on the performances of 1,079 deaf children and 1,074 hearing children. As noted earlier, both samples are inadequately described. And, the norms for the NTLA are badly out of date.

RELIABILITY

The only reliability data presented in the manual for the NTLA are split-half reliabilities for the standardization groups. Hiskey reports split-half reliabilities of .95 for the three- to ten-year-old deaf group, .92 for the eleven- to seventeen-year-old deaf group, .93 for three- to ten-year-old hearing children, and .90 for eleven- to seventeen-year-old hearing children. No data about the standard errors of measurement are included in the manual.

Hiskey does report data on the internal consistency of the test but does so in an effort to demonstrate validity for the measure. In citing evidence of content validity, Hiskey reports subtest intercorrelations and correlations of each subtest learning age with the median learning age for the entire test. There are no data on the reliabilities of the individual subtests. Hiskey states that "studies in the near future will provide additional evidence of reliability, based on re-test results after varying periods of time have elapsed" (p. 16). We have searched the literature and have failed to find these studies.

VALIDITY

Hiskey states that "the best evidence of the validity of a test is to be found in its successful use over a period of years. Research reported during the past twenty years indicates that the original scale has been a valid instrument" (p. 12). He provides very little empirical evidence to support his contention. Data on validity consist of reported concurrent validity and evidence about correlation of subtest learning ages with median learning ages for the total test.

Hiskey reports correlations between subtest learning ages and the median learning age for the total test ranging from .55 to .89 for three- to ten-year-old deaf children, from .59 to .67 for eleven- to seventeen-year-old deaf children, from .51 to .77 for three- to ten-year-old hearing children, and from .54 to .67 for eleven- to seventeen-year-old hearing children.

Most data about the concurrent validity of the NTLA are based on the earlier edition of the test. Hiskey does, however, report the following concurrent validity coefficients for the 1966 revision of the NTLA: .86 for ninety-nine hearing children (ages 3 to 10) between NTLA and Stanford-Binet IQs; .78 between the NTLA and Stanford-Binet IQs for fifty hearing children between 11 and 17 years of age; and .82 between WISC and NTLA IQs for fifty-two hearing children between 5 and 11 years of age.

SUMMARY

The NTLA is an individually administered measure of learning aptitude standardized on both deaf and hearing children. The test is administered by pantomime procedures for deaf children and by verbal instructions for hearing children. When administering the test, the examiner must be especially careful to use the appropriate set of normative data. The test was standardized using pantomime procedures for deaf children and verbal instructions for hearing children. The standardization samples are not described fully enough, and the norms are out of date.

Reliability data for the NTLA are limited. No subtest reliabilities are reported; only split-half reliabilities for the entire scale are included in the manual. Validity data consist of reported correlations between subtest learning ages and the median learning age for the total test, data on the earlier edition of the test, and concurrent correlations of the NTLA scores with scores of hearing children on the Stanford-Binet (old edition) and the WISC, not the WISC-R or the WISC-III.

The Nebraska Test of Learning Aptitude is the best available device for the assessment of the learning aptitude of deaf children between 5 and 12 years of age. Because of limited technical data and especially the datedness and inadequacy of the norm group, results on the test must be interpreted with considerable caution.

Arthur Adaptation of the Leiter International Performance Scale

*T*he Leiter International Performance Scale was first constructed by Russell Leiter in 1929 for the purpose of assessing the intelligence of children who might experience difficulty responding to a verbal test: the deaf, the hard of hearing, those who demonstrate speech difficulties, the bilingual, and those who do not speak English. The 1929 scale was an experimental edition; subsequent revisions were published in 1934, 1936, 1938, 1940, and 1948. In 1950, Grace Arthur published an adaptation (AALIPS) of the Leiter International Performance Scale.

The AALIPS is an untimed, nonverbal age scale containing sixty items ranging from the two-year to the twelve-year level. The 1948 edition of the LIPS contains additional items and can be used to assess the intelligence of persons 2 through 18 years of age. The test materials for the LIPS and the AALIPS are identical through the twelve-year level.

Materials for the AALIPS consist of a response frame with an adjustable card holder and two trays of response blocks with corresponding stimulus cards (see Figure 17.1). All tests are administered by placing a stimulus card on the response frame and pantomiming the directions. The child responds by placing blocks in the response frame. The actual tasks range from matching colors and forms to completing patterns, forming analogous designs, and classifying objects. Behaviors predominantly sampled, therefore, include discrimination, generalization, sequencing, analogies, and pattern completion. Most items require considerable perceptual organization and discrimination.

The directions for administering the scale that are included in the manual are confusing. They're illustrated by black-and-white pictures that, unfortunately, are of little assistance with items in which color is the discriminative feature in both administration and solution. Colored pictures would facilitate ease of administration; the use of black-and-white pictures necessitates reading an entire page of instructions in order to ascertain proper alignment of stimulus cards and pictures and to ensure correct standardized administration.

SCORES

A major shortcoming of the AALIPS is the fact that the correct answers to test questions (arrangements of blocks) are not included in the manual. Examiners must judge the correctness of a child's response on the basis of what they believe the correct response should be. We suggest that examiners solve

FIGURE 17.1   **An Item from the Leiter International Performance Scale**

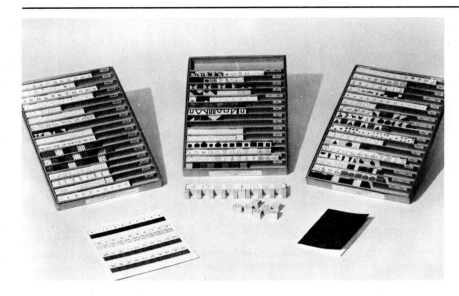

SOURCE: Photo courtesy Stoelting Company, Wood Dale, IL

the problems themselves before giving the test to children, that they obtain the consensus of other reasonably bright persons about the correctness of their responses, and that they then mark the blocks using a coding system to avoid scoring errors. Two scores, MA and a ratio IQ, are obtained by administering the AALIPS. There are four subtests at each age level of the test. The child earns a certain number of months credit for each subtest passed and the number of months are summed to produce a mental age. Only items between the child's basal and ceiling are administered. A basal is located by identifying the level at which a child answers all items correctly. The test involves a double ceiling: the child must fail all items at two consecutive year levels before testing is discontinued. Comparisons of the AALIPS with other intelligence tests (that is, the WISC and Stan-

ford-Binet) have consistently shown that scores on the AALIPS tend to be about 5 points lower than those earned on other scales. Arthur devised a bonus system that raises the basal and increases credit for subtests passed at the various year levels, thus bringing scores on the AALIPS into line with those on other tests.

NORMS

Normative data for the LIPS are not included in the AALIPS manual. The AALIPS, on the other hand, was standardized on only 289 children. All 289 came from a homogeneous middle-class, Midwestern, metropolitan background. There were few children at either extreme of the socioeconomic scale and apparently few or none who were the kind of children for whom the scale was originally developed—that is, children who experience difficulty responding to a verbal scale. The norms for the AALIPS are more than forty-five years old and are badly out of date. The test should not be used to make norm-referenced comparisons.

RELIABILITY AND VALIDITY

No reliability data are published in the manual for the AALIPS. Arthur reports a number of studies as evidence for the concurrent validity of the AALIPS. Correlations between performance on the AALIPS and on the Stanford-Binet Intelligence Scale for four-, five-, seven-, and eight-year-old children ranged from .69 to .93; for a sample of mentally retarded and brain-injured children these correlations were between .56 and .86. The AALIPS correlates more highly with the performance scale (from .79 to .80) than with the verbal scale (.40 to .78) of the WISC.

SUMMARY

The AALIPS is, in theory and design, a test that holds considerable promise for the intellectual assessment of children who have difficulty responding verbally. It lacks the necessary technical characteristics to make it psychometrically adequate. The test is inadequately standardized, the norms are dated, and few data about its reliability and validity are given in the manual. Until this test is made technically adequate, its use should be restricted to procurement of qualitative information by only the most experienced examiners.

Test of Nonverbal Intelligence–2

T he Test of Nonverbal Intelligence–2 (TONI-2) (Brown, Sherbenou, & Johnsen, 1990) is developed for use with individuals who require a language-free, motor-reduced, or culture-reduced test of abstract/figural problem solving. It is designed to be used in both screening and diagnosis with individuals between 5-0 and 85-11 years of age. The test is administered in pantomime, and those tested point to one of several responses presented in multiple-response array. Because no listening, speaking, reading, or writing is required in either the administration or scoring of this test, the test is especially useful with those who are unable to read or write or who may have impaired language abilities (for example, aphasic, non–English-speaking, culturally disadvantaged, mentally retarded, learning disabled, or deaf students). The TONI-2 should be given individually, even though the authors claim it can be administered to a group. They do not provide evidence for the reliability or validity of the test when it is group administered. The test is untimed and takes about 15 minutes.

There are two forms of the TONI-2; each has fifty-five items arranged in order of difficulty. The test is designed to assess one aspect of intelligence: abstract/figural problem solving. This aspect was selected because it was thought to be a general component of intelligence as well as a basic prerequisite of functional independence. All TONI-2 items require test takers to solve problems by identifying relationships among abstract figures. The subject must point to the one response among several alternatives that best fits a missing part in a pattern or matrix. There are five types of problem-solving items: simple matching, analogies, classification, intersections, and progressions. The test items shown in Figure 17.2 are examples of the kinds of items used in the TONI-2.

In item development for the original TONI, a pool of items had been reviewed by an unspecified number of professors, graduate students, school

FIGURE 17.2   **Representative Items from the TONI-2**

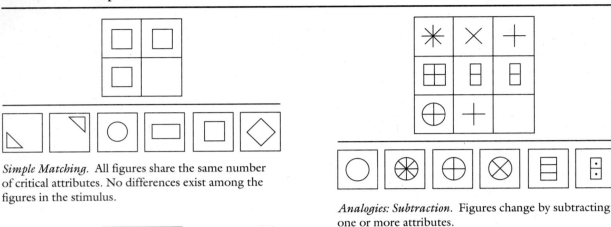

Simple Matching. All figures share the same number of critical attributes. No differences exist among the figures in the stimulus.

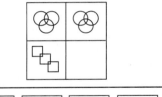

Analogies. The relationship among the figures in one of the rows or columns is the same as the relationship among the figures in the other rows and columns. The relationship varies in the following ways: *Matching.* No differences exist among figures.

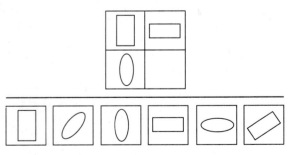

Analogies: Addition. Figures change by adding new attributes or additional figures.

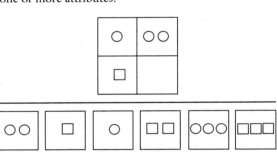

Analogies: Subtraction. Figures change by subtracting one or more attributes.

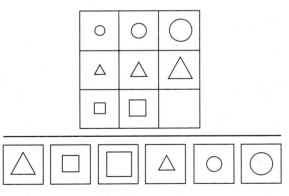

Analogies: Alteration. One or more of the attributes of a figure is changed or altered.

Analogies: Progressions. The same change continues between or among figures.

FIGURE 17.2 *(continued)*

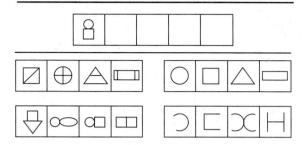

Classification. The figure in the stimulus is a member of one of the sets of figures in the response alternatives.

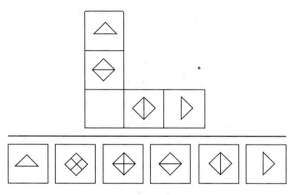

Intersections. A new figure is formed by joining parts of figures in the rows and columns.

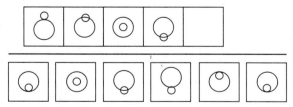

Progressions. The same change continues between or among figures.

SOURCE: Reprinted by permission of Pro-Ed, Inc.

psychologists, psychometrists, and special education teachers. Items that these experts thought were too ambiguous, symbolic, or that involved language were eliminated from the item pool. This left 183 items. These items were further reduced by giving the test to an unspecified sample of 322 students in grades K, 1, 3, 5, 7, and 9, and to young adults ages 18–35 and older adults ages 65–86. The number of items was reduced on the basis of indexes of item difficulty and item discriminating power, and 50 items were assigned to each of the two forms of the original TONI.

In developing the TONI-2, the authors wanted to put together a set of items that could be administered in pantomime and responded to by pointing. They also wanted items that were both abstract (nonmeaningful) and figural. An initial pool of one hundred test items was retained from the original TONI. The authors identified a pool of twenty-three additional potential items and administered them to fifty students enrolled in undergraduate courses at Baylor University in Waco, Texas. The authors selected bright students to participate because they wanted difficult items that could be placed at the ends of the two forms of the test. They selected ten items, five for each form of the test, developed by reviewing the content and format of other nonverbal and performance tests of intelligence

The authors of this test are careful to point out that the test is a measure of "only a small sliver" of the construct of intelligence. They are careful throughout the manual to point out that complete assessment of intelligence would usually be done with broad-based tests of intelligence or aptitude. They also rightfully point out, though, that all tests of intelligence measure samples of behavior from the domain of possible items or behavior samples. As we say so often in this text, one must never view tests as measures of constructs, but only as measures of samples of behavior that are thought to measure constructs. Thus, student performance on the TONI-2, as for other tests, should be described in terms of how the student performed on the kinds of behaviors sampled.

The authors of the TONI-2 do a nice job of cautioning users on how to use this measure. For example, they point out that the test is not diagnostic. They state that we know only what the examinee did on the measure. There are multiple explanations for poor performance on this test. The authors encourage users always to explore alternative explanations for poor performance and not to jump to interpretations like "Mitch earned a score of 60, indicating that he is mentally retarded." The authors set high standards for the TONI-2 and are careful to point out those few instances in which they are not sure they achieved their high standards.

SCORES

Two kinds of scores, percentile ranks and TONI quotients, may be obtained. TONI quotients are standard scores with a mean of 100 and a standard deviation of 15. Thus, they are like the IQs earned on other intelligence tests.

NORMS

The authors report that the TONI was standardized on 2,764 subjects from thirty states, ages 5-0 to 85-11. Subjects were selected randomly from the possible age range. The only individuals excluded were those who were profoundly retarded. Sixty-eight percent of the normative sample took the test (TONI) in 1981. The remaining 32 percent took the TONI-2 in 1989. Data on race, ethnicity, sex, and domicile indicate close approximation to 1986 U.S. census figures. Standardization was completed by administering the test to students individually or in groups of fewer than five.

The TONI-2 norms are based on the performance of two samples of individuals. The authors completed a confirmatory item discrimination study to make sure that the items were arranged in order of difficulty and to check the extent to which the original norms sample and the new one could be combined.

RELIABILITY

Data on internal-consistency and alternate-form reliability are reported in the test manual. Internal consistency was calculated by examining the performance of 900 subjects who participated in a factor analytic study. All but one of the reliability coefficients exceed .90.

The authors say they computed alternate-form reliabilities for the TONI by giving Form A and Form B of the test to 2,110 members of the normative group. Yet, the TONI and TONI-2 are not identical tests. Fewer than 1,000 subjects (654) were used for the standardization of the TONI-2. We assume the authors combined data from the two standardizations of the two different measures. Test-retest reliability was established by giving TONI-2 Form A to thirty-nine individuals from 7-9 to 15-9 years of age; it was estimated to be .86.

This is one of the few tests whose authors have conducted investigations of reliabilities for specific groups of persons with disabilities. This refreshing addition enables users to ascertain the extent to which the test provides consistent information on specific kinds of people.

VALIDITY

The authors report results of thirty validity studies. They illustrate that scores on the TONI (or TONI-2) correlate with chronological age, measures of achievement, other measures of aptitude, and general intelligence, and that the test discriminates between groups (such as normal students and those who are mentally retarded). Some studies are on the TONI, others on the TONI-2. In the introduction to the validity section Brown, Sherbenou, and Johnsen state, "For convenience, the acronym TONI-2 is used throughout this section; readers can tell by the date of the research which edition of the TONI was used" (p. 40). We had difficulty doing so. Of the thirty validity studies reported, six are dated 1990. The remaining twenty-four have earlier publication dates. We assume those with a 1990 date were TONI-2 studies and that earlier ones were on the TONI. It appears that the vast majority of the validity studies were completed on the TONI.

SUMMARY

The TONI-2 is an individually administered nonverbal measure of problem-solving ability. The test is the TONI with five items added to the upper end of each form. The norms are a combination of the norms for the TONI plus 885 additional individuals. Norms are adequately described in the manual, though cross-tabulations (for example, race by region) are not reported. Evidence for the reliability of this test is good. Data on validity are largely based on the previous edition of the measure. Given the small change in items (five new ones at the upper end), there is probably good evidence for validity. The authors of the TONI-2 have paid very careful attention to standards for test construction and are quick to call attention to any shortcomings of the test. They are to be commended for doing so. This nonverbal measure should prove especially useful given the fact that the normative samples for other nonverbal tests of problem solving and/or intelligence (Pictorial Test of Intelligence, Leiter International Performance Scale, Quick Test, Cattell Culture Fair Tests) all have norms that are so seriously out of date as to make them meaningless.

COPING WITH DILEMMAS IN CURRENT PRACTICE

The biggest difficulty encountered in trying to use individual intelligence tests is a problem of definition. What is intelligence? We noted in Chapter 6 that intelligence is an inferred construct. No one has seen a thing called *intelligence*. Yet there are many tests of this thing that no one has seen, and assessors are regularly required to assess it. Most of the definitions of conditions that indicate need or eligibility for special education include reference to cognitive functioning, intelligence, or capability. Students who are mentally retarded are said to have too little of it, students who are gifted have more than most. Students with learning disabilities are said to have average intelligence but fail to demonstrate school performance commensurate with the amount that they have.

Those who assess intelligence—and most diagnostic personnel are required to do so—must recognize that they can only infer intelligence from a sample of behavior derived through testing. Assessors must pay special attention to the kinds of behaviors sampled by intelligence tests. Two considerations are especially important. First, intelligence tests are usually administered for the purpose of making a prediction about future academic performance. In selecting an intelligence test, one must always ask, "What is the relationship between the kind(s) of behavior sampled by the test and the kind(s) of behavior I am trying to predict?" The closer the relationship, the better the prediction. It is wise to try to select tests that sample behaviors related as closely as possible to the behaviors one is trying to predict.

Second, one must always consider what behaviors or attributes are being assessed by intelligence test items. In particular, when different kinds of intelligence tests are used to assess students with disabilities, it is very important to be aware of the stimulus and response demands of the items. The descriptions of kinds of behaviors sampled by intelligence tests provided in the last chapter should be helpful. When we assess students' intelligence we want the test results to reflect intelligence, not sensory dysfunction.

It is important to remember that intelligence is not a fixed thing that we measure. Rather, it is an inferred entity, one that is understood best by evaluating the ways in which individuals who have different kinds of acculturation perform several different kinds of tasks. Intelligence tests differ markedly; individuals differ markedly. Evaluations of the intelligence of an individual must be understood as a function of the interaction between the skills and characteristics the individual brings to a test setting and the behaviors sampled by the test.

SUMMARY

Many different individually administered tests are currently used to assess intelligence. The tests differ considerably in their basic design, the kinds of behaviors they sample, and their technical adequacy. In evaluating performance on intelligence tests, it is especially important that teachers and examiners go beyond obtained scores to consider the specific tests on which the scores were obtained and the kinds of behaviors sampled by those tests. Detailed information facilitates that evaluation.

There are many individually administered tests designed to assess the intelligence of special populations. Individual intellectual assessment of children with specific disabilities should be carried out using tests designed to minimize the effects of the disabilities on their performances.

STUDY QUESTIONS

1. The Stanford-Binet Intelligence Scale IV and the Wechsler Intelligence Scale for Children–III are the two intelligence tests most frequently used with school-age children. Identify similarities and differences in the domains of behavior sampled by these two tests.
2. Why is it inappropriate to use the same intelligence tests with children who have sensory or physical disabilities as with children who do not have such disabilities?
3. Identify the major advantages of using the Stanford-Binet Intelligence Scale IV instead of the Slosson Intelligence Test–Revised.
4. In Chapter 16, we stated that IQs earned on different intelligence tests are not comparable. Using the Peabody Picture Vocabulary Test–Revised, the Test of Nonverbal Intelligence–2, and the Wechsler Intelligence Scale for Children–III as examples, support the statement.

5. The Performance sections for the Wechsler scales are the tests most commonly used today to assess the intelligence of deaf children. What are the major shortcomings of this practice? What alternatives exist?
6. Using the manual for any of the individual tests described in this chapter, characterize the domain or domains of behaviors sampled by any ten items. Use the domains described in Chapter 16.
7. Why would school personnel give individually administered intelligence tests?

ADDITIONAL READING

Gerweck, S., & Ysseldyke, J. E. (1974). Limitations of current psychological practices for the intellectual assessment of the hearing impaired. A response to the Levine Survey. *Volta Review, 77,* 243–248.

Sattler, J. (1988). *Assessment of children* (3rd ed.). San Diego: Jerome M. Sattler. (Chapter 4: Issues related to the measurement and change of intelligence; Chapter 5: Testing children; Chapter 11: Stanford-Binet Intelligence Scale: Fourth Edition)

Chapter 18

Assessment of Intelligence: Group Tests

*G*roup intelligence tests differ from one another in three ways. First, they differ in format. Whereas some group tests consist of a single battery to be administered in one sitting, others contain a number of subscales or subtests and are administered in two or more sittings. Second, they differ in the kinds of scores they provide. Some provide IQs and/or mental ages based on a global performance; others provide the same kinds of scores but differentiate them into subscale scores (for example, verbal, performance, and total; language, nonlanguage, and total). Third, some group intelligence tests are speed tests (timed), and others are power tests (untimed).

WHY DO WE ADMINISTER GROUP INTELLIGENCE TESTS?

Group intelligence tests are used for one of two purposes. Most often, they are routinely administered as screening devices to identify those who are different enough from average to warrant further assessment. Their merit, in this case, is that they can be administered relatively quickly by teachers to large numbers of students. Their drawback is that they suffer from the same limitations as any group test: They can be made to yield qualitative information only with difficulty, and they require that students be able to sit still for about 20 minutes, to mark with a pencil, and, often, to read.

Group intelligence tests are also used to provide descriptive information about the level of capability of students in a classroom, a district, or even a state. They are, on occasion, used in place of or in addition to achievement tests to track students. When used in this way, they set expectations; they are thought to indicate the level of achievement to be expected in individual classrooms or districts.

SPECIFIC GROUP TESTS OF INTELLIGENCE

Cognitive Abilities Test

*T*he Cognitive Abilities Test (CogAT) (Thorndike & Hagen, 1994) is a further development of the Lorge-Thorndike Intelligence Tests, which first appeared in 1954. The Iowa Tests of Basic Skills, the Tests of Achievement and Proficiency, and the CogAT comprise the Riverside Basic Skills Assessment Program. There are ten levels of the CogAT. Levels 1 and 2 make up the primary battery. Level 1 is appropriate for use in kindergarten and first grade, and level 2 is to be used in second and third grades. The other eight levels of the test (levels A through H) are published in a multilevel edition in a single test booklet. Items in the multilevel edition range from easy third-grade items to very difficult items at the twelfth-grade level. Examinees start and stop at different points, depending on the level being administered. The inclusion of eight levels of the test in a single multilevel edition allows teachers to administer levels of difficulty appropriate to the ability of their students. The scales increase in difficulty in very small steps. For students who attain little more than chance-level performance, the next easier level of the scale may be administered; for those who get nearly every item correct, the next more difficult level may be administered. Practice tests are available for all subtests in the scale.

Levels 1 and 2 are designed to assess the extent to which the child has developed the ability to reason inductively; the ability to solve problems; the ability to comprehend verbal statements; the ability to scan pictorial and figural stimuli to obtain either specific or general information; the child's store of general information and concepts; the ability to compare stimuli and detect similarities and differences in relative size; the ability to classify or order familiar objects; and the ability to use quantitative and special relationships and concepts.

The multilevel edition of the CogAT was constructed to provide a variety of tasks that require the student to discover and use relationships' to solve problems. The tasks use verbal, numerical, and nonverbal symbols.

Although both levels 1 and 2 and the multilevel edition include three separate batteries—verbal, quantitative, and nonverbal—the subtests included in the two editions differ. The various subtests are described below.

VERBAL BATTERY—LEVELS 1 AND 2

Oral Vocabulary The examiner reads a word or phrase aloud, and the student must mark the picture that illustrates it.

Verbal Reasoning Students are asked to make inferences, transformations, or judgments in response to common situations.

QUANTITATIVE BATTERY—LEVELS 1 AND 2

Quantitative Concepts The examiner asks the child to solve simple story problems or to solve a series problem based on a mathematical principle. All of the problems can be solved by using counting strategies that the majority of children develop before entering kindergarten.

Relational Concepts The examiner asks the child to mark the picture illustrating a particular relational concept (for example, biggest, tallest, beside) read aloud by the examiner.

NONVERBAL BATTERY—LEVELS 1 AND 2

Matrices The student must select from among four response choices the one that best completes a stimulus figure.

Figure Classifications   The child is shown three figures that are alike in some way and must select from four response possibilities the one figure that is like the three stimulus figures.

VERBAL BATTERY—MULTILEVEL EDITION

Sentence Completion   The student reads a sentence with a missing word and must select the response word that most appropriately fills the blank.

Verbal Classification   The student is given three or four words that are members of a conceptual category and must identify which response word best fits into the same category as the stimulus words.

Verbal Analogies   The student must complete verbal analogies of the form A:B::C: _____.

QUANTITATIVE BATTERY—MULTILEVEL EDITION

Quantitative Relations   The student must make judgments about relative sizes or amounts of material. Given two quantities (for example, 2 + 4 and 2 x 4), the student must identify which one is greater.

Number Series   Given a series of numbers that have a progressive relationship to one another, the student must select the number that best completes the relationship.

Equation Building   The student must construct correct equations using numbers and symbols for mathematical operations.

NONVERBAL BATTERY—MULTILEVEL EDITION

Figure Classification   Given three figures that are alike in some way, the student must identify the response figure that best fits into the same conceptual category.

Figure Analogies   The student must deduce the relationship between a pair of figures and must then select the last element of a second pair so that it accurately completes the analogy.

Figure Analysis   The student is given parts of figures and must identify the whole figure that could be formed by putting the parts together.

Levels 1 and 2 require no reading. These two levels are administered in three sessions ranging from 35 to 40 minutes each. Total working time is 98 minutes for each level. The multilevel edition is also administered in three sessions. Though administration time necessarily is longer, actual working time is 90 minutes for the three batteries of the multilevel edition.

SCORES

Four scores are provided for each level of the CogAT, one for each battery (Verbal, Quantitative, and Nonverbal) and a composite. Scores are not obtained for subtests within each battery. Among the scores available for each battery are number of items marked, raw score, standard age score, national grade and age percentile ranks, and grade and age stanines. Normal curve equivalent tables are provided in the norms booklet.

NORMS

The CogAT was standardized concurrently with the Iowa Tests of Basic Skills (Hoover et al., 1993) and the Tests of Achievement and Proficiency (Scannell et al., 1993). These measures were standardized on a carefully selected stratified national sample of about 170,000 students. All public school districts in the United States were stratified first on the basis of geographic region and then on the basis of size of enrollment. Districts were then stratified on the basis of socioeconomic status within the district, based on the percent of students in the district falling below the federal government poverty guideline. One district was randomly selected from each socioeconomic stratum. Once districts had been selected and had agreed to participate, further sample selection was accomplished by selecting buildings that would be representative of the distribution of achievement within the selected districts. Data provided in the test manuals show the breakdown of the sample by district size, region of the country, and district socioeconomic status. In addition to the public school norm sample, norms are provided for Catholic schools and for private non-Catholic schools. There are eight separate sets of norms —national, interpolated, local, large city, Catholic/private school, high socioeconomic, low socioeconomic, and international—so that student performance can be compared to different groups.

RELIABILITY

Data on internal-consistency reliability are reported for the Verbal, Quantitative, and Nonverbal batteries based on the performance of students in the fall and spring standardization sample. All reliability coefficients exceeded .80, with reliabilities higher for the multilevel edition than for Levels 1 and 2. There is good evidence for the internal consistency of the CogAT. No other reliability data are reported in the technical manual.

VALIDITY

There are no data on the validity of the 1993 CogAT. Perhaps these will appear in a research handbook, which the publishers indicate is yet to be published.

SUMMARY

The Cognitive Abilities Test consists of three batteries (Verbal, Quantitative, and Nonverbal) designed to measure the intelligence of students in kindergarten through grade 12. The procedures used in standardizing this test are exemplary. Evidence for internal-consistency reliability is good, but there are no data on other forms of reliability. There are no data on the validity of the CogAT.

Otis-Lennon School Ability Test

*T*he Otis-Lennon School Ability Test (OLSAT) (Otis & Lennon, 1989) is the latest in a series of intelligence tests that date back to 1918. The OLSAT requires a student to perform tasks such as detecting similarities and differences, solving analogies and matrices, classifying, and sequencing as a measure of those verbal, quantitative, and figural reasoning skills most closely related to scholastic achievement. The test is designed to assess "the examinees' ability to cope with school learning tasks, to suggest their possible placement for school learning functions, and to evaluate their achievement in relation to the talents they bring to school learning situations" (Otis & Lennon, 1989, p. 9).

Seven levels of the OLSAT (designated A through G) are used to assess abilities of students in K through grade 12. This most recent edition of the test includes two more subtests than previous editions. There is a separate test for each grade, K–3; thereafter, there is a multilevel edition of the test. At levels A and B (kindergarten and first grade) the entire test is dictated. Level C (second grade) contains two self-administered subtests, with the remainder of the test dictated. All other levels (D–G) are self-administered. The twenty-one different types of items that comprise the OLSAT fall into five clusters: Verbal Comprehension, Verbal Reasoning, Pictorial Reasoning, Figural Reasoning, and Quantitative Reasoning.

SCORES

Raw scores earned on verbal, nonverbal, and total test sections of the OLSAT may be converted to one or more derived scores: scaled scores, school ability indexes (with a mean of 100 and a standard deviation of 16), percentile ranks, stanines, or normal curve equivalents (NCE).

NORMS

The OLSAT was standardized in both fall and spring, 1988. The spring standardization sample consisted of 175,000 students from 1,000 school districts; the fall standardization used 135,000 students. The sampling of students took into account socioeconomic status (SES), region of the country, environment (urban or rural), and ethnicity. There was no specific stratification on the basis of age, grade, or gender. The sampling distribution is reported, but cross-tabulations are not. The sample is not a stratified sample; for example, we do not know how many students from the Northeast were from urban environments.

RELIABILITY

At each level, KR-20s are reported for each age and grade. All reliability coefficients exceed .76, with most ranging from .80 to .89. Reliability coefficients for the 1989 edition of the OLSAT are lower than those for previous editions. There are no data on test stability.

VALIDITY

The authors of the OLSAT argue that construct validity of the measure is shown by the high consistency of scores across all levels of the test. This is more a reliability than a validity argument. Evidence for validity is presented in the form of high correlations between the OLSAT and the Stanford Achievement Test. The authors show that scores on the verbal subtests of the OLSAT are better predictors of performance on verbal (language and reading) subtests of the SAT, and performance on the nonverbal section is more predictive of scores on the SAT mathematics subtests.

SUMMARY

The OLSAT is a quickly administered group test of intelligence for which there is reasonable evidence of internal consistency. There is no support for stability. Evidence for validity is limited. The authors do not report the stratification of the standardization sample.

COPING WITH DILEMMAS IN CURRENT PRACTICE

A number of specific limitations are inherent in the construction and use of group intelligence tests. The first limitation is that most tests have a number of levels designed for use in specific grades (for example, level A for kindergarten through third grade, level B for third through sixth grade). Tests are typically standardized by grade. Students of different ages are enrolled in the same grade; students of the same age are enrolled in different grades. Students with disabilities are often in ungraded programs. Test authors use interpolation to compute mental ages for students based on grade sampling. In earlier discussions, an age score was defined as the average score earned by individuals of a given age. Let us now consider a problem.

Suppose that an intelligence test has a level Q, which is designed to measure the intelligence of students in grades 6 through 9. As is typical of group intelligence tests, the test is standardized on students in grades 6 through 9, students who range in age from approximately 10 or 11 to 14 or 15 years old. Norms are based on this age range. The test is later administered to Stanley, age 10-8, who earns a mental age of 7-3. How can this be? Stanley, who is 10 years, 8 months old, could not possibly earn the same score as is typically earned on the test by students who are 7 years, 3 months old, since no students 7 years and 3 months old were included in the normative sample. The score is based on an extrapolation.

The second limitation is that most group intelligence tests, although standardized on large numbers of students, often are not standardized on representative populations. Most are standardized on school districts, not on individual students. An effort is made to select representative districts, but these may not necessarily include a representative population of individuals. Yet, the normative tables for group intelligence tests typically provide scores for individuals, not for groups.

The third limitation is that most group intelligence tests are standardized on volunteer samples. In the process of standardizing the test, representative districts are selected and are asked to participate. Districts that refuse, for any number of reasons, are replaced by "comparable" districts. This process of replacement may introduce bias into the standardization.

Finally, it must be remembered that when tests are standardized in public schools, those students who are excluded from school are also excluded from the standardization population. Students who are severely retarded, severely disturbed, or who have dropped out of school are excluded from the norms. Similarly, most authors of group intelligence tests do not describe the extent to which they included students enrolled in special education classes in their standardization samples. Exclusion of students with low IQs biases the norms; the range of performance of the standardization group is reduced, and the standard deviation is decreased. It is extremely important for the authors of group tests to provide tables in test manuals illustrating the composition of the standardization sample. Such tables should include descriptions of the kinds of individuals on whom a test was standardized, rather than descriptions of districts.

Many school districts have done away with the use of group intelligence tests for several reasons: The tests have been alleged to discriminate against members of racial and cultural minorities; they provide teachers with limited information for instructional planning; and teachers may form unrealistic or inaccurate expectancies or stereotypes based on the scores students receive on group intelligence tests.

In spite of limitations and problems, group intelligence tests are still used. Those who use the tests must recognize that they are sampling behaviors and must be aware of the behaviors sampled by the tests. School personnel give group intelligence tests to predict future performance, usually future achievement. It is wise, therefore, to use group intelligence tests and group achievement tests that have been standardized on the same population. We recommend that school personnel first select the group achievement test to be used and then choose the group intelligence test that has been standardized on the same population. The following pairs of tests have been standardized on identical groups of students: the Otis-Lennon School Ability Test and the Stanford Achievement Test; the Cognitive Abilities Test and the Iowa Tests of Basic Skills; the Otis-Lennon School Ability Test and the Metropolitan Achievement Tests; and the Cognitive Abilities Test and the Tests of Achievement and Proficiency.

SUMMARY

Group intelligence tests are used primarily as screening devices; they are designed to identify those whose intellectual development deviates significantly enough from "normal" to warrant individual intellectual assessment. Many different group intelligence tests are currently used in the schools. A review of the most commonly used group tests illustrates the many kinds of behaviors sampled in the assessment of intelligence. When teachers evaluate students' performances on group intelligence tests, they must go beyond obtained scores to look at the kinds of behaviors sampled by the tests. When selecting group intelligence tests, teachers must evaluate the extent to which specific tests are standardized on samples of students to whom they want to compare their pupils and the extent to which the tests are technically adequate for their own purposes.

STUDY QUESTIONS

1. Obtain a copy of any group intelligence test and identify the domains of behaviors sampled by at least ten items. Use the domains described in Chapter 16.
2. Identify at least four major factors a teacher must consider when administering a group intelligence test to students.
3. Why would school personnel give group intelligence tests to students?
4. Suppose you had to decide which group intelligence test to give in your school. What factors would you consider in selecting a test? Which test might you select? Justify your answer.
5. Of what value to classroom teachers are scores from group-administered intelligence tests?

ADDITIONAL READING

Kramer, J. J., & Conoley, J. C. (1992). *Buros eleventh mental measurements yearbook*. Lincoln, NE: University of Nebraska Press.

Chapter 19

Assessment of Sensory Acuity

*T*he *first* thing to check when a child is having academic or social difficulties is whether that child is receiving environmental information adequately and properly. In efforts to identify why children experience difficulties, we too often overlook the obvious in search of the subtle. Vision and hearing difficulties do interfere with the educational progress of a significant number of schoolchildren. The teacher's role in assessment of sensory acuity is twofold. First, the teacher must be aware of behaviors that may indicate sensory difficulties and thus must have at least an embryonic knowledge of the kinds of sensory difficulties children experience. Second, the teacher must know the instructional implications of sensory difficulties. Informed communication with vision specialists (ophthalmologists, optometrists, orientation and mobility specialists, and teachers of students with visual impairments) and hearing specialists (audiologists, speech and language pathologists, otolaryngologists, and teachers of students with hearing impairments) is the most effective way to gain such information. The teacher must have basic knowledge about procedures used to assess sensory acuity in order to comprehend and use data from specialists. This chapter, therefore, differs from previous chapters. It provides basic knowledge about the kinds of vision and hearing difficulties pupils experience as well as an overview of procedures and devices used to assess sensory acuity.

WHY DO WE ASSESS SENSORY ACUITY?

Difficulties in seeing or hearing are among the most obvious reasons that students experience academic and behavioral difficulties in school. They also generally are the kinds of difficulties most easily corrected or compensated for. The link between sensory difficulties and academic problems is easy to appreciate. The fact that sensory difficulties may cause behavioral problems, while not so obvious, has also been established.

VISUAL DIFFICULTIES

There are three ways in which vision may be limited: Visual acuity may be limited; the field of vision may be restricted; or color vision may be imperfect. The first two are the most significant.

Visual acuity refers to the clarity or sharpness with which a person sees. You probably have heard it said that a keen-sighted person has "perfect" vision— 20/20 in both eyes.[1] The person might more accurately be described as demonstrating "normal" vision; the numbers 20/20 simply indicate that the person is able to see a standard-sized object from a standard number of feet away. This method of measuring visual acuity is derived from the use of the Snellen Wall Chart. A person is described as having 20/20 vision if, at 20 feet from the chart, that person is able to distinguish letters that an average person can distinguish at 20 feet. A rating of 20/200 means that the person can distinguish letters at 20 feet that the average person can distinguish at 200 feet. Conversely, 20/10 vision means the person is able to distinguish letters at 20 feet that the average person can only distinguish at 10 feet. The former demonstrates limited vision, whereas the latter demonstrates better than average distance visual acuity.

One's field of vision may be restricted in two ways. A person may demonstrate normal central visual acuity with a restricted peripheral field; this is usually referred to as *tunnel vision*. Or a person may have a *scotoma*, a blind or dark spot in the visual field. If the spot occurs in the middle of the eye, it may result in central vision impairment.

Color vision is determined by the discrimination of three qualities of color: hue, saturation, and brightness. The essential difference between colorblind and normal persons is that hues that appear different to normal persons look the same to a colorblind person. Colorblind persons frequently do not know they are colorblind unless they have been tested and told so. Colorblindness is not an all-or-nothing condition. Most colorblindness is partial; the person has difficulty distinguishing certain colors, usually red and green. Total colorblindness is extremely rare. Colorblindness is an inherited trait found in about one out of twelve males and one out of two hundred females. There is no cure for colorblindness, but the condition is not usually regarded as a handicap.

Blindness may be either congenital or acquired. Congenital blindness or blindness acquired prior to age 5 has the most serious educational implications. Few people are totally blind; many have at least light perception and some object perception, either of which helps for mobility. Blindness, for legal purposes, is defined as

> central visual activity of 20/200 or less in the better eye, with correcting glasses, or central visual acuity of more than 20/200 if there is a field defect in which the peripheral field has contracted to such an extent that the widest diameter of visual field subtends an angular distance no greater than 20 degrees. (Hurlin, 1962, p. 8)

1. It is also said that hindsight is always 20/20.

It has been said that more people are blinded by definition (the legal definition cited above) than by any other cause (Greenwood, 1963, cited in Barraga, 1976). According to Taylor (cited in Barraga, 1976, p. 13),[2]

> the term *visually handicapped* is being used widely at present to denote the total group of children who have impairments in the structure or functioning of the visual sense organ—the eye—irrespective of the nature and extent of the impairment. This term has gained acceptance because the impairment causes a limitation that, even with the best possible correction, interferes with incidental or normal learning through the sense of vision.

When we deal with children, we are concerned primarily with the educational implications of reduced acuity. Educational needs resulting from low acuity get students declared eligible for special education services. Barraga differentiates among three categories of visual disabilities:

> *Blind.* This term [is] used to refer to children who have only light perception without projection, or those who are totally without the sense of vision (Faye, 1970) . . . . Educationally, the blind child is one who learns through braille and related media without the use of vision (Halliday, 1970), although perception of light may be present and useful in orientation and movement.
>
> *Low Vision.* Children who have limitations in distance vision but are able to see objects and materials when they are within a few inches or at a maximum of a few feet away are another subgroup. Most low-vision children will be able to use their vision for many school learning activities, a few for visual reading perhaps, whereas others may need to use tactual materials and possibly even Braille to supplement printed and other visual materials . . . Under no circumstances should low-vision children be referred to as "blind."
>
> *Visually Limited.* This term refers to children who in some way are limited in their use of vision under average circumstances. They may have difficulty seeing learning materials without special lighting, or they may be unable to see distant objects unless the objects are moving, or they may need to wear prescriptive lenses or use optical aids and special materials to function visually. Visually limited children will be considered for all educational purposes and under all circumstances as seeing children. (1976, p. 14)

Estimates of the number of schoolage children who experience visual difficulties range from 5 to 33 percent. Obviously, estimates differ as a function of the definition used and the screening devices employed.

Teachers must be consistently on the lookout for signs of visual difficulty. When children complain of frequent headaches, dizziness, sensitivity to light, or blurred vision, efforts must be made to evaluate the extent to which they are seeing properly. Obvious signs of possible visual difficulty include crossed eyes; turned-out eyes; red, swollen, or encrusted eyelids; constant rapid movement of

---

2. Quotations from Barraga's *Visual Handicaps and Learning: A Developmental Approach* used in this discussion are copyright 1976 by Wadsworth Publishing Company, Inc.

the eyes; watery eyes or discharges; and haziness in the pupils. These should receive special attention in the form of referral for vision screening (U.S. Public Health Service, 1971).

Certain behaviors also may indicate visual difficulties. According to the U.S. Public Health Service (1971), behaviors indicative of potential visual difficulties include holding books unusually close to or far from the eyes while reading; frequent blinking, squinting, or rubbing of the eyes; abnormal tilting or turning of the head; inattention in blackboard lessons; poor alignment in written work; unusual choice of colors in artwork; confusion of certain letters of the alphabet in reading (*o*s and *a*s, *e*s and *c*s, *b*s and *h*s, *n*s and *r*s); inability or reluctance to participate in games requiring distance vision or visual accuracy; and irritability when doing close work.

VISION SCREENING AND ASSESSMENT

Schools conduct vision screening, whereas vision testing is done clinically by ophthalmologists and optometrists. When youngsters experience learning difficulties, or when routine vision screening indicates visual difficulties, the child is referred for a clinical vision exam. If the clinical exam indicates 20/20 vision, no additional visual assessment needs to be done by educational personnel. Similarly, if visual acuity is limited but can be corrected by glasses, no visual assessments need be conducted by education personnel. However, if vision is 20/70 or less with best correction or if there is a limited visual field, educational personnel must ensure that a clinical low vision exam, functional vision assessment, or a learning media assessment is conducted. The purpose of these tests is intervention planning.

Most schools now have vision-screening programs, but the effectiveness of these programs varies. Two fundamentally different kinds of tests are used: those that screen only central visual acuity at a distance and those that assess both central visual acuity and a number of other visual capabilities. Most preschool screening programs include screening for amblyopia, often called *lazy eye*.

Basic Screening

The standard Snellen Wall Chart is the most commonly used screening test to assess visual acuity. The test consists simply of a wall chart of standard-sized letters that a child is asked to read at a distance of 20 feet. The test provides limited information about vision, assessing only central visual acuity at a distance of 20 feet. Specific difficulties may be encountered in using the test with some schoolage children. First, children may be unable to read the letters or to discriminate between letters like *F* and *P.* Second, children can often memorize the letters ahead of time. Third, the letters of the alphabet differ in legibility, which leads to guessing. The practical criterion for referral using this test is acuity of 20/40 or less in either eye for children in kindergarten through third grade, and 20/30 or less in either eye for those who are older (National Society for the Prevention of Blindness, 1961).

An adaptation of the Snellen Wall Chart, the Snellen E Test, is the most commonly used test with preschool children and those who are unable to read. The letter E is presented with its arms facing in one of four directions and the person being tested is asked either to name the direction, to point, or to hold up a letter E to match the stimulus. Again, this test assesses only central visual acuity.

Both Snellen tests fail to identify students with near vision problems, the kinds of problems often the most critical to reading. They also miss physical difficulties and problems in the internal structure of the eye (such as the retina). Some schools use the Keystone Telebinocular, a device that assesses fourteen different visual skills. Visual functioning is assessed at both a near point (16 inches) and a far point (20 inches). The distances are produced optically, and children remain seated in front of the instrument throughout testing.

Clinical Low-Vision Exams

More and more, educators are recognizing the limitations of assessing visual acuity with traditional measures. They note that low-vision students with similar ratings on measures of acuity vary considerably in their actual classroom functioning. For example, some children have vision but are unable to use it spontaneously. Others can use their vision in certain situations (for example, during one-to-one instruction in a controlled setting) but not for incidental learning. Still other students choose, consciously or unconsciously, not to use their vision (Corn, 1983). Corn (1983) outlined a theoretical model that could be used to think about vision and to assist professionals in eliciting visual behaviors or maximizing function in individuals with low vision. She points out that low vision results from differing visual disabilities (acuity, field, brain functions), and that these interact with other individual differences (such as cognition and physical makeup, including motor development and health) and also with environmental factors to influence visual functioning. She illustrates why so much of the assessment of students with visual impairments is individualized and clinical. In essence, educators use whatever methods they can to try to elicit visual behaviors in students who are not demonstrating them spontaneously. (For example, they might use a penlight, and if that didn't work, a large white dot on a television screen, to try to elicit a response to light.) And, they assess the extent to which educational adaptations (like large print) maximize the functioning of students with low vision.

Functional Vision Assessment

A significant effort is under way to develop in-school measures of residual vision and of functional vision. Unfortunately, most of the assessment procedures available are informal, nonstandardized sets of procedures or are more formal standardized procedures that are still under development (and have been for a very long time). Researchers at the University of Minnesota have been working on the Minnesota Functional Vision Assessment (MFVA) (Knowlton, 1988). They have produced eight subtests, each designed to assess an aspect of functional vision: acuity, binocular coordination, contrast, color, motion, functional fields, accommodation, and illusion. This assessment instrument is for use in the regular school environment.

Others have been working on assessment of functional vision. Jose, Smith and Shane (1988) outline a set of procedures for gathering information on the following aspects of functional vision: pupillary response; muscle imbalance (the tendency for the eyes to deviate); blink reflex; eye preference; central and peripheral fields; visual field preference; tracking ability; responses to lights and objects (reaching for or shifting attention to them); scanning ability; matching; ability to follow moving objects; imitation; object concept (response to objects and pictures); and object permanance. Langley and DuBose (1989) provide a set of procedures for functional vision testing and a checklist for diagnostic personnel to use in evaluating responses to visual stimuli, responses to objects on the basis of their size and distance, integration of visual and cognitive processing, and integration of visual and motor processing.

Mangold (1982) developed a form for teachers to complete after they have finished a functional visual assessment. The form becomes part of the student's record and is used to guide instruction or to make decisions about the kind(s) of instructional materials to use. The form is shown in Figure 19.1.

Learning Media Assessment

Learning media assessment is an objective process of systematically selecting learning and literacy media for students with visual impairments. Koening and Holbrook (1993), at the Texas School for the Blind and Visually Impaired, developed this informal assessment method for gathering data on general learning media and literacy media. General learning media include instructional *materials* (such as rulers, worksheets, pictures) and instructional *methods* (such as demonstration, modeling). Literacy media are the tools for reading and writing.

Koening and Holbrook (1993) indicate that three types of information are gathered on the student in learning media assessment:

FIGURE 19.1   **An Example of a Functional Vision Checklist**

Functional Vision Checklist Summary Sheet

Date _____

Student _____ Age ____ Grade ____ School _____

Vision Teacher _____ Contact Phone _____ Room _____

PHYSICAL INFORMATION

Nature of eye condition (describe in simple terms) _____

_____

Educational implications of eye condition _____

_____

Glasses prescribed _____ To be worn _____

Describe prescription (bifocal, aphakic, contact lens) _____

_____

Acuity (Near vision) _____ Field _____

Acuity (Far vision) _____ Color vision _____

Preferred eye _____ Child is/is not binocular _____

Preferred field of view _____ Best gaze posture, if any _____

_____ _____

Photophobia _____ Sunshade prescribed _____

CLASSROOM MODIFICATIONS: DISTANCE VISION

Child can use:

Overhead projectors _____ Flip charts _____

Filmstrips _____ Flashcards _____

Television _____ Wall clock _____

Blackboard: Child should be seated

In front row _____ Right front _____ Left front _____ Other _____

Distance aids used _____

Time adjustments (such as extra time to copy from the blackboard) _____

_____

_____

(continued)

391

FIGURE 19.1   **An Example of a Functional Vision Checklist (continued)**

CLASSROOM MODIFICATIONS: NEAR TASKS

1. Reading

    Optimum reading time ————————————————————————

    Child prefers to improve visual functioning by (finger pointing, marker, etc.)————

    Child's grade level when reading print————————————————————

    Print size   Reading ———————————   Mathematics ———————————

    Activity books ———————————   Ditto papers ———————————

    Dictionary ———————————   Other ———————————

    Adaptations of reading materials ————————————————————

    ————————————————————————————————————

2. Near vision devices

    Use of optical devices ————————————————————————

    Reading stand ——————— Marking pen ——————— Writing paper———————

    Ditto filters ——————————— Typoscope/marker ———————

    Closed-circuit television (CCTV):

    Best magnification ——————— Polarity ——————— Reading distance ———————

    Special lighting required ————————————————————

    Auditory (listening) program ————————————————————

    Child's grade level for auditory reading ————————————————

    Type of classwork to be read by ear ————————————————

EQUIPMENT ADAPTATIONS FOR CLASSES

    Will the student need special adaptations in:

    Cooking ——————— Sewing ——————— Shop ———————

    Laboratory——————— Physical education ————————————

    Testing situations: Modifications required (time and materials) ———————

    ————————————————————————————————————

TRAVEL SKILLS

    Student is oriented to: School ——— Bus ——— Community ———

    Can travel independently————————————————————

    Adaptations for independent travel————————————————

    Time adjustments for travel ————————————————————

    Additional notes:————————————————————————

SOURCE: Reprinted from Sally S. Mangold, ed., *A Teacher's Guide to the Special Educational Needs of Blind and Visually Handicapped Children* (New York: American Foundation for the Blind, 1982).

- The efficiency with which the student gathers information from various sensory channels
- The types of learning media the student uses or will use to accomplish learning tasks
- The literacy media the student will use for reading and writing

Braille Assessment Inventory

In Minnesota, teachers of students with visual impairments have been developing the Braille Assessment Inventory (Sharpe, McNear, & Bosma, 1993). This is an empirically based scale to be used by child study teams who are charged with the task of designing interventions for students with visual impairments. The scale is used to decide the appropriateness of Braille instruction for students who are blind and visually impaired. Composed of forty-three items grouped into five scales, the test is used to decide whether students should begin or continue to receive Braille instruction. The measure is complete, and data on technical adequacy should be available by late 1995.

ASSESSMENT OF COLOR VISION

As we indicated earlier, colorblindness is not usually an educationally disabling condition. Nevertheless, it is important that color vision be assessed, primarily so that colorblind children and their parents can know that the children have this condition.

Colorblindness is a stable trait, and one we ought to be able to assess with considerable reliability and validity. However, current devices used to assess color vision are not as reliable and valid as would be expected. Adam, Doran, and Modan (1967) state that "it has repeatedly been stressed by experts in the field of color vision (e.g., Franceschetti, 1928; Wright, 1947; Waardenburg et al., 1963) that an accurate diagnosis of color vision can be attained only by the use of an anomaloscope" (p. 297). An *anomaloscope* is a scientific instrument that presents two light spots simultaneously; the examinee must indicate whether the spots are of approximately equal brightness and whether they are the same color. Salvia and Ysseldyke (1972) investigated the validity of the results of four tests of colorblindness as compared to the findings using an anomaloscope with mentally retarded boys. Validities were low; the tests misdiagnosed from 7 to 30 percent of the boys.

If measures of colorblindness are used with students, we recommend that at least two different tests be given. If a student is identified as colorblind on both tests, there is a strong likelihood that the student is colorblind. A description of the tests most commonly used to assess color vision follows.

Farnsworth Dichotomous Test for Color Blindness

*T*he Farnsworth Dichotomous Test for Color Blindness (Farnsworth, 1947) consists of fifteen colored bottle caps that the student is asked to order with respect to a reference cap so that each cap is more like the preceding cap than any other. Diagnosis is made by plotting the order of the caps on a response sheet.

AO H-R-R Pseudoisochromatic Plates

*T*he AO H-R-R Pseudoisochromatic Plates test (Hardy, Rand, & Rittler, 1957) consists of twenty plates. Each plate is divided into four quadrants with identical background patterns and color (gray) in each quadrant on a given plate. In one or two of the quadrants, a symbol may appear, with no more than two symbols per plate. Subjects are asked to state what they see and where they see it.

Dvorine Pseudoisochromatic Plates

*T*he Dvorine Pseudoisochromatic Plates test (Dvorine, 1953) consists of fourteen number plates and seven trail plates with a number or trail formed of multicolor dots embedded in a background of dots of contrasting color. Subjects are asked to read the number or trace the trail with a fine brush.

Ishihara Color Blind Test

*T*he Ishihara Color Blind Test (Ishihara, 1970) consists of fourteen plates similar to those in the Dvorine Test. There are seven number plates and seven trail plates. Subjects are asked to name the number or trace the trail with a fine brush.

HEARING DIFFICULTIES[3]

Signs of Hearing Loss

Early detection of hearing problems is imperative in preschool and schoolage children so that appropriate remedial or compensatory procedures can be instituted. Children with hearing problems characteristically fail to pay attention, provide wrong answers to simple questions, frequently ask to have words or

---

3. This section was written especially for this book by Dr. Tom Frank, Professor of Audiology, Department of Communication Disorders, College of Health and Human Development, The Pennsylvania State University.

sentences repeated, and hear better in quiet conditions and when watching the teacher's face. Such children often function below their educational potential, are withdrawn, or exhibit behavior problems. Children who are repeatedly sick, have frequent earaches, colds, or other upper respiratory infections, allergies, or fluid draining from their ears may also have a concomitant hearing problem. Further, children who don't speak clearly or who show other types of speech or language problems and children who fail to discriminate between sounds or words with similar vowels but different consonants may also have hearing problems. Finally, some preschool and schoolage children are more at risk for hearing problems. These children include those with craniofacial anomalies such as cleft palate or Down syndrome, children from a lower socioeconomic class, Native Americans and Eskimos who may not be receiving appropriate and routine health care (Northern & Downs, 1991, pp. 22–24), and learning disabled or retarded children who cannot express that they have trouble hearing.

Any child, regardless of age, having one or more of the hearing-loss symptoms listed above or a child at risk for hearing loss should be referred for a hearing test. Depending on the school system, the hearing test may be given by the school nurse, speech-language pathologist, hearing therapist, audiologist, or a trained technician. These professionals have been trained to test hearing efficiently and accurately. In a preschool setting, additional support personnel for assessing hearing problems may not be available. Children in such a setting should be referred to their family physician or directly to a hearing specialist.

If a hearing problem is detected or the child is difficult to test, making the results questionable, the child should be referred to a doctor specializing in disorders of the ear, called an *otologist* or *otolaryngologist,* or to a specialist in hearing evaluation and rehabilitation, called an *audiologist.* The otologist and audiologist often work together as a team. An otologist has expertise in physical examination of the ears and in diagnosing and treating ear disorders. If a child has a correctable hearing loss, the otologist can provide the appropriate treatment (drug therapy or surgery). The audiologist has expertise in hearing assessment and rehabilitation. If a child has an educationally significant and noncorrectable hearing loss, the audiologist can prescribe, fit, and monitor the use of hearing aids. Further, the audiologist can make recommendations to teachers, hearing therapists, speech-language pathologists, and parents concerning the child's hearing ability in different listening environments.

Anatomy and Physiology

The assessment of hearing loss and hearing problems in preschool or schoolage children requires a basic understanding of the anatomy and physiology of the auditory system.

The auditory system can be divided into two parts, called the peripheral and the central auditory system. The peripheral auditory system can be further divided into three parts, known as the *outer, middle,* and *inner* ear. The outer ear contains the part we can see, known as the *pinna,* or *auricle,* and the *ear canal.* The outer ear functions as a resonator so that higher-frequency sounds are amplified and presented to the *eardrum,* or *tympanic membrane,* at a more intense level than their actual level in the environment. The middle ear is located within the temporal bone of the skull and contains the eardrum, or tympanic membrane; three connected bones known as the *malleus, incus,* and *stapes* (collectively called the *ossicles*); and the *Eustachian tube.* The Eustachian tube allows air into the middle ear so that the air pressure in the middle-ear cavity is the same as the pressure in the environment. When a sound strikes the eardrum, the eardrum moves back and forth and conveys that movement through the ossicles to the inner ear, with only a minimal loss in energy. The inner ear contains two parts and is the origin of the nerve of hearing called the *VIII cranial,* or *acoustic, nerve.* One part of the inner ear, the *vestibular system,* is responsible for balance, and the other part, the *cochlea,* is responsible for hearing. The cochlea is shaped like a snail and contains three fluid-filled portions; the middle portion, known as the *scala media,* contains the *organ of Corti* and is the most important, because it also contains a series of *outer* and *inner hair cells.* The function of the inner ear is to convert the movement of the cochlear fluid to a neural output. This process is initiated by the in-and-out movement of the stapes, which creates movement in the cochlear fluid that acts to stimulate the hair cells. The motion of the hair cells in turn sends a neural discharge to the acoustic nerve, which conveys the neural signal to the central auditory system.

The central auditory system can be divided into two parts, the *brainstem* and the auditory portion of the *temporal lobe,* or *cortex.* The neural output of the acoustic nerve, originating from the cochlea, is directed to the lower brainstem. Neural tracks within the brainstem convey the hearing-related neural activity to higher levels of the brainstem and then to the auditory area of the temporal lobe on each side of the brain. The function of the temporal lobe is to sample, analyze, and associate the hearing-related neural input with learned experiences to derive the sense of auditory receptioin, perception, and understanding and to appropriately change listening behaviors. This process is very complex and is not completely understood.

Modes of Hearing

The sensation of hearing can be initiated in two modes: air conduction and bone conduction.

Air-conduction hearing occurs when the sense of hearing is initiated by an airborne sound that enters the outer ear and passes through the middle and inner ear and the brainstem and is processed in the central auditory system. The vast majority of our everyday hearing experiences occur by air conduction; for example, listening to a teacher's voice or to television. To test hearing, air-conduction signals can be transmitted to the ear either via a loudspeaker, or, more commonly, via an earphone placed on the outer ear. *Bone-conduction* hearing occurs when the head is mechanically vibrated, so that the sense of hearing is initiated in the inner ear with little or no participation of the outer or middle ear. Hearing by bone conduction occurs when we listen to ourselves speak. To test hearing by bone conduction, signals are transmitted to the ear via a small vibrator commonly placed behind the outer ear on the mastoid bone. It is very important to note that normal hearing by air conduction depends on the normal functioning of the outer, middle, and inner ear and neural pathways, whereas normal hearing by bone conduction depends on the normal functioning of the inner ear and neural pathways.

Hearing screening tests initiate the sense of hearing using the air-conduction mode of hearing. Diagnostic hearing tests, which require the measurement of hearing thresholds, initiate the sense of hearing by both air and bone conduction. This is done to define the type and severity of a hearing loss, the severity of a hearing loss being generally defined as the average air-conduction hearing thresholds.

The Audiometer

Hearing screening, hearing-threshold testing, and other types of hearing tests are conducted with an electronic instrument called an *audiometer*. There are many types of audiometers, differentiated by their functions. Some audiometers are meant only for hearing screening, others are meant for very complex diagnostic hearing testing. Audiometers designed exclusively for hearing screening typically present discrete-frequency air-conducted pure tones through an earphone at a set output level, generally corresponding to the upper range of normal hearing. The type of audiometer most commonly used in school settings is known as a *pure-tone audiometer,* which can be used for both hearing screening and hearing threshold testing. A pure-tone audiometer equipped with earphones is shown in Figure 19.2. The American National Standards Institute (ANSI) has issued detailed specifications for audiometers and all pure-tone audiometers sold in the United States conform to these specifications.

All pure-tone audiometers produce signals at discrete frequencies called pure tones (hence the name) over the frequency range containing sounds used for understanding speech. The hertz (Hz), a unit named after a German physicist, Heinrich Rudolph Hertz, defines frequency as the number of events per second. Frequency can be described by the subjective impression it creates, known as *pitch*. A 125 Hz tone has a very low pitch, whereas an 8,000 Hz tone has a very high pitch. For hearing screening, testing is usually done from 500 to

FIGURE 19.2 **A Portable Pure-Tone Audiometer and Earphones**

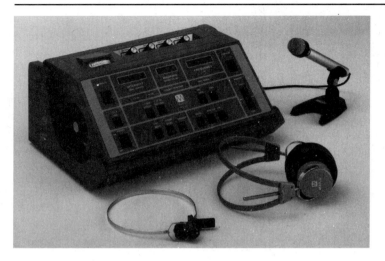

The power switch is located at the bottom left of the audiometer. The intensity (hearing level) of the pure tone is shown on the top left and the frequency is shown on the top right. The intensity and frequency can be changed by dials on the left and right side of the audiometer, respectively. When one of the stimulus switches on the top right and left of the audiometer is depressed, a pure tone will be presented. The ear selector switches are located at the bottom. The pulse, stimulation on, and FM switches can be used to control the presentation mode of a pure tone.

SOURCE: MA-41 portable audiometer courtesy of Maico Hearing Instruments, 7375 Bush Lake Road, Minneapolis, MN 55439

4,000 or 6,000 Hz. For diagnostic purposes, testing is usually done from 250 to 8,000 Hz.

The pure-tone audiometer also contains an amplifier and an attenuator that can be adjusted in discrete steps to increase or decrease the sound pressure level output of the earphones. Sound pressure level output can be quantified by a measurement unit known as a *decibel* (dB). Since a normal hearing ear does not have the same sound pressure level hearing thresholds at each frequency, audiometers are internally calibrated to a decibel scale called *hearing level* (HL). A HL of 0 dB represents average normal hearing for a pure tone at each frequency; −10 dB HL corresponds to better-than-normal hearing. The physical intensity of a sound creates a subjective impression known as *loudness*. A 0 dB HL is the threshold of normal hearing for pure tones at each frequency, 20 to 30 dB HL corresponds to the level of a whispered voice, 40 to 50 dB HL corresponds to the level of normal everyday speech, and 80 to 90 dB HL would correspond to a very loud shout.

Types of Screening and Assessment

The identification of preschool and schoolage children with hearing problems usually falls within the realm of a hearing-screening program, which may also be called a *hearing conservation* or a *hearing-loss identification program* or *identification audiometry*. All states have laws requiring hearing screening of schoolage children. Unfortunately, hearing screening for many children in preschool programs is not mandated by state or federal laws. Therefore, many preschool children who have educationally significant hearing losses are not being identified and may become educationally delayed. Hearing-screening programs generally have three components: the actual hearing screening, follow-up hearing-threshold tests for those who fail the screening, and referral.

Hearing Screening

The primary purpose of hearing screening in a school situation is to identify children with educationally significant hearing problems. Experience has indicated that teachers or parents may not be able to identify a child with an educationally significant hearing loss. Further, sometimes teachers and parents identify a normal child as having hearing loss. Thus, subjective estimates of a child's hearing ability are not always reliable and more objective testing must be conducted. This is the purpose of hearing screening.

At one time, group hearing-screening programs were very popular. However, research shows that group hearing tests have lower validity and reliability compared with individual testing. Therefore, hearing screening should be conducted for one child at a time. Screening a large number of children individually is more effective in identifying children with hearing problems and in the long run is more cost-efficient than screening groups of children.

The American Speech-Language-Hearing Association (ASHA) has recently developed guidelines for hearing screening (ASHA, 1990), based in part on earlier guidelines (ASHA, 1985a). The ASHA 1990 guidelines require that hearing screening be a three-step procedure including (1) documentation of case history and visual inspection of the outer ear, the ear canal, and the eardrum, (2) pure-tone hearing screening, and (3) tympanometry (to be discussed later). Further, the ASHA 1990 guidelines recommend that hearing be screened annually for children functioning at a developmental level of 3 years through third grade and high-risk children regardless of grade. High-risk children are those who have repeated a grade; require special education; are new to the school; are absent during the hearing screening (a technical category—an untested child is "at risk" per se); have failed previous hearing screenings; have speech, language, or communication problems; are suspected of having a hearing impairment or have a medical problem associated with hearing impairment (for example, chronic earaches or allergies); and those involved in course work around loud noise (such as band, woodworking, and auto repair). Some state laws mandate that children receive routine hearing screening. For example, Pennsylvania regulations require screening for all children in kindergarten, grades 1, 2, 3, 7, and 11, and those in special ungraded classes.

According to the ASHA 1990 guidelines, a case history and visual inspection of the outer ear, the ear canal, and the eardrum is the first step for hearing screening. This case history and visual inspection of the the ear must be done by a qualified individual such as a school nurse, speech-language pathologist, or audiologist. If a child has a significant case history for ear problems or if inspection of the ear reveals abnormalities (such as wax blocking the ear canal, fluid draining from the middle ear, or an eardrum perforation), the child is removed from the screening and should be referred for medical evaluation or treatment. It should be noted that even though the ASHA 1990 guidelines recommend case history and ear inspection as the first step in hearing screening, this step is often bypassed and hearing screening using air conducted pure tones becomes the first step.

When pure-tone hearing screening is conducted, the child is instructed to respond, even if the tone is very soft, by raising his or her hand. Older children may use a response button. Some preschool and younger schoolage children must be taught or be conditioned to respond. The tester then places earphones directly on the child's ears, making sure that there is no hair in between the earphone and the opening to the ear canal, that glasses have been removed, and that earrings are removed if they cause a problem. The child should be seated so that he or she cannot see the examiner. Because earphones are employed, the child's entire auditory system is being stimulated. That is, the child's hearing is being tested by air conduction.

For hearing screening, ASHA (1990) has recommended using the frequencies 500, 1,000, 2,000, and 4,000 Hertz (Hz) presented at a hearing level (HL) of 20 decibels (dB). However, if tympanometry screening is also conducted, screening at 500 Hz can be excluded. ASHA's choice of frequencies relates to the fact that hearing sounds in the range of 500 to 4,000 Hz is crucial for understanding speech. ASHA regards a 20 dB HL as the upper range of normal hearing for children. Many states have regulations pertaining to hearing screening that also specify hearing-screening frequencies and hearing levels. Needless to say, all hearing testing should be done in a very quiet room, separated not only acoustically but also by distance from noisy parts of the school. If hearing testing is done in the presence of excessive external noise, the noise will cover up, or mask, a pure tone. Consequently, many children who have normal hearing will fail the hearing screening because the external noise will prevent them from hearing the pure tone, especially in the lower pitches.

The ASHA (1990) criterion for failing is the failure to respond at the hearing-screening level at any frequency in either ear. However, state hearing-screening regulations may have different criteria for failure. Regardless of the failure criteria, all failures should be retested immediately, after giving a more careful set of instructions to the child.

Hearing-Threshold Testing

Children who fail the initial hearing screening and the repeat screening should receive a more detailed hearing test in school or be referred to an audiologist or an otologist. The more detailed test is known as a pure-tone threshold test, or pure-tone audiometry. The purpose of this test is to determine the child's hearing thresholds for different pitch pure tones in each ear. For this testing, hearing is measured using both earphones (air conduction) and a bone vibrator (bone conduction). However, bone conduction should never be assessed in a school setting because many variables may influence the results. A hearing *threshold* is usually defined as the lowest hearing level at which the child responds to a minimum of two out of three ascending (from inaudibility to audibility) tones.

In some situations, hearing thresholds must be obtained for one ear while a noise signal is directed to the other ear. This is called *masking*, and the resultant hearing threshold for the ear being tested is called a *masked threshold*. Masking is necessary so that the ear not being tested does not respond to a pure tone directed to the ear being tested. Masking is meant to produce an artificial temporary hearing loss in the nontest ear so that the true hearing threshold of the test ear can be obtained. Masked thresholds should only be obtained by an audiologist or otologist.

The hearing-threshold levels obtained as a result of the pure-tone threshold test can be expressed numerically. However, it is more common to plot the hearing thresholds on a graph called an *audiogram*, as shown in Figure 19.3. On the audiogram, frequency in Hertz (Hz) is shown along the top of the audiogram in octave intervals from 125 to 8,000 Hz; audiometric half-octave intervals at 750, 1,500, 3,000, and 6,000 Hz are also shown. Hearing level in decibels (dB) is shown along the side of the audiogram from −10 to 120 dB in 10-dB steps. The symbols plotted on the audiogram correspond to the hearing threshold for each ear at each frequency tested, using earphones (air conduction) or a bone vibrator (bone conduction) when the thresholds were unmasked or masked. Each audiogram contains an adjacent legend that defines the meaning of the symbols used on it. An audiogram legend is shown in Figure 19.4 (page 403). A circle indicates an unmasked air-conduction threshold for the right ear, and an X indicates an unmasked air-conduction threshold for the left ear. It is common practice to mark thresholds for the right ear in red and for the left ear in blue.

The criteria for failing a pure-tone threshold test are generally the same as for the hearing screening. Children who fail the air-conduction hearing-threshold test in school should be referred to an audiologist or an otologist for further testing and diagnosis of their suspected hearing loss.

Tympanometry Screening

Even though the pure-tone air-conduction screening and the threshold test are commonly used to identify children with educationally significant hearing loss,

FIGURE 19.3 **Audiogram Showing Frequency in Hertz (Hz) (top) and Hearing Level in Decibels (dB) (side)**

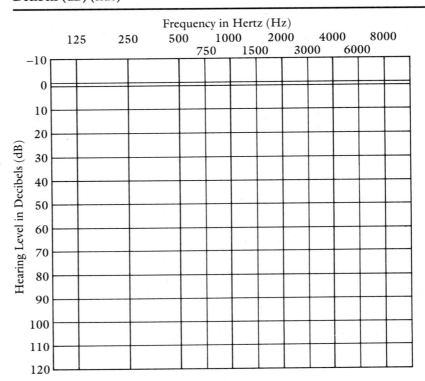

Average normal hearing is 0 dB HL at each frequency and the range of normal is from −10 to 20 dB, regardless of frequency.

SOURCE: American Speech-Language-Hearing Association. (1990). Guidelines for Audiometric Symbols, *ASHA, 32,* (Suppl. 2), 25–30. Reprinted with permission of the publisher.

they have a number of drawbacks. Both the amount of external noise in the test environment and the rapport between the child and the examiner influence the results. Also, some normal-hearing children might fail these tests because they are immature or inattentive or because they don't understand the instructions. Moreover, some children may pass these tests but have a minor hearing problem or a fluctuating hearing loss, usually due to abnormal conditions of the middle ear. Consequently, several school systems and states have initiated another type of screening test, used alone or in conjunction with pure-tone screening. This test, known as *tympanometry,* is the third step in the ASHA 1990 guidelines for hearing screening. Tympanometry has also been called *impedance audiometry, admittance audiometry, oto-admittance, middle-ear screening,* or *tympanometric screening.* Tympanometry can be defined as a method for detecting normal as

FIGURE 19.4   **Audiogram Legend Showing the Meaning of Symbols Plotted on an Audiogram**

Audiogram Legend

Modality	Ear		
	Left	Unspecified	Right
Air Conduction-Earphones			
Unmasked	✗		◯
Masked	☐		△
Bone Conduction-Mastoid			
Unmasked	>	⊓	<
Masked	]		[

This legend shows the symbols for air conduction unmasked and masked thresholds and for bone conduction unmasked and masked thresholds when a bone vibrator is placed on the mastoid bone behind the ear. It should be noted that there are many other symbols that can be used to plot hearing thresholds. The symbols shown in this figure are the most commonly used.

SOURCE: American Speech-Language-Hearing Association. (1990). Guidelines for Audiometric Symbols, *ASHA, 32,* (Suppl. 2), 25–30. Reprinted with permission of the publisher.

well as abnormal conditions of the eardrum and middle ear. Overall, tympanometry screening is designed to detect such abnormal conditions, not to detect educationally significant hearing losses. Disorders of the middle ear are the largest cause of educationally significant hearing loss in children, especially for preschool and young schoolage children.

Tympanometry is done using a specially designed instrument generically known as a *middle-ear screener, tympanogram screener, middle-ear analyzer,* or an *impedance or admittance meter.* Figure 19.5 shows a photograph of a middle-ear screening instrument. Many middle-ear screening instruments are automatic so that the procedure takes less than 10 seconds per ear.

The results of tympanometry are plotted on a graph known as a *tympanogram,* which shows eardrum movement in absolute or relative units on the *y*-axis as a function of air pressure in the ear canal on the *x*-axis. Figure 19.6 shows tympanograms for a normal middle ear and for middle ears that have various pathologic conditions.

FIGURE 19.5   **Middle-Ear Screening Instrument**

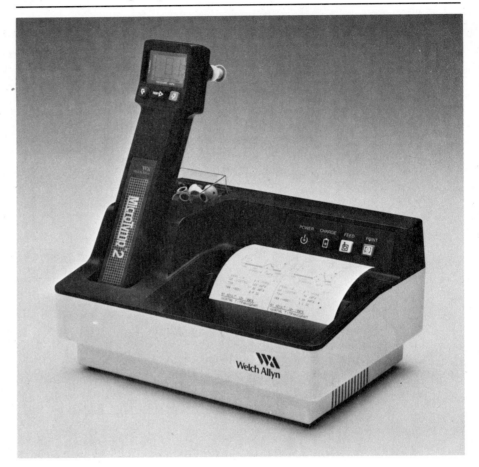

This is a hand-held instrument. When inserted into a child's ear canal and an air-tight seal is obtained, the instrument will automatically sample the immittance of the middle ear. When the instrument is inserted into its power charging stand, a tympanogram will automatically be printed.

SOURCE: Courtesy of Welch Allyn, Inc., 4341 State Street Road, Skaneateles Falls, NY 13153-0220

Children who fail tympanometry (abnormal tympanogram) but pass the pure-tone air-conduction screening should be rescreened (with both a pure-tone test and tympanometry) in four to six weeks. If they fail either rescreening procedure, they should be referred for additional testing and diagnosis. However, depending on the type of tympanogram, ASHA and some states require immediate referral for further diagnosis and/or treatment.

FIGURE 19.6   **Tympanogram Configurations for a Normal Middle Ear (a) and for Middle Ears Having a Pathologic Condition (b to e)**

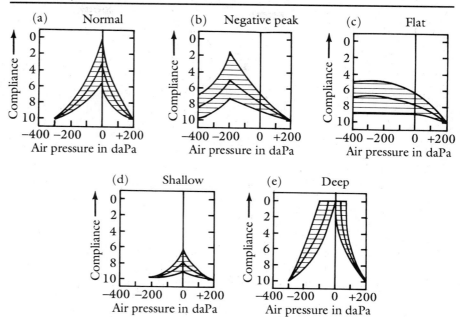

Each tympanogram shows compliance on the *y*-axis, air pressure on the *x*-axis, and a shaded area used for interpreting the tympanogram. Tympanogram (a) is normal. Tympanogram (b) is called negative peak and is observed in children having negative pressure in their middle ear. Tympanogram (c) is called flat and is commonly observed in children having middle ear fluid. Tympanogram (d) is called shallow and is observed when the middle ear is stiffer than normal but does not contain fluid. Tympanogram (e) is called deep and is observed in children who have a flaccid ear-drum or dysarticulation of the middle-ear bones.

SOURCE: Bess, F. H., and Humes, L. E., *Audiology: The Fundamentals* (Baltimore: Williams & Wilkins, 1990), Figure 4.15. Used with permission of the publisher and author.

It is important to recognize that screening for middle-ear disorders is not the same as screening for hearing loss since a child could have a middle-ear disorder but pass the pure-tone screening. To differentiate, note that the primary goal of pure-tone screening is to identify children with educationally significant hearing loss, whereas the primary goal of tympanometry screening is to identify children with middle-ear disorders. Even though some states only require pure-tone screening, it is in the best health interests of preschool and schoolage children to have both a pure-tone and tympanometry (middle-ear) screening in the same session. Further, criteria for failure and consequential referral should include the screening results for both air-conduction hearing (pure-tone screening) and middle-ear disorders (tympanometry).

Other Types of Hearing Testing

In addition to pure-tone audiometry and tympanometry, audiologists conduct several other hearing and middle-ear-function tests. These tests aid in diagnosis and hearing-aid fitting and are beyond the scope of this section. However, there are two important and routine tests that employ speech as the test signal. One test is used to determine a hearing threshold for speech, known as a *speech-recognition threshold* (SRT). The other test is used to determine word-recognition ability, known as a *word-recognition score* (WRS). (Word-recognition tests were once known as speech-discrimination or speech-intelligibility test.) Generally, both the SRT and WRS are obtained via earphones for each ear separately and via a loudspeaker located in an audiometric test booth. When testing is done via the loudspeaker, only the better-hearing ear responds. In cases where each ear hears at the same level, the advantage of binaural (both ears) hearing compared with monaural (one ear) hearing can usually be demonstrated.

The SRT is determined by having the child repeat back or point to printed bisyllabic words (for example, *hot dog, baseball, snowman*) spoken with a spondaic stress pattern (that is, equal stress on both syllables) while the hearing level is varied. The SRT is defined as the lowest hearing level at which the child responds to 50 percent of the words. The SRT is used to check the validity of the air-conducted pure-tone hearing thresholds, to provide an estimate of the child's threshold for speech, and when fitting hearing aids.

A WRS is usually determined by having the child repeat back or point to printed words when the words are presented at a hearing level loud enough to produce maximum recognition. A WRS is simply the percentage of words correctly heard. A WRS can also be determined by presenting the words through a loudspeaker at a hearing level corresponding to the level of normal conversational speech. This testing is very important for estimating the child's hearing handicap for speech. For example, if a child had a WRS of 90 percent in his or her better-hearing ear when speech was presented loud enough to be heard but only had a WRS of 20 percent when speech was presented at a normal level, the child would be very educationally handicapped for hearing speech. This result would also indicate that if speech were made louder through the use of hearing aids or if the hearing loss were medically corrected to normal, the child's WRS would increase from 20 percent to about 90 percent, drastically decreasing the educational significance of the child's hearing loss.

Types of Hearing Loss

As noted previously, the sense of hearing can be stimulated by both air and bone conduction. When hearing thresholds are obtained for both air- and bone-conducted pure tones, the type of hearing loss can be defined.

Normal hearing for preschool and schoolage children is usually defined within a range around 0 dB HL, from −10 to 20 dB HL. The audiogram in Figure 19.7 shows the air-conduction thresholds for a six-year-old girl having normal hearing in each ear from 250 to 8,000 Hz. Note that the right- and left-ear air-conduction symbols show about average normal hearing (0 dB HL) and lie within the normal range of −10 to 20 dB HL. In this case, bone-conduction thresholds were not measured, because the child had normal air-conduction hearing.

Conductive Hearing Loss

If a child has a hearing loss caused by an abnormal condition (pathology) in the outer ear, such as an excessive buildup of wax (*cerumen*) in the ear canal, or an abnormal condition of the middle ear, such as fluid in the middle ear (*otitis media*) or a perforation in the eardrum, bone conduction hearing will be normal because the inner ear is not affected. However, the child's hearing by air conduction will be abnormal, because the hearing problem (dysfunction) is due to a

FIGURE 19.7   **Audiogram for a Six-Year-Old Girl Having Normal Air-Conduction Hearing in Each Ear from 250 to 8,000 Hz**

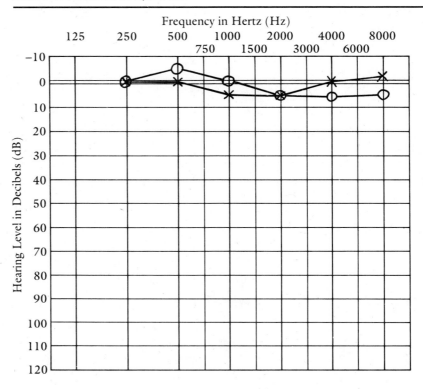

pathology in the outer or middle ear or both. This type of hearing loss (evidenced by normal bone-conduction but abnormal air-conduction hearing) is known as a *conductive hearing loss* because the pathology has affected the sound-conducting mechanisms of the outer or middle ear or both. The audiogram in Figure 19.8 shows the air- and bone-conduction thresholds of a five-year-old girl with a mild, bilateral (both ears), conductive hearing loss due to middle-ear fluid. Note that the bone-conduction masked thresholds are normal but the air-conduction thresholds are abnormal (>20 dB HL). This child failed the pure-tone screening and threshold test and had an abnormal tymponogram and was classified as having an educationally significant hearing loss in each ear. The child was referred to an audiologist for further testing and to an otologist for treatment. After the middle-ear fluid problem was resolved by medication, her air-conduction hearing and tympanogram returned to normal.

FIGURE 19.8 **Audiogram for a Five-Year-Old Girl Having a Mild, Bilateral (each ear), Conductive Hearing Loss Due to Middle-Ear Fluid**

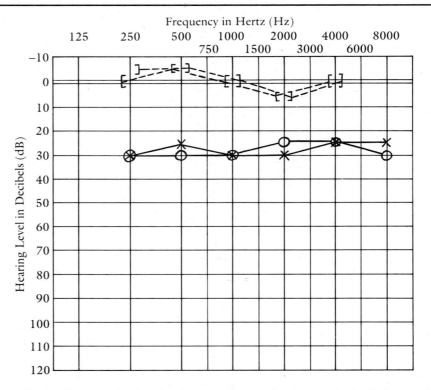

Note that her bone conduction thresholds were normal and were obtained when masking was directed to the nontest ear. However, her air-conduction thresholds were abnormal and demonstrated an educationally significant hearing loss.

The most common type of hearing problem in preschool and schoolage children is a conductive hearing loss due to the presence of middle-ear fluid. This condition is commonly called *otitis media with effusion* (fluid) and can have several causes. However, almost all the causes are related to dysfunction of the Eustachian tube. Some children have many episodes of otitis media and earaches, especially in early childhood. These children might be categorized as being otitis-media prone. Hearing loss due to otitis media is usually mild to moderate in degree, may fluctuate (with more hearing loss on some days than others), and is usually temporary until the fluid dissipates and the eardrum and middle ear return to normal. Generally, otitis media is treated by drug therapy. If this is not successful, the fluid can be removed surgically. This is done by making an incision in the lower part of the eardrum and removing the fluid and then placing a small plastic tube in the eardrum incision. This surgical procedure is called a *myringotomy with tubal insertion.* The small tube, called a *pressure-equalization (PE) tube,* temporarily takes over the function of the Eustachian tube by allowing air to enter the middle-ear space. A PE tube usually works its way out of the eardrum over time, and can be removed if necessary.

The associations between otitis media, speech and language development, attention, and learning ability are starting to be identified. Many researchers (Friel-Patti & Finitzo, 1990; Feagans et al., 1986; Northern & Downs, 1991, pp. 18–28) have suggested that children who have chronic otitis media have more speech and language, attention, and learning problems than children who do not suffer middle-ear disease. After appropriate treatment for conductive hearing loss, hearing ability can almost always be restored to normal. In cases when this is not possible and if the hearing loss is educationally significant, the use of hearing aids should be seriously considered. However, it should be noted that children with longstanding conductive hearing loss probably will need additional instruction to make up for what they missed when the hearing loss was present.

Sensorineural Hearing Loss

If a child has a hearing loss due to a dysfunction of the inner ear, bone- as well as air-conduction hearing will be equally abnormal. (The exception is very rare and need not be discussed.) This type of loss (abnormal bone and equally abnormal air-conduction hearing) is known as a *sensorineural, cochlear,* or *neurosensory hearing loss.* There are many causes of a sensorineural hearing loss, such as noise exposure, inheritance, ototoxic drugs, mumps, measles, and head trauma. The audiogram in Figure 19.9 is for a seven-year-old boy having a mild to moderate, bilateral, high-frequency, sensorineural hearing loss, probably due to a very high fever in infancy. Note that for the higher frequencies the bone- and air-conduction thresholds are equally abnormal (>20 dB HL). This child failed the pure-tone screening and threshold test and was classified as having an educationally significant hearing loss in each ear. Since the child's hearing loss was not due to an outer or middle-ear problem, the child passed the middle-ear

FIGURE 19.9 **Audiogram for a Seven-Year-Old Boy Having a Mild to Moderate, Bilateral, High-Frequency, Sensorineural Hearing Loss**

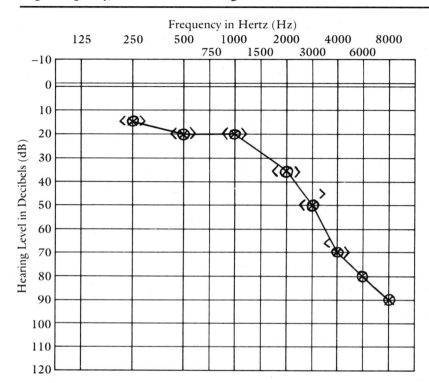

Note that his air and bone conduction thresholds were equally abnormal for the higher pitches.

screening (normal tympanogram). The child was referred to an audiologist and otologist and consequently fitted with a behind-the-ear hearing aid for each ear.

An educationally significant moderate or more severe sensorineural hearing loss will almost always be detected before a child enters a preschool. On the other hand, educationally significant, sensorineural hearing losses in just one ear (unilateral) or bilateral in the very high frequencies, or bilateral and very mild in all frequencies, are usually detected by hearing screening when a child enters kindergarten or first grade. A sensorineural hearing loss will not respond to medical or surgical treatment. For the vast majority of children with sensorineural hearing loss, hearing aids are very helpful.

Mixed Hearing Loss

A hearing loss can also be a combination of a conductive and sensorineural hearing loss. This type is known as a *mixed hearing loss* (abnormal bone- and even more abnormal air-conduction hearing). For example, a mixed loss could arise if a child had a problem with the middle-ear (middle-ear fluid) and with the inner ear (hair-cell dysfunction due to a very high fever). Generally, mixed hearing losses in children are the result of a pathology that creates a conductive loss on top of an existing sensorineural hearing loss. An otologist can usually alleviate the conductive part of the hearing loss by medical or surgical treatment. However, in some cases the conductive part of the mixed loss cannot be corrected. If a mixed hearing loss is educationally significant following medical or surgical treatment, the use of hearing aids is warranted.

Central Auditory Hearing Loss

Another type of hearing problem can occur in preschool and schoolage children with either normal hearing or hearing loss. This type of hearing problem is related to the function and processing capabilities of the central auditory system and is generally called a *central auditory processing dysfunction* or *central auditory hearing loss*. Children who have a central auditory processing dysfunction generally pass hearing screenings, threshold tests, and tympanometry because they have normal air-conduction hearing and middle-ear function. Further, they respond to whispers or speech spoken at a normal level with little background noise. However, these children may have difficulty understanding speech in a noisy background, as would occur in a classroom, and have problems with short- and long-term auditory memory, auditory sequential memory, sounding out words (phonetics), or reading comprehension. A central auditory processing problem can be very educationally significant and frustrating not only to the child but also to the teacher and parents. Any child who passes a hearing screening but is still suspected of having a hearing problem should be considered a candidate for central auditory processing testing. Testing for central auditory processing also should be considered for children with a reading or visual perception problem.

Several standardized tests have been developed for the sole purpose of determining a child's central auditory processing ability. Some of these tests can be administered by a school psychologist, a speech-language pathologist, or an audiologist. Testing for central auditory processing is very complex, and often the results are difficult to interpret. Children suspected of having a central auditory processing problem should be evaluated by a team of professionals representing many disciplines. If a central auditory problem is diagnosed, new teaching and learning strategies may need to be developed to reduce the educational significance of the problem. These strategies can be provided by special education teachers, speech-language pathologists, and school psychologists.

Severity of Hearing Loss

Besides providing a way to judge type of hearing loss, a pure-tone threshold test also provides valuable information regarding the severity of hearing loss for individual frequencies and frequency regions. This information is very important for understanding speech and fitting hearing aids. There are many ways to calculate hearing loss severity and many classification schemes. The most common method to determine severity is based on the average better-ear air-conduction hearing threshold. This is calculated by determining the lowest air-conduction hearing threshold, regardless of ear, at 500, 1,000, and 2,000 Hz, and then determining the average hearing level. This measure is usually referred to as the *better-ear three-frequency average.* The frequencies 500, 1,000, and 2,000 Hz, called the *speech frequencies,* were chosen because several speech sounds needed for understanding speech occur between 500 to 2,000 Hz. (However, it is important to realize that many speech sounds also needed for understanding speech are located in frequencies higher than 2,000 Hz. These speech sounds include many of the voiceless consonants, such as *f, s,* and *sh.*)

The average hearing loss can be described or classified in reference to a severity category and in relation to hearing and understanding speech. Figure 19.10 shows an audiogram that classifies hearing impairment by severity and handicap for hearing speech. For example, a child with an average hearing loss of 35 dB would be classified as having a mild hearing loss and would have difficulty hearing whispered or faint speech. A child with a hearing loss of 80 dB would be classified as having a severe hearing impairment and could only understand shouted or amplified speech.

Speech Understanding and Hearing Loss

Recall that children with a conductive hearing loss have a normal inner ear. Such children can perceive speech normally if it is loud enough to overcome the hearing loss. The effect of a 30- to 40-dB conductive hearing loss can be simulated by wearing a tight-fitting earplug in each ear. If you had such a loss, you would be able to hear normal conversational speech but at a very reduced level. You would have to strain to understand what had been said and would not be able to hear people talking at a distance. In addition, you might not be able to hear yourself walk or hear whispers. Imagine what it is like for a child to sit in a classroom all day every day, perhaps for months, unable to hear and understand everything that is being said!

Children with a sensorineural hearing loss have abnormal function of the inner ear, and the severity of the hearing loss usually increases as sound frequency increases. These children often report that they can hear someone talking but they cannot always understand what is said, sometimes even with the use of hearing aids. This occurs because the child can hear low-frequency vowel

FIGURE 19.10   **Classification of the Severity of Hearing Impairment in Relation to Hearing Handicap for Speech Recognition Shown on an Audiogram**

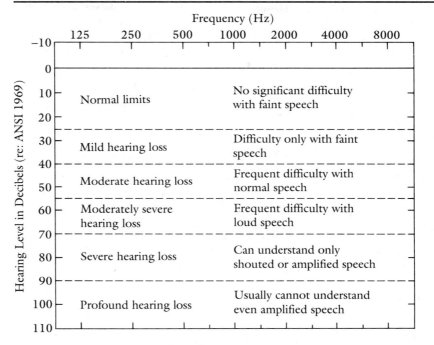

SOURCE: Bess, F. H., and Humes, L. E., *Audiology: The Fundamentals* (Baltimore: Williams & Wilkins, 1990), Figure 4.3. Used with permission of the publisher and author.

sounds, which carry the power of speech, but cannot hear the high-frequency consonant sounds, which carry the intelligibility of speech. It is difficult to simulate the effects of a sensorineural hearing loss. However, try listening to a radio station when your radio is slightly mistuned, then turn down the level and increase the bass. You will notice that you can hear speech but not understand what is being said.

Children who have sensorineural hearing loss have extreme difficulties hearing in a noisy environment. In most classrooms, the teacher's voice is only about 6 to 10 dB louder than the background noise. Research has clearly demonstrated that if the teacher's voice is about 15 to 20 dB louder than the classroom noise, children with sensorineural loss and, for that matter, normal-hearing children will have better speech understanding. In other words, improving the signal-to-noise ratio (teacher's voice to classroom noise) will improve speech understanding for all children in the classroom. There are many ways to improve the signal-to-noise ratio. One way is for the teacher simply to talk louder. Another way is to fit the classroom with carpeting, acoustic ceiling tile, and window drapes to reduce the level of classroom noise. An audiologist can recommend additional ways to improve the signal-to-noise ratio for increasing speech understanding. Research has also demonstrated that a child with sensorineural hearing loss will have improved understanding for speech when speech is better articulated, spoken directly to the child, and spoken at a slightly slower rate.

School Help for the Child

A preschool or schoolage child with a hearing problem should receive assistance from the teacher. The teacher should discuss classroom management of a hearing-impaired child with special support personnel such as a hearing therapist or speech-language pathologist. Preferential seating close to the teacher and the teacher's talking just a little louder and slower will improve the signal-to-noise ratio, thus maximizing a child's ability to hear and to read lips. Of course, if the teacher moves around the room and talks at a distance to the hearing-impaired child, the benefits of preferential seating are lost, especially for a child with a unilateral hearing loss. The teacher must be able to cope with children who have fluctuating hearing loss or permanent hearing loss and wear hearing aids. Sometimes children with fluctuating conductive hearing loss pass a pure-tone hearing and tympanometry screening. The teacher should arrange to have their hearing tested on a day such children demonstrate poor hearing in the classroom. For children who wear hearing aids, the teacher should ask the hearing therapist, speech-language pathologist, or audiologist for instruction on classroom maintenance of a hearing aid, especially for preschool and young schoolage children. This may require knowing how to put a hearing aid in an ear, adjust the volume control, and change the battery. Children with central auditory processing problems are hard to identify, and many require special instruction. Different teaching modes may be needed to maximize the hearing abilities of such children.

COPING WITH DILEMMAS IN CURRENT PRACTICE

Accurately assessing sensory acuity poses fewer difficulties than other kinds of assessment. Those who assess vision or hearing acuity are assessing relatively stable human characteristics. There are well-accepted objective standards of performance for making decisions about the nature and extent of vision or hearing difficulties. With the exception of color vision, the relationship between sensory difficulties and performance in the curriculum is well understood and established. And there are known treatments (corrective lenses or hearing aids) for most mild vision or hearing problems. There are also methods for coping with severe vision or hearing problems.

The major dilemma in assessment of sensory acuity is that, with the exception of routine screening, assessment is done by people outside the school. Students who have serious vision problems are assessed by optometrists or ophthalmologists. Those who have serious hearing problems are assessed by audiologists or ear, nose, and throat specialists. Communication between specialists outside the school and school personnel may be difficult—because specialists are not familiar with the curriculum, do not understand the educational relevance of their diagnoses, or do not take the necessary time to speak with school personnel about their findings for individual children. Difficulty may also arise when school personnel do not understand the vocabulary used by those who assess vision and hearing problems. Problems are most effectively overcome when there is very good communication and ongoing interaction among school personnel and out-of-school specialists.

SUMMARY

Vision and hearing difficulties can have a significant effect on the performance of children in educational environments. A basic overview of the kinds of vision and hearing difficulties children experience and of the procedures used to assess sensory acuity can help school personnel decide how to intervene. Screening tests of both visual and auditory acuity must be individually administered. This chapter reviewed individually administered screening tests that are appropriate and reasonably effective. The actual diagnosis of sensory difficulties must be completed by specialists: ophthalmologists, optometrists, audiologists, and otologists.

STUDY QUESTIONS

1. Identify several characteristics (behaviors) that a student might demonstrate that would make you question whether the student was seeing adequately.
2. Identify several characteristics (behaviors) that might make you question whether a student was hearing adequately.

ADDITIONAL READING

American-Speech-Language-Hearing Association. (1985a). Guidelines for identification audiometry. *ASHA 27,* 49–53.

American-Speech-Language-Hearing Association. (1985b). Guidelines for screening of hearing impairment and middle-ear disorders. *ASHA 32 (Suppl. 2),* 17–24.

Bess, F. H., & Hall, J. W. (1992). *Screening children for auditory function.* Nashville, TN: Bill Wilkerson Center Press.

Feagans, L., Sanyal, M., Henderson, F., Collier, A., & Appelbaum, M. I. (1986). The relationship of middle ear disease in early childhood to later narrative and attention skills. *Journal of Pediatric Psychology, 12,* 581–594.

Friel-Patti, S., & Finitzo, T. (1990). Language learning in a prospective study of otitis media with effusion in the first two years of life. *Journal of Speech and Hearing Research 33,* 188–194.

Northern, J. L., & Downs, M. P. (1991). *Hearing in children* (4th ed.) Baltimore, MD: Williams & Wilkins.

Sullivan, P. M., & Vernon, M. (1979). Psychological assessment of hearing impaired children. *School Psychology Review, 8,* 271–290.

Vernon, M., Bair, R., & Lotz, S. (1979). Psychological evaluation and testing of children who are deaf-blind. *School Psychology Review, 8,* 291–295.

Chapter 20

Assessment of Academic Achievement with Multiple-Skill Devices

*A*chievement tests are the most frequently used tests in educational settings. Multiple-skill achievement tests evaluate knowledge and understanding in several curricular areas (for example, in reading and math). They are intended to assess the extent to which students have profited from schooling and other life experiences compared to others of the same age or grade. Consequently, most achievement tests are norm-referenced, although some are criterion-referenced or performance measures. Norm-referenced, criterion-referenced, and performance tests are designed in consultation with subject-matter experts and are believed to reflect national curricula and national curricular trends in general.

Various kinds of tests were described in Chapter 2. Achievement tests can be classified along several dimensions; perhaps the most important one describes their specificity and density of content. Diagnostic achievement tests have dense content; they have many more items to assess specific skills and concepts and allow finer analyses to pinpoint specific strengths and weaknesses in academic development. Tests with fewer items per skill allow comparisons among test takers but lack a sufficient number of items to pinpoint strengths and weaknesses. These tests may be useful for estimating a student's current general level of functioning in comparison to other students; they estimate the extent to which an individual has acquired the skills and concepts that other students of the same age have acquired. Another important dimension is the number of students who can be tested at once. Tests are designed to be given to groups of students or to individual students. Generally, group tests require students to read and write or mark answers; individually administered tests may require an examiner to read questions to a student and may allow students to respond orally. The primary advantage of individually administered tests is that they afford examiners the opportunity to observe students working and solving problems. Therefore, examiners can glean valuable qualitative information in addition to the quantitative information that scores provide. Finally, it should be noted that a group test may be appropriately given to one student at a time, but individual tests should not be given to a group of students.

Table 20.1 shows the different categories of achievement tests. The Stanford Achievement Test is, for example, both a norm-referenced and a criterion-referenced (objective-referenced), group-administered screening test that samples skill development in many content areas. The Stanford Diagnostic Reading Test (SDRT) is both a norm-referenced, group-administered and a criterion-referenced, individually administered diagnostic test that samples skill-development strengths and weaknesses in the single skill of reading. The SDRT is intended to provide a classroom teacher with a more detailed analysis of students' strengths and weaknesses in reading, which may be of assistance in program planning and evaluation.

The most obvious advantage of multiple-skill achievement tests is that they can provide teachers with data showing the extent to which their pupils have acquired information and skills. By using group-administered, multiple-skill batteries, teachers can obtain a considerable amount of information in a relatively short time.

In selecting a multiple-skill achievement test, teachers must consider three factors. First, teachers must evaluate evidence for content validity, the most important kind of validity for achievement tests. Many multiple-skill tests have general content validity—the tests measure important concepts and skills that are generally part of most curricula. As such, their content is suitable for assessing general attainment. However, if a test is to be used to assess the extent to which students have profited from school instruction (that is, student achievement), more than general content validity is required: The test must match the instruction provided. Tests that do not match instruction lack content validity, and decisions based on such tests should be tempered. When making decisions about content validity for students with disabilities, it is very important always to consider the extent to which the student has had an opportunity to learn the content of the test. Many students with disabilities are assigned to a curriculum (often a functional curriculum) that differs from that to which students who are not disabled are exposed.

A second factor those who use achievement tests with students with disabilities need to consider is whether the stimulus/response modes of subtests may be difficult for students with physical or motor problems. Tests that are timed might be difficult for students whose reading or motor difficulties cause them to take more time on specific tasks. Many of these issues were described in greater detail in Chapter 9.

Third, teachers must evaluate the adequacy of each test's norms by asking whether the normative group is composed of the kinds of individuals to whom they wish to compare their students. If a test is used to estimate general attainment, a representative sample of students from across the nation is preferred.

TABLE 20.1   Categories of Achievement Tests

	Norm-Referenced		Criterion-Referenced	
	Single Skill	**Multiple Skill**	**Single Skill**	**Multiple Skill**
Group Administered Screening Devices	Gates-MacGinitie	California Achievement Test Iowa Tests of Basic Skills Metropolitan Achievement Tests (Survey Battery) Stanford Achievement Test Series	None	California Achievement Test Iowa Tests of Basic Skills Metropolitan Achievement Tests (Instructional Batteries) Stanford Achievement Test Series
Individually Administered Screening Devices	Test of Mathematical Abilities	Kaufman Test of Educational Achievement Peabody Individual Achievement Test–Revised Wide Range Achievement Test 3 Woodcock-Johnson Psycho-educational Battery–Revised Kaufman Assessment Battery for Children Basic Academic Skills Individual Screener	None	Basic Academic Skills Individual Screener
Group Administered Diagnostic Devices	Stanford Diagnostic Reading Test Stanford Diagnostic Mathematics Test	None	Prescriptive Reading Inventory Diagnostic Mathematics Inventory Stanford Diagnostic Mathematics Test	None
Individually Administered Diagnostic Devices	Gray Oral Reading Test-3 Durrell Analysis of Reading Difficulty Gates-McKillop-Horowitz Reading Diagnostic Tests Woodcock Reading Mastery Tests–Revised Test of Written Language Test of Written Spelling 2 Test of Reading Comprehension Formal Reading Inventory Test of Language Development 2 Test of Adolescent Language 2	Diagonostic Achievement Battery–2	Key Math–Revised Stanford Diagnostic Reading Test Standardized Reading Inventory	BRIGANCE® Diagnostic Inventories

However, if a test is used to estimate achievement in a school system, local norms are probably better. Finally, teachers should examine the extent to which a total test and its components have the reliability necessary for making decisions about what students have learned.

WHY DO WE ASSESS ACHIEVEMENT?

The very term *screening device* reflects the major purpose of achievement tests. These tests are used most often to screen students in an effort to identify those who demonstrate low-level, average, or high-level attainment in comparison to their peers. Achievement tests provide a global estimate of academic skill development and may be used to identify individual students for whom educational intervention is necessary either in the form of remediation (for those who demonstrate relatively low-level skill development) or in the form of academic enrichment (for those who exhibit exceptionally high-level skill development). However, screening tests have limited behavior samples and lower requirements for reliability. Therefore, students who are identified with screening tests should be further assessed with diagnostic tests to verify their need for educational intervention.

Although multiple-skill, group-administered achievement tests are usually considered to be screening devices, they are occasionally used in eligibility or entitlement decisions. In principle, such a use is generally inappropriate, although it may be justifiable and even desirable—when the group tests (for example, the Stanford Achievement Test Series or the Metropolitan Achievement Tests) contain behavior samples that are more complete than those contained in some individually administered tests of achievement used for placement (such as the Wide Range Achievement Test 3). Use of an achievement test with a better behavior sample is desirable if the tester goes beyond the scores earned to examine performance on specific test items.

Multiple-skill achievement tests may also be used for progress evaluation. Most school districts have routine testing programs at various grade levels to evaluate the extent to which pupils in their schools are progressing in comparison with some national standard. Scores on achievement tests provide communities, school boards, and parents with an index of the quality of schooling. Schools and the teachers within those schools are often subject to question when pupils fail to demonstrate expected progress.

Finally, achievement tests are used to evaluate the relative effectiveness of alternative curricula. Brown School may choose to use the Scott, Foresman Reading Series in third grade, while Green School decides to use the Lippincott Reading Program. If school personnel can assume that children were at relatively comparable reading levels when they entered the third grade, then achievement tests may be administered at the end of the year to ascertain the relative effectiveness of the Scott, Foresman and Lippincott programs. There are, of course, many assumptions in such evaluations (for example, that the quality of individual teachers and the instructional environment are comparable in the two schools) and many research pitfalls that must be avoided if comparative evaluation is to have meaning.

SPECIFIC TESTS OF ACADEMIC ACHIEVEMENT

The remainder of this chapter addresses specific multiple-skill devices and examines four popular group-administered multiple-skill batteries (the California Achievement Tests, the Iowa Tests of Basic Skills, the Metropolitan Achievement Tests, and the Stanford Achievement Test Series), four individually administered multiple-skill batteries (the Basic Achievement Skills Individual Screener, the Kaufman Test of Educational Achievement, the Peabody Individual Achievement Test–Revised, and the Wide Range Achievement Test 3), one individually administered, norm-referenced measure that is co-normed with intelligence tests (Wechsler Individual Achievement Test), one individually administered, criterion-referenced, multiple-skill battery (the BRIGANCE® Diagnostic Inventories) and one individually administered, norm-referenced, multiple-skill measure (Diagnostic Achievement Battery–2). Later chapters provide discussions of both screening and diagnostic tests that are devoted to specific content areas such as reading.

California Achievement Tests

*T*he California Achievement Tests (CAT/5) (CTB/Macmillan/McGraw-Hill, 1993) are a set of norm-referenced tests from which mastery scores for specific instructional objectives can also be obtained. The CAT/5 contains thirteen overlapping levels that measure academic achievement in grades K through 12. The tests include measures of skill development in reading, spelling, language, mathematics, study skills, science, and social studies. The CAT/5 has two test configurations: a Survey Battery and a Complete Battery. The Survey Battery is two-thirds as long as the Complete Battery and only provides norm-referenced information. The Survey can only be used in ten of the thirteen levels. The Complete Battery is available in two alternate forms and provides curriculum-referenced information as well as norm-referenced scores. The Complete Battery requires from 1 hour 27 minutes at level K to 5 hours 16 minutes at levels 14 to 21/22. The Survey requires 2 hours 47 minutes or less for each level.

A "locator test" is available; it may be used as a pretest to determine the appropriate level of the test to be administered. Use of the locator test facilitates functional level testing, that is, assessment of students at their functional level rather than their grade-placement level. The CAT/5 also has six practice exercises, which are designed to give students practice in taking standardized tests. The authors recommend giving the practice exercises a day or two before the first testing session. A class management guide is provided that includes instructions for norm-referenced and criterion-referenced use and interpretation of the test results, as well as selected instructional activities matched to the objectives assessed by the test. Technical information is included in separate technical bulletins.

The CAT/5 is organized into three broad areas: Reading/Language Arts, Mathematics, and Supplementary Content Areas. The subtests included in specific levels of the CAT are shown in Table 20.2. A description of each subtest follows.

READING/LANGUAGE ARTS

This content area was revised in the fifth edition of the CAT to reflect recent changes in education theory and practice regarding reading and language arts.

Visual Recognition   In this subtest, students must distinguish letters by recognizing single letters that are orally presented, recognizing uppercase and lowercase forms of the same letter, and matching letter groups.

Sound Recognition   This subtest assesses the students' skill in recognizing sounds in spoken words. Students must identify pictures of objects that have the same initial or final consonant sounds as words read by the examiner and identify pictures of objects whose names rhyme with words read by the examiner.

Word Analysis   This subtest measures the students' skill in decoding and in using structural clues to identify the proper pronunciation and meaning of unfamiliar words.

Vocabulary   This subtest measures the students' understanding of word meaning. Students must identify words that fit categories, that have the same meaning, or that have opposite meanings. Students are also re-

TABLE 20.2   Subtests at Each Level of the CAT/5

Test	K	10	11	12	13	14	15	16	17	18	19	20	21/22
Visual Recognition	X												
Word Analysis (Sound Recognition at Level K)	X	X	X	X	X								
Vocabulary	X	X	X	X	X	X	X	X	X	X	X	X	X
Comprehension	X	X	X	X	X	X	X	X	X	X	X	X	X
Spelling				X	X	X	X	X	X	X	X	X	X
Language Mechanics			X	X	X	X	X	X	X	X	X	X	X
Language Expression			X	X	X	X	X	X	X	X	X	X	X
Mathematics Computation			X	X	X	X	X	X	X	X	X	X	X
Mathematics Concepts and Applications	X	X	X	X	X	X	X	X	X	X	X	X	X
Study Skills						X	X	X	X	X	X	X	X
Science			X	X	X	X	X	X	X	X	X	X	X
Social Studies			X	X	X	X	X	X	X	X	X	X	X

SOURCE: CTB/Macmillan/McGraw-Hill. 1992. *The California Achievement Tests/5. Technical Bulletin 1.*

quired to use context clues to identify the intended meaning of words that have multiple meanings.

Comprehension This subtest assesses literal, inferential, and evaluative comprehension; students derive meaning from written sentences and passages.

Spelling The single subtest in this content area, which is not given at levels K, 10, or 11, assesses students' skill in identifying incorrectly spelled words used in sentences.

Language Mechanics This subtest measures capitalization and punctuation skills. Students are required to edit passages presented in differing formats.

Language Expression This subtest assesses the student's skill in effective written expression, including the use of various parts of speech and the formation and organization of sentences and paragraphs.

MATHEMATICS

The two subtests in this content area have been revised to meet the standards set by the National Council of Teachers of Mathematics (NCTM).

Mathematics Computation This subtest assesses students' skill in solving addition, subtraction, multiplication, and division problems involving whole numbers, fractions, mixed numbers, decimals, and algebraic expressions.

Mathematics Concepts and Applications This subtest assesses students' skill in understanding and applying a wide range of mathematical concepts involving numeration, number sentences, number theory, problem solving, measurement, and geometry.

SUPPLEMENTARY CONTENT AREAS

Study Skills Items in this subtest relate to parts of books, dictionary conventions, library skills, graphic

information, and study techniques. The subtest measures students' skill in finding and using information.

Science The subtest in this content area measures the student's understanding of scientific language, concepts, and methods of inquiry. Item content is drawn from each of the major areas of science.

Social Studies Items in the subtest in this content area measure understanding of the social sciences, including geography, economics, history, political science, and sociology.

SCORES

Five types of norm-referenced scores may be obtained for the CAT/5: percentile ranks, stanines, grade equivalents, normal curve equivalents, and scale scores (ranging from 000 to 999). Two types of curriculum-referenced information can be derived from the test. An objective performance index (OPI) is provided that describes a student's percentage correct on a specific test objective. A mastery band can be computed, based on the error of measurement of the test and the student's score; the mastery band is designed to give a graphical representation of students' actual level on each objective. An anticipated achievement score is provided if the CAT/5 is given along with the Test of Cognitive Skills (TCS/2).

The tests may be either hand-scored or submitted to the publisher for machine scoring. A variety of information systems are available, including individual test records, graphic frequency distributions, summary reports, error analyses, and class test records. Schools may obtain criterion-referenced data on objectives mastered by individuals or by classes, norm-referenced data comparing pupil performance to national norms, or demographic norm reports comparing class or school performance to the performances of schools of comparable demographic makeup.

NORMS

The CAT/5 has norms for the fall, winter, and spring. The test was standardized in January (winter norms), April (spring norms) and October (fall norms) of 1991. The winter standardization was for Level 11 only and consisted of 4,161 students. Stratification information was not provided for this group. The spring standardization involved 115,888 students and the fall standardization used 109,825 participants.

Three separate sampling designs were used in norming the CAT/5: public, private, and Catholic. The number of students from each setting was not reported in Technical Bulletin 1 (CTB/Macmillan/McGraw-Hill, 1992). Although the authors state that the public school samples were stratified on the basis of geographic region, community type (urban, rural, suburban), district size and socioeconomic status, the extent of stratification and counterbalancing could not be determined from the data provided. The norms are therefore questionable.

RELIABILITY

Data on reliability are restricted to KR-20 internal-consistency estimates. The authors provide internal-consistency coefficients for each of the subtests at each level of the CAT/5. The Survey is less reliable than the Complete Battery, and may not be suitable for screening. Several of the reliability coefficients for the subtests of the Survey are below .80. The reliability coefficients for the Complete Battery subtests are generally above .80. The exceptions are at grades 1 and 2 (Levels 11 and 12) for science and social studies, which fall below the .80 level. Data are not reported on test-retest reliability or alternate-forms reliability.

VALIDITY

Although the authors made an effort to ensure content validity and eliminate cultural bias from the test items, users must decide whether the CAT/5 measures the objectives of their curriculum. Data on other forms of validity of the CAT/5 are limited to an illustration that the percentage of students mastering objectives increases with age and a report of correlation of the CAT/5 with the Test of Cognitive Skills, a measure of learning aptitude.

SUMMARY

The California Achievement Tests is a group-administered, norm-referenced measure of pupils' skill development in reading, spelling, language, mathematics, science, and social studies. The tests are composed of a Survey and a Complete Battery. The information on standardization of the CAT/5 is incomplete. Data on reliability are limited to evidence of internal consistency and suggest that the CAT/5 Survey may not be suitable for screening. The Complete Battery appears to have sufficient reliability to support educational decisions about groups of students and reports of data on group performance. The reliabilities of some subtests are too low for use in making decisions about individual students. Data on validity are very limited.

Iowa Tests of Basic Skills and the Tests of Achievement and Proficiency

*T*he Iowa Tests of Basic Skills (ITBS) (Hoover, Hieronymus, Frisbie, & Dunbar, 1993) and the Tests of Achievement and Proficiency (TAP) (Scannell, Haugh, Lloyd, and Risinger, 1993) are norm-referenced and criterion-referenced tests designed to assess broad general functioning rather than specific facts and content. Both tests serve as continuous measures of growth in fundamental skills necessary to academic and later life success. The tests were designed to be used for multiple purposes, among which are (1) determination of students' developmental levels to assist in adapting instruction, (2) identification of specific qualitative strengths and weaknesses, (3) identification of readiness both to begin instruction and to proceed to the next step in instruction, (4) provision of data to assist in grouping students, (5) evaluation of strengths or weaknesses in entire group performance, (6) provision of information on pupil progress toward meeting instructional goals, and (7) provision to parents of objective, meaningful reports of their children's progress in learning basic skills.

The ITBS measures skills in vocabulary, reading, writing, listening, mathematics, science, and social studies. The ITBS is used in grades K through 9. The TAP measures advanced skills of the high school curriculum, assessing achievement in vocabulary, reading comprehension, written expression, mathematics, information processing, science, and social studies. Subtests of the ITBS and the TAP are listed in Tables 20.3 and 20.4 (pages 426 and 427). There are ten levels to the ITBS and four levels to the TAP. Levels 5 and 6 are the early primary battery used in kindergarten and first grade; levels 7 and 8 are the primary battery used in grades 1-7 to 3-5. Levels 9 to 14 make up the multilevel battery of the ITBS used in grades 3 through 9; levels 15 to 18 comprise the TAP. Levels are essentially equivalent to chronological age, and there are two forms at each level. There is a basic battery (nine of the fifteen subtests), which is a shorter version of the complete battery. Depending upon the level, the ITBS Complete Battery requires from 1 hour 53 minutes to 3 hours 20 minutes to administer. The ITBS Survey Battery takes 1 hour 50 minutes to complete at level 7 and 8, and 1 hour 40 minutes at levels 9 through 14. The TAP Complete Battery requires 2 hours 55 minutes at each level.

Following is a list of the subtests of the ITBS and the skills they assess.

Listening   The Listening subtest is included at levels 5 through 8 of the ITBS. Skills assessed include comprehending literal meaning and inferential meaning, following directions, understanding sequence, comprehending numerical, spatial, and temporal relationships, predicting outcomes, understanding linguistic relationships, and understanding a speaker's purpose, point of view, and style. An optional listening assessment is offered for levels 9 to 14, but the score for this subtest is not included in the composite score.

Writing   A supplemental writing subtest is available at levels 9 to 14. The test contains four different prompts to which students respond. The score on this supplemental subtest is not included in the composite score.

Word Analysis   This subtest is available only at the levels of the test intended for use in kindergarten through third grade. At the lower levels (levels 5 and 6), the subtest provides information on skill development in letter recognition and letter-sound correspondence. At levels 7 and 8, this subtest assesses students' knowledge of letter-sound relationships.

Vocabulary   At levels 5 and 6, this stand-alone subtest measures students' listening vocabulary. Reading vocabulary is assessed at levels 7 and 8. At the highest levels, the students' skill in identifying words in context is assessed.

Reading Comprehension   At level 6, this subtest assesses word recognition, word attack, and literal and inferential comprehension. At higher levels, the subtest assesses skill development in literal comprehension, inferential comprehension, and generalization.

Language Skills   This subtest assesses skills in four subareas: spelling, capitalization, punctuation, and usage. The spelling section is a measure of recognition, in which students identify one of four words as the correct spelling of a word read by the teacher. The capitalization section requires students to identify words that should be capitalized in sentences or

TABLE 20.3   Testing Times and Number of Items: Iowa Tests of Basic Skills, Forms K and L

Tests	Test Level:	Number of Items			Number of Items			Number of Items						
		5	6	Testing Time[a]	7	8	Testing Time[a]	9	10	11	12	13	14	Testing Time[a]
Practice Page		6	6	10										
Listening		29	29	30	31	31	25							
Word Analysis[b]		30	35	20	30	32	15							
Vocabulary		29	29	20	31	31	15	26	34	37	40	41	43	15
Reading/Reading Comprehension			50	43	40	43	35	36	38	41	44	46	49	40
Words			13	10										
Word Attack			7	5	7		5							
Pictures			13	8	19	23	10							
Sentences			13	10										
Stories			4	10	14	20	20							
Language		29	29	25	42	54	30(40)							
Spelling								27	31	34	36	39	41	12
Capitalization								24	27	27	28	29	30	12
Punctuation								24	27	27	28	29	30	12
Usage and Expression								31	36	40	41	41	43	24
Mathematics		29	35	25										
Mathematics Concepts					29	31	20	20	24	26	28	30	32	20
Mathematics Estimation								12	16	18	20	22	24	10
Mathematics Problem Solving					27	30	25	14	16	17	18	19	20	18
Mathematics Data Interpretation								10	11	13	14	16	16	12
Mathematics Computation[c]					27	30	25	34	37	39	41	42	43	20
Total:Core Battery					257	282	190(200)	258						195
Social Studies					31	31	25	30	35	40	42	44	46	30
Science					31	31	25	30	35	40	42	44	46	30
Sources of Information					28	34	30							
Maps and Diagrams								24	26	27	29	30	33	30
Reference Materials								28	30	32	34	36	38	25
Total:Complete Battery		146	207	173	347	378	270(280)	370	423	458	485	508	534	310
Listening Assessment								31	33	34	36	38	40	40
Writing Assessment[d]								4	4	4	4	4	4	40

[a] The testing time approximations are given in minutes. The total working time for Levels 5 and 6 includes the Practice Page, but Practice Page items are not included in the total number of items. The times in parentheses are for Level 8 only. Additional time is required for distributing and collecting materials and for completing answer sheet ID information and practice exercises.

[b] Word Analysis will not be included in either a Total Reading Score or a Total Language Score in the Complete or Core Batteries. A separate Word Analysis Score will be provided.

[c] The Mathematics Computation test is an optional test in all batteries. Mathematics Computation will not be included in the Math Total Score unless specifically requested.

[d] The optional Writing test has a choice of four different prompts (directions to the student) for Levels 9/10, Levels 11/12, and Levels 13/14.

SOURCE: Riverside Publishing Company. (1994). *Technical Summary 1: Riverside 2000*. Chicago: Riverside Publishing Company.

TABLE 20.4   **Testing Times and Number of Items: Test of Achievement and Proficiency, Forms K and L**

Tests	Test Level:	Testing Time[a]	Number of Items			
			15	16	17	18
Vocabulary		15	40	40	40	40
Reading Comprehension		40	58	60	62	63
Written Expression		40	60	60	62	64
Math Concepts and Problem Solving		40	48	48	48	48
Math Computation (optional)		20	40	40	40	40
Social Studies		40	61	62	62	62
Science		40	50	50	50	50
Information Processing		40	60	61	62	63
Totals		275	417	421	426	430

[a] Testing Time is given in minutes. Additional time is required for distributing and collecting materials and for completing answer sheet ID information and practice exercises.

SOURCE: Riverside Publishing Company. (1994). *Technical Summary 1: Riverside 2000.* Chicago: Riverside Publishing Company.

paragraphs. The punctuation section requires students to identify places in sentences that need specific punctuation marks. The usage section assesses knowledge of grammatical rules by requiring students to identify which of three alternative sentences employs correct usage.

Mathematics Skills   Three kinds of math tests are included in the ITBS. The first kind assesses knowledge of mathematical concepts, the second requires students to solve written problems and interpret data, and the optional third test requires students to solve computational problems. At lower levels of the test, the directions are read to the students; at upper levels, students must read the directions themselves.

Science   This subtest is available for levels 7 through 14 of the ITBS. It assesses the student's knowledge, understanding, and ability to evaluate facts and concepts in the content areas of life science, earth and space science, and physical science.

Social Studies   This subtest is available for levels 7 through 14 of the ITBS. It includes an assessment of students' knowledge, understanding, and ability to evaluate facts and concepts in economics, geography, history, political science, sociology, anthropology, and related social sciences.

Sources of Information   This subtest, included only at levels 7 to 14 of the ITBS, assesses generalized skill development in two areas: reading maps, charts and diagrams and demonstrating knowledge and uses of references. For the first area, students answer specific questions by reading maps, charts and diagrams. For the second area, students must demonstrate knowledge of how to alphabetize, read tables of contents, and use an index, dictionary, encyclopedia, and other general reference materials.

The subtests of the TAP and the skills they assess are as follows.

Vocabulary   This subtest assesses students' working vocabulary, free of contextual cues.

Written Expression   This subtest emphasizes complete composition and assesses the skills necessary for expressing ideas in writing. It includes questions on spelling, sentence structure, and the correct use of pronoun references.

Reading Comprehension   This subtest assesses students' skill in factual and inferential comprehension and in determining vocabulary in context.

Information Processing   This subtest assesses the extent to which students can read and use various types of maps, charts, and graphs and use references to locate information.

Mathematics   Two types of mathematics tests are included in the TAP. The first measures both the understanding of mathematical principles and the use of basic mathematics in managing the quantitative aspects of everyday living. The second, optional test assesses computational skills.

Social Studies   This subtest assesses students' knowledge of issues and problems associated with interactions among people and between people and the environment.

Science   This subtest measures problem solving and the interpretation of scientific information. Content is drawn from the life sciences and the earth and space sciences.

SCORES

The ITBS and the TAP provide six types of scores: raw scores, developmental standard scores, grade equivalents, national percentile ranks, national stanines, and normal curve equivalents. The developmental standard score provides an estimate of a student's location on an academic achievement continuum. The median standard score for each grade is computed and placed along the continuum of scores. The standard score can then be interpreted based on the typical performance of students in each grade. For example, the developmental standard score for students in grade 1 is 130, and the median score for students in grade 7 is 239. The ITBS and TAP can be hand- or machine-scored. A software package, Keyscore Norm Look-Up, is available to assist the hand-scoring process. The program will convert raw scores to each of the five other types of scores and provide interpolated norms and graphs of national percentile ranks.

NORMS

The ITBS and TAP were standardized concurrently in 1992 with the Cognitive Abilities Test (Thorndike & Hagen, 1993). These measures were standardized on a carefully selected stratified national sample of about 170,000 students. All public school districts in the United States were stratified, first on the basis of geographic region, and then on the basis of size of enrollment. Districts were then stratified on the basis of socioeconomic status, based on the percent of students in the district falling below the federal government poverty guideline. Within each socioeconomic stratum, one district was randomly selected. Once districts had been selected and had agreed to participate, further sample selection was accomplished by selecting buildings that would be representative of the distribution of achievement within the selected districts. Data provided in the test manuals show the breakdown of the sample by district size, region of the country, and district socioeconomic status.

In addition to the public school norm sample, norms are provided for Catholic schools and for private non-Catholic schools. Catholic schools were selected on the basis of geographic region and size of the diocesan school system of which they were members. Private non-Catholic schools were selected on the basis of region and type of school—Baptist, Lutheran, Seventh Day Adventist, other church-related, and non–church-related. There are eight separate sets of norms—national, interpolated, local, large city, Catholic/private school, high socioeconomic, low socioeconomic, and international—so that student performance can be compared to different groups.

RELIABILITY

Internal-consistency reliability data are based on the performance of the fall and spring 1992 standardization samples. Because major areas of the tests (for example, reading total and mathematics total) are most often used in norm-referenced interpretation, these are the reliabilities of greatest concern. Reliabilities for the ITBS raw scores range from .65 to .94 at the kindergarten and first-grade levels, and from .61 to .93 for the multilevel edition of the test. At the kindergarten level, the Language and Word Analysis subtests are the only subtests whose reliabilities are sufficient for the tests to be used in making screening decisions about individuals (that is, the reliabilities for these subtests exceed .80). At the first-grade level, only the Language, Word Analysis, and Mathematics subtests have reliabilities high enough for the tests to be used in making screening decisions about individuals. At the second- and third-grade levels, the reliability for the Listening, Mathematics Concepts, Social Studies, and Science subtests are too low for the tests to be used in making screening decisions about individuals.

Data on internal-consistency reliability of the TAP are based on the performance of the fall and spring 1992 standardization sample. The reliability coefficients for the TAP raw scores all exceed .80.

There are no data on the stability of raw scores on the 1993 edition of the ITBS or TAP.

VALIDITY

The authors of the ITBS and TAP attempted to ensure content validity by following a number of steps in the development of the tests. Curriculum guides, textbooks, and research were consulted in writing the items. Potential items were tried out on more than 100,000 students from thirty states plus Guam and the Virgin Islands. Item selection was based on the performance of this sample group, and selected items were reviewed for bias. There are no data on the construct validity or criterion validity of the 1993 editions of the ITBS or the TAP.

SUMMARY

The Iowa Tests of Basic Skills and the Tests of Achievement and Proficiency are a comprehensive battery designed to assess broad functional skills in grades K through 12. Development and standardization of the tests appear exemplary. From the internal-consistency data presented in the manual, reliability is variable. Test users should check the manual to ascertain the reliability for the grades and subtests they are considering. There are no data on the long-term stability (test-retest reliability) of either the ITBS or the TAP. Users must judge the content validity of these tests for their particular use. There are no data on either the construct validity or the criterion-related validity of the 1993 editions of the ITBS and the TAP.

Metropolitan Achievement Tests

*T*he Metropolitan Achievement Tests (7th Edition) (MAT7) (Balow, Farr, & Hogan, 1992) are standardized group achievement tests designed to measure student achievements in reading, language, mathematics, science, and social studies. The tests have been completely revised to address recent changes in school curricula. Leading textbooks, curriculum guidelines, and syllabi were analyzed to create test specifications and blueprints. The MAT7 is composed of fourteen levels, spanning kindergarten through twelfth grade. Two levels were created for kindergarten and one level for each remaining grade. Two forms were developed, one of which is a secure form and has limited release. Depending on the test level, the complete battery requires from 1 hour, 35 minutes to 4 hours, 10 minutes to administer (see Table 20.5). Besides the five content areas, the MAT7 also assesses Research Skills and Thinking Skills. The subtests of the MAT7 are described below.

Word Recognition   Skill in identifying consonant sounds, vowel sounds, and word parts is measured by this subtest.

Reading Vocabulary   This subtest, which must be read by the pupils, assesses skill in deriving meaning from words in context.

Reading Comprehension   This subtest assesses students' skill in recognizing detail and sequence; inferring meaning, cause and effect, main idea, and character analysis; and drawing conclusions.

Prereading   This subtest appears only at the preprimer and primer levels. All directions are read to the students. The test is a measure of auditory discrimination, visual discrimination, and letter recognition.

The NCTM standards were used in the development of the mathematics tests. Scores can be derived from the mathematics tests that reflect the NCTM core areas.

Concepts and Problem Solving   This subtest assesses the students' ability to determine which problem-solving strategies should be selected and used. The items require students to carefully analyze the problem, synthesize the information, and attend to detail.

Procedures   This subtest is optional and is not used at the preprimer, primer and secondary levels. The test includes traditional computation problems and word problems.

Mathematics   This subtest, which appears at the preprimer and primer levels only, assesses basic concepts of number and units, shapes, and money.

Prewriting/Composing/Editing   These subtests use a multiple-choice format that is designed to emulate the process of writing. Students must evaluate sections of a text and are asked questions related to the three stages of writing. Spelling items are also included in these subtests and begin at the Elementary 1 level.

Language   A single Language composite is produced for preprimer through primary 2. Skill development in listening comprehension and basic prewriting skills are measured at the lower levels of the test.

Science   This subtest assesses the students' knowledge of basic science facts and concepts derived from physical, earth and space, and life sciences. Also assessed are inquiry skills and skill in critical analysis.

Social Studies   This subtest assesses knowledge and comprehension of facts and concepts from the subject matter areas of geography, economics, history, political science, sociology, anthropology, and psychology.

Research Skills/Thinking Skills   These subtests, which are included in levels of the test intended for use beyond third grade, measure skill development in using library resources and other methods of collecting data and properly analyzing and applying information in a variety of contexts.

SCORES

Raw scores and several types of derived scores can be obtained for subtests and components of the MAT7. Derived scores include scaled scores, percentile ranks, grade equivalents, normal curve equivalents, functional reading levels, content cluster performance categories, proficiency statements, and predicted Scholastic Aptitude Test and American College Test performance ranges. Achievement-ability comparisons can also be derived if students are given the Otis-Lennon School Ability Test.

TABLE 20.5 Subtests and Levels of the MAT7

Subtest	PP Grade K-0-K-5		PR Grade K-5-1-5		P1 Grade 1-5-2-5		P2 Grade 2-5-3-5		E1 Grade 3-5-4-5		E2 Grade 4-5-5-5		I1 Grade 5-5-6-5		I2 Grade 6-5-7-5		I3 Grade 7-5-8-5		I4 Grade 8-5-9-5		S1 Grade 9		S2 Grade 10		S3 Grade 11		S4 Grade 12	
	K	T	K	T	K	T	K	T	K	T	K	T	K	T	K	T	K	T	K	T	K	T	K	T	K	T	K	T
Word Recognition					30	20	24	15																				
Reading Vocabulary					24	20	24	20	30	20	30	20	30	20	30	20	30	20	30	20	30	20	30	20	30	20	30	20
Reading Comprehension					40	35	45	40	55	50	55	50	55	50	55	50	55	50	55	50	55	50	55	50	55	50	55	50
Prereading/Total Reading	50	35	50	35	94	75	93	75	85	70	85	70	85	70	85	70	85	70	85	70	85	70	85	70	85	70	85	70
Concepts and Problem Solving					32	35	36	35	40	40	40	40	48	50	54	50	54	50	54	50								
Procedures					20	20	20	20	24	25	24	25	24	25	24	25	24	25	24	25								
Mathematics/Total Mathematics	30	30	38	40	52	55	56	55	64	65	64	65	72	75	78	75	78	75	78	75	52	50	52	50	52	50	52	50
Prewriting									15		15		15		15		15		15		15		15		15		15	
Composing									15		15		15		15		15		15		15		15		15		15	
Editing									24		24		24		24		24		24		24		24		24		24	
Language	40	30	40	30	46	40	46	40	54	45	54	45	54	45	54	45	54	45	54	45	54	45	54	45	54	45	54	45
Science					30	25	30	25	35	25	35	25	40	30	40	30	40	30	40	30	40	30	40	30	40	30	40	30
Social Studies					30	25	30	25	35	25	35	25	40	30	40	30	40	30	40	30	40	30	40	30	40	30	40	30
Research Skills									31		36		41		42		42		42		41		41		43		43	
Thinking Skills									78		83		100		103		103		110		116		117		119		120	
Basic Battery	120	95	128	105	192	170	195	170	203	180	203	180	211	190	217	190	217	190	217	190	191	165	191	165	191	165	191	165
Complete Battery					252	220	255	220	273	230	273	230	291	250	297	250	297	250	297	250	271	225	271	225	271	225	271	225
Total Testing Time	1 hr. 35 min.		1 hr. 45 min.		3 hrs. 40 min.		3 hrs. 40 min.		3 hrs 50 min.		3 hrs. 50 min.		4 hrs. 10 min.		4hrs. 10 min.		4 hrs. 10 min.		4 hrs. 10 min.		3 hrs. 45 min.		3 hrs. 45 min.		3 hrs. 45 min.		3 hrs. 45 min.	

K = Number of items
T = Time in minutes

SOURCE: Balow, I. H., Farr, R. C., & Hogan, T. P. (1992). *Metropolitan Achievement Tests, Seventh Edition.* San Antonio, TX: Psychological Corporation.

Content cluster performance indicators are used to describe the student's performance on each content cluster of the MAT7, relative to the performance of a nationwide sample of students at the same grade level. Three types of functional reading level are provided: instructional, independent, and frustration. Instructional reading levels are indexes of the highest level at which pupils can read without experiencing frustration. Independent reading levels are criterion-referenced scores indicating the level of material students can read with ease and efficiency. Frustration reading levels are criterion-referenced scores showing the level at which students will find materials too difficult to comprehend even with instruction. Proficiency statements describe what type of tasks students should be able to complete based on their MAT7 scores.

The MAT7 may be hand-scored or submitted to the publisher for computerized scoring. The scoring service may be used to obtain class summary reports, norm-referenced analyses for classes and for individual pupils, and criterion-referenced analyses for classes and for individuals.

NORMS

The MAT7 was standardized during the spring and fall of 1992. The spring standardization consisted of 100,000 students from 300 schools; the fall standardization contained 79,000 students. The authors state that the sample was stratified originally by geographic region, socioeconomic status (SES), community type (urban or rural), and ethnicity, and then statistically weighted to match the 1990 Census data when they became available.

RELIABILITY

Three forms of internal-consistency reliability data were computed. Alternate-form, KR-20, and KR-21 reliability coefficients generally exceed .80 across the fourteen levels of the test, although several cluster scores drop well below the .80 mark. The test appears to be adequate for group reporting and screening but should not be used to make decisions about individuals. Test-retest data were not reported.

VALIDITY

Although the content validity of an achievement test must ultimately be determined by the user, the authors of the MAT7 rigorously attempted to match the test with current school curricula. An effort was also made to eliminate cultural bias from the test items, mostly by asking individuals from different cultural groups to review the items. Data on the construct validity of the MAT7 are limited to an illustration that growth occurs across levels of the test and that items can discriminate across grade levels.

SUMMARY

The Metropolitan Achievement Tests (7th edition) is a norm-referenced and criterion-referenced achievement test designed for use in grades K through 12. The test was adequately standardized and is reliable for group reporting and screening purposes. The test was redesigned to match current school curricula. Judgments about content validity must be made by users, who must consider the extent to which the test samples what they teach.

Stanford Achievement Test Series

*T*he Stanford Achievement Test Series is made up of three separate measures. The Stanford Early School Achievement Test (SESAT) (Psychological Corporation, 1992b) is in its third edition and is intended for use in kindergarten and first grade. The Stanford Achievement Test (SAT) (Psychological Corporation, 1992a) is in its eighth edition and is used in first grade through ninth grade. The Test of Academic Skills (TASK) (Psychological Corporation, 1992c) is in its third edition and is used in ninth grade through community college. All forms and levels of the test are group administered. The test is both norm-referenced and criterion-referenced.

There are thirteen levels of the Stanford Achievement Test Series and five to thirteen subtests at each level. Subtests at each level of the series as well as number of items per subtest and the administration time are listed in Table 20.6 (on the following page). No subtest occurs at all levels.

Assessors must decide whether to use a Basic Battery or a Complete Battery. At all levels, the Basic Battery includes all subtests except the Environment, Science and Social Science subtests. Assessors may also decide to assess students in only reading or mathematics. The publishers have provided separate booklets including all reading tests and all mathematics tests. Total administration time for the Basic Battery ranges from 1 hour, 45 minutes to 5 hours. Administration time for the Complete Battery ranges from 2 hours, 15 minutes to 6 hours.

Ten special reports are also available. These reports describe the content of the various subtests and include descriptions of ways in which the tests may be used to improve instruction.

Following is a description of subtests of the Stanford series and behaviors they sample.

Sounds and Letters   This subtest is included only in SESAT 1 and 2 and primary levels 2 and 3 in the SAT. It is an assessment of the abilities to match beginning or ending sounds in words, to recognize letters, and to match sounds to letters.

Word Study Skills   This subtest measures students' skills in decoding words and identifying relationships between sounds and letters. This subtest is at the primary levels only.

Word Reading   This subtest measures students' ability to recognize words by (1) matching spoken words to pictures, (2) identifying printed words that name particular illustrations, and (3) identifying printed words that describe or are associated with a picture. This subtest is at the SESAT and primary 1 levels only.

Reading Vocabulary   In this subtest, students are asked to select words that best fit definitions read by the examiner. The measure thus provides an assessment of students' word knowledge independent of their ability to read definitions.

Sentence Reading   This subtest, used at the SESAT 2 level only, assesses students' skill in identifying pictures that illustrate sentences they read.

Reading Comprehension   In this subtest, students read passages that assess textual, functional, and recreational reading skills and then answer questions at the end of each passage, which assess literal and inferential comprehension.

Listening to Words and Stories   This subtest assesses students' ability to remember details, follow directions, identify cause and effect, identify main ideas, and understand aspects of language structure. Students must demonstrate knowledge of word meanings and skill in comprehending what is read to them.

Listening Comprehension   This subtest assesses students' ability to process information that is read to them.

Language Arts   The language arts subtest measures students' achievement in understanding and using the mechanics of language, forming complete sentences, locating and organizing information, and applying the conventions of spelling.

Language Mechanics   This subtest assesses students' knowledge of the conventions of capitalization and punctuation and their use of grammatical concepts.

Language Expression   Students' skill in manipulating words, phrases, and clauses and in evaluating style and organization are assessed in this subtest.

TABLE 20.6 Content and Structure: Full-Length Edition of the Stanford Achievement Test Series, Eighth Edition (Forms J, K, L, and M)

Subtest/Total	SESAT 1 Items	Time*	SESAT 2 Items	Time	PRIMARY 1 Items	Time	PRIMARY 2 Items	Time	PRIMARY 3 Items	Time	INTERMEDIATE 1 Items	Time	INTERMEDIATE 2 Items	Time	INTERMEDIATE 3 Items	Time	ADVANCED 1 Items	Time	ADVANCED 2 Items	Time	TASK 1 Items	Time	TASK 2 Items	Time	TASK 3 Items	Time
Grade (Content)[1]	1st half K		2nd half K / 1st half 1		1		2		3		4		5		6		7		8		9		10		11-12	
Recommended Administration Points	K-0-K.5		K.5-1.5		1.5-2.5		2.5-3.5		3.5-4.5		4.5-5.5		5.5-6.5		6.5-7.5		7.5-8.5		8.5-9.9		9.0-9.9		10.0-10.9		11.0-12.9	
Sounds & Letters/	48	30	40	25																						
Word Study Skills	30	15	40	25	36	20	48	25	48	25																
Word Reading/			30	30	30	20																				
Reading Vocabulary[3]							40	30	40	25	40	25	40	25	40	25	40	25	40	25	40	25	40	25	40	25
Sentence Reading/																										
Reading Comprehension					40	35	40	35	54	45	54	50	54	50	54	50	54	50	54	50	54	40	54	40	54	40
Total Reading	78	45	110	80	106	75	128	90	142	95	94	75	94	75	94	75	94	75	94	75	94	65	94	65	94	65
Language Mechanics									30	20	30	20	30	20	30	20	30	20	30	20						
Language Expression									30	25	30	25	30	25	30	25	30	25	30	25						
Language/English/					44	40	44	40													54	30	54	30	54	30
Total Language[2]									60	45	60	45	60	45	60	45	60	45	60	45						
Study Skills									30	25	30	25	30	25	32	25	32	25	32	25	34	25	34	25	34	25
Spelling					30	20	30	20	36	15	50	15	50	15	50	15	50	15	50	15	40	15	40	15	40	15
Listening[3]	45	30	45	30	45	30	45	30	45	30	45	30	45	30	45	30	45	30	45	30						
Concepts of Number					34	20	34	20	34	20	34	20	34	20	34	20	34	20	34	20						
Mathematics Computation					26	30	36	30	44	35	44	40	44	40	44	40	44	40	44	40						
Mathematics Applications[4]	21**	30	22**	30	30	30	35	25	38	35	40	35	40	35	40	35	40	35	40	35	18**	35	18**	35	18**	35
Mathematics/	42	30	44	30																	48	40	48	40	48	40
Total Mathematics					90	85	105	75	116	90	118	95	118	95	118	95	118	95	118	95						
Environment	40	30	40	30	40	30	40	30																		
Science									50	30	50	30	50	30	50	30	50	30	50	30	50	25	50	25	50	25
Social Science									50	30	50	30	50	30	50	30	50	30	50	30	50	25	50	25	50	25
Chapter 1 Edition[7]					70	65	75	60	92	80	94	85	94	85	94	85	94	85	94	85						
Basic Battery[6]	165	105	199	140	315	250	352	255	429	300	387	285	397	285	399	285	399	285	399	285	270	175	270	175	270	175
Complete Battery[5]	205	135	239	170	355	280	392	285	529	360	487	345	497	345	499	345	499	345	499	345	370	225	370	225	370	225
Using Information[8]									X		X		X		X		X		X		X		X		X	
Thinking Skills[8]									X		X		X		X		X		X		X		X		X	

1 For fall testing, we recommend use of the previous grade level. For example, use Primary 2 for testing in the fall of grade 3, since most students will not have been exposed to the content on Primary 3 (3rd Grade).

2 A total Language score is also available that includes Spelling, which can be substituted for the regular Total Language score.

3 Auditory Vocabulary is included in the Listening subtest.

4 The Mathematics Applications subtest is available with or without calculator norms.

5 Complete Battery includes all subtests. Basic Battery excludes Environment, Science, and Social Science.

6 Basic Battery excludes Environment, Science, and Social Science.

7 Chapter 1 Edition includes only Reading Comprehension and Mathematics Applications subtests.

8 Using Information and Thinking Skills are "embedded subtests" that do not require additional administration time. They are available from the Basic or Complete Battery (Stanford 8) or Complete Battery (Stanford Abbreviated).

* Time for each subtest is in minutes.

** A separate Mathematics Applications score is available for these items embedded in the SESAT and TASK Mathematics subtests.

SOURCE: Copyright © 1992 by The Psychological Corporation. All rights reserved. Printed in the U.S.A.

Study Skills   This subtest measures the skills used in the process of investigation.

Spelling   Students must identify the correct spelling of words in this subtest.

Mathematics   The SAT contains three separate subtests in mathematics: Concepts of Number, Mathematics Computation, and Mathematics Applications. In the SESAT and TASK, these subtests are combined into a single Mathematics subtest.

Concepts of Number   This subtest measures understanding of basic number concepts.

Mathematics Computation   Students are required to solve computation problems in this subtest.

Mathematics Applications   This subtest assesses students' ability to apply mathematics skills to the solution of problems.

Science   Students' understanding of the facts and concepts of the biological and physical sciences is measured. The subtest also assesses inquiry skills in science.

Social Science   This subtest measures skill development in geography, history, anthropology, sociology, political science, and economics, as well as students' ability to interpret data presented in graphic form.

Environment   The Science and Social Science subtests are combined at the early levels of the test in an assessment of concepts about the social and natural environment.

In addition to scores from the subtests listed, scores indicating skills in using information and thinking skills may be obtained. The using information score is obtained by separately scoring selected items from the Mathematics Applications, Study Skills, Science, and Social Science subtests. The score provides an index of a student's ability to use reference materials and to read graphs and charts.

There are two special editions of the Stanford Achievement Test: one for assessing blind or partially sighted students and one for assessing deaf students. The edition for use with blind or partially sighted students can be obtained in either Braille or large print from the American Printing House for the Blind, and the edition for hearing-impaired students may be obtained from Gallaudet College. Both special editions were standardized on the respective populations of individuals with disabilities.

SCORES

A variety of transformed scores are obtained for the Stanford series: stanines, grade equivalent scores, percentiles, and various standard scores. The tests may be scored by hand or submitted to the publisher for machine scoring. When protocols are submitted to the publisher's scoring service, the publisher can provide record sheets for individual students, forms for reporting test results to parents, item analyses, class profiles, profiles comparing individual achievement with individual capability, analyses of each student's performance in attainment of specific objectives, local norms, and so forth.

NORMS

The eighth edition of the Stanford Achievement Test Series was standardized simultaneously with the Otis-Lennon School Ability Test in both the fall and spring of 1991. Separate norms are thus provided for schools whose students must be tested at specific times of the year. Standardizing the series along with the Otis-Lennon enabled the authors to account for the ability levels of the students in the standardization population and also to develop a set of tables for comparison of ability level to achievement.

Sample selection was based on several variables including geographic region, socioeconomic status, community type (urban or rural), and public/nonpublic status. About 190,000 students participated in the standardization of the series. The technical manual includes a table showing the percentages of different types of students who participated and comparing those percentages to national census data. There is close correspondence between standardization sample makeup and the makeup of the 1990 census.

RELIABILITY

Reliability data for the SESAT, SAT, and TASK consist of KR-20 and KR-21 internal-consistency coefficients and alternative-forms coefficients for each level of the test. KR-20 coefficients ranged from .72 to .99. KR-21 coefficients, which represent the lower bound of internal consistency, ranged from .60 to .96. Most coefficients are between .85 and .90. The majority of the low coefficients are for the Language Mechanics and the Environment subtests. Alternative-forms reliability estimates ranged from .71 to .95. Extensive tables listing reliability coefficients and standard errors of measurement are included in the technical manual for the test. With only a few exceptions, the scores for subtests are reliable enough for group decision making and reporting.

VALIDITY

As for any achievement test, the validity of the Stanford series rests primarily on its content validity. Items for the series were originally written by the test authors and submitted to a group of subject-matter experts to establish the content accuracy. Measurement experts examined and edited the items, and the items were reviewed by general editors for writing clarity. The test items were submitted to a group of people representing minority groups, who screened the items in terms of the appropriateness of content for various cultural groups. In addition, teachers from the schools participating in the standardization process evaluated the clarity of both the instructions and the items.

Empirical validity was established on the basis of three factors: the increasing difficulty of items with higher grade levels, a moderate to high relationship with the seventh edition of the Stanford series, and intercorrelations between Stanford subtests and the Otis-Lennon School Ability Test.

SUMMARY

The Stanford Achievement Test Series is composed of the SESAT, SAT, and TASK. The tests provide a comprehensive continuous assessment of skill development in a variety of areas. Standardization, reliability, and validity are adequate for screening purposes.

Basic Achievement Skills Individual Screener

*T*he Basic Achievement Skills Individual Screener (BASIS) (Sonnenschein, 1983) is an individually administered achievement test that assesses pupil skills in reading, mathematics, spelling, and writing. The test takes less than one hour to administer and provides both norm- and criterion-referenced interpretation. Normative scores are available for pupils in grades 1 to 12. Criterion-referenced use involves assessment of pupil performance on clusters of test items. Each cluster reflects the curriculum of a specific grade, and grade-referenced placement scores are obtained that describe achievement in basic skills. These scores are used to derive classroom and textbook placement suggestions.

BASIS may be administered by teachers, resource teachers, or school psychologists. Examiners do not give all items of the test but instead administer clusters of items appropriate to the student's developmental level. Clusters of items range from readiness to grade 8 in reading and mathematics, and from grade 1 to grade 8 in spelling. Testing starts with administration of relatively easy clusters and proceeds until the student fails to reach criterion on one of the more difficult graded clusters. Behaviors sampled by subtests of BASIS are described below.

Reading   This subtest measures comprehension of graded passages. At upper levels the student supplies missing words in paragraphs. At early levels, the student reads words and sentences; at the readiness level, the student must identify letters.

Mathematics This subtest measures computational skill. The student completes paper-and-pencil computation problems and word problems that are read to the student.

Spelling The student must write words dictated by the examiner.

Writing The student must write for 10 minutes on a subject assigned by the examiner and intended to elicit descriptive writing.

SCORES

Both norm-referenced and criterion-referenced scores are obtained for BASIS. Both grade and age scores are expressed as standard scores, percentile ranks, stanines, grade equivalents, age equivalents, and normal curve equivalents. Criterion-referenced scores, called grade-referenced placements, may also be obtained. These scores are used to recommend the grade or textbook level at which a student should be instructed in each subject.

NORMS

In developing items for the test, the authors reviewed the most commonly used textbooks in each subject-matter area, selected the objectives that formed the essence of the curriculum, and developed items to measure those objectives. The authors focused on computation and problem solving in mathematics, on comprehension in reading, and on production from dictation in spelling. An item analysis was conducted in spring 1981 by administering the test to between 1,900 and 2,000 students. BASIS was standardized in the fall of 1982 on more than 3,200 students who were representative of students in grades 1 to 12. The sample was stratified on the basis of grade, sex, geographic region, socioeconomic status, and ethnic representation. The authors report characteristics of the sample in comparison to 1970 educational census figures. Sample distribution was very close to population distribution on all characteristics.

RELIABILITY

Several different indexes of reliability were derived using the standardization group as a sample. Internal-consistency coefficients for the math, reading, and spelling subtest at each grade level all exceed .85. All but four coefficients exceed .90. Test-retest reliabilities were computed for a subsample (about 20 percent) of the standardization group. All test-retest reliabilities exceed .80.

VALIDITY

Content validity was established by initial selection of items and later demonstration that item difficulty increased with grade level. Validity was also investigated by correlating performance on the BASIS with performance on unspecified achievement tests. Correlations ranged from .30 to .72. All correlations except one were greater than .43. Correlations between BASIS scores and report card grades consistently exceeded .40.

The author of BASIS also conducted a number of studies on the validity of the test for use with special populations of children. First, the author established correlations between performance on the BASIS reading subtest and scores on two reading achievement tests (the Metropolitan Achievement Test and the Degrees of Reading Power) using forty-nine mainstreamed students. Correlations were .61 and .64. Instructional reading levels (from MAT) were in consistent agreement with the grade-referenced placements on BASIS. For thirty-five third-grade learning-disabled students, correlations between BASIS subtests and comparable content subtests of the MAT and the Wide Range Achievement Test (WRAT) ranged from .40 to .74. For twenty-nine severely learning-disabled seventh and eighth graders, BASIS reading correlated .60 with Woodcock Reading Mastery Test scores. BASIS correlated .44 to .57 with Metropolitan Achievement Test scores for thirty-four gifted fourth- and fifth-grade students. BASIS subtests correlations with WRAT subtests were 44 (Math), .19 (Reading), and .90 (Spelling) for twenty-six educable mentally retarded junior high school students. Correlations between BASIS, WRAT, and California Achievement Test scores for twenty-five emotionally handicapped sixth-, seventh-, and eighth-graders ranged from .51 to .81. For twenty-two hearing-impaired students in grades 4, 5, and 6, correlations between BASIS scores and comparable content CAT scores ranged from .71 to .83.

SUMMARY

BASIS is an individually administered achievement test that samples behaviors in reading, mathematics, spelling, and writing. The test is norm-referenced and offers limited criterion-referenced interpretation. The test norms may now be outdated. Reliability is suitable for screening purposes, and validity is adequate.

Kaufman Test of Educational Achievement

*T*he Kaufman Test of Educational Achievement (KTEA) is an individually administered norm-referenced multiple-skill achievement test that can be used with students in the first through twelfth grades. The KTEA comes in two quite different forms: the Comprehensive Form (CF) (Kaufman & Kaufman, 1985a, c) and the Brief Form (BF) (Kaufman & Kaufman, 1985a, b). The BF requires from 10 to 35 minutes to administer and the CF from 20 to 75 minutes, depending on a child's grade. Both forms use the easel-kit format.

Both forms of the KTEA are intended for use in program planning, program evaluation, placement decision making, self-appraisal, and personnel selection. They are also recommended by the Kaufmans for use in estimating "social adaptive" functioning and assisting governmental social agencies in "their decision making process regarding adoption, welfare, court cases, vocational rehabilitation, and the like" (1985b, p. 11). In addition, the BF is recommended for screening, and the CF can be used to assess a pupil's strengths and weaknesses.

Although the tests bear the same name and have some similarities in content, they are quite different. Consequently, we will for the most part treat the forms separately.

The Comprehensive Form (CF) contains five subtests.

Reading Decoding This sixty-item subtest requires a student to identify letters and then to read phonetic and nonphonetic words of increasing difficulty.

Reading Comprehension This subtest contains two types of items. For twelve questions, the student must respond gesturally or orally to commands given in printed sentences. For the remaining thirty-eight questions, the student must read material and then answer literal and inferential questions about it. The complexity and variety of language structures increase over the course of the subtest.

Mathematics Applications This subtest assesses a student's "ability to solve real-world problems by the application of mathematics knowledge" (1985c, p. 196). The sixty items are of two types: math concepts and applications in practical situations. All problems are read to the student, who can refer to various visual materials (illustrations, graphs, and so forth).

Mathematics Computation This sixty-item subtest assesses a student's skill in solving problems involving basic operations, exponents, symbols, abbreviations, and algebraic equations.

Spelling This subtest assesses a student's ability to spell fifty words. The tester says each word and uses it in a sentence. (A student who is unable to write is allowed to spell orally.)

The Brief Form (BF) includes three subtests that provide global assessment of skill in reading, mathematics, and spelling.

Reading This subtest contains fifty-two items. The first twenty-three items require letter identification and word decoding; the remaining items are similar to those on the CF Reading Comprehension subtest.

Mathematics This subtest contains fifty-two items that assess arithmetic concepts, applications, reasoning, and computational skill. The first twenty-five problems require written computation. The remaining problems are read to the student, who can refer to various visual materials (such as illustrations, graphs, and so forth).

Spelling This forty-word subtest is similar in form to the CF Spelling subtest.

SCORES

For individual subtest scores and composite scores (reading, mathematics, and battery), normalized standard scores are available by grade or age and can be compared to either the spring or the fall norm sample. (For the CF, mean = 100 and standard deviation = 15; the values are approximately the same for the BF). Composites are based on raw score totals; thus, subtests are not equally weighted within composites. Percentile ranks, stanines, and normal curve equivalents are also available, as are age and grade equivalents.

Finally, a teacher can conduct an error analysis of each subtest of the CF. Errors made consistently by a student are noted, and the number of errors is compared to the number made by students in the norm sample.

NORMS

For the Comprehensive Form, separate norms are provided for spring and fall. The spring sample consisted of 1,409 students and the fall sample contained 1,067, with no fewer than 100 students per grade. The authors have done an exemplary job of describing and documenting the characteristics of the normative samples. The samples were stratified within each grade level by sex, geographic region, socioeconomic status, and racial/ethnic group to represent the proportions in the 1983 or 1984 census report.

Comprehensive tables document the correspondence of the standardization samples to the population on each of the stratification variables. Overall, geographic representation is good, although the Northeast is overrepresented (and the Northcentral region and the South underrepresented) in the eleventh and twelfth grades. The socioeconomic composition of the sample (represented by parental education) varies somewhat across grades from the national average, but never by more than 8 percent and usually by much less. The racial/ethnic composition of the sample closely approximates that of the U.S. population at all grades.

The norms for the Brief Form were equated to the norms for the Comprehensive Form by testing 589 students (from 49 to 61 per grade) with both forms and equating their scores. The BF sample "was carefully selected to match the demographic characteristics of the nationally representative Comprehensive Form norm group" (Kaufman & Kaufman, 1985b, p. 96); it was also stratified within each grade level with respect to sex, geographic region, socioeconomic status, and racial/ethnic background.

RELIABILITY

For the Comprehensive Form, averages of the spring and fall split-half estimates of reliability are presented for each subtest and composite at each grade level. Reliabilities for the five subtests, corrected by the Spearman-Brown formula, range from .87 to .96; eleven of the sixty grade-by-subtest coefficients are in the .80s, and the remainder are in the .90s. The reliabilities for the reading, math, and battery composites all exceed .92. Stability data are based on the performances of 172 students who were retested between one and thirty-five days after their first testing. Data were combined for grades 1 to 6 and grades 7 to 12. All correlations for subtests and composites exceed .90, although these coefficients should be considered inflated estimates. The correlations of achievement with grade are confounded with stability.

For the Brief Form, split-half estimates of reliability, corrected with the Spearman-Brown formula, were computed for each subtest and composite at each grade level and at each age level from 6 to 18. For the subtests by grades, these estimates range from .72 to .97; of the thirty-six coefficients, only seven equal or exceed .90. For the composites by ages, only one coefficient ($r_{xx} = .89$) falls below .90. Stability data are based on the performances of 153 students who were retested between one and twenty-five days after their first testing. As with the Comprehensive Form, data were combined for grades 1 to 6 and grades 7 to 12. For subtests, stability coefficients ranged from .84 to .90; only one of the six coefficients equaled .90. Of the composites, both coefficients exceeded .90, although these coefficients should also be considered inflated estimates.

VALIDITY

The validity of both forms was established in essentially the same way. First, the content of the KTEA was carefully selected to assess the general domains covered by the tests. Because content varies considerably from curriculum to curriculum, however, the test user must verify that the content of the KTEA subtests and composites is appropriate for the particular curriculum being used by the students who are being tested.

To demonstrate construct validity, the authors show increases of subtest and composite scores across grades and ages. Some evidence of criterion-related validity is presented in the form of correlations between the KTEA forms and the Wide Range Achievement Test or the Peabody Individual Achievement Test. Correlations with the Kaufman Assessment Battery for Children and the Peabody Picture Vocabulary Test are presented, but it is unclear why these correlations would help establish validity.

Finally, for the CF, data from previously administered group achievement tests are reviewed. Although there are some methodological problems with these data, they do demonstrate the expected relationships with the KTEA.

No data are offered to establish that either form is effective for program planning, program evaluation, placement decisions, self-appraisal, personnel selection, or estimating "social adaptive" functioning.

SUMMARY

The Kaufman Test of Educational Achievement forms are individually administered, norm-referenced tests. The content of subtests on the CF appears well selected. The content of the BF is less well defined; the reading and mathematics subtests seemed to have been formed by combining the two reading subtests and the two mathematics subtests on the CF. Thus their content demands vary considerably across grades and are not conceptually homogeneous.

The technical characteristics of the KTEA vary in adequacy. The normative samples are adequate. Internal consistencies for subtests vary from adequate for screening to adequate for more important decisions. The composites have good internal consistency. Stability cannot be accurately assessed from the data presented. Sufficient evidence for the test's validity is offered to make the case for general adequacy. As with any achievement test, however, the most critical concern is content validity. Users must be sensitive to the correspondence of the KTEA's content with a student's curriculum.

Peabody Individual Achievement Test-Revised

T he Peabody Individual Achievement Test–Revised (PIAT-R) (Markwardt, 1989) is a norm-referenced, individually administered test designed to provide a wide-range screening measure of academic achievement in six content areas. The test can be used with students in kindergarten through twelfth grade. PIAT-R test materials are contained in four easel kits—one for each volume of the test. Easel-kit volumes present stimulus materials to the student at eye level; the examiner's instructions are placed on the reverse side (see Figure 20.1). The student can see one side of the response plate, whereas the examiner can see both sides. The test includes a test record and a separate response booklet for written expression. The author lists the following as recommended uses for the PIAT-R: individual evaluation, guidance and counseling, admissions and transfers, grouping students, progress evaluation, and personnel selection.

FIGURE 20.1   **Easel Kit for the Peabody Individual Achievement Test–Revised**

SOURCE: *Peabody Individual Achievement Test–Revised* (*PIAT-R*) by Frederick C. Markwardt. Jr. Circle Pines, MN: American Guidance Service. Copyright 1989. All rights reserved. Photo courtesy American Guidance Service, Inc.

The original PIAT (Dunn & Markwardt, 1970) included five subtests. The Written Expression subtest is new to the revised edition of the test. Other changes made in revising the test included development of updated norms, addition of test items, and inclusion of more contemporary content. About 65 percent of the items are new to the PIAT-R. Behaviors sampled by the six subtests of the PIAT-R follow.

Mathematics This subtest contains one hundred multiple-choice items ranging from items that assess such early skills as matching, discriminating, and recognizing numerals to items that assess advanced concepts in geometry and trigonometry. The test is a measure of the student's knowledge and application of math concepts and facts.

Reading Recognition This subtest also contains one hundred items ranging in difficulty from preschool level through high school level. Items assess skill development in matching letters, naming capital and lowercase letters, and recognizing words in isolation.

Reading Comprehension This subtest contains eighty-one multiple-choice items assessing skill development in understanding what is read. After reading a sentence the student must indicate comprehension by choosing the correct picture out of a group of four.

Spelling This subtest consists of one hundred items sampling behaviors from kindergarten level through high school level. Initial items assess the student's ability to distinguish a printed letter of the alphabet from pictured objects and to associate letter symbols with speech sounds. More difficult items assess the student's ability to identify, from a response bank of four words, the correct spelling of a word read aloud by the examiner.

General Information This subtest consists of one hundred questions presented orally that the student must answer orally. Items assess the extent to which the student has learned facts in social studies, science, sports, and the fine arts.

Written Expression This subtest assesses written-language skills at two levels. Level I, appropriate for students in kindergarten and first grade, is a measure of prewriting skills such as skill in copying and writing letters, words, and sentences from dictation. At level II, students write a story in response to a picture prompt.

SCORES

All but one of the PIAT-R subtests are scored in the same way: The student's response to each item is scored pass-fail. On these five subtests raw scores are converted to grade and age equivalents, grade and age-based standard scores, percentile ranks, normal curve equivalents, and stanines. The Written Expression subtest is scored differently from the other subtests. The examiner uses a set of scoring criteria included in an appendix in the test manual. At level I the examiner scores the student's writing of his or her name and then scores eighteen items pass-fail. For the more difficult items at level I, the student must earn a specified number of subcredits to pass the item. Methods for assigning subcredits are specified clearly in the manual. At level II the student generates a free response, and the assessor examines the response for certain specified characteristics. For example, the student is given credit for each letter correctly capitalized, each correct punctuation, and absence of inappropriate words. Scores earned on the Written Expression subtest include grade-based stanines and developmental scaled scores (with mean = 8 and standard deviation ≈ 3).

Three composite scores are used to summarize student performance on the PIAT-R: Total Reading, Total Test, and Written Language. Total Reading is described as an overall measure of "reading ability" and is obtained by combining scores on Reading

Recognition and Reading Comprehension. The Total Test score is obtained by combining performance on the General Information, Reading Recognition, Reading Comprehension, Mathematics, and Spelling subtests. A third composite score, the Written Language composite score, is optional and is obtained by combining performance on the Spelling and Written Expression subtests.

NORMS

The PIAT-R was standardized on 1,563 students in grades K through 12 in thirty-three communities nationwide. An additional 175 kindergarten students took the test to establish fall norms. The standardization plan called for assessing 159 students at each grade K–2, 125 at each grade 3–8, and 100 students at each grade 9–12. Minor deviations from this plan were a result of attrition. The standardization sample was stratified within geographic region on the basis of sex, socioeconomic status, and race or ethnic group. Percentages in each of these stratification cells are reported in the manual. For the most part, the sample proportions approximated census proportions. The norms are not representative of geographic region at grade 12, where there is overrepresentation of students from the Northeast. The norms are not representative of sex at grade 1 and of race at grade 11.

RELIABILITY

Several kinds of reliability data are presented in the manual for the PIAT-R and are based on the performance of students in the standardization sample. Reliability data are reported separately for the Written Expression subtest and the other five subtests.

Excluding the Written Language subtest, split-half reliabilities for the PIAT-R are high. All exceed .90 with the exception of the Math and Spelling subtests at kindergarten level and the Spelling subtest at

grade 11. All internal-consistency coefficients exceeded .90 with the exception of Math and Spelling at kindergarten level. Test-retest reliabilities are generally high; 66 percent exceed .90, and 90 percent exceed .80.

Internal-consistency and interrater reliability are reported for the Written Expression subtest. At level I the internal consistencies range from .61 to .69. For level II they range from .69 to .91. All except two internal-consistency coefficients for Written Expression are below .90. Interrater reliability was .56 for level I and .58 for level II.

Except for Written Language, the subtests of the PIAT-R are reliable enough to be used in making screening decisions. The reliability of the Written Expression subtest is such that it should be used only for experimental purposes.

VALIDITY

Information on two kinds of validity, content validity and construct validity, is reported in the manual. Content validity is largely a matter of expert opinion.

Concurrent validity was said to be established by correlating scores on the PIAT-R, an achievement test, with scores on the Peabody Picture Vocabulary Test–Revised, a measure of receptive vocabulary. These data cannot be considered particularly relevant to the test's validity.

SUMMARY

The Peabody Individual Achievement Test–Revised is designed to provide screening information on development of skills in six academic areas. Its standardization appears good. Internal consistencies are generally adequate for use in making important educational decisions. Validity of the PIAT rests on its content validity. Teachers need to assess its appropriateness for the curricula they use.

Wide Range Achievement Test 3

*T*he Wide Range Achievement Test 3 (WRAT3) (Wilkinson, 1993) is designed to measure the "codes which are needed to learn the basic skills of reading, writing, spelling and arithmetic" (p. 10). The author states that an attempt was made to eliminate the effect of comprehension. This was done to enable diagnosticians to determine whether an academic problem is caused by an inability to learn specific codes or by an inability to derive meaning from the codes.

The WRAT3 is a single-level, individually administered test that can be used with individuals aged 5 to 75. Two forms were developed; these can be used individually or combined to give a more comprehensive evaluation. The author suggests using the alternate forms for pre- and post-testing situations. The test is composed of three subtests.

Reading This subtest assesses skill in letter recognition, letter naming, and pronunciation of words in isolation.

Spelling This subtest assesses skills in copying marks onto paper, writing one's name, and writing single words from dictation.

Arithmetic This subtest assesses skills in counting, reading numerals, solving problems presented orally, and performing written computation of arithmetic problems.

SCORES

Six scores can be derived from the WRAT3: raw, absolute, standard, grade equivalent, percentiles and normal curve equivalents. The absolute score provides an interval-based estimate of an individual's performance level that can be used to make comparisons across scales or between individuals. The standard scores have a mean of 100 and a standard deviation of 15. A Profile Analysis Form is provided that can be used to compare WRAT3 scores with intelligence test scores; it gives a picture of the degree of difficulty of the items passed by the test taker.

NORMS

The WRAT3 was standardized on 4,443 individuals. The sample was stratified and counterbalanced by age, regional residence, gender, and ethnicity based on 1990 U.S. census data. Socioeconomic level was controlled for based on the occupational category of the individual or his or her caregiver. The author states that a minimum of four states per region were used, but the total number of states and setting (rural, urban, suburban) is not reported.

RELIABILITY

The WRAT3 appears to be internally consistent. Three forms of internal consistency were provided. Coefficient alphas for each of the twenty-three age groups were computed for each form. The median coefficient alpha for the individual forms ranged from .85 to .91. The combined-form coefficients all exceeded .90. Alternate-forms correlations were also computed. The median correlations for the Reading, Spelling, and Arithmetic subtests are .92, .93, and .89, respectively. Rasch Person Separation indexes, a form of internal consistency, ranged from .98 to .99. (See Appendix 6.) The stability of the WRAT3 appears to be more than adequate. Corrected test-retest reliability coefficients for a sample of 142 individuals between the ages of 6 and 16 were all greater than .91.

VALIDITY

Although the WRAT3 has questionable content validity, strong evidence for the test's construct validity is provided. The author argues that since the Rasch Item Separation indexes are all 1.00, the test has content validity. Information is not provided regarding the match between the WRAT3 content and that of a typical curriculum; therefore the content validity is questionable. Several forms of support for construct validity are provided. The mean scores of the subtests increase with age, which is in accordance with the developmental nature of basic academic skills. Moderate correlations exist between the WRAT3 and two measures of intelligence: the WISC-III and the WAIS-R. Moderate correlations were found between the WRAT3 and three standardized group achievement tests: the California Achievement Test–Form E, the California Test of Basic Skills–4, and the Stanford Achievement Test. The WRAT3 was able to discriminate among 222 regular and special education students. The test was able to group students labeled gifted, learning disabled, educably mentally handi-

capped, and general education with 68 percent success.

SUMMARY

The Wide Range Achievement Test 3 is an individually administered achievement test designed to assess the basic academic skills necessary in reading, spelling, and arithmetic. The test is well standardized and has adequate reliability. There are two forms of the test. Data on standardization are incomplete. The test has sufficient reliability to be used in making decisions about individuals. Several forms of construct validity are provided in the manual that accompanies the test, but the test's content validity is questionable.

Wechsler Individual Achievement Test

*T*he Wechsler Individual Achievement Test (WIAT) (Psychological Corporation, 1992d) is an individually administered, norm-referenced achievement test designed to be used with students in grades K through 12 who are between 5 to 19 years old. The WIAT was co-normed with the Wechsler series of intelligence tests: the WPPSI-R, the WISC-III, and the WAIS-R. This characteristic makes the WIAT especially useful for educational planning and placement decisions that use ability-achievement discrepancies. The use of co-normed ability and achievement tests provides more reliable estimates of a student's aptitude-achievement discrepancy. Another unique characteristic of the WIAT is its design. The test's authors created subtests that parallel and comprehensively cover the seven areas of learning disability specified in Public Law 94-142: basic reading skill, reading comprehension, mathematics reasoning, mathematics calculation, listening comprehension, oral expression, and written expression. These seven domains, plus spelling, comprise the eight subtests of the WIAT. Three of the subtests, Basic Reading, Mathematics

Reasoning, and Spelling, comprise the WIAT Screener, which is a 10 to 15 minute academic achievement screening instrument. The WIAT can be completed in 30 to 50 minutes for younger children and approximately 55 minutes for adolescents. The behaviors sampled by the WIAT subtests are described in Table 20.7.

SCORES

Five types of scores—standard, percentile rank, age equivalent, normal curve equivalent, and stanines—can be derived from each of the subtests and six composites. The Reading, Mathematics, Language, and Writing composites are each based on two subtests. Three subtests form the Screening composite, and the Total composite is based on all of the subtests. The standard score, which has a mean of 100 and a standard deviation of 15, can be computed by age or grade. Ability-achievement scores based on the WIAT standard scores and one of the three Wechsler ability tests, (WPPSI-R, WISC-III, or WAIS-R) are also provided. The test authors provide

TABLE 20.7   **Description of the WIAT Subtests**

Subtest	Description
Basic Reading	A series of pictures and printed words for assessing decoding and word-reading ability. For early items the child is to point to responses; later items require the child to respond orally.
Mathematics Reasoning	A series of problems for assessing the ability to reason mathematically. Many items include visual stimuli (e.g., graphs). The text for each item is orally presented and in most cases is also printed on the child's Stimulus Booklet page. The child is to respond in a variety of ways.
Spelling	A series of dictated letters, sounds, and words for measuring encoding and spelling ability. The child is to write responses.
Reading Comprehension	A series of printed passages and orally presented questions designed to tap skills such as recognizing stated detail and making inferences. Passages consist of one or more sentences, some of which are accompanied by a picture. The child is to respond orally.
Numerical Operations	Sets of problems for assessing the ability to write dictated numerals and solve calculation problems and equations involving all basic operations (addition, subtraction, multiplication, and division). The child is to write responses.
Listening Comprehension	A series of items for assessing listening comprehension skills such as listening for detail. Items focus on the child's ability to identify the picture that corresponds to an orally presented word and on the child's comprehension of orally presented passages accompanied by pictures. For early items the child is to respond by pointing; for later items the child is to respond orally.
Oral Expression	A series of items focusing on the ability to express words, describe scenes, give directions, and explain steps. Items consist of pictures accompanied by orally presented instructions. The child is to respond orally.
Written Expression	For Grades 3–12 only, writing prompts for assessing various writing skills such as development and organization of ideas, capitalization, and punctuation. Two prompts are provided, but only one is used in any one WIAT administration. The child's response can be evaluated analytically and holistically.

two methods of computing discrepancy scores, Simple-Difference and Predicted Achievement, and provide information regarding the limitations of each approach.

NORMS

The WIAT was standardized on 4,252 children in grades K through 12. A sample of 1,289 children was used to link the WIAT with the WPPSI-R, WISC-III, and WAIS-R. The information collected from the linking studies was used to develop the ability-achievement discrepancy statistics. The sample selection was based on 1988 U.S. Census Bureau data. The sample was randomly selected and stratified on age, grade, gender, race/ethnicity, geographic region, and parent education. Economic status was not used as a stratification variable. The extent of stratification and the national representativeness of the sample cannot be determined from the information provided in the technical manual.

RELIABILITY

Three forms of reliability data were calculated for the WIAT. Split-half reliability coefficients based on age and grade standard subtest scores generally exceed .80. The Basic Reading coefficient for the fall norm group and coefficients for Numerical Operations and Written Expression for certain ages fall below .80. The split-half coefficients for the six composites are all greater than .80. A sample of 367 students in grades 1, 3, 5, 8, and 10 was selected to determine the test-retest reliability of the WIAT. The subtest scores are generally above .80, but scores for Oral Expression and Written Expression are below .80 for most of the grades in the sample. Scores on the Language composite for grades 5, 8, and 10 are the only composite test-retest scores below .80. Interrater agreement was calculated with fifty protocols for the four subtests that require subjective scoring. The correlation between raters for Reading Comprehension and raters for Listening Comprehension ranges

from .89 to .99, with an average correlation of .98. The interrater agreement for Oral Expression was .93. Interrater agreement for Prompt 1 of the Written Expression subtest was .89 and for prompt 2 it was .79.

VALIDITY

The WIAT has excellent content, construct, and criterion-related validity. Expert judgment and a large-scale item tryout were used to establish the content validity of the instrument. Experts analyzed the extent to which the items measured specific curriculum objectives and were related to current instructional methodology and content. Empirical item analysis was used to eliminate poorly constructed items and to prevent gender or race bias. The construct validity of the WIAT was documented through analysis of subtest intercorrelations, correlations with ability measures, and expected developmental differences across age and grade groups. Several forms of support of criterion validity are provided. There are moderate correlations between the WIAT and the Kaufman Test of Educational Achievement (KTEA), the Basic Achievement Skills Individual Screener (BASIS), the Wide Range Achievement Test–Revised (WRAT-R), the achievement test of the Woodcock-Johnson Psychoeducational Battery–Revised (WJ-R ACH), the Differential Ability Scales (DAS), and the Peabody Picture Vocabulary Test–Revised (PPVT-R) The WIAT was also correlated with several group-administered achievement tests which, produced moderate correlations. The correlation between the WIAT and school grades was generally low, but this is no different than expected given the low reliability of school grades.

SUMMARY

The Wechsler Individual Achievement Test is an individually administered achievement test that is conormed with the Wechsler series of intelligence tests. The subtests are designed to measure the seven areas of learning disability defined in Public Law 94-142. The test has an adequate standardization sample and appears to be very reliable and valid. Two

methods and statistical tables for computing ability-achievement discrepancies are provided, along with a description of the limitations of each method.

BRIGANCE® Diagnostic Inventories[1]

T he BRIGANCE® Diagnostic Inventories consist of three batteries: The Diagnostic Inventory of Early Development (Brigance, 1991), which is intended for use with individuals with developmental ages less than 7 years, the Diagnostic Inventory of Basic Skills (Brigance, 1977), which is intended for use with children from kindergarten through sixth grade, and the Diagnostic Inventory of Essential Skills (Brigance, 1980), which is intended for use in secondary programs. Each inventory is a criterion-referenced multiple-skill battery.

The three inventories are highly similar in purpose and format. Each inventory is intended to assess mastery of the skill or concept; consequently, testers are urged to adapt the testing procedures as necessary to ensure valid assessment. Administering the inventories thus requires some professional judgment, although no special training is required. Figure 20.2 (pages 450 and 451) illustrates an assessment from the early development inventory. The child's page contains the test stimuli. The examiner's page contains the suggested directions for administering the items, the rule for discontinuing the test, the criteria for scoring, the instructional objective for the item being assessed, and several other useful bits of information.

Each inventory assesses observable behavior or products and is scored objectively except for some rating forms in the essential-skills inventory. Each inventory is comprehensive: The early development inventory assesses more than 200 skill sequences; the basic-skills inventory, 140 skill sequences; and the essential-skills inventory, 165 skill sequences. As is true of most criterion-referenced systems, the in-

ventories provide the educator with lists of mastered and unmastered skills from which strengths and weaknesses as well as potential instructional objectives can be inferred.

DIAGNOSTIC INVENTORY OF EARLY DEVELOPMENT

In addition to being criterion-referenced, the Diagnostic Inventory of Early Development is also "normative-referenced." Developmental skills are assigned developmental ages, not by norming the items, but by consulting several texts in which age norms for the skills are published. Moreover, the texts are referenced to each skill so that the user can check the sources for any skill of particular interest. Eleven subscales make up the early development inventories; following is a list of the skills assessed by these subscales.

1. Four preambulatory motor skills (for example, lying supine, lying prone, sitting, and standing)
2. Ten gross motor skills (for example, walking, catching, running)
3. Six fine motor skills (for example, eye/ finger/ hand manipulative skills, cutting with scissors)
4. Eleven self-help skills (for example, feeding/ eating, unfastening, toileting, performing household chores)
5. Eleven speech and language skills (for example, demonstrate the use of prespeech receptive language, recognize picture vocabulary, respond to sentences of different lengths)
6. Nine general knowledge and comprehension skills (for example, knowledge of body parts, colors, shape concepts, use of objects)

1. BRIGANCE® is a trademark of Curriculum Associates, Inc., North Billerica, Mass.

7. Three social and emotional development skills and behaviors (general social and emotional development, play skills and behaviors, work-related skills and behaviors)
8. Four readiness skills (performing visual discrimination, reciting alphabet, recognizing uppercase letters and lowercase letters)
9. Ten basic reading skills (for example, reading number words, reading common signs, performing auditory discrimination)
10. Seven manuscript-writing skills (for example, printing capital letters sequentially, printing simple sentences)
11. Twelve math sequences (for example, rote counting, writing dictated numerals, recognizing money)

DIAGNOSTIC INVENTORY OF BASIC SKILLS

In addition to being criterion-referenced, the Diagnostic Inventory of Basic Skills is "text-referenced." Grade levels are determined by the level at which the material is first taught, not by the level at which half of the students have learned the material. This inventory is composed of four subscales.

Readiness This subscale contains twenty-four sequences ranging from developmental skills (such as recognizing colors, identifying body parts, articulating sounds) to more academic enabling skills (among them, recognizing uppercase and lowercase letters, recognizing numbers, writing letters).

Reading This subscale contains four subparts.

1. Six word-recognition sequences (for example, basic sight vocabulary)
2. Three reading sequences (oral reading comprehension, literal comprehension, or recall, oral reading rate)
3. Nineteen word-analysis sequences (such as auditory discrimination, initial sounds aurally and visually, prefixes and suffixes, syllabication)

4. Five vocabulary sequences (context clues, classification, analogies, antonyms, and homonyms)

Language Arts This subscale contains four subparts.

1. Three handwriting sequences (cursive lowercase, cursive capitals, personal data)
2. Three grammar sequences (capitalization, punctuation, and parts of speech)
3. Four spelling sequences (initial consonants, initial clusters, suffixes, and prefixes)
4. Nine reference skills (such as dictionary use, maps)

Mathematics This subscale has four parts.

1. Thirteen number sequences (for example, rote counting, writing numbers from dictation, decimals)
2. Seventeen operation sequences (such as addition combinations, division by decimals)
3. Twenty-five measurement sequences (four dealing with money; nine with time; four with the calendar; three with linear measurement; three with weight or thermometers; and two with liquids)
4. Eight geometry sequences (for example, two-dimensional squares, three-dimensional cylinders)

DIAGNOSTIC INVENTORY OF ESSENTIAL SKILLS

The Diagnostic Inventory of Essential Skills focuses on "skills which have been identified as essential for mastery if the student is to be able to function successfully and with the greatest degree of independence as a citizen, consumer, worker, and family member" (Brigance, 1980, p. v). Unlike the other two inventories, this one has two forms (A and B) for several parts; it also contains nine rating scales to assess health practices and attitudes, self-concept, general attitude, personality, responsibility and self-discipline, job interview preparation, job interview,

FIGURE 20.2   Sample from **BRIGANCE**® Diagnostic Inventory of Early Development

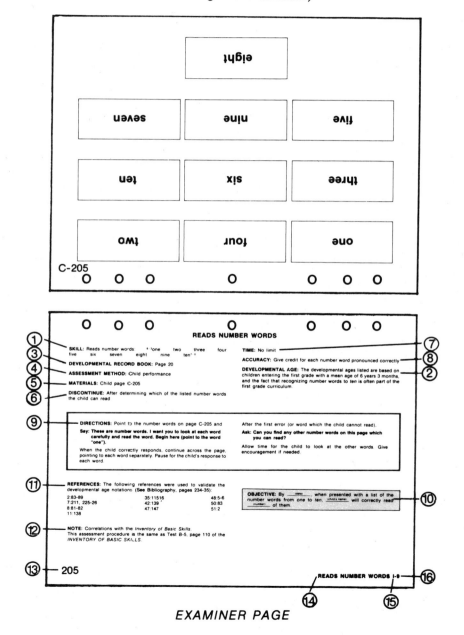

CHILD PAGE
(Oriented for the child facing the examiner.)

EXAMINER PAGE

FIGURE 20.2   **(continued)**

MODEL OF FORMAT
FOR AN ASSESSMENT PROCEDURE
WITH A CHILD PAGE

1. **SKILL:** A general statement of the skill being assessed. When appropriate, the skill sequence in the *Developmental Record Book* is also listed.

2. **DEVELOPMENTAL AGE NOTATION:** The numbers preceding a sequence indicate the year and month the child usually begins to learn or master that skill. Those following indicate when mastery is usually accomplished. Example: for ⁴⁻⁷, read 4 years and 7 months developmental age.

   In addition, the developmental ages are explained or discussed in a separate note where necessary.

3. **DEVELOPMENTAL RECORD BOOK:** The page on which this skill is listed in the *Developmental Record Book.*

4. **ASSESSMENT METHODS:** The means recommended for assessing.

5. **MATERIALS:** Materials which are needed for the assessment.

6. **DISCONTINUE:** Indicates the number of items the child may fail before you discontinue the assessment of skills in this sequence.

7. **TIME:** Time limits suggested for the child's response.

8. **ACCURACY:** Explanation of scoring criteria.

9. **DIRECTIONS:** The recommended directions for assessing the skills sequence. Recommended phrasing of instructions or questions is clearly labeled, indented and printed in bold face type.

10. **OBJECTIVE:** The objective for the skills being assessed is stated, and is a valuable resource for developing individualized education programs (IEP's).

11. **REFERENCES:** the numbers listed correspond to the sources used to establish and validate the skill sequences and developmental ages. References are found in the *Bibliography* on page 246-7.

12. **NOTES:** Helpful notes on observations, resources or diagnosing are listed here.

13. Examiner's page number.

14. Skill assessed.

15. The first letter, "I," indicates the section, where all basic reading skills are located.

16. This number indicates the ninth of the skills sequenced in the basic reading section of the *Inventory.*

SOURCE: BRIGANCE® Diagnostic Inventory of Early Development. Copyright © 1991, Curriculum Associates, Inc. Reprinted by permission.

auto safety, and communication skills. The 165 skill sequences are divided into two parts: academic skills and applied skills. The academic skills include:

1. Oral reading (graded from second to eleventh grade)
2. Reading comprehension (graded from third to eleventh grade)
3. Functional word recognition (basic sight vocabulary, directions, abbreviations, signs, numbers)
4. Word analysis (such as vowel sounds, digraphs, diphthongs, prefixes, and suffixes)
5. Reference skills (for example, alphabetizing, using library card catalog)
6. Graphic representations (understanding a TV schedule, graphs, and the like)
7. Writing (including cursive letter formation, punctuation, letter writing)
8. Filling out forms
9. Spelling (for example, calendar words, initial consonants)
10. Numbers (recognizing, writing from dictation)
11. Arithmetic functions (basic operations)
12. Computation of whole numbers
13. Fractions
14. Decimals
15. Percent

16. Measurement (money, time, metric, English, temperature, reading meters and gauges)
17. Metrics
18. Math vocabulary

The applied skills include:

1. Health and safety
2. Vocational
3. Food and clothing (for example, reading directions or labels, selecting by best price for quantity)
4. Communication and telephone

Too comprehensive to be administered in its entirety, the essential-skills inventory should be administered selectively. Grade-placement tests are intended to provide a way to identify starting places for detailed assessments in word recognition, writing, spelling, and math.

SCORES

Skills on each sequence from the diagnostic inventories are scored as either mastered or unmastered. These scores can be displayed on pupil record forms and class record forms. No summary scores are obtained. The normative-referenced and test-referenced features should not be thought of as scores.

NORMS

The inventories are criterion-referenced, so norms are not required.

RELIABILITY

No reliability data are provided. At a minimum, alternate-forms reliability estimates should be provided on tests with two forms, and interrater agreement should be provided on the rating scales.

VALIDITY

The content validity of the inventories is the overriding concern. Although there are subtle differences in the content of the three devices, they are highly similar. All were developed by review of appropriate literature, and all were submitted to field testing. A detailed description of these procedures is absent. Nonetheless, inspection of the content of the inventories indicates comprehensive coverage, careful preparation, and meticulous selection of items.

SUMMARY

The BRIGANCE® Diagnostic Inventories offer comprehensive criterion-referenced assessment of important skills, concepts, and behavior. They are appropriately used with individuals ranging from infants through adolescents. The content validity of the devices is most acceptable. However, in the absence of information about reliability, the usefulness of the scales in planning and evaluating instruction for pupils with disabilities is undetermined.

Diagnostic Achievement Battery–2

The Diagnostic Achievement Battery–2 (DAB-2)(Newcomer, 1990) is an individually administered measure of childrens' skills in listening, speaking, reading, writing, and mathematics. Although the test is called *diagnostic*, it is essentially similar to the PIAT-R, WRAT3, and KTEA. One does not use this test to "diagnose" skill strengths and weaknesses in individual content areas, but to profile scores across areas. The test is designed to meet four purposes: (1) identification of students who are significantly below their peers in spoken language (listening and speaking), written language (reading and writing), and mathematics, (2) to ascertain an individual student's skill development strengths and weaknesses, (3) to document intervention progress for individual students, and (4) research.

The DAB-2 is based on a specific conceptual model of academic achievement; that model is shown in Figure 20.3. (You may find it helpful to refer to the figure while reading the description below of the individual subtests and composites.) Subtests are divided into five areas: listening (Story Comprehension, Characteristics), speaking (Synonyms, Grammatic Completion), reading (Alphabet/Word Knowledge, Reading Comprehension), writing (Capitalization, Punctuation, Spelling, Writing Composition), and mathematics (Mathematics Reasoning and Mathematics Calculation). Behaviors sampled by the subtests are as follows.

Story Comprehension   The student must listen to the examiner read a story and then answer questions about the story presented orally.

Characteristics   After listening to the examiner read brief statements, the student must indicate whether the statements are true or false.

Synonyms   The student must provide synonyms for words read by the examiner.

Grammatic Completion   The student must supply missing words or phrases in sentences read by the examiner.

Alphabet/Word Knowledge   The student must read letters or words.

Reading Comprehension   The student must read short stories silently and then answer questions about them.

Capitalization   The student must indicate appropriate placement of capital letters in a set of thirty sentences.

FIGURE 20.3.   **Conceptual Model Underlying the DAB-2**

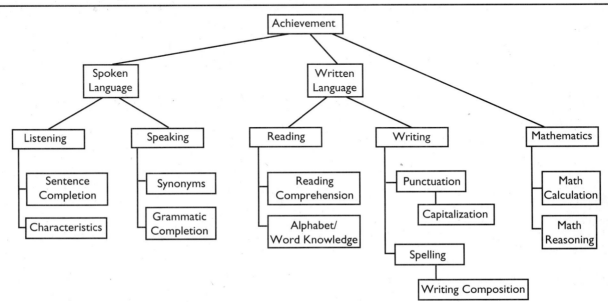

Punctuation   The student must indicate appropriate punctuation in a set of thirty sentences.

Spelling   The student must write and spell correctly twenty dictated words.

Writing Composition   The student must write a story in response to three pictures that represent a modified version of the classic fable "The Tortoise and the Hare." The story is evaluated for the presence of words that have seven or more letters and for thematic content.

Mathematics Reasoning   The student is presented with mathematical information in the form of pictures (for a young child) or statements presented orally and must use the information to solve math problems.

Mathematics Calculation   The student must solve thirty-six written calculation problems.

The DAB-2 is an untimed test. The examiner begins and ends the test using specific rules for basals and ceilings. The test takes from one to two hours to administer. The DAB-2 is a mixture of eight subtests that were retained from the original DAB (Newcomer, 1983) and four new subtests. The new subtests consist of three revised DAB subtests (Capitalization, Punctuation, and Reading Comprehension) and one new subtest (Writing Composition). Items for DAB-2 were tried out and selected on the basis of the performance of a limited and geographically restricted sample of one hundred children in San Antonio, Texas.

NORMS

The DAB-2 norms are a mixture of new norms and norms retained from the standardization of the DAB. The total standardization population was 2,623 students from forty states. The norms were obtained by (1) keeping the 1983 norms for the eight subtests that are unchanged and (2) adding data on these original eight and the four new subtests. The new data were obtained by asking users of the test to administer the test to twenty to thirty children representative of children in their area. The author argues that a population representative of the 1985 census was obtained. Comparative percentages are shown, but there is no information on cross-tabulations. That is, we do not know, for example, if all of the black children were from urban areas in the Northeast, rural areas in the South, and so forth.

SCORES

Four kinds of scores are obtained for performance on the DAB-2. The examiner can compute standard scores (with mean = 10 and standard deviation = 3), composite scores (quotients with mean = 100 and standard deviation = 15) for each of the composites, percentile ranks for subtests and composites, and grade equivalents.

RELIABILITY

Data on reliability are for either the DAB or the DAB-2. Most of the data are for the DAB. Data on internal consistency of the DAB-2 were computed by examining performance on fifty protocols at each age level. Of the ninety-nine coefficients reported for subtests, ninety-one exceed .80. All reliability coefficients for composite scores exceed .80. Information on test-retest reliability of the DAB-2 is limited to the performance of fifty-two children in a private school in Los Angeles on three of the four new subtests of the DAB-2. Reliability coefficients for Capitalization, Punctuation, and Written Composition exceeded .80.

VALIDITY

The author reports considerable data on validity of the DAB-2. Criteria for content and item selection are specified, and evidence for construct and criterion-related validity is presented. There is good evidence for the validity of this test.

SUMMARY

The DAB-2 is a revision of the 1983 DAB, which was changed by modifying three subtests and adding one new one. The test was standardized on a population of students drawn in 1982–1983 and 1988. The norm sample is described in the manual, but evidence on the extent to which it was stratified is limited. There is limited evidence for the reliability of this test, but good evidence for its validity.

GETTING THE MOST OUT OF AN ACHIEVEMENT TEST

The achievement tests described in this chapter provide the teacher with global scores in areas such as word meaning and work-study skills. Although global scores can help in screening children, they generally lack the specificity to help in planning individualized instructional programs. Merely knowing that Emily earned a standard score of 85 on the Mathematics Computation subtest of the Metropolitan Achievement Tests does not tell us what math skills Emily has. In addition, a teacher cannot rely on test names as an indication of what is measured by a specific test. For example, a reading score of 115 on the Wide Range Achievement Test tells a teacher nothing about reading comprehension or rate of oral reading.

A teacher must look at any screening test (or at *any* test, for that matter) in terms of the *behaviors* sampled by that test. Let's take a case in point. Suppose Richard earned a standard score of 70 on a spelling subtest. What do we know about Richard? We know Richard earned enough raw score points to place him two standard deviations below the mean of students in his grade. That is *all* we know without going beyond the score and looking at the kinds of behaviors sampled by the test. The test title tells us only that the test measures skill development in spelling. But we still do not know *what* Richard did to earn a score of 70.

First, we need to ask, "What is the nature of the behaviors sampled by the test?" Spelling tests can be of several kinds. Richard may have been asked to write a word read by his teacher, as is the case in the Spelling subtest of the Wide Range Achievement Test. Such a behavior sampling demands that he recall the correct spelling of a word and actually produce that correct spelling in writing. On the other hand, Richard's score of 70 may have been earned on a spelling test that asked him to recognize the correct spelling of a word. For example, the Spelling subtest of the Peabody Individual Achievement Test presents the student with four alternative spellings of a word (for example, *empti, empty, impty, emity)*, and the teacher asks a child to point to the word *empty*. Such an item demands recognition and pointing rather than recall and production. Thus, we need to look first at the nature of the behaviors sampled by the test.

Second, a teacher must look at the specific items a student passes or fails. This requires going back to the original test protocol to analyze the specific nature of skill development in a given area. We need to ask, "What kinds of items did the child fail?" and to look for consistent patterns among the failures. In trying to identify the nature of spelling errors, the teacher needs to ask such questions as "Does the student consistently demonstrate errors in spelling words with long vowels? with silent *e*s? with specific consonant blends?" and so on. The search is for specific patterns of errors, and the teacher tries to ascertain the student's relative degree of consistency in making certain errors. Of course, finding error patterns requires that the test content be sufficiently dense to allow a student to make the same error at least two times.

Similar procedures are followed with any screening device. Quite obviously, the information achieved is not nearly as specific as the information obtained from diagnostic tests. Administration of an achievement test that is a screening test gives the classroom teacher a general idea of where to start with any additional diagnostic assessment.

Coping with Dilemmas in Current Practice

Two limitations affect the use of achievement tests as screening devices. As was noted earlier, unless the content of an achievement test reflects the content of the curriculum, the obtained results are meaningless. If students are instructed in new math but tested with traditional math achievement tests, they may well perform poorly. Yet the obtained results cannot be said to reflect accurately and validly those students' level of skill development in math. Jenkins and Pany (1978) compared the contents of four separate reading achievement tests with the contents of five commercial reading series at grades 1 and 2. Their major concern was the extent to which students might earn different scores on different tests of reading achievement simply as a function of the degree of overlap in content between tests and curricula. Jenkins and Pany calculated the grade scores that would be earned by students who had mastered the words taught in the respective curricula and who had correctly read those words on the four tests. Grade scores are reported in Table 20.8. It is apparent that different curricula result in different performances on different tests. Those charged with the selection of achievement tests must go beyond a casual inspection of test items. They should construct a table of specifications for each area of the curriculum to be tested and compare prospective tests on that table. Only then will they be able to make valid judgments about the relative correspondence of test content and curriculum.

A second limitation is inherent in the way most achievement tests are administered. Most achievement tests are group administered, and teachers giving a group-administered test are unable to observe individual pupil performance. They may lose valuable information about how a student goes about solving problems, analyzing words, and spelling because they cannot observe individual behavior directly. Then, because most screening devices provide global scores by

TABLE 20.8   **Grade-Equivalent Scores Obtained by Matching Specific Reading Test Words to Standardized Reading Test Words**

Curriculum	PIAT	MAT		SDRT	WRAT
		Word Knowledge	**Word Analysis**		
Bank Street Reading Series					
Grade 1	1.5	1.0	1.1	1.8	2.0
Grade 2	2.8	2.5	1.2	2.9	2.7
Keys to Reading					
Grade 1	2.0	1.4	1.2	2.2	2.2
Grade 2	3.3	1.9	1.0	3.0	3.0
Reading 360					
Grade 1	1.5	1.0	1.0	1.4	1.7
Grade 2	2.2	2.1	1.0	2.7	2.3
SRA Reading Program					
Grade 1	1.5	1.2	1.3	1.0	2.1
Grade 2	3.1	2.5	1.4	2.9	3.5
Sullivan Associates Programmed Reading					
Grade 1	1.8	1.4	1.2	1.1	2.0
Grade 2	2.2	2.4	1.1	2.5	2.5

SOURCE: From "Standardized Achievement Tests: How Useful for Special Education?" by J. Jenkins & D. Pany, *Exceptional Children, 44,* (1978), 450. Copyright 1978 by The Council for Exceptional Children. Reprinted with permission.

content areas, teachers must return to a student's test blank or answer sheet to investigate the kinds of errors made. Otherwise, teachers are left with a score but little information about how the score was obtained and no systematic analysis of skill-development strengths and weaknesses.

SUMMARY

Screening devices used to assess academic achievement provide a global picture of a student's skill development in academic content areas. Screening tests must be selected on the basis of the kinds of behavior each test samples, the adequacy of its norms, its reliability, and its validity. When selecting an achievement test or when evaluating the results of a student's performance on an achievement test, the classroom teacher needs to take into careful consideration not only the technical characteristics of the test but also the extent to which the behaviors sampled represent the goals and objectives of the student's curriculum. The teacher can adapt certain techniques for administering group tests and for getting the most mileage out of the results of group tests.

STUDY QUESTIONS

1. State at least three different reasons for administering the screening tests described in this chapter.
2. Differentiate between screening tests and diagnostic tests.
3. Identify at least four important considerations in selecting a specific achievement test for use with the third-graders in your local school system.
4. Identify similarities and differences in the domains of behavior sampled by the California Achievement Tests, the Iowa Tests of Basic Skills, and the Peabody Individual Achievement Test–Revised.
5. Ms. Epstein decides to assess the achievement of her fifth-grade pupils. She believes her pupils are unusually "slow" and estimates that, in general, they are functioning on about a third-grade level. She decides to use primary level III of the SAT. What difficulties will she face in doing so?
6. Mr. Spencer, a fourth-grade teacher in Bemidji, Minnesota, wants to group students in his class for reading instruction. He administers the reading recognition subtest of the Wide Range Achievement Test 3 and assigns students to groups on the basis of the grade scores they earn on the test. Which of the basic assumptions underlying assessment has Mr. Spencer violated? How might he make this grouping decision?

ADDITIONAL READING

Conoley, J. C., & Kramer, J. J. (1993). *Buros eleventh mental measurements yearbook*. Lincoln, NE: University of Nebraska Press.

Gronlund, N. E. (1982). *Constructing achievement tests*. Englewood Cliffs, NJ: Prentice-Hall.

Chapter 21

Assessment of Reading

*I*n Chapter 19 we described multiple-skill achievement tests, which provide global information about a student's achievements. Often, school personnel need more specific information. In this chapter we give detailed descriptions of the kinds of behaviors sampled by reading tests and then describe commonly used reading tests, both norm-referenced and criterion-referenced, or performance, measures.

WHY DO WE ASSESS READING SKILLS?

Reading is thought to be the most fundamental skill that students acquire through the process of schooling. Students who experience difficulty reading can be expected to have difficulty with nearly all academic curriculum content. It should not surprise you to learn that "difficulty reading" is the most frequently stated reason for referring students for psychoeducational evaluation.

Diagnostic tests are designed to help school personnel pinpoint students' strengths and weaknesses in reading and plan appropriate educational interventions. They are used to give teachers a systematic, detailed picture of where pupils stand in their development of specific reading skills.

Reading tests are also used to spot common problems within groups of children. One of the authors recently consulted at a school in which pupils consistently performed above grade level in all areas of the curriculum but one: reading. Nearly all of the students in that school earned below-average scores on the reading subtests of the Metropolitan Achievement Test. A diagnostic reading test was used to pinpoint skill deficiencies that the students consistently demonstrated. When specific deficiencies were identified, teachers were able to explore alternative explanations for the deficiencies. They learned that the skills were not systematically taught in the reading curriculum used by the school. Teachers then identified skills that they thought were very important to teach and added those skills to the curriculum.

Norm-referenced diagnostic reading tests provide information about relative standing in development of reading skills. This information might be used for making classification or placement decisions and for making program evaluation decisions. However, when norm-referenced diagnostic reading tests are used in instructional planning, users must go beyond the derived scores to analyze error patterns on items sampled by the test; knowledge of grade scores, age scores, percentile ranks, and stanines is of limited value in instructional planning. For example, knowing where Heather stands relative to other students does not help a teacher decide how to teach Heather to read.

Skills Assessed by Diagnostic Reading Tests

Reading is a complex behavior composed of many skills. No one diagnostic reading test assesses all aspects of reading completely. Rather, each test samples specific reading or reading-related behaviors. The particular behaviors assessed by any one test are simply those behaviors that the test authors believe are most important to assess. In a broad sense, several different categories of behaviors are sampled by diagnostic reading tests. Specific tests or subtests assess oral reading skills, comprehension skills, word-attack skills, and rate of reading. A variety of supplementary subtests are included in a number of diagnostic reading tests.

Assessment of Oral Reading Skills

A number of tests or parts of tests are designed to assess the accuracy and fluency of a student's oral reading. Oral reading tests consist of a series of paragraphs arranged sequentially, from very easy paragraphs to relatively difficult ones. The student reads aloud while the examiner notes both the kinds of errors made and the behaviors that characterize the student's oral reading. Two commonly used tests—the Gray Oral Reading Test–3 and the Gilmore Oral Reading Test[1]—are designed specifically to assess skill development in oral reading. Four other commonly used tests—the Formal Reading Inventory, the Gates-McKillop-Horowitz Reading Diagnostic Tests, the Durrell Analysis of Reading Difficulty, and the Standardized Reading Inventory—include oral reading subtests.

Different oral reading tests record different behaviors as errors or miscues in oral reading. Following are descriptions of the behaviors demonstrated as each specific kind of error takes place.

Aid If a student either hesitates for a time without making an audible effort to pronounce a word or appears to be attempting for ten seconds to pronounce the word, the examiner pronounces the word and records an error. The error is recorded by an underlined bracket.

---

1. The Gilmore Oral Reading Test was reviewed in earlier editions of this text. We do not review it here because its norms now are out of date.

Hesitation   The student hesitates for two or more seconds before pronouncing a word. The error is recorded as a check (√) over the word. If the examiner then pronounces the word, it is recorded as √p.

Gross Mispronunciation of a Word   A gross mispronunciation is recorded when the pupil's pronunciation of a word bears so little resemblance to the proper pronunciation that the examiner must be looking at the word to recognize it. An example of a gross mispronunciation is the pupil reading the word *encounters* as "actors." The examiner records the error phonetically above the mispronounced word.

Partial Mispronunciation of a Word   A partial mispronunciation can be one of several different kinds of errors. The examiner may have to pronounce part of a word for the student (an aid); the student may phonetically mispronounce specific letters (for example, by reading the word *red* as "reed"); or the student may omit part of a word, insert elements of words, or make errors in syllabication, accent, or inversion. Such errors are recorded phonetically and scored as partial mispronunciations.

Omission of a Word or Group of Words   Omissions consist of skipping individual words or groups of words. The examiner simply circles the word or group of words omitted.

Insertion of a Word or Group of Words   Insertions consist of the student's putting one or more words into the sentence being read. The student may, for example, read *the dog* as "the mean dog." Insertions are recorded by placing a caret (^) in the sentence and writing in the word or words inserted.

Substitution of One Meaningful Word for Another   Substitutions consist of the replacement of one or more words in the passage by one or more meaningful words. The student might read *dense* as "depress." Students often replace entire sequences of words with others, as illustrated by the replacement of *he is his own mechanic* with "he sat on his own machine." The examiner records substitutions by underlining the word or words substituted and writing in the substitutions. Some oral reading tests require that examiners record the specific kind of substitution error. Substitutions are classified as meaning similarity (the words have similar meanings), function similarity (the two words have syntactically similar functions), graphic/phoneme similarity (the words sound alike), or a combination of the above.

Repetition   Repetition is repeating words or groups of words while attempting to read sentences or paragraphs. In some cases, if a student repeats a group of words to correct an error, the original error is not recorded but a repetition error is. In other cases, such behaviors are recorded simply as spontaneous corrections. Repetitions are recorded by underlining the repeated word or words with a wavy line. Errors due to stuttering are not recorded as repetition errors.

Inversion, or Changing of Word Order   Errors of inversion are recorded when the child changes the order of words appearing in a sentence; for example, *house the* is an inversion.

Disregard of Punctuation   The student may fail to observe punctuation—that is, may not pause for a comma, stop for a period, or indicate by vocal inflection a question mark or exclamation point. These errors of disregard of punctuation are recorded by circling the punctuation mark.

In addition to making a systematic analysis of oral reading errors, the examiner can note the behaviors that characterize a student's oral reading. Although any characteristics may be observed, the most frequently looked for indicators of difficulty include head movement, finger pointing, loss of place, word-by-word reading, poor phrasing, lack of expression, reading in a monotonous tone, and reading in a strained voice.

Assessment of Comprehension Skills

Diagnostic reading tests assess six kinds of comprehension skills: literal comprehension, inferential comprehension, listening comprehension, critical comprehension, affective comprehension, and lexical comprehension.

Assessment of *literal comprehension* is usually accomplished by asking a number of factual questions based directly on the content of a paragraph or story the student has read. The answers to such questions appear explicitly in the story or paragraph. Such comprehension tests require specific recall of material read and, for that reason, are sometimes characterized as memory tests (unless, of course, the passage is available for the student to refer to when responding to the questions).

Inferential comprehension tests require interpretation and extension of what has been read. The student must demonstrate an ability to derive meaning from printed paragraphs or stories. Assessment of *listening comprehension* is accomplished by reading a story or paragraph to a student and then asking questions requiring recall and understanding of the material read. Listening comprehension tests can measure both literal and inferential comprehension. *Critical comprehension* tests assess the student's skill in analyzing, evaluating, or making judgments about what is read, whereas *affective comprehension* tests involve personal and emotional responses to the text. *Lexical comprehension* tests pertain to knowledge of key vocabulary words. Though students can answer the questions correctly without reading the text, these tests do give examiners information on the extent to which poor performance is a function of lack of knowledge of the meanings of specific words.

In the process of assessing the development of comprehension skills, it is absolutely necessary for the teacher or diagnostic specialist to examine critically how those skills are assessed. The method by which comprehension skills are assessed may muddy the waters, in that pupil performance may depend more on other traits or skills than on comprehension of what is read. When literal comprehension is assessed by asking students to read a passage and recall, without observing the passage, what has been read, performance may depend more on memory than on reading comprehension. Similarly, for students to infer meaning on the basis of what they have read requires as much cognition as comprehension. In our opinion, the best way to assess comprehension is to ask students to state or paraphrase what they have read.

Assessment of Word-Attack Skills

Word-attack, or word-analysis, skills are those used "to derive the meaning and/or pronunciation of a word through phonics, structural analysis, or context clues" (Ekwall, 1970, p. 4). Students must be able to decode words before they can gain meaning from the printed page. Since word-analysis difficulties are among the principal reasons students have trouble reading, a variety of subtests of commonly used diagnostic reading tests specifically assess word-analysis skills.

Subtests that assess word-analysis skills range from such basic assessments as analysis of skill in associating letters with sounds to tests of syllabication and blending. Generally, for subtests that assess skill in associating letters with sounds, the examiner reads a word aloud and the student must identify the consonant, vowel, consonant cluster, or digraph that has the same sound as the beginning, middle, or ending letters of the word. Syllabication subtests present polysyllabic words, and the student must either divide the word into syllables or circle specific syllables. Blending subtests, on the other hand, are of three types. In the first method, the examiner may read syllables out loud ("wa - ter - mel - on," for example) and ask the student to pronounce the word. In the second type of subtest, the student may be asked to read word parts and pronounce whole words. In the third method, the student, may be presented with alternative beginning, middle, and ending sounds and asked to produce a word. Figure 21.1 illustrates the third method used with the Stanford Diagnostic Reading Test.

FIGURE 21.1   **An Item that Assesses Blending Skill**

Assessment of Word-Recognition Skills

Subtests of diagnostic reading tests that assess a pupil's word-recognition skills are designed to ascertain what many educators call *sight vocabulary*. A student learns the correct pronunciation of letters and words through a variety of experiences. The more exposure a student has to specific words and the more familiar those words become, the more readily he or she recognizes those words and is able to pronounce them correctly. Well-known words require very little reliance on word-attack skills. Most readers of this book immediately recognize the word *hemorrhage* and do not have to employ phonetic skills to pronounce it. On the other hand, words like *nephrocystanastomosis* are not a part of the sight vocabulary for most of us. Such words slow us down; we must use phonetics to analyze them.

Word-recognition subtests form a major part of most diagnostic reading tests. Some tests use paper tachistoscopes to expose words for brief periods of time (usually one-half second). Students who recognize many words are said to have good sight vocabularies or good word-recognition skills. Other subtests assess letter recognition, recognition of words in isolation, and recognition of words in context.

Assessment of Rate of Reading

Reading rate is generally played down in the diagnostic assessment of reading difficulties. There are, however, some exceptions. Two levels of the Stanford Diagnostic Reading Test have subtests to assess rate of reading. On the other hand, tests such as the Gray Oral Reading Test–Revised are timed, with time affecting the score a pupil receives. A pupil who reads a passage on the GORT-R slowly but makes no errors in reading can earn a lower score than a rapid reader who makes one or two errors in reading.

Assessment of Other Reading and Reading-Related Behaviors

A variety of subtests that fit none of the above categories are included in diagnostic reading tests as either major or supplementary subtests. Examples of such tests include oral vocabulary, spelling, handwriting, and auditory discrimination. In most cases, such subtests are included simply to provide the examiner with additional diagnostic information.

GENERAL READING TESTS

Gates-MacGinitie Reading Tests

*T*he third edition of the Gates-MacGinitie Reading Tests (MacGinitie & MacGinitie, 1989) is the most recent in a series that began with publication of the Gates Silent Reading Test and the Gates Primary Reading Tests in 1926. The series consists of norm-referenced screening tests designed to assess skill development in reading from prekindergarten through twelfth grade. The Pre-Reading Evaluation Level (PRE) is new to the third edition and is used to help teachers identify what each student knows about the concepts on which beginning reading development is based. It assesses repetitions understanding of literacy concepts, relational concepts, oral language concepts, and letters and letter-sound correspondence. Level R, also new to the third edition, measures beginning reading achievement in grade 1. Subtests at that level include knowledge of initial consonants and consonant clusters, final consonants and consonant clusters, and vowels and sentence context. There are seven additional levels of the tests, with at least two forms at each level; there are three forms for use in grades 4 through 9. Testing time is about 55 minutes for each level. For levels PRE, R, 1, 2, and 3, the student records his/her answers in the test booklet, and these answers may be scored by hand or machine. For the remaining levels, the student's answers are recorded on a separate sheet and are scored by hand.

Following is a description of the specific subtests and the behaviors they sample:

Vocabulary This subtest assesses reading vocabulary. The actual demand of the task varies with grade level. The Vocabulary subtest for grades 1, 2, and 3, for example, presents the student with four printed words and a picture illustrating one of the words. The student must circle the word that best corresponds to the picture. From grade 4 through grade 12, the student is presented with a stimulus word and five additional words. The student must identify the response word that has the same meaning as the stimulus word.

Comprehension This subtest assesses ability to read and understand whole sentences and paragraphs. In grades 1 and 2, the student must read a selection and choose the picture that best describes its content. In grade 3, the student reads a paragraph and then selects from four response choices the best answer to specific questions about the paragraph. In grades 4 through 12, the student is presented with paragraphs in which there are a number of blank spaces. The student must select from five response alternatives the word or phrase that best fits in the blank.

SCORES

Raw scores for the Vocabulary and Comprehension subtests are simply the number of items correct. Raw scores are not obtained for the level of the test used in grades 1-0 to 1-9 (level R) because the subtests are very short. For level R, normative information is given descriptively (low, average, or high). Raw scores for the other levels of the test may be transformed to normal curve equivalents, percentile ranks, stanines, grade equivalents, and extended scale scores.

NORMS

The Gates-MacGinitie Reading Tests were standardized in October 1976, February 1977 (level A only), and May 1977. The sample was selected to correspond to 1970 census data: geographic region, district enrollment size, and the school district's so-

TABLE 21.1   **Alternate-Form Reliabilities for the Gates-MacGinitie Reading Tests**

Level	Vocabulary	Comprehension	Total
A	.88–.90	.89	.92–.94
B	.88–.90	.86	.92
C	.89–.90	.85–.86	.93
D	.86–.89	.83–.84	.91–.92
E	.86–.90	.82–.87	.89–.93
F	.86–.87	.77–.83	.89–.91

cioeconomic status (median family income and median years of education completed by adults). A total of 65,000 students (approximately 5,000 per grade) were assessed. The authors state that districts were selected within each region that exhibited a representative proportion of black and Hispanic students. There are no demographic data in the manuals that accompany this test that describe the specific characteristics of the sample or that contrast sample proportions with population proportions.

RELIABILITY

Three kinds of reliability data—internal-consistency, alternate-form, and test-retest—are reported in the technical manual for the Gates-MacGinitie Reading Tests. Internal-consistency coefficients based on the performance of pupils in the standardization sample

are all greater than .85, with most being greater than .90. Alternate-form reliabilities are reported for all levels. These are summarized for levels A to F in Table 21.1. Alternate-form reliability for the total test at level R was .91; for subtests, however, alternate-form reliability ranged only from .57 to .78. Test-retest reliability, based on correlations between pupils' performances in October and May, ranged from .77 to .89.

VALIDITY

Two indexes of validity are reported for the Gates-MacGinitie Reading Tests. The authors report correlations ranging from .74 to .94 with the first edition of the test. They also report correlations with corresponding subtests of the Metropolitan Achievement Test at grades 5-8 and 8-8. Correlations at grade 5-8 were .88 (Vocabulary), .83 (Comprehension), and .91 (Total); at grade 8-8, correlations were .86 (Vocabulary), .80 (Comprehension), and .88 (Total).

SUMMARY

The third edition of the Gates-MacGinitie Reading Tests provides a comprehensive assessment of reading skills in two domains: vocabulary and comprehension. Data on the specific makeup of the standardization group are not provided. Evidence for reliability and validity of the tests is adequate.

ORAL READING TESTS

Gray Oral Reading Test, Third Edition

*T*he Gray Oral Reading Test–3 (GORT-3) (1992) is the second revision of the Gray Oral Reading Test by Wiederholt and Bryant. The GORT-3 remains an individually administered, norm-referenced measure of oral reading and comprehension. Each of the two forms (A and

B) of the GORT-3 contain thirteen reading passages of increasing difficulty. Students are required to read paragraphs orally and to respond to a set of five comprehension questions for each paragraph. The test is intended for use with students between the ages of 7-0 and 18-11. Specific basal and ceiling rules are used to limit time, which typically ranges from 15 to 30 minutes.

The authors of the GORT-3 state four purposes for the test: "(a) to help identify those students who are significantly below their peers in oral reading proficiency and who may profit from supplemental help; (b) to aid in determining the particular kinds of reading strengths and weaknesses that individual students possess; (c) to document students' progress in reading as a consequence of special intervention programs; and (d) to serve as a measurement device in investigations where researchers are studying the abilities of school-age students" (Wiederholt & Bryant, 1992, p. 6).

In the manual, the authors go into considerable detail in describing the extensive care with which the oral reading passages for the GORT-3 were developed. They describe the great care taken to ensure that the comprehension questions that follow each passage were written to assess literal, inferential, critical, and affective comprehension. In fact, the two forms of the GORT-3 are identical in every way to the two forms of the GORT-R, which are, in turn, identical to Forms B and D of the Formal Reading Inventory (FRI) (Wiederholt, 1986). The FRI differs from the GORT-R in that the FRI examiner obtains only a classification of oral reading miscues; the GORT-R examiner can obtain a composite Oral Reading Quotient, separate indexes of oral reading and comprehension, and a percentage score for each of the specific kinds of miscues. The GORT-3 differs from the GORT-R in that the GORT-3 provides separate percentiles and standard scores for rate and accuracy, whereas GORT-R provides percentiles and standard scores for rate and accuracy combined.

SCORES

The examiner records the number of seconds that the student required to read the passage aloud and tallies the number of deviations from the test (that is, any deviation from print is scored as an oral reading miscue, unless the deviation is the result of normal speech variations). At the bottom of the test protocol is a matrix. The top row of the matrix has a six-point scale (0 through 5); the next row of the matrix has six time ranges corresponding to the six-point scale; and the third row has six error ranges that also correspond to the six-point scale. The examiner awards points (0 through 5) for the speed and for the accuracy with which the passage is read. For each passage, the sum of the rate and accuracy scores is called a passage score. The rate, accuracy, passage, and comprehension scores are then summed for the stories read to yield total scores for rate, accuracy, passage, and comprehension. From these total scores, corresponding grade equivalents, percentiles, and standard scores (mean = 10, standard deviation = 3) can be found in various tables in the manual. The passage and comprehension standard scores are added and then transformed into a standard score called the Oral Reading Quotient, which has a mean of 100 and a standard deviation of 15.

The examiner also records both the number and kinds of miscues (the kinds are identical to those scored on the FRI). The number is also converted into a percentage. (On the FRI, the examiner simply records the number of errors of a given type.)

NORMS

The GORT-R was standardized on 1,401 students from fifteen states. The GORT-3 combines 1,259 of the original 1,401 students tested in the 1980s with 226 newly tested students.[2] The GORT-3 norms are better described than the GORT-R norms and appear to be generally representative of the U.S. population in terms of sex, place of residence (urban, rural), race, ethnicity, and geographic region; no data describing the socioeconomic status of the standardization sample are provided.

2. The norms for the two editions are, therefore, almost identical. Approximately 85 percent of the 1992 norm group (1,259 of 1,485) came from the 1986 normative sample. The manual offers no explanation for the deletion of these 142 students from the 1986 standardization.

RELIABILITY

The internal consistency for five scores (rate, accuracy, passage, comprehension, and Oral Reading Quotient) at twelve ages (6 to 7 through 17 to 18) were estimated from the performances of fifty students in each age group who were randomly selected from the standardization sample. The ninety-six alphas for subtests ranged from .79 to .96; fifty-four of the ninety-six coefficients equaled or exceeded .90. Alpha for the Oral Reading Quotient equaled or exceeded .95 at all ages. Test-retest reliability using the alternate forms was also estimated. These coefficients ranged from .62 to .90, but users should understand that these estimates include error attributable to content sampling as well as error attributable to different rates. Overall, the Oral Reading Quotient of the GORT-3 appears sufficiently reliable for making important decisions for individual students; use of other scores for this purpose will depend on the age of the student and the particular score.

VALIDITY

Early in the manual for the GORT-3, the authors list several purposes of the test. They do not provide evidence of the validity of the scale for those purposes. Rather, data are provided on the general context, criterion-related, and construct validity of the test. The authors argue that the test has good content validity because of the procedures followed in test construction. Specifically, they argue that the reading passages were written to control for "density of words, length of words and sentences, complexity of sentence structure, structure of sentences, logical connections between sentences and clauses, and coherence of topics" (p. 37).

With two exceptions, the concurrent validity of GORT-3 is based on studies previously reported on GORT-R. Relying on the validity of a previous edition is often problematic; in this case, however, this reliance is appropriate because the content of the test is unchanged and the norms are essentially unchanged. In the GORT-R studies, concurrent validity was examined by taking scores earned on other tests from the files of students who participated in the standardized population. Thus, the other test scores are for students from a variety of school districts who took the tests at various points in time. The GORT-R scores of thirty students were correlated with their scores on Form C of the Formal Reading Inventory; correlations ranged from .44 to .66. Three elementary teachers rated the overall reading of thirty-seven students on a five-point scale. The correlations between their judgments and GORT-R scores ranged from .47 to .78. Data are reported on the correlation of the scores of 108 students in grades 9 through 12 on the GORT-R and the Iowa Tests of Educational Development. Correlations ranged from .28 to .47. The Form A GORT-3 scores earned by seventy-four students in grades 3 and 4 were correlated with their reading subtest scores on the California Achievement Test; the correlations ranged from .35 to .60. A final study reported in the manual involved the scores of thirty-four students who were tested with Form A and also tested with the reading subtest of the Screening Children for Related Early Educational Needs and the reading subtests of the Diagnostic Achievement Battery–Second Edition. In all, approximately 180 correlation coefficients were calculated, the median of which was .57.

The authors examined the construct validity of the GORT-3 by showing that GORT-3 scores increase with age and are highly correlated with measures of other language abilities and total achievement. GORT-3 also distinguishes groups of students identified as having reading deficits from groups of students without deficits.

SUMMARY

The GORT-3 is an individually administered, norm-referenced measure of oral reading and comprehension for use with students between the ages of 7-0 and 18-11. Multiple scores are derived from a student's reading (rate, accuracy, and rate plus accuracy); a single score is derived for comprehension; and a composite score based on rate, accuracy, and comprehension can be calculated. The standardization sample used for the GORT-3 appears to be generally representative of the U.S. population in terms of sex, place of residence (urban, rural), race, ethnicity, and geographic region; there were no data on the socioeconomic status of that standardization sample. Overall, the Oral Reading Quotient of the GORT-3 appears sufficiently reliable for making important decisions for individual students; use of other scores for this purpose will depend on the age of the student

and the particular score. The GORT-3 appears to have satisfactory validity.

Although we have used the authors' terminology in calling the test the GORT-3, the GORT-3 is the same test as the GORT-R. Test users would have been better served by the publication of modified test protocols and a brief supplement to the GORT-R manual. The supplement to the manual might have included (1) separate standard scores and percentiles for rate and accuracy, (2) better described norms with eighty-four more students, and (3) better descriptions of the test's reliability.

Formal Reading Inventory

*T*he Formal Reading Inventory (FRI) (Wiederholt, 1986) is an individually administered, norm-referenced measure of a student's skill development in oral and silent reading. The test is appropriate for use with students in grades 1 through 12 (ages 6-6 through 17-11). There are four forms of the test. Forms A and C are read silently; Forms B and D are read orally. Forms B and D are identical in every respect to the two forms of the Gray Oral Reading Test–Revised. Materials for the FRI consist of a reusable student book of reading passages, an examiner's manual, and examiner's worksheets. Each form of the test contains thirteen reading passages, each of which is followed by five multiple-choice comprehension questions. It takes about 15 minutes to administer each form of the test.

In developing the stories for the FRI, the author made a specific effort to control for density of words, length of words and sentences, complexity of sentence structure, structure of sentences, logical connections between sentences and clauses, and coherence of topics. The readability levels of the paragraphs were assessed by five different readability formulas: Flesch, Fry, Dale-Chall, Farr-Jenkins-Patterson, and Danielson-Bryan. Three separate word lists were used to control the vocabulary level of words in the FRI passages. In developing the comprehension questions, the author used special

care to ensure that the level of vocabulary in the questions did not exceed that used in the stories. Four kinds of reading comprehension are assessed: literal, inferential, critical, and affective. The questions were written so as to be passage dependent—an effort was made to eliminate the possibility that the correct response would be chosen primarily on the basis of similarities in text features.

By administering the FRI, the examiner obtains two kinds of information: (1) an analysis and classification of the kinds of oral reading miscues the student makes and (2) a silent reading comprehension quotient. Miscues are further examined and categorized as to type only if they are substitutions. The following categories of substitution miscues are recorded:

Meaning Similarity   Miscues are scored in this category when the examiner judges that the miscue consisted of the student's substituting one word for another having essentially the same meaning (for example, the student read *menace* as "threat").

Function Similarity   These are miscues in which one word is substituted for another having a "syntactically similar function." The number of such miscues is a measure of the student's use of correct grammatical forms in reading. The examiner must judge whether a substituted word has the same grammatical function as the original printed word.

Graphic/Phonemic Similarity Miscues are scored in this category when the examiner decides that the word substituted looks like and/or sounds like the original word (for example, the student read *thought* as "through").

Multiple Sources Miscues are scored in this category when they fit more than one of the types of miscues listed above.

Self-Correction Miscues are scored in this category when the student corrects all errors in oral reading. These miscues are recorded to differentiate readers who correct their errors from those who do not.

In addition to recording the five kinds of oral reading miscues described above, examiners make note of other kinds of miscues. These include errors of dialect, reversals, omissions, and additions. The examiner also makes note of such oral reading behaviors as slow reading rate, word-by-word reading, poor phrasing, lack of expression, pitch too high or low, voice too soft or strained, poor enunciation, disregard of punctuation, head movement, finger pointing, loss of place, holding the book far away or very close, nervousness, and poor attitude.

The kinds of miscues students make are recorded directly on the FRI worksheet. Figure 21.2 illustrates the recording procedure. The student's responses to the five multiple-choice comprehension questions are simply scored pass-fail.

SCORES

Scores obtained from administering the FRI include a silent reading comprehension quotient, a percentile score for silent reading comprehension, and a classification of oral reading miscues. Because the two forms of the test read orally (Forms B and D) are identical to the Gray Oral Reading Test–3 (Wiederholt & Bryant, 1992), the GORT-3 manual can be used to obtain an oral reading comprehension score and an oral reading quotient for the FRI.

The silent reading comprehension quotient has a mean of 100 and a standard deviation of 15. For the categorical analysis of oral reading miscues, the examiner notes the total number of miscues made and the number of each type.

NORMS

The FRI was standardized on 1,737 children from twelve states (Florida, Iowa, Illinois, Kansas, Louisiana, Missouri, Mississippi, New York, Ohio, South Carolina, Texas, and Washington). The author reports a breakdown of the normative sample in terms of sex, area of residence (urban, rural), race, geographic area, and ethnicity, although no indication is given of how the sample was stratified. The percentages for students in the sample are reasonably close to the percentages for the population as revealed by census data, but these figures may be misleading. For example, although the percentage of the sample coming from the Western United States (20 percent) was identical to the percentage of the population in that region according to census data, the only Western state from which standardization data were collected was Washington. The author does not provide data on the socioeconomic status of those who make up the standardization group.

RELIABILITY

Two kinds of reliability data are provided in the FRI manual. Reported data on the internal consistency of the test are based on twenty-five protocols selected at random for each age level in the standardization population. All internal-consistency coefficients exceeded .92. Alternate-form reliability was computed by correlating scores of the standardization sample for Forms A and C of the test. The correlation was .75.

VALIDITY

Two studies were conducted to ascertain the concurrent validity of the FRI. In the first study, 190 children in grades 1 through 6 in Tacoma, Washington took the FRI and the Comprehensive Tests of Basic Skills. In a second study, 114 children in grades 4, 5, 6, 8, and 10 from a school district in Westlake, Texas took the FRI and the California Achievement Test. Correlations between the FRI and the total reading score on the CTBS ranged from .21 for Form A to .46 for Form D. Correla-

FIGURE 21.2 **An Illustration of the Recording Procedure for the Formal Reading Inventory**

Story 10

1. For days the zoologist had scoured the protected area for a coyote den.

2. Unless she could stake one out for field study, it would be impossible to docu-

3. ment her theory that a coyote is a social creature staunchly devoted to its family

4. and clan, not the loner of popular imagination. The wildlife sanctuary had

5. seemed the ideal setting for tracking coyotes, for there the detested adversary

6. of sheep ranchers was afforded refuge from the wholesale onslaughts of trap-

7. ping, shooting, and poisoning. But years of this guerilla warfare had conditioned

8. in the species a wariness that made coyote sightings a rarity. Seasoned by com-

9. bat, the species had evolved a highly suspicious nature that honed its survival

10. instincts and thwarted efforts aimed at its extermination. Yet this same trait, as

11. the zoologist was forced to acknowledge with frustration, had endowed it with

12. the uncanny ability to elude scientific scrutiny.

---

1. ✓_____   2. _____   3. _____   4. _____   5. _____

SOURCE: J. L. Wiederholt, *Formal Reading Inventory, Examiner's Manual* (p. 51) (Austin, TX: Pro-Ed, 1986). Reprinted by permission of Pro-Ed.

tions between the FRI and the total reading score for the CAT ranged from .37 for Form A to .69 for Form B. To establish construct validity, the author shows that FRI scores increase with age, that the stories become progressively more difficult throughout the test, that children with subnormal reading comprehension performance on the Comprehensive Test of Basic Skills earn low scores on the FRI, and that correlations between the FRI and a measure of intelligence are high. This latter finding is based on a very small sample (seventeen adolescent females) and on correlations with only one test (the Detroit Tests of Learning Aptitude–2). Yet the correlations with intelligence are as high as or higher than the correlations with other measures of reading.

SUMMARY

The Formal Reading Inventory (FRI) is an individually administered, norm-referenced measure that provides users with an assessment of silent reading comprehension and an analysis of the kinds of oral reading miscues students make. Forms B and D of this scale, which are used to assess oral reading, are identical to the Gray Oral Reading Test–Revised. The FRI requires students to read paragraphs orally or silently and then answer comprehension questions. The extent to which the norms for this test are based on a representative sample of students is questionable. However, evidence for reliability is restricted to internal consistency, which is very good.

DIAGNOSTIC READING TESTS

Gates-McKillop-Horowitz Reading Diagnostic Tests

*T*he Gates-McKillop-Horowitz Reading Diagnostic Tests (Gates, McKillop, & Horowitz, 1981) are a revision of the Gates-McKillop Reading Diagnostic Tests (Gates & McKillop, 1962). The tests consist of a battery of fourteen individually administered subtests and parts of subtests designed to assess skill development in reading. The tests are used with students in grades 1 through 6. No set battery of subtests must be given to each child; rather, the examiner selects those subtests thought necessary.

The manual for the Gates-McKillop-Horowitz states no specific qualifications as necessary for administering the tests. Most subtests are easy enough for a classroom teacher with little testing experience to administer. Scoring and interpretation are, however, complex and difficult for even the most experienced examiner.

The following behaviors are sampled by the Gates-McKillop-Horowitz Reading Diagnostic Tests.

Oral Reading The Oral Reading subtest of the Gates-McKillop-Horowitz is similar to the Gray and Gilmore oral reading tests. The errors recorded for this subtest include hesitations, omissions, additions, repetitions, and mispronunciations. Mispronunciations are scored in terms of the kind of error made, including directional errors (inversions); words pronounced with wrong beginnings, wrong middles, or wrong endings; words pronounced incorrectly in several parts; and accent errors.

Words: Flash This subtest purports to assess sight vocabulary. A cardboard tachistoscope is provided to the examiner to use to expose single words for one-half second. The student reads the words aloud.

Words: Untimed This subtest is said to be a measure of word-attack skills. The student reads words without time restriction.

Knowledge of Word Parts: Word Attack This subtest has the following six parts, all of which assess skill development in word attack.

1. *Syllabication*. The pupil is shown nonsense words divided into syllables and is asked to read the words aloud. The examiner records errors phonetically.

2. *Recognizing and blending common word parts.* This part of the subtest is complex, both in administration and in scoring. The examiner asks the student to read nonsense words like *drack* and *glebe*. When the pupil reads a nonsense word incorrectly, the word is presented in two parts ("dr-ack") and the pupil is asked to pronounce the parts and to blend them to pronounce the nonsense word.

3. *Reading words*. The student is shown nonsense words and is required to read them. The examiner records errors phonetically.

4. *Giving letter sounds*. The pupil is shown letters and is asked to give their sounds.

5. *Naming capital letters*. The student is shown capital letters and is asked to name them.

6. *Naming lowercase letters*. The student is shown lowercase letters and is asked to name them.

Recognizing the Visual Form of Sounds This subtest contains a part called Vowels. The examiner reads nonsense words, and the student is asked to identify the vowel that produces the vowel sound in each word.

Auditory Blending The examiner pronounces words part by part; for example, "z-ip." The student must blend the parts to say the word.

Auditory Discrimination This subtest assesses skill in discriminating among common English phonemes.

Written Expression Two measures comprise the Written Expression subtest:

1. *Spelling*. The student writes words dictated by the examiner.

2. *Informal writing sample*. The pupil writes on any topic. There are no formal criteria for scoring performance; rather, the examiner evaluates the pupil's performance on the basis of expression of ideas and handwriting.

SCORES AND NORMS

A number of normative tables appear in the Gates-McKillop-Horowitz manual, but there is no information about the nature of the group on whom the test was standardized. Pupil performance is evaluated in two ways. For four subtests, grade scores are provided. These scores are, in turn, assigned a rating of high, medium, low, or very low relative to the student's grade. For the rest of the tests, there are no scoring standards; the authors simply provide guidelines for interpretation. Ratings for grade scores are based on the authors' opinions.

We commented earlier on the educational meaninglessness of scores that compare students to one another; transformed scores earned on the Gates-McKillop-Horowitz have little meaning. Normative comparisons provide very limited help in teachers' attempts to differentiate instruction. That process is further complicated by the use of grade scores—the kinds of scores that are most frequently misinterpreted. The value of the Gates-McKillop-Horowitz is limited to its clinical use. It may provide a skilled examiner with a sample of items that can be used to identify specific skill-development strengths and weaknesses in reading; however, to accomplish this, the examiner will have to go beyond scores and look at performance on individual items.

RELIABILITY

The authors report the results of two reliability studies. The first was completed on an unspecified group of twenty-seven students who took the Oral Reading subtest twice. Scores on the first administration correlated .94 with scores on the second administration. The other study was one of interscorer reliability. In our opinion, the reliability of this measure has not been established.

VALIDITY

The authors report an investigation of the measure's validity by correlating pupil performance on this test with performance on the Gates-MacGinitie and the Metropolitan Achievement Tests. Only a range of coefficients is given (.68–.96), and the user is not told the number of coefficients for specific levels. The sample is not satisfactorily described. There is no evidence for the validity of the scale.

SUMMARY

The Gates-McKillop-Horowitz Reading Diagnostic Tests are a widely used diagnostic instrument in spite of significant limitations. The manual provides normative tables without including a description of the population on whom the test was standardized. The many scores obtained on the tests are subject to misinterpretation. Evidence for reliability and validity is unsatisfactory.

Durrell Analysis of Reading Difficulty

*T*he Durrell Analysis of Reading Difficulty (DARD) (Durrell & Catterson, 1980) is designed to assist diagnostic personnel in estimating a general level of reading achievement and identifying specific strengths and weaknesses in reading. The test covers a range of reading ability from the nonreader, or prereading, level to the sixth-grade level. The 1980 edition of the test is the third edition in a series that was originally published in 1937.

The DARD is administered individually and is designed to be used by experienced teachers. The authors state that the administration of the test is best learned under the direction of a person who has had experience in analyzing and correcting reading difficulties. Test materials include a booklet of reading paragraphs to be used in the major subtests, a manual of directions, an individual record book, and a cardboard tachistoscope with accompanying test cards and word lists. Test administration takes about 30 to 90 minutes. The DARD subtests sample several different reading and reading-related behaviors, as described below.

Oral Reading   This subtest consists of eight paragraphs of increasing difficulty that the student is required to read aloud. The subtest is scored in much the same manner as the Gray, the Gilmore, and the Oral Reading subtest of the Gates-McKillop-Horowitz. The student responds to literal comprehension questions following the reading of each paragraph.

Silent Reading   The Silent Reading subtest contains eight paragraphs of difficulty comparable to those in the Oral Reading subtest. The examiner tests and records voluntary memory (simple recall), prompted memory (responses to specific questions), and eye movement.

Listening Comprehension   The examiner reads the six paragraphs of this subtest aloud and asks specific comprehension questions. The most difficult paragraph for which the student misses no more than one comprehension question is identified by grade and score as the student's listening comprehension level.

Word Recognition and Word Analysis   This subtest contains several parts. The examiner uses a cardboard tachistoscope, exposing words for one-half second, to assess word-recognition skills. When the student is unsuccessful in reading a word, the same word is presented in an untimed format. The student is then asked to name the letters seen and is given an opportunity to sound out the word.

Listening Vocabulary   This subtest contains the same words as those listed in the Word Recognition and Word Analysis subtest. The student must point to pictures to indicate an understanding of words read by the examiner. The examiner can compare performance on this subtest (a measure of words understood in speech) with performance on the Word

Recognition and Word Analysis subtest (a measure of words understood in print).

Pronunciation of Word Elements This subtest measures the pupil's skill in pronouncing sounds (letters, blends, digraphs, phonograms, and affixes) in isolation.

Spelling This subtest measures the pupil's skill in correctly writing and spelling words read by the examiner.

Visual Memory of Words The student is required to remember the visual pattern of words long enough to circle them (for students whose oral reading level is grade 3 or below) or to write them down.

Auditory Analysis of Words and Elements The student is required to identify sounds in words (for students whose oral reading level is grade 3 or below) or to spell words phonetically.

Prereading Phonics Abilities Inventories Two new measures (syntax matching and identifying letter names in spoken words) have been added to three subtests—identifying phonemes, naming letters, and writing letters—from previous editions of the DARD. Together they form a measure of prereading abilities. These measures are designed to help evaluate the prereading phonics skills necessary for success in learning to read.

SCORES

Most subtests of the DARD provide raw scores that can be converted to grade scores. However, the greatest emphasis in interpreting pupil performance is placed on the checklist of instructional needs that is completed by the examiner following administration of each subtest.

NORMS

The DARD was standardized on "carefully selected populations in six school systems in different geographic regions" (Durrell & Catterson, 1980, p. 8). The names of the school districts are listed in the test manual, but we know little more than that about the normative population. A total of 1,224 students participated in the standardization of the test. Students were selected because they were enrolled in districts chosen by university personnel in graduate reading programs. The authors state that "factors such as language backgrounds, socioeconomic status, ethnic characteristics, and curriculum emphasis were taken into consideration in choosing the particular schools and classrooms from which the children were selected for testing" (p. 56).

Students in the six school districts were given the Metropolitan Achievement Tests. Forty children in each grade who earned average scores (fourth, fifth, or sixth stanine) on the MAT were given the Durrell. The authors do not provide data on the sex, ages, socioeconomic status, or nature of reading curriculum for the standardization group.

RELIABILITY

Reliability was assessed in several ways. For the Oral Reading and Silent Reading subtests, the authors correlated reading time for adjacent paragraphs. Correlations were .85 for oral reading and .80 for silent reading. These are not reliability data. What is needed is information on consistency over time on the same, similar, or parallel levels of passages. For each of the additional subtests, the authors computed internal consistency using the Kuder-Richardson 21 formula. Reliabilities ranged from .63 to .97. Reliabilities exceeded .80 for eight of the thirteen subtests. No data are reported on test-retest reliability.

VALIDITY

The section on validity in the DARD manual consists primarily of a discussion of the concept of validity, with little actual data presented. Initially, the authors make the case for expert opinion, stating that the device has been used and modified since 1937 and that the "stability of the content of the test from revision to revision attests to current professional confidence in its general validity" (Durrell & Catterson, 1980, p. 2). Stability of test content, of course, reflects only the fact that the authors have not made major changes in the test.

The authors do report one validity study. They correlated September measures of first-grade pupils' scores on the prereading inventory with their reading achievement at the end of first grade. Correlations ranged from "about .55," to "about .65." The authors do not say how many students participated in the study, do not describe those who participated, and do not say what test was used to measure reading achievement.

SUMMARY

The DARD is designed to assist classroom teachers in delineating specific skill-development strengths and weaknesses in reading. As long as the examiner and user of the test data place little emphasis on scores obtained and look instead at the qualitative information afforded by the test, the results may be useful in making tentative hypotheses about the nature of a student's reading difficulties. The norm-referenced use of the test is hindered by inadequate standardization, absence of a description of the norm group, limited data on reliability, and limited validity.

Stanford Diagnostic Reading Test

*T*he 1984 Stanford Diagnostic Reading Test (SDRT) (Karlsen & Gardner, 1985) is the third edition of a test originally published in 1966. The SDRT is a group-administered diagnostic test designed to identify specific strengths and weaknesses in reading. It provides detailed coverage of skills in decoding, vocabulary, comprehension, and reading rate. Because the test is intended for use with low achievers, it contains easier questions than do most achievement tests.

There are four overlapping levels of the SDRT, with two parallel forms (G and H) at each level. The Red Level is designed to be used at the end of grade 1, in grade 2, and with low achievers in grade 3. The Green Level is intended for use in grades 3 and 4 and with very low achievers in grade 5. The Brown Level is to be used in grades 5 through 8 and with very low-achieving high school students. The Blue Level is intended for use from the end of grade 8 through the community college level.

The SDRT can be group administered by a classroom teacher. Four skill domains are sampled by the test, although not all domains are sampled at all levels. Subtests and skill domains sampled by the SDRT are reported in Table 21.2. Behaviors sampled are as follows.

Auditory Vocabulary This subtest assesses the language competence of students without requiring them to read. Words were selected from three general content areas: reading and literature, mathematics and science, and social studies and the arts. At the Red Level, students must identify pictures of words read by the examiner. At the Green and Brown levels, pupils select the word or words that best fit the meaning of a sentence read by the examiner.

Vocabulary This subtest appears only at the Blue Level. Words included in the test were selected from lists of words that are encountered most commonly in a high school curriculum. Students must recognize the meanings of words in the context of passages from the areas of reading and literature, mathematics and science, and social studies and the arts.

Auditory Discrimination This subtest appears at the Red and Green levels only. The subtest assesses skill in hearing similar and different sounds in words. Students are asked to determine whether two dictated words have the same beginning, middle, and ending sounds.

TABLE 21.2   Subtests and Skill Domains of the Stanford Diagnostic Reading Test

Decoding

Red Level	Green Level	Brown Level	Blue Level
TEST 2: Auditory Discrimination Consonants (15 items) Vowels (15 items)	TEST 2: Auditory Discrimination Consonants (15 items) Vowels (15 items)		
TEST 3: Phonetic Analysis Consonants (24 items) Vowels (16 items)	TEST 3: Phonetic Analysis Consonants (15 items) Vowels (15 items)	TEST 3: Phonetic Analysis Consonants (15 items) Vowels (15 items)	TEST 4: Phonetic Analysis Consonants (15 items) Vowels (15 items)
TEST 4: Structural Analysis Word Division (24 items) Blending (24 items)	TEST 4: Structural Analysis Word Division (24 items) Blending (24 items)	TEST 4: Structural Analysis Word Division (48 items) Blending (30 items)	TEST 5: Structural Analysis Affixes (15 items) Syllables (15 items)

Vocabulary

Red Level	Green Level	Brown Level	Blue Level
TEST 1: Auditory Vocabulary (36 items)	TEST 1: Auditory Vocabulary (40 items)	TEST 1: Auditory Vocabulary (40 items)	
		TEST 2: Vocabulary (30 items) TEST 3: Word Parts (30 items)	

Comprehension

Red Level	Green Level	Brown Level	Blue Level
TEST 4: Word Reading (30 items)			
TEST 5: Reading Comprehension	TEST 5: Reading Comprehension	TEST 2: Reading Comprehension (items measure two skills)	TEST 1: Reading Comprehension (items measure two skills)
Sentence Reading (28 items) Paragraph Comprehension (20 items)	Literal Comprehension (24 items) Inferential Comprehension (24 items)	Literal Comprehension (30 items) Inferential Comprehension (30 items) and Textual Reading (20 items) Functional Reading (20 items) Recreational Reading (20 items)	Literal Comprehension (30 items) Inferential Comprehension (30 items) and Textual Reading (20 items) Functional Reading (20 items) Recreational Reading (20 items)

Rate

Red Level	Green Level	Brown Level	Blue Level
		TEST 5: Reading Rate (33 items)	TEST 6: Scanning and Skimming (32 items)
			TEST 7: Fast Reading (30 items)

SOURCE: *Stanford Diagnostic Reading Test: Third Edition*. Copyright © 1984 by The Psychological Corporation. Reproduced by permission. All rights reserved.

Phonetic Analysis   This subtest appears at all levels of the SDRT. At the Red Level, students must identify letters that represent beginning and ending sounds of words. At the Green and Brown levels, the task is to identify sounds in words and match these to common or variant spellings of the sound. At the Blue Level, focus is on unusual letter-sound combinations.

Structural Analysis   This subtest appears at all but the Red Level of the test. At the Green Level, the subtest includes two parts. Students must identify the first syllable of two-syllable words, and they must identify common word parts and blend them into words. At the Brown and Blue levels, the subtest requires students to divide three-syllable words into syllables.

Word Parts   This vocabulary subtest is at the Blue Level only. It assesses students' knowledge of word parts such as prefixes, suffixes, root words, and word roots.

Word Reading   This subtest, which is at the Red Level only, measures skill in recognizing and attaching meaning to words.

Reading Comprehension   There is a reading comprehension subtest at each level of the SDRT, but the methods of sampling the behaviors differ at the various levels. At the Red Level, students must identify the pictures that best represent sentences they read, and they must read and understand sentences and paragraphs presented in a multiple-choice cloze format.[1] At the Green Level, literal and inferential comprehension are assessed by requiring students to respond to multiple-choice questions in cloze format. At the Brown and Blue Levels, literal and inferential comprehension are assessed by means of textual, functional, and recreational reading passages followed by questions.

Reading Rate   This subtest, which is at the Brown Level only, assesses skill in reading easy material quickly.

Scanning and Skimming   This subtest is at the Blue Level only. There are two parts to the subtest. The first measures skill in scanning an article or chapter for specific information. In the second part, students must extract both general and specific information from an article in a short period of time.

Fast Reading   Used at the Blue Level only, this subtest measures skill in reading easy material quickly with comprehension.

SCORES

The SDRT is both norm referenced and criterion referenced. It can be used to assess a pupil's performance relative to the performance of others, and it can be used to pinpoint individual pupils' strengths and weaknesses in specific reading skills.

Students respond either in the test booklets or on machine-readable answer sheets. The test can, therefore, be either hand scored or machine scored. Six kinds of scores can be obtained; which scores are useful depends on the purpose for which the test has been administered.

Raw scores are obtained for each subtest and can be transformed into "Progress Indicators," percentile ranks, stanines, grade equivalents, and scaled scores. Progress Indicators are criterion-referenced scores, whereas the other four scores are norm referenced. Progress Indicators are + or − indications as to whether a pupil achieved a predetermined cutoff score in a specific skill domain; they show whether a pupil demonstrates mastery of specific skills impor-

---

1. The cloze procedure is a technique in which words are omitted from a sentence. To close the sentence correctly, the student must comprehend the story. Many programmed texts use a cloze format. The modified cloze format used in the SDRT gives the student a choice of several words, as illustrated below.

Elephants are well known as animals that never forget. But Henry was a strange elephant who, unlike other elephants, always _____ things. (a) wanted (b) forgot (c) remembered (d) liked

tant to the various stages in the process of learning to read effectively. The manual reports that

> . . . in setting the Progress Indicator cutoff scores, the SDRT authors were guided by the relative importance of each skill to the reading process, by the location of these skills in the developmental sequence, and by the performance of students at different achievement levels on the items measuring these skills. (Karlsen & Gardner, 1985, p. 13)

The manual for each level of the SDRT includes an appendix that lists specific instructional objectives assessed by each level of the test.

The norm-referenced scores obtained by administering the SDRT can be used for a variety of purposes. The authors suggest that comparisons to national norms be made using percentile ranks, stanines, or normal curve equivalents. Detailed procedures for the use of stanines to group students for instructional purposes are included in the manuals. Scaled scores, because they are comparable across both grades and levels, are most useful in evaluating pupil growth and in interpreting the performance of pupils who are tested out of level (for example, the scores of a fifth grader who has taken the Red Level).

A number of reports can be generated from the SDRT by making use of the publisher's computer-scoring service. Examiners can obtain an Individual Diagnostic Report, which contains a detailed analysis of the performance of a single pupil. They can also obtain a Class Summary Report. This report shows the average scores earned by the pupils on each of the subtests. It also provides an analysis of skill development for the class by indicating the number of students in the class who obtained a Progress Indicator of + and the number who obtained a Progress Indicator of −. Examiners can obtain a Master List Report, which consists of a listing of scores for all students in a class. They can obtain a Parent Report, classified specifically for sending test results home to parents. Or they can obtain a Pupil Item Analysis, showing the raw scores earned by a particular student on each subtest and cluster, as well as the student's response to each item.

NORMS

In selecting the standardization sample for the SDRT, the authors used a stratified random-sampling technique. Socioeconomic status, school-system enrollment, and geographic region were the stratification variables. School-system data were obtained from the U.S. Office of Education's 1970 census tapes. The tapes were used to generate a random sample of 3,000 school districts. A composite socioeconomic-status index for each system was determined by weighting family income twice and averaging it with the median years of parental schooling. Age and sex were not controlled in standardizing the SDRT.

School districts within each of the stratified cells were invited to participate in standardization of the test. A random sample of consenting districts within each cell was selected. The SDRT was standardized during the fall of 1983 and spring of 1984. Thirty-three school systems participated in the fall standardization, and forty-eight participated in the spring standardization. The test was standardized on about 30,000 students in grades 2 through 12 in the fall; it was standardized on about 34,000 students in grades 1 through 12 in the spring.

RELIABILITY

Two kinds of reliability data are provided for the SDRT. Data on internal consistency are provided for all but the speeded subtests. Data on alternate-form reliability are reported for the speeded subtests. All but two of the internal-consistency coefficients exceed .80. The reliability of the Auditory Vocabulary subtest is .79 at grade 2 and .76 at grade 3. Alternate-form reliabilities for the rate measures are generally lower. These range from .66 to .78.

VALIDITY

Data are provided on content validity and criterion-related validity. The authors state that the test's content validity, like the content validity of any other measure of academic achievement, must be based on an evaluation of the extent to which the test content reflects local curricular content. Criterion-related validity was established by correlating performance on subtests of the SDRT with performance on their counterparts on the Stanford Achievement Test. The correlations range from .67 to .88 at the Red Level, from .68 to .87 at the Green Level, from .69 to .87 at the Brown Level, and from .64 to .74 at the Blue Level.

SUMMARY

The Stanford Diagnostic Reading Test is a group-administered device that is both norm referenced and criterion referenced. The device was exceptionally well standardized and is reliable enough to be used in pinpointing specific domains of reading in which pupils demonstrate skill-development strengths and weaknesses. Validity for the SDRT, as for any achievement measure, must be judged relative to the content of local curricula.

Diagnostic Reading Scales

*T*he Diagnostic Reading Scales (Spache, 1981) are a series of individually administered tests designed to provide standardized evaluations of oral and silent reading skills and of auditory comprehension. The tests consist of three lists of words to be recognized, twenty-two reading passages of graduated difficulty, and twelve supplementary word-analysis and phonics tests. The scales can be used with students in grades 1 through 7 and, according to the author, with junior and senior high school students who are functioning below normal in reading.

The word lists are administered as an assessment of a student's skill in pronouncing words in isolation. According to the author, the word lists serve three purposes: to estimate the instructional level of reading, to reveal the student's methods of word attack and word analysis, and to evaluate sight vocabulary. The reading passages are used to assess literal and inferential comprehension of material read orally or silently by the student and of material read to the student. The author states that the passages are useful in identifying suitable reading material for the student and in determining the nature and extent of the student's reading errors, reading speed, and reading potential.

The twelve word-analysis and phonics tests cover initial consonants, final consonants, consonant di-graphs, consonant blends, initial-consonant substitution, initial-consonant sounds recognized auditorily, auditory discrimination, short and long vowel sounds, vowels with *r*, vowel diphthongs and digraphs, common syllables, and blending. The subtests are designed to give the examiner a detailed analysis of phonic knowledge and word-analysis skills. Total administration time for the Diagnostic Reading Scales is about 60 minutes, and all student responses are oral.

SCORES

The word lists are administered to determine which of the several reading passages should be used as a starting point for the assessment of oral, silent, and auditory comprehension skills. The author states that on the basis of a pupil's score in oral reading the teacher can ascertain the pupil's instructional level—that is, the level at which instruction in reading should be given. Performance in comprehension of passages read silently is used to ascertain the pupil's independent level, which is the grade level at which the pupil can read recreational and supplementary reading materials. Performance in auditory comprehension is used as an assessment of the pupil's potential reading level.

As is the case with most diagnostic reading tests, the most valuable information is obtained by careful analysis of the kinds of errors the pupil makes in oral reading and on the six supplementary subtests.

NORMS

The Diagnostic Reading Scales were originally standardized in 1963 on an unspecified population of students. The test was revised in 1972 and again in 1981. As part of each revision, the author conducted a study and used the results of pupils' performance to rearrange the items on the test. The 1981 version of the Diagnostic Reading Scales is not identical to the 1963 edition. As part of revising the scales, in 1981 the test was given to a sample of 534 students. In a section of the manual entitled "Validity," the author describes the 534 students as having attended grades 1 through 8 in sixty-six school districts in thirty-two states. He says that there were approximately equal numbers of males and females and a representative number of black and Hispanic students. The norms are not described enough that a user would know the nature of those to whom an examinee is being compared.

RELIABILITY

Data on reliability of the Diagnostic Reading Scales are reported in a separate technical manual. With minor exceptions, reliability data are on earlier versions of the test. The author does say that alternate-form reliabilities were computed on an unspecified number of students in grades 1 through 8. He does not report correlation coefficients by grade level but says they averaged .89.

Data on test-retest reliability are reported only for grades 1 and 2, and only for the word-analysis and phonics subtests. Data are on an unspecified number of students. Correlation coefficients ranged from .09 (initial-consonant sounds recognized auditorily) to .93. Only half of the twenty-four coefficients exceed .80.

Data on internal consistency are reported only for an unspecified number of students in grades 1 and 2. All but three of the twenty-four coefficients reported exceed .80. No data on reliability are reported for students in upper grades. The author argues that these students earn a ceiling too easily.

VALIDITY

Much space in the technical manual is devoted to a discussion of validity. Again, nearly all data reported are on the 1963 and 1972 editions of the test. Only one validity study is reported on the 1981 scale. The author reports that test scores are higher with increases in grade level, teacher estimates of reading level, level of classroom reader, and scores on reading tests. The latter information is derived from a number of different reading tests. Data on validity are not convincing. The author reports that the sample on whom validity and reliability data were based included more older than younger students and an excessive number of cases scoring at the high end of the scale.

SUMMARY

The Diagnostic Reading Scales are an individually administered series of scales designed to assess oral and silent reading skills and auditory comprehension. The manual includes normative tables but does not provide an adequate description of the nature of the group on whom the test was standardized. A separate technical manual includes data on reliability and validity, although most of this information is on earlier versions of the test. Evidence for the technical adequacy of the 1981 scales is very limited. At best, the scales are useful for screening purposes.

Woodcock Reading Mastery Tests–Revised

*T*he Woodcock Reading Mastery Tests–Revised (Woodcock, 1987) is a battery of six individually administered tests used to assess development of readiness skills, basic reading skills, and reading-comprehension skills in students from kindergartners to college seniors and in adults up to 75 years of age. The test is also used in clinical assessment and diagnosis, planning of programs, and research. The complete materials for the test are contained in an easel kit similar to the easel kit illustrated earlier for the Peabody Individual Achievement Test (Figure 20.2). There are two forms of the test, G and H. Form G includes all six tests; Form H includes only the four reading-achievement tests (it does not include the readiness measures). The six tests that make up the WRMT-R battery are described below.

Visual-Auditory Learning   In a miniature learning-to-read task, the student is required to associate unfamiliar visual stimuli (rebuses) with familiar oral words and to translate sequences of rebuses into sentences. The test is the same as the Visual-Auditory Learning subtest of the Woodcock-Johnson Psychoeducational Battery.

Letter Identification   This test assesses skill in naming or pronouncing (the student is permitted to do either) letters of the alphabet. Both upper- and lowercase letters are used, and the letters are presented in a variety of type styles.

Word Identification   This test measures skill in pronouncing words in isolation.

Word Attack   This test assesses skill in using phonic and structural analysis to read nonsense words.

Word Comprehension   Three subtests make up this test: Antonyms, Synonyms, and Analogies. In the Antonyms subtest, the student must read a word and then provide a word that means its opposite; in the Synonyms subtest, words with similar meanings to the stimulus words must be provided. In the Analogies subtest, the student must read a pair of words, ascertain the relationship between the two words, read a third word, and then supply a word that has the same relationship to the third word as exists between the initial pair of words read. Separate scores can be obtained for comprehension of words in different content areas: General Reading Vocabulary, Science-Mathematics Vocabulary, Social Studies Vocabulary, and Humanities Vocabulary.

Passage Comprehension   This test uses a modified cloze procedure. The student's task is to read silently a passage that has a word missing and then tell the examiner a word that could appropriately fill the blank space. The passages are passages drawn from actual newspaper articles and textbooks.

The six tests of the WRMT-R are organized into three clusters. The Readiness Cluster is composed of the Visual-Auditory Learning and Letter Identification tests. The Word Identification and Word Attack tests make up the Basic Skills Cluster. The Word Comprehension and Passage Comprehension tests make up the Reading Comprehension Cluster.

There are several differences between the WRMT-R and the 1973 edition of the tests. A readiness section has been added to the battery, and the Word Comprehension test has been expanded to include three different samples of behavior finding analogies, antonyms, and synonyms. Reading vocabulary is assessed in four content areas, listed previously in the description of the Word Comprehension test. More sample items have been incorporated into the WRMT-R. A Short Scale has been developed that allows only the administration and scoring of the Word Identification and Passage Comprehension tests. Several diagnostic aids have been added, which, in addition to facilitating error analysis, enable the examiner to compare performance on the WRMT-R with performance on either the Goldman-Fristoe-Woodcock Auditory Skills Test or the

Woodcock-Johnson Psychoeducational Battery—Revised. Scoring, procedures for recording scores, and procedures for creating visual displays of score have been simplified.

A special microcomputer-scoring program, AS-SIST, can be used to compute and report all derived scores for the WRMT-R. Also available is a report to parents, which conveys test results, explains student performance, and describes each of the WRMT-R tests.

SCORES

Woodcock (1987) describes three options for interpreting the WRMT-R, four levels of interpretive information for the WRMT-R (or any other test), and nine kinds of derived scores.

The three options for interpreting the WRMT-R are designed to provide differing degrees of precision. At the lowest level, examiners can simply plot raw scores from the WRMT-R, the Goldman-Fristoe-Woodcock Auditory Skills Test Battery, and the Woodcock-Johnson Psychoeducational Battery on an Instructional Level Profile and/or on three diagnostic profiles. When the Instructional Level Profile has been completed, approximate grade equivalents and instructional ranges can be observed, and strengths and weaknesses across the WRMT-R and subtests of the other two tests can be seen. An Instructional Level Profile from the WRMT-R Test Record is shown in Figure 21.3. At a middle level of interpretation, the examiner goes to the norm tables and gets the total reading score as well as percentile ranks and relative performance indexes (RPIs) for each of the subtests. At the highest level, the examiner uses the norm tables to get exact grade equivalents, age equivalents, a variety of standard scores, confidence bands for RPIs, and percentile ranks.

Woodcock describes four levels of interpretive information for the WRMT-R. The examiner can analyze errors in the responses that a student makes to individual items; the examiner can describe the student's level of development by reporting such derived scores as grade equivalents and age equivalents; the examiner can describe the quality of the student's performance by reporting Relative Performance Indicators, difference scores, or instructional ranges; or the examiner can report the student's standing in a group by reporting percentile rank or standard scores.

Many derived scores can be obtained for the WRMT-R. Some (for example, W-scores) are complex, and a reasonably sophisticated knowledge of measurement is required to understand them.[2] We have chosen not to describe those scores here. The kinds of scores obtained from the WRMT-R include grade equivalents, age equivalents, relative performance indexes, instructional ranges, percentile ranks, and standard scores. The RPI provides an index of a student's expected quality of performance on tasks of a given level of difficulty. According to Woodcock (1987),

> An RPI is like the index used with the Snellen Chart to describe visual acuity. On the Snellen Index, 20/20 vision indicates a person can distinguish at a distance of 20 feet what people with normal vision can see at 20 feet. A person with 20/100 vision has to be at 20 feet to see what people with normal vision can see at 100 feet. (p. 40)

RPIs are used to indicate percentage mastery and therefore are indicative of quality of performance rather than standing within a group.

Instructional range is designed to provide a guide to the level of instruction that would be appropriate for a student. The range includes that interval between instructional activities or materials that are too easy and those that are too difficult and therefore frustrating. Instructional levels are indicated by the shaded areas in Figure 21.3.

In addition to obtaining scores, examiners can complete a number of visual profiles of scores: the Instructional Level Profile noted above, a Percentile

---

2. See Appendix 6 for a general description of Rasch scaling and item-response theory.

FIGURE 21.3 **Instructional Level Profile from the WRMT-R Test Record**

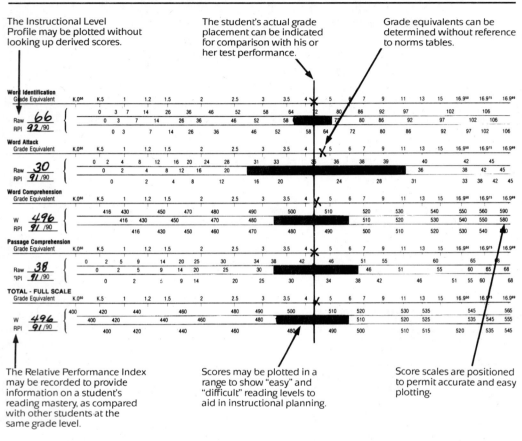

The Instructional Level Profile may be plotted without looking up derived scores.

The student's actual grade placement can be indicated for comparison with his or her test performance.

Grade equivalents can be determined without reference to norms tables.

The Relative Performance Index may be recorded to provide information on a student's reading mastery, as compared with other students at the same grade level.

Scores may be plotted in a range to show "easy" and "difficult" reading levels to aid in instructional planning.

Score scales are positioned to permit accurate and easy plotting.

SOURCE: Richard W. Woodcock, *Woodcock Reading Mastery Test–Revised*. (Circle Pines, MN: American Guidance Service, 1987).

Rank Profile, and three diagnostic profiles (a Diagnostic Readiness Profile, a Diagnostic Basic Skills Profile, and a Diagnostic Comprehension Profile). Completion of these profiles enables examiners, teachers, and parents to visualize the strengths and weaknesses of the student's performance on the six tests and to compare the student's performance on the WRMT-R with his or her performance on the Goldman-Fristoe-Woodcock and the Woodcock-Johnson Psychoeducational Battery.

NORMS

The WRMT-R was standardized on 6,089 students in sixty geographically diverse communities. Subjects were randomly selected using a sampling design stratified on the basis of geographic region, community size, sex, race, and ethnic origin. The college sample was stratified on the basis of type of college (public, private, university, two-year college, four-year college), in addition to the above factors. The adult sample was stratified on the basis of number of years of education, occupational status, and occupational type, in addition to the core factors noted above. A table in the manual compares the proportion of the sample in each of the stratification categories with the proportion of the U.S. population in that category. Standardization data were gathered throughout the school year, and continuous-year norms are provided.

RELIABILITY

Data are provided on the internal-consistency reliability of the WRMT-R. These data are for all tests and clusters and are provided separately for grades 1, 3, 5, 8, and 11 and for college and adult groups. Reliabilities for clusters exceed .80; in all but three cases they exceed .90. With one exception, reliabilities for the six tests exceed .80; most exceed .90. There are no data on the test-retest reliability of the WRMT-R.

VALIDITY

Several kinds of validity are discussed in the manual for the WRMT-R. The case for content validity is made on the basis of expert judgment and the Rasch scaling procedures used in constructing the test. Users of the test will have to make judgments about the extent to which the test measures mastery of the content of their curriculum. Evidence for concurrent validity is good. Data are presented showing correlations of the WRMT-R with the reading subtests of the Woodcock-Johnson Psychoeducational Battery. Correlations among subtests measuring similar behaviors are high. There is good evidence for the convergent validity of the scale; that is, performance on specific tests correlates more highly with performance on other measures of similar reading behaviors than with performance on measures of different reading behaviors.

SUMMARY

The Woodcock Reading Mastery Tests-Revised, a revision of a scale that was originally published in 1973, includes six separate measures of pupil skill development in reading and reading comprehension. The WRMT-R has expanded and updated norms and now includes a readiness component. The test is also normed on college students and adults. The several new diagnostic aids that have been developed appear to be useful. The test is appropriately and adequately normed, and evidence for internal-consistency reliability is good. There are no data on test-retest reliability. Evidence for validity of the tests is good.

MEASURES OF READING COMPREHENSION

Test of Reading Comprehension

*T*he Test of Reading Comprehension: Revised Edition (TORC) (Brown, Hammill, & Wiederholt, 1986) is an individually administered, norm-referenced measure of students' understanding of written language. The authors of the TORC identify six purposes for using the test:

(1) To determine a student's relative reading comprehension status in relation to a normative group;

(2) to determine how well a student or group of students can comprehend written language when a program-independent measure is needed; (3) to examine strengths and weaknesses from one subtest to another for diagnostic purposes; (4) to compare relative performance in reading-comprehension tasks with other conceptual abilities when appropriate measures are available; (5) to compare TORC performances with other language behaviors to determine relative strengths

and weaknesses; and (6) to investigate behaviors related to reading comprehension and to study the construct itself. (p. 15)

The test may, on occasion, be given to groups of three to five students; it is appropriate for use with students of ages 7-0 to 17-11. In developing the TORC, the authors set out to construct a measure of comprehension of written language that was independent of any instructional program; to use multiple formats or styles to assess reading comprehension; to minimize the likelihood of obtaining correct responses solely as a result of general information, memorization, or guessing; to use a silent rather than an oral reading format; and to avoid overuse of vocabulary from any specific content area. For the most part, they were successful. The authors clearly state that any results obtained from this measure are to be treated as instructional hypotheses to be confirmed through more individualized, behaviorally focused strategies.

The TORC is made up of eight subtests. Four of the subtests are combined to form a General Reading Comprehension Core, three are measures of content-specific vocabularies, and one subtest is a measure of the student's skill in reading directions in schoolwork. The names of the subtests and a brief description of each follow.

General Vocabulary The student is required to read three stimulus words that are related in some way and then select from four response words the two that are related to the three stimulus words.

Syntactic Similarities The student is given five sentences and must select the two that are most closely related in meaning.

Paragraph Reading The student is required to read paragraphs and then answer five multiple-choice questions for each paragraph. The questions differ in their demands: One question requires the selection of a "best title" for the paragraph, two require the literal recall of story details, one requires

the inference of meaning, and one requires the making of a negative inference.

Sentence Sequencing Each item consists of five randomly ordered sentences, which the student must order in such a way that they make a meaningful story.

Mathematics Vocabulary The format of this subtest is identical to that of the General Vocabulary subtest. The words are taken from recent mathematics textbooks.

Social Studies Vocabulary The format of this subtest is identical to that of the General Vocabulary subtest. The words are taken from recent social studies textbooks.

Science Vocabulary The format of this subtest is identical to that of the General Vocabulary subtest. The words are taken from recent science textbooks.

Reading the Directions of Schoolwork This subtest is designed for younger and remedial readers. The student must read a set of directions and then carry them out on an answer sheet.

The TORC contains a relatively limited number of items for a measure spanning a ten-year age range. Six of the subtests contain twenty-five items each, the Sentence Sequencing subtest contains ten items, and the Paragraph Reading subtest contains six reading passages, each of which is followed by five questions. Item selection was based on the performance of 120 elementary school students in grades 2 through 6 in one school district in Austin, Texas. The authors used the performance of these students to reduce the test from an initial 358 items to the 185 items that make up the test.

SCORES

Raw scores, percentiles, and standard scores may be obtained for each subtest. In addition, an overall

Reading Comprehension Quotient may be calculated. Standard scores have a mean of 10 and a standard deviation of 3. The Reading Comprehension Quotient is obtained by adding the standard scores for the General Vocabulary, Syntactic Similarities, Paragraph Reading, and Sentence Sequencing subtests. These four subtests comprise the General Reading Comprehension Core. The Reading Comprehension Quotient has a mean of 100 and a standard deviation of 15.

The TORC was standardized on a sample of 2,492 children from thirteen states. The Revised Edition of this test is basically an expanded-norm edition; that is, the authors added to the original 1978 normative sample by obtaining data on an unspecified number of additional students. These data were obtained by getting users of the scale to submit twenty protocols each and by sending a team of personnel into selected areas to administer the TORC. The authors do not indicate the extent to which this approach resulted in a representative sample. They do provide data on sex, residence (urban, rural), and geographic area for students in the normative sample, and they demonstrate that on two of these three factors (sex and residence) the sample distribution closely matches the population as characterized by census data. No data are provided on the race or socioeconomic status of those who participated in the standardization of this test. Also, no data are provided on the crosstabulations of sample characteristics. For example, data are not provided on the number of females who were from urban environments in the West. These data are necessary to make judgments about the representativeness of the norm group.

RELIABILITY

The authors of the TORC provide data on two kinds of reliability: internal consistency and test-retest. Internal-consistency coefficients were computed for each of the individual subtests at each age. Eight percent of those coefficients exceed .90, and all but one of the ninety-six coefficients exceed the desirable standard of .80.

VALIDITY

The authors have not done a convincing job of demonstrating that the TORC is, indeed, a measure of reading comprehension. First, the rationale for inclusion of the eight subtests as measures of reading comprehension is not convincing. This is especially true for the subtests that measure content-specific vocabulary in mathematics, social studies, and science. Also, the results of five criterion-related validity studies reported by the authors raise some major questions. The investigations were conducted with very specific samples (for example, fifty-four boys and girls attending second and third grade in Norman, Oklahoma; twenty-eight adolescent girls attending a residential treatment center in Austin, Texas). Sample size ranged from twenty-eight to ninety-four, and performance on the TORC was correlated with performance on other measures of reading, intelligence, mathematics, and language arts. Correlations of TORC subtests with measures of intelligence and measures of mathematics achievement are as high as correlations with other measures of reading, language arts, and reading comprehension.

SUMMARY

The Test of Reading Comprehension is a norm-referenced measure designed to provide an evaluation of students' comprehension of written language. In addition to a Reading Comprehension Quotient, which is based on pupil performance on four subtests, the test provides users with an assessment of pupil performance in content-specific vocabulary and in following the directions of schoolwork. There is some question about the adequacy of the norms. In general, TORC appears sufficiently reliable for making important individual decisions about students, but the extent to which the test measures reading comprehension is uncertain.

CRITERION-REFERENCED TESTING IN READING

The tests we have discussed to this point are norm-referenced tests, which are designed to compare individuals to their peers. Criterion-referenced diagnostic testing in reading is a practice that dates from the late 1960s. Criterion-referenced diagnostic reading tests are designed to analyze systematically an individual's strengths and weaknesses without comparing that individual to others. The principle objective of criterion-referenced tests is to assess the specific skills a pupil has, to determine those skills the pupil does not have, and to relate the assessment to curricular content. Criterion-referenced assessment is tied to instructional objectives, and individual items are designed to assess mastery of specific objectives.

Although all criterion-referenced reading tests are based on task analyses of reading, the particular skills assessed and their sequences differ from test to test. This is because different authors view reading in different ways and see the sequence of development of reading skills differently. For this reason, it is especially important with criterion-referenced tests (as with norm-referenced tests) that teachers pay special attention to the behaviors and sequences of behaviors sampled by the tests.

Because normative comparisons are not made in criterion-referenced assessment, no derived scores are calculated. For that reason, many authors of criterion-referenced tests downplay the importance of reliability for their scales. But reliable assessment is important in criterion-referenced tests. Although we are not concerned with the consistency of derived scores, we are concerned with the consistency of responses to items when all items in the domain are assessed. If a different pattern of item scores is obtained each time an individual takes the test, we begin to question the reliability of the device. Because criterion-referenced devices generally contain relatively limited samples of behavior, it is important that test authors report the consistency with which their tests assess each specific behavior. Test authors can and should report test-retest reliabilities for each item. It is important to note the consistency with which the test samples the domain of possible test items when the domain is not exhausted. When alternate forms of a criterion-referenced test are available, the authors should report correlations between performances on the two forms.

Standardized Reading Inventory

The Standardized Reading Inventory (SRI) (Newcomer, 1986) is an individually administered measure of skill development in oral and silent reading, appropriate for use with students whose reading competence does not exceed the eighth-grade level. The test provides information on both word recognition and reading comprehension and is designed to be used to diagnose the nature of reading difficulties of students who are experiencing reading problems. The author indicates that the test can be administered in 15 to 45 minutes but recommends that users allot 1 hour for testing. Materials for this scale consist of a test manual; a student booklet containing word lists, reading passages, and comprehension questions; and summary/record sheets. After reading the word lists, the student reads passages orally and then silently. There are two forms of the test, Form A and Form B.

In administering the SRI, the examiner first asks the student to read the words from the graded word list that is two grades below the student's estimated reading level. If the student misreads three or more words, the examiner drops down to an easier list. The student continues reading words in isolation until three or more words on a list are misread. The student then is required to read passages, beginning with the passage that corresponds to the highest grade level at which the student attained an independent level in reading the word lists. The student reads each passage aloud, while the examiner records errors in oral reading. The student then reads the same passages silently and responds to a set of comprehension questions for each passage.

SCORES

The SRI is scored in such a way that examiners obtain an indication of whether word-recognition skills and reading comprehension are at an independent, instructional, or frustration level. An instructional level is defined as a score that is plus or minus one standard deviation from the mean; an independent level is defined as a score that is more than one standard deviation above the mean; and a frustration level is defined as a score that is more than one standard deviation below the mean. In practice, for word-recognition skills, an independent level is the level at which the student misreads fewer than two words; the instructional level is the level at which two words are misread; the frustration level is the level at which the student misreads three or more words. For the oral reading passages, there are specified criteria for independent, instructional, and frustration levels for both word recognition and comprehension.

In developing the SRI, the author first compiled lists of new words that are included as typical words in five popular basal reading series: Scott Foresman Basics in Reading, Houghton Mifflin Reading Series, HBJ Bookmark Reading Program, Macmillan Reading Series, and Ginn Reading Series. Words presented at the same grade level in two or more reading series were designated as key words, and these words were then used in writing the reading passages. The author states, "In composing the passages, the total number of words, total number of sentences, and the number of words per sentence were held relatively constant for the forms of the passages at each grade level; but the number of key words and novel words varied" (p. 6).

NORMS

There are no norms for the SRI. The author argues that the SRI is a criterion-referenced test that is standardized. She uses Hammill's definition of standardized assessment instruments as instruments that possess "(a) set administration procedures, (b) objective scoring criteria, and (c) specified guidelines for interpreting results" (Newcomer, 1986, p. 1).

RELIABILITY

Three types of reliability are presented for the SRI: test-retest, alternate form, and interscorer. Test-retest reliability data are based on the performance of thirty third-grade students in a single school district at levels 2, 3, and 4 of the SRI. The test was given twice at an interval of one week. Test-retest reliabilities ranged from .83 for level 2 of Form A to .92 for level 4 of Form B.

Alternate-form reliability was established by correlating performance on Forms A and B for the 288 children who took the test as part of the standardization process. This sample included twenty-four students reading at the preprimer level, twenty-four at the primer level, and thirty each at levels 1 through 8. The students took the test so that the difficulty of the passages could be calibrated. Alternate-form coefficients ranged from .70 to .97 for Word Recognition and from .71 to .96 for Reading Comprehension. For Word Recognition, acceptable levels of reliability were obtained only after the grade-1 level.

To establish interscorer reliability, the author and a colleague scored thirty completed protocols. There was ninety-seven percent agreement for both Word Recognition and Reading Comprehension. The author and a colleague also scored tape-recorded performances of twenty students. Interscorer agreement on the instructional level exceeded 90 percent.

The reliability coefficients for the SRI indicate satisfactory reliability, although the coefficients are based on limited samples of students.

VALIDITY

The author goes to considerable trouble to demonstrate the content validity of the SRI. This is as it should be for criterion-referenced measures. Yet, passages were selected for the test and placed at specified grade levels based on the performances of 288 children from a single school district in suburban Philadelphia. Designated reading levels were established by getting data on the performance of students on end-of-book tests at specified levels and, in some instances, performance on the Stanford Achievement Test.

Criterion-related validity was established by correlating results of performance on the SRI with the results of performance on the reading section of the Stanford Achievement Test. Subjects were thirty fifth graders from a suburban Philadelphia school district. Correlation of the SAT reading score was .74 with the SRI Word Recognition score and .74 with the SRI Reading Comprehension score.

Further evidence for validity of the test is provided: Scores on the SRI increase with age, performance on the test is highly correlated with intelligence, and good readers perform significantly better than poor readers.

SUMMARY

The Standardized Reading Inventory is a criterion-referenced measure of pupil skill development in both oral and silent reading. The test provides users with an assessment of the nature of oral reading errors and of comprehension of material read silently. There are no norms for this test; the author argues that the test is a standardized criterion-referenced measure. Reliability coefficients are variable, so test users must consult the manual with regard to specific ages to determine the test's suitability for various educational decisions. There is good evidence for the validity of the test.

Prescriptive Reading Inventory

*T*he Prescriptive Reading Inventory/ Reading System (PRI/RS) (CTB/McGraw-Hill, 1980) is a criterion-referenced assessment and instruction program, incorporated into a reading system, for use in planning and managing instruction in reading and language arts in grades K through 9. The system is designed to be used by teachers in placing students at appropriate instructional levels, diagnosing specific instructional strengths and weaknesses, prescribing appropriate

materials and activities, and monitoring pupil progress toward mastery of instructional objectives.

The PRI/RS assesses skills in four discrete skill areas of reading and language arts: Oral Language and Oral Comprehension, Word Attack and Usage (including Word Analysis, Vocabulary, and Word Usage), Comprehension (literal, interpretive, and critical), and Reading Applications (Study Skills and Content Area Reading). There are five overlapping levels of the test, intended for use at specific grade levels: A (grades K through 1), B (grades 1 through 2), C (grades 2 through 3), D (grades 4 through 6), and E (grades 7 through 9).

Three kinds of criterion-referenced assessment can be carried out with the PRI/RS. The examiner can conduct a skill-area assessment, a category-objectives assessment, or an instructional-objectives assessment. Skill-area assessments are broad diagnoses of skill mastery in areas such as Vocabulary or Word Analysis. Assessment of category objectives consists of assessment of terminal reading objectives such as sound and symbol correspondence. Examiners also can use the PRI/RS to access mastery of very specific instructional objectives such as mastery of sounds of single consonants. The entire PRI Reading System assesses mastery of 171 objectives across the five levels. Objectives may be assessed at more than one level.

Examiners choose one of two systems when using the PRI/RS: System 1 or System 2. Each of these systems represents a unique approach to reading instruction. "System 1, the graded approach to reading assessment, deals with students' reading abilities in all skill clusters at a particular level. System 2, the multigraded approach to reading assessment, deals with proficiency in a particular skill cluster across several levels" (CTB/McGraw-Hill, 1980, p. 3). System 1 of the PRI Reading System includes three assessment instruments ranging from very broad to very specific. The broadest measure is the Skill-Areas Survey, and the most precise is the Instructional-Objectives Inventory. Midway between these is the Category-Objectives Test. When System 2 is used, the examiner goes through two activities in assessing the student. First, a PRI Reading System Placement Test is given to identify the student's instructional level in each of the skill areas. Then, a Skill Diagnostic Test is administered to ascertain whether the student has mastered specific instructional objectives within the specific skill area.

The PRI/RS is indexed to kits of instructional materials. There are five kits for System 1 and four kits for System 2. The kits include, among other things, a teacher's guide, teacher resource files, tutor activities, student worksheets, mastery tests, and continuous logs.

SCORES

Traditional derived scores such as grade equivalents and age scores are not provided for the PRI. Because the device is criterion-referenced, scores consist of detailed analyses of objectives mastered. Five kinds of reports are used for the purpose of interpreting pupil and class performance on the PRI.

1. *Individual diagnostic maps* show the extent to which a student has mastered specific reading objectives at age and grade level.
2. *Class diagnostic maps* summarize the performance of each pupil in a class on items assessing each of the specific objectives.
3. *Class grouping reports* identify groups of students who share common reading difficulties and who may be grouped together for instructional purposes.
4. *Individual study guides* cross-reference reading objectives assessed in the PRI/RS with page numbers in basal reading series where the objectives are taught.
5. *Program reference guides* cross-reference each basal reading series in its entirety to each of the objectives assessed by the PRI/RS.

This battery is cross-referenced to basal readers. In addition, an *Interpretive Handbook* is provided, which identifies numerous specific instructional exercises that can be used to teach to areas of deficiency.

NORMS

Normative scores can be obtained for the PRI/RS, but basing conclusions on them is relatively risky. Scores on the PRI/RS earned by an unspecified number and kind of students in a norm group were correlated with scores they earned on Form C of the

California Achievement Test (CAT). These correlations for the norm group are used to estimate the scores other students would have earned had they taken the CAT. In addition, the information is for a previous edition of the CAT. We recommend that users restrict themselves to criterion-referenced use of the PRI/RS.

RELIABILITY AND VALIDITY

No data on consistency of student performance are provided for the PRI. The developers do report a study of the validity of the device. The PRI and the reading section of the California Achievement Test were administered to the students who participated in the field testing. This procedure was used in an effort to check the extent to which the performance of the sample of students was comparable to that of a representative national sample. Although no specific data are reported on the relationship of pupil performance on the two tests, the developers stated that no adjustments to the PRI/RS were deemed necessary. Validity rests largely on expert opinion.

There are no data in the manual on the validity of the recommended grouping of students for instructional purposes.

SUMMARY

The Prescriptive Reading Inventory/Reading System is a criterion-referenced assessment and instruction program designed to address mastery of pre-reading behaviors and desired reading behaviors in grades K through 9. Five kinds of reports are available that may be of considerable assistance in pinpointing individual pupil strengths and weaknesses, evaluating individual pupil progress, grouping students for instructional purposes, and evaluating program effectiveness.

The cross-referencing of this system to the most widely used basal readers has two specific advantages: Those who use the test do not have to purchase an entire curriculum, and teachers can readily shift materials for individual students who experience difficulty learning in specific curricula.

COPING WITH DILEMMAS IN CURRENT PRACTICE

There are four major problems in the diagnostic assessment of reading strengths and weaknesses. The first is the problem of curriculum match. Students enrolled in different reading curricula have different opportunities to learn specific skills. Reading series differ in the skills that are taught, in the emphasis placed on different skills, in the sequence in which skills are taught, and the time at which skills are taught. Tests differ in the skills they assess. Thus, it can be expected that pupils studying different curricula will perform differently on the same reading test. It can also be expected that pupils studying the same curriculum will perform differently on different reading tests. Diagnostic personnel must be very careful to examine the match between skills taught in the student's curriculum and skills tested. Most teachers' manuals for reading series include a listing of the skills taught at each level in the series. Many authors of diagnostic reading tests now include in test manuals a list of the objectives measured by the test. At the very least, assessors should carefully examine the extent to which the test measures what has been taught. Ideally, assessors would select specific parts of tests to measure exactly what has been taught. To the extent that there is a difference between what has been taught and what is tested, the test is not a valid measure.

A second problem is the selection of tests that are appropriate for making different kinds of educational decisions. We noted that there are different types of diagnostic reading tests. In making classification decisions, educators must administer tests individually. One may either use an individually administered test or give a group test to one individual. In making instructional planning decisions, the most precise and helpful information will be obtained by giving individually administered criterion-referenced measures. One can, of course, systematically analyze pupil performance on a norm-referenced test, but the approach is difficult and time-consuming. It may also be futile, since norm-referenced tests usually do not contain a sufficient number of items on which to base a diagnosis.

When evaluating individual pupil progress, the assessor must consider carefully the kinds of comparisons he or she wants to make. If one wants to compare pupils to others their age, norm-referenced measures are useful. If, on the other hand, one wants to know the extent to which individual pupils are mastering curriculum objectives, criterion-referenced measures are the tests of choice.

The third problem in the assessment of reading strengths and weaknesses is that there are few technically adequate tests. We have noted that for many norm-referenced reading tests there is no description, or an inadequate description, of the groups on which the tests were standardized. Other tests were inadequately standardized. There is no evidence of the reliability and/or validity of many diagnostic reading tests. The reliability of other tests is not sufficient to allow valid decisions about individuals. Diagnostic personnel should refrain from using technically inadequate measures. At the very least, they must operate with full awareness of the technical limitations of the devices they use.

The fourth problem is one of generalization. Assessors are faced with the difficult task of describing or predicting pupil performance in reading. Yet, reading itself is difficult to describe, being a complex behavior composed of subskills. Those who engage in reading diagnosis will do well to describe pupil performance in terms of specific skills or subskills (such as recognition of words in isolation, listening comprehension, specific word-attack skills, and so on). They should also limit their predictions to making statements about probable performance of specific reading behaviors, not probable performance in reading.

SUMMARY

In this chapter we have reviewed the kinds of behaviors sampled by diagnostic reading tests. Several specific norm-referenced and criterion-referenced tests have been evaluated in terms of the kinds of behaviors they sample and their technical adequacy. Most of the norm-referenced devices clearly lack the technical characteristics necessary for use in making specific instructional decisions. Many do not present evidence of reliability and validity. In fact, some tests (Gates-McKillop-Horowitz, Durrell, and Diagnostic Reading Scales) present the assessor with numerous normative tables for interpreting test data without describing the nature of the normative population.

The criterion-referenced tests described in this chapter are designed to pinpoint skill-development strengths and weaknesses, provide teachers with instructional objectives, and direct teachers to materials that help teach to those objectives. We do not yet have sufficient empirical evidence to judge the extent to which criterion-referenced tests meet their stated objectives. Teachers need to judge for their own purposes the adequacy of the behavior samplings and the sequences of behaviors sampled. The systems still contain many rough spots that need to be smoothed out.

How, then, do teachers and diagnostic specialists assess skill development in reading and prescribe developmental, corrective, or remedial programs? Reliance on scores provided by diagnostic reading tests is indeed precarious. Teachers and diagnostic specialists must rely on the qualitative information obtained in testing. Some tests provide checklists of observed difficulties, and these may be of considerable help in identifying an individual pupil's reading characteristics.

In assessing reading strengths and weaknesses, teachers must first ask themselves what kinds of behaviors they want to assess. Specific subtests of larger batteries may then be used to assess those behaviors. Teachers should choose the subtests that are technically most accurate. Interpretation must be in terms of behaviors sampled rather than in terms of subtest names.

STUDY QUESTIONS

1. For what purpose are diagnostic reading tests given?
2. What are the relative merits and limitations of using criterion-referenced diagnostic reading tests? Of using norm-referenced tests?
3. Several shortcomings have been noted for each of the specific norm-referenced diagnostic reading tests described in this chapter. What shortcomings do most of the tests have in common?
4. Deirdre, a student in Mr. Albert's fifth-grade class, has considerable difficulty reading. Mr. Albert wants to know at what level to begin reading instruction. Given the state of the art in diagnostic testing in reading, describe some alternative ways for Mr. Albert to identify a starting point.
5. You are teaching reading to a third-grade class. The school psychologist assesses one of the children in your class and reports that the child earned a grade score of 1.6 in reading. What additional information would you ask the psychologist to give you?

6. When teachers use criterion-referenced reading tests, they often find that the sequence in which specific individuals learn reading skills differs from the sequence of skills assessed by the test. How might this be explained?
7. It has been argued that norms are more important for screening tests than for diagnostic tests. Why?

ADDITIONAL READING

Buros, O. K. (Ed.). (1968). *Reading tests and reviews.* Highland Park, NJ: Gryphon Press.

Kramer, J. J., & Conoley, J. C. (1992). *Buros eleventh mental measurements yearbook.* Lincoln, NE: University of Nebraska Press.

Salvia, J., & Hughes, C. (1990). *Curriculum-based assessment: Testing what is taught.* New York: Macmillan. (Chapter 6: CBA in reading)

Taylor, B., Harris, L. A., & Pearson, P. D. (1988). *Reading difficulties: Instruction and assessment.* NY: Random House.

Chapter 22

Assessment of Mathematics

*D*iagnostic testing in mathematics is designed to identify specific strengths and weaknesses in skill development. We have seen that all major achievement tests designed to assess multiple skills include subtests that measure mathematics skills. These tests are necessarily global and attempt to assess a wide range of skills. In most cases, the number of items assessing specific math skills is insufficient for diagnostic purposes. Diagnostic testing in mathematics is more specific, providing a detailed assessment of skill development within specific areas.

There are fewer diagnostic math tests than diagnostic reading tests, but math assessment is more clear-cut. Because the successful performance of some mathematical operations clearly depends on the successful performance of other operations (for example, multiplication depends on addition), it is easier to sequence skill development and assessment in math than in reading. Diagnostic math tests generally sample similar behaviors. They sample various contents, mathematical concepts, operations, and applications of mathematical facts and principles.

WHY DO WE ASSESS MATHEMATICS?

There are several reasons to assess mathematics skills. First, we are often interested in evaluating a student's attainments in math. We may use diagnostic tests in mathematics to assess a student's readiness for instruction (in mathematics and other subjects) or to determine eligibility for employment. Second, all public school programs, with the exception of programs for students with profound disabilities, teach mathematical facts and concepts. Thus, teachers need to know if pupils have mastered particular facts and concepts. Diagnostic math tests are intended to provide sufficiently detailed information that teachers and intervention-assistance teams can plan and evaluate instructional programs. Finally, diagnostic math tests are occasionally used to make exceptionality and eligibility decisions. Individually administered tests are usually required for eligibility and placement decisions. Therefore, we often see diagnostic math tests used to establish special learning needs and eligibility for programs for children with learning disabilities in mathematics.

BEHAVIORS SAMPLED BY DIAGNOSTIC MATHEMATICS TESTS

Behaviors sampled by diagnostic math tests have been classified by Connolly, Nachtman, and Pritchett (1976) and are described below.

Content

A number of content areas are assessed by diagnostic math tests. Facts, knowledge, and concepts necessary for the successful performance of mathematical operations and for meaningful applications of math are assessed in each of the following content areas.

Numeration   Diagnostic math subtests assess knowledge of the number system. Items include those that assess identification of quantities and set value, rounding, identification of missing numbers in sequences, and counting.

Fractions   In nearly all cases and especially in tests designed to be used with students beyond fourth grade, understanding of basic concepts about fractions, decimals, and percentages is assessed.

Geometry   Items that assess knowledge of geometry typically measure skill in recognizing specific shapes and, in some cases, understanding of theorems.

Algebra   Some diagnostic math tests include subtests or items designed to assess knowledge and understanding of principles involved in the solution of linear and quadratic equations.

Operations

Subtests and items designed to assess students' skill in carrying out fundamental arithmetic operations include measures of counting, computation, and arithmetic reasoning.

Counting   Items designed to assess skill in counting usually require the student to count dots or objects and to select or write numerals to represent the number of objects counted.

Computation Items and subtests designed to assess computational skills range from those that sample the traditional arithmetic operations of addition, subtraction, multiplication, and division to those that require the student to complete as many as four computational operations in problem-solving tasks. Items designed to assess specific operations generally range from those that require use of the operation in solving word problems to those that require the written solution of relatively complex computational problems.

Arithmetic Reasoning Arithmetic-reasoning subtests require the solution of problems with missing number facts.

Applications

Diagnostic math tests assess students' skills in applying mathematical facts and concepts to the solution of problems. Tasks generally include the following kinds of behavior samplings.

Measurement Items assessing measurement require the recognition and application of common measurement units and the practical application of length, weight, and temperature measures.

Reading Graphs and Tables The application of mathematical skills and concepts may be assessed by requiring the student to read graphs and tables in the solution of problems.

Money and Budgeting The application of mathematical skills and concepts may be assessed by requiring the student to solve money problems. Items include those that assess the extent to which the student can make value judgments about purchasing articles, interpret budgets, and comprehend checks and checking accounts.

Time The application of mathematical facts and concepts to the solution of problems involving time includes test items requiring the student to read clocks and to identify time intervals, holidays, and seasons.

Problem Solving Problem-solving tasks require students to solve story problems that are read to them or that they read themselves. Four kinds of problems are generally included: (1) those requiring only a one-step mathematical operation; (2) those requiring more than one computational operation; (3) those requiring the student to differentiate between essential and nonessential information in solving problems; and (4) those requiring the student to demonstrate logical thinking by solving problems with missing elements.

SPECIFIC DIAGNOSTIC MATHEMATICS TESTS

This chapter reviews four diagnostic mathematics tests: the KeyMath–Revised, the Stanford Diagnostic Mathematics Test, the Test of Mathematical Abilities, and the Diagnostic Mathematics Inventory/Mathematics Systems.

KeyMath–Revised

K eyMath–Revised: A Diagnostic Inventory of Essential Mathematics (KeyMath-R) (Connolly, 1988) is an individually administered, norm-referenced device. The basic testing materials consist of two easels that contain testing items and directions for presenting and scoring items. Four uses are suggested for the test: instructional planning, comparison of students, evaluation of educational progress, and curriculum evaluation.

There are two forms of KeyMath-R (Forms A and B), and each contains 258 items. Total math performance is divided into three areas. The area of Basic Concepts is composed of three subtests: numeration, rational numbers, and geometry. The Operations area consists of addition, subtraction, multiplication, division, and mental computation. The area of Applications contains items assessing measurement, time and money, estimation, interpretation of data, and problem solving. Each subtest is in turn composed of domains, or subtests. There are three or four domains per subtest for a total of 43 domains. For example, the subtest of rational numbers consists of three domains (fractions, decimals, and percents). Written computation is permitted only on some of the subtests in Operations.

SCORES

Both percentiles and standard scores with a mean of 10 and a standard deviation of 3 are available for each subtest. For area and total test performance, six derived scores are provided: standard scores (with a mean of 100 and standard deviation of 15), normal curve equivalents, stanines, percentiles, age equivalents, and grade equivalents. Finally, KeyMath-R provides a rather unusual score for domains. (A domain is a subdivision of a subtest; for example, in the measurement subtest, there are four domains: comparisons, using nonstandard units, using standard units of length and area, and using standard units of weight and capacity.) Domain Performance scores divide student performances into strong (top quartile), average (middle quartiles) or weak (bottom quartile); the usefulness of domain scores for instructional planning is unclear. A computer program is available to convert raw scores and construct profiles.

NORMS

A total of 1,798 students (873 in the fall and 925 in the spring) from kindergarten through eighth grade were tested for the national standardization. The sample was stratified on the basis of geographic region, grade, sex, socioeconomic status (inferred from the educational attainment of the parents), and racial/ethnic status. For each grade, the demographic characteristics of KeyMath-R's sample is compared to the U.S. population. Regional representation is quite close to the census figures although the standardization sample was drawn from only twenty-two locations in sixteen states; Pennsylvania and Texas had the most testing sites (four and three, respectively). Representation by educational attainment is quite close to the national proportions; representation by racial or ethnic group slightly overrepresents minorities, but this overrepresentation should have little, if any, practical effect. Finally, minor differences in the norms of Forms A and B were removed statistically.

RELIABILITY

Alternate-form reliability was estimated by retesting about 70 percent of the students in grades K, 2, 4, 6, and 8 at two- and four-week intervals. However, Connolly does not report estimated reliability by grade; rather, he reports pooled (across-grade) coefficients. Only the total score may be sufficiently reliable for making important educational decisions for students; all subtest and area estimates of reliability are less than .85.

Split-half reliabilities (using all odd-even split and Spearman-Brown correction) were also estimated by grade and age.[1] For students in kindergarten through the second grade, total scores are consistently reliable enough to make decisions for individuals; area subtests fluctuate so the test user must determine if a particular age-area combination is sufficiently reliable for interpretation. After second grade, area scores have acceptable reliability, and total scores have excellent reliability; however, because basal and ceiling rules were applied to the test scores, the obtained split-half estimates are likely to be inflated.

A third method of estimating reliability based on item-response theory was used. The results of this analysis are essentially the same as those obtained using split-half estimates.

1. We believe that the reliability estimates based on age are somewhat misleading because several age groups are contained within any grade. Consequently, the range of ability would likely be extended.

No reliability data are provided for domain scores. No stability coefficients are reported, although stability can be inferred from the alternate-form reliability coefficients.

VALIDITY

Little evidence of construct validity is presented. What is offered is a demonstration of mean-score progressions from grade to grade. No evidence of concurrent validity is presented. However, for most achievement tests, these indexes of validity are less important than evidence of content validity. Limited evidence for KeyMath-R's content validity comes from the careful development of a table of specifications to guide item development. As is always the case, however, test users should inspect the test's content to make sure that it conforms to the curriculum followed by the students who are being assessed.

SUMMARY

From its title and claims made in its manual, Key-Math-R is intended as a diagnostic test. The standardization of the test appears to be generally adequate. Before third grade, only the total score is sufficiently reliable for diagnostic purposes; for third grade and later, area and total scores are sufficiently reliable. Because of the low reliabilities of subtests and the absence of reliability information for domains, users should avoid making inferences about a student's instructional strengths and weaknesses based on subtest and domain scores. Of the four uses that are proffered for the test, no evidence of KeyMath-R's validity for instructional planning, evaluation of educational progress, or curriculum evaluation is presented. Some evidence for the validity of comparing students' global performances is presented.

Stanford Diagnostic Mathematics Test

*T*he Stanford Diagnostic Mathematics Test (SDMT) (Beatty, Gardner, Madden, & Karlsen, 1985) is the third edition of this group-administered, norm-referenced device intended for use with pupils in the second through twelfth grades. The test comes in four booklets for overlapping levels red, green, brown, and blue (see the first column of Table 22.1, page 502).

The SDMT has two purposes: It serves both as a diagnostic test for classroom teachers and as a test for program evaluation for school administrators. The content is arranged in the following three subtests.

Number System and Numeration The tasks included in this subtest range from identifying numerals and comparing sets to working with fractions and more complex arithmetic operations. The items are noncomputational; they are designed to assess pupils' understanding of numbers and their properties.

Computation This subtest assesses knowledge of the primary facts and algorithms of addition, subtraction, multiplication, and division, as well as methods for solving simple and compound number sentences.

Applications This subtest assesses skill in applying basic mathematical facts and principles. Items range in difficulty from those that require students to solve simple story problems and to select correct models for solving one-step problems to those that require students to solve multiple-step and measurement problems and to read tables and graphs.

SCORES

Content-referenced and norm-referenced scores are available for each subtest, and norm-referenced scores are available for the total test. Content-referenced scores are raw scores (the number correct) and Progress Indicators. Progress Indicators, expressed as + and −, are intended "to identify those pupils who have demonstrated sufficient competence in specific mathematics skills to make satisfactory progress in the regular mathematics program" (Beatty et al., p. 10). The basis of these scores is not made explicit.

Norm-referenced scores consist of percentiles, stanines, normal curve equivalents, grade equivalents, and scaled scores that are standardized across grades. The scaled scores create some problems because "each subtest and total score has its own system" (Beatty et al., p. 12); scaled scores are not equivalent across subtests and totals.

NORMS

Norms are provided for spring and fall testing. However, the characteristics of the sample and specifics of the sampling plan used to select the normative sample are not discussed in the technical manuals.

Data from the school census conducted in 1970 by the U.S. Office of Education were used to stratify schools on the basis of the districts' socioeconomic levels (family income and educational attainment of adults in the community) and pupil enrollments. An unspecified number of SES-by-enrollment cells were created for each grade level, and from four to six school districts per cell were chosen at random to participate. The final sample contains an unspecified number of students from an unspecified number of school districts. The sample does closely approximate the population (as reflected in the 1983 school census) with respect to district size (within 5 percent) and ethnic group (6 percent); however, with respect to geographic area, the fall sample overrepresents the Southeastern United States by 24 percent.

TABLE 22.1   KR-20 Estimates of Internal Consistency of the Subtests of the Stanford Diagnostic Math Test

Level/Grade/Form	Subtest 1	Subtest 2	Subtest 3	Total
Red Level				
Grade 2				
Form G	.86	.88	.82	.94
Form H	.87	.87	.83	.94
Grade 3				
Form G	.84	.84	.82	.92
Form H	.86	.82	.83	.93
Grade 4				
Form G	.74	.82	.78	.89
Form H	.78	.80	.71	.88
Green Level				
Grade 4				
Form G	.85	.91	.88	.95
Form H	.86	.92	.87	.95
Grade 5				
Form G	.86	.91	.88	.95
Form H	.85	.91	.88	.95
Grade 6				
Form G	.84	.86	.88	.93
Form H	.85	.91	.88	.94
Brown Level				
Grade 6				
Form G	.86	.92	.90	.96
Form H	.86	.91	.88	.96
Grade 7				
Form G	.87	.90	.90	.95
Form H	.86	.91	.88	.95
Grade 8				
Form G	.88	.91	.89	.95
Form H	.87	.89	.87	.95
Blue Level				
Grade 8				
Form G	.89	.92	.85	.96
Form H	.89	.92	.86	.96
Grade 9				
Form G	.90	.93	.89	.96
Form H	.90	.92	.87	.96
Grade 10				
Form G	.90	.91	.87	.96
Form H	.90	.91	.87	.96
Grade 11				
Form G	.90	.92	.88	.96
Form H	.90	.91	.88	.96
Grade 12				
Form G	.91	.92	.87	.96
Form H	.91	.92	.89	.96

RELIABILITY

KR-20 estimates of internal consistency are presented for all combinations of subtests and totals, forms and grades. These values are shown in Table 22.1. For the total score, only the reliability coefficients for grade 4 fail to exceed .90. For the individual combinations of form, grade, and subtest, the eighty-four KR-20s are lower: Four coefficients are less than .80; fifty coefficients are less than .90; and the remaining thirty equal or exceed .90. Thus, most of the subtests are not sufficiently reliable for use in making important educational decisions.

No stability data are presented, and no data are presented on the reliability of Progress Indicators.

VALIDITY

The absence of a description of how items were selected or developed makes evaluation of the SDMT's content validity difficult. The content validity, as with any achievement test, depends on the match between curriculum and test; test users themselves must evaluate the content validity.

Limited evidence of concurrent validity is presented. The subtests and total of the SDMT are highly correlated with the corresponding subtests and total of the Stanford Achievement Test in grades 2 through 8; rs range from .64 to .89. For the upper grades, the authors report only the correlation of the total scores ($r = .84$).

Finally, no evidence is presented to show that Progress Indicators are valid. Evidence is presented to show that the SDMT correlates with the Otis-Lennon School Ability Test, but it is not clear why these correlations would establish the validity of the SDMT as a diagnostic achievement test.

SUMMARY

The Stanford Diagnostic Mathematics Test is a group-administered achievement test intended for use as a diagnostic test by classroom teachers and as a test for program evaluation by school administrators. The norms are inadequately described. The subtests lack sufficient reliability for the SDMT to be used as a diagnostic tool. Its validity for use in program evaluation will depend on its relevance to the particular program being evaluated.

Test of Mathematical Abilities

*T*he Test of Mathematical Abilities (TOMA) (Brown & McEntire, 1984) is a norm-referenced device intended for use with students in grades 3 through 12 or between the ages of 8-6 and 18-11. The TOMA provides information about students' skills in computation and in solving word problems, as well as about attitudes toward mathematics, mathematical vocabulary, and general cultural application of information. It is intended to identify students who are significantly ahead of or behind their agemates in mathematical ability, to determine strengths and weaknesses of the students, to document progress, and to serve as a useful research tool. Four of the subtests may be group administered; general information must be individually administered. The 107 test items are grouped into the following five subtests.

Attitude Toward Math The fifteen items in this subtest are based on the Estes Attitude Scales. Students use a three-point scale to rate their feelings about mathematics

Vocabulary The student must define twenty terms in writing.

Computation Students solve twenty-five problems in their answer booklets.

General Information   Each of the thirty questions in this subtest requires an oral response to "cultural-social-practical applications of mathematics."

Story Problems   Students solve seventeen word problems in their answer booklets.

Scores

Derived scores are reported by ages (half years from 8-0 to 10-0, then one-year intervals from 100 to 18-11), not by grades. Standard scores have a mean of 10 and a standard deviation of 3. A math quotient is obtained by adding the standard scores from each subtest. Math quotients have a mean of 100 and a standard deviation of 15. Percentile ranks, as well as age and grade equivalents, are also available.

Norms

The TOMA was standardized on 1,560 students living in five states. Although five states seems few, the final sample is within 7 percent of the 1980 census proportions for urban-rural residence, race, and region of residence. However, no data are presented for socioeconomic status (education or income) of the parents of the students in the sample.

Reliability

The subtest scores are of considerably greater interest than total scores (which do not seem to us to be readily interpretable). Coefficient alphas for each of the fifty combinations of ten age groups and five subtests ranged from .57 for computation at age 11 to .97 for computation at ages 8-6 to 8-11. Only twelve of the fifty coefficients equaled or exceeded .90. Two studies examined the stability of TOMA. One study used twenty-three normal eleven-year-old students; reliabilities ranged from .71 (Attitude Toward Math) to .81 (General Information). In the second study, learning-disabled students between ages 9 and 17 were tested. However, crossing so many age levels tends to seriously inflate estimates of reliability. (Indeed, for the norming sample, age correlated with test scores about .60.) SEMs (standard errors of measurement) based on internal-consistency estimates are also reported.

Validity

No evidence of content validity is presented. Criterion-related validity was established by correlating the TOMA scores with the math subtests of the PIAT-R and the WRAT-R, as well as with the Key-Math Diagnostic Arithmetic Test. Given these three tests as the criteria, the TOMA subtests of Computation and Story Problems are of particular interest, as their behavior samples are similar. The TOMA Computation correlates .45 with the PIAT-R but is nonsignificant with the WRAT-R. Story Problems correlates .36 with the PIAT-R but .37 with the WRAT-R, despite the fact that there are no word problems on the WRAT-R. None of the criterion measures seems appropriate for Attitude Toward Math. (Indeed, correlations between math attitudes and achievement might better be construed as construct validity.) All of the TOMA subtests correlate modestly with Key-Math-R total scores.

Construct validity was established by showing that the TOMA scores increased with age, that the four subtests requiring cognitive skills were correlated with the WISC-R and the Slosson IQs, and that learning-disabled students earned significantly lower scores than normal students on the TOMA.

Summary

The TOMA is a group-administered and an individually administered norm-referenced test that assesses several aspects of mathematical ability. The quality of the norms is difficult to assess. They appear representative on the dimensions of urban-rural residence, geographic region, and race. No data are presented on social status of the parents of children in the normative sample or on the curricula in which the students were enrolled. The internal-consistency reliability is adequate for screening decisions and occasionally adequate for important educational decisions. Stability is unknown for all but one subtest.

No evidence of content validity is presented, and only limited evidence of criterion-related and construct validity is provided.

Diagnostic Mathematics Inventory/Mathematics Systems

*D*iagnostic Mathematics Inventory/Mathematics Systems (DMI/MS) (Gessell, 1983) is a criterion-referenced assessment and instruction program incorporated into a set of systems for use in mathematics instruction. There are two systems: System 1 is a graded system, and System 2 is an ungraded, objectives-based system. The two systems include identical material packaged in different ways. The systems are used to place students at their instructional level, diagnose specific strengths and weaknesses in mathematics, prescribe appropriate instructional materials and activities, and monitor pupil progress. The test is designed for use with students in grades K-6 through 8-9. The test component is accompanied by an instructional program, but the test is also cross-referenced to a wide range of basal mathematics series.

The DMI/MS is used to provide teachers with an assessment of skill development in four major content areas of mathematics: Whole Numbers, Fractions and Decimals, Measurement and Geometry, and Problem Solving and Special Topics. Materials included with the test provide teachers with a very detailed list of the specific skills assessed in each of these content areas. The areas are divided into twenty-nine categories of objectives, which are then subdivided into eighty-two instructional objectives. The Whole Numbers domain includes an assessment of students' concepts of whole numbers as well as their skill in performing operations using whole numbers. The Fractions and Decimals domain includes an assessment of students' concepts of fractions as well as their skill in performing arithmetic operations using fractions and decimals. The Mathematics and Geometry domain includes items assessing knowledge of metric and customary units of

measurement as well as those assessing geometric concepts and operations. The Problem Solving and Special Topics domain is a set of items assessing the ability to apply mathematics skills to the solution of word problems and problems involving graphs, basic statistics and probability, and prealgebra. The DMI/MS has seven levels: A (grades K-6 through 1-5), B (grades 1-6 through 2-5), C (grades 2-6 through 3-5), D, (grades 3-6 through 4-5), E (grades 4-6 through 5-5), F (grades 5-6 through 6-5) and G (grades 6-6 through 8-9 and up). Content of the DMI/MS was selected based on a review of the content of fourteen basal mathematics series. The DMI/MS is available on computer disks.

SCORES

Scores on the DMI/MS are available in the following five report formats.

Objectives Mastery Report   This report identifies those objectives mastered and not mastered by each student in a class.

Common Error Report   This report, available for individual students and for a class of students, provides information on errors made frequently. It is used by the teacher to identify aspects of instruction that many students are not mastering.

Individual Diagnostic Report   This report, available for individual students, provides a listing of objectives mastered and not mastered as well as an analysis of the common errors made.

Class Grouping Report   This report is a list of the students who demonstrate mastery of each of the objectives in the system.

Estimated Norms Report   This report consists of a set of estimated normative scores for students who took the DMI/MS.

NORMS

Normative scores can be obtained for the DMI/MS, but basing conclusions on them is relatively risky. Scores on the DMI/MS earned by an unspecified number and kind of students in a norm group were correlated with the scores they earned on Form C of the California Achievement Test and Form U of the Comprehensive Tests of Basic Skills. These correlations for the norm group are used to estimate the scores other students would have earned had they taken the CAT or the CTBS. Previous editions of the CAT and CTBS were used in the process of develop-

ing estimated norms. We recommend that users restrict themselves to criterion-referenced use of the DMI/MS.

RELIABILITY AND VALIDITY

The DMI/MS is a criterion-referenced mathematics test. Traditional reliability and validity data are not included in the manuals for the DMI/MS.

SUMMARY

The DMI/MS is one of the most complete diagnostic-prescriptive inventories we have seen. The system can be used to assess pupil mastery of objectives in twenty-nine instructional categories. Objectives are cross-referenced to mathematics textbooks and supplementary materials. The DMI/MS should be extremely useful to teachers and other educational personnel in planning specific individualized educational programs in mathematics.

COPING WITH DILEMMAS IN CURRENT PRACTICE

There are three major problems in the diagnostic assessment of mathematical skills. The first problem is the recurring issue of curriculum match. There is considerable variation in math curricula. This variation means that diagnostic math tests will not be equally representative of all curricula or even appropriate for some commonly used ones. As a result, great care must be exercised in using diagnostic math tests to make various educational decisions. Assessment personnel must be extremely careful to note the match between test content and curriculum. This should involve far more than a quick inspection of test items by someone unfamiliar with the specific classroom curriculum. For example, a diagnostician could inspect the teacher's manual to ensure that the test assesses only material that has been taught and that there is reasonable correspondence between the relative emphasis placed on teaching the material and testing the material. To do this, the diagnostician might have to develop a table of specifications for the math curriculum and compare test items to that table. However, once a table of specifications has been developed for the curriculum, a better procedure would be to select items from a criterion-referenced system to fit the cells in the table exactly.

The next problem is selecting an appropriate test for the type of decision that needs to be made. School personnel are usually required to use individually administered norm-referenced devices in classification decisions. Decisions about a pupil's eligibility for special services, however, need not be based on detailed information about the pupil's strengths and weaknesses, as provided by diagnostic tests; diagnosticians are interested in a pupil's relative standing. In our opinion, the best achievement survey tests are subtests of group-administered tests. A practical solution is not to use a diagnostic math test for eligibility decisions but to administer individually a subtest from one of the better group achievement tests.

The third problem is that most of the diagnostic tests in mathematics do not test a sufficiently detailed sample of facts and concepts (although the DMI/MS may be an exception). Consequently, one must generalize from a student's performance on the items tested to his or her performance on the items that are not tested. The reliabilities of the subtests of diagnostic math tests are often not high enough for educators to make such a generalization with any great degree of confidence. As a result, these tests are not too useful in assessing readiness or strengths and weaknesses in order to plan instructional programs. We believe that the preferred practice in diagnostic testing in mathematics is for teachers to develop criterion-referenced achievement tests that exactly parallel the curriculum being taught.

SUMMARY

In this chapter we have reviewed the kinds of behaviors sampled by diagnostic mathematics tests and have evaluated the most commonly used tests in terms of the kinds of behaviors they sample and their technical adequacy. The four tests reviewed in this chapter are designed to provide teachers and diagnostic specialists with specified information on those math skills that pupils have and have not mastered. Compared to diagnostic testing in reading, diagnostic testing in math puts less emphasis on scores.

The tests described in this chapter differ in their technical adequacy for use in making instructional decisions for students. Knowledge of pupil mastery of specific math skills gained from administration of one or more of the tests, along with knowledge of the general sequence of development of math skills, can help teachers design curricular content for individual students.

STUDY QUESTIONS

1. Identify four ways a teacher can interpret the performance of a pupil on Key-Math-R.

2. The Stanford Diagnostic Mathematics Test is both norm-referenced and criterion-referenced. Under what circumstances would a teacher want to use the norms for the SDMT?

3. Given the state of the art in diagnostic assessment in math, identify at least two ways a classroom teacher can pinpoint a starting place for teaching math to an individual pupil.

4. You are teaching arithmetic to a third-grade class. The local school psychologist assesses one of the students in your class and reports that the student earned a grade equivalent of 5-6 in arithmetic. What additional information would you ask the psychologist to give you?

ADDITIONAL READING

Kramer, J. J., & Conoley, J. C. (1992). *Buros eleventh mental measurements yearbook*. Lincoln, NE: University of Nebraska Press.

Reisman, F. (1982). Strategies for mathematics disorders. In C. Reynolds and T. Gutkin (Eds.), *Handbook of school psychology*. New York: Wiley.

Chapter 23

Assessment of Oral Language

*T*here are many ways of defining language. Educators, psychologists, linguists, and speech-language pathologists often have different perspectives on which skills comprise language. Not surprisingly, these differing perspectives on language have resulted in the plethora of language assessment instruments currently on the market, each with an apparently unique (or oblique) method of assessing language. Because of these different perspectives, the nature of oral language can be rather elusive. Indeed, one could argue that certain kinds of tasks touted as oral language tasks actually fall outside of the construct. As you read about the currently available instruments used to assess oral language, bear in mind that theoretical perspectives on the nature of language have been changing dramatically over the past three decades. Similarly, the technology used to assess language has mirrored the theoretical shifts. Yet new instruments do not displace established tests in the way that new theories replace older theoretical models. Rather, the new instruments typically are squeezed into an already crowded field. In order to meaningfully compare instruments arising from quite different theoretical models, the reader must have some understanding of the theoretical underpinnings of each particular instrument. A detailed presentation of a wide variety of theoretical perspectives is beyond the scope of this chapter; instead we present (1) a current definition of language and (2) a brief description of several of the major theories of language that have been adapted to assess oral language.

This chapter was written by Stephen Camarata, Vanderbilt University. Parts of the chapter are based on a previous version prepared by Ed Klein.

Definition of Oral Language

Linguistic Aspects

In a way, the definition of language has come full circle. Language theorists have long been interested in describing the various structural aspects of language (see Bloomfield, 1933). This emphasis was followed by a shift to explanatory mechanisms (for example, Osgood, 1963) and a fragmentation of the study of language with an emphasis on specific dominant components (for example, sentence structure; see Chomsky, 1957). More recently, there has been a return to descriptive kinds of structural analyses (for example, Lahey, 1988). In the current literature, there is a consensus on a broad, cross-disciplinary, basic definition of language: *language can be defined as a code for conveying ideas* (Bloom & Lahey, 1978; Fromkin & Rodman, 1978; Reich, 1986). Although there is some variation, language theorists also propose five basic components to describe the code: phonology, semantics, morphology, syntax, and pragmatics. Figure 23.1 presents a graphic representation of these aspects of language.

In order to examine the basic parts of oral language, consider a typical sentence such as "The girl is running away." At the most basic level, such a sentence includes speech sounds. For example, the word *is* includes a consonant sound /s/ and a vowel sound /I/. This aspect of oral language is defined as *phonology* (see Fromkin & Rodman, 1978). Note that many speech-language pathologists also use the term *articulation* to describe speech sound production. Although there are some subtle differences in how these terms are used (see Ingram, 1976) the term *articulation* is considered to be synonymous with the term *phonology* in this chapter. In addition to speech sounds, the above sentence also contains words (such as *the* and *girl*). The study of word meanings is defined as *semantics*. Although the scope of the term *semantics* can extend beyond individual words to include sentence meaning (see Filmore, 1968), the term generally applies to word-level meaning.

FIGURE 23.1   **Linguistic Aspects of Language**

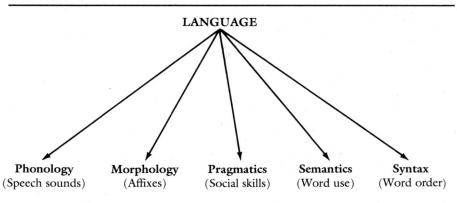

| Phonology | Morphology | Pragmatics | Semantics | Syntax |
| (Speech sounds) | (Affixes) | (Social skills) | (Word use) | (Word order) |

Closer examination of the sentence indicates that some of the words contain affixes (suffixes and/or prefixes). For example, the word *running* includes the root word *run* and the progressive suffix *ing*. The description of such affixes falls within the domain of *morphology*. Morphology also includes auxiliary and copula (connecting) forms of the verb *be* (for example, the auxiliary verb *is*) and function words such as *the* in the sentence example. In addition to containing sounds and words, the example sentence follows a specific word order. This aspect of oral language is known as *syntax;* it includes the rules for arranging words into a sentence. Another name for the combination of syntax and morphology that may be more familiar to educators is *grammar*. The term *grammar* will be used in this chapter to denote a combination of *syntax and morphology*.

Finally, the example sentence occurred within a certain linguistic context (in this case, providing an example within this chapter). The social context in which a sentence occurs is defined as *pragmatics*. To understand how pragmatics applies to oral language, consider the sentence "Can you close the door?" spoken in two different contexts. First, imagine that a professor has spoken this sentence to a student sitting next to an open door. In this example, the sentence clearly is a request to close the door. Second, imagine that a patient is receiving physical therapy, and the therapist is trying to determine the extent of the patient's residual physical capabilities. In this example, the question should be interpreted literally ("are you able to close the door?"). In each of these cases, the phonology, semantics, morphology, and syntax are precisely the same, yet the sentence means different things depending on the context. It should be noted that pragmatics has only recently appeared on the oral language scene (see Prutting & Kirshner, 1987) and there are few standardized assessments available to evaluate this aspect of language. However, it will become increasingly important within assessment, as the ultimate communicative success of oral language users is predicated upon using language correctly within a shifting social context.

Thus, language is defined as a code for conveying ideas—a code that includes phonology, semantics, morphology, syntax, and pragmatics. One of the advantages of adopting this descriptive framework is that widely divergent theoretical models for assessment can be encompassed. For example, for Bloom and Lahey (1978) the term *content* is included in semantics, and *form* can be captured within phonology, morphology, and syntax. Similarly, *sound blending* within an information-processing model (Osgood, 1962) is a part of the phonological domain. Because of this, the definition given above is well-suited to evaluating assessment instruments constructed with different kinds of theoretical underpinnings. Therefore, the following review of standardized assessment instruments will be organized with respect to this basic framework for defining oral language.

Finally, a question to address here is whether this particular definition has any advantages over explanatory or component-specific definitions of language. One can argue that the construct validity of any of the competing models of language is directly related to the degree to which the model captures actual language behavior. The parts of the definition given here represent well-established areas of language inquiry; each of the basic levels of analysis can be applied to any conversation involving oral language. Although many of the tests reviewed herein assess only one aspect of language, some will include tasks designed to assess several aspects of oral language.

Metalinguistic Aspects

A final concept that requires explanation within the definition of oral language, *metalinguistic*, refers to the direct examination of the structural aspects of language. For example, a metalinguistic analysis of the phonological structure of the example sentence reveals that it includes sixteen phonemes. Similarly, a metalinguistic analysis of the syntactic structure of the example sentence indicates that its basic structure is simple-active-declarative. The phonics approach to reading could be considered metalinguistic: The child is taught that each letter represents a sound and these sounds can be compiled into words, which are then compiled into sentences, and so on. Many of the assessment instruments used with older children involve metalinguistic tasks.

Expressive and Receptive Language

Oral language includes both speaking and listening. Speaking can be considered an output modality, whereas listening involves receiving and analyzing input. Therefore, each of the preceding components of language consists of both receptive and expressive aspects. A synonym for receptive language is *comprehension*; a synonym for expressive language is *production*. Many tests assess only one of these modalities. However, it is important to note that although a child can have difficulties with both the expressive and the receptive aspects of oral language, it is not unusual for a child to have problems in only one of these areas (For example, expressive skill problems with normal abilities in the receptive domain). Therefore, performance within one modality does not always predict performance in the other. For example, for a child to have normal comprehension does not necessarily mean that the child will have normal production abilities. Although less common, a child with relatively normal expressive skills may have problems with receptive language. Therefore, a complete oral language assessment will include examination of both modalities. A schematic of these modalities across the basic language domains is presented in Table 23.1.

WHY ASSESS ORAL LANGUAGE?

There are two primary reasons for assessing oral language abilities. First, well-developed language abilities are desirable in and of themselves. The ability to converse and express oneself is a goal of most individuals. Those who have difficulties with various aspects of language are often eligible for special services from speech and language specialists or from special educators (usually special-

TABLE 23.1   **A Model of Language Subskills**

Channels of Communication	Phonology	Morphology and Syntax	Semantics	Pragmatics	Ultimate Language Skill
Reception	Hearing and discrimination of speech sounds	Understanding grammatical structure of language	Understanding vocabulary, meaning, concepts	Understanding speaker's intentions	Understanding spoken language
Expression	Articulation of speech sounds	Using the grammatical structure of language	Using vocabulary, meaning, concepts	Using awareness of social aspects of language	Talking

ists in learning disabilities). Second, various language processes and skills are believed to underlie subsequent development. For example, recent research indicates that difficulties in oral language are related to the incidence of behavior disorders (Camarata, Hughes, & Ruhl, 1988). Similarly, it appears that children with speech and language disabilities are at a much greater risk for learning disabilities (King, Jones, & Lasky, 1982). Finally, there have been a number of studies indicating that *phoneme awareness*, the ability to identify phonemes in words and segment words into their phoneme constituents, is related to subsequent reading competence (see Mann, 1993). Consequently, the identification and subsequent remediation of oral language disorders are believed to have a broad, general, positive effect on personal and academic development.

A HISTORICAL PERSPECTIVE ON ORAL LANGUAGE

As noted earlier, instruments designed to assess oral language have mirrored the shifting theoretical positions on the nature of oral language. At the risk of oversimplifying the evolution of test development, in general it has included instruments designed to test specific aspects of language to the exclusion of others (such as syntax); information-processing capabilities; cognitive capabilities; and a combination of two or more of the basic language areas (phonology, semantics, morphology, syntax, and pragmatics). It is important to note that although the models that were used to construct these instruments have been discarded or modified extensively, the actual instruments may have remained relatively intact. Indeed, an instrument may possess some utility that was not evident in the theoretical model (for example, digit span, the delayed imitation of numerical sequences, may no longer be thought to be a precursor to language development, but it may identify language-impaired children). However, it is important to determine what aspect of language a particular instrument actually assesses. Therefore, let us examine the evolution of test development in a bit more detail.

Specific Components Models

For many years, the assessment of oral language simply meant the assessment of expressive phonology, or more precisely, articulation (Van Riper, 1939). Consequently, early oral language assessment instruments included no other information about language (for example, the Templin-Darley Test of Articulation). This period was followed by a shift to syntax. Chomsky (1957) spearheaded the movement to new models of grammar, and instruments to assess syntax soon appeared (for example, the Northwestern Syntax Screening Test). This work had a profound effect on language assessment, extending it beyond speech sounds. However, although phonology and syntax are still an important part of oral language assessment, a comprehensive evaluation covers more than just these specific abilities.

Information-Processing Models

The work of Lashly (1951), Miller (1951), and Osgood (1963) led to models of language that paralleled the development of the computer. These models outline a series of processing levels needed to complete language comprehension and production. For example, language comprehension requires that a listener detect sounds as they travel across the air, filter the relevant signals, and assign meaning to the message. Such models do not focus on the structural aspects of language; rather they describe the mechanisms for processing the linguistic signal. Oral language assessment instruments designed using this type of model include a series of tasks designed to assess each of the processing levels thought to contribute to normal language use (for example, the Illinois Test of Psycholinguistic Abilities).

Cognitive Models

Piaget (1955) and Vygotsky (1962) have stressed the cognitive bases of language; they argue that oral language arises from the development of more general cognitive structures. Brown (1973) argued that early word use arises from the Piagetian cognitive structure of object permanence. Assessment instruments generated from this theoretical perspective include cognitive tasks thought to relate to language performance (for example, the Early Language Inventory). Most intelligence assessment instruments also include items and/or subtests that assess oral language (for example, the Weschler Intelligence Scale for Children). Indeed, several are exclusively language oriented (such as the Peabody Picture Vocabulary Test–Revised).

CONSIDERATIONS IN THE ASSESSMENT OF ORAL LANGUAGE

Cultural Diversity

Certain factors outside of test content or construction must be considered when undertaking a valid assessment of a child's language competence. First, a child's *cultural background must be considered*. Although most children in the United States learn English, the form of English that they learn depends on where they were born, who their parents are, and so on. For example, in central Pennsylvania, a child might say, "My hands need washed," rather than the more standard "My hands need to be washed." In New York City, a child learning Black English might say "birfday" instead of "birthday" or "he be running" instead of "he is running." These and other culturally determined alternative constructions and pronunciations are not incorrect or inferior; they are just different. Indeed, they are appropriate within the child's surrounding community. For example, a number of studies of Black English have shown that it has its own rules of pronunciation, structure, and meaning—and that those rules are at least as complex as those of Standard American English (Wolfram, 1971).

For many years, all nonstandard U.S. dialects were viewed as inferior. Children who did not speak or write in Standard American English were diagnosed as having language disorders. This error has been recognized. Children should be viewed as having a language disorder only if they exhibit disordered production of their own primary language or dialect. If the latter is not the case, then they are simply producing an acceptable language variation. This is not meant to imply that children with language variations should not be taught Standard American English. Knowledge of Standard American English is vital if a person is to progress academically, socially, and economically. Thus, a child should be taught Standard American English, not because other dialects are inherently inferior, but because it allows that child greater access to the general U.S. cultural community (Salvia & Ysseldyke, 1978). However, children who speak nonstandard dialects should not be viewed as language disordered.

Cultural background becomes particularly important when considering the language assessment devices that are currently available, including those listed in Tables 23.2 through 23.5. Ideally, a child should be compared with others in the same language community in order to determine the existence or nonexistence of a language disorder. Again, ideally, there should be separate norms for each language community, including Standard American English. Unfortunately, the normative samples of most language tests are heterogeneous. Thus, scores on these tests may not be valid indicators of a child's language ability. As a final example, consider plate 25 of the original Peabody Picture Vocabulary Test (PPVT). This plate contained four pictures, and the examiner was supposed to say, "Show me the wiener." There are many places in this country where the only word for that item is *hot dog* or *frankfurter*. Yet, because the test was standardized using *wiener*, the examiner was required to use that term. If the child

TABLE 23.2   **Tests Discussed in this Book that Provide Information About Auditory Discrimination, Letter-Sound Associations, Sound Blending, and Other Receptive Skills**

California Achievement Tests–5
Diagnostic Reading Scales
Durrell Analysis of Reading Difficulties
Gates-McKillop-Horowitz Reading Diagnostic Tests
Iowa Tests of Basic Skills
Kaufman Assessment Battery for Children
Metropolitan Achievement Tests
Stanford Achievement Tests
Stanford Diagnostic Reading Test
Woodcock-Johnson Psychoeducational Battery–Revised

TABLE 23.3   **The Most Frequently Used Articulation-Assessment Tests**

Name of Test	Author	Publisher	Date of Publication
Arizona Articulation Proficiency Scale	J. Fudala & W. Reynolds	Western Psychological Services Los Angeles, CA	1991
Fisher-Logemann Test of Articulation Competence	H. Fisher & J. Logemann	The Riverside Publishing Company Chicago, IL	1971
Goldman-Fristoe Test of Articulation[a]	R. Goldman & M. Fristoe	American Guidance Service, Inc. Circle Pines, MN	1986
Phonological Process Analysis[a]	F. Weiner	University Park Press Baltimore, MD	1979
Photo Articulation Test	K. Pendergast, S. Dickey, J. Selmar, & A. Soder	Interstate Printers & Publishers Danville, IL	1969
Predictive Screening Test of Articulation, 3rd ed.	C. Van Riper & R. Erickson	Continuing Education Office Western Michigan University Kalamazoo, MI	1973
Templin-Darley Tests of Articulation, 2nd ed.	M. Templin & F. Darley	Bureau of Educational Research University of Iowa Iowa City, IA	1969

[a] Reviewed in this chapter

had never heard the word *wiener*, he or she was penalized and received a lower score, even though the error is cultural and not a semantic or intellectual deficiency. If there are a number of such items on a test, a child's score can hardly be considered a valid indicator of language ability.

TABLE 23.4   **Tests Discussed Elsewhere in this Book that Provide Information About Grammatical Usage**

California Achievement Tests–5	Metropolitan Achievement Tests
Diagnostic Reading Scales	Peabody Individual Achievement
Durrell Analysis of Reading Difficulties	Test–Revised
Gates–MacGinitie Reading Tests	Stanford Achievement Tests
Gray Oral Reading Test–3	Stanford Diagnostic Reading Test
Iowa Tests of Basic Skills	Woodcock Reading Mastery Tests–Revised

TABLE 23.5   **Tests Discussed Elsewhere in this Book that Provide Information About a Child's Vocabulary**

Boehm Test of Basic Concepts–Revised	Peabody Individual Achievement
California Achievement Tests–5	Test–Revised
Cognitive Abilities Test	Peabody Picture Vocabulary Test–Revised
Diagnostic Reading Scales	Stanford Achievement Tests
Durrell Analysis of Reading Difficulties	Stanford-Binet Intelligence Scale–IV
Gates–MacGinitie Reading Tests	Stanford Diagnostic Reading Test
Gates–McKillop-Horowitz Reading	Test of Adolescent Language–3
Diagnostic Tests	Tests of Basic Experiences–2
Gray Oral Reading Test–3	Test of Nonverbal Intelligence
Iowa Tests of Basic Skills	Wechsler Intelligence Scale for
Kaufman Assessment Battery for Children	Children–III
Metropolitan Achievement Tests	Woodcock-Johnson Psychoeducational
Metropolitan Readiness Tests	Battery–Revised
Otis-Lennon School Ability Test	

Developmental Considerations

A second major consideration in the assessment of language is the child's *age*, especially if the test being used is criterion-referenced rather than norm-referenced. It is important to be aware that language acquisition is developmental; some sounds, linguistic structures, and even semantic elements are correctly produced at an earlier age than others. Thus, it is not unusual or an indication of language disorder for a two-year-old child to say "Kitty house" for "The cat is in the house," although the same phrase *would* be an indication of disorder in a three-year-old. It is important to be aware of the developmental norms for language acquisition and to use those norms when making judgments about a child's language competence.

Similarly, it is important to note that some oral language assessment tasks are developmental in nature. For example, most two-year-old children can repeat only one or two digits, whereas older children can repeat much longer number strings. However, a task such as repeating digits should not be viewed as a precursor to language acquisition. Rather, such skills develop in conjunction with language. Therefore, many of the tasks used to assess oral language may not be useful for planning treatment.

GOALS OF A LANGUAGE ASSESSMENT SESSION

The chapter thus far has laid the groundwork for an evaluation of oral language assessment instruments. However, a description of the goals of a language assessment session must be provided in order to put the use of standard assessment instruments into proper perspective. According to Lahey (1988), the basic objectives of an oral language assessment session include: (1) to determine whether the child is language disordered, (2) to determine the goals of intervention, (3) to plan procedures for intervention, and (4) to determine prognosis (adapted from Table 6-1 in Lahey, 1988, p. 125). As noted earlier, standardized oral language assessments may not be directly useful for determining the goals of treatment or planning intervention because the instruments may not directly reflect the child's everyday language use. Rather, such instruments are of particular use in meeting the first objective: determining whether the child is language disordered. That is, a psychometrically valid oral assessment instrument that meets a majority of the criteria for standardization is particularly well suited for comparing a child's performance to that of the normal population. Indeed, one could argue that standardized instruments are the only reliable and valid method of doing this.

Conversely, standardized oral language assessment instruments are not constructed to assess a child's conversational abilities. Yet, such information is needed to provide input into determining treatment goals and for planning intervention (the second and third objectives). Conversational language assessment is conducted using nonstandardized procedures such as those outlined by Lee (1974), Miller (1981), or Tyack and Gottsleben (1974). Therefore, in order to meet all of the goals of oral language assessment, a session should include both nonstandard assessment of conversational language abilities and administration of a psychometrically sound standardized instrument. A discussion of these methods of language assessment will be presented later in this chapter.

OBSERVING LANGUAGE BEHAVIOR

There has been some disagreement among language professionals concerning the most valid method of evaluating a child's language performance, especially in the expressive channel of communication. In all, there are three procedures used to gather a sample of a child's language behavior: spontaneous, imitative, and elicited.

Spontaneous Language

One school of thought holds that the only valid measure of a child's language abilities is one that studies the language that the child produces spontaneously (for example, see Miller, 1981). Using this approach, the examiner records fifty to one hundred consecutive utterances produced as the child is talking to an adult or playing with toys. With older children, conversations or storytelling tasks are often used. The child's utterances are then analyzed in terms of phonology, semantics, morphology, syntax, and pragmatics in order to provide information on the child's conversational abilities. Because the construct of pragmatics has been developed only recently, there are few standard assessment instruments available to sample this domain. Therefore, spontaneous language sampling procedures are widely used to evaluate pragmatic abilities (see Prutting & Kirshner, 1987). Although analysis of a child's spontaneous language production is not the purpose of any standard oral language assessment instruments, some interest has been shown in standard assessment of handwriting and spelling skills in an uncontrived, spontaneous situation (for example, the Test of Written Language by Hammill and Larsen).

Imitation

Imitation tasks require a child to repeat directly the word, phrase, or sentence produced by the examiner. One might predict that such tasks bear little relation to spontaneous performance, but there is some evidence to suggest that such tasks are valid predictors of spontaneous production. In fact, many investigators have demonstrated that children's imitative language is essentially the same in content and structure as their spontaneous language (Brown & Bellugi, 1964; Ervin, 1964; Slobin & Welsh, 1973). Evidently, the children translate adult sentences into their own language system and then repeat the sentences using their own language rules. Thus, a young child might imitate "The boy is running and jumping" as "boy run and jump." Therefore, imitation seems to be a valuable tool for providing information about a child's language abilities. One caution should be noted, however. Features of a child's language systems can be obtained using imitation only if the stimulus sentences are long enough to tax the child's memory, as a child will imitate perfectly any sentence *if the length of that sentence is within memory capacity* (Slobin & Welsh, 1973).

The use of imitation does not preclude the need for spontaneous sampling, because the examiner also needs information derived from direct observation of conversational skills. Rather, imitation tasks should be used to augment the information obtained from the spontaneous sample, as such tasks can be used to elicit forms that the child did not attempt in the conversations. Standardized imitation tasks are widely used in oral language assessment instruments (such as the Test of Language Development and the Illinois Test of Psycholinguistic Abilities). Assessment devices that use imitation usually contain a number of grammatically loaded words, phrases, or sentences that children are asked to imitate. The examiner records and transcribes the children's responses and then analyzes their phonology, morphology, and syntax. (Semantics and pragmatics are rarely assessed using an imitative mode.) Finally, imitation generally is used only in assessing expressive oral language.

Elicited Language[1]

Using a picture stimulus to elicit language involves no imitation on the part of the child but cannot be classified as a totally spontaneous procedure. In this type of task, the child is presented with a picture or pictures of objects or action scenes and asked to do one of the following: (1) point to the correct object (a receptive vocabulary task), (2) point to the action picture that best describes a sentence (receptive language, including vocabulary), (3) name the picture (expressive vocabulary), or (4) describe the picture (expressive language, including vocabulary).

There are advantages and disadvantages to all three methods of language observation. The use of spontaneous language samples has two major advantages. First, a child's spontaneous language is undoubtedly the best and most natural indicator of everyday language performance. Second, the informality of the procedure often allows the examiner to assess children quite easily, without the difficulties sometimes associated with a formal testing atmosphere. The disadvantages associated with this procedure relate to the nonstandard nature of the data collection. Although some aspects of language sampling are stable across a variety of parameters, there is much wider variability than is seen with other standardized assessments. Additionally, language sampling requires detailed analyses across language domains, which are relatively more time-consuming than administering a standardized instrument. Finally, because the examiner does not directly control the selection of target words and phrases, he or she may have difficulty understanding a young child, or there may be several different interpretations of what a child intended to say. Moreover, the child may have avoided, or may not have had an opportunity to attempt, a particular structure that is of interest to the examiner.

The use of imitation overcomes many of the disadvantages inherent in the spontaneous approach. An imitation task will often assess many different language elements and provide a representative view of a child's language system. Also, because of the structure of the test, the examiner knows at all times what elements of language are being assessed. Thus, even the language abilities of a child with a severe language disorder (especially a severe phonological disorder) can be quantified. Finally, imitation devices can be administered much more quickly than spontaneous language samples. Unfortunately, the advantages of the spontaneous approach become the disadvantages of the imitative method. First, a child's auditory memory may have some effect on the results. For example, an

1. Although only stimulus pictures are described in this section, some tests use concrete objects rather than pictures to elicit language responses.

echolalic child may score well on an imitative test, without demonstrating productive knowledge of the language structures being imitated. Second, a child may repeat part of a sentence exactly because the utterance is too simple or short to place a load on the child's memory. Therefore, accurate production is not necessarily evidence that the child uses the structure spontaneously. However, inaccurate productions often do reflect a child's lack of mastery of the structure. Thus, one should draw conclusions only about a child's errors from an imitative test. A third disadvantage of imitative tests is that they are often quite boring to the child. Not all children will sit still for the time required to repeat fifty to one hundred sentences without any other stimulation such as pictures or toys.

The use of pictures to elicit language production is an attempt to overcome the disadvantages of both imitation and spontaneous language. Pictures are easy to administer, are interesting to children, and require minimal administration time. They can be structured to test desired language elements and yet retain some of the spontaneity of spontaneous language samples, because children have to formulate the language on their own. Because there is no time limit, results are not dependent on the child's word retention skills. Despite these advantages, a major disadvantage limits the usefulness of picture stimuli in language assessment: It is difficult to create pictures guaranteed to elicit specific language elements. Even though it is probably easiest to create pictures for object identification, difficulties arise even in this area. Thus, the disadvantage seen in spontaneous sampling is evident with picture stimuli as well—the child may not produce or attempt to produce the desired language structure.

To summarize, all three methods of language observation have advantages and disadvantages. The examiner must decide which elements of language should be tested, which methods of observation are most appropriate for assessing those elements, and which assessment devices satisfy these needs. It should not be surprising that more than one test is often necessary to assess all aspects of language (phonology, semantics, morphology, syntax, and pragmatics), both receptively and expressively. As noted, standardized instruments should be supplemented with measures of conversational abilities within any oral language assessment. Additionally, the different language domains are often best assessed by different procedures. For example, picture stimuli are particularly well suited for assessment of phonological abilities, because the examiner should know the intended production. Similarly, imitation tasks are often employed to assess morphological abilities, as the child having difficulty with this domain will often delete suffixes and prefixes during imitation. Finally, because assessment of pragmatics involves determining the child's conversational use of language, this domain should be assessed with spontaneous production.

SUMMARY

Language is defined as a code for conveying ideas, consisting of phonology, semantics, morphology, syntax, and pragmatics. Additionally, language includes both input and output modalities. A comprehensive oral language assessment will gather information on all of these domains across both modalities. Finally, standardized oral language assessment instruments are typically used to identify a child as language disordered and to indicate areas of weakness. The structure of the standardized assessment instrument is predicated on the model of language that was used to construct the test. Therefore, the following review of specific oral language tests will include references to the underlying models.

SPECIFIC TESTS OF EXPRESSIVE AND RECEPTIVE LANGUAGE
Goldman-Fristoe Test of Articulation

Language Component Assessed   Phonology
Communication Channel   Expressive

*T*he Goldman-Fristoe Test of Articulation (GFTA) (Goldman & Fristoe, 1986) is one of the more popular tools developed to assess phonology. It is an individually administered, norm-referenced device in which most consonant sounds and eleven common consonant blends (*st*, for example) are elicited in differing levels of complexity (word, sentence) and in a variety of word positions (beginning, middle, and end of word). Familiarity with the International Phonetic Alphabet (IPA) and experience in identifying and transcribing disordered speech are useful for administering and scoring the GFTA. Although the device does not specifically measure vowels, the examiner can observe the child's vowel production, because all vowels and diphthongs are used at least once within the stimulus words. However, vowel production is not included in the normative data. The GFTA is divided into three sections.

Sounds-in-Words   In this subtest, thirty-five pictures of familiar objects are presented to the child, who must either name the picture or answer questions pertaining to it. In all, forty-four responses are elicited, including eleven common consonant blends and all single consonant sounds (except *zh*); medial position *h*, *w*, *wh*, and *y*; and final position voiced *th* (as in *bathe*).

Sounds-in-Sentences   This subtest is designed to elicit a sample of a child's speech in a more complex, spontaneous context. The examiner reads two stories aloud to the child while presenting four or five pictures illustrating each story. After the story is read, the examiner again presents the pictures to the child, who recounts the story. The story is loaded with sounds most commonly misarticulated by children, and the examiner appraises the child's speech-sound production in the more complex context of sentences.

Stimulability   After the first two subtests are completed, the examiner returns to the sounds the child has misarticulated and tries to stimulate correct production by means of a three-step procedure explained in the instructions. The purpose of this subtest is to find out how stimulable a child is to intervention. This clinical information then leads to a decision regarding prognosis for and length of intervention.

Unlike some other articulation tests, the GFTA assesses more than one speech sound in many of the test items. This places a greater load on the listening abilities of the examiner, although many individuals using this test seem to have no problem listening for more than one sound in a given word. The stimulus pictures are large and colorful, making the test very motivating for young children. However, older children might find the device too juvenile, especially compared with the black-and-white pictures of a test such as the Arizona Articulation Proficiency Scale (Fudala, 1970).

SCORES

Percentile ranks (based on the National Speech and Hearing Survey conducted by Hull, Meilke, Timmons, & Willeford, 1971) are available for schoolage students for the Sounds-in-Words and Stimulability subtests (ages 6-6 through 16-0). Percentile ranks are also available for children between 2 and 6 years of age. These norms are from the 1983 sample used to standardize the Khan-Lewis Phonological Analysis. Pertinent characteristics of the children making up these norms are not described.

RELIABILITY

Percent agreement data are presented in the manual for three types of reliability. The stability of a child's correct production of each sound on two subtests (Sounds-in-Words and Sounds-in-Sentences) was assessed with a one-week interval between assessments. Data were collected on thirty-seven children between the ages of 4 and 8 who were assessed by eight certified (Certificate of Clinical Competence) clinicians. Only median stabilities for each subtest are presented; neither data for each sound nor ranges of values are reported. For Sounds-in-Words, the median reliability was .95; for Sounds-in-Sentences, it was .94; and for the specific type of error made (such as omission or distortion) on Sounds-in-Words, it was .89.

Intrarater agreement (stability of the rater over time) was assessed by having six judges, described only as having had "at least one semester of experience" using the test, evaluate the tape-recorded responses of four individuals who had articulation problems judged to range from mild to severe. Only medians are presented. For presence or absence of error and for the type of error, the median stability was .91.

Interrater agreement was also assessed for Sounds-in-Words. Six judges, described only as having had "at least one semester of experience" using the test, evaluated the tape-recorded responses of four individuals who had articulation problems judged to range from mild to severe. Again, only medians are presented for percentage agreement. For presence or absence of error for the sounds, the median was .92; for type of error, the median was .88.

VALIDITY

Only content validity is discussed in the manual. The authors argue that the test is a valid sampling of English consonants and that the productions are representative of the child's use. Although the test items include an adequate sample of consonant speech sounds, there are no objective measures of validity reported. This lack of validity data is a weakness in the instrument.

SUMMARY

The GFTA is an individually administered norm-referenced device that has supplemental norms. The norms are more than sixteen years old for all ages except the two- to six-year-olds. Reliability data are inadequately reported, but do appear adequate for at least half of the sample. Validity data are lacking.

Phonological Process Analysis

Language Component Assessed   Phonology

Communication Channel   Expressive

*T*he Phonological Process Analysis (PPA) (Weiner, 1979) was one of the first attempts to assess a child's articulation abilities other than by examining the child's isolated speech-sound production. Instead, the PPA assumes that there are speech production rules or patterns that cut across single sounds. These rules, or processes, "are based on such factors as sound environment, syllable structure" and differences in the distinctive features of sounds (Weiner, 1979, p. 1). The PPA is an individually administered, criterion-referenced device that assesses sixteen such phonological rules that might explain a child's speech production problems. Although no norms are provided and no specific age range of applicability is presented, the author implies that the instrument would be most appropriate for two- to five-year-olds: "The unintelligible child is usually between 2 and 5 years of age . . ." (p. 1).

For each rule tested, there are four to eight stimulus words. Each word is elicited twice from the child. The first mode of elicitation used is delayed imitation, in which the examiner shows the child an action picture and reads an incomplete sentence. For example, "Uncle George is running fast. Uncle George, be careful; you are running too _____." The child must complete the sentence. Then, the examiner elicits the same stimulus word a second time by asking, "What is Uncle George doing?" The desired response is "running too fast." If the child does not respond correctly to these modes of elicitation, immediate imitation might be required. The examiner transcribes both responses for each stimulus word tested onto a process profile and analyzes the data to determine whether a child is having problems with any particular phonological rules. All responses should be tape-recorded for verification and better analysis of the live transcription.

Although the PPA takes 45 minutes to complete with a cooperative child, it is not necessary to complete the entire assessment in one session. In fact, the examiner might not want to assess all phonological rules with every child.

SCORES

Because the PPA is an un-normed, criterion-referenced device, there is no attempt to assign scores to a child's responses. The examiner does, however, indicate the percentage of times the child has correctly used the given rule. If the percentage is less than 100 percent, the examiner must determine the extent to which the misuse of that rule is con-

tributing to the child's speech problems. If the examiner decides that the child's misuse of the rule is a significant factor, a program of intervention should be developed to teach the given rule to the child.

RELIABILITY

No reliability data accompany the PPA.

VALIDITY

The content validity of the PPA is derived from the detailed descriptions of the phonological processes (rules) included in the instrument and the procedures for selecting these items. However, the content validity in turn rests on the construct validity of phonological processes, a construct that has come under increasing criticism in recent years (Camarata, in press; Camarata & Gandour, 1984; Gierut, 1989; McReynolds & Elbert, 1981). As evidence of content validity, Weiner (1979) states that the 136 test items included in the PPA were those that most often assessed the desired phonological rules in a group of one hundred children with phonological disorders. It should be noted that neither the severity nor the type of these children's phonological problems was described. Also, there is no information on whether some of the instructions and presentations might be too difficult for younger children.

The types of items included seem an appropriate measure of the test domain. The sample of items seems extensive enough to measure satisfactorily the sixteen phonological rules. Note, however, that controversy continues regarding the number of processes that should be sampled: Shriberg and Kwiatkowski (1980) include eight, whereas Ingram (1981) includes twenty-seven, and Hodson and Paden include forty-two. Again, construct validity analysis should be completed in order to evaluate the number and type of processes that should be included in the instrument. Finally, the items assess the rules using two elicitation modes, delayed imitation and recall.

SUMMARY

The PPA is an individually administered, criterion-referenced test intended to assess the child's use of the phonological rules inherent in the production of speech. The lack of reliability and validity data are important weaknesses in the instrument's construction that limit applicability.

Auditory Discrimination Test

Language Component Assessed   Phonology

Communication Channel   Receptive

The Auditory Discrimination Test (ADT) (Wepman, revised 1973) is an individually administered, norm-referenced device intended to measure the auditory discrimination abilities of five- to eight-year-old children. The procedure used to equate the two forms of the ADT is not specified in the technical information. Each form contains forty pairs of words, ten of which are identical and thirty of which differ from each other in only one phoneme. In the different-word pairs, the location of the differing phoneme is the medial position for vowels and the initial and/or final position for consonants. To administer the device, the examiner reads each word pair. The child must indicate whether the two words are the same or different.

SCORES

The child receives one point for each correct recognition of different-word pairs, for a possible raw score of 30. The technical manual provides tables with which the examiner can convert raw scores to a five-point rating scale. The scale appears to be based on percentile ranks, but it is not clear how these percentile ranks were derived. (Presumably they were based on the performance of a normative sample.) The test is deemed invalid if the child scores below 10 on the different-word pairs or below 7 on the same-word pairs.

NORMS

No data are given concerning either the children in the normative sample or any of their characteristics.

RELIABILITY

Two types of reliability data are presented for the ADT. Test-retest reliability was undertaken twice, with good stability coefficients of .91 and .95. In addition, alternate-forms reliability was estimated as .92. Neither the sample used to estimate the reliability coefficients nor the time interval between test administrations is discussed in the manual.

VALIDITY

Of eight studies presented in the manual that purport to establish the validity of the ADT, only seven are truly studies of validity. These seven studies provide information regarding construct validity.

Three of the seven validity studies indicate that there is a significant relationship between age and auditory discrimination score. As children get older, their auditory discrimination scores increase.

Two studies attempt to establish a relationship between auditory discrimination (as measured by the ADT) and reading. In fact, these studies report significant differences in reading scores between those students with adequate auditory discrimination and those with inadequate auditory discrimination. However, upon closer study of the data, some curious facts emerge. The first-graders showing adequate auditory discrimination had a mean reading score of 2.2, whereas the other group (inadequate) had a 1.9 reading grade level. Both of these groups are well above normal reading ability.

Another validity study compared the scores of first-graders on the ADT and the Metropolitan

Achievement Tests (MAT). Wepman reports significant correlations between subtests of the MAT and the ADT and implies a causative connection between school achievement and auditory discrimination. However, the correlations found were only between .235 and .348, which are statistically significant but trivial.

In a final study, Wepman reports a significant difference between the auditory discrimination abilities of children with articulation problems and those without. However, there have been many studies in this same area, and Rees (1973), in a thorough examination of research on this relationship, did not find any that proved the connection between auditory discrimination and speech ability.

No evidence of content or criterion-related validity is presented in the manual. It is questionable whether the items appropriately and completely measure the domain. For example, the two words in the different-word pairs differ only in placement of the articulators. There is no pair that tests discrimination of acoustic characteristics (such as a stop-burst sound *t* versus an affricate *ch*), or voicing of the sound versus nonvoicing (*z* versus *s*, for example). Also, some of the more frequently misarticulated sounds (*r, l, w, y*) are not even included in the test. Winitz (1975) concludes that the Auditory Discrimination Test does not provide the information needed to validly assess a child's auditory discrimination abilities.

SUMMARY

The purpose of the ADT is to assess the auditory discrimination skills of children 5 to 8 years of age. It is individually administered and norm-referenced, although the sample on which the norms are based is not described in the manual. Reliability is satisfactory, although the sample used is not described and there is no information concerning the time interval between test administrations. The construct validity of the ADT seems very questionable, and content validity seems quite poor. No mention is made of criterion validity. The ADT should be used only with caution and with a thorough knowledge of its shortcomings.

Comprehensive Receptive and Expressive Vocabulary Test

Language Component Assessed   Semantics (vocabulary)

Communication Channels   Receptive and expressive

*T*he Comprehensive Receptive and Expressive Vocabulary Test (CREVT) (Wallace & Hammill, 1994) is a newly developed norm-referenced instrument designed to assess receptive and expressive vocabulary in children aged 4-0 to 17-11 (5-0 to 17-11 for expressive vocabulary). It combines receptive and expressive vocabulary assessment into one instrument, communication channels that have traditionally been assessed using two instruments, such as the PPVT-R and the Expressive One-Word Picture Vocabulary Test–Revised (EOWVT-R). High quality photographs are included in the stimulus materials. Two forms of the test (A and B) are available.

Receptive Vocabulary   In this subtest, the child points to one of six pictures in response to the verbal presentation of words by the examiner. Sixty-one items are included in this subtest. Unlike the PPVT-R, or the Test of Auditory Comprehension of Language–Revised (TACL-R), which require one response per page (plate), from four to seven responses are required on each plate for the CREVT.

Therefore, the sixty-one items are represented on ten plates (pages).

Expressive Vocabulary This subtest uses a format similar to that on the Test of Language Development 2, Primary (TOLD-P2). The child is required to tell the examiner "what a word means" in response to a verbal presentation of the word. This subtest includes twenty-five items.

SCORING

The CREVT yields standard scores with a mean of 100 and a standard deviation of 15 for each subtest. A composite score (General Vocabulary) is generated by combining the two subtests and yields a transformed standard score with identical parameters (mean = 100, standard deviation = 15). Normative data are provided at six-month intervals for each year from 4-0 to 12-11 and one-year intervals from 13-0 through 17-11 for receptive vocabulary and at six-month intervals from 5-0 through 10-11 and one-year intervals from 11-0 through 17-11 for expressive vocabulary.

RELIABILITY

Coefficient alpha was computed for forms A and B for each level for each subtest and for the composite. In contrast with the standard scores, coefficients are reported at one-year intervals for all age levels. Also unlike the standard scores, a coefficient for 4-0 is provided for expressive vocabulary. This yields a total of eighty-four alpha coefficients (fourteen age groups with two forms across two subtests and one composite). All are above .80, with sixty above .90 (twenty-four between .80 and .90). Composites (General Vocabulary) at all age levels are above .90. Also, alpha coefficients are presented for children with learning disabilities, speech-language disabilities, and mental retardation. Although many of these were pooled across age levels, so that it is difficult to determine what proportion of subjects was at

each age level, these coefficients are routinely high (ranging from .83 to .98). Alternate-forms reliability was assessed by computing correlations at each age level for test forms A and B in the entire normative sample. The results of this analysis indicate that r_{AB} ranged from .84 (age 6) to .97 (age 17) with a mean of .92 for receptive vocabulary; r_{AB} ranged from .74 (age 6) to .96 (age 16 and 17) with a mean of .90 for expressive vocabulary. Test-retest reliability was assessed by readministering the instrument to twenty-seven kindergartners after two months and to twenty-eight twelfth-graders after two weeks. Both groups were selected from the Austin, Texas area. Coefficients are reported for each group for both forms (A and B) of the expressive and receptive subtests and for the composite (General Vocabulary) scores. These correlations ranged from .79 to .87 for the kindergarteners and from .79 to .94 for the twelfth-graders. Although this test-retest reliability is lower than the alpha coefficients, which is somewhat surprising given the likelihood of both samples being derived from presumably homogeneous populations, all reliability coefficients are within acceptable ranges.

VALIDITY

The manual includes sections on content, concurrent, and construct validity. (Although the authors say that the concurrent validity is criterion-related, no predictive validity assessments are included.) Content validity was evaluated qualitatively by simply reporting the rationale for selecting the test format and the procedures for selecting the pool of items that ultimately were included in the test. This section would be strengthened if some form of quantitative evaluation, such as results from a survey of experts on receptive and expressive vocabulary, were included in the manual. The content validity of the categories selected for the receptive subtest (such as, animals, transportation, occupations, and foods) also should be examined. Item analysis and a table of "median discriminating powers" are included in the manual. These are relatively high at the upper age ranges and relatively low at the lower age ranges (ages 4 through 9). Also, given the relatively limited number of items in each subtest, particularly for the expressive subtest (twenty-five items) which are distributed over a relatively large age range (4 to 17 years), certain individual items may have a disproportionate discriminating power. Because Table 7.2 in the manual includes median scores, it is difficult to evaluate the relative contribution of individual items.

Concurrent validity was evaluated by correlating the scores on the CREVT with the PPVT-R, the EOWPVT-R, the Clinical Evaluation of Language Function–Revised (CELF-R), and the TOLD-P2. Although the authors indicate that these correlations are based upon a subset of children in the normative sample who were also assessed using one or more of these other instruments, it is not clear what the sample size or selection criteria were for these data. Because of this, it is difficult to interpret the correlation coefficients presented in Table 7.4 on page 35 of the manual. Also, it was not clear why the TOLD-P2 subtests that are most relevant for evaluating the concurrent validity of the CREVT were not included in addition to the composite scores. That is, the TOLD-P2 includes receptive and oral vocabulary subtests. We view this as a serious omission. Although a number of the correlation coefficients would suggest a high degree of concurrent validity, there are also a number that are surprisingly low. For example, the correlation between the CREVT Expressive Vocabulary subtest and the EOWPVT-R is .36 for form A and .44 for form B. Although one could argue that the different formats (one-word responses for the EOWPVT-R, multiword descriptions for the CREVT) result in a lower correlation, it would appear that this is a relatively minor difference in response format as compared to tests with higher correlations (for example, TOLD-P2 syntax composite has correlations of .75 and .76 for forms A and B respectively). Similarly, one would expect very high correlations between the PPVT-R and the Receptive Vocabulary subtest of the CREVT. Although

these were in the acceptable range (.76 and .72 for forms A and B of the CREVT), one would expect these to be somewhat higher if these tests are sampling identical domains (receptive vocabulary). Thus, additional information, including sampling procedures, correlations with relevant subtests, and a more detailed explanation of the observed coefficients (particularly for the EOWPVT-R) are required before one can be assured that the CREVT displays adequate concurrent validity.

Evidence of construct validity is also included in the manual. Four basic constructs underlying the CREVT are presented and evaluated. These constructs are as follows: (1) The test is constructed to be developmentally ordered. (2) Expressive and receptive vocabulary should be highly related to one another. (3) The CREVT is designed to differentiate normal children and adolescents from those with deficiencies in vocabulary skills. (4) Each item within the subtests should relate to the overall score for that subtest. Although one could argue that a larger language construct should be included because vocabulary is an essential building block for overall language competence, these four constructs are reasonable. The evidence for construct validity includes (1) presentation of correlational relationships between chronological age and CREVT scores; (2) intercorrelations between the subtests (Receptive and Expressive); (3) comparison to the normative sample for mean performance on the CREVT for three groups of children with disabilities (thirty-two with mental retardation, thirty-three with speech and language problems, and thirty-seven with learning disabilities); and (4) reference to item analysis data. With the exception of the data on group differentiation, this evidence of construct validity appears to be adequate. In addition to the group means, information on the percentage of students who actually fell below the normal range on the CREVT would be helpful to researchers and practitioners. Speech pathologists, special educators, and psychometricians often identify children as qualifying for services if their score on one or more standardized instruments falls below a cut-off score. Given the relatively high means evident on the CREVT for the children with speech and language disabilities and with learning disabilities, it is not clear that this instrument would, in practice, be useful in distinguishing these groups from the normal population. Presentation of individual scores, or at least median and range values, would be useful.

SUMMARY

The CREVT is an individually administered receptive and expressive vocabulary test. It has clear pictures and is simple to administer and score. A primary strength of the instrument is that expressive and receptive vocabulary can be assessed in a relatively short time across a wide age range of children and adolescents. Psychometric data on reliability and validity are provided. Weaknesses include a lack of information on key psychometric parameters and a potential lack of sensitivity due to the relatively low number of items on the instrument (particularly on the Expressive subtest). Because the CREVT is a relatively new instrument, data from practitioners are not currently available. Despite these weaknesses, the CREVT appears to be potentially useful as a quickly administered vocabulary screening instrument, to be followed up with more detailed vocabulary assessment as needed. Hopefully, additional applied information will be forthcoming as the instrument is used with clinical populations.

Test of Adolescent Language–3

Language Components Assessed   Semantics, morphology, and syntax

Communication Channels   Receptive and expressive

*T*he third revision of the Test of Adolescent Language: A Multidimensional Approach to Assessment (TOAL-3) (Hammill, Brown, Larsen, & Wiederholt, 1994) is a norm-referenced device designed for adolescents between the ages of 12 and 25. It is intended to identify areas of relative strength and weakness, document academic progress, and identify those who might profit from programs of language intervention. Six of the subtests may be administered to groups; two (Speaking/Vocabulary and Speaking/Grammar) must be administered individually. The TOAL-3 was designed to assess receptive and expressive spoken and written vocabulary (semantics) and grammar (morphology and syntax). These abilities are assessed through the following eight subtests:

Listening/Vocabulary   In this thirty-five-item picture vocabulary subtest, the adolescent must select two pictures that relate to the stimulus word read by the examiner. Credit for an item is awarded only if both correct items are selected.

Listening/Grammar   Each of the thirty-five items in this subtest contains three sentences that are read aloud to the adolescent, who must select the two sentences that have the same meaning.

Speaking/Vocabulary   In this subtest, the examiner reads a stimulus word and the adolescent must say a meaningful sentence that includes appropriate use of the target word. The subtest contains twenty-five stimulus words.

Speaking/Grammar   In this subtest, the examiner reads a sentence to the adolescent, who must then repeat it. There are thirty stimulus items.

Reading/Vocabulary   The adolescent is presented with up to thirty items in this subtest. Each item consists of three stimulus words and a multiple-choice array containing four additional words. The adolescent must select from the array two words that go with the stimulus words.

Reading/Grammar   The adolescent is presented with up to twenty-five items, each of which contains five sentences. The adolescent must read all five sentences and then find the two sentences that mean "almost the same thing."

Writing/Vocabulary   The adolescent is required to read a stimulus word and write a meaningful sentence using that word. The stimulus word must be used correctly in the exact form in which it is given. The subtest contains thirty items.

Writing/Grammar   Each of the thirty items in this subtest contains two to six sentences of varying complexity. The adolescent is instructed to combine the sentences into one. The simple sentences prompt grammatically more complex constructions. This subtest is analogous to the Sentence Combining subtest of the Test of Language Development, Intermediate 2 (TOLD-I2), but requires written rather than verbal responses.

Scores

Several types of scores are available. The eight subtest scores can be transformed into standard scores (mean = 10, standard deviation = 3). Standard scores (mean = 100, standard deviation = 15) are also available for each of the following eleven composite scores:

- Listening (Listening/Vocabulary and Listening/Grammar)
- Speaking (Speaking/Vocabulary and Speaking/Grammar)
- Reading (Reading/Vocabulary and Reading/Grammar)
- Writing (Writing/Vocabulary and Writing/Grammar)

- Spoken Language (Listening/Vocabulary, Listening/Grammar, Speaking/Vocabulary, and Speaking Grammar)
- Written Language (Reading/Vocabulary, Reading/Grammar, Writing/Vocabulary, and Writing/Grammar)
- Vocabulary (Listening/Vocabulary, Speaking/Vocabulary, Reading/Vocabulary, and Writing/Vocabulary)
- Grammar (Listening/Grammar, Speaking/Grammar, Reading/Grammar, and Writing/Grammar)
- Receptive Language (Listening/Vocabulary, Listening/Grammar, Reading/Vocabulary, and Reading/Grammar)
- Expressive Language (Speaking/Vocabulary, Speaking/Grammar, Writing/Vocabulary, and Writing/Grammar)
- General Language

Norms

The TOAL-3 was normed on a total of 3,056 adolescents between 12 and 25 years of age selected from twenty-six states. Of this total, 1,512 were from the original TOAL sample, 957 were added for the TOAL-2, and 587 were added for the TOAL-3. All of the subjects in the latter group were from 18-0 to 24-11 years old and were added to extend the TOAL-3 norms upward from the 18-year-level on the TOAL-2. Because each version of the TOAL has included some modifications (for example, the TOAL-3 includes extensive modifications of the Writing/Grammar subtest), combining norms from three different versions may not be appropriate. These adolescents make up twelve normative groups: half-year intervals for ages 12-0 to 16-11, a combination group of ages 17-0 through 18-11, and a combination group for 19-0 through 24-11. Because the original norms included one-year samples, the number and demographics for the groups in these norms are unknown. The manual includes sample characteristics of the normative group, but these data are reported for two-year intervals so that the information is not consistent with the scoring norms and it is impossible to determine whether adequate sample sizes were included in the scoring norms. For example, a total of 319 thirteen-year-olds were included in the normative sample, but the authors do not indicate how many were in the 13-0 to 13-6 and 13-7 to 13-11 age ranges that are included in the scoring norms. Tables on pages 48 and 49 of the TOAL-3 manual show that the normative sample corresponds closely to the overall population of adolescents at the time of the 1990 census. There is no more than a 3-percent difference between the TOAL-3 sample and the population with respect to sex, residence (urban/rural), race, ethnicity, and geographic region (four U.S. regions). A table also includes data on the educational status of the nineteen- to twenty-five year-olds included in the normative sample.

RELIABILITY

Three types of reliability data are presented. First, coefficient alpha was computed for each subtest, each composite, and the total score for each age group. Again, these data are not presented for the age groups for the reported standard scores; rather, data are given for 12, 13, 14, 15, 16, 17/18, 19/20, 21/22, and 23/24 age groups for each subtest. Of the seventy-two age-by-subtest coefficients (nine age groups for eight subtests), twenty-two are less than .90, but none is lower than .80. All ninety-nine of the composite-by-age coefficients (nine age groups over eleven composites) exceed .90.

Second, two stability coefficients were computed. The first was on fifty-two adolescents attending different grades in a parochial school in Kansas City, Missouri. These adolescents took TOAL, not the revised version (TOAL-3), and nineteen of the subjects were below the normative age range. In this sample, coefficients for three subtests (Listening/Vocabulary, Listening/Grammar, and Speaking/Grammar) were greater than .70 but less than .80. On four subtests (Speaking/Vocabulary, Reading/Vocabulary, Reading/Grammar, and Writing/Grammar) coefficients were greater than .80 but

less than .90. On one (Writing/Vocabulary) the coefficient was .90. The Listening and Speaking composites were greater than .80 but less than .90, whereas the remaining composites exceeded .90. The second measure of stability was completed on fifty-nine college students from Austin, Texas who were retested following a two-week interval. These college students ranged in age from 19 to 24 years. The results indicated that stability coefficients for two subtests (Reading/ Grammar and Writing/Grammar) were greater than .70 but less than .80, and for the remaining subtests they fell between .80 and .90. The Listening, Speaking, Reading, and Writing composites all fell between .80 and .90, and the remaining composites were greater than .90.

Finally, reliability data are presented on interscorer agreement of six raters on the three subtests that use subjective scoring. For Writing/Vocabulary, the correlations between raters ranged from .70 to .95; for Speaking/Vocabulary, correlations ranged from .86 to .99; and for Writing/Grammar, they ranged from .91 to .99. Calculations of the percentage of interscorer agreement, based on the same data, yielded different results. Only the Speaking/Vocabulary subtest attained a minimum of 90 percent agreement among all raters. Because several items presented difficulties in scoring, the authors revised the criteria for scoring these items. Unfortunately, the revised scoring criteria were not empirically tested, and the revised items were not identified. Also, these data appear to have been gathered on an earlier version of the TOAL.

VALIDITY

The authors provide a discussion of the selection of formats for subtests. Content validity is discussed in terms of the procedures and theoretical rationale for test construction. No empirical studies of content validity are presented. It would be useful to see the results of survey data from professionals, as was presented for the related tests in the series (TOLD-P2 and TOLD-I2). Evidence of criterion-related validity for the first edition of the test is presented. Moderate correlations are reported between TOAL and the Peabody Picture Vocabulary Test, a subtest of the Detroit Tests of Learning Aptitude, the reading and language totals from the Comprehensive Test of Basic Skills, the total score from the Test of Written Language, and the Test of Language Competence. It is interesting that the Listening/Vocabulary subtest and the PPVT-R correlate only at .49, when both of these instruments theoretically measure the same construct. No explanation for this low correlation is provided in the manual. Because the TOAL, TOAL-2, and TOAL-3 are very highly correlated, the authors assume these correlations are for TOAL-3 as well as for TOAL and TOAL-2. Additionally, the authors note that the TOAL correlated with intelligence and that students previously identified as mentally retarded or learning disabled attained lower scores. Six additional studies completed independently replicate the group differentiation findings. Group differentiations reported in the manual include: learning disabilities versus emotional disturbance; learning disabled subjects versus normal controls (two studies); high and low "job performing" juvenile delinquents, and skilled and poor readers of college age. No data are provided to indicate that the TOAL-3 is sufficiently sensitive to monitor a student's progress, and no data are provided to demonstrate that the TOAL-3 identifies students who might profit from programs of language intervention (predictive validity).

SUMMARY

TOAL-3 is a norm-referenced device that assesses three aspects of language (semantics, morphology, and syntax) via both the receptive and the expressive channels. Expressive and receptive skills are sampled using both oral and written modes of communication. The composite scores have good internal consistency, and the reported stability and interscorer reliability are adequate, although it is difficult to interpret these data because different versions of the test are pooled in the normative sample and the standard score groups are not consistent with normative sample information. Evidence of criterion-related validity is presented as well. Despite the limitations noted, the TOAL-3 appears to be a useful instrument and is used widely.

Test of Auditory Comprehension of Language–Revised

Language Components Assessed   Morphology, syntax, and semantics (vocabulary)

Communication Channel   Receptive

The Test of Auditory Comprehension of Language–Revised (TACL-R) (Carrow-Wolfolk, 1985) is an individually administered, norm-referenced test designed to assess the language comprehension of children between the ages of 3 years, 0 months and 9 years, 11 months. TACL-R consists of 120 test items in which a child selects, from a set of three pictures, the one picture that best represents a word or sentence read to the child by the examiner. An oral response is not required. Basal and ceiling criteria speed the administration of the test.

Test items are arranged in three categories. Category I assesses the literal meaning of various words and basic word relations (for example, "riding a little bicycle"). Category II assesses grammatical morphemes (for example, past tense, noun and verb agreement). Category III assesses the ability to derive meaning from spoken sentences (for example, active and passive voices, direct and indirect objects).

The author states that TACL-R scores are useful for identifying children with language problems, for measuring school readiness, for program planning, and for program monitoring.

SCORES

Various tables are provided in the examiner's manual (Carrow-Wolfolk, 1985) for converting raw scores to percentile ranks and age equivalents. A student's performances are compared to those of one of ten age groups: six six-month norm groups (from 3 years, 0 months to 5 years, 11 months) and four one-year norm groups (from 6 years, 0 months to 9 years, 11 months). In addition, a table is presented for converting percentile ranks to z-scores, T-scores, deviation quotients (mean = 100, standard deviation = 15), and normal curve equivalents. This table is based on the assumption that the raw scores are normally distributed. However, no data are presented to indicate whether this assumption is valid.

NORMS

A stratified sample of 1,003 children was selected to correspond to the population at the time of the 1980 U.S. census. Stratification variables within each age group included family occupation, ethnic/racial background, sex, and geographical factors (such as region of the United States and community size). The obtained sample was differentially weighted (some children were counted as more than one child) to adjust the norm characteristics so that they would correspond exactly to the census data.

RELIABILITY

Forty split-half estimates of internal consistency (corrected by the Spearman-Brown formula) were computed (ten age groups on three category scores and a total score). For Category I, coefficients ranged from .73 to .95, with half of the coefficients equaling or exceeding .90. Category II coefficients ranged from .82 to .95; four of the ten coefficients were less than .90. For Category III, the coefficients ranged from .86 to .96, with only two coefficients less than .90. As expected, the reliability of the total score was higher; except for one group—8 years, 0 months to 8 years, 11 months—all coefficients exceeded .91. The reliability for this age group was consistently low. Stability coefficients for the four scores equaled or exceeded .90, except for Category III (r_{xx} = .89).

VALIDITY

Evidence is presented for the content validity of TACL-R. A wide variety of language elements are assessed. The author also presents evidence for construct validity by demonstrating that the TACL-R is correlated with age and hence is developmental. Also, performances of the children in the normative sample corresponded to the expected progression of subtest difficulty (Category I was easier than Category II, which in turn was easier than Category III). The performances of the children in the norm sample also were better than the performances of children with language disorders. The results of several studies are presented to establish the criterion-related validity of the TACL-R. However, the data in these studies are difficult to interpret.

Finally, no data are presented to demonstrate that TACL-R scores are useful for identifying children with language problems, for determining school readiness, for planning educational or therapeutic programs, or for monitoring the therapeutic program of an individual student.

SUMMARY

TACL-R is an individually administered device intended to assess receptive morphological, syntactic, and semantic abilities of children between 3 and 12 years of age. Reliability data for total scores are high, but category-score reliability is variable. Some evidence of validity is presented. The total score appears to be the most reliable and valid indicator of comprehension ability.

Test of Language Development, Primary 2 (second edition)

Language Components Assessed   Semantics, morphology, syntax, and phonology

Communication Channels   Expressive and receptive

T he Test of Language Development, Primary 2 (TOLD-P2) (Newcomer & Hammill, 1988) is a norm-referenced, individually administered device intended to identify children with language problems, to ascertain a child's language strengths and weaknesses, to evaluate pupil progress in language programs, and to facilitate research. TOLD-P2 can be administered to children between the ages of 4-0 and 8-11. Various aspects of language are assessed by the seven subtests. The second edition of the TOLD-P2 includes a new phonology quotient, which is a combination of the previously developed Word Discrimination and Word Articulation subtests.

Picture Vocabulary   This twenty-five-item subtest requires a child to point to the one picture in a group of four that best represents the stimulus word read by the tester.

Oral Vocabulary   This thirty-item subtest requires a child to describe words orally. The individual word items are presented orally. No pictures or other stimulus support are provided.

Grammatic Understanding   This twenty-five-item subtest requires a child to select from a group of three pictures the one that best represents a sentence read by the tester.

Sentence Imitation   This thirty-item subtest requires a child to repeat, verbatim, sentences that vary in length from five words to twelve words and that vary considerably in grammatical form.

Grammatic Completion   This thirty-item subtest uses a cloze prompting procedure and requires the child to complete sentences by supplying appropriate plurals, possessives, tenses, adjectival comparisons, and so forth.

Word Discrimination   This twenty-item subtest requires a child to say whether two words read by the examiner are the same or different. The words differ from each other in only the beginning, middle, or ending phoneme. Six "foil" items with identical words are also included to ensure the child is not simply responding "different" to all items.

Word Articulation   This twenty-item subtest uses pictures of familiar things to prompt speech. Phonetic transcription of the child's production of the words are completed and speech errors are noted on each item.

SCORES

Subtest raw scores can be transformed into Language Ages (based on mean performances), percentiles, and standard scores (mean = 10, standard deviation = 3). Subtests can also be combined into six composites:

- Phonology (Word Discrimination and Word Articulation)
- Syntax (Grammatic Understanding, Sentence Imitation, and Grammatic Completion)
- Semantics (Picture Vocabulary and Oral Vocabulary)
- Speaking (Oral Vocabulary, Sentence Imitation, and Grammatic Completion)
- Listening (Picture Vocabulary and Grammatic Understanding)
- Spoken Language (all subtests)

Composites are appropriately obtained by adding the subtest scaled scores and converting this sum to a scaled score with a mean of 100 and a standard deviation of 15. The composites are based on only fifty children at each age (250 children), however, rather than the entire sample (1,836 children).

NORMS

The TOLD-P series (TOLD-P, TOLD-P2, and TOLD-P2, second edition) was normed on a total of 2,436 children between 4 and 8 years of age. Because each successive version of the instrument included changes, it is not clear whether all normative information can be validly applied to this version of the test. The distribution of children at each age is reported and is well over one hundred for each age level (range = 315 to 622). Children came from twenty-nine states and British Columbia, Canada. A table on page 43 of the TOLD-P2 manual shows that the normative sample approximates the population derived from the *1985 Statistical Abstract of the United States*. The difference between TOLD-P2 and the population with respect to sex is 2 percent; residence (urban/rural), 3 percent; race, 1 to 5 percent; geographic region (four U.S. regions), 4 to 7 percent; and occupation of parents, 2 to 11 percent. Nonetheless, additional data would be helpful for interpreting the adequacy of the normative sample. Norms are important because they are used to derive standard scores for each age group. Therefore, correspondence between the sample and the population *at each age* is important. This problem has persisted in each version of the TOLD-P series.

The norms for age 4 for several subtests (and hence composites) are less useful for identification because of restriction of range difficulties. For example, a child who completes no items correctly on the Oral Vocabulary subtest receives a standard score of 7, but a child who completes only one item correctly scores within the normal range. This problem is also evident on the Word Discrimination, Word Articulation, and Grammatical Completion Subtests.

RELIABILITY

Split-half reliability estimates are presented that are based on the performance of part of the standardiza-

tion sample (fifty children at each age). For the seven subtests at the five age groups, seventeen of the thirty-five corrected coefficients equal or exceed .90. For the composites, thirty-four of the thirty-five corrected coefficients equal or exceed .90. Lower coefficients are reported from other studies that assessed special samples.

Stability (within a five-day interval) was estimated from the performances of twenty-one children who ranged in age from 4 to 8. All but two subtests had stabilities in excess of .90. However, because raw scores were used to estimate stability and raw scores on the TOLD-P2 are correlated with age (see the section on Validity below), the obtained coefficients are systematically inflated. A more recent study by McNeilly (1987) of test-retest stability over a two-week period (and corrected for attenuation) yielded stability coefficients that were consistently lower that those reported by Newcomer and Hammill (and calculated for the original TOLD-P in 1977). The coefficients reported by McNeilly ranged from .74 to .95, with three greater than .70 but less than .80, three greater than .80 but less than .90, and one greater than .90. Given the wide use of the TOLD-P series, one would expect future editions to include updated stability coefficients using a larger sample of children.

VALIDITY

Several types of validity data are presented for TOLD-P2. The authors establish content validity by arguing that their subtests measure the same things as subtests of other devices used to assess language and by collecting survey data showing that a group of experts felt that the items included in the test were measuring the appropriate domains. However, no data are presented to show that the subtests sample the intended domains systematically or completely. Also, one could argue that although these expert raters agreed that specified domains were sampled (for example, listening or speaking), content validity as it relates to the content validity of the underlying model should also be examined. For example, the authors should not only have experts rate whether Word Discrimination and Word Articulation are parts of phonology, but also have these experts indicate whether these subtests are an important, central part of phonology and whether these subtests assess important aspects of phonological competence. This type of question should be included for all subtests and all domains.

To establish criterion-related validity, the authors discuss several studies showing that various TOLD-P2 subtests correlate with other appropriate language measures at each age. Evidence offered for construct validity is in the form of correlations of TOLD-P2 scores with age, intelligence, academic achievement, and school readiness. Further evidence offered is in the form of intercorrelations of subtests and factor analyses. Finally, TOLD-P2 differentiates handicapped students from nonhandicapped students.

SUMMARY

TOLD-P2 is an individually administered, norm-referenced test designed to assess expressive and receptive semantics, syntax, and phonology. Norms are provided, but problems in interpreting these norms that were evident in earlier versions still remain. The reliability is at least adequate or better for screening and for classification decisions. The item sample seems too sparse for the test to be used for either program planning or program evaluation. Validity appears adequate for general purposes. The TOLD-P2 appears to be most appropriate for identifying children with speech and language disabilities, but intervention plans should include data from other measures to ensure adequate domain sampling.

Test of Language Development, Intermediate 2

Language Components Assessed   Semantics, morphology, syntax, and phonology

Communication Channels   Expressive and receptive

*T*he Test of Language Development, Intermediate 2 (TOLD-I2) (Hammill & Newcomer, 1988) is a norm-referenced, individually administered device designed for use with children between the ages of 8-6 and 12-11. In addition to facilitating research, TOLD-I2 is intended to identify children with language problems, to ascertain a child's language strengths and weaknesses, and to evaluate pupil progress in language programs. Various aspects of language are assessed by the following six subtests.

Sentence Combining   In this twenty-five-item subtest, a child must combine two or more simple sentences into a compound, complex, or compound-complex sentence that incorporates all the essential information from the original simple sentences.

Vocabulary   This thirty-five-item subtest requires the child to make judgments about the relationship between words presented in pairs. Specifically, the child must identify whether the word pairs represent opposites (for example, *thin-thick*), similar (same) meanings (for example, *foolish-stupid*), or are unrelated (neither) (for example, *gleam-league*).

Word Ordering   In this twenty-five-item subtest of syntactic ability, a sentence in which the words have been scrambled is presented orally. The child must reorder the words to make a correct English sentence (for example, *party, fun, was, the*).

Generals   This twenty-five-item subtest requires a child to find a superordinate semantic classification for three words that are read by the examiner (for example, *perch, bass, trout* are read to the child, who is expected to identify these as *types of fish*).

Grammatic Comprehension   In this forty-item subtest, a child must state whether a sentence presented orally is grammatically correct. Ten sentences are correct (foils), and thirty are incorrect.

Malapropisms   The child is required to identify an incorrect word in each of the thirty sentences on this subtest and supply the correct form. (For example, the child is required to tell the examiner that the word *photograph* should have been used in the sentence "John took a phonograph of his family.") As with the previous subtests, the items are read to the child by the examiner.

SCORES

Subtest raw scores can be transformed into percentiles and standard scores (mean = 10, standard deviation = 3). Subtests can be combined into five composites:

- Syntax (Grammatic Comprehension, Sentence Combining, and Word Ordering)
- Semantics (Vocabulary, Generals, and Malapropisms)
- Speaking (Sentence Combining, Word Ordering, and Generals)
- Listening (Vocabulary, Grammatic Comprehension, and Malapropisms)
- Spoken Language (all subtests)

Composites are appropriately obtained by adding the subtest scaled scores and converting this sum to a scaled score with a mean of 100 and a standard deviation of 15. The composites are based on fifty children at each age, rather than the entire sample.

NORMS

The TOLD-I2 was normed on 1,214 children between the ages of 8-6 and 12-11. The distribution of children at each age is reported in Table 5 on page 31 of the manual. Well over 200 children are included at the 9, 10, 11, and 12 year levels. Only sixty-six children were included at the 8 year level.

Children came from twenty-one states. A table on page 31 of the TOLD-I2 manual shows that the normative sample approximates the population extracted from the *1985 Statistical Abstract of the United States*. There is no difference between the TOLD-I2 norm group and the population with respect to sex. The difference with respect to residence (urban/rural) is 5 percent; for race, 6 percent; for geographic region (four U.S. regions), 1–4 percent; and for occupation of parents, 2–6 percent. It is difficult to interpret these norms, however, because samples were pooled from previous versions of the TOLD-I, and because there have been substantial changes from earlier versions. (The original TOLD-I included a Characteristics subtest that is deleted in the current versions and the Vocabulary and Malapropisms subtests were not included in the original version.)

RELIABILITY

Coefficient alpha was computed from the performances of 150 children from the standardization sample. Although internal consistency is reported for each age level, the number of children at each age level (of the 150 total) is not reported. For the six subtests within the five age groups (for thirty coefficients), fourteen of the coefficients equal or exceed .90, fifteen exceed .80 but are less than .90, and one is .78. For the composites, all thirty coefficients equal or exceed .90. Stability from the original TOLD-I sample for the four subtests from that version (with a one-week interval) was estimated from the performances of thirty fifth- and sixth-grade students. Two subtests had stabilities of less than .90; all composites exceeded .90. No stability data are provided for other grades or ages. The manual also cites a study by Fodness (1987) of test-retest reliability on fifty-six children over a two-week period. The ages of these children were not reported and Fodness used the first edition of the TOLD-I2. Stability coefficients ranged from .77 to .96, with three greater than .90, two falling between .80 and .90, and one (Vocabulary) between .70 and

.80. No stability data were presented for the TOLD-I2 second edition.

VALIDITY

Three types of validity are discussed in the TOLD-I2 manual. First, expert opinion about what the items might be measuring is offered to support content validity. Hammill and Newcomer (1988) report that the results of this survey of experts indicate high content validity. However, the expert opinion does not attest to the completeness of the domain. For example, the content area of "vocabulary" is measured using a task that requires identification of antonyms, synonyms, or unrelated words. Although this may represent one aspect of the content of the construct "vocabulary" (and be rated as such by judges), few would argue that this represents the entire construct, and many would argue that such a task represents a tertiary skill in the domain. A similar argument could be applied to all subtests. Therefore, although the data presented in the manual are important, additional evaluation of content validity is important and the results from this test should be evaluated with a firm understanding of this limitation.

Criterion-related validity was investigated by correlating TOLD-I2 scores and scores from the Test of Adolescent Language for a group of thirty students. The obtained correlations were corrected to determine the maximum possible correlation between the scores if they were all completely reliable. The median correlation was .56. This information was generated from earlier versions of the TOLD-I and the TOAL. It would be useful to see concurrent validity on other tests, such as the PPVT-R, the CELF-R, the EOWVT-R, and the TACL-R for a more thorough evaluation of the criterion-related validity.

Finally, several types of evidence of construct validity are presented. Language scores are associated with chronological age, TOLD-I2 scores are associated with achievement, and TOLD-I2 differentiates groups of handicapped students (who might be expected to have poorer language skills) from nonhandicapped students. Again, these data were generated, at least in part, using earlier versions of the instrument and they may not apply to the revised version (second edition), which included two subtests not used in the original TOLD-I.

SUMMARY

TOLD-I2 is an individually administered, norm-referenced test designed to assess expressive and receptive semantics, morphology, syntax, and phonology. The internal consistency of the composites is high, as is the stability for the sampled grade levels. Some evidence of construct validity, criterion-related validity, and content validity is presented. As with the other tests in this series (the TOAL-3 and TOLD-P2), the TOLD-I2 meets a higher number of psychometric criteria than many tests designed to evaluate oral language. However, there are limitations in the validity assessment and some concern about the accuracy of the psychometric assessments completed on the original TOLD-I, which is substantially different from the current version.

Carrow Elicited Language Inventory

Language Components Assessed   Morphology and syntax

Communication Channel   Expressive

he Carrow Elicited Language Inventory (CELI) (Carrow, 1974) is one of the few formal tests designed to give the examiner information about a child's expressive grammatical competence. Although quantification of a child's abilities is possible and normative data are provided, the CELI is best used as a criterion-referenced device that allows the examiner to determine which specific elements of language the child is producing incorrectly.

The CELI is an individually administered device consisting of fifty-one grammatically loaded sentences and one phrase. The lengths of the stimuli range from two to ten words, with an average length of six words. Within these sentences, the following grammatical forms are tested: forty-one pronouns (of six different types), fourteen prepositions (in four contexts), seven conjunctions, forty-one articles (in two contexts), nine adverbs, five *Wh* questions (who, what, where, when, and why), thirteen negatives (in three contexts), fifty-nine nouns (both singular and plural), seven adjectives, 103 verbs (of twenty types), eight infinitives, and one gerund.

To administer the test, the examiner presents a stimulus sentence and asks the child to imitate that sentence. Ideally, the child's responses should be taped so that there can be two levels of analysis: one immediate and one after listening to the tape. The scoring sheet is in the form of a matrix, with the grammatical categories listed horizontally and the sentences listed vertically in the order in which they are presented to the child. The examiner identifies and analyzes any elements in a sentence that the child has produced incorrectly. A second score sheet, called the verb protocol, allows for a detailed analysis of the verb errors a child is making. This is helpful because a large percentage of grammatical errors made by children involve verbs. The verb protocol is suggested if the child's verb score falls below the tenth percentile. However, it can be used profitably with children above that cut-off point.

The test itself takes about 20 to 30 minutes to administer, depending on the child's attention span (which can be a problem, as the only stimuli are the orally presented sentences). The analysis, however, can take up to 45 minutes. Detailed training of prospective examiners, including use of a training tape and case studies of "practice children" included

in a kit, is recommended. Although the CELI was developed for use by speech-language pathologists, the manual states that any examiner with a language background will be able to administer and use the test.

Finally, the manual warns that the test should not be used with children with such severe misarticulation that the examiner cannot understand what is being said or children with echolalia.

SCORES

The number of grammatical errors a child makes is summed to provide the total error score, from which other kinds of scores may be obtained. An error score in each of the grammatical subcategories can also be obtained. Percentile ranks are given that correspond to the child's total and subcategory error scores. Stanines have been provided for each age level and subcategory.

As stated above, the CELI is best used as a criterion-referenced device. In fact, the normative scores provided have some problems that are not explained in the technical manual. For example, from age 36 months to 79 months, the expected error score decreases. This is unsurprising. However, from 79 months to 95 months, the error score begins to rise again. Although the author claims that perhaps a test ceiling has been reached at 79 months and that the increased error score is due to random factors, this hypothesis has not been tested.

A second problem with the scores provided is the instability of both of the subcategory error scores. The author states, "With the exception of the verb subscore in the grammar categories . . . the performance of the five, six, and seven year old children in the subcategories was relatively homogeneous within each age group. Consequently, the percentile scores must be interpreted with caution" (Carrow, 1974, p. 20). Thus, a seven-year-old child who makes no contraction errors will be at the one-hundredth percentile, whereas one who makes just one error will be at the fifteenth percentile. Also, because the scores of each of the groups are so homogeneous, a child can achieve a score of 31 at age 3-11 and be placed in the seventy-sixth percentile, and yet one month later, if the child achieves the same score at 4-0, he or she is placed in the twenty-eighth percentile. It seems, then, that the range of the age groups used in computing the scores (one year) is too large to trace the development of language accurately.

NORMS

The CELI was standardized on a restricted group of 475 white middle-class children aged 3-0 to 7-11 from homes where only Standard American English was spoken. The author acknowledges that this is a narrowly defined group and indicates the intent to gather additional data on language-disordered children and children speaking the major dialects of English. All children in the original norming group were selected from day-care centers and church schools in middle-income neighborhoods in Houston, Texas. Children who had any speech or language disorders were eliminated from the sample.

RELIABILITY

Three measures of reliability are provided for the CELI. Test-retest reliability was determined for twenty-five children (five each across five age levels) selected at random and retested after two weeks. The same examiner performed both tests. The stability coefficient obtained was .98.

Two measures of interrater reliability were obtained. First, two examiners listened to and scored ten randomly selected tapes of children's responses, with a resulting reliability coefficient of .98. Second, two examiners administered the test to twenty children, ten of whom were diagnosed as having language disorders. Taped responses were transcribed and scored, with a resultant correlation coefficient of .99.

VALIDITY

Because the CELI is best used as a criterion-referenced test, much of its validity rests on its content validity. Although the author makes little reference to content validity in the test manual, the wide variety of language structures sampled appears to indicate that the test's content is valid. However, it also appears that certain structures are inadequately sampled; for these structures, more caution is desirable when making conclusions about a child's language abilities.

Evidence of concurrent validity is presented in the technical manual. First, the CELI was compared with the Developmental Sentence Scoring (DSS) procedure (Lee and Canter, 1971), a widely used procedure for analyzing children's language abilities. The correlation between the two measures was −.79. (Because the CELI uses error scores and the DSS uses "correct" scores, the correlation is negative.) Content validity was tested by obtaining scores on the CELI for twenty children. These scores were ranked from highest to lowest and then compared with a ranking of these children according to the external clinical judgment of expert observers. The number of judges conducting this evaluation was not reported in the manual. The rank order correlation (rho) between the CELI and the ranking of the children by the judges was .77.

Finally, Carrow presents some evidence of construct validity. The correlation coefficient between total error score and age was −.62. Also, the manual presents some evidence that the CELI successfully separates children with language disorders from those with normal language.

SUMMARY

The CELI is an individually administered device designed to measure the expressive morphological and syntactic abilities of children between 3 and 8 years of age. Reliability and validity data appear adequate, and the test appears to be useful to identify children with language disorders (Camarata, Nelson, & Camarata, in press).

Expressive One-Word Picture Vocabulary Test–Revised

Language Component Assessed   Semantics (Vocabulary)

Communication Channel   Expressive

Languages   English and Spanish

The Expressive One-Word Picture Vocabulary Test–Revised (EOWPVT-R) (Gardner, 1990) is one of the few formal expressive vocabulary tests that has a standardized form for Spanish in addition to one for English. It provides a standard estimate of a child's spoken vocabulary in a relatively quick assessment and provides norm-referenced information that is particularly useful for identifying strengths and weaknesses within this construct. It is important to note that the EOWPVT-R is domain specific for expressive vocabulary and should not be used to make more general descriptions of the child's language skills. For example, Whitehurst, Fischel, Arnold, and Lonigan (1992) described children with low EOWPVT-R scores as having "expressive language delay," although the instrument samples only one expressive language domain. Gardner recognizes this when he states

> "It is this author's (Gardner) opinion that tests of this type are valuable when used for the purpose for which the test was intended, and while the EOWPVT-R can be used by itself for obtaining an estimate of the child's expressive one-word picture vocabulary ability, it becomes more useful and meaningful when used as part of a battery of other well-standardized and well-normed psychological tests (1990, p. 5).

The EOWPVT-R is an individually administered device consisting of four training items and one hundred test pictures. The stimulus items are developmentally ordered to allow establishment of basal and ceiling levels so that the entire set of test pictures need not be administered. To administer the test, the examiner presents a stimulus picture and asks the child to name that item. Ideally, the child's responses should be taped so that there can be two levels of analysis: one immediate and one after listening to the tape. This latter method is advised if one wishes to perform secondary phonological analysis on the named pictures (as suggested by Gardner on page 1 of the test manual).

The test itself takes about 20 to 30 minutes to administer, depending on the child's attention span and level of cooperation. Scoring is relatively quick and straightforward, particularly for users who are already familiar with the Peabody Picture Vocabulary Test–Revised (Dunn & Dunn, 1981), which uses a similar format.

SCORES

The number of correctly named pictures is used as a raw score. If a basal score is obtained (eight consecutive correct responses), items falling below the basal level are assumed to be correct and are added to the number of correct items to yield the raw score. This raw score is then transformed to a standard score (mean = 100, standard deviation = 15) or a scaled score (mean = 10, standard deviation = 3) appropriate for the child's age level. These can then be converted to stanines and/or percentile ranks if desired. A table for converting the raw scores to age equivalencies is also provided.

NORMS

The EOWPVT-R was standardized on a restricted group of 1,118 children aged 2-0 to 11-11 residing in the San Francisco Bay area. Approximately equal proportions of males and females were included in the sample at each age level. More than one hundred children were included in the normative sample from age 4 years through age 11 years, but only 53 children were included at 2 years and only 77 were included at 3 years. No information was provided regarding the ethnic background of the standardization sample, nor were data on socioeconomic status provided. It is presumed that the standardization sample included only English-speaking children; no standardization data are provided for administration of the instrument in Spanish. It appears that applying the EOWPVT-R to Spanish-speaking individuals requires use of the norms for English speakers, which limits, the usefulness of the norms in this group.

RELIABILITY

Split-half reliability was computed for each age level in the standardization sample and reliability coefficients were generated using the Kuder-Richardsen formula (KR-20). These range from .84 at age 2 to .92 at age 9, with a median reliability coefficient of .90. The manual also includes conversion of reliability to standard error of measurement (SEM) at each age interval for standard scores and for scaled scores. No other reliability data were reported.

VALIDITY

Evidence of concurrent validity is presented in the technical manual. The EOWPVT-R was compared with the various subtests of the WPPSI-R, Vocabulary and Similarities subtests of the WISC-R, Word Opposites subtest of the DTLA-2, various subtests of the the Test of Auditory-Perceptual Skills, and the Reading subtest of the Test of Academic Achievement Skills. These comparisons generally yielded low to moderate correlations (ranging from .19 to .59). In addition it should be noted that the concurrent validity was completed on a restricted age range of the EOWPVT-R because the comparison tests did not uniformly overlap with regard to applicability across age ranges. This is particularly noteworthy for the lower age ranges of the EOWPVT-R, as no concurrent validity was completed for the 2 and 3 year levels.

Content validity was not assessed directly, but the author indicates that the procedures for test construction ensured that items were selected to reflect general English use for expressive vocabulary. The author also indicates that item analysis was completed on a larger pool of pictures to ensure that included items were maximally discriminative within and across age groups and to ensure that appropriate items were included.

No additional information on construct or criterion-related validity was provided.

SUMMARY

The EOWPVT-R is an individually administered device designed to measure the expressive vocabulary of children between 2 and 11 years of age. This instrument is useful in providing specific data from the the expressive semantics language domain. Reliability and validity data are provided for application to English speaking four to eleven-year-olds. Interpretations of results from two- and three-year-olds and from Spanish-speaking children should be made with caution because of limited normative and validity data.

COPING WITH DILEMMAS IN CURRENT PRACTICE

Three issues are particulary troublesome in the assessment of oral language: (1) ensuring that the elicited language assessment is a true reflection of the child's general spontaneous language capacity, (2) using the results of standardized tests to generate effective therapy, and (3) adapting assessment to individuals who do not match the characteristics of the standardization sample. All of these dilemmas stem from the limited nature of the standardized tests and must be addressed in practice.

From a practical standpoint, the clinician must use standardized tests to identify a language impaired child. Yet, as noted earlier in this chapter, such instruments may not directly measure a child's true language abilities. Thus, the clinician must supplement the standard tests with nonstandard spontaneous language sampling. Additionally, if possible, the child should be observed in a number of settings outside the formal testing situation. After the spontaneous samples have been gathered, the results of these analyses should be compared to the performance on the standardized tests.

Selection of targets for intervention is one of the more difficult tasks facing the clinician. Many standardized tests that are useful for identifying language disorders in children may not lend themselves to determining efficient treatment. The clinician must evaluate the results of both the standard and nonstandard assessment procedures and decide which language skills are most important to the child. Although it is tempting simply to train the child to perform better on a particular test (hence boosting performance on that instrument), the clinician must bear in mind that such tasks are often metalinguistic in nature and will not ultimately result in generalized language skills. Rather, the focus of treatment should be on those language behaviors and structures that are needed for improved language competence in the home and in the classroom.

Finally, in today's oral language assessment environment, with a plethora of multicultural and socioeconomic variation in caseloads, a clinician is bound to encounter many children who differ in one or more respects from the standardization sample of a particular test. Indeed, clinicians are likely to see children who do not match the standardization sample of *any* standardized test. When this occurs, the clinician must interpret the scores derived from these tests conservatively. Information from nonstandard assessments becomes even more important and the clinician should obtain reports from parents, teachers, and peers regarding their impressions of the child's language competence. Additionally, the clinician should determine whether local norms have been developed for the standard and nonstandard assessment procedures. As noted earlier, it is inappropriate to treat multicultural language differences as if they were language disorders. However, the clinician performing an assessment must judge whether the child's language is disordered within his or her language community and what impact such disorders may have on classroom performance and communication skills generally.

SUMMARY

The primary function of standard oral language tests is to identify language disorders. Assessment sessions should include nonstandard measures such as language sampling to augment the results obtained from standard instruments. The assessment session should include measures of all aspects of oral language, including phonology, semantics, morphology, syntax, and pragmatics across both receptive and expressive channels.

This chapter's review of standardized tests indicates a general lack of application of psychometric principles to the construction of these instruments. Such a conclusion has been supported in the literature (see McCauley & Swisher, 1984). Although more recent tests have generally included more detailed psychometric data, the basic challenge of upgrading standardized tests remains. Additionally, the mismatch between the standard instruments and the content of the field remains large. Standard measures of language sampling are needed, as are reliable and valid instruments designed to measure pragmatics. The commercial success of the TOLD series suggests that professionals in the field would welcome new instruments that meet a majority of the psychometric criteria outlined elsewhere within this book.

Finally, a review of the first edition of this book indicates that the theoretical basis of language has changed dramatically over the past decade. The earliest version of this book included only three components of language. The "new" areas of language represent new constructs that fill gaps in the earlier models of language. As noted elsewhere, testing technology lags behind the theoretical frontiers. The reader should be aware that new instruments will be designed to assess these domains and that such instruments may change the manner in which oral language is assessed.

STUDY QUESTIONS

1. Define *oral language* and identify the five components of language.
2. Define *metalinguistic* and describe a task that is metalinguistic in nature.
3. Why should a standard assessment instrument be used to identify language disorders?
4. Why should language sampling procedures be included in the assessment session?
5. What are the three techniques for obtaining a sample of language from a child?
6. Design an assessment session that includes information on all aspects of language for both comprehension and production. Be sure to include a list of specific tests required to complete the session. Don't forget to include language sampling.

ADDITIONAL READING

Lahey, M. (1988). *Language disorders and language development*. New York: Macmillan.

Miller, J. (1981). *Assessing language production in children*. Austin: Pro-Ed.

Reed, V. (1986). *An introduction to children with language disorders*. New York: Macmillan.

Chapter 24

Assessment of Written Language

*W*ritten expression is the end product of a considerable amount of intellectual activity: the formation of ideas, their elaboration, their sequencing, and so forth. Much of what we consider to be writing is a creative endeavor. One's ability to use words to excite, to depict vividly, to imply is far more than a set of mechanical skills that can be taught, although they can be polished and honed. However, several aspects of written language can be thought of as skills that can be taught and mastered. These skills have been separated from those discussed in Chapter 23 on oral language because they are routinely taught in school. Within most educational settings, writing is the primary means by which students demonstrate their knowledge. The written encoding of language requires that we observe certain conventions, or rules. These conventions are taught in school and learned by students. Several components of written language are assessed: spelling, punctuation and capitalization, grammar, word usage, penmanship, and, occasionally, outlining and organizing.

Spelling is assessed as part of several standardized tests: the California Achievement Tests, the Iowa Tests of Basic Skills and Tests of Achievement and Proficiency, the Metropolitan Achievement Tests, the Stanford Achievement Test, the Wide Range Achievement Test–III, the Peabody Individual Achievement Test–Revised, the BRIGANCE® Diagnostic Inventory of Basic Skills, the Durrell Analysis of Reading Difficulty, and the Woodcock-Johnson Psychoeducational Battery–Revised. However, the spelling words that students are to learn vary considerably from curriculum to curriculum. For example, Ames (1965) examined seven spelling series and found that they introduce an average of 3,200 words between the second and eighth grades. However, only about 1,300 words were common to all the series; about 1,700 words were taught in only one series. Moreover, the words taught in several series varied considerably in their grade placement, sometimes by as many as five grades.

Mechanics (capitalization and punctuation) are also assessed on several achievement batteries: the California Achievement Tests, the Iowa Tests of Basic Skills and Tests of Achievement and Proficiency, the Metropolitan Achievement Tests, the Stanford Achievement Test, the BRIGANCE® Diagnostic Inventory of Basic Skills, and the Woodcock-Johnson Psychoeducational Battery–Revised. Again, standardized tests are not well suited to measuring achievement in these areas, since the grade level at which these skills are taught varies so much from one curriculum to another. To be valid, the measurement of achievement in these areas must be closely tied to the curriculum being taught. For example, pupils may learn that a sentence always begins with a capital letter in either kindergarten, first grade, second grade, or later. They may learn that commercial brand names are capitalized in the sixth grade or several grades earlier. Students may be taught that the apostrophe in "it's" makes the word a contraction of "it is" in the second or third grade but may still be studying "it's" in high school. Finally, in assessing word usage, organization, and penmanship we must take into account the emphasis that individual teachers place on these components of written language and when and how students are taught.

The more usual way to assess written language is to conduct an informal evaluation of a student's written work and to develop vocabulary and spelling tests that parallel the curriculum. In this way teachers can be sure that they are measuring precisely what has been taught. Most teachers' editions of language arts series contain scope and sequence charts that specify fairly clearly the objectives that are taught in each unit. From these charts teachers can develop appropriate criterion-referenced tests.

WHY DO WE ASSESS WRITTEN LANGUAGE?

Written language and spelling are regularly taught in school, and these areas are singled out for assessment in Public Law 94-142 and IDEA. We assess written language and spelling for the same reasons we assess any achievement area. We may use tests to screen for pupils who exhibit difficulties in various aspects of written language. We may use tests to ascertain eligibility for special educational services for the language-impaired or learning-disabled. We may use language tests as aids in planning instructional programs. Finally, we may use language tests to evaluate the progress of individual pupils.

TESTS OF WRITTEN EXPRESSION AND SPELLING

Test of Written Language–2

*T*he Test of Written Language–2 (TOWL-2) (Hammill & Larsen, 1988) is a norm-referenced device designed to assess written-language competence of students between the ages of 7 years, 6 months and 17 years, 11 months. Although designed to be administered to individual students, the authors claim that it can be given to groups; the only proviso given for group administration is to "stop testing when the vast majority of the individuals in the group have attained a ceiling" (p. 13). Because the test scores are based on individual administration, great care should be exercised in interpreting the results of group administration. The recommended uses of TOWL-2 include identifying students with writing difficulties, determining strengths and weaknesses of individual students, evaluating student progress, and doing research.

TOWL-2 is published with two alternate forms, A and B. On each form, ten subtests are combined into three composite scores: Overall Written Language (a composite of all subtests), Contrived Writing (a composite based on five subtests), and Spontaneous Writing (a composite based on the other five subtests). Contrived Writing is defined by the test authors as "the ability to write when measured by tests having contrived formats" (Hammill & Larsen, 1988, p. 6). Later in the test manual contrived formats are defined as "traditional, standardized test formats" (p. 46). Following are brief descriptions of the five contrived-writing subtests and their formats.

Vocabulary This area is assessed by having a student write correct sentences using stimulus words.

Spelling The TOWL-2 assesses spelling by having a student write sentences from dictation.

Style Competence in this aspect of writing is assessed by evaluating the punctuation and capitalization of words in sentences written from dictation.

Logical Sentences Competence in this area is assessed by having students rewrite illogical sentences so that they make sense.

Sentence Combining TOWL-2 requires students to write one grammatically correct sentence based on the information in several, short sentences presented visually.

Spontaneous Writing is assessed from a "free, spontaneously produced essay" (p. 46). On the TOWL-2, a student is asked to write a story using one of two pictures as a story starter. After the story has been written (and the other five subtests administered), the story is scored on five dimensions. Each dimension is treated as a subtest. Following are brief descriptions of how these subtests are scored.

Thematic Maturity This aspect is assessed by evaluating a student's story on the basis of thirty different elements (for example, paragraph usage, naming objects depicted in the stimulus, definite story ending, presence of a moral or philosophic theme, and so forth).

Contextual Vocabulary This area is evaluated by counting the number of different seven-letter words contained in the story.

Syntactic Maturity TOWL-2 evaluates this factor by counting the number of grammatical errors in the story. Spelling and punctuation errors are not counted as grammatical errors.

Contextual Spelling Competence on this subtest is evaluated by counting the number of different words that have been spelled correctly.

Contextual Style This subtest is evaluated on the basis of the number of different punctuation and capitalization rules used in the story. Rules are given different point values. For example, a period at the end of sentence and capitalizing the first word of a sentence each are awarded one point; a comma after an introductory clause and capitalizing proper adjectives (for example, *American*) each are awarded three points.

SCORES

Raw scores for each subtest can be converted to percentiles or standard scores. The standard scores have a mean of 10 and a standard deviation of 3. Composite quotients are standard scores with a mean of 100 and a standard deviation of 15. Percentiles may be obtained.

Raw-score conversions are based on age rather than grade. However, written expression is not a trait that develops independently of schooling;

much of TOWL-2's content (for example, spelling, punctuation, and paragraph usage, among others) is systematically taught in school. Therefore, grade conversions are more appropriate. Furthermore, students of the same age may receive instruction in two or three different grades. Because skill levels should be more closely related to grade than age, age norms will likely be more variable than grade norms, and estimates of reliability may be somewhat inflated.

NORMS

TOWL-2 was standardized on 2,216 students from nineteen states. Overall, the sample approximates the characteristics of people living in the United States on selected demographic variables. Urbanites and Hispanics are slightly overrepresented; Westerners are substantially overrepresented (they are 25 percent of people in the norm group versus 20 percent of the U.S. population), whereas Southerners are substantially underrepresented (29 versus 34 percent). Because the test authors have provided demographic data only for the entire sample, the representativeness of the normative sample at each age is unknown. However, because the data from the total sample are averages, the samples at specific age groups are probably less representative than the total sample.

RELIABILITY

Three types of reliability are discussed in the TOWL-2 manual: interscorer reliability, internal-consistency reliability, and stability with alternate forms. Interscorer reliability was estimated by having two scorers each evaluate twenty protocols selected to represent short, medium, and long stories written by third, seventh, and tenth graders. With the exception of an anomalous value for sentence combining on Form A, all interscorer correlations exceed .90.

Internal-consistency (that is, split-half and coefficient-alpha) estimates of reliability are incompletely reported. Coefficient alpha was computed for the five Contrived Writing subtests; split-half estimates, corrected by the Spearman Brown formula, were computed for the five Spontaneous Writing subtests. The data reported in the test manual are based on the performances of twenty-five students randomly selected from each age group. Adjacent age groups between the ages of 7 and 14 were then combined to create groups of fifty students (for example, seven- and eight-year-olds); the fifteen-, sixteen-, and seventeen-year-olds were combined into one group of seventy-five students. Combining age groups is undesirable for two reasons. First, because raw scores must be used to estimate both alpha and split-half coefficients, the combined ranges of ability underlying the correlations are needlessly extended. Therefore, these estimates of reliability are likely inflated. Second, reliability estimates should be reported for each score at each age. Because TOWL-2 subtest reliability coefficients seem to increase with age, test users should be cautious when interpreting subtests with students younger than 10 years old. Conclusions about the internal consistency of TOWL-2 must be tempered; reliability estimates appearing in the test manual are probably maximum values. In general, TOWL-2 subtests probably have adequate internal consistency for screening purposes; composite scores probably have adequate reliability for decisions about individual students.

Alternate-form reliability (with an average testing interval of two days) is based on seventy-seven students who lived in Austin, Texas. Because standard scores were used in the analysis, the range of ability underlying the correlation should not be affected. All the obtained coefficients are less than .90. Moreover, the internal-consistency estimates that are presented often contradict the notion that A and B are truly alternate forms. The data from the 7- to 8-year-old age group readily illustrate the problem: The Form A vocabulary subtest has a reliability of .83 whereas the Form B vocabulary subtest has a reliability coefficient of .95; Form A contextual spelling has an estimated reliability of .97 whereas Form B contextual spelling has an estimated reliability of .70.

Stability was estimated by statistically removing the average error associated with internal consistency from the alternate-form estimate of reliability. However, because there is considerable variation in the internal-consistency estimates between the two forms of the test, the average internal consistency for any subtest or composite will overestimate the stability on one form while underestimating the stability on the other form. Given this problem, TOWL-2 scores should not be considered sufficiently stable for purposes other than screening.

VALIDITY

Some claim for content validity can be made from the way the test was developed, the completeness of the dimensions of written language, and the methods by which competence in written language is assessed. Those major aspects of written language that lend themselves to objective appraisal are assessed. However, more subjective aspects (for example, content generation, cohesion, audience considerations) are not. The subtest and total scores are intuitively interpretable. The interpretation of the Contrived Writing and Spontaneous Writing composites is more problematic because they represent testing format rather than test content. Moreover, the results of factor-analytic studies (discussed later) suggest that TOWL-2 subtests assess only one general factor—that is, general written language.

Evidence for TOWL-2's criterion-related validity comes from two studies. The first study relates the TOWL-2 performance of sixty-eight students of unknown demographic characteristics to their performance on the Language Arts subtest of the SRA Achievement Test. The obtained correlations support a claim for the criterion-related validity of the Contrived Writing subtests but offer less support for the validity of the Spontaneous Writing subtests. The second study evaluated TOWL-2 essays of fifty-one private school students from Austin, Texas, who were enrolled in grades two through seven. The essays were graded holistically and with the TOWL-2 criteria. The correlation of holistic ratings with the total TOWL-2 score was .61; all other correlations were less than .50. However, because it is unclear if raw or standard scores were used in the statistical analyses, the correlations may be inflated.

Several types of evidence for TOWL-2's construct validity are offered in the test manual. In our opinion, three studies give support to a claim for TOWL-2's construct validity. First, the test correlates modestly with grade. Second, a subsample of learning-disabled students who participated in the standardization of the test earned substantially lower scores on TOWL-2. Third, different procedures were used in factor analysis of the test. The different procedures resulted in different factoral structures; this finding suggests that the factor structure of TOWL-2 is not robust. However, neither procedure found more than two factors, and in both factor analyses the factors identified were consistent with the test's structure.

SUMMARY

The content and structure of TOWL-2 appear appropriate. The representativeness of the test's norms at each age cannot be evaluated with the data presented in the test manual, and age norms are used rather than grade norms. Interscorer reliability is excellent. The internal consistencies of composite and total scores are probably high enough to use in making individual decisions. Although the means and standard deviations of forms A and B appear equivalent, the internal consistencies of subtests within forms do not support the hypothesis that the forms are equivalent. Because of the lack of equivalence of the two test forms, stability data are not readily interpretable. Because of the difficulties with the presentation of norms and reliability data, the validity of TOWL-2 scores is unclear. Although the validity of the test's content appears acceptable, the validity of the quantification of student performance should not be assumed. Consequently, the validity of TOWL-2's ability to identify students with writing difficulties is not established. The data presented in the test manual do not support the contention that TOWL-2 can be used to determine strengths and weaknesses of individual students or to evaluate the progress of individual students.

Test of Written Spelling–2

*T*est of Written Spelling–2 (TWS-2) (Larsen & Hammill, 1986) is the most recent edition of this individually administered, norm-referenced test, intended to assess the spelling ability of students ranging in age from 6-6 to 18-5. TWS-2 is based on the realization that some words are spelled phonetically and need not be taught or learned by memorization, whereas other words are irregular and must be memorized individually. Consequently, there are two subtests on TWS-2.

Predictable Words   This subtest contains fifty words whose spellings are consistently governed by the rules of Standard American English.

Unpredictable Words   This subtest contains fifty words that could not be spelled by computer even after more than two thousand rules of English spelling were applied.

A three-step process is used to administer TWS-2. The examiner reads the word, uses the word in a sentence, and reads the word a second time in isolation. The student then writes the word. Basal and ceiling levels (five consecutive correct responses and five consecutive incorrect responses, respectively) speed administration, which can usually be accomplished in less than 25 minutes. Guidelines for group administration are also given (p. 6).[1]

SCORES

For each subtest and for the total score, raw scores are converted into percentiles and standard scores (called quotients) that have a mean of 100 and a standard deviation of 15.

1. The number of words is fixed for the group; thus, basals and ceilings may not be obtained for all students.

NORMS

The TWS-2 was normed on over 3,800 students from fifteen states. The plan used to obtain the normative sample is not discussed. However, the sample is quite close (within 5 percent) to the general U.S. population as revealed by the 1985 census with respect to sex, residence, race, and ethnicity. The Northcentral region of the United States is underrepresented in the norms (18 percent of the sample but 25 percent of the national population).

RELIABILITY

Internal consistency was estimated with coefficient alpha by examining the responses of fifty students from the standardization sample. A total of thirty-nine coefficients were obtained (two subtests and a total score for thirteen age groups). Only two subtests had coefficients less than .90: Predictable Words and Unpredictable Words for the six-year-old group. Stability (two-week interval) was estimated from the performances of 160 students in the first through eighth grades at one school in Michigan. Again, the coefficients were extremely high. Only one coefficient was less than .90 (Predictable Words for second graders).

VALIDITY

Content validity is of the greatest importance. The TWS-2 is one of only a few tests that precisely relate test content to the content taught in various curricula. Each of the words included in the original TWS appeared in ten basal spelling series. Additional words were added to the TWS-2 to test students between the ages of 13 and 18 and to strengthen the test for younger students. New words for the TWS-2 were selected from the reading core vocabulary in the EDL Core Vocabularies in Reading, Mathematics, Science, and Social Studies. Evidence of criterion-related validity is offered in the form of correlations between the TWS and the spelling subtests of the Durrell Analysis of Reading Difficulty, the Wide Range Achievement Test, the California Achievement Tests, and the SRA Achievement Series. (Because the TWS and the TWS-2 are highly correlated—$r > .90$—correlations between the TWS-2 and those tests can safely be assumed.) These studies are poorly described, however, and the large correlations between measures must be interpreted cautiously. The correlation of TWS-2 scores with age and the poor performance of learning-disabled students are cited as evidence of construct validity.

SUMMARY

The Test of Written Spelling–2 is a norm-referenced, individually administered device designed to assess spelling ability in students between the ages of 6-6 and 18-5. The test has adequate norms, good reliability, and content validity.

COPING WITH DILEMMAS IN CURRENT PRACTICE

The most serious problem in the assessment of written language is identifying a match between what is taught in the school curriculum and what is tested. The great variation in the time at which various skills and facts are taught renders a general test of achievement inappropriate. This dilemma also attends diagnostic assessment of written language. Commercially prepared tests have doubtful validity for planning individual programs and evaluating the progress of individual pupils. We recommend that teachers and diagnosticians construct criterion-referenced achievement tests that closely parallel the curricula followed by the students being tested.

In cases where normative data are required, there are three choices. Diagnosticians can select the devices that most closely parallel the curriculum, develop local norms, or select individual students for comparative purposes.

Care should be exercised in selecting methods of assessing language skills. For example, it is probably better to test pupils in ways that are familiar to them. Thus, if the teacher's weekly spelling test is from dictation, then spelling tests using dictation are probably preferable to tests requiring the student to identify incorrectly spelled words.

SUMMARY

Written language and spelling are regularly assessed in the schools. Teachers routinely assess these skills with informal and criterion-referenced tests. Most standardized test batteries include subtests that assess language and spelling. Very few individually administered tests have been published that deal with these content areas. Two are reviewed in this chapter.

STUDY QUESTIONS

1. Why is it important to teach Standard American English in the public schools?
2. List and explain five components of written language.
3. Why is it important for spelling tests to correspond closely to the spelling words that teachers assign to their students?
4. List and explain three limitations on analyzing a pupil's English composition to assess skill in spelling, grammar, and punctuation.

ADDITIONAL READING

Cooper, C., & Odell, L. (1977). *Evaluating writing: Describing, measuring, judging*. Urbana, IL: National Council of Teachers of English. (Chapter 1: Holistic evaluation of writing; Chapter 2: Primary trait scoring)

Graves, D. (1981). A new look at research on writing. In S. Haley-James (Ed.), *Perspectives on writing in grades 1–8*. Urbana, IL: National Council of Teachers of English.

Hillerich, R. L. (1985). *Teaching children to write, K–8*. Englewood Cliffs, NJ: Prentice-Hall. (Selected chapters on the evaluation of writing)

Isaacson, S. (1988). Assessing the writing product: Quantitative and qualitative measures. *Exceptional children, 54,* 528–535.

Moss, P., Cole, N., & Khampalikit, C. (1982). A comparison of procedures to assess written language skills at grades 4, 7, and 10. *Journal of Educational Measurement, 19,* 37– 47.

Chapter 25

Assessment of Perceptual-Motor Skills

*E*ducators and psychologists have operated for quite some time under the assumption that adequate perceptual-motor development is important both in and of itself and as a prerequisite to the development of academic skills. A wide variety of devices designed to assess children's perceptual-motor functioning are in use in the public schools today. Many measures of learning aptitude include items designed to assess perceptual or motor skills, and many readiness tests assess aspects of perceptual-motor development. However, this chapter focuses on those devices designed specifically and exclusively to assess perceptual-motor skills.

WHY DO WE ASSESS PERCEPTUAL-MOTOR SKILLS?

Perceptual-motor assessment typically takes place for one of several purposes. In some cases, the perceptual-motor skills of entire classes of students are assessed in an effort to identify those with perceptual-motor difficulties so that training programs can be instituted to prevent incipient learning difficulties from worsening. Students who perform poorly on perceptual-motor devices are said to demonstrate perceptual-motor problems thought to contribute to or cause learning problems. In other cases, students having academic difficulties are assessed by means of perceptual-motor tests in an effort to identify whether perceptual-motor difficulties may be causing the academic difficulties. In both instances, efforts are made to identify perceptual-motor problems so that training programs can be prescribed. Finally, perceptual-motor tests are widely used to diagnose brain injury.

THE INTERESTING PAST AND PROBLEMATIC PRESENT OF PERCEPTUAL-MOTOR ASSESSMENT

The practice of perceptual-motor assessment, while relatively new, has an interesting history. In the early 1900s gestalt psychology was born with the publication of a paper by Max Wertheimer that reported the work of Wertheimer, Kurt Koffka, and Wolfgang Kohler on perceptual phenomena such as apparent movement and afterimages. In 1923 Wertheimer put together a set of empirical statements known as the *principles of perceptual organization*. Gestalt psychologists, although certainly concerned with other aspects of psychology, made perception their major study. The early work of Wertheimer and his associates is apparent even today in the assessment of perceptual-motor development.

Hallahan and Cruickshank (1973) traced the history of the study of perceptual-motor problems in children who are mentally retarded, brain-injured, and learning disabled. According to Hallahan and Cruickshank, the historical roots of current practices in perceptual-motor assessment can be traced to the early work of Goldstein and of Werner and Strauss. Goldstein (1927, 1936, 1939) was engaged in the study of soldiers who had suffered traumatic head injuries during World War I. According to Hallahan and Cruickshank (1973), "Goldstein . . . found in his patients . . . the psychological characteristics of concrete behavior, meticulosity, preseveration, figure-background confusion, forced responsiveness to stimuli, and catastrophic reaction" (p. 59).

In the mid-1930s the two German psychologists Heinz Werner and Alfred Strauss began to study the behavioral pathology evidenced by people who were brain-injured. In a series of studies at the Wayne County Training School in Detroit, Michigan, Werner and Strauss studied two kinds of brain-injured subjects: brain-injured retardates and nonretardates who had experienced traumatic head injury from an automobile accident, a fall, a gunshot wound, or other similar incident. Their early research resulted in a list of behavioral characteristics said to differentiate people who were and were not brain-injured. The tests that were constructed to assess these behavioral characteristics are used today for that purpose.

Hallahan and Cruickshank state that "for Werner and Strauss it became a major concern to learn whether the psychological manifestations of brain injury found in adults by Goldstein would also be observable in children" (p. 60). Despite this interest in children, it must be remembered that the subjects studied in early investigations and on whom early tests were developed differ significantly from the children we currently assess using perceptual-motor tests. Subjects in early investigations were primarily adults who exhibited focal brain injury in the form of tissue damage, lesions, or tumors. To generalize characteristics of such persons to children with "diffuse brain injury" ignores neurological differences as well as developmental differences between children and adults. Many current perceptual-motor tests were developed using a criterion-group approach; they were developed to differentiate between *groups* of persons known to have sustained brain injury and people who were non–brain-injured. The tests are currently used to differentiate between *individuals* whose problems may be due to brain injury and those who have no proven injury to the central nervous system.

Although perceptual-motor tests have been used for some time to diagnose brain injury, recently there has been a dramatic and significant increase in the use of various perceptual-motor devices to diagnose learning disabilities. According to Hallahan and Cruickshank (1973), the early leaders in the field of learning disabilities, who were responsible for its origin and development and for the development of the major perceptual-motor tests, were at one time associates or students of Werner and Strauss or were at least significantly influenced by their work. William Cruickshank, Samuel Kirk, and Newell Kephart were all associated with the Wayne County Training School at the time Werner and Strauss were engaged in their early investigations. Gerald Getman, an optometrist, later worked with Kephart at Purdue University; Ray Barsch worked with both Getman and Strauss. Marianne Frostig, although not a direct associate of Werner and Strauss, has stated that she was significantly influenced by their early investigations (Hallahan & Cruickshank, 1973).

The associates of Werner and Strauss went on to apply their early work to the study of behavioral pathology in nonretarded children who were experiencing learning difficulty. Kirk emphasized psycholinguistic disabilities and with his students constructed the Illinois Test of Psycholinguistic Abilities; the others stressed perceptual problems. Cruickshank focused on children with brain injury and children with cerebral palsy, and Kephart, Getman, Barsch, and Frostig focused on the academic correlates of perceptual-motor problems.

Out of the long history of interest in perception and perceptual problems among adults and brain-injured retardates has grown today a particular concern for the perceptual and motor problems of children who are not retarded but who fail academically. The thinking underlying this concern is illustrated by this statement made by Frostig, Lefever, and Whittlesey (1966).

> It is most important that a child's perceptual disabilities, if any exist, be discovered as early as possible. All research to date which has explored the child's general classroom behavior has confirmed the authors' original finding that kindergarten and first-grade children with visual perceptual disabilities are likely to be rated by their teachers as maladjusted in the classroom; not only do they frequently find academic learning difficult, but their ability to adjust to the social and emotional demands of classroom procedures is often impaired. Identification and training of children with visual perceptual disabilities during the preschool years or at the time of school entrance would help prevent many instances of school failure and maladjustment *caused* [emphasis added] by visual perceptual difficulties. Although some children may overcome these difficulties at a later age, there is as yet no method to predict whether a child will be able to do so without help . . . The authors' research has shown that visual perceptual difficulties, regardless of etiology, can be ameliorated by specific training. Pinpointing the areas of a child's visual perceptual difficulties and measuring their severity is helpful and is often necessary

in designing the most efficient training program to aid in overcoming the disabilities. (p. 6)

The writers of the preceding paragraphs (who are also the authors of the first edition of the Developmental Test of Visual Perception) do not cite empirical support for their contentions. We would argue that the claims made are unwarranted. The majority of the research does not support the contention that children with visual-perceptual disabilities are likely to be rated as maladjusted. At most, it can demonstrate simply that children who are rated as maladjusted also perform poorly on perceptual-motor tests. Furthermore, the authors recommend assessment of perceptual-motor difficulties under the assumption that remediation of identified disabilities will lead to greater academic success, and yet reviews of the efficacy of perceptual-motor training demonstrate that it is grossly ineffective in improving academic performance (Mann, 1971; Hammill & Wiederholt, 1973; Ysseldyke, 1973).

What the majority of the research *has* shown is that most perceptual-motor tests are unreliable. We do not know what they measure, because they do not measure anything consistently. Unlike the majority of intelligence and achievement tests, the tests used to assess perceptual-motor skills in children are technically inadequate. And for the most part they are neither theoretically nor psychometrically sound. For example, they are designed to assess perceptual-motor abilities under the assumption that such abilities cause academic success or academic failure (see Ysseldyke & Salvia, 1974). Or they are designed to assess hypothetical constructs like figure-ground perception and body image and differentiation but do not do so with consistency (see Ysseldyke, 1973; Ysseldyke & Salvia, 1974). Or they may be based on criterion keying, an approach that can lead to logical fallacies of undistributed middle terms (all canaries eat birdseed; Esmeralda eats birdseed; therefore, Esmeralda is a canary).

In short, the majority of devices currently used to assess children's perceptual-motor skills are extremely inadequate. The real danger is that reliance on such tests in planning interventions for children may actually lead to assigning children to activities that do them absolutely no good. Having said that few currently available perceptual-motor devices approach either theoretical or psychometrical adequacy, we review those that are most often used.

SPECIFIC TESTS OF PERCEPTUAL-MOTOR SKILLS

Bender Visual Motor Gestalt Test

*T*he Bender Visual Motor Gestalt Test (BVMGT), consisting of nine geometric designs to be copied on paper, was originally developed by Loretta Bender in 1938. The designs in the test were first used by Wertheimer in 1923 to illustrate the perceptual principles of gestalt psychology. Bender used the designs in a test to differentiate brain-injured from non–brain-injured adults and to detect signs of emotional disturbance. The test has gained widespread popularity among clinical psychologists and has become one of the most frequently administered psychometric devices.

Administration of the BVMGT simply consists of presenting nine geometric designs, one at a time, to a subject who is asked to copy each of them on a plain sheet of paper. Although Bender provided criteria for scoring the test, a variety of other scoring systems were developed by Elizabeth Koppitz in 1963. The impetus for Koppitz's work arose from her experience in a child guidance clinic, where she was reportedly impressed with the frequency of perceptual problems among children with emotional difficulties.

The Koppitz scoring system, restricted to use with children between 5 and 11 years of age, is the system most often used by psychologists in school settings. In 1963, Koppitz published a text describing the scoring system, the various uses of the BVMGT with children, normative data for the scoring system, and limited information about reliability and validity. In 1975, Koppitz published volume II of *The Bender Gestalt Test for Young Children,* a compilation and synthesis of research on the BVMGT between 1963 and 1973. This latter text is a commendable effort that eliminates the need to search the literature for research on the test. Our discussion of the BVMGT is based entirely on use of the Koppitz scoring system.

SCORES

When scoring according to the Koppitz system, the examiner records the number of errors on each of the nine separate geometric forms. Four kinds of errors are recorded.

- *Distortion of Shape* Errors are scored as distortion of shape when a child's reproduction of the stimulus design is so misshapen that the general configuration is lost. If a child converts dots to circles, alters the relative size of components of the stimulus drawing, or in other ways distorts the design, errors are recorded.
- *Perseveration* Perseveration errors are recorded when a child fails to stop after completing the required drawing—for example, a child is asked to copy eleven dots in a row and then copies significantly more than eleven.
- *Integration* Integration errors consist of a failure to juxtapose correctly parts of a design, as illustrated in Figure 25.1. In drawing a, the components of the design fail to meet. In drawing b, they overlap.
- *Rotation* Rotation errors are recorded when a child rotates a design by more than 45 degrees or rotates the stimulus card and then copies the rotated drawing correctly. Reversals are 180-degree rotations and are scored as rotation errors.

More than one error can be scored on each drawing. The total number of possible errors is twenty-five. The examiner adds the number of errors to obtain a total raw score for the test. The higher the total raw score, the poorer the performance.

The Koppitz manual (1963) contains a normative table reporting means and standard deviations of error scores for specific age levels in half-year intervals. This normative table, based on the 1963

FIGURE 25.1 **Two Integration Errors in Koppitz's Scoring of the Bender Visual Motor Gestalt Test**

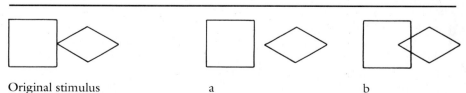

Original stimulus   a   b

standardization of the test, is used to transform error scores to developmental ages. The 1975 publication reporting research on the BVMGT from 1963 to 1973 includes two features. A new set of examples for scoring individual items has been included to eliminate the scoring difficulties that examiners reported to the author. The publicaton also includes a new set of normative tables based on a 1974 renorming of the test. This set of tables can be used to convert error scores to age equivalents and to percentile ranks.

NORMS

Two sets of norms are now available for the Koppitz scoring system. The test was originally standardized on 1,104 children from forty-six classes in twelve public schools. The schools were reportedly selected from rural, urban, and suburban areas in unspecified proportions. The original normative sample included 637 boys and 467 girls. There are no data in the 1963 manual on the geographic areas the sample was drawn from or their demographic characteristics. In volume II (1975), Koppitz reports that 98 percent of the original sample was white.

Koppitz renormed the test in 1974 in an effort to achieve a more representative sample of American schoolchildren. The 1974 normative sample included 975 children between the ages of 5 and 11. A geographic cross section was not attained; 15 percent of the children were from the West, 2 percent were from the South, and 83 percent were from the Northeast. Racial balance is more nearly representative: 86 percent of the sample was white, 8.5 percent was black, 4.5 percent was either Mexican-American or Puerto Rican, and 1 percent was Asian. There is no indication of the socioeconomic level of the sample; Koppitz states that research has demonstrated that socioeconomic status is not an important variable in children's performance on the BVMGT. Community size is adequately described: 7 percent were from rural communities, 31 percent were from small towns, 36 percent from suburbs, and 26 percent were from large metropolitan areas.

The sample sizes for half-year-interval age groups in both the 1963 and 1974 norms are unevenly distributed. For the 1963 norms, the norm groups ranged in size from 27 children at ages 10-0 to 10-5 to 180 children at ages 6-6 to 6-11. For the 1974 norms, the norm groups ranged in size from 47 children (at ages 5-0 to 5-5, 7-6 to 7-11, and 9-6 to 9-11) to 175 children at ages 6-0 to 6-5. Another major difficulty was present in the 1963 standardization: After age 8-6 the standard deviations for raw scores exceeded the means. For the 1974 norms, the standard deviations after age 8-6 are about equal to the means.

Those who use the BVMGT as a norm-referenced test are comparing the individuals they assess to an unknown group. Clearly, such comparisons are unwarranted.

RELIABILITY

Two kinds of reliability data are reported for the BVMGT. Koppitz (1975) summarizes twenty-three studies of the interscorer reliability for her scoring system. Interscorer reliabilities ranged from .79 to .99, with 81 percent exceeding .89. The revised set of scoring examples, published by Koppitz in 1975 after test users reported scoring difficulties, facilitate interscorer agreement in scoring a child's performance.

In her 1975 addition to the 1963 manual, Koppitz reports research on factors she believes may affect performance on the scale. Her review of research on the effects of motivation, task familiarization, verbal labeling, tracing and copying, and specific perceptual-motor training led to the conclusion that the BVMGT does indeed serve mainly as a measure of children's level of maturation in integration of perceptual and motor functions. Only secondarily does it reflect their various learning experiences with specific perceptual-motor tasks.

The 1975 manual also summarizes the results of nine test-retest reliability studies with normal elementary school children. Reliability coefficients ranged from .50 to .90 (mean = 71.48; mode = .76). On the basis of her review, Koppitz made a claim for the essential reliability of the BVMGT scores for normal children. Yet five of the nine reliability studies she reports are on kindergarten children only; and only one of twenty-five reported coefficients exceeds the standard of .90 recommended for tests used to make important decisions. As Koppitz wisely cautions, "Certainly no diagnosis or major decision should ever be made on the basis of a single scoring point, nor for that matter on the basis of a youngster's total Developmental Bender Test score" (p. 29).

VALIDITY

The construct of *visual-motor perception* is never adequately defined in either Koppitz manual. There is no evidence about the extent to which the test assesses visual-motor perception; the copying of nine designs is believed to be a measure of visual perception because some experts say it is one.

Koppitz (1975) cites several uses for the BVMGT and reports research on each of the suggested uses. She reports correlations of performance on the BVMGT and performance on measures of intelligence, academic achievement, and visual perception. She also cites evidence for use of the test in diagnosing minimal brain dysfunction and emotional disturbance. The paragraphs that follow describe some of her findings and recommendations.

In her 1963 manual, Koppitz reported results of tests of the relationship between scores earned on the BVMGT and scores earned on intelligence tests. She concluded that the BVMGT may be substituted "with some confidence" for a screening test of intelligence. She stated:

> In clinical and school settings psychologists are constantly faced with the problem of how to use their limited time most economically. A full scale intelligence test usually requires so much time that only a brief period is left for other tests or an interview. The author has used the Bender Test frequently with young children of normal intelligence who primarily seemed to show emotional problems and revealed no hearing difficulties. The Bender test not only gives the examiner a rough measure of the youngster's intellectual ability, but also serves as a nonthreatening introduction to the interview. Children tend to enjoy copying the Bender designs, and in some cases the Bender figures evoke associations and spontaneous comments which can lead to further discussions. In most cases the Bender Test will suffice to rule out mental retardation or serious perceptual problems associated with neurological impairment and the examiner can use most of his/her time for projective tests and an interview rather than spending it on a lengthy intelligence test which offers little insight into the dynamics of the child's emotional problems. (p. 51)

In the 1975 addition to the 1963 manual, Koppitz continues to support the use of the BVMGT as a rough test of intelligence:

> The statement "The Bender Gestalt Test can be used with some degree of confidence as a short nonverbal intelligence test for young children, particularly for screening purposes" (Koppitz, 1963, p. 50) has been supported by a number of recent studies. But as I previously suggested, the Bender Test should if possible be combined with a brief verbal test. (p. 47)

The BVMGT is *not* an intelligence test but a measure of a child's skill in copying geometric designs. It provides a very limited sample of behavior; in fact, of the thirteen kinds of behaviors described in Chapter 16 as being regularly sampled in intelligence tests, the Bender samples only one. In our opinion, the BVMGT should never be used as, or substituted for, a measure of intellectual functioning.

Koppitz (1975) reviews numerous investigations of the relationship between children's performance on the BVMGT and their academic achievement. Good students and poor students, she concludes, tend as groups to make significantly different total scores on the test. Furthermore, the scores normal children earn show a positive correlation with their academic achievement. Koppitz uses observed differences to conclude that scores earned on the BVMGT appear to be most successful in predicting overall school functioning and rate of progress in total achievement. A child with a marked discrepancy between IQ and Bender Test scores usually has specific learning difficulties. LD pupils and slow learners mature at a significantly slower rate in visual-motor integration, as measured on the Bender Test, than do well-functioning children. Scores from repeated administrations of the Bender Test are good indicators of progress a child is making, and they are helpful in planning an individualized educational program. (p. 70)

Children who perform well in school may in fact do better on the BVMGT than children who experience academic difficulty. But as Koppitz herself states, the test cannot be used to predict the academic performance of *individual* children (1975, p. 70). Moreover, Koppitz has not provided evidence to support the contention that the test facilitates individualization of instruction. To do so would require demonstration of an interaction between test performance and success under different methods or techniques of instruction—demonstration, in other words, of evidence for aptitude-treatment interactions.

Koppitz (1975) reviewed many studies of the use of the BVMGT to diagnose minimal brain dysfunction in school children. She concluded that the test is a valuable aid for this purpose but should never be used in isolation. Rather, she believes test results are valuable when combined with other medical and behavioral data.

Koppitz (1975) also claims that recent research gives additional validity to the ten indicators of emotional problems that she delineated in her 1963 text. Although she again provides notes of caution indicating that not all children with poor Bender protocols have emotional problems, she does state that "the presence of three or more emotional indicators on a Bender Test protocol tends to reflect emotional difficulties that warrant further investigation" (p. 92).

Koppitz (1975) provides evidence to support the contention that performance on the BVMGT is significantly related to performance on other visual-perceptual measures. She does not report the extent to which pupils who achieve low scores on the BVMGT perform well on these other tests or vice versa.

The BVMGT is, quite simply, a measure of skill development in copying geometric designs. It is *not* designed as a measure of intelligence, a predictor of achievement, or a measure of emotional disturbance or minimal brain dysfunction. Using it for any of these purposes is risky and unwarranted.

SUMMARY

The BVMGT requires the child to copy nine geometric designs. The test was originally developed by Bender, who used designs developed earlier by Wertheimer. Koppitz has developed a scoring system for the test, and her system is designed to be used with children ages 5 to 11. The BVMGT is today one of the most widely used psychometric devices. The most recent standardization of the test was in 1974, so the norms are more than twenty years old.

Reliability for the BVMGT is relatively low, at least too low for use in making eligibility decisions. Yet, performance on the test is used as a criterion in the differential identification of children as brain injured, perceptually handicapped, or emotionally disturbed. Validity for the BVMGT is currently not clearly established. The author has not empirically demonstrated that the test measures visual-motor perception or that it discriminates individual cases of brain injury, perceptual handicap, or emotional disturbance. The test certainly provides a very limited sample of perceptual-motor behavior, and, for this reason if for no other, one would have to be extremely cautious in interpreting and using its results.

A statement by Koppitz is a fitting conclusion to our discussion of her test. "The very fact," she writes, "that the Bender Test is so appealing and is easy to administer presents a certain danger. Because it is so deceptively simple, it is probably one of the most overrated, most misunderstood, and most maligned tests currently in use" (1975, p. 2).

Developmental Test of Visual Perception, Second Edition

*T*he revised Developmental Test of Visual Perception (DTVP-2) (Hammill, Pearson, and Voress, 1993) is an individually administered, norm-referenced test designed for use with children between the ages of 4 and 10. In several ways, the second edition of the DTVP is different from the first edition published in the 1960s. Two new composite scores have been added (motor-reduced perception and visual-motor integration), the age range of the test has been extended to age 10, and the technical characteristics (and their reporting) have been substantially improved. Requiring 30 to 60 minutes to administer, the DTVP-2 has eight subtests, all of which have demonstration items.

Eye-Hand Coordination   Four items require children to draw a line on a band that progressively narrows and curves from item one to item four. Each band is segmented, and the child receives a point for each segment in which performance is acceptable. Thus, although there are only four items, the child may earn up to 52 points for staying on the band and not picking up the pencil.

Position in Space   Twenty-five items require children to match a figure from an array containing the same figure in three to five different rotations.

Copying   Twenty items require a child to copy a sample figure of increasing difficulty in a 1.75 inch box. Each drawing is awarded 0, 1, or 2 points on the basis of clear scoring standards.

Figure-Ground   Eighteen items require children to identify two or more figures embedded in a stimulus composed of overlapping and over-drawn figures. Each item is scored pass (1) or fail (0). For example, in item 10 of this subtest, the child must find all of the figures shown in the boxed area that are included in the stimulus drawing at the top of the item.

Spatial Relations   Ten items require children to connect some dots in an array of dots to reproduce a stimulus pattern.

Visual Closure   In these twenty items, children are shown a stimulus picture and required to select (from a multiple-choice array) the option that could match the stimulus picture if that option were completed. The child does not need to draw the stimulus from the option but need only recognize the one option that could be completed.

Visual-Motor Speed   On this timed subtest children are shown four stimuli (large circle, small circle, large square, and small square). The large circle contains two parallel, horizontal lines and the small square contains two diagonal lines connecting opposite corners. Below these stimuli are 128 figures (32 large circles, 32 small circles, etc. in random order) that do not contain the internal lines. Children must add the lines to as many other appropriate figures as they can in one minute. One point is awarded for each figure correctly completed without drawing outside the figure.

Form Constancy   The twenty items in this subtest each contain a stimulus (a geometric form) and an array of response options. For each item, children are required to identify the two options that are the same shape as the stimulus. However, correct response options may be different from the stimulus in size, rotation, color, or shading.

SCORES

All subtests except Visual-Motor Speed have ceiling rules. Subtest raw scores may be converted to age equivalents, percentiles, and normalized standard scores (mean = 10, standard deviation = 3). Subtest standard scores can be summed and converted to three different composite standard scores (each with a mean of 100 and standard deviation of 15): General Visual Perception Quotient (based on all eight subtests), Motor Reduced Visual Perception Quotient (based on the four subtests that only require a pointing response), and Visual-Motor Integration Quotient (based on the four subtests that require drawing).

NORMS

To obtain a normative sample, the authors of the DTVP-2 asked those who had purchased other Pro-Ed perceptual-motor tests to test children in their immediate geographic vicinity. The resulting sample of 1,972 children, from twelve states, appears representative of the United States (1990 census) in terms of race, ethnicity, gender, residence, geographic area, and handedness. Approximately 3 percent of the sample were children with disabilities. The number of children at each age appears to be more than sufficient, except for four-year-olds.[1]

RELIABILITY

Alphas for individual subtests range from .80 (Figure-Ground at three ages) to .97 (Spatial Relations at two ages). Of the fifty-six subtest-by-age alphas, thirty are in the .80s and twenty equal or exceed .90. Thus, individual subtests generally do not have sufficient reliability for making important educational decisions for individual students. The alphas of the three composites are all excellent, ranging from .93 to .98. Similar patterns of results were

found for stability. Eighty-eight students, ranging in age from 4 through 10 years, were tested and retested two weeks later.[2] Reliabilities for subtests range from .71 to .86; stabilities for the composites range from .89 to .95. Thus, the composites are quite stable. Finally, interscorer agreement, estimated from the protocols of eighty-eight students, is excellent for subtests and composites.

VALIDITY

The selection of specific subtests is based on classic research and theory in visual perception, and careful and thoughtful item development closely approximates the theoretical constructs on which the subtests are based. Thus, there is strong rationale for the DTVP-2's content validity. Strong evidence of criterion-related validity is also presented in the manual. DTVP-2 scores were correlated with scores from the Motor Free Visual Perception Test (MFVP) and the Developmental Test of Visual Motor Integration (VMI) (a test that requires copying). The correlations between the DTVP-2 subtests and these measures range from .27 to .95. As should occur, DTVP-2 subtests that have a motor component generally correlate more highly with the VMI, whereas subtests without a motor component generally correlate more highly with the MVPT. This pattern is even more pronounced for the composite scores of the DTVP-2. Some evidence of construct validity is provided by the DTVP-2's relationship with age (as should be expected). More compelling are the results of factor analytic studies that suggest that two related factors, approximately the same as Motor Reduced Visual Perception and Visual-Motor Integration, underlie the test. In addition, the DTVP-2 appears to differentiate between groups of children known to be normal and those known to below average in visual perceptual ability. Finally, the DTVP-2 has low correlations with cognitive measures, which supports the notion that visual perception is a distinct ability.

1. Raw scores are converted to derived scores by six-month intervals; for example, the scores of children from 4-0 through 4-5 are converted using one table; scores of children from 4-6 through 4-11 are converted using a different table. The number of children in whole year groups (for example, 4-0 through 4-11) is reported, not the number of children in each half-year group. Nonetheless, assuming even a 60 percent-40 percent division of children into the two age subgroups, all age subgroups would have at least one hundred children, except the four-year-old subgroups, each of which would have around fifty students per subgroup.

2. The authors report stabilities with the effects of age correctly controlled.

SUMMARY

The revised Developmental Test of Visual Perception is an individually administered, norm-referenced test suitable for use with children between the ages of 4 and 10. The DTVP-2 has eight subtests: (1) Eye-Hand Coordination, (2) Position in Space, (3) Copying, (4) Figure-Ground, (5) Spatial Relations, (6) Visual Closure, (7) Visual-Motor Speed, and (8) Form Constancy. Raw scores can be converted to age equivalents, percentiles, or normalized standard scores; subtest standard scores can be combined to form three composite scores: General Visual Perception Quotient, Motor Reduced Visual Perception Quotient, and Visual-Motor Integration Quotient. The second edition of the DTVP represents a significant improvement over the first edition in all technical aspects. The norms appear representative and the test is internally consistent, stable, and has good interscorer reliability. The considerable amount of information presented by the authors strongly suggests the DTVP-2 is a valid measure of visual perception.

Developmental Test of Visual-Motor Integration

The Developmental Test of Visual-Motor Integration (Beery, 1989) is designed to assess visual perception and motor coordination in students ages 2 to 19. It is intended for use primarily with pre-kindergarten children and those enrolled in the early grades. The test may be administered individually or to groups. The test consists of twenty-four geometric designs of increasing difficulty to be copied with a pencil on paper. The test can be administered and scored by a classroom teacher and usually takes about 15 minutes. Scoring is relatively easy, as the designs are scored pass-fail, and individual protocols can be scored in a few minutes.

SCORES

The manual for the VMI includes two pages of scoring information for each of the twenty-four designs. The child's reproduction of each design is scored pass-fail, and criteria for successful performance are clearly articulated. A raw score for the total test is obtained by adding the number of reproductions copied correctly before three consecutive failures. Normative tables provided in the manual allow the examiner to convert the total raw score to a developmental age equivalent. Scoring procedures for the VMI were changed in 1989. The twenty-four forms were weighted according to their developmental difficulty. The range of possible scores was expanded from 1–24 to 1–50. The author argues that new scores correlate highly with scores earned using the previous scoring procedures, and that the technical data for earlier versions of the test still apply to the most recent (1989) edition.

NORMS

The VMI was originally standardized on 1,030 children in rural, urban, and suburban Illinois. In 1981 the test was cross-validated with samples of children "from various ethnic and income groups in California" (Beery, 1982, p. 10). In 1988 the test was again cross-validated with an unspecified group of students "from several Eastern, Northern and Southern states" (Beery, 1989, p. 10). The 1988 norm sample is not representative of the U. S. population with respect to ethnicity and residence of the students. The norms are based on the performance of an unspecified group of 5,824 individuals. Norm-referenced use of the test should be discouraged, as the tester cannot know the nature of the group to whom tested individuals are being compared.

RELIABILITY

The author summarizes the results of many different reliability studies conducted by others since initial publication of the VMI. Ten studies of interscorer reliability are listed, and the manual reports that reliability coefficients ranged from .58 to .99 with a median of .93. Five studies of test-retest reliability are mentioned, and a range of .63 to .92 is reported. Four studies of split-half reliability are reported, with coefficients ranging from .66 to .93 and a median of .79. The samples for these studies are not described.

VALIDITY

The author summarizes studies by many different investigators but does not describe these studies specifically. He reports that scores on the VMI correlate .42 with a measure of handwriting, about .50 with readiness tests, .89 with chronological age, .41 to .82 with performance on the Bender Visual Motor Gestalt Test, and .37 to .59 with mental age. Studies of the relationship between performance on the VMI and later achievement show mixed results. Some investigators have found moderately strong relationships; others report little relationship.

SUMMARY

The VMI is designed to assess the integration of visual and motor skills by asking a child to copy geometric designs. As is the case with other such tests, the behavior sampling is limited, although the twenty-four items on the VMI certainly provide a larger sample of behavior than is provided by the nine items on the Bender Visual Motor Gestalt Test. The VMI has relatively high reliability and validity in comparison to other measures of perceptual-motor skills.

COPING WITH DILEMMAS IN CURRENT PRACTICE

The assessment of perceptual-motor skills is incredibly problematic. There are many obvious problems. First, it is very difficult to define perception and therefore difficult to come up with measures of it. Yet school personnel assume, and in fact insist, that adequate perceptual-motor development is a necessary prerequisite to acquiring reading skills. Often, assessors are asked to find out whether students have perceptual-motor problems. Without adequate definition of perception, with few technically adequate tests to measure it, and with no evidence that there are specific, effective interventions for students with perceptual-motor problems, the assessor is in a difficult bind.

We are of the opinion that if assessments cannot be done properly, they should not be done at all. We believe that this is one domain in which formal assessment using standardized tests is of little value. Rather, we encourage those who are concerned about development of perceptual-motor skills to engage in direct systematic observation in the natural environment in which these skills actually occur.

Summary

Educational personnel typically assess perceptual-motor skills for one of three reasons: prevention, remediation, and differential diagnosis. The use of perceptual-motor tests to identify children who demonstrate perceptual motor difficulties is based on the assumption that without special perceptual-motor training, these children will experience academic difficulties. The tests are used to try to ascertain whether perceptual-motor difficulties are causing academic difficulties and must therefore be remediated. Third, perceptual-motor tests are used diagnostically to identify brain injury and emotional difficulties.

In this chapter we reviewed the most commonly used perceptual-motor tests. Most lack the reliability needed in making important instructional decisions. Likewise, they lack demonstrated validity; we simply cannot say with much certainty that the tests measure what they purport to measure.

The practice of perceptual-motor assessment is linked directly to perceptual-motor training or remediation. There is a tremendous lack of empirical evidence to support the claim that specific perceptual-motor training facilitates the acquisition of academic skills or improves the chances of academic success. Perceptual-motor training will improve *perceptual-motor* functioning. When the purpose of perceptual-motor assessment is to identify specific important perceptual and motor behaviors that children have not yet mastered, some of the devices reviewed in this chapter may provide useful information; performance on individual items will indicate the extent to which specific skills (for example, walking along a straight line) have been mastered. There is no support for the use of perceptual-motor tests in planning programs designed to facilitate academic learning or to remediate academic difficulties.

Study Questions

1. Homer, age 6-3, takes two visual-perceptual tests, the Developmental Test of Visual Perception (DTVP) and the Developmental Test of Visual-Motor Integration (VMI). On the DTVP he earns a developmental age of 5-6, and on the VMI he earns a developmental age of 7-4. Give two different explanations for the discrepancy between the scores.
2. Original measures of perceptual-motor characteristics were shown to discriminate between brain-injured and non–brain-injured adults. Identify at least two major problems in the current use of these tests to diagnose brain injury in school-age children.
3. Briardale School District decides to implement a preschool screening program to identify children with perceptual-motor problems. School personnel decide to evaluate all four-year-olds in the community with the Developmental Test of Visual Perception, the Developmental Test of Visual-Motor Integration, and the Bender Visual Motor Gestalt Test. You are on the team

charged with implementation of this screening project. Would you object to the proposed screening, and if so, why?

4. Identify at least three major problems in current perceptual-motor assessment practices.

5. A local school district in Boston, Massachusetts, uses the Bender Visual Motor Gestalt Test to screen kindergarten youngsters for potential perceptual-motor problems. To whom are these children being compared?

6. Performance on the Bender Visual Motor Gestalt Test is used as a criterion in the differential identification of children as brain-injured, perceptually handicapped, or emotionally disturbed. Why must the examiner use caution in interpreting and using BVMGT test results for this purpose?

ADDITIONAL READING

Arter, J., & Jenkins, J. R. (1979). Differential diagnosis—prescriptive teaching: A critical appraisal. *Review of Educational Research, 49,* 517–556.

Kramer, J. J., & Conoley, J. L. (1992). *Buros eleventh mental measurements yearbook.* Lincoln, NE: University of Nebraska Press.

Mann, L. (1971). Perceptual training revisited: The training of nothing at all. *Rehabilitation Literature, 32,* 322–335.

Yates, A. J. (1954). The validity of some psychological tests of brain damage. *Psychological Bulletin, 51,* 359–379.

Ysseldyke, J. E., & Algozzine, B. (1979). Perspectives on assessment of learning disabled students. *Learning Disability Quarterly, 2,* 3–15.

Chapter 26

Assessment of Social-Emotional Behavior

S ocial-emotional behavior is an enigma for educators and psychologists. No area has burgeoned faster than assessment of the social-behavioral domain (Reynolds & Kamphaus, 1992). Many more students now act out and challenge teachers and schools in very aggressive ways. "Among children with disabilities, those with emotional/behavioral disorders are already known to be the least welcome in . . . school" (Guetzloe, 1993, p. 304). However, the practices used in the assessment of students for possible emotional-behavioral difficulties have been less than adequate in the opinion of many educators (Guetzloe, 1993; Wood, 1987) often because of the perception that students who truly need services are being *underidentified* (National Mental Health Association, 1993). How can this be? In part it is because social-emotional assessments have not been very successful in identifying students who internalize behavior and withdraw from their environment.

Estimates of the percentage of students with emotional/behavioral disorders come from multiple sources, use multiple definitions, and are therefore difficult to compare. Officially, .89 percent of students with special needs are receiving services for emotional/behavioral disorders (U.S. Department of Education, 1993). Estimates of the number of students in need of services are sometimes five to six times greater than the official number reported (National Mental Health Association, 1993). One study by Rubin and Balow (1978) estimated that nearly 60 percent of students are identified by their teachers as having behavior problems at least some time in their elementary school years!

Besides underidentification, there is also concern that social-emotional assessments do not always lead to the types of services students need because of

This chapter was written by James G. Shriner, Clemson University.

misidentification or misdiagnoses (Center, 1989). The fact is that the assessment of social-emotional behavior is a very difficult enterprise and not as well developed as cognitive, aptitude, and achievement testing (Martin, 1988). On the whole, assessments of personality and social-emotional behavior are not as sound technically as measures in other areas. During the past decade there has been a significant renewal of interest in social-emotional behavior, and there is a "new generation" of tests (Morgan & Jensen, 1988, p. 60) specifically designed to bridge assessment and intervention—a criticism of the utility of such assessments in the past.

AN OVERVIEW OF SOCIAL-EMOTIONAL ASSESSMENT

Social-emotional behavior is often influenced by each specific environment the student encounters (Bronfenbrenner, 1979). Suppose we want to observe a student to see how he or she is "behaving." When the student is observed in one environment, we see a contextually defined sample of behavior. It is possible that what we are seeing *is* representative of all of the student behavior, but it is more likely that we are seeing an incomplete picture. Thus, some unknown amount of "error" is part of the observation. To minimize the error we see, it is often recommended that we aggregate data by some method, perhaps by observing the student more than once. Additionally, we could access another source of information or use a method other than observation. Martin (1988) refers to the aggregation process and subsequent broadening of available information as "multi-setting, multi-source, multi-instrument assessment" (p. 86). Witt, Heffer, and Pfeiffer (1990) also think that error would be reduced using these tactics because "the best measurement science has to offer in defining truth is the convergence of data from multiple sources" (p. 366). The assessment should consist of some combination of method, context, and source of data. For example, we could gather data by observing a student on the playground, by having the teacher rate the behavior of the student in the classroom, or by having a parent report on the student's behavior at home. Table 26.1 shows some of the possible breakdowns of each category of a multifactored assessment.

Proponents of the multifactor approach assert that it is essential. There are no shortcuts; behavior is unstable and environmentally specific, and different data collection techniques yield valuable information (McConaughy, Achenbach, & Gent, 1988; Martin, 1988). There is an opposing view, however, that multiple data sources may increase error and confusion when incongruent information is obtained (Merrell, 1994). Reconciling contradictory information is a particularly difficult task, one that is sometimes mentioned by authors proposing a multifactor approach (Achenbach, 1991a). As we shall see, authors of some rating scales that employ multiple raters acknowledge the low cross-informant

TABLE 26.1   **Methods, Contexts, and Sources of Data for Social-Emotional Assessment**

Method	Context	Source of Data
Rating scales	Classroom	Child
Self-reports	Playground	Parent/Surrogate
Situational measures	Home	Members of extended family
Observation procedures	Work	Teachers
Projective techniques	Social	Other school personnel
		Peers/Classmates
		Co-workers

agreement across measures. Such low reliability sometimes occurs when raters have different backgrounds and frames of reference and are asked to observe the same student. Same-type raters (e.g., two teachers) tend to agree more than different-type raters (e.g., a teacher and a counselor). With these concepts and issues in mind, we turn to the different methods of gathering social-emotional data.

Rating Scales

There are several types of rating scales; generally a parent, teacher, peer, or "significant other" in a student's environment must rate the extent to which that student demonstrates certain desirable and/or undesirable behaviors. Raters are often asked to determine the presence or absence of a particular behavior and may be asked to quantify the amount or frequency of the behavior. Rating scales are popular because they are easy to administer and useful in providing basic information about a student's level of functioning. They offer structure to an assessment or evaluation and can be used in almost any environment to gather data from almost any source (refer to Table 26.1). The important concept to remember is that rating scales provide an index of someone's *perception* of a student's behavior. Different raters will likely have different perceptions of the same student's behavior and are likely to provide different ratings of the student; each is likely to have different views of acceptable and unacceptable expectations and/or standards. Gresham and Elliott (1990) point out that rating scales are inexact and should be supplemented by other data collection methods.

Observational Procedures

Most observational procedures used to assess emotional characteristics are systematic. "The most direct and desirable way to assess child and adolescent behavior in most cases is through naturalistic observation" (Merrell, 1994).

Walker (1983) claims that observation of natural situations reduces the chance of making incorrect assumptions. We most often observe students in school, but there are times when home or work environments are more appropriate settings. Sometimes it is necessary to contrive a situation for an observation of a student. Such an observation is called an *analogue* and serves to control the environment to increase the probability that the behavior of concern will be exhibited. In analogue observations, however, some degree of inference is imposed, and interpretations of what is observed must be adjusted.

Self-Report Measures

A technique commonly used in social-emotional assessment is the self-report measure. Individuals being assessed are asked to reveal common behaviors in which they engage or to identify inner feelings. Martin (1988) maintains that self-reports of "aspirations, anxieties, feelings of self-worth, attributions about the causes of behavior, and attitudes about school are [important] regardless of the theoretical orientation of the psychologist" (p. 230). Self-reports are usually part of a more comprehensive assessment plan and often involve the use of interviews to obtain data.

Interview Techniques

Interviews are most often used by *experienced professionals* as a source of information about a student's perspective on a variety of issues and to gain insight into overall patterns of thinking and behaving. There are many variations on the interview method—most distinctions are made along a continuum from structured to unstructured or from formal to informal. Regardless of the format, Merrell (1994) suggests that most interviews probe for information in one or more of the following areas of functioning and development: medical/developmental history, social-emotional functioning, educational progress, and community involvement. Increasingly, the family as a unit (or individual family members) is the focus of interviews that seek to identify salient home environment factors that may be having an impact on the student (Broderick, 1993).

Situational Measures

Situational measures of social-emotional behavior can include nearly any reasonable activity (Walker, 1973), but two well-known methods are peer acceptance nomination scales and sociometric ranking techniques. Both types of measures provide an indication of an individual's social status and may help describe the attitude of a particular group (e.g., the class) toward the target student. Peer nomination techniques require that students identify other students whom they prefer on some set of criteria (e.g., students they would like to have as study partners). Pictorial representations of the results, called *sociograms*, can be created. Overall, sociometric techniques provide a contemporary point of reference for comparisons of a student's status among members of a specified group.

Projective Methods

To delve more deeply into an individual's personality, projective measures are sometimes used. Projective methods grew out of psychoanalytic and Gestalt psychology. In this method, ambiguous stimuli (e.g., inkblots) are presented, and individuals are asked to describe what they see. Theoretically, the inner feelings of the students are engaged by the stimuli, and they will project aspects of their personality in their responses. Information about their thoughts, beliefs, expectations, and needs is obtained. Sometimes, projective techniques involve responses requiring a lower level of inference. For example, measures using sentence-completion stimuli may be used to probe about a particular event or time period. In this case, projectives are somewhat like interviews but still require a great deal of interpretation on the part of the examiner.

The Concept of Multiple-Gating

The current status of social-emotional assessment is ambiguous and largely reliant on subjective methods. Wehby (in press) reiterates this point in his discussion of the need for accurate and efficient assessment and identification of students in need of emotional or behavioral services. To accomplish this end, a process known as *multiple-gating* is being used increasingly. Walker et al. (1988) define multiple-gating as a procedure "that consists of a series of progressively more precise assessments or 'gates' that provide for the sequential assessment and cross-validation of multi-method forms of child assessment that establish a decision-making structure for the aggregation of information produced by different assessment sources" (p. 10). Multiple-gating procedures can be community based, but the focus here is on school-based assessment. Table 26.2 is a listing of the basic components of the process.

Essentially, all students are initially in the pool of students who may be at risk for some learning or behavior problem(s). Multiple-gating progressively narrows the larger pool, until those individuals who are "highly likely to exhibit the [learning or behavior problems] in question are identified" (Merrell, 1994, p. 37). The selection is accomplished through the use of more sensitive (and thus more time-consuming and expensive) procedures and measures. Almost all of the methods of assessment discussed above could be used in multiple-gating systems; however, projective measures are not likely to be part of such a plan.

This chapter introduces several measures of social-emotional functioning of children and youth; there are many others, and we could not hope to cover

TABLE 26.2   **Multiple-Gating Procedures**

Gate	Who Is Involved	What Is Done
1 (Primary)	All classroom students	Teacher screening/ranking of all students for problem behavior
2 (Secondary)	Students who ranked highest on problem behaviors	Teacher rating on specific behavior
3 (Tertiary)	Students who exceed established criteria	Direct observation of behavior in different settings
Completed Screening	Students with observed behavioral deficits or excesses who pass through all gates	Pre-referral intervention or formal evaluation

them all. You will see the range of options available and be informed about some possibilities for particular assessment purposes. Keep in mind that not all assessment instruments are created equal; it will be up to you to make your own judgments about the usefulness of particular instruments.

SPECIFIC TESTS OF SOCIAL-EMOTIONAL BEHAVIOR

Attention-Deficit Disorders Evaluation Scale–School Version

The Attention-Deficit Disorders Evaluation Scale–School Version (ADDES-SV) (McCarney, 1989a) is a rating scale consisting of sixty items divided into three subscales (Inattentive, twenty-seven items; Impulsive, eighteen items; Hyperactive, fifteen items). The test was designed to measure the three constructs of ADD posited in DSM III-R. The ADDES-SV is administered individually; it takes about 20 minutes for an educator familiar with the target student to complete the scale. It is intended for students aged 4 or 5 years to 21 years. The author lists the following uses for the scale: screening for attention-deficit disorder (ADD), providing a measure of ADD for any referred student, contributing information to the diagnosis of ADD, developing program goals and objectives, and identifying intervention areas for ADD.

Items from the Inattentive scale include "Loses place when reading" (e.g., leaves out words or sentences when reading) and "Does not listen to what others are saying." Examples of Impulsive items are "Grabs things away from others" and "Moves about while seated, fidgets, squirms, etc." The Hyperactive scale includes items like "Cannot wait appropriately for assistance from instructor" and "Talks beyond what is expected or at inappropriate times." All items on all scales are to be completed; if an item is not appropriate for a particular student, it is scored as "Does not engage in the behavior."

SCORES

Raters are provided guidelines for making judgments about student behavior. Each subscale yields a raw score that is the sum of all quantifiers (0 to 4) chosen for the items of the subscale. The guidelines and quantifiers are logically linked, as a score of 0 means the subject has *never* been seen exhibiting the behavior being rated; a score of 1 means the behavior occurs several (three or four) times per month; a score of 2 means the behavior occurs several times per week; a score of 3 means the behavior occurs several times a day; a score of 4 means the behavior occurs several times per hour. Subscale raw scores are convertible to gender and age-specific standard scores (mean = 10, standard deviation = 3) provided in an appendix. A percentile score for the ADDES-SV total scale is obtained by adding all subscale standard scores and using a similar gender-age conversion chart. Percentiles for the subscales are not provided.

NORMS

The ADDES-SV was normed on 4,876 students from ages 4-5 years to 21 years. These students were rated by 1,567 teachers. The sample included both students with ADD and students without ADD, although the author does not describe the proportion of either in the norms description section. Eighty-seven percent of the norm sample students were in grades K–6. No other educational information on the sampled students is provided. General demographic data are provided for the student sample. Overall, the sample is evenly split by gender and appears representative of the nation. Using the 5 percent differential guideline, there is an underrepresentation of students of white-collar parents and an overrepresentation of an unspecified category of "other" (McCarney, 1989a, p. 10). The author also lists the numbers of participating teachers at each age level but provides no details for comparison purposes.

RELIABILITY

Three types of reliability data are provided; all are from studies involving subsamples of the normative population. Test-retest reliability over a thirty-day period is provided for a random sample of 481 students for subscales and Total score (Inattentive, .97, Impulsive, .89, Hyperactive, .92, and Total, .92). Internal-consistency coefficients using the Kuder-Richardson 20 formula for dichotomous data are reported for the subscales. All coefficients are .97 or

above; however, the subsample size is not specified. Item-total and item-subscale correlations are presented as evidence of validity but are considered here as measures of internal consistency. These correlation coefficients are .60 or greater, high enough to ensure that the test is internally consistent.

Finally, interrater-reliability correlations on 462 students rated by 237 pairs of educators are reported by age levels. Coefficients range from .81 to .90. Because the normative data produced significant gender and age differences on the ADDES-SV, the author's decision to provide interrater reliability by age level is to be commended. The same strategy for other measures and reports of reliabilities found by other investigators would provide better support for the overall reliability of the instrument.

VALIDITY

Evidence for the content validity of the ADDES-SV consists of the author's description of the item selection process. Initially, the author conducted a literature search and sought input from diagnosticians. Items on a field version of the test were reviewed and item analysis (see the Reliability section above) was used to reduce the list to "the most educationally relevant indicators" (McCarney, 1989a, p. 13) of ADD behavior.

Factor-analytic studies are presented to describe the extraction of the three subscales of the ADDES-SV and to support its construct validity. Factor loadings indicate significant overlap, and only the Hyperactive scale emerges as a unique measure. These findings, coupled with the high correlations among subscales (.77 to .95), suggest that the ADDES-SV is a measure of the construct of ADD but raise questions about the need for the specification of three subscales. As the author notes, "Students with behavior problems in one area also have problems in other areas" (McCarney, 1989, p. 12).

One study is presented as support for discriminant validity. Subscale raw scores and total percentile score were found to be statistically different for students previously diagnosed as ADD (N =

102) compared to a similarly sized sample of students without ADD (ages 4-5 years to 21 years). Results are presented for male and female subjects but are not differentiated by age level. No data on discriminations among different disabling conditions are provided.

Criterion-related concurrent validity data also emanate from a single study. Two hundred students (ages 4-5 to 21 years) identified as ADD were rated on the ADDES-SV and *Conners Teacher-Rating Scale–Revised*. All resulting subscale correlations were above .35, with the strongest relationship between the Inattentive subscales of the two devices.

SUMMARY

The Attention-Deficit Disorders Evaluation Scale–School Version is a sixty-item rating scale for use with students aged 4-5 to 21 years. There are three subscales (Inattentive, Impulsive, and Hyperactive) from which raw scores and standard scores are obtained. The ADDES-SV norms have adequate numbers of subjects but are heavily weighted at the lower age levels. Students with and without ADD were included in the sample, but the proportions of students in each group are not provided. Reliability data are limited to the author's own studies but appear adequate for screening decisions. The same is true for validity. Most of the data are promising; however, more evidence of the test's appropriateness for purported uses other than screening are needed. The ADDES-SV appears to be a useful measure of the overall construct of ADD. The ADDES-SV should be used for screening rather than diagnostic purposes. It should not be used as the sole basis for ADD classification.

Attention-Deficit Disorders Evaluation Scale–Home Version

T he Attention-Deficit Disorders Evaluation Scale–Home Version (ADDES-HV) (McCarney, 1989b) is a counterpart of the Attention-Deficit Disorders Evaluation Scale–School Version (ADDES-SV) that is packaged as a separate assessment instrument. The author says the test was "specifically designed as a relevant assessment tool in the home environment" (McCarney, 1989b, p. 6), but the text of the manual, the format, and item content are virtually identical to the school version. Intended uses of the device are the same as the ADDES-SV, except that the home is the target environment for intervention planning.

Items on the ADDES-HV are scored on a five-point rating scale:

0   Does not engage in the behavior

1   1 to several times per month

2   1 to several times per week

3   1 to several times per day

4   1 to several times per hour.

The forty-three-item test is divided into three subscales: Inattentive (nineteen items, such as "Has a short attention span"), Impulsive (fifteen items, such as "Grabs things away from others"), and Hyperactive (twelve items, such as "Cannot remain seated"). Although the ADDES-HV contains fewer items than the school version, item content is similar and is designed to reflect the DSM III-R definition of attention-deficit disorder (ADD).

SCORES

Raw scores are obtained for each subscale by summing the ratings assigned to each item. Subscale raw scores are convertible to gender- and age-specific standard scores (mean = 10, standard deviation = 3).

A total score percentile rank can be obtained by adding all subscale standard scores and using a conversion chart provided in an appendix. Percentile scores are not available for the subscales.

NORMS

Students ($N = 1,754$) and parents ($N = 3,172$) from twelve states were involved in the normative process. Basic demographic data for the sample and national averages for comparison are provided. There is an overrepresentation of students from city and suburban locations in comparison to the national average (83 percent versus 73 percent) and, therefore, an underrepresentation from rural locations (17 percent versus 27 percent). Students ranged from 4 years to 20 years of age, and most (70 percent) were in grades K–6. Some students with ADD and some without ADD were included in the norm sample, but the author does not report the proportions of each student type. The manual provides conflicting data on the number of students at specific ages. For example, the author reports in the norms section that 130 six-year-old students were included (p. 10). Later, in the section on standard error of measurement, he reports that 67 females and 102 males aged 6 years are in the sample (p. 13). Also, the manual does not provide an indication of how the student sample was selected or any relevant educational characteristics.

The author provides only the numbers of parents in the norm sample, at each student age level, and, although the size of the sample is adequate, there is no description of relevant characteristics.

RELIABILITY

Test-retest reliability on a subsample of 148 children at an interval of thirty days was computed for each subscale and total score. All coefficients are .90 or above. Data for each of the age-gender groups developed from the norm sample are not provided.

Interrater reliability results from a study involving 172 pairs of parents with "equal knowledge of the child's behavior" (McCarney, 1989b, p. 11) who rated a subsample of eighty-six students reveal lower total-score reliability for older students.

The interrater correlations for each scale on an unknown sample are Inattentive, .80, Impulsive, .81, and Hyperactive, .88. Internal consistencies of the scales are all above .93. Again, no indications of sample size or internal-consistency reliability by the gender-age groupings are provided. Item-total correlations, although presented as validity data, support the internal consistency of the ADDES-HV. Most coefficients are in the .70s and .80s. Standard errors of measurement are provided for the nine gender-age normative groups, but the reader is reminded of the discrepancy in reports of numbers of subjects noted earlier. No data from studies other than those conducted by the test author on the normative sample are offered in support of the reliability of the ADDES-HV.

VALIDITY

The ADDES-HV was developed using the same procedures as the school version. Content validity is based on literature reviews and input from diagnosticians and parents of children with ADD. As was the case with the school version, the Inattentive subscale contains six items that may not be appropriate for children under 5 years of age. In addition, the response distributions show strong positive skew. More than half of the subjects were rated as "not engaging in the behavior" on nearly half of the forty-three items on the ADDES-HV. The content validity of the test under such circumstances must be interpreted with caution, especially for the youngest students for whom it is intended.

Construct validity of the home version is argued on the basis of factor-analytic studies. An examination of the factor loadings indicates that although the Inattentive and Hyperactive subscales each load primarily on a single factor, every item of the Impulsive subscale has a factor loading of .30 or greater on at least two separate factors. Interrelations among subscales are moderate to high (.67 to .79). Thus, the data seem to support ADDES-HV as a measure of the construct of ADD, but the discriminations among subscales are not convincing. Diagnostic validity is suggested by a comparative study of students with and without ADD.

Some evidence of convergent validity[1] is found in one criterion-related validity study. The ADDES-HV and Conners Parent Rating Scale–48 were administered to a subsample of 170 students previously diagnosed with ADD. Correlations ranged from moderate to strong among the tests' subscales.

SUMMARY

The ADDES-HV is a forty-three-item rating scale designed for use with children and students 4 to 20 years of age. The instrument consists of three subscales: Inattentive, Impulsive, and Hyperactive, each of which is supposed to assess ADD characteristics.

Like the ADDES-SV, this instrument was standardized using sufficient numbers of subjects in the norm samples, and normative scores are provided for different age levels by gender. Reliability and validity data are limited to studies on subsamples from the norm group. Although three subscales are presented, convincing evidence of the need for all three is not provided. The ADDES-HV appears to measure the overall construct of ADD and, because of promising initial data, is best used as a screening instrument that may, in conjunction with other supporting data, indicate the need for more comprehensive assessment. Insufficient evidence of validity for clinical or treatment use is provided for the current version, and thus some of the proposed uses of the instrument may be inappropriate until additional (and preferably independent) supporting evidence is provided. In light of these concerns, Merrell (1994) recommends research use of the ADDES-HV and ADDES-SV at this time.

Autism Screening Instrument for Educational Planning, Second Edition

The Autism Screening Instrument for Educational Planning, Second Edition (ASIEP-2) (Krug, Arick, & Almond, 1993) is an assessment consisting of five separate subtests. Each subtest is designed to assist in one or more of the following areas: screening, diagnosis, placement, program planning, and progress monitoring. The Autism Behavior Checklist (ABC), Sample of Vocal Behavior (SVB), and Interaction Assessment (IA) are listed as screening and diagnostic scales; Educational Assessment (EA) and Prognosis of Learning Rate (PLR) may be used in conjunction with the diagnostic tests as part of a complete intervention-planning battery. The ABC is designed

for use with any individual who may have autism, whereas the other subtests are appropriate for individuals functioning at a language and social age between 3 months and 49 months.

The Autism Behavior Checklist (ABC) consists of fifty-seven differentially weighted behavior statements grouped into five symptom areas: sensory, relating, body and object use, language, and social/self help. The rater (a professional educator or parent) circles the number (weight) that most accurately describes the student or client with respect to a given behavior statement.

The Sample of Vocal Behavior (SVB) is used to evaluate expressive speech at the preverbal and emerging language levels. The authors recommend that two people share responsibility for conducting this subtest—one to elicit utterances and one to make a verbatim recording. The subtest lasts 30 minutes or until fifty vocalizations are recorded.

---

1. Convergent validity is the correlation between measures of the same construct using different measurement techniques. Ideally, scores on different measures of the same attribute should be highly correlated.

The Interaction Assessment (IA) uses a 10 second time-sampling procedure under three conditions (active modeling, passive/no initiation, direct cues), each of which lasts 4 minutes. Student behaviors are categorized as interactions, independent play, no response, or negative aggressive. Two adults (an observer and an interacting adult) are needed for this subtest, which measures spontaneous social reactions and the responses to requests.

The Educational Assessment (EA) probes the student's functioning level in five areas: in-seat behavior, receptive language, expressive language, body concept, and speech imitation. All subparts except in-seat behavior have twelve items. The assessor presents various materials (e.g., toys, foods, and blocks) and gives cues to the student to elicit certain responses. The EA probes the individual's adaptive-language concepts and requires that the child have some entry-level behaviors (e.g., staying seated and looking at objects). The authors state also that "an individual must have no disruptive behaviors that are incompatible with test taking" (Krug, Arick, & Almond, 1993, p. 5). The EA takes about 20 minutes and is meant to be useful in intervention planning.

The Progress of Learning Rate (PLR) subtest is used to examine an individual's rate of learning by training the individual on a discrete trial, direct-instruction task, using a differential reinforcement strategy. The learning task in which the student is trained, placing a chip on a tray, consists of three phases: pretraining, random presentation of objects (black circle chip, white circle chip, white square chip) and post-testing for shape and color discriminations. Optional training steps that vary the positioning of the objects may be used.

SCORING PROCEDURES AND SCORES

The ABC is scored by summing the weighted values first within symptom areas and then across all areas for a total score. Raw scores are plotted on summary profiles that show the area means for the standard-ization sample. The total score mean of the total sample on the ABC is 77, (standard deviation = 20), and the authors suggest a cutoff score of one-half standard deviation below this point (67) as indicating a high probability of autism (p. 27).

The SVB appears rather complicated to administer and score. The author's suggestion to tape record each subtest should be followed. All of the nine possible speech characteristics are summed individually, and the total score is calculated as the sum of four areas: Repetitive, Noncommunicative, Unintelligible, and Babbling. This total score is also called the Autistic Speech Characteristics score. All scores are plotted on a summary profile. A Language Age Equivalency (LAE) score is obtained by first summing some of the characteristics. Percentile scores are available in the IA profile for the Autistic Speech Characteristics total only.

The IA yields raw scores in four areas: Interaction, Independent Play, No Response, and Negative Aggressive. These are plotted on a summary profile, showing mean performance levels of an autistic and nonautistic subgroup. Raw scores are converted to percentiles using one of two charts defining the two groups by ABC total score, Language Age, and chronological age. An Autistic Social Score is computed by following a formula on the record form. Care must be used in using IA scores because two areas are positively oriented (Interaction and Independent Play) and two are negatively oriented (No Response and Negative Aggressive).

The EA is summarized by raw scores in five areas: In-Seat, Receptive Language, Expressive Language, Body Concept, and Speech Imitation. The total score is the sum across these areas. Each raw score is plotted on a summary profile and can be converted to percentiles for either subgroup. The total raw score is converted to percentiles for the IA profile.

The PLR raw scores (number of trials to criterion) for each step of the subtest are translated to percentiles according to the autistic-nonautistic breakdown. The raw score from the first random position task is used on the IA profile and is converted to a percentile.

NORMS

Autism Behavior Checklist   The ABC was normed on three samples of individuals. Sample 1 consisted of persons selected by members of the American Association for the Education of the Severely/ Profoundly Handicapped, "teachers of trainable mentally retarded children throughout Oregon, and attenders of several conference presentations in the western United States and Canada" (Krug, Arick, & Almond, 1993, pp. 41–42). Although 3,000 ABCs were distributed, Sample 1 consisted of 1,049 individuals ranging in age from 18 months to 35 years. Reported diagnoses of the total sample were 172 autistic, 423 severely mentally retarded, 254 emotionally disturbed, 100 deaf-blind, and 100 nondisabled. No other demographic information on these persons is provided, except that the male-to-female ratio across all ages was 2.5 to 1.

Sample 2 consisted of sixty-two individuals aged 3 years to 23 years, all of whom had a diagnosis of autism. The individuals were selected by professionals throughout the U.S. and Canada. Sample 3 consisted of 953 adults aged 21 years to 68 years. Ninety-five percent of these individuals were diagnosed with severe mental retardation. It is not clear how these individuals were selected. No further information about Samples 2 and 3 is presented in the manual.

Given the limitations surrounding these low-incidence populations, the ABC norm samples may be somewhat representative of the autistic, deaf-blind, and severe mental retardation groups. However, the remaining groups are inadequately sampled. Because very gross age breakdowns are given (e.g., 21–68 years for Sample 3) and because no other descriptives are provided, one must be very cautious in making interpretations based on the ABC standardization.

Sample of Vocal Behavior   For the SVB, eighty-one examiners collected data on 157 subjects aged 2 years, 4 months to 20 years. Sixty-one of these persons had autism, and ninety-six had severe disabilities without autism. Forty of these individuals (twenty-four with autism, sixteen without autism) were selected for subgroup analysis to define representative summary profiles on the SVB. Preschool and school-age profiles were developed from samples of nine and fourteen students, respectively. No other information about any of these students is provided.

Interaction Assessment   Sixty professionals gathered data for the standardization study of the IA. Subjects were fifty-two students with autism (as defined by the combination demographics of ABC scores, Language Age, and chronological age) and sixty-three individuals who were nonautistic but severely disabled. Profiles based on the total sample are provided. No other identifying information on the IA standardization subjects is provided.

Educational Assessment   The EA is a criterion-referenced subtest. Standardization was conducted by eighty examiners on forty-one students who met the defined demographic criteria for autism and ninety-one students who were severely disabled but not autistic. A summary profile on each group was developed.

Prognosis of Learning Rate   The PLR was standardized on 124 students who were assessed by eighty-one examiners. Diagnostic profiles for autistic and nonautistic groups are provided.

Summary   The norms for the ASIEP-2 are tenuous at best. The ABC is the best normed subtest; however, the reader is given very little information other than numbers of subjects per diagnostic group. Hammill, Brown, and Bryant (1992) have suggested that seventy-five or more subjects in *most* one-year age intervals with which the test is intended to be used, could be considered appropriate for constructing useful norms. The representativeness of the ABC norm sample along demographic characteristics (e.g., gender, domicile, parental education, geographic region, and ethnicity) is also largely unknown. The remaining four subtests were standardized on not more than 157 students, whose characteristics are mostly unspecified.

RELIABILITY

Two reliability statistics for the ABC are provided. On the full Sample 1 group, split-half reliability was .87. On a subset of fourteen children rated by forty-two people, 95 percent interrater agreement was reached. No information is provided on the type of raters used.

Test-retest reliabilities on five areas of the SVB (Repetitive, Babbling, Noncommunicative, First Use, Communication) for twenty subjects over a three-day period were all above .81. Split-half reliability determined by separation of odd-even utterances was .95. Interrater agreement across the Repetitive, Babbling, Noncommunicative, and Unintelligible categories averaged 90 percent.

Eighty-seven observers who watched a videotape of the IA administration obtained a median agreement of 89 percent match to a criterion defined as the ratings of six professionals already familiar with the subtest. A Kuder-Richardson test of item reliability yielded a coefficient of .85.

A test-retest evaluation over an unspecified time period was conducted for the EA. Agreement ranged from 84 to 100 percent, with an average across all data points of 95 percent.

In summary, reliability evidence for the ASIEP-2 is potentially strong; most reported coefficients are above .80. Some reliability studies were on small samples of subjects, and some interrater agreement studies are not described in enough detail for a reader to be able to tell who is doing what comparisons. Finally, no reliability for the PLR is reported in the manual. The evidence on reliability is not strong enough to consider the ASIEP-2 reliable for all of the purposes presented by the authors.

VALIDITY

Evidence for the validity of the ABC begins with the procedures used to establish content validity. The authors first examined many sources (e.g., instruments, checklists, and literature reviews) for relevant behavior descriptors. Second, twenty-six experts in the field of autism reviewed an initial ABC device. A revised version containing fifty-seven items was subjected to chi-square analysis using individuals' reported autism as the criterion variable. Results were used to assign the weights for items by forming groups of items with similar predictive coefficients.

Two criterion-related validity studies are reported for the SVB. The Autistic Speech Characteristics scores from the SVB were correlated with the Total ABC scores for 185 subjects. Correlations ranged from .32 to .46. The SVB Language Age raw score was correlated with the language age provided by examiners. This correlation was .81. The authors (Krug, Arick, & Almond, 1993) report that examiner-identified language ages were "generally from the *Sequenced Inventory of Communication Development*" (p. 46), although no summary of the examiners' reports is provided. Profiles of performance for the two groups are offered for the SVB.

Arguments for the content validity of the EA are based on the reviews of existing curricula, assessments, and literature related to the needs of individuals with autism. Specific validity studies are not presented for the IA or PLR subtests. Several studies showing differences between students with autism and students with severe disabilities on ASIEP-2 subtests are presented, and cross-validity data are discussed by the authors. It is sometimes unclear which sample participated in these studies. Matched sample studies usually had fewer than twenty-five students per group (some had four or five). Cross validity, in this case, refers to correlations among subtests of the instrument and not analyses of performance of distinct groups on items from the subscales. Because validity for all subtests and their intended purposes must be demonstrated, the authors' treatment of validity issues in the manual provides only limited support for their claims for the instrument and its subscales.

SUMMARY

The ASIEP-2 was developed for use by professionals in identifying persons with autism and in making appropriate educational plans. Five subtests are included: the Autism Behavior Checklist, Sample of Verbal Behavior, Interaction Assessment, Educational Assessment, and Prognosis of Learning Rate. Of these, the Autism Behavior Checklist is the best-developed, best-normed scale and may be useful for screening purposes. Reliability data for the subtests are sparse, and validity is inadequately demonstrated for the most part. Validity of an instrument is demonstrated over time; the authors have sound theoretical bases for the instrument and its components, but to date they have not documented enough evidence to support some of the suggested uses for particular scales. Skilled professionals may still gain useful information from administrations of the ASIEP-2, as the complete battery does yield a great deal of qualitative information about the examinee.

OVERVIEW OF THE CHILD BEHAVIOR CHECKLIST

One of the most frequently used assessments of child and adolescent emotional/behavioral functioning is the Child Behavior Checklist (CBCL) series by Achenbach and his colleagues (Achenbach, 1991a, McConaughy, 1993b). The following overview draws on these sources. Table 26.3 summarizes the domains, groupings, and syndromes of the six forms of the CBCL.

The six forms of the CBCL are the Child Behavior Checklist (CBCL) and 1992 Profile for Ages 2–3, the CBCL and 1991 Profile for Ages 4–18, the Youth Self-Report (YSR) and 1991 Profile for Ages 11–18, the Teacher's Report Form (TRF) and 1991 Profile for Ages 5–18, the Direct Observation Form (DOF), and the Semistructured Clinical Interview for Children and Adolescents (SCICA). The need for data on children's functioning from multiple sources has led to the development of multiaxial, empirically based assessment (Achenbach, 1991a). Therefore, each Achenbach scale seeks to document the strengths and weaknesses of the same child in different contexts. The instruments are designed to provide behavioral descriptions of students as opposed to diagnostic inferences. Data from the multiple sources are the basis for empirically derived cross-informant syndromes for the CBCL, TRF, and YSR (McConaughy, 1993a). A syndrome is composed of items that tend to co-occur within one instrument. The cross-informant syndromes are composed of items that were found to be in a syndrome for at least two of these three instruments. All scoring profiles have two levels of problem scales: broad scales (Internalizing, Externalizing) and syndrome scales. As you read the descriptions of the Achenbach scales included here, keep in mind that the different scales share many items. Still, each form has its own research base, protocols, and technical manual. Achenbach also publishes overviews and integrative guides to assist professionals in using the various scales.

TABLE 26.3 **Domains, Groupings, and Syndromes of the CBCL**

Test Form	Sections/Domains	Groupings and Syndrome Scales (numbered)
CBCL/4–18	I. Competence items	Extracurricular Activity Social Interaction School Functioning

	II. Problem items	Internalizing
		    (1) Withdrawn
		    (2) Somatic Complaints
		    (3) Anxious/Depressed
		Externalizing
		    (4) Delinquent Behavior
		    (5) Aggressive Behavior
		(6) Social Problems
		(7) Thought Problems
		(8) Attention Problems
		(9) Sex Problems

CBCL/2–3		Internalizing
		    (1) Anxious/Depressed
		    (2) Withdrawn
		Externalizing
		    (3) Aggressive Behavior
		    (4) Destructive Behavior
		(5) Sleep Problems
		(6) Somatic Problems

TRF	I. Academic Performance II. Adaptive Characteristics	Working hard Behaving appropriately Is learning Is happy

	III. Problem items	Internalizing
		    (1) Withdrawn
		    (2) Somatic Complaints
		    (3) Anxious/Depressed
		Externalizing
		    (4) Aggressive Behavior
		    (5) Delinquent Behavior
		(6) Social Problems
		(7) Thought Problems
		(8) Attention Problems

(continued)

TABLE 26.3   (continued)

Test Form	Sections/Domains	Groupings and Syndrome Scales (numbered)
YSR	I. Competence	Activities
		Social
		Total Competence
	II. Problem items	Internalizing
		(1) Withdrawn
		(2) Somatic Complaints
		(3) Anxious/Depressed
		Externalizing
		(4) Delinquent Behavior
		(5) Agressive Behavior
		(6) Social Problems
		(7) Thought Problems
		(8) Attention Problems
		(9) Self-Destructive/Identity Problems
DOF		On Task
		Problem Behaviors
		Internalizing
		(1) Withdrawn/Inattentive
		(2) Nervous/Obsessive
		(3) Depressed
		Externalizing
		(4) Hyperactive
		(5) Attention Demanding
		(6) Agressive

Child Behavior Checklist and 1991 Profile for Ages 4–18

*T*he Child Behavior Checklist and 1991 Profile for Ages 4–18 (CBCL/4–18) (Achenbach, 1991b) is an individually administered parent (or surrogate) assessment checklist of a child's competence and problem behaviors. The primary purpose of the CBCL/4–18 is to provide a set of standardized procedures for assessing behavioral and emotional disorders. The current CBCL is a revision of the *Manual for the Child Behavior Checklist and Revised Child Behavior Profile* (Achenbach & Edelbrock, 1983). The CBCL /4–18 can be completed within 10 to 20 minutes. It assumes the administrator has fifth-grade reading ability and may be self-administered or read by the parent without modifying the results.

The CBCL/4–18 is composed of two main sections: Competence items and Problem items. Discriminations are made between children who are adapting successfully and those in need of additional support to deal with behavioral and emotional problems. The Competence scale includes twenty items that parents rate according to the amount and quality of their child's participation along three dimensions: (1) extracurricular activities (e.g., participation in sports, hobbies, clubs, and friendships), (2) social interactions, and (3) school functioning. The Problems section includes 118 specific problem items and two open-ended items. Problem items include statements such as "Argues a lot," "Deliberately harms self," or "Likes to be alone." On some items, parents are asked to describe the problem behavior; for example, "Hears sounds or voices that aren't there (describe)," or "Nervous movements or twitching (describe)." Two broad groupings of Internalizing and Externalizing problems, nine syndrome scales, and a Total Problem score are presented on the CBCL/4–18. The first grouping scale, Internalizing, includes three syndrome scales: Withdrawn, Somatic Complaints, and Anxious/Depressed. The Externalizing grouping consists of two syndrome scales: Delinquent Behavior and Aggressive Behavior. Four additional syndrome scales—Social Problems, Thought Problems, Attention Problems, and Sex Problems, (scored only for ages 6–11)—are provided but are categorized as neither Internalizing nor Externalizing.

SCORES

The Competence items are scored by having parents estimate their child's engagement (both type and quality) across the twenty items and three scales. A four-point comparative scale ("Don't know," "Less than average," "Average," "More than average") is used to make judgments on a child's engagement in comparison to same-age peers. Problem items are scored using a three-point response scale: 0, Not true; 1, Somewhat or sometimes true; 2, Very true or often true. Problem scores are computed by summing the item scores for each syndrome (Competence and Problem Behaviors). Internalizing, Externalizing, and Total Problem scores are also computed. A child's score is then evaluated according to percentile ranks and normalized T-scores to classify scores within a normal, borderline, or clinical

range. Decision rules and scoring criteria are included in the manual. The CBCL/4–18 can be scored by hand or computer.

NORMS

The norms for the CBCL/4–18 consist of a national sample that includes children aged 4 years through 18 years (N = 2,368). Normative data for the CBCL/4–18 are based on children who had not received mental health or special education services within one year of standardization. Subjects were recruited to produce a standardization sample representative of the forty-eight contiguous states with respect to SES, geographic region, and urban, suburban, and rural demographic characteristics. The CBCL/4–18 scales are normed separately for each gender for ages 4–11 and 12–18. Ethnic distribution averaged across gender/age groups was 73 percent white, 16 percent black, 7 percent Hispanic, and 3 percent other.

The CBCL/4–18 syndrome scales were derived from principal components analyses of clinical samples of boys and girls ages 4–18. These children were from fifty-two clinical settings located in the Eastern, Southern, and Midwestern areas of the United States. The author claims that a broad distribution of SES, demographic, and other client characteristics was obtained; however no data are provided to substantiate the claim.

RELIABILITY

Data are reported on inter-interviewer reliability, test-retest reliability, and internal consistency. Achenbach uses intraclass correlation coefficients (ICCs) for several reliability measures. ICCs reflect the proportion of total variance present in item scores and are sensitive to differences in rank order and magnitude of scored items. It should be noted that a significant portion of supporting reliability information from earlier versions of the CBCL is not presented in the 1991 manual.

Inter-Interviewer Reliability To assess differences that may result if the CBCL/4–18 is self-administered or used as a questionnaire, inter-interviewer reliability was computed on results obtained by three interviewers. A total of 241 children were matched for gender, age, ethnicity, and SES to establish matched triads. ICCs obtained for the twenty Competency items and for the 118 specific Problem items were .93 and .96, respectively.

Test-Retest Reliability A single interviewer visited mothers of seventy-two nonreferred four- to sixteen-year-old children two times, one week apart. Reliabilities were .99 for the twenty competency items and .95 for the 118 problem items.

Mothers' ratings of eighty children (the above-mentioned seventy-two subjects plus an additional eight subjects) were compared at two points, seven days apart. Mean correlation for all Competency items was .87, and mean correlation for Problem Behavior items was .89.

CBCLs were completed by mothers during a longitudinal study that included low birthweight and normal birthweight children (ages 6 to 7 years and 7 to 8 years) at one- and two-year intervals. Across all Competence items, average mean correlations ranged from .56 to .63. Mean correlations across Problem items ranged from .71 to .74.

The author reports a study of parents' ratings of clinical and general population samples in a longitudinal investigation. Interparent agreement from four age groups ranged from .48 to .79 for the various syndromes. The mean *r* for Total Competence was .79.

Internal consistency Internal consistency, using Cronbach's alpha for Total Competence scales, ranged from .57 to .64. For Total Problems, alpha was .96 for both boys and girls at both age levels.

VALIDITY

Several types of validity data are reported on the CBCL/4–18. The primary concern in the development of the CBCL/4–18 was to ensure content validity by assembling items that represented a broad range of competencies and problem items of clinical concern. Selection of the original item pool and evaluation of item content were extremely rigorous and included clinical research and literature reviews. In addition, consultations with clinical experts, developmental psychologists, psychiatrists, and psychiatric social workers were completed. The initial item pool was then pilot tested. Empirical evidence and professional feedback were used to improve the final measure.

Criterion-Related Validity The CBCL/4–18, Conners Parent Questionnaire (1973), and Quay-Peterson Revised Behavior Problems Checklist (1987) were administered to parents of sixty clinically referred students 6 to 11 years old. The children were being seen in sixty separate outpatient settings across the United States and Canada. Correlations between the CBCL and the other measures are reported for scales that are similar or that correspond. Correlations between the CBCL and the Conners syndromes ranged from .56 to .86; Total Problem scores correlated .82. Correlations between the CBCL and the Quay-Peterson ranged from .52 to .88, with Total Problem scores correlating at .81.

Achenbach states that a key index of criterion validity is the ability of a measure to identify individuals whose problems arouse enough concern that they are referred for professional help. Criterion validity of the CBCL/4–18 was assessed by determining the degree to which each scale discriminated among children selected from the clinical sample and demographically matched nonreferred children. All Competence scales were scored higher for nonreferred than for referred persons and all Problem scales were scored lower for nonreferred than for referred persons.

Achenbach also presents relative-risk odds ratios to indicate the odds of an individual's having a particular condition, given a particular risk factor. This ratio is compared to the odds for individuals who do not have the particular risk factor. For the sake of this comparison, individuals who were scored in the clinical range were identified as having a risk factor. The odds ratios provide evidence that the CBCL/4–18 can help distinguish between these two groups of individuals.

Construct Validity The CBCL/4–18 syndromes were derived empirically using a principal-components analysis to construct a taxonomy of childhood disorders. Results of discriminant analyses are presented for total scores, scale scores, and individual items. Probabilities for total *T*-scores and referral status are also provided. On the whole, the evidence suggests that if both total Competence and total Problem scores are in the same range (normal or clinical), then the CBCL/4–18 is very effective in making group discriminations. In addition, clinical cutoff points were used to evaluate the discriminant ability of the CBCL/4–18. Overall, 61 percent of the referred children score in the clinical range on the total Competence scale compared to 16 percent of the nonreferred children. Additionally, 68 percent of the referred children scored in the clinical range on the total Problem score compared to 18 percent of the nonreferred sample. These data provide evidence that the CBCL/4–18 discriminates between referred and nonreferred children.

SUMMARY

The CBCL/4–18 is used to record in a standardized manner children's competence and problem behaviors as reported by a parent or other informant. Internalizing and Externalizing dimensions are used to classify children's emotional and behavioral problems. Nine syndrome scales were derived empirically. Norms are adequate and more representative of the national population than previous versions of the CBCL. Some of the reliability measures, although described in detail, were conducted on a small subset of the standardization sample. Validity is supported by content, criterion-related, and construct data within the manual. In addition, the author provides a reference to the *Bibliography of Published Studies Using the Child Behavior Checklist and Related Materials* (Achenbach & Brown, 1991), which is a resource that describes the numerous studies identifying correlates of CBCL syndromes and other variables. The 1991 revision advances the CBCL assessment system, which continues to be one of the best available assessments for use by clinicians and psychologists.

Child Behavior Checklist and 1992 Profile for Ages 2–3

*T*he Child Behavior Checklist and 1992 Profile for Ages 2–3 (CBCL/2–3) (Achenbach, 1992) provides information on behavioral and emotional problems evidenced by young children as seen by parents or other respondents who interact with them. The CBCL/2–3 is a two-page form modeled after the CBCL/4–18. In fact, fifty-nine problem items were taken from the CBCL/4–18. An additional forty problem items were developed to meet the specific needs of children aged 2–3 years. Informants are asked to rate each item as either representing the child's current behavior or describing the child's behavior over the previous two months.

The CBCL/2–3 yields information on six empirically derived syndromes. These syndromes provide a profile of a child's problem behaviors along two broad groupings of behavior: Internalizing and Externalizing. The Internalizing grouping comprises the Anxious/Depressed and Withdrawn scales. The Externalizing grouping is composed of the Aggressive Behavior scale and the Destructive Behavior scale. Two additional scales, Sleep Problems and Somatic Problems, which are part of neither the Internalizing nor the Externalizing groupings, are provided. Unlike the other Achenbach behavioral scales, the CBCL/2–3 does not include a separate section of scored competence items for extracurricular activities, social interactions, or school functioning.

SCORING

The CBCL/2–3 can be scored by hand or by computer. Detailed scoring procedures are described in the manual. Scale scores are computed by summing the scores of items that comprise a separate behavioral grouping or scale. In addition, a Total Problems score is presented on the CBCL/2–3. Percentile ranks and *T*-scores can be obtained from a profile. Explicit decision rules and scoring criteria are provided in the manual for classifying a child's score on the Internalizing or Externalizing grouping, and for determining whether the child falls within the normal, borderline, or clinical range.

NORMS

A national sample was obtained by identifying siblings aged 2 to 3 years of children who were part of the original standardization sample for the CBCL/4–18. Because gender and age distributions from this sampling procedure were unequal, children were also "randomly selected" from a previous CBCL sample recruited from Massachusetts. A total sample of 368 children was obtained (183 from the national sample and 185 from Massachusetts), with 92 children at each age level for both boys and girls. The author provides demographic breakdowns of the total sample; however, the degree to which these children are representative of the U.S. population at large may be questionable. Whereas the original standardization sample was recruited to produce a representative sample of the forty-eight contiguous states, no census data are provided to substantiate the author's claim that a representative sample was achieved. It does appear that the Northeastern U.S. is overrepresented and the West is underrepresented.

The six syndromes for the 1992 profile were derived from (1) the original (1986) Massachusetts sample, (2) characteristics of children from a longitudinal study, and (3) characteristics of children receiving mental health or special education services in seven different states. This clinical sample consisted of 367 boys and 273 girls who were initially recruited from the previously named sites. However, to provide an equal number of boys and girls by age, a random sample of 273 boys was selected to produce a final clinical sample of 546 children.

RELIABILITY

Interparent Agreement   The CBCL/2–3 was administered to both parents of sixty-four children at age 2 and fifty-nine children at age 3. All CBCL scales were evaluated for interparent agreement correlations. Results indicate that interparent correlations were significant at the .01 confidence level at both ages and that mean correlations were similar (.63 for age 2 and .60 for age 3).

Test-Retest Reliability   Mothers' ratings of sixty-one nonreferred two- and three-year-old children from Massachusetts were compared seven days after their initial rating. Comparisons were calculated to examine the degree to which rank orders and magnitude of scores remained stable. Correlations for all six syndromes, Internalizing and Externalizing groupings, and total Problem scale were significant at the .001 confidence level, with a mean *r* of .85.

Long-Term Stability   Seventy-five children participating in a longitudinal study were rated by their mothers one year after having completed an initial rating. Stability correlations ranged from .50 to .78, with a mean correlation of .64.

Internal Consistency   Internal consistency using Cronbach's alpha was calculated for the matched referred and nonreferred children. The alphas for the six syndrome scales ranged from .65 (Somatic Problems) to .92 (Aggressive Behavior). For Internalizing items, Cronbach's alpha was .88, and for Externalizing items, .93. The total Problems alpha was .96.

VALIDITY

Content Validity   The CBCL/2–3 is an empirically derived scale based on assessment data of actual samples of children. A total of ninety-nine problem items appear on the CBCL/2–3, with fifty-nine items from the CBCL/4–18 plus forty additional items selected to provide differentiating data on emotional and behavioral problems in young children. These additional items were developed from interviews with parents and previous research. Children who had been referred to a clinic for mental health services obtained higher total scores than demographically similar, nonreferred children. The author cautions users of the instrument to judge for themselves whether the content is appropriate for their particular purpose.

Criterion-Related Validity   A study of 642 children (321 children from the clinical standardization and 321 children from the general normative sample) who were matched on demographic characteristics revealed that children who were clinically referred scored significantly higher on all Problem scales than nonreferred children.

Construct Validity   Convergent validity was examined in a study comparing scores obtained on the CBCL/2–3 and the Richman Behavior Checklist (Richman, Stevenson, & Graham, 1982), a British measure of problem behavior. Although the structure of the RBCL is different from that of the CBCL/2–3, correlations ranged from .56 to .77.

A second correlational study was conducted to assess the divergent validity of the CBCL/2–3 and common developmental measures. A total of eighty-six children participating in a low birthweight study were examined on the Bayley Mental Scale at age 2, the McCarthy General Cognitive Index at age 3, and the Minnesota Child Development Inventory (MCDI) (Ireton & Thwing, 1974). The results of

this study indicate no concurrent correlations between the CBCL/2–3 and the Bayley, the McCarthy, or the MCDI. These studies provide support of the CBCL/2–3 as a measure of the construct of early childhood problem behavior.

Further support of construct validity is found in the procedural studies in which the six syndromes and two primary groupings of problem behavior on the CBCL/2–3 were derived empirically using a principal-components analysis. A clinical sample of 546 boys and girls from seven sites was recruited to obtain CBCL/2–3 data. Three sets of discriminant analyses were performed for each gender-age group. First, Internalizing and Externalizing scores were used as predictors. Second, the six syndrome scales were used as predictors, followed by all Problem items. For boys, Externalizing items discriminated between clinically referred and nonreferred children. Although Externalizing items were seven times more powerful than Internalizing items, the latter also accounted for a significant amount of variance between the two groups. For girls, Internalizing items accounted for a majority of the variance. These results suggest that specific items, groupings, and syndromes from the CBCL/2–3 can discriminate between clinically referred and nonreferred children, but the author points out that the degree of influence sample specificity may have exerted is unknown.

SUMMARY

The CBCL/2–3 is a two-page parent rating form of young children's emotional and behavioral problems. A total of ninety-nine items are scored using a three-point scale. Some items are designed so that parents provide additional written descriptions to add clarity to behavioral concerns. The standardization sample, norms, reliability, and validity are not as well developed as they are for other Achenbach instruments. The author cites the *Bibliography of Published Studies Using the Child Behavior Checklist and Related Materials* (Achenbach & Brown, 1991) as a resource to validate the CBCL/2–3. This reference describes the numerous studies identifying correlates of CBCL syndromes and other variables. Overall, the CBCL/2–3 appears to be an adequate adaptation of a well-known system of evaluation and should contribute greatly to the identification and monitoring of young children in need of additional emotional and behavioral supports. As the author mentions, however, the CBCL/2–3 should not be used as the sole data source when making individual diagnostic or placement decisions.

Teacher's Report Form and 1991 Profile for Ages 5–18

*T*he Teacher's Report Form and 1991 Profile for Ages 5–18 (TRF) (Achenbach, 1991c) is modeled on the CBCL/4–18 and is designed to obtain a description of a pupil's behavior as observed by teachers in school environments. Like all the Achenbach instruments, the TRF is not meant to be used as the sole basis for diagnostic inferences. Practitioners are encouraged to verify that the teacher is familiar with the student being evaluated and that the student has been enrolled in the class for at least a two-month period.

DESCRIPTION OF THE SCALES

The TRF is composed of three major sections. In the first section, a student's Academic Performance relative to grade level is rated by the teacher for specific content areas. In the second section, ratings of four Adaptive Characteristics (Working Hard, Behaving Appropriately, Is Learning, and Is Happy) compare the target student to typically developing peers of the same age. Examples of Adaptive items include "How hard is he/she working?" and "How happy is he/she?"

The third section consists of 118 items indicative of childhood and adolescent behavior problems. Problem items include statements such as "Acts too young for his/her age," "Destroys property belonging to others," "Overconforms to rules," and "Withdrawn, doesn't get involved with others." As with the CBCL/4–18, several items require additional information from the teacher to provide a description of the problem behavior—for example, "Behaves irresponsibly (describe)" and "Stores up things he/she doesn't need (describe)." Two groupings (Internalizing and Externalizing), eight syndrome scales, and a total Problems score are presented on the TRF. The first grouping, Internalizing, is composed of three scales: Withdrawn, Somatic Complaints, and Anxious/Depressed. The Externalizing grouping is composed of the Aggressive Behavior scale and a Delinquent Behavior scale. Three additional scales, Social Problems, Thought Problems, and Attention Problems, are not categorized as part of the Internalizing or Externalizing groupings.

SCORES

The Academic Performance items are scored on a five point scale from "far below grade level" to "far above grade level." Adaptive Characteristics are rated on a seven-point comparative scale. Problem Behaviors are scored on a three-point scale (0, Never; 1, Somewhat or sometimes true; and 2, Very true or often true). Scale scores are computed by summing the item scores for each domain (Academic, Adaptive, Problems). Scores are plotted by gender and age (5–11 years and 12–18 years) to provide a graphic display for each scale. Percentiles based on nonreferred pupils and *T*-scores are obtained from the profile. Internalizing, Externalizing, and total Problems scores are also computed. Decision rules and scoring criteria are included in the manual. The TRF can be scored by hand or by computer.

NORMS

A subset of subjects assessed on the CBCL/4–18 in 1989 was used to standardize the TRF. Students aged 7 to 18 years were chosen to provide a representative sample of the forty-eight contiguous states with respect to socioeconomic status, ethnicity, region, and urban, suburban, and rural areas. The authors refer the user of the TRF to journal articles that define the census information. Children aged 5 to 6 years were siblings of those in the seven- to eighteen-year-old sample. A total of 2,113 children were ultimately recruited, and complete data were obtained for 1,613 (76 percent) of these children. Students who had received special education or mental health services were removed from this group to provide a normative sample ($N = 1,391$) of "healthy" individuals (Achenbach, 1991c, p. 15). The TRF scales are normed on each gender for ages 5–11 and 12–18. Ethnic distributions are similar to those of the CBCL/4–18.

A clinical sample of 2,550 students was obtained from a recruited sample of 2,815 children who were receiving either special education services for severe emotional disturbances or mental health services outside of school. The author reports that these students came from fifty-eight settings that were diverse enough to "minimize selective factors affecting the caseloads of individual services" (p. 26); however, no supporting data are presented. This clinical sample was used to derive the TRF syndrome scales and in validation studies.

RELIABILITY

Test-Retest Reliability Teachers completed TRF ratings twice on forty-four eight- and nine-year-old students following a waiting period of between seven and thirty days. All test-retest correlations were found to be significant at the .01 confidence level except for one scale (Thought Problems for girls). Mean correlations between first and second assessments were .90 for Adaptive scales and .92 for all Problem Behaviors scales.

Stability Teachers completed TRF ratings at two- and four-month intervals for nineteen boys who were referred for special services relating to behav-

ioral and emotional problems. Mean correlation was .75 at the two-month interval and .66 at the four month interval.

Interrater Agreement A total of 207 children aged 5–18 years were rated by two teachers who were familiar with each student. The mean correlation was .61 for the total Adaptive scale and .60 for the total Problems scale. A second study compared a primary teacher's rating of a child with that of a teacher's aide who worked with the child under similar conditions. Mean correlations were .65 for the total Adaptive and .57 for the total Problem scale.

Internal Consistency Internal-consistency reliability coefficients were reported for total Problems and Externalizing and Internalizing groupings. In addition, coefficients are provided for each of the eight syndrome scales by gender and age. Coefficients for both boys and girls (aged 5–11 years and 12–18 years) on the total Problems scale were approximately .97; on Externalizing, the coefficient was .96; on Internalizing, the coefficient was .90 for boys and .91 and .92 for girls at each age level. For boys, coefficients ranged from .70 (Delinquent Behavior) to .96 (Aggressive Behavior) on syndrome scales; for girls, coefficients ranged from .63 (Thought Problems) to .97 (Aggressive Behavior).

VALIDITY

Content Validity All scale items on the TRF are statements of a student's competencies and problems that are identified concerns of parents, mental health providers, and educators. The scales have been subjected to extensive research and clinical application. Most of the Problem Behavior items on the TRF are taken directly from the CBCL/4–18. A total of twenty-five Problem Behavior items were replaced with items that are more appropriate for teachers to rate, and an unspecified number of Problem items were altered to make them more appropriate for teachers. Academic Performance and Adaptive Characteristics items were evaluated during field testing for their usefulness in judging children's functioning in schools.

Criterion-Related Validity   In a study to establish criterion-related validity, forty-five students (thirty-eight boys, seven girls) aged 5–16 years were rated by teachers on the TRF and the Conners Revised Teacher Rating Scale (Goyette, Conners, & Ulrich, 1978). TRF scales correlated from .80 to .83 with the Conners Conduct Problems, Inattention-Passivity, and total Problem scores. The TRF Aggressive Behavior (r = .67) and Externalizing (r = .63) scales were the closest counterparts of the Conners Hyperactivity scale. In addition, the closest counterpart of the Conners Hyperactivity Index was the TRF total Problems score (.71). Criterion validity of the TRF instrument was also assessed by evaluating two samples of demographically matched referred and nonreferred students who were rated by teachers. Nonreferred students were rated higher on Academic and Adaptive scales and lower on Problem scores when compared to the referred sample. All comparisons were significant at the .01 confidence level with the exception of Somatic Complaints for twelve to eighteen-year-old males.

Achenbach also presents relative risk odds ratios to indicate the odds of having a particular condition given that an individual has a particular risk factor. Odds-ratio analyses were conducted on TRF scores and referral status. Students from the matched referred and nonreferred sample were identified as scoring in the clinical range on any of the TRF scales. Next, calculations were made to determine the odds that a clinical score was obtained by a student from the referred sample. All odds ratios were significantly greater than 1.0, and the percent of children scoring in the clinical range was statistically significant between the two samples at the .01 confidence level.

Construct Validity   A study that compared 1,275 students referred for behavioral and/or emotional problems with 1,275 demographically matched nonreferred students was conducted to evaluate the discriminative validity of the TRF. With referral status as the criterion, results indicated that nonreferred students were rated significantly higher on all items of Adaptive functioning and lower on nearly all TRF Problem items. These data suggest the TRF content is able to discriminate adequately between referred and nonreferred students.

One of the most efficient and effective ways to discriminate clinical from nonclinical subgroups is to classify students as deviant if their Academic, total Adaptive, and total Problem scores are in the clinical range. Additional findings are presented in the manual that will help practitioners select the most powerful combinations of scale and items to differentiate between clinical and normal samples. Evidence of criterion validity is taken from independent studies of the TRF scores and children with clinical diagnoses. All evidence is provided on the pre-1991 measure. Children classified as having attention deficit/hyperactivity disorder were found to produce higher scores on the TRF Attention problem items than a control group of other clinically diagnosed children. In a comparison of special education students, children classified as learning disabled scored significantly lower than those classified as emotionally disordered on Problem scales.

Overall, the TRF appears to be a useful measure of the construct of emotional/behavioral functioning. The TRF appears relatively successful at discriminating among groups of referred and nonreferred students and students with different disability conditions.

SUMMARY

The TRF is a well-developed, empirically based instrument designed to obtain information about a student's performance on Academic, Adaptive, and Problem items in a standardized manner that can be compared to norms established by gender and age. The standardization sample was selected from the overall CBCL/4–18 sample. Three types of reliability data were reported. Test-retest coefficients were within an acceptable range, stability and interrater reliability are marginal, and internal consistency of scale items is based on factor-analytic studies. Validity rests primarily on CBCL/4–18 validity.

Overall, the TRF is a well-researched instrument that appears to measure what it is supposed to measure—the overall emotional/behavioral status of children and youth. The TRF is an important component of assessment that will serve professionals in the field well as part of Achenbach's five-axis assessment systems.

Youth Self-Report and 1991 Profile for Ages 11–18

*T*he Youth Self-Report (YSR) (Achenbach, 1991d) is a self-administered rating scale designed to be completed in approximately 15 minutes by adolescents aged 11 to 18 years with at least a fifth-grade reading level. The YSR was developed primarily to assess a student's interests, feelings, and behaviors. It is a revision of the *Manual for the Youth Self-Report and Profile* (Achenbach & Edelbrock, 1987). The current revision incorporates new national norms and changes in the scoring profile and includes new provisions for integrating self-report data with the CBCL/4–18 and the TRF.

DESCRIPTION OF SCALES

Two broad areas are assessed: Competence and Problem Behaviors. The Competence scales include Activities (e.g., sports, hobbies, and extracurricular activities), Social (e.g., total number of friends and activities with friends), and Total Competence, which includes self-ratings of academic performance. Problem scales include two groupings of syndromes: Internalizing (Withdrawn, Somatic Complaints, Anxious/Depressed) and Externalizing (Delinquent Behavior, Aggressive Behavior). Four additional syndromes are not part of either Internalizing or Externalizing (Social Problems, Thought Problems, Attention Problems, and Self-Destructive/Identity Problems). (The Self-Destructive/Identity Problems syndrome is relevant for boys only.)

The Problem Behaviors items are very similar to the items from the CBCL/4–18 but are written in the first person. An additional sixteen items that were deemed to reflect socially desirable behavior are also included on the Problem items scale. For example, items include statements such as "I argue a lot," "I destroy my own things," and "I set fires." Some items provide open-ended questions that allow the student to list additional physical problems or to provide further descriptions of scored items. Examples include "I do things other people think are strange (describe)" and "I have trouble sleeping (describe)." Respondents are encouraged to provide descriptions of these items so that the items will not be scored improperly.

SCORES

Detailed scoring procedures are provided in the administration manual. Students rate their competence across different points of interest using a three-point scale—that is, they determine whether the amount of time or number of activities are "Less than average," "Average," or "More than average" as compared to their same-age peers. The 102 Problem items plus an open-ended item are rated on a three-point scale (0, Not true; 1, Somewhat or sometimes true; 2, Very true or often true).

Raw scores are tallied for all items within individual scales and are plotted on the YSR profile by gender. Percentile rank and normalized *T*-scores are presented for all scales; no differentiation is made by gender or age. As with the other Achenbach instruments, scores may be classified within the normal, borderline, or clinical range.

NORMS

A subsample of the CBCL (1989) standardization sample was recruited by targeting children and adolescents between 11 and 18. To create a normative sample that was representative of regular education students, students who had not received mental health services or special education services within the preceding twelve months were selected from this group; the resulting YSR normative sample contained 1,315 subjects. Ethnic distributions were similar to those of the CBCL/4–18. The YSR scales are normed separately for each gender for ages 11–18. A clinical sample of 709 boys and 563 girls aged 11–18 years was also assessed on the YSR. These subjects were from twenty-six settings, primarily in the Eastern United States. The author claims that a wide distribution of socioeconomic, demographic, and other client characteristics were obtained on all samples, although no national census data are provided for comparison.

RELIABILITY

Test-Retest Reliability   Fifty subjects completed the YSR two times with a seven-day time lapse. Correlations between the two administrations are presented for each scale by gender and age. Most scale correlations were significant at the .05 confidence level, although ratings by eleven- to fourteen-year-olds were somewhat less reliable. The range of coefficients was from .37 (Activities for boys and Thought Problems for ages 11–14) to .91 (Internalizing, Externalizing, and total Problems for ages 15–18). The total Competence mean correlation was .80 and the total Problems scale mean correlation was .79.

Long-Term Stability   Children selected from the general population sample completed the YSR on two occasions, seven months apart. A total of 111 children (forty-nine boys, sixty-two girls) aged 11–14 years participated. Results are presented by gender and age groupings. Total Competence scores produced a mean correlation of .62, and the total Problems scale produced a mean correlation of .56. In a study of a nondefined clinical sample of twelve- to seventeen-year-olds, total Problems scores correlated at .69 over a 6-month interval (Achenbach & Edelbrock, 1987).

Internal Consistency   Internal consistency for the total Competence scale was .46; for total Problems, alpha was .95. Both the Internalizing and Externalizing groupings had internal consistencies of .89. Alphas for syndrome scales range from .59 (Withdrawn) to .86 (Aggressive Behavior and Anxious/Depressed).

VALIDITY

Content Validity   A majority of YSR items were taken directly from the previously validated CBCL/4–18. The author describes the process used to revise some items and to delete others from certain scores.

Criterion-Related Validity   As with the other measures, referral status is used as the validity criterion. In a study of 2,108 subjects, the author evaluated the relationship between scale scores and concurrent referral status. Significantly higher Competence scores and lower Problem scores were obtained by the nonreferred group compared to the referred group. For both girls and boys, the largest effects of referral status were found for Delinquent Behavior and total Problems. The Problem scales appear to function well in discriminating between referred and nonreferred students; however, the YSR Competence scales are not strong discriminators of referral status.

Construct Validity   Achenbach does not present explicit evidence of construct validity for the YSR as he does for other measures. He offers the current lack of suitable (and similar) measures to employ in convergent and divergent validity studies as the reason for limited available evidence. Some indirect evidence is provided in the form of correlations among the other Achenbach instruments. The mean coefficient is .50 (with a range of .27 to .62). Ratings such as these are not unexpected and fall in the low to moderate range for validity coefficients.

SUMMARY

The YSR is a self-administered report on an adolescent's competence and problem concerns. The instrument's scales provide indications of the student's overall emotional/behavioral status. Because of the empirical underpinnings of the YSR, its technical features are advanced for this particular type of assessment. However, they are not sufficiently defined and described to warrant extensive trust in the device. Reliability and validity studies are mixed but generally supportive. Still, the YSR should be considered a useful adjunct for use in screening and a key component in multiaxial assessment process.

The Direct Observation Form

*T*he Direct Observation Form (DOF) (Achenbach, 1986) is designed to record behavior problems exhibited by a child during 10-minute observations. No age range guidelines are given although the clinical sample included children aged 5–14 years. Observations are conducted in group settings such as in classrooms and at recess. A detailed list of ninety-six specific problem behaviors and an open-ended item for entering additional problems are provided. In general, observers are asked to describe a child's behavior in a narrative during a 10-minute observation. The observer is advised to refer to the DOF items during the observation to organize the narrative description. In addition, a child's on-task behavior is recorded and included in the final description of his or her performance. After watching a child and completing the narrative, an observer rates each of the ninety-six items and provides information on the open-ended question. Whereas the DOF provides supplemental information on a child's performance, direct links with the other Achenbach instruments are enhanced by the fact that seventy-two of the ninety-six Problem items have counterparts on the CBCL/4–18 and eighty-five items directly correspond to items on the TRF. Examples of Problem items include "Acts too young for age," "Argues," "Disturbs other children," "Shows off or clowns," and "Unhappy, sad, or depressed."

Like the other Achenbach instruments, the DOF can be scored by hand or by computer. Detailed rules for scoring each item are printed on the DOF form. Scores are provided on four broad scales and six syndromes. Broad scales include On Task, total Problems, Internalizing and Externalizing. The syndromes include Withdrawn/Inattentive, Nervous/Obsessive, Depressed, Hyperactive, Attention Demanding, and Aggressive. Unlike those for other instruments, the syndrome scores for the DOF can be obtained only when using the computer-scoring program because of the complexity of producing these scores.

SCORES

The On-Task intervals are tallied at the end of the observation and reported as a score ranging from 0 to 10. The ninety-six Problem behaviors are also rated by the observer along a four-point scale (0 to 3). This four-point scale is different from those used in the other Achenbach instruments in that the author claims the additional gradation of the scale allows for "a slight or ambiguous occurrence" of a behavior to be scored as a 1, "a definite occurrence with a mild to moderate intensity and less than three minutes duration" to be scored as a 2, and "a definite occurrence with severe intensity or greater that three minutes duration" to be scored as a 3.

Mean scores are computed based on the number of observations conducted. Scores can be plotted on the DOF profile, and percentile and *T*-scores can be obtained to determine whether a target student's performance is within clinical or normal ranges. The same scoring profile is used for both boys and girls. The author suggests that the DOF should be completed on three to six occasions to obtain a stable index of a child's performance. In addition, to provide direct peer comparisons, it is suggested that two randomly selected peers be observed immediately prior to and immediately after observing the target child. The two peer observations can be averaged to provide a standard to which the target child's performance can be compared.

NORMS

All scale scores and syndromes identified on the DOF are empirically derived using principal components analyses on data obtained from a sample of 212 clinically referred individuals (5–14 years old). The DOF was then normed on 287 regular education students recruited from forty-five schools located in three states (Vermont, Nebraska, and Oregon). No additional demographic characteristics are provided.

RELIABILITY AND VALIDITY

Reliability and validity information are not provided in a separate manual for the DOF. Rather, users of

the DOF are referred to the following sources for technical data in support of the scale: Achenbach and Edelbrock (1983), McConaughy, Achenbach, and Gent (1988), and Reed and Edelbrock (1983).

SUMMARY

The DOF provides practitioners with an observational tool that can be used to record on-task behavior and problem behaviors across ninety-six items that are highly similar to those included in other Achenbach instruments. Although the correspondence of items across the CBCL/4–18 and the TRF may be helpful in coordinating data, the overall technical adequacy of the DOF by itself is not well substantiated. The norms of the DOF are not well defined, and users of the scale who want information on reliability and validity must seek outside references to obtain this evidence. Overall, the DOF should be considered as an ancillary tool to substantiate behavioral problems in classroom or group settings rather than as an independent instrument.

The Behavior Evaluation Scale–2

*T*he Behavior Evaluation Scale–2 (BES-2) (McCarney & Leigh, 1990) is a seventy-six-item rating scale developed for students enrolled in kindergarten through grade 12. The manual provides a brief description of the rationale for and importance of assessing emotional/behavioral disorders. The manual also provides clear administration, scoring, and interpretation guidelines, as well as technical information about the standardization process. Five scale scores are provided on the BES-2: Learning Problems, Interpersonal Difficulties, Inappropriate Behavior, Unhappiness/Depression, and Physical Symptoms/Fears. Educators who have had at least one month of interaction with a student may complete the BES-2 rating scale. Estimated time to complete the rating form is 15 to

20 minutes. The author suggests six primary uses of this scale:

1. To screen for behavior problems
2. To assess the behavior of students who are referred
3. To assist in the diagnosis of behavior disorders or emotional disturbance
4. To contribute to the development of individual educational programs
5. To document progress resulting from behavioral interventions
6. To collect data for research purposes

All items on the BES-2 are stated in observable and measurable terms. In addition, great effort has been made to link behavioral descriptions to federal guidelines established by Public Law 94-142 as well as to Bower's (1981) widely used definition of emotionally disturbed/behaviorally disordered children. To reduce the subjective nature of teachers' ratings, a seven-point scale is provided: 1, Never or not observed; 2, Less than once a week; 3, Approximately once a month; 4, Approximately once a week; 5, More than once a week; 6, Daily at various times; 7, Continuously throughout the day. The authors claim that rating the frequency of behaviors can reduce the need for more expensive methods of direct and continuous observation by school personnel.

SCORES

Five types of scores can be obtained from the BES-2: weighted scores of individual items, subscale raw scores, subscale standard scores, a quotient representing performance on the total scale, and percentile ranks for each subscale and total scale. Scale scores are computed by transferring ratings for each of the seventy-six items to a data summary sheet on the rating protocol. Each subscale lists the specific item numbers that comprise the five individual scales. Item ratings are multiplied by a pre-established weighting factor and summed by scale. The sums of the weighted scores for each of the five subscales are converted to standard scores (mean = 10, standard deviation = 3) and percentile ranks. A Total Quotient score (mean = 100, standard deviation = 15) and percentile rank are computed by summing the five subscale standard scores and using appropriate conversion tables provided in the appendix.

NORMS

The BES-2 was standardized on a completely new standardization sample. A total of 2,272 students from thirty-one states were selected to represent four geographic regions of the United States. A sample of 568 regular education teachers administered the BES-2 to randomly selected students from their classes. The number of participating children was distributed fairly equally across the K–12 grade levels (range = 137–207). Demographic characteristics of the sample provide a good match to the U.S. (1980) census data for gender, race, ethnicity, geographic area, and educational status of parents. A notable exception appears to be an underrepresentation within the standardization sample of Hispanic and Asian students.

RELIABILITY

Two types of reliability data are offered for the BES-2: internal consistency and test-retest.

Internal-consistency coefficients range from .75 to .95, with twenty of twenty-four calculated coefficients exceeding a coefficient alpha of .88. Total-scale coefficients were either .97 or .98 across all grade levels.

Stability of scores obtained on typically developing children ($N = 82$) from ten states and emotionally disturbed/behaviorally disordered children ($N = 108$) from thirteen states was assessed at an interval of ten to fourteen days. Spearman correlation coefficients between two sets of obtained scores (test and retest) exceed or round to .90 (range = .89–.97). All correlations were found to be statistically significant at the .001 level of confidence.

No other reliability data (e.g., interrater reliability and/or interrater agreement) are provided.

VALIDITY

Studies were conducted to provide evidence of validity for the BES-2. Three types of validity are presented: content validity, criterion-related validity, and construct validity.

Appropriateness of scale items was initially evaluated by a large sample of classroom teachers and special education personnel with expertise in the area of behavioral disorders. In addition, during the revision process a sample of 675 professionals from thirty-one states reviewed each item to determine its appropriateness for describing educational behavioral problems. All items on the final version were judged by 95 percent of the experts as appropriate descriptors of problem behavior.

To evaluate concurrent criterion-related validity, the BES-2 was compared to the Teacher Rating Scale of the Behavior Rating Profile (BRP; Brown & Hammill, 1978). Twenty-six students from elementary and secondary grades, identified as behaviorally disordered and receiving special education services in Missouri, were assessed on both measures. Five of six scores on the BES-2 produced coefficients that were statistically significant at the .01 and .05 confidence levels (Range = .44–.81). One subscale, Learning Problems, did not correlate at all with the BRP (r = .01). In another study, teachers' professional judgments were compared to BES-2 results. A total of 190 teachers rated students from regular (N = 82) and special education (N = 108) classrooms (K–12) on the BES-2 after having answered the question, "Relative to other students of this age, how would you generally rate this student's classroom behavior?" A nine-point scale was used by the teachers to rate students. Behavioral descriptions were provided for 1, "Student has significant behavior problems in comparison to others"; 5, "Student's behavior is about the same as that of others"; and 9, "Student has excellent classroom behavior in comparison with others." No additional guidelines on how to rate students on the nine-point scale were provided to teachers. The five BES-2 subscales and total score produced significant correlation coefficients at the .01 level of confidence except for emotional/behavioral disordered students rated on Physical Symptoms/Fears. Correlations ranged from .45 to .75 for regular education students and from .15 to .59 for behavioral disordered students.

Evidence for construct validity is based on studies showing that students identified as behaviorally disordered exhibited significantly more psychopathology across all five subscales.

SUMMARY

The Behavior Evaluation Scale–2 is a seventy-six-item rating scale for children enrolled in kindergarten through grade 12. Three subscales produce raw scores that are converted to standard scores (mean = 10, standard deviation = 3). The total score is the only score that can be represented as a percentile rank. The standardization procedures appear to be appropriate (norm tables are provided by age-gender groups), although reliability measures were not reported in this manner. Validity studies support the criterion-related and construct validity of the BES-2 as a device that is adequate for screening purposes.

Early Childhood Behavior Scale

*T*he Early Childhood Behavior Scale (ECBS) (McCarney, 1992) was developed to assess children 36 to 72 months of age. The ECBS consists of fifty-three items divided into three subscales: Academic Progress (ten items), Social Relationships (twelve items), and Personal Adjustment (thirty-one items). Estimated time to complete the ECBS is approximately 15 minutes. The primary purpose of the ECBS is to facilitate the identification of children with emotional and behavioral disturbances in preschool environments. In addition, the author claims that the information gathered from this rating scale can be translated directly into goal statements and behavioral objectives for a child's educational programming.

Each scale consists of a series of behavioral items that are rated by educators familiar with the child of concern. For example, items from the Academic Progress scale include "Is unable to perform tasks independently" and "Requires repeated drill and practice to learn what other children master easily." Examples from the Social Relationship scale include "Fights with others" and "Will not share possessions or materials." Finally, examples of items from the

Personal Adjustment scale include " Exhibits extreme mood changes" and "Does not accept changes in established routines."

Educators rate each item according to a six-point scale of perceived frequency to quantify their concerns: 0, Not in my presence; 1, One time; 2, Several times; 3, More than one time a month, up to one time a week; 4, More than one time a week, up to once a day; 5, More than once a day, up to once an hour; 6, More than once an hour. A sound rationale for and further description of the six-point scale can be found in the technical manual.

SCORES

Scores on three individual scales are computed by tabulating teacher ratings for each item within a specific subscale. Raw scores are converted to standard scores using conversion tables provided in the appendix. Standard scores have a mean of 10 and a standard deviation of 3. In addition, a total score is calculated by adding standard scores across all three subscales. The total score is then converted to a percentile rank. Because of the different outcomes evidenced by the standardization sample, three separate norm tables are provided for males by age: 36–47 months, 48–59 months, and 60–71 months. Females required only two age clusters: 36–47 months and 48–71 months. A summary table on the front of the scoring protocol provides an area for scores and the percentile rank to be plotted.

NORMS

The standardization sample consisted of 1,314 children, aged 3 to 6 years. The author provides additional data on the number of children by age in three-month increments. The standardization sample is distributed across these age groups, with each age group having one hundred children or more, with the exception of ages 45–47 months ($N = 91$), 48–50 months ($N = 98$), and 51–53 months ($N = 82$). For all age groups N ranged from 82 to 127. Students were enrolled in both regular and be-havioral-disordered classrooms. Rating scales were completed by 289 teachers from sixty-eight public schools across seventeen states. Characteristics of the standardization sample were compared to actual percentages of the U.S. census. In general, it appears that the author has provided a sample representative of the U.S. population with regard to race/ethnicity, region, and socioeconomic status. However, the sample does appear to overrepresent the Northeast and underrepresent the South by 8 percent and 11 percent, respectively.

RELIABILITY

Three types of reliability data are provided: test-retest, internal consistency, and interrater agreement. All reliability studies involve random samples drawn from the standardization sample. Test-retest reliability results are provided by subscale but not by sex or age. This is a concern because of the author's own claims of differential effects found for the different gender-age groupings. Reliability coefficients for the different scales were .88 for Academic, .81 for Social Relationships, and .91 for Personal Adjustment.

Internal-consistency coefficients exceed .90, but the sample on which these results are based is not clearly described. Item-total and item-subscale correlations are presented in the technical manual with correlations ranging from .28 to .85.

Interrater agreement was based on the ratings of two educators with equal knowledge of each child rated. A total of 101 pairs of teachers rated 237 children on the ECBS. The author presents extensive results of Pearson product moment correlations across three-month age intervals; however, once again, results are not presented separately by gender. Coefficients ranged from .81 to .88, with a mean of .85.

VALIDITY

Content validity of the ECBS is based on a comprehensive review of the literature as well as input from experienced practitioners who helped produce an initial pool of scale items. The author reports that the literature review supports the five-category definition of emotionally disturbed/behaviorally disordered children on which the ECBS is based. However, the ECBS collapses these five categories into a three-scale format (Academic, Social, and Personal Skills) to address the National Mental Health and Special Education definitions of the emotionally disturbed/behaviorally disordered. Finally, an item analysis was conducted to assess whether adequate differentiation occurs across items. The fifty-three-item rating scale is the result of this process.

Criterion-related validity data are reported from a single study on fifty-seven students previously identified as behaviorally disordered and receiving special education services. Teachers with the most knowledge of the child's behavior rated each of the fifty-seven children on the ECBS and the corresponding form of the Child Behavior Checklist for ages 2–3, and ages 4–18 (Achenbach, 1991b, 1992d). All correlations were significant at the .001 confidence level. Once again, results were not differentiated by age or gender.

A principal-components analysis and a factor–analytic procedure were used to verify whether the three theoretically separate subscales could be empirically confirmed. The ECBS appears to measure the overall construct of behavior disorders, but the results from the factor analysis do not support the definition of three subscales. Further evidence of a unitary construct is found in the high intercorrelations of the subscales.

A sample of 196 students randomly selected from the standardization sample was compared to a corresponding group of identified behaviorally disordered students from eleven school districts who were receiving program services. Mean total subscale scores and percentile scores were significantly different at the .001 confidence level. However, it should be noted that the previously identified subsample scored within one standard deviation on all subscales except for Personal Adjustment. Children aged 36–47 months were the only subgroup that consistently scored one standard deviation below the mean on all three subscales.

SUMMARY

The Early Childhood Behavior Scale is a fifty-three-item rating scale for children aged 36–72 months. Three subscales produce raw scores that are converted to standard scores (mean = 10, standard deviation = 3). The total score is the only score that can be represented as a percentile rank. The standardization procedures appear to be well controlled; demographic characteristics and distribution of age groups are well documented. Although norm tables are provided by gender-age groups, reliability measures were not reported in this manner. Initial data indicate that the test is adequate for screening purposes. Questions still remain about the usefulness of the ECBS for diagnostic purposes. Specifically, the inability of the three subscales of the ECBS to differentiate previously identified emotionally disturbed/behaviorally disordered students from regular education students may call into question the relevance of the three subscales for diagnostic purposes. Ultimately, the true test of the effectiveness of the ECBS will be the extent to which it leads to better diagnostic and educational program planning for emotionally disturbed/behaviorally disordered students. Although support may accrue over time, additional evidence of technical adequacy and diagnostic precision are needed.

Behavior Rating Profile, Second Edition

*T*he Behavior Rating Profile, Second Edition (BRP-2) (Brown & Hammill, 1990) is a multirater, multicontext instrument designed for use with students aged 6-6 to 18-6 years. The BRP-2 consists of three Student Rating scales (Home, SRS:H; School, SRS:S; and Peers, SRS:P), a Teacher Rating scale (TRS), a Parent Rating scale (PRS), and a Sociogram. The three student scales are printed in a single booklet and are administered simultaneously.

The authors propose that the BRP-2 be used to help identify students with emotional, behavioral, personal, or social adjustment problems in home, school, or social-interpersonal settings. The ecological framework is depicted in Table 26.4.

Each Student Rating scale has twenty items that are answered as either true or false. Representative Home items include "I don't listen to my parents when they are talking to me" and "I have lots of nightmares and bad dreams." School items include "My teachers give me work that I cannot do" and "I can't seem to stay in my desk at school." Peer items include "Other children are always picking on me" and "I seem to get into a lot of fights." The Teacher Rating scale has thirty items that include statements about the student's school behavior. These statements are negatively oriented and are rated on a four-point scale (1, Very much like the student; 2, Like the student; 3, Not much like the student; 4, Not at all like the student). Examples of items from the TRS include "Swears in class" and "Tattles on classmates." The Parent Rating Scale contains thirty negatively worded items describing behaviors that may be observed at home. These are rated on the same four-point scale as the TRS. Examples of the PRS items include "Is verbally aggressive to parents" and "Violates curfew."

The Sociogram uses a peer-nomination technique to get peer perceptions of the target student. Pairs of stimulus questions selected from the manual or devised by the examiner are given to the students; for example, "Which students in your class would you like most to have as a class officer?" and "Which students would you least like to have as a class officer?" Students then nominate three of their peers whom they would "like most" and "like least". The examiner then rank-orders students based on their acceptance and rejection rates.

SCORES

All five scales of the BRP-2 yield raw scores, standard scores, and percentile ranks. Scoring of the rating scales is straightforward; however, scoring the Sociogram involves a more complex six-step computation and ranking procedure. Standard error of measurement (SEM) data are complicated. An SEM of 1 is printed on the BRP-2 profile form for all scales. However, SEMs actually vary by subtest and grade level from 0.4 to 1.6. Thus, the example of how to use the SEM provided in the manual is not easy to follow.

NORMS

Three norm samples (1978, 1983, 1989) have been integrated for the BRP-2. A total of 2,682 students aged 6-6 to 18-6 from twenty-six states are included in the complete group. Data to support the representativeness of the norm sample are provided. Students at the anchor points (ages 6 and 18 years) are

TABLE 26.4   **Ecological Orientation of the BRP-2**

BRP-2 Scale	Respondent				Ecology		
	Student	Teacher	Parent	Peer	Home	School	Social
Student Rating Scale: Home	X				X		
Student Rating Scale: School	X					X	
Student Rating Scale: Peer	X					X	X
Teacher Rating Scale		X				X	
Parent Rating Scale			X		X		
Sociogram				X			X

SOURCE: Brown, L., and Hammill, D. D. (1990). *Behavior Rating Profile, 2nd ed.* Austin, TX, Pro-Ed.

underrepresented, and the educational attainment of students' parents is biased toward the high end. A notable exclusionary practice of the BRP-2 is the authors' decision *not* to assess students with social-emotional disturbances (SED) in the normative process. Salvia and Ysseldyke (this edition) consider it inappropriate to exclude students with particular characteristics from the norm group of a test designed to help identify them. Readers are cautioned that in using the BRP-2 they will be making normative comparisons are to a sample presumably less prone to behavior problems.

Norm data for the PRS were gathered from 1,948 parents in nineteen states. Procedures for gathering parent data included sending BRP-2 scales home, asking those attending PTA meetings to fill out the scales, and asking parents at school conferences to complete the instrument. Again, no students with SED were rated in these processes.

For the TRS, data are available from 1,452 teachers from twenty-six states. Teachers were asked to rate every fifth student on their class rosters, *except* students with SED. Overall demographics for the PRS and TRS appear to closely match national averages.

No norm sample data on the Sociogram are presented, because the target student's own classmates serve as the normative comparison. Normative scoring information for the Sociogram was prepared by examining normalized distributions of student ranks for different class sizes.

RELIABILITY

Two types of reliability data are offered to support the BRP-2: internal consistency using coefficient alpha and test-retest stability. Reliability coefficients are reported for five grade levels for the five rating scales. Each scale's internal consistency was calculated for a sample size of about 200 across these grade levels. Coefficients ranged from .77 to .98 and are adequate for the test's intended purpose as a screening device. Internal-consistency estimates with special populations (emotionally disturbed elemen-

tary and learning-disabled secondary students) ranged from .76 to .97. Overall, these also are of adequate magnitude for the BRP-2's intended use.

Test-retest reliability is presented from several studies. For a group of thirty-six high school students, their teachers, and their parents, reliability coefficients ranged from .78 to .91 across a two-week interval. The TRS was the most stable scale. Another study of 198 students in grades 1 through 12, including 212 parents and 176 teachers, yielded test-retest reliability ranging from .43 to .96. (Coefficients for grades 1 and 2 were lowest (SRS:H = .43, SRS:S = .58, SRS:P = .52, PRS = .69, TRS = .94.) No explanation for or speculation about these coefficients is provided; however, the capriciousness of self-reports by young children and their reading difficulties may be partial explanations. Ninety-seven secondary students with emotional disturbances, their parents, and their teachers provided test-retest data on the BRP-2 scales. Coefficients for these subjects ranged from .76 to .82.

Information on an important type of reliability data for rating scales, interrater reliability, is missing from the BRP-2 technical manual. The authors' discussion of interpretation of scores from an ecological perspective includes issues of multiple raters and possible discrepancies among their scores. Still, some indication of interrater agreement can be gleaned from their discussion of patterns across student, teacher, and parent ratings. Students tend to give themselves the highest scores, whereas parents usually assign the lowest scores. Omission of direct interrater reliability data, however, weakens the overall data support for the instrument.

VALIDITY

The authors believe validity is not easily discussed along traditional lines of content, criterion-related, and construct validity data. Evidence of overall validity is provided for "more punctilious readers" (Brown & Hammill, 1990, p. 48) in sections devoted to relationships among BRP-2 items and/or scales and other variables or criteria.

Content validation was approached through the authors' examination of the professional literature, existing checklists, rating scales (e.g., Walker Problem Behavior Identification Checklist, Quay-Peterson Behavior Problem Checklist), and other assessments. Parents of students with emotional and learning problems provided written input about behavior concerns. Longer, experimental versions of the BRP scales were reduced to a more manageable length through empirical-item analyses.

Criterion-related concurrent and construct validity data are supplied in several sections describing the relationship of BRP-2 scales to measures of achievement, aptitude, and affect. Correlations with tests of achievement and aptitude produce low (near-zero) coefficients, as was expected by the authors. Stronger correlations between the BRP-2 and measures of affect were expected as evidence that these criterion variables were measuring the same construct.

The strongest evidence for validity rests on data from a study conducted in Kansas of 108 students (twenty-seven in each of four groups: normal, learning disabled, public school socially/emotionally disturbed, and institutionalized socially/emotionally disturbed). All BRP-2 scales except the Sociogram were correlated with the Walker Problem Behavior Identification Checklist, the Quay-Peterson Behavior Problem Checklist, and the Vineland Social Maturity Scale. Inspection of the data shows that sixty-four of seventy-two resulting correlations were significant and exceeded their target magnitude of .35. The results were weakest for the students with SED who received services in the public schools. There is some confusion, however, in the reporting of these data. The authors' explanations of the data account for only sixty of the seventy-two reported correlations, and this research is not discussed in sufficient detail.

Other studies correlate BRP-2 scales with the Test of Early Socioemotional Development, the Behavior Evaluation Scale, the Devereaux Elementary School Behavior Rating Scale II, the Children's Manifest Anxiety Scale, and the Index of Children's Personality Characteristics. These data support the concurrent and construct validity of the BRP-2 as a measure of overall behavior and social adjustment.

Support for the discriminative validity of the BRP-2 scales (except the Sociogram) is provided in a section listing fifteen studies reporting BRP-2 scores for different student groups. (Some of the studies were conducted by the authors.) As a whole, these studies reveal the expected differences in group means. Students with social/emotional disturbance and mental retardation score lower than learning disabled and nondisabled students, who tend to receive average scores. Gifted students tend to score higher than all other groups. Several of the studies are described in some detail. The statistical significance of the findings in these studies, however, is not detailed.

SUMMARY

The BRP-2 is designed to assess students' behavior in different ecologies and is intended to identify students with emotional, behavioral, and social adjustment problems. The device is made up of five rating scales and a Sociogram. The rating scales require true-false responses of the students and Likert-type ratings from teachers and parents. Norms for the BRP-2 exclude students with SED but otherwise appear well defined. Users of the BRP-2 must recognize this design characteristic and adjust their interpretations accordingly. Reliability for the scales is supported by adequate internal-consistency and test-retest data. No interrater reliability data are provided. Content validity of the BRP-2 scales was ensured by a well-planned development process. The tests appear to have high criterion-related concurrent and construct validity. There is some question of the instrument's ability to discriminate between students with learning problems and students with behavior problems. The BRP-2 should be used with confidence as a screening tool but should not be used as the primary data source for classification or diagnostic decisions.

The Walker-McConnell Scale of Social Competence and School Adjustment

*T*he Walker-McConnell Scale of Social Competence and School Adjustment (W-M) (Walker & McConnell, 1988) is a norm-referenced rating scale of social skills for use with elementary-aged children. The instrument consists of three subscales (Teacher-Preferred Social Behavior, Peer-Preferred Social Behavior, and School Adjustment Behavior) intended to be used for "screening and identification of social skills deficits" (Walker & McConnell, 1988, p. 1). The W-M was "not designed as either a diagnostic or classification instrument" (p. 3). Information on students' social competence and school adjustment that can be used as part of referral or child-study team processes, as well as for program planning, is obtained from item subscale and total scores and through normative comparisons. The authors suggest that in addition to the national norms provided in the manual, a classroom normative reference can be gained by assessing typical peers of the target student on the W-M. This procedure also helps validate the ratings of the target student.

The W-M consists of forty-three positively worded descriptions of social skills. Subscale 1 (Teacher-Preferred Behavior) consists of sixteen items that assess sensitivity, empathy, cooperation, self-control, and maturity. Examples of items include "Shows empathy" and "Cooperates with peers." Subscale 2 (Peer-Preferred Behavior) has seventeen items that address peer values and relations in social situations. Items include "Invites peers to play or share activities" and "Compromises when the situation calls for it." Subscale 3 (School Adjustment) has ten items that assess competencies in academic settings. Sample items include "Displays independent study skills" and "Listens carefully to teacher directions." All items are rated on a five-point Likert scale from "Never occurs" to "Frequently occurs." The upper anchor point is defined in somewhat vague terminology ("Frequently occurs" is defined as "a high rate"), and a rationale for the scaling choice is not provided. More explicit definitions may help raters make more objective evaluations of student behavior.

SCORES

The W-M yields raw scores (subscale and total) by adding the numerical Likert ratings. Raw scores are converted to standard scores for the subscales (mean = 10, standard deviation = 3) and for the total scale (mean = 100, standard deviation = 15). Standard scores are converted to percentile rankings.

NORMS

Normative data for the W-M are based on a sample of 1,812 students from grades K–6. Sixty percent of these students were in grades 1, 2, and 4, but there were at least 125 students per grade. Data were collected over a two-year period from 1985 to 1987. Students were from fifteen states, with three states (Alabama, Montana, and Oregon) supplying 48 percent of the sample. The authors provide data to show that the mean score of subjects from the four geographic regions were all within one standard error of measurement. Other demographics (e.g., urban-suburban and ethnicity) appear representative of the nation.

RELIABILITY

The authors supply three types of reliability data: test-retest, interrater, and internal consistency. In addition, item-total correlations (considered by Salvia and Ysseldyke to be reliability data) are found in the manual's section on item validity.

Test-retest reliability is supported by data from several studies, some of which were conducted by other investigators. Coefficients range from .67 to .97 for studies with test-retest intervals of between two to four weeks. A study of test-retest stability with antisocial and normal boys over a six-month period produced slightly lower correlations.

Interrater reliability studies produced what the authors call "modest agreement levels" (p. 33). What is missing is an estimate of interrater reliability using two same-type raters (e.g., two teachers or two teacher's aides). Such data provide an estimate of the consistency of assessments of student-functioning from a common frame of reference.

Internal-consistency data are presented in the form of alpha coefficients for the total norm sample. All subscales were above .95, and all coefficients by grade level were above .94. Collectively, these data support the claim that the W-M has adequate reliability for its intended purposes.

VALIDITY

Twenty-four pages of the fifty-page manual for the W-M are devoted to text, tables, and figures on validity data (including the item-total correlations discussed above). The authors report their own studies and those of other investigators using the W-M in research.

Content Validity The authors of the W-M examined the professional literature, existing teacher-rating instruments, and materials from other national projects to develop an initial item pool of one hundred descriptors of school-related social skills. Eighty-three items were selected for testing, and the final forty-three items were chosen based on (1) item means, (2) item variances, (3) item-total correlations, and (4) item loadings from first- and second-order factor analyses. Clearly, the authors have employed empirical processes for the identification of the items included in the W-M.

Criterion-Related and Discriminative Validity Several studies are presented to support the criterion-related validity of the W-M. These are mostly supportive of concurrent validity. In a study using the Walker Problem Behavior Identification Checklist (WPBIC) as the criterion, thirteen elementary students who had been referred for resource room services and seventeen nondisabled students who had been referred for counseling were rated by teachers and by their parents. The WPBIC and W-M are scaled in opposite ways; thus the resulting validity coefficients were negative and significant (range = −.69 to −.89).

In another study using teacher ratings of social adjustment, peer sociometrics, and academic achievement variables as criteria, sixty-five elementary students were also rated on the W-M. Moderate to high correlations were found between the teacher ratings and the W-M subscale and total scores. Low to moderate correlations were found for peer sociometrics and achievement data. The W-M does not appear to correlate with measures of academic engagement.

Correlations with the Social Skills Rating System for Teachers (SSRS-T) provides potentially strong evidence of concurrent validity. The SSRS-T is an earlier version of the teacher scale of the Social Skills Rating System (Gresham & Elliott, 1990). Unfortunately, the authors do not report the number of subjects or population(s) involved in the validity study. The total scores of the W-M and the SSRS-T correlated. The subscales of the W-M and factors of the SSRS-T correlated in the expected directions.

Discriminative validity of the W-M is supported by studies designed to document the sensitivity of the instrument in discriminating groups defined by researchers or based on school district classifications. Other discriminative validity studies involved research-defined groups of antisocial and normal students, students categorized under a two-dimensional model of behavior (disciplinary problems and peer acceptance), sociometrically defined groups (e.g., popular and rejected), and school-identified groups of at risk and disabled students. In most cases, the W-M appears sensitive to group differences and predicts membership or performance in expected directions. Subscales 1 and 2 scores and total score on the W-M appear to discriminate better than Subscale 3 scores.

Standard scores between 7 and 13 on the W-M are within "normal" limits. In plotting the "characteristic profiles" of five student groups (normal, learning disabled, residential severely emotionally disturbed, resource room, antisocial), the normal group scored highest, and the scores of the other four groups were lower. However, there is very little differentiation among these four groups, and, although the authors say these students show moderate to severe deficits on the W-M, nearly all subscale standard scores of these groups are within one standard deviation of the mean. The W-M, as the authors state, is not to be used for differential diagnoses among disability groups.

Construct Validity The authors report evidence of construct validity and factorial validity. Subscale 2 is specifically supported by longitudinal research on one hundred boys at risk for antisocial behavior. The construct validity of the W-M is also argued on the basis of data showing near-zero correlations with student age and very low correlations with student gender, although one might expect to find gender differences favoring females.

SUMMARY

The Walker-McConnell Scale of Social Competence and School Adjustment is a forty-three-item rating scale for screening and identification of social skills deficits in elementary school students. The W-M is easy to administer and score; it yields raw scores, standard scores, and percentiles. The norms for the W-M are adequate, although there is some overrepresentation of Western states. Reliability data to support its use include test-retest, interrater, and internal-consistency coefficients. Coefficients are generally above .80. Content, criterion-related, and construct validity data are convincing for the intended purposes of the device. Though three subscales are identified, the W-M is best used for normative comparisons as a global measure of social competence. Subscales and items within subscales may provide teachers with indications of specific areas of skills deficits for individual students. One must remember, however, that item-reliability data are not provided, and the authors' suggestions of remediation based on individual item data need further research support.

Behavior Assessment System for Children

*T*he Behavior Assessment System for Children (BASC) (Reynolds & Kamphaus, 1992) is "a multimethod, multidimensional approach to evaluate the behavior and self-perception of children 4 to 18 years of age" (p.1). This comprehensive assessment system is designed to assess the numerous aspects of behavior and personality, including both adaptive and maladaptive behavior. The BASC is composed of five main measures of behavior: (1) Teacher Rating Scale, (2) Parent Rating Scale, (3) Self-Report of Personality, (4) Structured Developmental History Inventory, and (5) Student Observation System.

BEHAVIORS SAMPLED

The Teacher Rating scale (TRS) is a comprehensive measure of both adaptive and problem behaviors that children exhibit in school settings. Three different forms are available—Preschool (4–5 years), Child (6–11 years), and Adolescent (12–18 years)—with the behavior items specifically tailored for each age range. Teachers or school personnel rate students on a list of behavioral descriptions using a four-point scale of frequency (N, Never; S, Sometimes; O, Often; A, Almost always). Estimated time to complete the TRS is 10 to 20 minutes. The TRS for preschool is composed of 109 items, the TRS for children 148 items, and the TRS for adolescents 138 items; items are tailored to the specific age groups. Examples of general items in the TRS include "Bullies others," "Refuses to talk," "Adjusts well to new teachers," "Stares blankly," "Changes moods quickly," "Uses illegal drugs," "Uses foul language," and "Is good at getting people to work together."

The Parent Rating Scale (PRS) is a comprehensive measure of a child's adaptive and problem behavior exhibited in community and home settings. The PRS uses the same four-point rating scale as the TRS. In addition, three forms are provided by age groups, as defined previously. Estimated time to complete this measure is 10 to 20 minutes.

The Self-Report of Personality (SRP) contains short statements that a student is expected to endorse or reject by marking true or false on the rating form. Because of the nature of the task, only two forms are available by age level: child (8–11 years) and adolescent (12–18 years). Estimated time per administration is 30 minutes.

The Structured Developmental History Inventory (SDH) is a broad-based developmental history instrument developed to obtain information on the following areas: social, psychological, developmental, educational, and medical. The SDH may be used either as an interview format or as a questionnaire. The organization of the SDH may help in conducting interviews and obtaining important historical information that may be beneficial to the diagnostic and treatment processes.

The Student Observation System (SOS) is an observation tool developed to facilitate diagnosis, treatment planning, and monitoring of intervention programs. Both adaptive and maladaptive behaviors are coded during a 15-minute classroom observation. It is important to note, however, that the SOS is a nonnormed instrument, and therefore may not be best used for diagnostic decisions, as the authors suggest.

The SOS is divided into three parts. The first section, Behavior Key and Checklist, is a list of sixty-five specific behaviors organized into thirteen categories (four categories of positive behavior and nine categories of problem behavior). Following a 15-minute observation, the coder rates the child on the sixty-five items according to a three-point frequency gradation (NO, Never observed; SO, Sometimes Observed; and FO, Frequently observed).

The second part, Time Sampling, requires the informant to decide whether a behavior is present during a 3-second period following a 30- second interval of observation. Observers place a check mark in separate time columns next to any of the thirteen categories of behavior that occur during any one interval. The third section, Teacher's Interaction, is completed following the 15-minute observation. The observer scores the teacher's interactions with the students on three aspects of classroom interactions: (1) teacher position during the observation, (2) teacher techniques to change student behavior, and (3) additional observations that are relevant to the assessment process.

SCORES

A hand-scored response form is used for the first three instruments (TRS, PRS, and SRP). The protocols are constructed in a unique format, using pressure-sensitive paper, that provides the examiner with an immediate translation of ratings to score. After administration of the different rating forms, the administrator removes the outer page to reveal a scoring key. Scale and composite scores are totaled easily, and a behavior profile is available to represent the data visually. Validity scores are tabulated to evaluate the quality of completed forms and to guard against response patterns that may skew the data profiles positively or negatively. Detailed scoring procedures that use a ten-step procedure for each of these scales are described in the administration manual.

Raw scores for each scale are transferred to a summary table for each individual measure. *T*-scores (mean = 50, standard deviation = 10) and percentiles are obtained after selecting appropriate norm tables for comparisons. In addition, a high/low column is provided to allow the assessor a quick and efficient method for evaluating whether differences among composite scores on one individual are statistically significant.

Types of Scores The TRS produces three composite scores of clinical problems: Externalizing Problems, Internalizing Problems, and School Problems. Externalizing Problems include aggression, hyperactivity, and conduct problems. Internalizing Problems include anxiety, depression, and somatization.

School Problems are broken down into attentional and learning deficits. A broad composite score of overall problem behaviors is provided on the Behavioral Symptoms Index (BSI). In addition, positive behaviors are presented on an Adaptive Skills Profile scale. These include leadership, social skills, and study skills. The PRS provides the same scoring categories and subscales, with the exception that the School Problems composite scores, composed of subscales for learning problems and study skills, are omitted.

The Self-Report of Personality (SRP) produces four composite scores: Clinical Maladjustment, School Maladjustment, Personal Adjustment, and an overall composite score referred to as an Emotional Symptoms Index (ESI). The composite ESI score includes both negative and adaptive scales. Clinical Maladjustment includes anxiety, atypicality, locus of control, social stress, and somatization subscales. School Maladjustment subscales are attitude toward school, attitude toward teachers, and sensation seeking. Personal Adjustment subscales include relations with parents, interpersonal relations, self-esteem, and self-reliance. There is also a category of "other problems" that includes depression and sense of inadequacy. Three validity scores are provided. To detect either consistently negative bias or positive bias in the responses provided by the student, there is an F index (fakes bad) and an L index (fakes good). The V index incorporates nonsensical items (e.g., "Superman is a real person") such that a child who consistently marks these items true may be exhibiting poor reading skills, may be uncooperative, or may have poor contact with reality. The Structured Developmental History Inventory and Student Observation System are not norm-referenced measures and do not provide individual scores of comparisons. Rather, these instruments provide additional information about a child that may be used to describe his or her strengths and weaknesses.

NORMS

Standardization and norm development for the general and clinical norms on the TRS, PRS, and SRP took place between the fall of 1988 and the spring of 1991. A total of 116 testing sites were used to obtain general standardization data. The number of children who received behavioral ratings across the different measures were, for the TRS, $N = 2,401$; for the PRS, $N = 3,483$; and for the SRP, $N = 9,861$. Efforts were made to ensure that the standardization sample was representative of the U.S. population of children aged 4–18, including exceptional children. The standardization sample was compared to census data for geographic region, socioeconomic status, culture, and ethnicity. The authors present data to support mostly balanced norms; however, the Northwest appears to be underrepresented for preschool-aged children, and the Midwest is overrepresented for the PRS. The authors claim that children with behavioral-emotional disturbances are represented appropriately at each grade level of each instrument, and the data provided in the manual support this claim. Finally, children with mild mental retardation are underrepresented on the SRP, given their difficulty in completing a self-report questionnaire the nature of the tasks.

Clinical population sample norms consist of data collected on children receiving school or clinical services for emotional or behavioral problems. Special education students (e.g., those with learning disabilities) were not included unless coexisting emotional or behavioral problems were identified. Thirty-six sites in the United States and Canada were used as settings for gathering data. Sample sizes were, for the TRS, $N = 693$; for the PRS, $N = 401$; and for the SRP, $N = 411$. The authors state that the clinical sample was not controlled demographically because this subgroup is not a random set of children. For example, significantly more males were included than females.

RELIABILITY

The manual has a chapter devoted to the technical information supporting reliability and validity for each normed scale (TRS, PRS, and SRP). Three types of reliability are provided within the technical manual: internal consistency, test-retest, and interrater agreement. Results are generally reported for three age levels: preschool (4–5 years), child (6–11 years), and adolescent (12–18 years).

Internal Consistency: TRS Across all three age groups of the general population (preschool, child, and adolescent), median internal-consistency coefficients for all scales were above .80. In general, externalizing dimensions produced higher reliability compared to internalizing dimensions.

Internal Consistency: PRS Internal-consistency coefficients for each PRS scale and composite score for general norm samples are presented in a table by gender and age. Internal consistency at all three age levels of the PRS forms for both genders ranged from .56 to .94. A majority of the coefficients are in the .70 to .80 range. The Behavior Symptoms Index (BSI) coefficients ranged from .88 to .94. On average, the clinical sample produced higher PRS internal-consistency coefficients. Reported reliability scores by age ranged from .72 to .94.

Internal Consistency: SRP Internal consistency coefficients computed for each SRP by age and gender averaged about .80 (range = .54–.97). The clinical norm sample demonstrated similar internal consistency (range = .64–.96). Composite reliability coefficients are very high, ranging from .85 to .97.

Test-Retest Reliability TRS test-retest reliability was computed by having teachers rate the same child after a period of between two and eight weeks. A total of 246 students were selected from across the three age levels. Median test-retest correlations of .89, .91, and .82 were found for the preschool, child, and adolescent age levels, respectively. Long-term stability (seven months) was computed on ratings produced for fifty-five children classified as emotionally/behaviorally disordered. A median correlation of .69 was obtained.

Test-retest reliability of the PRS was examined by looking at correspondence between same-parent ratings with an interval of two to eight weeks between ratings. Median correlation values were .85,

.88, and .70 for preschool, child, and adolescent levels, respectively.

SRP test-retest reliability was evaluated by administering this instrument one month after the initial presentation. Median correlations were .76 at each age level (child and adolescent). Test-retest correlations for composite scores ranged from .78 to .86. This suggests that children and adolescents are relatively consistent in their interpretation of items.

Interrater Reliability Two types of interrater data are presented for the TRS-Preschool and TRS-Child. First, a total of forty-eight preschool children were scored by four pairs of teachers. Interrater correlations represent the similarity of rankings by a few teachers on many children across the various scales. Correlation values of the scales and composites ranged from .60 to .91. Second, eighty-seven children (preschool and child forms) were rated across different teacher informants. Correlations suggest moderate to high agreement with a median scale value of .83 (range = .29–.93). Interrater reliability is not reported for the TRS-Adolescent form.

PRS interrater reliability was computed by examining both parents' ratings of their child at the same point in time. The most notable difference produced is that mothers tend to rate children higher on the social skills scale than fathers do. Median interparent correlation values were .46, .57, and .67 at the preschool, child, and adolescent age levels, respectively. Overall, parents demonstrated higher concordance on externalizing dimensions of behavior than on internalizing factors. No interrater reliability correlations are provided on the SRP, as it is a self-report instrument.

In an attempt to examine reliability across measures of the BASC, correlations were computed between the TRS and the PRS on a subsample of 1,423 children selected from the standardization sample. Correlations are low to moderate and increase with age. Across all three age levels, like-named scales correlated highest across instruments. Furthermore, correlations were found to be highest among externalizing scales and lowest among internalizing dimensions.

VALIDITY

Content Validity   For the TRS, PRS, and SRP development process, the authors reviewed behavior ratings, self-report measures, and literature on social/emotional assessment, and drew upon their clinical and consultation work in an effort to identify the most important content and constructs for the BASC. In item development and tryouts the authors relied on data-based decision making to revise, delete, or add items and alter formats. The BASC went through three item selection/tryout phases, and the final sets of items per form appear to include appropriate content and to be of high validity. Composite scales were developed through factor-analytic studies and inspection of scale intercorrelations. Data appear to support the three-factor preschool and four-factor child and adolescent composite scores.

The authors also describe their efforts to test BASC items for bias against different subject groups on the basis of factors such as gender and ethnicity. Several items were found to be unsatisfactory in this regard and were dropped. The development of the validity scales (F, L, and V) is also described. Overall, users of the BASC system can be confident of the content and representativeness of the instrument and its scales.

Criterion-Related and Construct Validity   The authors of the BASC do not describe validity along traditional criterion-related and construct breakdowns. Factor-analytic studies to support the structure of composite scales are provided, as are a series of studies of correlations among BASC scales and other measures. Construct validity of the BASC is supported by the extensive factor modeling used to define the scales and subscales. Intercorrelations among components and scales support the overall test as a measure of social/emotional status. Diagnostic validity data are also presented.

Criterion-related validity was evaluated by examining correlations of the TRS with five separate standardized measures. Correlations between externalizing scales approach .90 for both children and adolescents. Correlations between internalizing scales produced lower coefficients of .73 and .81 for children and adolescents, respectively.

A third study compared the Conners Teacher Rating Scale (CTRS-39; Conners, 1989b) with the TRS for children aged 4 and 5 years ($N = 91$). Correlations were low to moderate, suggesting that the two measures do not have a close match between these scales. The highest correlation ($r = .69$) was found between the TRS Depression scale and the CTRS-39 Emotional Indulgent scale. Correlations between the TRS Hyperactivity scale and the Conners Hyperactivity scale and Hyperactivity Index were more modest ($r = .57$ and .54, respectively).

Finally, a validity study comparing scores produced on the Teacher Rating scale of the Behavior Rating Profile (BRP; Brown & Hammill, 1983) and the TRS for children enrolled in regular education classrooms ($N = 37$) is reported. The BRP provides a profile of problem-behavior excesses; therefore, positive correlations were expected on the TRS Adaptive scale and negative correlations on problem behavior. Overall, correlations were low to moderate in strength. The correlations were highest on measures of school problems and, given the characteristics of the sample, provided only limited correlation support for overall validity.

Criterion-related validity for the PRS was evaluated by examining correlations of the PRS with four separate standardized measures. Correlations for externalizing composites were higher than for internalizing composites.

A second study compared scores of thirty-nine children aged 4–5 years on the PRS and the Personality Inventory for Children–Revised (PIC-R; Lachar, 1982). Correlation levels are moderate at best, with the highest correlation between PRS Withdrawal and PIC-R Withdrawal scales at .57. Also, scores were obtained on the PRS and the Conners Parent Rating Scale (CPRS-39; Conners, 1989b) for a total of forty-six children aged 6–11 years who were rated by their parents on both scales. Children who scored high on the PRS externalizing scale produced high scores on the CPRS-39 scales of Conduct Disorder, Antisocial, and Learning Problems ($r = .78, .71,$ and .67, respectively). Internalizing scales produced lower overall correlations with internalizing PRS; correlations were $r = .51$ on the Anxious/Shy profile and $r = .45$ on the Psychosomatic.

The final comparison examined correspondence between the PRS and the Behavior Rating Profile (BRP; Brown & Hammill, 1983). A total of thirty-five children between the ages of 6 and 11 years were rated by parents on both scales. The BRP scores correlate at a low to moderate level with all three PRS composite scores and the BSI composite.

Criterion-related validity of the SRP was evaluated across a series of correlation studies with other self-report measures of personality. The first study examined a comparison of scores produced on both the SRP and the Minnesota Multiphasic Personality Inventory (MMPI; Hathaway & McKinley, 1970).

Also examined was a concordance of scores produced on the SRP and the Children's Personality Questionnaire, Form A (CPQ; Porter & Cattell, 1975). The CPQ scales reflect normal dimensions of personality. Correlations with the MMPI were high, but the CPQ appears to function differently as a measure of personality, although a few strong relationships exist among scales.

Diagnostic Validity Diagnostic validity in the form of differential group profiles for clinical groups is provided for the TRS, PRS, and SRP. The purpose is to help in interpretation of scale scores and to provide empirical support for BASC scales and composites. The following clinical classifications were used to select a clinical sample: Conduct Disordered, Behavior Disordered, Depression, Emotional Disturbance, Attention Deficit/Hyperactivity Disordered, Learning Disordered, Mild Mental Retardation, and Autism. Overall, the three BASC measures were able to provide moderate evidence of diagnostic/ discriminant validity; however, because of small sample sizes for many of the clinical classifications, these results should be considered with care.

SUMMARY

The Behavior Assessment System for Children (BASC) is a comprehensive instrument that may be used to evaluate the behavior and self-perception of children 4 to 18 years of age. This integrated system is composed of five separate measures of behavior: (1) Teacher Rating Scale, (2) Parent Rating Scale, (3) Self-Report of Personality, (4) Structured Developmental History Inventory, and (5) Student Observation Scale. Although the multimethod and multidimensional approach should be commended, the TRS, PRS, and SRP are the only scales for which normative data are provided on which any classification or interpretative statements can be made. Norms for the BASC are more than adequate, with general and clinical norm data provided. Reliability of the instruments' scales and composites is very good, although the Conduct Problems scale yields somewhat lower reliability coefficients. As with other rating scales, the BASC appears better able to differentiate externalizing dimensions than internalizing dimensions of emotional disturbance. Moreover, in evaluating previously identified clinical samples, the BASC did not appear to adequately differentiate between diagnostic categories of referred and nonreferred samples. In conclusion, the BASC, like the CBCL (Achenbach, 1991a), provides one of the most comprehensive assessment tools on the market today. Support is presented for content, criterion-related, and construct validity. Although the BASC is a relatively new instrument, it already has an impressive foundation of support.

Systematic Screening for Behavior Disorders (SSBD)

*T*he Systematic Screening for Behavior Disorders (SSBD) (Walker & Severson, 1992) is a series of three interrelated measures of behavior for children in grades 1 to 6. This three-stage sequential screening system incorporates a procedure known as *gating*. Gating is discussed in the introductory section of this chapter and refers to the progressively more detailed and precise assessment procedures that identify students who may be at risk, in this case for behavioral problems. Stages One and Two of the SSBD rely solely on teacher judgments of child behavior across externalizing and internalizing dimensions. The final assessment step, Stage Three, consists of repeated observations conducted by a trained observer (someone other than the teacher) to validate teacher concerns about students who have passed through the previous two gating procedures.

The authors state that "the SSBD provides for mass screening of all students enrolled in a regular classroom. The system also gives each child an equal chance to be screened and identified for either externalizing or internalizing behavior disorders and problems" (p. 3). Referral for further assessment is contingent on a child's passing through the entire multiple-gating process. A description of the three-stage process follows.

STAGE ONE: RANK-ORDERING ALL STUDENTS ENROLLED IN REGULAR CLASSROOMS

Teachers rate (for a minimum of thirty days) all students enrolled in their classroom on both Externalizing and Internalizing dimensions of problem behavior. Clear operational definitions are provided to facilitate teacher ratings of children's behavior. Initially, teachers nominate ten children according to the Externalizing and Internalizing descriptions provided. Next, teachers rank-order the ten students from 1 to 10 for each dimension. The three top-ranked students who best match the behavioral profile for either the Internalizing or Externalizing dimension may be passed through to Stage Two.

STAGE TWO: TEACHER RATING SCALES

The teacher rating scales include a thirty-three-item Critical Events Index (CEI) to rate low-frequency, high-intensity events. For example, items include "Steals," "Sets fires," or "Damages property." Two open items are provided on the CEI scale so that teachers can provide information on critical events that may not appear on the prepared list. Although these teacher-provided critical events are included in the total score, no criteria or guidelines are provided to teachers on acceptable or unacceptable items. This may invite an unnecessary degree of subjectivity that could skew results and/or decisions.

The second part of the Stage Two procedure produces a Combined Frequency Index (CFI), which is calculated by summing scores on Adaptive and Maladaptive Behavior scales. The Adaptive Behavior section is a twelve-item scale with specific behaviors that are rated by a teacher to describe a child's current functioning. Items include statements like "Follows established classroom rules" and "Initiates positive social interactions with peers." The Maladaptive Behavior scale is composed of eleven items. Examples from this scale include statements like "Refuses to participate in games and activities with other children at recess" and "Creates a disturbance during class activities."

STAGE THREE: OBSERVATIONS OF ACADEMIC AND SOCIAL BEHAVIOR

All students who pass through Stages One and Two are further observed using two different observational measures. The purposes of these observations are to (1) verify teachers' rankings of student behavior, (2) provide a direct measure of behavior adjustments that children are required to make to teachers and peers, and (3) evaluate students' normative levels of performance regarding their adjustment to teachers and peers.

The first measure is a record of a child's Academic Engaged Time (AET). An observer using a stopwatch records the total amount of time a child is engaged on an instructional task. The second measure is a rating of Peer Social Behavior (PSB) during playground interactions using a 10-second interval recording system. Coders are asked to record children's social behavior according to five categories: Social Engagement, Participation, Parallel Play, Alone, and No Code. Each observation is scheduled for a total of 15 minutes and the recording of behavior on the two measures occurs across two days. A significant amount of training is required for observers of Stage Three measures. Quizzes and videotaped practice observations are used to train observers to "expert" criterion.

SCALE DEVELOPMENT

The development of the SSBD and the collection of data to support its technical adequacy involved five years of research. Instrument development and preliminary testing were conducted during an initial phase. Extensive research on the reliability and validity of the measures was done in a secondary phase. Normative studies were conducted in the latter phase. A technical development section of over fifty pages is included in the manual. Interested readers should consult this source for the complete report on all research and development activities.

SCORES PRODUCED

Stage One produces no scores, as teachers rank-order children on Internalizing and Externalizing dimensions of problem behavior.

Stage Two is composed of two indexes of behavior, the Critical Events Index (CEI) and the Combined Frequency Index (CFI). The CEI is scored by adding the number of items endorsed. The range of scores on the CEI is from 0 to 35. The CFI is composed of two scales of Adaptive and Maladaptive Behavior. These two scales use a 1 to 5 continuous rating scale (1, Never; 3, Sometimes; 5, Frequently). Although these anchor points are not defined further, teachers are encouraged to choose any number between 1 and 5 that best describes the frequency of a child's behavior during the last six months. In addition, teachers are instructed to endorse items that

they may not have witnessed but that can be confirmed by a reliable source. Total subscale scores are computed by summing the points assigned to all items within the subscale. The ranges of scores are from 12 to 60 for the Adaptive scale and from 11 to 55 for the Maladaptive scale.

In Stage Three, the score for the Academic Engaged Time (AET) measure is calculated by recording the total seconds a child is engaged on instructional tasks. An average of the two observations is computed and compared to separate norm scores by group (normal, externalizers, internalizers, and combined) and grade (1–3, 4–6).

Scores for the five social behavior categories on the Peer Social Behavior (PSB) measure are transferred to an Observation Summary sheet. Summary scores are reported as a percentage of intervals observed. Both individual code categories and summary scores (composed of code category combinations) are reported on this summary form.

DECISION RULES

Decision rules for determining whether a child continues to progress through Stages One, Two, and Three are described thoroughly in the administration manual for each level. Straightforward criteria are presented separately for children rated on the Externalizing and Internalizing dimensions of problem behavior. Flowcharts are presented in the manual with separate cutoff scores for all scales (by behavioral dimension). Stage Three decision rules for the PSB scale are provided by grade level. The authors suggest that an additional level of evaluation can be conducted at Stage Three by collecting comparable observation data on a same-sex, nonreferred peer. In this manner, peer-referenced norms can be created for specific classrooms.

ADDITIONAL SCORE COMPARISONS

Means, standard deviations, and standard errors for Stage Two and Stage Three are presented in the administration manual. Additional conversions of raw scale scores to *T*-scores and percentile ranks are also available for these measures. All norm tables are provided separately for children initially ranked by teachers on Externalizing and Internalizing dimensions. Norms are presented separately for males and females for AET and PBS measures. Finally, norm tables are provided for nonranked students from the standardization sample for Stage Three measures.

NORMS

The SSBD was normed on a national sample of children enrolled in regular education classrooms from eighteen school districts across eight states. Stage Two included 4,463 students, with 72 percent of the sample coming from three states (Kentucky, Oregon, and Utah). Stage Three observations were conducted on 1,275 students, with 70 percent of the sample drawn from the same three states. No additional information is provided on the gender, age, grade distribution, or educational classifications of subjects participating in the national sample. Demographic data are included for only 66 percent of the standardization sample. In addition, demographic data are reported only by the total enrollment of participating school districts, not the actual students included in the standardization sample.

RELIABILITY

Test-retest, internal-consistency, and interrater reliability data were collected during both phases of development of the SSBD. Data on these reliabilities are summarized below.

Test-Retest Reliability   For Stage One measures (teacher rankings), stability of behavioral classifications (Internalizing, Externalizing) was calculated during early tests of the SSBD. In a study involving 168 students, 78 percent of the students were classified in the same category on two occasions.

For Stage Two measures (ratings on the CEI and CFI), short-term stability coefficients are provided.

Reported correlations are in the .80s; however, the authors warn about possible inflation of these values because categories of students were collapsed for data analysis. No test-retest data for the Stage Three (observational) measures are provided in the technical manual.

Internal Consistency Reliability   Data related to the internal consistency of Stage Two measures are reported. Reliability coefficients for the CFI Adaptive scale range from .85 to .94 and for the Maladaptive scale, from .82 to .92.

Item-total correlations are provided for the scales of the CFI. Coefficients obtained in early testing of the measures were lower than those obtained during the standardization/validation studies.

Interrater Agreement   The authors made extensive use of interrater agreement data in the development of the Stage One measures. Rankings of students by two teachers, or a teacher and a teacher's aide, on early versions of the SSBD yielded coefficients ranging from .60 to .94 for Externalizing students and from .35 to .72 for Internalizing students. For the final version (after group membership definitions were clarified), coefficients obtained by eight pairs of raters were .89 to .94 for externalizers and .82 to .90 for internalizers.

Stage Three measures by trained observers have repeatedly resulted in high interrater agreement. The authors state that "interrater agreement levels have not been as yet established for Stage Two measures" (Walker & Severson, 1992, p. 34).

Overall, the reliabilities of the SSBD measures are adequately supported by appropriate data from multiple-trial testing and validation studies. Some gaps in evidence are noticeable, and the potential user of the SSBD is not provided with comprehensive reliability data for all measures and for the full range of ages for which the SSBD is intended (grades 1–6). Because some portions of the device are age sensitive (e.g., Stage Three), reliability of these measures for these ages would be better substantiated if supporting data were made available.

VALIDITY

Content Validity Publication of the SSBD was preceded by extensive development and research procedures. The selected behavioral items and the Internalizing and Externalizing scales have undergone a thorough testing, refinement, and validation process that has included both regular and special education teachers. For the Stage Three observation codes, a previous observation code developed by Walker, Hops, and Greenwood (1984) served as a model. The authors provide adequate data to support their claim that these observation codes have been used and validated across numerous school settings.

Criterion-Related Validity Two types of criterion-related validity (concurrent and predictive) are referred to in the technical manual. Support for concurrent validity is provided by a series of correlational studies conducted during the instrument development phase and the research phase of the development process. In one such study, correlation coefficients between the SSBD-CFI scales and the Child Behavior Checklist (CBCL) were calculated. On two occasions, correlations between the CBCL externalizing scale and the SSBD Adaptive scale were −.63 and −.68, and for the Maladaptive scale, .81 and .77 (compared at two different times). All correlations were significant at the .001 confidence level.

In addition, Stage Two measures were correlated with the Walker-McConnell Scale of Social Competence and School Adjustment (W-M; Walker & McConnell, 1988) and the Classroom Adjustment Code (CAC; Walker, Block-Pedego, McConnell, & Clark, in press). Total score correlations were computed between the W-M and the CEI and the Adaptive and Maladaptive scales. All three comparisons were found to be statistically significant at the .001 confidence level (correlations were −.57, .79, and −.44 respectively). Correlations obtained between the CAC scales of on-task and unacceptable behavior with the CEI were −.45 and .15, respectively. The

Adaptive and Maladaptive scales correlated in the low to moderate range in expected directions with the CAC measures.

To assess the predictive validity of the SSBD, a total of 155 students (grades 1–5) were assessed on all measures and reassessed one year later by different raters and observers. Students initially rated as externalizers were found to be rated in the top three externalizers one year later, 69 percent of the time. Internalizers were rated among the top three at a lower level one year later 52 percent of the time. Correlations between year-one and year-two scores on Stage Two measures for combined Internalizing and Externalizing groups ranged from .32 (CEI) to .70 (Maladaptive scale). Overall, correlations between time one and time two were in the low to moderate range. In addition, the criterion of teacher ratings at different times that was used to suggest predictive validity seems more appropriate for long-term stability evidence. It may have served consumers better if an independent standard of comparison had been included.

Construct Validity To establish construct validity, the authors present data explaining factor-analytic and discriminant function analyses conducted on the SSBD. Evidence of construct validity in the form of convergent and divergent correlational studies is also presented. Correlations between the CBCL Internalizing and Externalizing scales and Stage Three (AET and PSB scales) were calculated. Stage Three AET correlated −.42 with the CBCL at a .01 confidence level, and the PSB produced two significant correlations with the CBCL: negative social interaction and positive social interaction, with correlations of .29 and −.35, respectively. No SSBD observation measures were found to be significantly correlated with the CBCL Internalizing scales.

In another study, a total of seventy-six students from Washington enrolled in grades 1, 3, and 5 were assessed on the SSBD Stage Two measures. Additional instruments were used to collect information regarding the children's status on sociometrics, direct observation, school records, and social skills ratings. The authors created a "deviance index" (p. 59) by combining selected variables from within the SSBD and from other measures judged to be best evidence variables for each group. Then, Stage One rankings of the students were compared to the deviance index. Correlations between Stage One rankings and these multiple instruments for internalizers and externalizers were .71 and .76 ($p < .001$); these students were correctly identified most of the time (82 percent and 73 percent, respectively).

The authors also describe a study in which a total of forty regular education teachers, who had been assigned fifty-four children identified previously as severely behaviorally disordered (forty-five externalizers, and nine internalizers), completed the SSBD. The teachers, having no prior knowledge of the students' educational history, were able to identify all fifty-four students by using the SSBD gating procedures. Overall, these correlations and classifications appear to be in the moderate to high range and provide support for the SSBD as a measure of school adjustment problems.

Discriminant Validity Discriminant validity of the SSBD system and its component measures is very important to the authors, given that one of the main constructs of the SSBD is the notion of differentiating children on a bipolar continuum of Externalizing and Internalizing problem behaviors. In prevalidation studies of the SSBD, almost 90 percent of students were correctly classified as internalizers or externalizers using Stage Two and Stage Three measures.

In one validation study, 170 teachers (for grades 1 to 5) completed Stage One and Stage Two measures for students enrolled in classrooms in Oregon. Analysis of variance on group differences for Stage Two measures were highly significant. Post hoc *T*-tests indicated that all possible combinations of comparisons among three groups (internalizers, externalizers, and controls) were significant at the .01 confidence level.

In a second study conducted to replicate the first, a total of forty regular education teachers from the state of Washington completed Stage One and Stage Two measures for 270 students. All post hoc *T*-tests identified mean differences among all comparisons of these groups that were significant at the .05 level of confidence. These two studies suggest that the SSBD has sufficient discriminant power to differentiate among these three groups.

An additional study examined a more clinical sample of 106 students who were assigned to a residential facility serving severely disturbed and/or abused children in kindergarten through grade 12. Students were enrolled in four different programs that included two residential and two day treatment programs: Secure unit ($N = 17$), Residential ($N = 52$), Day treatment ($N = 20$), and Community-based ($N = 17$). Separate one-way ANOVAs were conducted for the Critical Events Index, the Maladaptive scale, and Adapative scale. Results indicated significant differences among the four categories of students on the CEI. No statistical differences were observed on the Maladaptive or Adaptive rating scale. Post hoc *T*-tests identified differences between the Secure unit and Residential students. No other mean differences were found to be significant. This may suggest that although the SSBD has sufficient discriminant power to differentiate classification between clinical and general population samples, further specificity within clinical populations is not as well established.

Taken together, discriminant validity studies demonstrate that the SSBD is effective at distinguishing internalizing and externalizing students from the larger population of students without behavioral and adjustment problems. Students classified as externalizers on the SSBD were found to engage in less adaptive behavior and more maladaptive behavior than controls and internalizers. In addition, this group spent less time academically engaged and more time in negative interactions than did internalizers and control children. Children rated as internalizers on the SSBD were found to engage in less adaptive behavior and more maladaptive behavior and to spend more time alone than control students.

SUMMARY

The SSBD is a well-conceived and researched instrument for screening and identifying children in need of further assessment for behavioral disorders. In fact, the SSBD has been nominated as an example of an effective instrument by the Program Effectiveness Panel of the U.S. Department of Education. However, to date, the SSBD has been used largely in a research capacity that has consistently produced discrete evidence of reliability and validity. Normative and demographic data and defining characteristics of the students who participated in the standardization sample are difficult to discern. The authors provide substantial evidence of the SSBD scales' ability to differentiate between students exhibiting Internalizing or Externalizing problem behavior and well-adjusted students. Although reported reliability and validity studies appear adequate, there are gaps in some areas (e.g., interrater reliability and grade-specific reliabilities). These gaps may ultimately restrict the types of interpretations that can be made from the results of the SSBD instrument. The essential strength of the SSBD is the conceptual framework of multiple-gating procedures, which serves to organize and standardize what teachers and practitioners have been doing informally for years.

COPING WITH DILEMMAS IN CURRENT PRACTICE

The field of social/emotional assessment has advanced significantly over the past decade. However, certain dilemmas still arise in discussions of assessment and testing of students' social/emotional functioning. One of the dilemmas involves the problem that is being evaluated. Very often, the presenting problem that is mentioned during pre-referral meetings is not the actual problem requiring attention. A system that provides multiple perspectives on the same perceived problem is very helpful in problem definition. In some cases, one can be reasonably sure of the need for service and of the focus of intervention if convergent data are obtained from multiple respondents. If, however, very divergent views are discovered, then more detailed examination of the situational variables, of the classroom ecology, and of the perspectives of the respondents may be indicated.

Other issues are potential sources of challenge in social/emotional assessment. With regard to rating-scale technology, the scales themselves may be a source of response error. Sometimes, as Witt, Heffer, and Peiffer (1990) point out, rating scales are constructed with very poorly defined quantifiers. Subjectivity is increased, and misinterpretation becomes more probable. Scales that use more objectively defined quantifiers provide a better source of data by allowing observers to better operationalize the behavior(s) of concern. These same authors also point out that halo effects are sometimes an issue. When halo effects are active, the respondent tends to overgeneralize about the subject and be less objective about the situational or contextual specificity of the subject's behavior. The possibility of central tendency bias is also a dilemma to be confronted. In this case, the respondent does not evaluate the student's behavior in terms of the extremes of the scale but systematically selects the rating scale quantifiers that are in the middle of the scale.

Scores from rating scales or checklists do not correlate highly with external criteria or measures of behavior. In particular, rating scales that have Internalizing dimensions are not very good at identifying students with depressive disorders and do not agree with clinical or interview data. (B. Egeland, personal communication, March 30, 1994). Therefore, students suspected of being at risk for internalizing disorders such as childhood depression are best served via a comprehensive clinical evaluation.

Finally, all social-emotional assessment is linked to the idea that effective interventions and treatments will be available for the students whom we identify as being in need of service. Some of the instruments reviewed in this chapter have companion manuals that describe interventions based on specific items or groups of items assessed by the ratings scales or checklists. Some of these ideas are tried-and-true methods that fit into most useful social skills training programs. Others are less well documented and lack effective instructional or intervention strategies. Social-emotional and behavioral assessment practices are neatly summed up by Brown and Hammill (1990) with the phrase "caveat utilitor." Interventions with students must be based on sound assessment data, and it is up to the users of these devices to evaluate the instruments and plan for instruction. Assessments and rating scales are only as good as the practitioners who use them. It is essential that any sort of treatment based on information gleaned from rating scales or other social/emotional assessment be evaluated in terms of its positive and negative impact upon student behavior and social/emotional progression.

Summary

The assessment of the social-emotional behavior of students has become more frequent in recent years. There are more students coming to school with problem behaviors. These behaviors can be internalizing or externalizing. An important concept in testing is that of the multifactor approach to assessment, in which the *method* of measurement, *context* of behavior, and *source of data* must all be considered. It is often some combination of these factors that provides the most accurate and reliable assessment of student behavior.

The concept of multiple-gating involves procedures whereby progressively more precise measures are used systematically to narrow the number of students assessed. Multiple-gating also provides a structure for the decisions made in social-emotional assessment. Most often, assessment is considered for children at risk for emotional/behavioral disorders; however, children with academically based deficits may also be referred for social skills or behavioral evaluations. Common methods of measurement include rating scales, teacher questionnaires, and direct observation. Assessment of social-emotional behavior, like most academic assessment, should be conducted with the intention of providing assessment-based interventions to ameliorate identified problems.

STUDY QUESTIONS

1. Define the term "multifactor assessment". Why do many people consider it essential to social-emotional assessment?
2. What is "multiple-gating," and how does it assist in the assessment of social-emotional behavior?
3. Design an assessment session that incorporates the concept of multifactor evaluation. Why might some portions of the session be more relevant to particular concerns than others? Which type(s) of measurement do you believe results in the best assessment data?
4. What are the major concerns in using rating scales to describe a student's social-emotional behavior?

ADDITIONAL READING

Bronfenbrenner, U. (1979). *The ecology of human development.* Cambridge, MA: Harvard University Press.

Martin, R. P. (1988). *Assessment of personality and behavior problems: Infancy throughout adolescence.* New York: Guilford Press.

Merrell, K. W. (1994). *Assessment of behavioral, social, and emotional problems.* New York: Longman.

National Mental Health Association. (1993). *All systems failure: An examination of the results of neglecting the needs of children with serious emotional disturbance.* Alexandria, VA: Author.

Ninness, H. A., Glenn, S. S., & Ellis, J. (1993). *Assessment and treatment of emotional or behavioral disorders.* Westport, CT: Praeger.

Chapter 27

Assessment of Adaptive Behavior

*A*daptive behavior is the way individuals adapt themselves to the requirements of their physical and social environment (Schmidt & Salvia, 1984). In part, adaptation means survival: Adaptive behaviors are those that allow individuals to continue to live by avoiding dangers and taking reasonable precautions to ensure their safety. Yet, adaptivity refers to more than mere survival; it implies the ability to thrive in both good and adverse times.

Adaptive behavior also requires more than an appropriate response to the demands of the immediate environment; it also requires preparation for responses to probable future environments. Certain current behaviors (for example, smoking or high-risk sexual activity) can have life-threatening future consequences. Similarly, acquiring more education or job training and saving money increase the likelihood that one can thrive in later years. Adaptive behavior, in the present and future, must also take into account the demands of a person's physical surroundings and the expectations of that person's culture.

DEFINING ADAPTIVE BEHAVIOR

Physical Environment

The knowledge and skill required to avoid danger (or to react appropriately when in danger) vary considerably from environment to environment. For example, different environments require different protective clothing and different precautions against climate. Living in the desert Southwest requires guarding against dehydration and heat stroke, whereas living in New England in the winter requires guarding against hypothermia and frostbite. Different environments have different dangerous wildlife: alligators in southeastern swamps, scorpions and gila monsters in the Southwest, rats in many urban areas, and so forth. In addition to natural hazards, different environments present man-made hazards: automobiles, electrical appliances, cutting tools, chemicals, and so forth.

Social and Cultural Expectations

Social expectations vary considerably from culture to culture, and the ability to thrive in a culture requires some degree of conformity to that society's cultural norms. Societal expectations manifest themselves in language usage (for example, polite or respectful language, speaking distance, speaking volume), role performance, personal responsibility, and independence.

Age and Adaptation

Sociocultural expectations are also a function of the person's age. In the United States, we have different expectations for infants, children, adolescents, and adults. For infants and young children, expectations center on maturational processes; at some points in these processes, reflexive behavior (for example, sucking) is a necessary component of survival. After infancy, maturational processes merely enable behavior. "Thus, goodness of vision and hearing, intactness of motor skills, neuromotor integrity, and similar characteristics are not adaptive behaviors of the individual; they are biological characteristics of the human species and provide the basis for behavior" (Salvia, Neisworth, & Schmidt, 1990, p. 57). Thus, for older individuals, adaptive behavior is learned behavior.

We expect youngsters to use language socially, to play appropriately, to assume limited responsibilities (for example, picking up toys), and to function in increasingly independent ways (for example, self-feeding, self-dressing, going about their homes and neighborhoods). As children get older, the expectations for independence and responsibility increase both at home and in school. With adolescence come demands for making the transition to adulthood (for example, preparing for employment, accepting more complete personal responsibility, and so forth).

Performance Versus Ability

Adaptive behavior is not synonymous with the *ability* to behave in expected ways. Knowing how to survive and thrive does not ensure that one will behave accordingly. For example, children may know that they should look both ways before crossing streets, and they may know how to do so; however, the important consideration is whether they do look both ways. Not only must a behavior be performed regularly (habitually and customarily), it must be performed without prompting or assistance.

Maladaption

In their definitions of adaptive behavior, some theorists include an absence of marked maladaption. Although such a position may have intuitive appeal, there are at least two conceptual problems with including maladaptive behavior on formal tests. First, the absence of maladaptive behavior does not imply the presence of adaptive behavior. Second, except for suicidal behavior and a very few universally taboo behaviors (for example, smearing oneself with human excrement), maladaptive behavior is determined by context as well as frequency and amplitude.

Context

The context of behavior refers to both social tolerance and the specific situation in which a behavior occurs. Social tolerance is an important qualifier because so few behaviors are universally taboo. For example, certain types of hallucinations may be prized as religious experiences in some societies but seen as psychotic in others; homosexuality is accepted in some societies but punished in others. The list of potential examples is very long. Within a society, taboo behavior is codified by custom, religion, and law.

Some behaviors are evaluated solely on the basis of context. For example, disrobing is usually considered deviant in a classroom full of students but normal before bathing; failure to disrobe is normal in classrooms but abnormal before bathing. Even when certain behaviors are proscribed, the circumstances in which those behaviors are demonstrated is important. For example, in the United States, killing another person is not necessarily murder. The context in which the death occurred determines if it is a crime (murder or voluntary manslaughter) or not (justifiable homicide or accidental death).

Finally, to be considered deviant, either the behavior or its consequence must be observed. If no one witnesses the act or its consequence, it will not be considered maladaptive. Moreover, the person observing the behavior (or consequence) must be willing and have the authority to label the behavior as deviant.

Frequency and Amplitude

The frequency and amplitude of behavior are also important in labeling a behavior as maladaptive. Some behavior will be tolerated or condoned if it occurs infrequently. For example, occasional drunkenness may be ignored, but chronic drunkenness is considered alcoholism. The boundaries separating tolerated occasional misbehavior from deviance vary with context, status of the person, and consequences of the behavior. The amplitude of behavior also affects social and cultural tolerance. For example, biting one's fingernails is seldom, in and of itself, considered significant. However, when biting one's fingernails produces bleeding, scarring, and deformity, the behavior has crossed a line into self-mutilation.

ASSESSING ADAPTIVE BEHAVIOR

Historically, the assessment of adaptive behavior has relied on the report of a third person (typically designated as a *respondent*). Thus, we do not assess an individual's adaptive behavior directly; an examiner does not test or observe the individual being assessed. Instead, the examiner relies on the cumulative observations of a respondent who is both truthful and sufficiently familiar with the subject of the assessment to make a judgment about that subject's behavior.

This method of administration is susceptible to a variety of errors and biases. The student being evaluated may generally conceal behavior that is culturally taboo, or the student may conceal behavior from the respondent if the student knows the respondent disapproves of the behavior. The student being evaluated may selectively demonstrate the behavior. For example, when the respondent (a parent or teacher) is present, the student may behave appropriately; when the respondent is absent, the student may not. Finally, when respondents have a stake in the outcome, they may be less than truthful or objective. For example, if a parent respondent does not want a student classified as mentally retarded, that parent may give the child the benefit of the doubt in every response.

WHY DO WE ASSESS ADAPTIVE BEHAVIOR?

There are two major reasons for assessing adaptive behavior. The first is that mental retardation is generally defined, in part, as a failure of adaptive behavior. In theory, in order to classify a pupil as mentally retarded, for example, one needs to assess adaptive behavior. More important, however, are the federal regulations and state school codes requiring that adaptive behavior be assessed before a pupil can be considered mentally retarded.

The second reason for assessing adaptive behavior is for program planning. Educational objectives in the domain of adaptive behavior are frequently developed for moderately and severely retarded individuals. Adaptive behavior is often important in planning habilitative and transition services for students with other disabilities. Thus, scales of adaptive behavior are often the source of educational goals.

SPECIFIC TESTS OF ADAPTIVE BEHAVIOR

The six devices reviewed in the pages that follow are used most often in assessment of handicapped individuals.

Vineland Adaptive Behavior Scale

*T*he Vineland Adaptive Behavior Scale (VABS) is an individually administered scale given to someone, such as a parent, caregiver, or teacher, who is familiar with the person who is the subject of the assessment. The VABS has been termed the 1984 revision of the Vineland Social Maturity Scale (VSMS). As would be expected, the revision entailed conversion of the old VSMS from an age scale to a much more modern point scale and complete restandardization. The revision is far more sweeping, however; thus, the new VABS might better be considered a new device.

The VABS is available in three forms that have three separate technical manuals. Two forms are termed interview editions: the Expanded Form (Sparrow, Balla, & Cicchetti, 1984a) and the Survey Form (Sparrow, Balla, & Cicchetti, 1984b). The third form is the Classroom Edition (Harrison, 1985). The three forms vary in the number and types of items included as well as in the respondent who completes the form. The Survey Form contains 297 items and is intended to provide a general appraisal of the individual; it requires about 20 to 60 minutes to administer to a parent or caregiver. The Expanded Form contains 577 items and is intended to provide a comprehensive appraisal suitable for planning educational programs; it requires 60 to 90 minutes to administer to a parent or caregiver. The Classroom Edition contains 244 items and requires about 20 minutes for a teacher to complete.

Individual items form subdomains, and subdomains form domains. All three editions assess Communication, Daily Living Skills, Socialization, and Motor Skills domains. The two interview editions also assess the Maladaptive Behavior domain.

Communication   This domain consists of three subdomains: Receptive (for example, listens to a story for at least 20 minutes), Expressive (for example, uses *around* as a preposition in a phrase), and Written (for example, addresses letters correctly).

Daily Living Skills   This domain consists of three subdomains: Personal (for example, dresses self completely, except for tying shoelaces), Domestic (for example, puts clean clothes away without assistance), and Community (for example, states current date when asked).

Socialization   This domain consists of three subdomains: Interpersonal (for example, shows desire to please caregiver), Play and Leisure Time (for example, shares toys or possessions without being told to do so), and Coping Skills (for example, does not talk with food in mouth).

Motor Skills   This domain consists of two subdomains: Gross (for example, can jump over small objects) and Fine (for example, can unlock key locks).

Maladaptive Behavior   This domain consists of thirty-six behaviors. Part 1 contains twenty-seven maladaptive behaviors that are termed minor (for example, sucks thumb or finger, bites fingernails, is stubborn or sullen, and so forth); Part 2 contains nine behaviors that are considered more serious (for example, displays inappropriate sexual behavior, uses bizarre speech, rocks back and forth when sitting or standing).

The subdomains are not evenly distributed throughout the domains. For example, in Communication, the Receptive subdomain is assessed, with one exception, totally in the first half of the domain, and the Written subdomain is assessed exclusively in the second half of the domain.

SCORES

Within the Communication, Daily Living Skills, Socialization, and Motor Skills domains, items between basal and ceiling are scored 2 (yes or usually), 1 (sometimes or partially), or 0 (no or never). Items may also be scored "DK" (respondent does not know) or "N" (no opportunity). In Part 1 of the Maladaptive Behavior domain (minor maladaptive behaviors), items are scored 2 (usually), 1 (sometimes), or 0 (never or very seldom). In Part 2, items are scored for their intensity (severe, moderate, or absent). Subdomain scores are combined into domain scores, and the Communication, Daily Living Skills, Socialization, and Motor Skills domains can be combined into an Adaptive Behavior Composite.

Domain and composite scores can be transformed to standard scores (mean = 100, standard deviation = 15), percentile ranks, age equivalents, and adaptive levels. The adaptive levels are high (more than two standard deviations above the mean), moderately high (between one and two standard deviations above the mean), adequate (between one standard deviation above and one below the mean), moderately low (between one and two standard deviations below the mean), and low (more than two standard deviations below the mean).

NORMS

Several sets of norm groups are available. For the two interview editions, a national sample of 3,000 individuals ranging in age from newborn to 18 years, 11 months was tested. The sample is quite similar to the population at the time of the 1980 census in terms of geographic region, racial/ethnic group, parental education, and community size. For the Classroom Edition, 1,984 children between the ages of 3 and 12 years, 11 months were tested. The sample resembles the population at the time of the 1980 census with respect to racial/ethnic group. It appears unrepresentative with respect to geographic region (overrepresenting the Northcentral region and underrepresenting the others), parental education (overrepresenting college educated and underrepresenting those with only a high school education or less), and community size (overrepresenting central city and underrepresenting rural areas). Supplementary samples are also available: institutionalized and non-institutionalized mentally retarded adults and institutionalized children who were either emotion-

ally disturbed, visually handicapped, or hearing impaired. The supplementary norms are not carefully described, but must be used for Part 2 of the Maladaptive Behavior domain.

RELIABILITY

Interview Editions Internal consistency of the Survey Form was estimated by odd-even correlations corrected by the Spearman-Brown formula. For Communication, coefficients for the different age groups range from .73 to .94; only six of the fifteen coefficients equal or exceed .90. For Daily Living Skills, coefficients for the fifteen age groups range from .83 to .92; eight of the fifteen coefficients equal or exceed .90. For Socialization, the fifteen coefficients range from .78 to .94; only two of the fifteen coefficients equal or exceed .90. For Motor Skills, the six coefficients range from .70 to .95; only for the 0 to 0-11 age group is the reliability greater than .89. The estimated reliabilities for the Adaptive Behavior Composite are generally higher; the lowest coefficient is .89 for the 14-0 to 15-11 age group. Finally, the ten coefficients for Maladaptive Behavior (Part 1) ranged from .77 to .88. As could be anticipated, the estimated reliabilities for the subdomains are considerably lower.

The split-half correlations from the Survey Form were used "to estimate split-half reliability coefficients for the Expanded Form" (Sparrow, Balla, & Cicchetti, 1984a, p. 30).[1] For Communication, the reported coefficients for the fifteen age groups range from .84 to .97; only five of the fifteen coefficients are less than .90. For Daily Living Skills, coefficients for the fifteen age groups all exceed .90. For

---

1. The procedure used rests on several assumptions; one is that the "items in the Expanded Form constituted the complete universe from which a representative sample of about 48 percent was used to develop the Survey Form" (Sparrow, Balla, & Cicchetti, 1948a, p. 30). Of course, if this assumption were met, then there would be no need to *estimate* reliability. Because the entire domain is supposedly tested by the Expanded Form, by most definitions the obtained scores must equal true scores. The amount of bias introduced by violating the assumption is unknown.

Socialization, the fifteen coefficients range from .88 to .97; only two of the fifteen coefficients are less than .90. For Motor Skills, the six coefficients range from .83 to .97; half of the coefficients are .90 or larger. The estimated reliabilities for the Adaptive Behavior Composite all exceed .93. The ten coefficients for Maladaptive Behavior (Part 1) range from .77 to .88. As we would anticipate, the estimated reliabilities for the subdomains are considerably lower.

Stability is estimated by correlating raw scores for age groups. The fifteen age groups were combined into just six, however. Consequently, stability coefficients are inflated by the degree to which chronological age correlates with the raw scores. For Communication, the estimated stabilities for the six age groups ranged from .80 to .98; two coefficients were less than .90. For Daily Living Skills, the estimated stabilities ranged from .87 to .96; half of the coefficients were less than .90. For Socialization, they ranged from .77 to .92; only one exceeded .89. For the three combined age groups for Motor Skills, two stability coefficients were below .90. Stability for the domain of Maladaptive Behavior ranged from .84 to .89 for the four age groups for which this domain is appropriate. The stability of composite scores is not reported.

Interrater agreement was assessed for 160 individuals who varied in age from 0-6 to 18-11. In these computations, the effect of chronological age on the correlations between rates was removed statistically.[2] For Communication and Daily Living Skills, interrater agreement exceeded .90; for Socialization and Motor Skills, it was less than .87.

Classroom Edition   Coefficient alpha was used to estimate internal consistency for subdomains and domains for ten age groups (a combined 3-0 to 4-11 group and nine one-year groups between 5-0 and 12-11). For Communication, alphas ranged from .88 to .95, with only one coefficient less than .89. For Daily Living Skills and Socialization, alphas ranged from .91 to .96. For Motor Skills, the two

coefficients were .84 and .77. The Adaptive Behavior Composite exceeded .95 at each age.

VALIDITY

Evidence of the validity of the Classroom Edition and the Survey Form comes from several sources. Content validity is difficult to assess because a precise definition of the domain to be assessed is never offered. The authors state that they conducted an intensive review of the child development literature and drew on their own clinical and research experiences to determine the four behavioral domains (Communication, Daily Living Skills, Socialization, and Motor Skills). How daily activities are related to adaptive behavior is unclear.

Evidence of construct validity comes from the correlation of VABS scores and chronological age. Results of factor analyses only partially confirm the subdomains, however. The differential performances of supplementary norm groups are also used to support the construct validity of the scale. In addition, correlations between VABS and intelligence-test scores are reported. Evidence for criterion-related validity comes from the correlation of the VABS with the original Vineland Social Maturity Scale, the Adaptive Behavior Inventory for Children, and the AAMD Adaptive Behavior Scale.

No independent evidence of criterion-related validity is offered for the Expanded Form. Rather, validity is estimated from correlations between the VABS Survey Form and the criterion measures discussed in the preceding paragraph.

SUMMARY

The Vineland Adaptive Behavior Scale is an individually administered, norm-referenced device intended to assess the adaptive and maladaptive behaviors of individuals under 19 years of age. Norming appears quite good. Reliability of the scale varies considerably, however, and only sometimes are the domains and subdomains suitable for use in making important individual decisions. Validity data are adequate.

---

2. First-order partial correlations were computed. Because this procedure was used for interrater agreement, it seems inconsistent not to have used it with stability estimates.

AAMR Adaptive Behavior Scale: Residential and Community Scale (Second Edition)

*T*he AAMR Adaptive Behavior Scale: Residential and Community Scale, Second Edition (ABS-RC2) (Nihira, Leland, & Lambert, 1993) is an individually administered, norm-referenced scale designed for use with individuals between 18 and 79 years of age. Since its introduction in 1969, this scale has undergone numerous modifications. For this latest version, items from previous editions were selected because of their interrater reliability and effectiveness in discrimination among various levels of adaptation.

The scale is divided into two parts. Part I focuses on ten domains related to independent and responsible functioning, physical development, language development, and socialization. Three factors underlie these domains: Personal Self-Sufficiency, Community Self-Sufficiency, and Personal-Social Responsibility. Two administration formats are used in this part. In the first format, responses to items consist of a series of statements denoting increasingly higher levels of adaptation. These items are scored by circling the highest level of functioning demonstrated by the client. For example, in the domain of physical development, the response to item 25 (vision) has four levels: Has no difficulty seeing, Has some difficulty seeing, Has great difficulty seeing, and Has no vision at all. In the second format, each item consists of a series of statements that are answered either yes or no. A socially desirable response is awarded 1 point. For example, item 62 (persistence) in the Self-Direction domain consists of five statements: Cannot organize task, Becomes easily discouraged, Fails to carry out tasks, Jumps from one activity to another, and Needs constant encouragement to complete task. For this item, "No" is the socially desirable response; each time a statement does not apply to the subject, the subject is awarded 1 point. Thus, a subject may receive between 0 and 5 points on this item. Students can earn from 3 to 9 points on each item scored in this format.

The items in Part II of the scale are concerned with maladaptive behaviors that are manifestations of personality and behavior disorders. These items are grouped into eight domains, and only one administration format is used. Two factors underlie these eight domains: Social Adjustment and Personal Adjustment. Each item consists of multiple statements and is scored on a three-point scale (Never, 0; Occasionally, 1; or Frequently, 2). (See Table 27.1 for a list of domains and factors.)

SCORES

All raw scores from the ABS-RC2 can be converted to percentiles, standard scores for domains (mean = 10, standard deviation = 3), and quotients for factors (mean = 100, standard deviation = 15). Age equivalents are also available for scores from Part I; Part II scores are not related to age so no age equivalents are available. Derived scores for an adaptive behavior total or composite are not available.

Domain scores provide measures of relative standing in each topical domain. In addition, five factor scores (based on previous research and a confirmatory factor analysis) can be obtained for the three factors in Part I (Personal Self-Sufficiency, Community Self-Sufficiency, and Personal-Social Responsibility) and two factors in Part II (Social Adjustment and Personal Adjustment). The factor scores are obtained by summing item raw scores and converting the totals to derived scores.

NORMS

The ABS-RC2 was standardized on 4,103 individuals with developmental disabilities. Participants in the standardization were stratified on living arrangements: those living in the community (for example, living at home or in small community-based residences) and those living in institutions. Some subjects were selected by site coordinators in Connecticut, Florida, Ohio, and California; other subjects were located through a mailing to members of the

TABLE 27.1   **Domains and Factors in Parts I and II of the ABS-RC2**

	Domains (number of items in each)	Factors
Part I	1. Independent Functioning (24)	Personal Self-Sufficiency
	2. Physical Development (6)	Community Self-Sufficiency
	3. Economic Activity (6)	Personal-Social Responsibility
	4. Language Development (10)	
	5. Numbers and Time (3)	
	6. Domestic Activity (6)	
	7. Prevocational/Vocational Activity (3)	
	8. Self-Direction (5)	
	9. Responsibility (3)	
	10. Socialization (7)	
Part II	11. Social Behavior (7)	Social Adjustment
	12. Conformity (6)	Personal Adjustment
	13. Trustworthiness (6)	
	14. Stereotyped and Hyperactive Behavior (5)	
	15. Sexual Behavior (4)	
	16. Self-Abusive Behavior (3)	
	17. Social Engagement (4)	
	18. Disturbing Interpersonal Behavior (6)	

American Association on Mental Deficiency who were asked to participate in the standardization.

These techniques for finding subjects resulted in a sample drawn from forty-six states and the District of Columbia. Subjects in the normative sample were predominantly between the ages of 18 and 39; there were 1,339 individuals between 18 and 29, 1,254 individuals between 30 and 39, 759 individuals between 40 and 49, 418 individuals between 50 and 59, and 333 individuals 60 or older. The sample is generally representative of the nation in terms of geographical region, race, and ethnicity; it overrepresents males and individuals living in urban areas. The extent to which this sample represents the population of individuals with mental retardation is unclear: 18 percent of the sample had IQs less than 20, 43.2 percent had IQs between 20 and 49, and 38.8 percent had IQs between 50 and 70.

Professionals who conduct assessments with the ABS-RC2 must be very aware that the percentiles and standard scores are based on the performances of individuals with mental retardation. Thus, the usual score interpretations are not correct. A person earning a percentile of 50 on this test has performed equal to or greater than 50 percent of the retarded individuals in the normative sample.

RELIABILITY

Reliability of the ABS-RC2 was estimated for items (using coefficient alpha), for times (stability), and for raters.[3] In Part I, alphas for domains ranged from a low of .80 (for ages 18–29 on Prevocational/Vocational Activity) to a high of .98 (Independent Functioning for ages 18–29 and 30–39); of the fifty domain alphas, forty-one equaled or exceeded .90.

3. The authors provide information about what they call interscorer reliability. In the study they cite, two graduate students tabulated completed protocols. Because the tabulation of scores is not particularly complicated on this scale, the high correlations obtained are not surprising.

Alphas for Part I factors were all quite high, ranging from .96 to .99. In Part II, alphas for domains ranged from a low of .80 (Sexual Behavior of ages 60 and older and Self-Abusive Behavior for ages 30–39 and 40–49) to a high of .95 (Social Behavior for ages 18–29 and 50–59). Of the forty alphas for Part II domains, only thirteen equaled or exceeded .90. Alphas for Part II factors all exceeded .90. The reason alphas were higher for factor scores than for domain scores is probably because there are more items in factor scores and the factor scores are more homogeneous than domain scores.

Two-week stability was estimated based on scores of forty-five individuals working in a sheltered workshop. The individuals ranged in age from 24 to 61, but it is unclear if standard scores or other methods of controlling for age range were used. Uncorrected correlations between test and retest for Part I domains ranged from .86 to .98; seven of the ten coefficients equaled or exceeded .90. Uncorrected correlations for factors ranged from .93 to .98. For Part II, uncorrected correlations ranged from .81 to .97 for domain scores; four of the eight coefficients equaled or exceeded .90. Part II factor scores were .94 and .82.

The authors also provide information about inter-rater agreement (which they term *ecological validity*) for forty-five employees of a sheltered workshop. Supervisors and the parents of the employees were independently rated. For Part I domain scores, agreement ranged from .31 (Prevocational/Vocational) to .87 (Physical Development); the agreement for Part I factor scores ranged from .47 (Personal-Social Responsibility) to .88 (Personal Self-Sufficiency). For Part II domain scores, agreement ranged from .07 (Social Behavior) to .85 (Sexual Behavior); for Part II factors, agreement was .31 (Social Adjustment) and .39 (Personal Adjustment).

VALIDITY

Content Validity   The content of the revised scale remains quite similar to the content of previous versions of this device. In previous editions of this text we questioned the content validity of the scale because the authors presented no conceptualization of the domain used to guide inclusion and exclusion of items. We were also troubled because many of the items assess physical and emotional states (not behavior) and because many items that appeared in Part II probably should not be considered maladaptive (for example, "Gossips about others," "Is always in the way," "Bites fingernails"). We still find the rationale for item selection and the scale's content to be troubling.

Criterion-Related Validity   Two criterion-related validity studies are reported. In the first, sixty-three individuals were tested using the ABS-RC2 and the Vineland Adaptive Behavior Scales. In the second study, thirty individuals were tested using the ABS-RC2 and the Adaptive Behavior Inventory.[4] In both studies, the correlations between the Part I ABS-RC2 scores and the other measures were generally moderate to high; the correlations between Part II ABS-RC2 scores and the other measures were generally not significantly different from zero. These findings strongly suggest that Part II is not measuring what is typically measured on other measures of adaptive behavior. They also provide some support for the criterion-related validity of Part I scores.

Construct Validity   Although several indexes of construct validity are provided in the ABS-RC2 manual, three seem most pertinent to our discussion. The first evidence comes from the relationship between age and Part I and Part II of the scale. As expected for a valid measure of adaptive behavior, Part I scores show some relationship to age for normally developing children and youth, but no relationship to age for adults with mental retardation.

4. The same study appears to have been reported in the examiner's manual for the school version of the ABS. (Identical correlations are reported and the subject description is similar.) In that manual, the subjects are described as attending school. At worst, these individuals fall outside of the age range with which the ABS-RC2 is intended to be used; at best, these individuals represent only one extreme of the age range with which the ABS-RC2 is intended to be used.

Part II scores are unrelated to age—also as would be expected of a valid measure.

Second, the empirical factor structure of the ABS-RC2 supports the hypothesis of three factors for Part I (as is typically found in factor analytic studies of adaptive behavior) and two factors for Part II. Thus, not only do Parts I and II measure different things, but Part I appears to be measuring constructs similar to those assessed by other measures of adaptive behavior. The meaning of Part II is not clarified by these results.

Third, scores on the ABS-RC2 differentiate youngsters with and without disabilities, and both of these groups of youngsters perform differently from adults with mental retardation. Although these results are suggestive of the construct validity of the scale, we note that the ABS-RC2 is not intended for use with children and youth. As expected, scores frequently discriminated individuals living in community placements from those living in residential settings.

SUMMARY

The ABS-RC2 is an individually administered, norm-referenced scale designed for use with individuals between 18 and 79 years of age. The scale is divided into two parts. Part I focuses on ten domains that assess three factors: Personal Self-Sufficiency, Community Self-Sufficiency, and Personal-Social Responsibility. Part II focuses on eight domains that assess (the lack of) Social Adjustment and Personal Adjustment. The ABS-RC2 represents a substantial improvement over previous editions. The norming is far more comprehensive and appears much more representative. However, given the elusive nature of mild retardation, the identification of which is affected by economic and social circumstances, conclusions about the population of reference must be tentative. The information about the scale's reliability is far more extensive than in previous editions. The internal consistency of factor scores on both parts of the scale is excellent; the domain alphas are not nearly as high. The factor scores also appear to be quite stable. Interrater agreement (called ecological validity by the authors) is weak, however. Thus, examiners should expect the ABS-RC2 to produce internally consistent scores that are stable over time but that vary according to who provides the information. Evidence of the scales' validity is emerging. The content of specific items is troubling, but there is no indication that the scale lacks criterion-related or construct validity.

AAMR Adaptive Behavior Scale–School 2[5]

*T*he revised school version of the AAMR Adaptive Behavior Scale (ABS-S2) (Nihira, Leland & Lambert, 1993) is an individually administered, norm-referenced scale designed for use with children and youth ages 3 to 21. The 1993 revision is the latest version of the 1969 and 1974 AAMD Adaptive Behavior Scales. Like the Residential and Community version of this scale, the ABS-S2 has undergone numerous modifications since its introduction in 1969. In this edition, items from previous editions were selected because of their interrater reliability and effectiveness in discrimination among various levels of adaptation.

The items and scoring procedures of the school version of the ABS are identical to those used with the residential and community edition, with two exceptions. On the school version one domain has been deleted from each part of the scale: Domestic Activity from Part I and Sexual Behavior from Part II. Otherwise the two scales appear to be identical. (Readers familiar with the community and residen-

5. The ABS-RC2 and the ABS-S2 are highly similar devices. Even though much of the material is redundant, we have treated them as separate scales to facilitate the use of this text as a reference work.

tial version of the ABS should skip to the sections dealing with technical characteristics of this version.) Thus, the scale is divided into two parts. Part I focuses on nine domains related to independent and responsible functioning, physical development, language development, and socialization. Three factors underlie these domains: Personal Self-Sufficiency, Community Self-Sufficiency, and Personal-Social Responsibility. In this part, two administration formats are used. In the first format, items that consist of a series of statements denoting increasingly higher levels of adaptation. These items are scored by circling the highest level of functioning demonstrated by the client. For example, in the domain of Physical Development, item 25 (vision) has four levels of functioning: has no difficulty seeing, has some difficulty seeing, has great difficulty seeing, and has no vision at all. In the second format, each item consists of a series of statements that are answered either yes or no. A socially desirable response is awarded 1

point. For example, item 62 (persistence) in the Self-Direction domain consists of five statements: Cannot organize task, Becomes easily discouraged, Fails to carry out tasks, Jumps from one activity to another, and Needs constant encouragement to complete task. For this item, "No" is the socially desirable response; each time a statement does not apply to the subject, the subject is awarded 1 point. Thus, a subject may receive between 0 and 5 points on this item. Students can earn from 3 to 9 points on each item scored in this format. The items in Part II of the scale are concerned with maladaptive behaviors that are manifestations of personality and behavior disorders. These items are grouped into seven domains that form two factors: Social Adjustment and Personal Adjustment. Only one administration format is used in Part II. Each item consists of multiple statements and is scored on a three-point scale (never = 0, occasionally = 1, and frequently = 2). (See Table 27.2 for a list of domains and factors.)

TABLE 27.2   **Domains and Factors in Parts I and II of the ABS-S22**

	Domains (number of items in each)	Factors
Part I	1. Independent Functioning (24)	Personal Self-Sufficiency
	2. Physical Development (6)	Community Self-Sufficiency
	3. Economic Activity (6)	Personal-Social Responsibility
	4. Language Development (10)	
	5. Numbers and Time (3)	
	6. Prevocational/Vocational Activity (3)	
	7. Self-Direction (5)	
	8. Responsibility (3)	
	9. Socialization (7)	
Part II	10. Social Behavior (7)	Social Adjustment
	11. Conformity (6)	Personal Adjustment
	12. Trustworthiness (6)	
	13. Stereotyped and Hyperactive Behavior (5)	
	14. Self-Abusive Behavior (3)	
	15. Social Engagement (4)	
	16. Disturbing Interpersonal Behavior (6)	

SCORES

Raw scores from the ABS-S2 can be converted to standard scores and percentiles for domains (mean = 10, standard deviation = 3), or to quotients for factors, (mean = 100, standard deviation = 15) and factor standard scores can be converted to percentiles on the basis of the normal curve. Age equivalents are also available for scores from Part I; Part II scores are not related to age so no age equivalents are available. Derived scores for an adaptive behavior total or composite are not available.

NORMS

Like the ABS-RC2, two different sampling procedures were used to develop norms for the ABS-S2. First, standardization sites were established in Connecticut, Florida, Ohio, and California. A site coordinator with experience in collecting standardization data was selected for each location and trained with the ABS-S2. Second, individual educators were contacted and asked to complete ten to twenty evaluations. Individuals selected under either procedure were pooled into two normative samples. One sample consisted of 2,074 individuals with mental retardation; these individuals ranged in age from 3 to 21 and resided in forty different states. The second sample consisted of 1,254 individuals without mental retardation who ranged in age from 3 to 18 and resided in forty-four states and the District of Columbia.

Both samples adequately approximate the demographic makeup of the United States in terms of race, ethnicity, sex, and geographic region. Both normative samples are more urban than the nation is. Table 27.3 indicates the number of individuals from each group at each age. About two-thirds of the time, the number of people in the age groups is less than 100. Thus, some care must be exercised when interpreting derived scores based on these samples. They are too small to allow a full range of scores.

The authors offer no guidance on when an examiner should use one set of norms or the other. However, it seems logical to use the norms based on individuals without retardation when the purpose of assessment is to establish entitlement to services. Interpretations based on the norm group of individuals with retardation should be made most carefully because these individuals have very limited intellectual ability (that is, 60 percent have IQs below 50).

RELIABILITY

Reliability of the ABS-S2 was estimated separately for each normative group. The authors present reliability estimates for items (coefficient alpha), for times (stability), and for raters.[6] For the sample with mental retardation, alphas for the 171 domain-age

TABLE 27.3 **Norm Samples Used for the ABS-S2**

Age	Individuals without Retardation	Individuals with Retardation
3	72	74
4	65	74
5	96	91
6	79	90
7	83	83
8	110	98
9	85	143
10	108	134
11	85	133
12	93	132
13	81	123
14	69	146
15	69	123
16	66	126
17	48	94
18	45	114
19		101
20		105
21		90

6. The authors provide information about what they call interscorer reliability. In the study they cite, two graduate students tabulated completed protocols. Because the tabulation of scores is not particularly complicated on this scale, the high correlations obtained are not surprising.

reliabilities in Part I ranged from a low of .81 to a high of .98; 42 of the 171 coefficients (primarily associated with the Prevocational/Vocational and Responsibility domains) were below .90. The reliability of factor scores at all ages equaled or exceeded .95. In Part II, alphas for the 133 domain-age reliabilities ranged from a low of .80 to a high of .96; 49 of the 133 coefficients were below .90. With one exception, the reliability of factor scores at all ages equaled or exceeded .90. For the sample without mental retardation, in Part I, alphas for the 144 domain-age reliabilities ranged from a low of .79 to a high of .97; 100 of the 144 coefficients were below .90. The reliability of the factor scores at the sixteen ages ranged from .80 to .97, and fourteen of the thirty-two coefficients were below .90. In Part II, alphas for the 112 domain-age reliabilities ranged from a low of .80 to a high of .98; 69 of the 112 coefficients were below .90. Reliability of the factor scores was higher. Only seven of the thirty-two factor-age alphas were below .90. In summary, for both samples, domain scores should be used with some caution because their reliabilities frequently are below .90, especially for the normative sample without mental retardation. Factor scores had more consistently acceptable reliability. The reason alphas were higher for factor scores than for domain scores is probably because there are more items in factor scores and the factor scores are more homogeneous than domain scores.

Two-week stability was estimated based on scores of forty-five students with emotional disturbance in ninth through eleventh grades. Uncorrected correlations between test and retest for Part I domains ranged from .42 to .79; none of the nine coefficients equaled or exceeded .90. Uncorrected stability estimates for factors ranged from .61 to .72. For Part II, uncorrected test-retest correlations ranged from .72 to .89 for domain scores; Part II factor scores were .84 and .81. Thus, none of the stabilities reach .90.

The authors also provide information about inter-rater agreement for fifty students with emotional disabilities (they call this *ecological validity*). The students' teacher and the teacher's aide each completed an ABS-S2. For Part I domain scores, agreement ranged from .51 (Physical Development) to .92 (Numbers and Time); the reliability of only one domain score reached .90. For Part I factor scores, the reliabilities were .80, .66, and .76. For Part II domain scores, agreement ranged from .55 (Social Engagement) to .88 (Conformity); for Part II factors, agreement was .61 (Social Adjustment) and .53 (Personal Adjustment).

VALIDITY

Content Validity   The content of the revised scale remains quite similar to the content of previous versions of this device. In previous editions of this text we questioned the content validity of the scale because the authors presented no conceptualization of the domain used to guide inclusion and exclusion of items. We were also troubled because many of the items assess physical and emotional states (not behavior) and because many items that appeared in Part II probably should not be considered maladaptive (for example, "Gossips about others," "Is always in the way," "Bites fingernails"). We still find the rationale for item selection as well as the scale's content itself to be troubling.

Criterion-Related Validity   One criterion-related validity study dealing specifically with the ABS-S2 is reported. In this study, thirty students with mental retardation were tested using the ABS-S2 and the Adaptive Behavior Inventory (ABI). The correlations between the Part I ABS-S2 scores and the ABI were generally moderate to high; the correlations between Part II ABS-S2 scores and the ABI were generally not significantly different from zero. These findings strongly suggest that Part II is not measuring what is typically measured on other measures of adaptive behavior. They also provide some support for the criterion-related validity of Part I scores.

Construct Validity   Although several indexes of construct validity are provided in the ABS-S2 manual, three seem most pertinent to our discussion.

The first evidence comes from the relationship between age and Part I and Part II of the scale. As expected for a valid measure of adaptive behavior, most scores from Part I show some relationship to age for normally developing children and youth; however, they do tend to flatten out around age 15 or 16, depending on the particular score. Part II scores show a much weaker developmental trend to about age 15 or 16, but then tend to decline. This observation suggests that students with maladaptive behavior were lost, possibly because they dropped out of school. These data generally appear consistent with the developmental domains being assessed.

Second, the factor structure of the ABS-S2 supports the notion of three factors for Part I (as is typically found in factor analytic studies of adaptive behavior) and two factors for Part II. Thus, not only do Parts I and II measure different things, but Part I appears to be measuring constructs similar to those assessed by other measures of adaptive behavior. The meaning of Part II is not clarified by these results.

Third, scores on the ABS-S2 differentiate children and youth with and without mental retardation. Thus, individuals with mental retardation earn lower scores than individuals without mental retardation.

SUMMARY

The ABS-S2 is an individually administered, norm-referenced scale designed for use with individuals between 3 and 18 years of age. The scale is divided into two parts. Part I focuses on nine domains that assess three factors: Personal Self-Sufficiency, Community Self-Sufficiency, and Personal-Social Responsibility. Part II focuses on seven domains that assess (the lack of) Social Adjustment and Personal Adjustment. The ABS-S2 represents a substantial improvement over previous editions. The norming is far more comprehensive and appears much more representative. The information about the scale's reliability is far more extensive than in previous editions. The internal-consistency estimates vary by norm group, score, and age. Surprisingly, the scale is more reliable with the sample of individuals with mental retardation; generally reliability estimates based on the performance of extreme populations are lower. One can only speculate as to why this might be the case. For all subjects, factor scores are generally more reliable than domain scores. However, examiners are cautioned that specific age-score combinations frequently fail to meet minimum standards (.90) recommended when making important educational decisions. Similarly, neither the domain or factor scores appear to be sufficiently stable to be used as the basis for important educational decisions. Inter-rater agreement (called ecological validity by the authors) is weak. Evidence of the scales' validity is emerging. Specific content items are troubling, but there is no indication that the scale lacks criterion-related or construct validity.

Adaptive Behavior Inventory

*T*he Adaptive Behavior Inventory (ABI) (Brown & Leigh, 1986a) is a norm-referenced scale appropriate for use with students who range in age from 6-0 to 18-11. The ABI is intended to be used to provide information about adaptive behavior during the diagnosis of mental retardation, to compare various components of adaptive behavior exhibited by one individual, and to evaluate instructional programs designed to affect a student's adaptation. Like other adaptive behavior measures, it is administered by having a respondent answer questions about the subject being assessed. The preferred respondent for the ABI is "the classroom teacher or other professional who has relevant contact with the student being assessed" (Brown & Leigh, 1986b, p. 4). It is particularly praiseworthy that ABI users are urged to postpone administration of the device if a rater cannot be found who has had sufficient contact with the student to provide complete and reliable information.

The ABI consists of five subtests that can be given independently in about 5 minutes each.

Self-Care Skills   This subtest contains thirty items that range from going from one school area to another to grooming to being aware of social-service agencies.

Communication Skills   This subtest contains thirty items that range from communicating one's needs orally to describing abstract ideas in writing.

Social Skills   This subtest contains thirty-two items that range from referring to others by name to sharing to organizing and leading groups.

Academic Skills   This subtest contains thirty items that range from identifying alphabet letters and one's own name to taking adequate notes to performing advanced mathematical tasks.

Occupational Skills   This subtest contains twenty-eight items that range from being punctual to supervising the work of others.

A short form of the ABI is also available. It contains a sample of items from each subtest.

SCORES

Individual items are scored using a four-point scale, with which the respondent indicates that the subject does not perform the behavior (0 points), is beginning to perform the behavior (1 point), performs the behavior most of the time (3 points), or has mastered the behavior (4 points).

Raw scores on each subtest can be converted into percentiles and standard scores (mean = 100, standard deviation = 15). If four or five subtests are administered, a weighted composite deviation score can also be obtained.

NORMS

Two sets of norms are available. One set, the normal intelligence sample, is intended to be representative of students in the general U.S. population; the other set is intended to be representative of mentally retarded pupils in special educational programs and residential facilities. Sampling plans are not provided for either normative sample, and the samples are poorly described.

The normal intelligence sample was composed of about 1,300 individuals who ranged in age from 5-0 to 18-11 and resided in twenty-four states. This sample, as a whole, corresponds to the population at the time of the 1980 census in terms of sex, race, ethnicity, geographic area, and socioeconomic status. However, the correspondence of each age group with these characteristics is not described.

The mentally retarded sample was composed of about 1,100 individuals from the same age range drawn from the same twenty-four states. This sample, as a whole, corresponds to the population at the time of the 1980 census in terms of sex and measured IQ. The sample underrepresents students in special day schools.

RELIABILITY

Internal consistency was estimated by coefficient alpha. Adjacent age groups were combined (five- and six-year-olds, seven- and eight-year-olds, and so forth), and the responses for fifty individuals at each age level in the two standardization groups were randomly selected. For the normal intelligence groups, forty-two coefficients were computed (five subtests and total score for the seven ages). The thirty-five subtest-by-age coefficients ranged from .86 (for the 5- and 6-year-old group) to .97; twenty-five of the thirty-five coefficients equaled or exceeded .90. All of the coefficients for the total ABI score exceeded .90. The internal consistency of the ABI short form also exceeded .90 for each of the age groups. Stability was estimated by test-retest reliability using thirty-nine students of normal intelligence who ranged in age from 5 to 18 and fifty-six mentally retarded students who ranged in age from 6 to 18. The effects of age were held constant statistically.[7] Estimated stabilities for the subtests, the composite, and the short-form composite all exceeded .90.

VALIDITY

Reports on validity data are superficial. Thus, most of the evidence provided is difficult to evaluate. Inspection of the items included in the ABI may provide some evidence of content validity. Some items are too subjective, however, and criteria for scoring/marking each item may not be clear to the person completing the form. For example, teachers are asked to rate a student's performance on *intermediate* reading tasks, understanding of *basic* measurement concepts, knowledge of the *approximate* cost of common items, and so forth.

As evidence of criterion-related validity, the authors provide correlations with teacher judgments of adaptive behavior and modest to high correlations with the AAMD Adaptive Behavior Scale and the Vineland Adaptive Behavior Scale. These studies are incompletely described, however, so it is difficult to evaluate the ABI's criterion-related validity.

As evidence of construct validity, the authors offer the correlations of the ABI with achievement tests, intelligence tests, and age, as well as the intercorrelations of the ABI's subtests. Finally, to show construct validity, the performances of retarded and normal students in the standardization samples were compared. "In every instance, there were significant differences between each of the pairwise comparisons of the groups, with higher ABI means attributed to students in less restrictive classroom environments" (Brown & Leigh, 1986b, p. 40).

SUMMARY

The ABI is a norm-referenced scale that assesses five aspects of adaptive behavior through ratings by a student's teacher. The norms appear adequate, and the device appears to have adequate reliability and validity.

Scales of Independent Behavior

*T*he Scales of Independent Behavior (SIB) (Bruininks, Woodcock, Weatherman, & Hill, 1984) is an individually administered, norm-referenced device suitable for use with individuals ranging in age from infancy through adulthood. The SIB's primary use is "'to identify individuals who lack adaptive functional independence in particular settings" (Bruininks et al., 1984, p. 3). Additional uses include aiding in the development of individualized education plans (IEPs) and individually prescribed programs (IPPs), in the selection and placement of individuals within programs of education and training, in guidance, in the assessment of individual gains following intervention, in program management and evaluation, and in research. Like other measures of adaptive behavior, the SIB is administered to a respondent who is thoroughly familiar with the subject being assessed.

Adaptive behavior items are arranged into fourteen subscales; subscales are grouped into four clusters. The Motor Skills cluster consists of two subscales: Gross Motor Skills and Fine Motor Skills. The Social Interaction and Communication Skills cluster consists of three subscales: Social Interaction, Language Comprehension, and Language Expression. The Personal Living Skills cluster consists of five subscales: Eating and Meal Preparation, Dressing, Toileting, Personal Self-Care, and Domestic Skills. The Community Living Skills cluster consists of four subscales: Time and Punctuality, Money and Value, Work Skills, and Home and Community Orientation. The clusters can be combined into a total score called Broad Independence. Also included in the SIB are four maladaptive behavior indexes: General Maladaptive Behavior, Internalized Maladaptive Behav-

---

7. Partial correlation was used. In essence, this procedure gives the average test-retest correlation at each age.

ior, Asocial Maladaptive Behavior, and Externalized Maladaptive Behavior (Bruininks et al., 1984, pp. 11–12). Two short-form options are available, the Short Form Scale and the Early Primary Scale.

SCORES

A variety of norm-referenced scores are available for adaptive behavior: age equivalents, percentile ranks, standard scores (mean = 100, standard deviation = 15), and normal curve equivalents. Also available are instructional ranges, relative performance indexes,[8] functioning levels (*very superior* to *severe deficit*), and adjusted adaptive behavior scores (comparisons with Woodcock-Johnson IQs). Three different scores are available for the maladaptive indexes: stanines, maladaptive behavior indexes, and levels of seriousness.

NORMS

Norms, developed using Rasch scaling techniques, were based on interviews for over 1,700 subjects who ranged in age from 3 months to 44 years.[9] A detailed sampling plan is provided. The normative sample was intended to approximate the U.S. population in terms of sex, race, community size (urban and urban fringe, outside urban area, rural), geographic region (eleven states in nine regions), and socioeconomic status. In the construction of the norms, individual subjects were weighted so that the figures would correspond exactly with those of the national census.

RELIABILITY

Corrected split-half estimates of reliability are provided for each subscale and scale for thirteen age

8. The RPI is a fractional index (for example, 75/90) indicating "the percent of independence predicted for a given subject on a set of tasks that a reference group can perform with 90% accuracy" (Bruininks et al., 1984, p. 14).

9. See Appendix 6 for a general description of Rasch scaling and item response theory.

groups ranging from 0-3/0-11 to 29 years and older. The 182 reliability coefficients range from .00 to .95, with fourteen equaling or exceeding .90. Many of the lowest reliabilities are the result of floor and ceiling effects. For example, the coefficients that equaled 0 were found for the 0-3/0-11 age group for behaviors such as domestic skills and time and punctuality. When reliabilities are estimated across all age levels, however, no subscale has a reliability equal to or greater than .90. Cluster reliabilities are substantially higher: reliabilities for Motor Skills range from .64 to .93; for Social and Communication Skills, from .85 to .93; for Personal Living Skills, from .85 to .95; and for Community Living Skills, from .67 to .94. The total score Broad Independence is very reliable, equaling or exceeding .95 for all age groups. Internal-consistency estimates are not provided for the maladaptive indexes.

Stability estimates are provided for two age groups (6 to 8 years old and 10 to 11 years old) for the adaptive subscales, clusters, Broad Independence, and maladaptive indexes. For the 6-8 age group, subscale stabilities ranged from .67 to .94; only two subscales had coefficients equal to or greater than .90. For the 10-11 age group, stabilities ranged from .51 to .88. The clusters, as expected, had higher coefficients. Only for Motor Skills was the coefficient less than .90 for the younger group; for the older group, coefficients for Motor Skills ranged from .71 to .88. Stabilities for Broad Independence for the older and younger groups were .96 and .87, respectively. The maladaptive indexes for the two age groups ranged from .75 to .90.

Finally, data are provided on rater agreement and inter-interviewer agreement. Correlations were very high—.90 or higher.

VALIDITY

Content validity was established through delineation of the domain and careful item selection. Criterion-related validity was investigated by correlating SIB scores with scores on the AAMD Adaptive Behavior Scale (School edition). Correlations between SIB cluster scores and ABS-S2 factor scores ranged from .59 to .91. Also, the SIB scores correlate moderately with Woodcock-Johnson Psychoeducational Battery Broad Cognitive scores. Maladaptive indexes were correlated with results of the Revised Problem Behavior Checklist (RPBC) (Quay & Peterson, 1987); the pattern of correlations supports the validity of the SIB (for example, the Asocial Maladaptive Behavior Index of the SIB correlates better with scores on the Socialized Aggression, Attention Problems, and Motor Excess scales of the RPBC than with scores on the other subscales of the RPBC).

Construct validity was established in several ways. Adaptive behavior was demonstrated to increase with age (although maladaptive behavior was essentially unrelated to age). Several studies were conducted in which the scores of special populations (for example, trainable mentally retarded individuals) in several age ranges were compared to those of nonhandicapped persons drawn at random from the normative sample. The comparisons showed that the SIB consistently assigned lower adaptivity to handicapped persons. Moreover, differences in adaptive behavior were on expected dimensions. For example,

hearing-impaired individuals earned significantly lower scores on the Social Interaction and Language Comprehension subscales and on the Social Interaction and Communication Skills cluster.

SUMMARY

The Scales of Independent Behavior is an individually administered, norm-referenced adaptive behavior scale that is useful with individuals ranging in age from infancy through adulthood. The SIB includes four clusters of adaptive behavior (Motor Skills, Social Interaction and Communication Skills, Personal Living Skills, and Community Living Skills) and four maladaptive behavior indexes (General Maladaptive Behavior, Internalized Maladaptive Behavior, Asocial Maladaptive Behavior, and Externalized Maladaptive Behavior). Norms appear to be representative of the general U.S. population. Evidence for the SIB's reliability is mixed. Subscales and scales often have relatively poor reliability, although Broad Independence is highly reliable at all ages. Evidence for the validity of the scale is excellent.

Responsibility and Independence Scale for Adolescents

T he Responsibility and Independence Scale for Adolescents (RISA) (Salvia, Neisworth, & Schmidt, 1990) is an individually administered, norm-referenced device intended to assess the adaptive behavior of adolescents between the ages of 12 and 19. The scale contains 136 items, in question format. A respondent (for example, a parent or spouse, in the case of older adolescents) answers each question with yes or no to indicate if the adolescent performs various actions. To facilitate comprehension of the questions, each item is illustrated by a line drawing that is shown to the respondent as the question is asked. These drawings (with the question written at the bottom) are spiral-bound into a book. Although no specialized training is required to administer RISA, the authors provide

practice exercises for individuals who are not experienced in the use of this type of instrument.

The 136 items are arranged in two subtests named Responsibility and Independence. Items assessing maladaptive behavior were not included. Responsibility consists of fifty-two items that assess "a broad class of adaptive behaviors that meet social expectations and standards of reciprocity, accountability, and fairness that enable personal development . . ." (p. 2). The items are clustered in three areas. Self-Management contains seventeen items that deal with topics such as resisting peer pressure, using constructive criticism, and following household rules (for example, regarding phone use). Social Maturity contains twenty-one items dealing with topics such as friendships and appropriate public behavior. Social

Communication contains fourteen items dealing with polite listening and speaking, asking permission to borrow things, and using the telephone to obtain information.

Independence consists of eighty-four items that assess "behaviors that allow individuals to live separately and free from the control or determination of others, and to conduct themselves effectively . . . " (p. 2). The items are clustered in five areas. Domestic Skills contains nine items dealing with such topics as following laundry care labels, maintaining a supply of frequently used foods, and using safety equipment and clothing when necessary. Money Management contains twenty-three items dealing with such topics as realistically estimating the cost of common household items, saving money for the future, using coupons, and using unit pricing. Citizenship contains five items related to voting, political awareness, and civic responsibility. Personal Organization contains fifteen items dealing with topics such as using lists, making preparations for the future, and taking actions to improve one's health. Transportation Skills contains eighteen items dealing with behavior related to safe driving, asking for directions when lost, and using public transportation. Career Skills contains fourteen items dealing with job training, securing employment, and career advancement.

SCORES

Responsibility, Independence, and Total scores can be converted to percentiles and standard scores (mean = 100, standard deviation = 15). A table is also available to convert differences between Responsibility and Independence standard scores.

NORMS

A two-stage cluster sampling technique was used to select the normative sample. First, the United States was divided into four regions (Northeast, Northcentral, West, and South) and clusters of communities within regions were identified. Several community characteristics guided selection: degree of urbanization (central cities, urban fringe, cities with populations between 2,500 and 49,999 located at least fifty miles from the central city, and rural communities with populations less than 2,500); community educational attainment; community income; community employment status; and community occupational type. Seventy target communities that were broadly representative of the United States at the 1980 census were selected. Adolescents were selected at random from public and private schools and agencies that served high, middle, and low socioeconomic sections of their communities. The norms are based on the ratings of 1,900 adolescents from nine age groups. The largest sample ($N = 291$) consisted of fifteen-year-olds, and the smallest sample ($N = 124$) consisted of nineteen-year-olds. Each age group was weighted (using sex, community size, educational attainment of parents, and geographic region) so that the standardization sample closely approximated the most recent census data. Students with disabilities were included in the norms for each age group, although their proportions are not reported.

RELIABILITY

Three types of reliability data are presented. Corrected split-half estimates of reliability are presented for each age and are based on the ratings of the adolescents who were the normative sample. All subtest reliabilities equaled or exceeded .90 at every age except for Responsibility at age 14, where r_{xx} equaled .83. Corrected split-half estimates for the Total exceeded .90 at every age. Test-retest correlations were computed to estimate stability for three age groups: ages 12 and 13 ($N = 40$), ages 15 and 16 ($N = 45$), and ages 18 and 19 ($N = 34$). All subtest and total score coefficients exceeded .90. The reliability of the difference between Independence and Responsibility scores was also estimated. These estimates ranged from a low of .76 (at age 19) to a high of .89 (at both 12 and 13). Thus, differences between subscales are not sufficiently reliable to allow use of the subscales in making important educational decisions.

VALIDITY

Evidence for content, criterion-related, and construct validity is presented in RISA's technical manual. The authors can lay some claim to content validity based on their careful generation and selection of items. Moreover, most of the test's items assess behavior that would be appropriate for high-school students or young adults. Correlations with two other measures of adaptive behavior (the Vineland Adaptive Behavior Scale and the Scales of Independent Behavior) are presented as evidence for RISA's concurrent validity. Total scores of these other two measures correlate as well with RISA Total scores as they do with each other (that is, about .50). Finally, several studies support RISA's construct validity.

First, RISA scores increase with age. Second, the factor analysis supports the use of two subtests and the factors identified are consistent with those identified in studies of other adaptive behavior measures. Third, there is a relative absence of differences in the performances of different racial and ethnic groups. Finally, adolescents previously and independently identified as mentally retarded earned substantially lower scores than nonhandicapped peers.

SUMMARY

RISA, a scale intended for use only with adolescents, assesses two major components of adaptive behavior: Responsibility and Independence. The technical manual provides clear evidence of a representative norm group and reliability. Some evidence of the scale's validity is also presented.

COPING WITH DILEMMAS IN CURRENT PRACTICE

There are three severe problems in the use of currently available instruments to assess adaptive behavior. The first problem is the internal consistency of the adaptive behavior scales. There is no theoretical reason why adaptive behavior scales should not be internally consistent. That some scales are not homogeneous can reasonably be attributed to the lack of a clear definition of adaptive behavior, a problem to which we alluded earlier in this chapter. There is no professional consensus about the types of behavior that are indicative of adaptation. Indeed, inspection of the behaviors sampled by the various devices suggests a lack of agreement about what adaptive behavior is—there is a broad range of behaviors sampled and orientations toward measurement. Without a more precise concept of adaptive behavior, one should expect heterogeneous operationalizations of the definition (that is, heterogeneous scales of adaptive behavior). One solution to this problem is for test authors to rely more heavily on factor analytic studies of adaptive behavior. If scores on adaptive behavior scales represent underlying factors, the scores will be more homogeneous and, therefore, more reliable. This point is clearly illustrated by the ABS-RC2, for which domain scores are less reliable than factor scores. Therefore, whenever possible, test users should rely on scores that represent the underlying factors that make up adaptive behavior rather than using scores that describe interrelated surface performances (for example, eating or dressing).

The second problem is that scales of adaptive behavior frequently are poorly normed (sometimes only on individuals with disabilities). If its norm samples are unrepresentative, a scale should not be used. An alternative to using unrepresentative norms is simply to identify one or two students to use for social comparison. Teachers or parents can be asked to nominate individuals of the same age and sex as those in the norm group, whom they believe have "adapted" successfully. The behavior of these adaptive peers can then be used to make rather simple comparisons. Although one or two children certainly are no substitute for a normative sample, they may prove adequate for some comparisons.

A most vexing problem, both theoretically and practically, is the lack of agreement among raters. When reported at all for adaptive behavior scales, interrater agreement is often poor. The interpretation of such findings can proceed along two lines. First, poor agreement can suggest lack of reliability. Thus, one would suspect at least three potential problems: (1) The specific items are difficult to understand or interpret; (2) the criteria used to rate the behavior are subjective; or (3) one or both of the raters are insufficiently familiar with the student. Lack of interrater agreement can also suggest lack of validity in addition to lack of reliability. Thus, one would suspect at least two potential problems: (1) One of the raters may have distorted perceptions or may not be entirely truthful; or (2) the student's behavior may vary in different contexts. In practice, examiners have few options for dealing with rater disagreement. One should select as the respondent the person who is most familiar with the student, who has seen the student in the most contexts, and who will provide truthful responses. Examiners should also guard against conveying their own expectations to the respondent. Finally, when behavior clearly varies across contexts, examiners should consider elements in those contexts that may set the occasion for behavior, because such elements may have importance in educational interventions.

SUMMARY

In the assessment of adaptive behavior we are interested in what an individual regularly does, not what the individual is capable of doing. Ultimately, the behaviors of interest in adults are those that allow individuals to manage their affairs sufficiently well that they do not require societal intervention to protect them or others. The behaviors that are believed to be important vary from time to time and from theory to theory. In general, in the United States, adults are expected to take reasonable care of themselves (by managing their own health, dressing, eating, and so on), to work, and to engage in socially acceptable recreational or leisure activities. In children and adolescents, the behaviors of interest are those that are believed to enable the desired adult behaviors and skills.

The assessment of adaptive behavior usually takes the form of a structured interview with a person (for example, a parent or teacher) who is very familiar with the person being assessed (the subject of the interview). The assessment of adaptive behavior has been plagued by inadequate instruments—scales that lack reliability and are poorly normed. One must select scales (or parts of scales) with great care.

STUDY QUESTIONS

1. How does the assessment of adaptive behavior differ from the assessment of academic achievement?
2. What criteria would be appropriate to classify a behavior as maladaptive?
3. With the introduction of computers and robots to American industry, what do you think will happen to current definitions of adaptive behavior?
4. Do you think adaptive behavior ranges from absent to highly developed, or does it range from absent to adequate? Why?

ADDITIONAL READING

Reschly, D. (1982). Assessing mild mental retardation: The influence of adaptive behavior, sociocultural status, and prospects for nonbiased assessment. In C. Reynolds and T. Gutkin (Eds.), *Handbook of school psychology* (pp. 220–236). New York: Wiley.

Schmidt, M., & Salvia, J. (1984). Adaptive behavior: A conceptual analysis. *Diagnostique, 9*(2), 117–125.

Chapter 28

Diagnostic Systems

*E*arlier in this text we noted that tests are samples of behavior. Most tests sample behaviors from a single domain (for example, intelligence, achievement, or adaptive behavior). Two tests that sample behaviors from the same domain may actually differ significantly because they sample different behaviors from that domain.

In the late 1970s test publishers began to develop measures that sample behaviors from several domains. Whereas other chapters in Parts 3 and 4 of this text are restricted to specific domains (although achievement covers multiple domains), the measures reviewed in this chapter are entire diagnostic systems. One diagnostic system, the system of Multicultural Pluralistic Assessment was reviewed in earlier editions of this text. Components of SOMPA (specifically the WISC-R) are no longer published. SOMPA, therefore, is no longer of much use.

WHY DO WE USE DIAGNOSTIC SYSTEMS?

Diagnostic systems were designed to provide a comprehensive testing instrument to link students' learning abilities to their school achievement in one continuous system of measurement. Teachers can use these interrelated findings as the basis for instructional planning. Diagnostic systems offer two major advantages. The first is technical. The same normative sample provides derived scores for all measures in the various domains assessed in the diagnostic system. As you recall from Chapter 6, differences between test scores may be a function of differences in normative samples. Thus, if an intelligence test shows that Sam's IQ is 115 and his standard score on an achievement test is 106 (mean = 100, standard deviation = 15), part of the difference between 115 and 106 may be attributable to differences in the norms of the two tests. Diagnostic systems provide more accurate comparisons of a person's performances in different domains because the derived scores in the different domains are based on the same norm group.

The second advantage of diagnostic systems is that they may be more convenient for the assessor to use than several tests of single domains. For example, the time it takes to administer tests may be reduced because redundancies in several domains may be lessened. In addition, it may take assessors less time to put together the necessary materials for testing.

SPECIFIC DIAGNOSTIC SYSTEMS

Kaufman Assessment Battery for Children

*T*he Kaufman Assessment Battery for Children (K-ABC) (Kaufman & Kaufman, 1983) is an individually administered norm-referenced battery intended to provide a comprehensive assessment of intelligence (learning potential and preferred learning style) and achievement for children between the ages of 2-5 and 12-5. Kaufman and Kaufman claim that the test is useful for the following purposes: (1) psychological and clinical assessment (including projective interpretation of personality and inferences about impulsivity-reflectivity, perseverative behavior, rigidity-flexibility, and tolerance for frustration); (2) psychoeducational evaluation of exceptional children, particularly the learning disabled; (3) educational placement and planning; (4) assessment of minorities (especially blacks, Hispanics, and bilingual children); (5) preschool assessment; and (6) neuropsychological assessment.

Sixteen subtests are combined into three regularly administered scales and one supplementary scale. Intelligence is assessed on three scales: the Simultaneous Processing Scale, the Sequential Processing Scale, and the optional Nonverbal Scale. Simultaneous and Sequential Processing scales are combined to form the Mental Processing Scale. Achievement is assessed with the Achievement Scale.

The K-ABC draws heavily on the information-processing theories of Das (for example, Das, Kirby, & Jarman, 1975) and Luria (1966) as well as the neuropsychological research of Cohen (1972). In these theories the processing of information is viewed dichotomously. One may act upon information sequentially or simultaneously. Many examples of tasks that are essentially sequential in nature are provided in the K-ABC manuals, such as memorization of number facts, spelling, application of stepwise

procedures in arithmetic (for example, the division algorithm), word-attack skills, and so on. The other method of acting on information is simultaneous processing. In many tasks separate elements are not handled sequentially; rather, the elements are handled (processed) at once, as a whole. For example, skilled readers seldom ponder individual letters in a word; they grasp the word as a whole.

Kaufman and Kaufman are also concerned with the assessment of culturally atypical children. The optional Nonverbal Scale combines subtests that can be administered gesturally and to which students can respond nonverbally. The Nonverbal Scale is believed to be "a good estimate of intellectual potential for . . . deaf, hearing-impaired, speech- or language-disordered, autistic, and non–English-speaking children" (Kaufman & Kaufman, 1983, p. 35).

Achievement is conceptualized as "the ability to integrate the two types of mental processing and apply them to real-life situations" (p. 33). The "Achievement Scale is intended to assess factual knowledge and skills usually acquired in a school setting or through alertness to the environment" (p. 33).

Brief descriptions of each subtest follow and are based on the descriptions provided by Kaufman and Kaufman in the Interpretative Manual. Unless otherwise indicated, each subtest can be administered to children between 2-5 and 12-5.

SEQUENTIAL PROCESSING SCALE

- *Hand Movements* Requires a child to copy a sequence of taps made by the tester with the fist, palm, or side of the hand

- *Number Recall* Requires a child to repeat a series of digits read by the tester
- *Word Order* (ages 4-0 to 12-5) Requires a child to point to silhouettes of common objects in the order named by the tester

SIMULTANEOUS PROCESSING SCALE

- *Magic Window* (ages 2-6 to 4-11) Requires a child to identify a picture that the tester rotates behind a narrow slit, exposing only a part of the picture at any one time
- *Face Recognition* (ages 2-6 to 4-11) Requires a child to recall one or two faces that have been presented briefly by selecting the correct face(s), in a different pose, from a group photograph
- *Gestalt Closure* Requires a child to complete an inkblot drawing and to name or describe it
- *Triangles* (ages 4-0 to 12-5) Requires a child to assemble triangles (one side blue, one side yellow) to match an abstract design
- *Matrix Analogies* (ages 5-0 to 12-5) Requires a child to select the picture or design that completes a 2-by-2 visual analogy.
- *Spatial Memory* (ages 5-0 to 12-5) Requires a child to remember where pictures were arranged on a page
- *Photo Series* (ages 6-0 to 12-5) Requires a child to organize photographs that illustrate an event and to place them in proper chronology

ACHIEVEMENT SCALE

- *Expressive Vocabulary* (ages 2-6 to 4-11) Requires a child to name objects from photographs
- *Faces and Places* Requires a child to name famous persons, fictional characters, or places shown in pictures
- *Arithmetic* (ages 3-0 to 12-5) Requires a child to name numbers, to count, to compute, and to understand mathematical concepts
- *Riddles* (ages 3-0 to 12-5) Requires a child to name a concrete or abstract concept when given several of its characteristics

- *Reading/Decoding* (ages 5-0 to 12-5) Requires a child to name letters and to read words orally
- *Reading/Understanding* (ages 7-0 to 12-5) Requires children to act out commands given in sentences that they read

NONVERBAL SCALE

The composition of the Nonverbal Scale varies with a child's age. For four-year-olds, the scale consists of Face Recognition, Hand Movements, and Triangles. For five-year-olds, the scale consists of Hand Movements, Triangles, Matrix Analogies, and Spatial Memory. For children 6 years old and older, the scale consists of Hand Movements, Triangles, Matrix Analogies, Spatial Memory, and Photo Series.

SCORES

A variety of transformed scores are used. Scaled scores (mean = 10, standard deviation = 3) are available by chronological age for the Mental Processing subtests. Mental Processing subtests are combined into Sequential Processing, Simultaneous Processing, Mental Processing Composite, and Nonverbal scales (mean = 100, standard deviation = 15). Raw scores on the Achievement Scale yield standard scores (mean = 100, standard deviation = 15). Percentile ranks are available for each subtest and scale. Age equivalents are available for each subtest of the Mental Processing Scale, and grade equivalents are available for each of the Achievement subtests.

NORMS

National norms and sociocultural norms are available for comparisons. The national norms consist of one hundred students at each half-year of age from 2-6 to 12-5. A representative sample was obtained by stratifying on sex, education of the parent, ethnic status (white, black, Hispanic, other), geographic considerations, and school placement. In addition, sociocultural norms are provided to compare a child to others of similar racial and ethnic background and socioeconomic status on the Mental Processing Scale and Achievement subtests (except Expressive Vocabulary). The standardization procedures were excellent.

RELIABILITY

Both split-half and test-retest reliability coefficients, based on the standardization sample, are provided. Split-half coefficients, corrected with the Spearman-Brown formula, range from a high of .92 (Triangles at age 5) to a low of .62 (Gestalt Closure at age 7) on the Mental Processing subtests. Of the eighty coefficients reported, only one equaled or exceeded .90. Corrected split-half coefficients on the Mental Processing Scale (including the Nonverbal Scale) range from a high of .95 (for several ages on the Composite Mental Processing Scale) to a low of .84 (for ages 2 and 3 on the Simultaneous Processing Scale). As would be expected, the composites are more reliable than the subtests; of the forty-two coefficients, thirty equal or exceed .90. On the achievement subtests, corrected split-half reliabilities range from .97 (Reading/Decoding at age 6) to .70 (Faces and Places at age 3). Of the forty-eight age-subtest coefficients, twelve equal or exceed .90. The reliability of the composite Achievement Scale exceeds .90 at all ages.

Test-retest reliabilities (two- to four-week interval between tests) were obtained by retesting 246 children from the standardization sample. The correlations were, however, based on several combined ages. Stabilities for the Mental Processing subtests range from .86 (Gestalt Closure for age range 9-0 through 12-5) to .59 (Hand Movements for age range 9-0 through 12-5). Of the twenty-three stability coefficients, none equals or exceeds .90. Stabilities for the Mental Processing Scale range from .93 (Composite for age range 9-0 through 12-5) to .77 (Sequential Processing and Simultaneous Processing for age range 2-6 through 4-11). Of the twelve coefficients, two equal or exceed .90. Stabilities on the Achievement subtests range from .98 (Reading/Decoding for age range 5-0 through 8-11) to .72

(Riddles for age range 2-6 through 4-11). Of the fourteen age range-subtest coefficients, eight equal or exceed .90; the composite Achievement Scale exceeds .90 at the three age ranges.

VALIDITY

Forty pages of the Interpretative Manual, describing numerous unpublished studies, are devoted to the validity of the K-ABC. Several types of evidence are presented to demonstrate construct validity. Scores on each subtest of K-ABC increase with age. The subtests are internally consistent (although this type of information is better considered as evidence of reliability). The results of several factor analyses that partially support the theorized factor structure of the K-ABC are also discussed. Convergent/discriminant validity is reported.

Criterion-related validity is also examined by correlating the K-ABC with several other tests. To support the contention that the K-ABC measures intelligence, correlations between the K-ABC scales and various intelligence scales were examined. Correlation with the WISC-R Full-Scale IQ and the Mental Processing Composite was .70. The WISC-R Full-Scale IQ and the individual scales making up the Mental Processing Scale were moderately correlated: correlations with the Simultaneous Processing and Nonverbal Scales, were in the .60s; correlation with Sequential Processing was .47. Correlations with the 1970 Stanford-Binet using various samples of children ranged from .36 to .72 for the Mental Processing Composite, from .15 to .65 for the Simultaneous Processing Scale, from .27 to .63 for the Sequential Processing Scale, and from .31 to .70 for the Nonverbal Scale. Other tests of intelligence that were used as criteria include the McCarthy Scales, the Cognitive Abilities Test, the Woodcock-Johnson Cognitive Ability subtests, the Columbia Mental Maturity Scale, and the Slosson Intelligence Test. Finally, several studies examined the relationship of the K-ABC with the Peabody Picture Vocabulary Test. The sixty coefficients ranged from .21 (for Sequential Processing) to .75 (for the Mental Processing Composite).

K-ABC scores were also used to predict achievement. Generally the correlations were unimpressive. For example, correlations between the PIAT-R subtests and the Sequential Processing Scale ranged from .12 (Spelling) to .64 (Math); with the Simultaneous Processing Scale, from .02 (Reading Recognition) to .62 (Math); with the Nonverbal Scale, from .12 (Reading Recognition) to .51 (Math). Correlations with various subtests from the Iowa Tests of Basic Skills, the California Achievement Tests, and the SRA Achievement Series are comparable to the PIAT-R correlations.

Validation of the Achievement Scale is less persuasive, largely because of the definition of achievement employed: "factual knowledge and skills usually acquired in a school setting or through alertness to the environment" (Kaufman & Kaufman, 1983, p. 33). (Achievement is usually defined as the consequence of direct instruction.) The issue is further complicated by the way the achievement subtests are described. For example, "Expressive Vocabulary is a direct adaptation of the Stanford-Binet Picture Vocabulary task" (p. 51) or "Riddles probably comes closest to a Wechsler or Stanford-Binet Vocabulary subtest in terms of what it measures" (p. 54). The problem is that the Weschler scales and the Stanford-Binet are used by the Kaufmans to validate the achievement components of their scale. This is not the same as proving that the scale measures achievement. In addition, the K-ABC provides no linkages to curricula; there is no table of specifications. Numerous correlations between the Achievement Scale and various achievement tests are presented. However, the composite achievement score is not meaningful because it mixes such disparate contents.

Although the manuals present considerable evidence to indicate the K-ABC assesses two different types of mental processing, there is little convincing evidence that the K-ABC can be substituted for more traditional measures of intelligence or achievement. No data are presented to validate the K-ABC as a measure of learning potential, for use in educational placement and planning, for clinical assessment, or for neurological assessment.

SUMMARY

The K-ABC is designed to assess the way children process information and the amount of information they have obtained compared to others of similar age and background. The battery was adequately standardized. The composite scales are generally reliable; the subtests are not. Although there is considerable indication that the battery measures different mental processes, the validity of the battery for the purposes for which it is intended is not established.

Woodcock-Johnson Psychoeducational Battery–Revised (WJ-R)

*T*he Woodcock–Johnson Psychoeducational Battery–Revised (WJ-R) (Woodcock & Johnson, 1989) is an individually administered, norm-referenced assessment system intended to assess the intellectual and academic development of individuals from preschool through adulthood.[1]

In addition to the technical manuals that accompany the test, the WJ-R provides four easel kits for presenting stimulus materials: one for the standard cognitive subtests, one for the supplementary cognitive subtests, one for the standard achievement subtests, and one for the supplementary achievement subtests.

The revision represents a substantial modification of the first edition. Some of the new features are ten new tests added to the cognitive battery, four new tests added to the achievement battery, alternate forms for the achievement tests, and the

1. Basal and ceiling rules are used so that no subject is administered all of the items. These rules have been changed in the WJ-R. Some scoring criteria are not found in the easel used to present test stimuli. Thus, testers must refer to the examiner's manual during the administration to find the criteria.

availability of computerized scoring. The tests of interest were dropped from the 1989 edition. The batteries require a skillful examiner to administer and score the subtests.

TESTS OF COGNITIVE ABILITY

The Cognitive Battery is composed of twenty-one cognitive subtests and is based on the Horn-Cattell theory of Fluid (Gf) and Crystallized (Gc) intelligence. To date, nine broad intellectual abilities have been identified in the work of Cattell, Horn, and others working on the Gf-Gc theory. The WJ-R measures eight of the nine abilities. The nine factors in the Horn-Cattell model are Comprehension Knowledge (Gc), Fluid Reasoning (Gf), Visual Processing (Gv), Auditory Processing (Ga), Correct Decision Speed (CDS), Processing Speed (Gs), Short-term Memory (Gsm), Long-term Retrieval (Glr), and Quantitative Ability (Gq). The Standard Battery consists of the following seven subtests, each of which corresponds to a hypothesized factor of intelligence.

Memory for Names   This subtest consists of auditory/visual tasks in which the individual learns the names of nine pictured space creatures.

Memory for Sentences   This subtest consists of phrases and sentences that are presented individually on audiotape and that must be repeated by the individual.

Visual Matching   This subtest consists of seventy sets of numbers; each set consists of six numbers that range from single digits to three-digit numbers. An individual's score is based on the number of sets that are matched correctly in 3 minutes.

Incomplete Words   This subtest has words with one or more missing phonemes that the individual must identify.

Visual Closure   Forty-nine visual stimuli are presented for identification in this subtest. The pictures are distorted, incomplete, or have patterns superimposed on them.

Picture Vocabulary   In this subtest, the individual must name pictures of objects.

Analysis-Synthesis   This learning task requires the individual to determine what components are missing from an incomplete logic puzzle.

The supplementary battery consists of the following fourteen subtests, which are designed to provide additional information about the factors measured by the standard intellectual battery.

Visual-Auditory Learning   In this subtest, the individual associates visual symbols with words and make sentences out of the symbols.

Memory for Words   In this subtest, the individual repeats lists of unrelated words; the lists range in length from one to eight words.

Cross Out   This subtest consists of timed, match-to-sample tasks. The individual must locate five drawings that match the stimulus, out of a set of twenty.

Sound Blending   In this subtest, the individual synthesizes syllables into words.

Picture Recognition   In this subtest, the individual must recognize a subset of pictures that have been presented among a set of distracting pictures.

Oral Vocabulary   The individual gives synonyms or antonyms in response to stimulus words read by the examiner.

Concept Formation   This subtest consists of a set of materials that contains instances and noninstances of concepts and the individual must specify the concepts.

Delayed Recall—Memory for Names   This subtest requires the individual to recall, after from one to eight days, the names of the space creatures learned in the first test.

Delayed Recall—Visual-Auditory Learning This subtest requires the individual to recall, after from one to eight days, the symbols learned in the eighth test (Visual-Auditory Learning).

Numbers Reversed In this subtest, the individual repeats a series of digits backward.

Sound Patterns In this subtest, the individual listens to two complex sound patterns and must tell if they are the same or different.

Spatial Relations The individual matches shapes in this subtest.

Listening Comprehension In this oral cloze task, the individual listens to a passage and supplies the last word.

Verbal Analogies This subtest requires the individual to complete progressively more difficult analogies.

As shown in Figure 28.1, these tests can be combined into seven Cognitive Factor Clusters (Long-Term Retrieval, Short-Term Memory, Processing Speed, Auditory Processing, Visual Processing, Comprehension-Knowledge, and Fluid Reasoning), four Scholastic-Aptitude clusters (Reading Aptitude, Mathematics Aptitude, Written Language Aptitude, and Knowledge Aptitude), two Oral Language Clusters (Oral Language Ability and Oral Language Aptitude), and three total scores: Early Development Scale (which uses subtests appropriate for young children), Broad Cognitive Ability (based on the standard battery) and Broad Cognitive Ability (based on the extended battery).

TESTS OF ACHIEVEMENT

The Achievement Battery is composed of fourteen achievement subtests. The first nine make up the standard achievement battery.

Letter-Word Identification This subtest assesses the identification of letters in isolation and in words.

Passage Comprehension This modified cloze procedure assesses comprehension of short passages.

Calculation This subtest assesses prowess in solving whole and mixed-number problems involving basic operations, as well as problems requiring higher mathematics (for example, trigonometry and calculus).

Applied Problems This subtest assesses skill in solving practical mathematics problems.

Dictation This subtest assesses an individual's spelling, capitalization, punctuation, and word usage based on written answers to questions.

Writing Samples In this subtest, individuals respond to a variety of questions by writing answers that range from very simple (for example, writing one's name) to more difficult (for example, writing a correct sentence describing a stimulus picture and using specified vocabulary).

Science These questions assess knowledge in biology and physical science and are answered orally.

Social Studies These questions assess knowledge in economics, history, geography, and related subjects and are answered orally.

Humanities These questions assess knowledge in art, music, and literature and are answered orally.

The supplementary battery consists of the next five subtests, which are designed to provide additional information about a student's achievement.

Word Attack In this subtest, individuals read low oral-frequency and nonsense words. It assesses skill in applying rules of phonics and structural analysis.

Reading Vocabulary The individuals read words and give synonyms or antonyms in this subtest.

FIGURE 28.1   Relationship Between WJ-R Cognitive Tests and Composite Score

TESTS OF COGNITIVE ABILITY	Early Development Scale	Standard Scale	Extended Scale	Long Term Retrieval (Glr)	Short Term Memory (Gsm)	Processing Speed (Gs)	Auditory Processing (Ga)	Visual Processing (Gv)	Comprehension Knowledge (Gc)	Fluid Reasoning (Gf)	Oral Language	Reading	Mathematics	Written Language	Knowledge	Intra-Cognitive Discrepancies	Oral Language
STANDARD BATTERY																	
1. Memory for Names	●	●	●	●												●	
2. Memory for Sentences	●	●	●		●						●	●			●	●	
3. Visual Matching		●	●			●						●	●	●		●	
4. Incomplete Words	●	●	●				●									●	
5. Visual Closure	●	●	●					●							●	●	
6. Picture Vocabulary	●	●	●						●		●					●	
7. Analysis-Synthesis		●	●							●			●			●	
SUPPLEMENTAL BATTERY																	
8. Visual-Auditory Learning	○		●	●										●		●	
9. Memory for Words	○		●		●											●	
10. Cross Out			●			●										●	
11. Sound Blending	○		●				●					●		●	●	●	
12. Picture Recognition	○		●					●								●	●
13. Oral Vocabulary			●						●		●	●	●			●	
14. Concept Formation			●							●			●	●	●	●	●
15. Delayed Recall — Memory for Names				○													
16. Delayed Recall — Visual-Auditory Learning				○													
17. Numbers Reversed					○												●
18. Sound Patterns							○										●
19. Spatial Relations								○		○							
20. Listening Comprehension									○		●						
21. Verbal Analogies									○	○	●						

● = Tests to administer for a cluster score
○ = Tests which can supply additional information

SOURCE: Reprinted from the Woodcock-Johnson Tests of Cognitive Ability–Standard and Supplemental Batteries Examiner's Manual (Woodcock & Mather, 1989a, p. 12). Used with permission of The Riverside Publishing Company, Chicago, Illinois.

Quantitative Concepts   This subtest assesses knowledge of mathematical concepts and vocabulary.

Proofing   This subtest assesses individuals' ability to recognize and correct errors in capitalization, diction, punctuation, and spelling.

Writing Fluency   This timed subtest presents individuals with either stimulus pictures or three words; the individuals must write appropriate responses to these. Separate scores are obtained for punctuation and capitalization, spelling, usage, and handwriting.

As shown in Figure 28.2, these subtests can be combined into five Achievement Clusters (Broad Reading, Broad Mathematics, Broad Written Language, Broad Knowledge, and Skills) and six skill areas (Basic Reading Skills, Reading Comprehen-

FIGURE 28.2   **Relationship Between WJ-R Achievement Tests and Composite Score**

TESTS OF ACHIEVEMENT	Early Development	Reading: Broad Reading	Reading: Basic Skills	Reading: Comprehension	Mathematics: Broad Mathematics (Gq)	Mathematics: Basic Skills	Mathematics: Reasoning	Written Language: Broad Written Language	Written Language: Basic Skills	Written Language: Expression	Written Language: P.S.U	Written Language: Handwriting	Broad Knowledge	Skills	Wide Achievement Discrepancies
STANDARD BATTERY															
22. Letter-Word Identification	●	●	●											●	●
23. Passage Comprehension		●		●											●
24. Calculation					●	●									●
25. Applied Problems	●				●		●							●	●
26. Dictation	●							●	●					●	●
27. Writing Samples								●		●	●				●
28. Science	●												●		●
29. Social Studies	●												●		●
30. Humanities	●												●		●
SUPPLEMENTAL BATTERY															
31. Word Attack			●												
32. Reading Vocabulary				●											
33. Quantitative Concepts							●								
34. Proofing										●		●			
35. Writing Fluency											●				

SOURCE: Reprinted from the Woodcock-Johnson Tests of Achievement—Standard and Supplemental Batteries Examiner's Manual (Woodcock & Mather, 1989a, p. 12). Used with permission of The Riverside Publishing Company, Chicago, Illinois.

sion, Basic Mathematics Skills, Mathematics Reasoning, Basic Writing Skills, and Written Expression).

SCORES

Raw scores from the subtests are converted to *W*-scores, and *W*-scores are combined into cluster scores. *W*-scores, or derived Rasch scores, are equal-interval scores with a mean of approximately 500 for fifth-graders.[2] The psychometric basis for this score, item-response theory, is still not well understood by many practitioners. Thus, *W*-scores may not be readily interpretable.

Although conversion to age or grade equivalents[3] is easier for the WJ-R than for the first edition, these

scores have severe limitations. Percentiles and standard scores are readily understood and used by most practitioners and should be stressed. Conversion to age or grade scores still appears to be tedious, time-consuming, and so complex that examiners may be prone to error. In addition, the WJ-R uses Relative Mastery Indexes (RMIs). These scores predict success as a ratio; for example, a relative mastery index of 60/90 means that an individual will probably achieve 60 percent success on tasks on which peers will achieve 90 percent. Finally, normative data for a variety of differences are available. Interpretation of

2. See Appendix 6 for a general description of Rasch scaling and item-response theory.

3. The WJ-R uses an extended age- and grade-score scale that provides a hybrid of percentiles and equivalents. A superscript denotes the percentile rank for a person attaining the highest or lowest equivalent. For example, an age equivalent of 33[75] indicates that 33 is the highest age equivalent that can be determined and the raw score is at the 75th percentile for that age equivalent.

a difference is based on the actual performance of individuals rather than being estimated mathematically. For example, in evaluating a difference between cognitive ability and achievement, the average achievement of individuals with the same cognitive ability is used to compare the obtained achievement of a student with the expected achievement.

NORMS

WJ-R norms are based on the performances of 6,359 individuals living in more than one hundred communities. A stratified random sampling plan was used to locate individuals. The sample was weighted, and the total sample corresponds closely (within 2 percent) to the 1980 U.S. census on relevant characteristics such as region, community size, sex, race, and so forth. Correspondence of the sample at specific ages to the census data is not presented.

RELIABILITY

Information about the WJ-R's reliability is incompletely reported. Except for the timed subtests, no data on score stability are reported.[4] The reliability information that is reported is for selected ages (2, 4, 6, 9, 13, and 18) and age ranges (30–39, 50–59, and 70–79). Odd-even correlations, corrected by the Spearman-Brown formula, were used to estimate reliability for each untimed subtest, and test-retest correlations were used to estimate the stability of timed subtests. All the reliabilities for the Broad Cognitive and Achievement Clusters exceed .90, so it is probably a safe assumption that the Broad Clusters are also reliable enough at the missing ages to facilitate decision making for individual students. However, the same assumption should not be made for subtests and other cluster scores. The specific estimates of reliability are variable and often fall below the desirable minimum of .90. Moreover, we could not recognize consistent patterns of increasing or decreasing relia-

bility by age within subtests and other clusters. Therefore, one should not presume that the reliabilities of subtests and other clusters at missing ages are sufficient for making important educational and psychological decisions about individual students.

Cognitive Battery Of the 157 age-by-subtest reliabilities reported, 54 percent are less than .90, and 22 percent are less than .80. The stability of the two timed tests equaled or exceeded .80 at only three ages. Consequently, the subtests generally are not sufficiently reliable for making important decisions for individuals. On the extended scale, the scores for specific abilities are more reliable. Of the fifty-six age-by-subtest reliability coefficients reported for this scale, sixteen are less than .90, and of these sixteen only three are less than .80.

Achievement Battery All the reliability information is presented by age, even though reliability by grade is usually more relevant. Of the seventy-four age-by-subtest reliabilities reported for the Standard Battery, 46 percent are less than .90, and 4 percent are less than .80. Of the twenty-nine age-by-subtest reliabilities reported for the Supplementary Battery, 44 percent are less than .90, and 3 percent are less than .80. Of the twenty-eight age-by-subtest stability coefficients, 75 percent are less than .90, and 21 percent are less than .80. Four of the forty-four reliabilities for the clusters based on the Supplementary Battery are below .90.

VALIDITY

Careful item selection is consistent with claims for the content validity of both the Cognitive Battery and the Achievement Battery.[5] The items within subtests appear appropriate and carefully prepared.

The evidence of concurrent validity comes from studies using three-, nine-, and seventeen-year-olds.

---

4. Neither the length of time between test and retest nor the expected change in scores between retests is indicated.

5. As is the case for all commercially prepared achievement measures, test users must exercise great caution in applying test scores to specific curricula.

For the Cognitive Battery, scores on the WJ-R Broad Cognitive Clusters were compared with performances on other intellectual measures appropriate for individuals at the ages tested. For example, at age 3 the criterion measures included the Stanford-Binet (fourth edition) and the Boehm Tests of Basic Concepts, among others. The correlations between the WJ-R and criterion measures were in the range of .46 to .73. For the Achievement Battery, scores on the WJ-R Broad Achievement Clusters were also compared to scores on appropriate achievement measures (for example, BASIS, K-ABC, KTEA, WRAT-R, and so forth). The pattern and magnitude of correlations suggest that the WJ-R is measuring skills similar to those measured by other achievement tests.

To establish construct validity, the authors examined the intercorrelations among subtests within each battery. As expected, subtests assessing the same broad cognitive ability or achievement area usually correlated more highly with each other than with subtests assessing different cognitive abilities or areas of achievement. Further evidence of construct validity comes from comparisons of groups of exceptional persons (that is, gifted, learning-disabled, and mentally retarded individuals) with nonexceptional persons. The means for each group of exceptional persons are arrayed as expected for the cognitive and achievement clusters: Gifted individuals earn higher scores than normal individuals who, in turn, earn higher scores than learning-disabled individuals; learning-disabled individuals earn higher scores than mentally retarded individuals.

Summary

The WJ-R (Woodcock & Johnson, 1989) provides a comprehensive assessment of cognitive and academic ability throughout the life span. There are sixteen standard subtests and nineteen supplementary subtests. A variety of scores are available, although conversion is often awkward. WJ-R norms are based on a large and representative sample of the United States. No data on interscorer agreement are reported; except for the timed subtests, no data on score stability are reported. Reliabilities reported are for selected ages, not for grades. All the reliabilities reported for the Broad Cognitive and Broad Achievement Clusters exceed .90, so these scores are probably reliable at all ages. The reliabilities of subtests and other clusters are variable, so scores on these subtests probably should not be used in educational decision making. For a new device, the WJ-R appears to have adequate validity.

Coping with Dilemmas in Current Practice

The general problems raised by diagnostic systems are often the same as those raised in the measurement of the domains that are included in the systems. Methods for coping with the problems are also the same. For example, when a diagnostic system examines achievement, the question of curriculum match must be addressed.

One problem is particularly noteworthy. The theoretical constructs on which diagnostic systems are based often force the assessor to interpret behavior samples in novel and unusual ways. The K-ABC provides an example. Simultaneous and sequential processing are proposed as measures of intelligence. However, such an orientation to intellectual assessment is quite revolutionary. For many diagnosticians, a considerably larger base of research support is necessary before they can accept the K-ABC's orientation. We believe it is preferable to defer acceptance of novel theoretical orientations until a firm base of research indicates their validity. Until such research is available, patience and skepticism may serve the tester well.

SUMMARY

Two diagnostic systems—assessment devices sampling behaviors in multiple domains—were reviewed in this chapter: the K-ABC and the WJ-R. Each system offers the advantage of being standardized on one sample for all its domains. Therefore, differences between domains within a particular diagnostic system do not result from differences in standardization samples, and the tester is freed from a previously uncontrolled source of error in the examination of intraindividual differences. Other than sharing this common advantage, the diagnostic systems considered in this chapter differ sharply from each other.

The Kaufman Assessment Battery for Children has four components: a Sequential Processing Scale, a Simultaneous Processing Scale, an Achievement Scale, and an optional Nonverbal Scale. The first two scales are derived from a model of intellectual function that stresses how people process information; this model is different from the models on which many other measures of intelligence are based (a general intellectual factor, g).

The Woodcock-Johnson Psychoeducational Battery–Revised (WJ-R) is a comprehensive system designed to assess cognitive functioning and achievement. The cognitive battery is based on the Horn-Cattell theory of fluid and crystallized intelligence. Although the domains assessed and their interpretations are well within the mainstream of modern testing, the methodology used to develop the test is quite different from that used to develop most other tests. The WJ-R uses Rasch's model of item-response theory. In this model, selection of test items and the development of norms are based on a set of assumptions and procedures that are quite different from the assumptions and methods used in the more traditional models discussed earlier in this book. Thus, much of the technical discussion of test development and some of the derived scores that are available may be unfamiliar to traditionally trained readers.

Each diagnostic system is intended by its authors to be used in its entirety, but some practicing psychologists use only parts of a system. For example, it is not uncommon for a psychologist to use the Wechsler Intelligence Scale for Children–Revised in conjunction with the achievement battery from the Woodcock-Johnson Psychoeducational Battery–Revised or the achievement scale from the Kaufman Assessment Battery for Children. Although such practices do not give a diagnostician the advantage of a shared normative sample, they do make sense; relevant domains are assessed in a way that provides the tester with technically adequate and meaningful information. In the final analysis, diagnostic systems provide additional ways and domains for assessment.

STUDY QUESTIONS

1. What instructional implications can you derive from the K-ABC?
2. To what extent does the K-ABC provide a nondiscriminatory assessment?
3. Identify three potential difficulties that users may face in using the Woodcock-Johnson Psychoeducational Battery–Revised.

ADDITIONAL READING

Journal of Special Education, Fall 1984 issue. (The entire issue is a symposium on the Kaufman Assessment Battery.)

McGrew, K. S. (1994). *Clinical interpretation of the Woodcock-Johnson Tests of Cognitive Ability–Revised*. Boston: Allyn and Bacon.

Woodcock, R. (1990). Theoretical foundations of the WJ-R measures of cognitive ability. *Journal of Psychoeducational Assessment, 8*, 244–246.

Chapter 29

Developmental Appraisal

*I*nfants, toddlers, and preschoolers present special challenges to examiners both in terms of how they should be assessed and in terms of what should be assessed. Traditional assessment practices in which an examiner asks a question and the student responds can be very difficult for very young children. Their language development may be limited; thus, they may not completely understand even simple questions and oral requests. In addition, very young children are frequently too uncooperative to be tested—they may be frightened of strangers and too shy to respond, or they may simply refuse to respond. The assessment process is further complicated because, obviously, young children are not simply miniature adults. Their behavior is molar and undifferentiated. The typical domains in which youngsters are assessed (that is, communication and language, motor development, social behavior, and self-help skills) are not independent. Babies fuss with their bodies as well as their voices. Although downward extensions of many measures may be used with children, the practice of assessing infants, toddlers, and preschool children is unique, because infants and preschool children are qualitatively different from children of elementary school age.

To engage in accurate assessment at this level requires a good working knowledge of three areas. First, examiners must understand the course of normal development for infants and preschoolers. They must also know about the organization and meaning of infant behavior. Many of the assessments are based on developmental milestones (that is, significant developmental accomplishments such as using oral language, walking, and so forth). Although children's development is variable, when children are delayed in their attainment of developmental milestones, they are usually thought of as being at risk for later problems. Second, examiners must understand the environments in which infants, toddlers, and preschool children spend their time. Thus, those who assess infants and preschool children must understand family systems and functioning, and they must understand the role of culture in child rearing. In short, examiners must be able to work with families and caregivers from a variety of backgrounds in gathering assessment information. Finally, examiners must be flexible in how assessment information is gathered. Rather than relying on tests, examiners often must use direct observation, parent interviews, rating scales, and structured play situations to gather information.

THE IMPETUS FOR ASSESSMENT OF INFANTS, TODDLERS, AND PRESCHOOL CHILDREN

School systems are playing an increasingly important role in assessment and intervention with infants, toddlers, and preschool children. Much of this activity is in direct response to legislation mandating that schools serve very young students with disabilities. In the recent past, very young children with disabilities received services from physicians, hospitals, developmental achievement centers in communities, or from community mental health centers. Public schools now have responsibility for delivering services to these children and are now seen as legitimate providers of service.

Two factors have contributed to the push for early intervention and the assessment activities associated with it. First, developmental psychologists increasingly have shown the importance of early experience in human development. More importantly, they have shown that early experience is malleable and demonstrated the developmental plasticity of intelligence. (Earlier, psychologists thought that intelligence was fixed, so there was little reason to intervene in children's development to try to influence their later accomplishments.) Second, the federal government now sponsors early intervention programs, especially those designed for poor children, and federal legislation has mandated early intervention for students with disabilities.

The Handicapped Children's Early Education Assistance Act, passed by Congress in 1968, established the Handicapped Children's Early Education Model Program, which led to establishment of Child Service Demonstration Centers designed to show the effectiveness of early-intervention programs. In 1975, as part of Public Law 94-142, schools were required to serve children as young as age 5.

Major advances occurred with passage of Public Law 99-457 in 1986. This law has two major provisions, Part B and Part H, that pertain to assessment of infants, toddlers, and preschool children who are handicapped. Part B of the law required that states have available by 1990–1991 services for children ages 3 to 5 who are handicapped. This part of the law extended Public Law 94-142 to children as young as age 3. States can serve any child who meets the criteria for one or more conditions specified in Public Law 94-142, but they do not have to assign the child to a category. That is, they do not have to label preschool children in order to serve them. Part H extends services to children from birth to 3 years of age who:

- Have a physical or mental condition (such as cerebral palsy or Down syndrome) that has a high probability of resulting in developmental delay
- Are at risk medically or environmentally for developmental delay
- Have delays in one or more of the following areas: cognitive, physical, language and speech, psychosocial, or self-help

Part H also requires the development of an Individual Family Service Plan (IFSP) by a multidisciplinary team who meet with the parents. The IFSP is used to guide intervention with an infant, toddler, or preschool child and must include eight components:

1. A statement of the child's present levels of development (cognitive, speech and language, psychosocial, motor, and self-help)
2. A statement of the family's strengths and needs relating to enhancing the child's development
3. A statement of major outcomes expected to be achieved by the child and family
4. The criteria, procedures, and time lines for determining progress
5. The specific early-intervention services necessary to meet the unique needs of the child and family, including the method, frequency, and intensity of service
6. The projected dates for initiation of services and their expected duration
7. The name of the case manager
8. The procedures for transition to early intervention in the preschool program

Entitlement for Infants, Toddlers, and Preschoolers

We use developmental tests with young children much as we use achievement and intelligence tests with students who are enrolled in schools, as measures of attainment before formal schooling. Since special education services are frequently available for preschoolers, some form of assessment is needed to ascertain whether a child needs or is entitled to some form of special service.

The Early and Periodic Screening, Diagnosis, and Treatment (EPSDT) program is a nationwide screening and referral-to-service program established in 1972. The goals of the program are (1) early identification of young children with special needs and (2) connection of children from low-income families with medical services. Those who screen young children are often part of "Child Find" activities. Child Find is defined as "A systematic process of identifying infants and children who are eligible or potentially eligible for enrollment in intervention programs" (Wolery, 1989, p. 120).

Neurobiological Appraisal

Early-childhood special educators now are required to assess and develop interventions for newborn infants. Such assessment typically involves neurobiological

TABLE 29.1   **Tests Used in Assessment of Newborns**

Assessment of Preterm Infant Behavior (Als, Lester, Tronick, & Brazelton, 1982)
Graham-Rosenblith Behavior Test for Neonates (Rosenblith, 1961)
Neurological Assessment of the Preterm and Full Term Newborn Infant (Dubowitz &
    Dubowitz, 1981)
Neonatal Behavioral Assessment Scale (Brazelton, 1984)
Naturalistic Observation of the Preterm Infant (Als, 1984)

appraisal, which has its origins in medicine (specifically in pediatrics and neurology) rather than in education. Neurobiological appraisal involves assessment in four areas: neurological integrity, behavioral organization and needs, temperament, and state of consciousness. When assessors examine neurological integrity, they look for signs of brain injury by looking at reflexes, postural responses, and developmental level. They assess behavioral organization by looking at the infant's competence in attending and responding to social stimuli. They examine temperament by looking at how infants relate to their caregivers (mothers or others). In doing so, they look at sensitivity, involvement, and responsiveness. The tests listed in Table 29.1 are used to assess such things as a neonate's heart rate, color, respiratory regularity, visceral signs, posture, muscle tone, movements, states, attention, and quality of responsiveness. The fourth major area assessed in appraisals of infants is state of consciousness. Prechtl (1974) describes six states: quiet sleep, active sleep, drowsy, quiet awake, active awake, and distress. Infants are not assessed when they are asleep; the other states are defined in Table 29.2.

TABLE 29.2   **Infant States of Consciousness**

State	Description
Drowsy	Eyes open and close; eyes are "heavy-lidded" and have dull, glazed appearance. Infant may respond to sensory stimuli although responses are usually delayed.
Quiet Awake	Eyes wide open; limited motor activity, child is quite alert to environment, primarily through visual modality.
Active Awake	Eyes wide open with accompanying motor activity; occasional periods of fussiness; increased sensitivity to disturbing contextual stimuli.
Distress	Characterized by crying, grimacing, and increased motor activity

SOURCE: From Bailey, D. B., & Rouse, T. L. (1989), Procedural considerations in assessing infants and preschoolers with handicaps. In D. B. Bailey & M. Wolery (Eds.), *Assessing infants and preschoolers with handicaps.* Columbus, OH: Merrill. pp. 48–49. Copyright © 1989 by Merrill Publishing.

People who assess infants must take into account the infant's state. They should contact nursery attendants or parents and find out when the infant is alert and then arrange to test the infant at that time. Those who assess infants must be careful not to disturb them unduly. Infants show distress when approached by strangers. Bailey and Rouse (1989) report that "beginning at developmental age 6–8 months and continuing through approximately 18 months, infants show varying degrees of distress when approached by unfamiliar adults" (p. 49). Distance matters—so keep your distance. Infants show a better response to strangers when held by their caregivers. It is generally recommended that parents be present when infants are assessed. It is also strongly recommended that preschoolers be assessed in the *absence* of their parent(s). The exception, of course, is when toddlers or preschoolers are extremely fearful or shy. Many other factors must also be considered in assessing infants and preschoolers. Bailey and Rouse (1989, p. 50) state that "infants and preschoolers may have high activity levels, be easily distracted, display variable states and attention spans, be wary of strangers, and display inconsistent performance in strange situations."

Instructional Planning

Early-childhood special educators now find themselves involved in the planning of instructional programs, treatments, or interventions with two new populations of children: medically high-risk infants (for example, low-birth-weight infants) and special-needs infants and toddlers (for example, drug addicted or HIV positive infants or those with developmental disabilities). When examiners assess newborn infants, they do so in order to provide information to (and to receive information from) physicians, parents, and community early-intervention programs—for the express purpose of developing interventions for these very young children.

Program Evaluation

Many measures currently available for use with very young children were developed exclusively for measuring attainment of goals in Head Start programs. Kelley and Surbeck (1985) report that well over two hundred assessment instruments were constructed and published during between 1960 and 1980. In the 1960s Congress authorized the establishment of a set of programs known collectively as the Handicapped Children's Early Education Program. Each of these programs was required to have an evaluation plan. The shortage of instruments that could be used to assess student gains led to the development of many new measures.

Assessment of Readiness

School personnel frequently evaluate the school readiness of incoming students. The information from these evaluations may lead educators to recommend delaying school entrance for unready students or to track pupils into various programs. Readiness is usually considered essential for initial entry into school, although the concept of readiness can be appropriately applied at all levels of instruction.[1] Readiness for first grade or even kindergarten is generalized readiness and refers to both academic and social readiness. Academic readiness is most often thought of in terms of reading readiness but properly includes readiness for all academic instruction. We must also consider a child's readiness for the social milieu of school. In school, children must follow the directions of an adult other than their parent or guardian, must enter into cooperative ventures with their peers, must not present a physical threat to themselves or others, must have mastered many self-help skills such as toileting, and so on.

Readiness for school entry is further complicated because there are two different orientations toward the topic. The first, a *skill orientation,* was implicit in the foregoing discussion. It holds that readiness involves having developed the skills and knowledge prerequisite to *beginning* instruction. Academic and social instruction present sequential skills and knowledge that are built on previously mastered skills and knowledge. From this perspective, skills learned in school build on skills learned at home. The second orientation, a *process orientation,* is further removed from direct instruction. Readiness is viewed in terms of underlying processes (intelligence, discrimination, and so on) that are believed to be necessary for the acquisition of skills and knowledge. If the processes are mature or developed, the child is ready to learn, to acquire skills in developmentally appropriate ways.

Traditionally, formal readiness assessment has dealt with academic-process testing. For the most part, the tests have been norm-referenced, and the abilities that are thought to underlie all, or at least most, academic skills are the most typically tested. Thus, intelligence, or learning aptitude, which is believed to underlie all school subjects, is often a component of a readiness assessment. Indeed, intelligence tests were developed to predict school success and are often validated against achievement tests or teacher ratings. Entry into formal school programs is often predicated on a mental age of 6 or more years. Intellectual readiness can be assessed by any of the tests discussed in Chapters 17 and 18. Perceptual-motor development is also thought to underlie school achievement, particularly reading (see Chapter 25). Readiness tests often contain many items or subtests that assess perceptual-motor factors. Although these items and tests are usually less predictive of school achievement than are intelligence tests, many

---

1. For example, to be ready for algebra instruction, the student must have mastered more basic mathematical concepts and operations. Readiness for higher-level academic instruction is usually conceptualized as mastery of prerequisite material.

people believe they are an important component of readiness. Language development (see Chapter 23) is obviously important for school success. Children must be fluent in the idiomatic English of their peers; they must also understand and use standard (formal) English.

The assessment of school readiness is *not* a unique kind of measurement. What makes a test a readiness test is not what the test measures or how the measuring is done; rather, three distinctive features make a test a readiness test. First, readiness tests are typically administered before school entry or during kindergarten. Second, the tests are used to predict initial school success and to identify children who perform so poorly that they need either remedial–compensatory educational programs or delayed school entry. Third, readiness tests often contain the word *readiness* in the test name.

TECHNICAL CONSIDERATIONS IN SCHOOL READINESS

School readiness is a deceptively simple concept. Knowledge of a child's readiness can provide the teacher with invaluable information that may ensure that the child enters an instructional sequence at an appropriate level—but knowledge of a child's lack of readiness can create a destructive self-fulfilling prophecy that may actually hamper a child's development. Since decisions made on the basis of readiness tests are so important, the validity of the tests is crucial. The purpose of readiness tests is twofold:

1. To predict who is not ready for formal entry into academic instruction
2. To predict who will profit from either remedial or compensatory educational programs in which readiness skills or processes are developed

The academic development of many children must be followed and documented. When the same children are followed and their progress is recorded, the data are called *longitudinal*. Readiness data used in both standardization and validation *must* be longitudinal. Specifically, to validate a readiness test, a large number of children must be tested before they enter school and then be retested after they have received instruction in school (generally at the end of the first grade). Only in this way can we determine if children with poor scores on the readiness test perform poorly during actual schooling.

When readiness tests do identify accurately which children will do poorly in school, the educator is faced with a choice of admitting a child to the regular school program or taking another action. If the child is admitted to the regular school program, the only justification for having administered the test is that it gave the classroom teacher sufficient information to take steps to overcome the child's lack of readiness. Such a use of readiness tests is not justified when one views readiness as physiological maturation. However, if readiness is viewed as having skills or processes susceptible to environmental manipulation, there is some justification for using readiness tests before placing children in regular school programs.

If the child is not admitted to the regular school program, the educator can choose either to delay entry into the regular program or to provide remedial or compensatory preschool or kindergarten programs. These alternatives should be considered only in light of research data indicating that readiness tests are effective predictors of differential programming. In essence, aptitude-treatment interaction (ATI) research is required to validate these uses. As an illustration of how ATI research might be accomplished, consider a school district that wants to learn if it is a good practice to delay school entry for children who score poorly on a readiness test. It would be necessary to administer the test to a large number of children before admission to school, identify those children who scored poorly enough to warrant delayed entry, and then divide these children randomly into two groups, admitting one group to school and delaying the entry of the other for, say, one year. After both groups had completed their first year of regular schooling (kindergarten or first grade), the groups would be compared on some measure of school success.

Two of several possible outcomes are presented in Figure 29.1. In part a, no matter what their readiness score, children perform better if their school entry is delayed. For children earning low scores on the readiness measure, subsequent school achievement is better when their school entrance is delayed than when their entrance occurs immediately (that is, A' is greater than A); for children earning high scores on the readiness measure, subsequent school achievement is also better when their school entrance is delayed (that is, B' is greater than B). Thus, in this hypothetical example, delaying school entrance is better for children regardless of their scores on the readiness test. In part b, a different hypothetical outcome is illustrated. Here, for children earning low scores on the readiness measure, subsequent school performance is better when their school entrance is delayed than when their entrance occurs immediately (that is, A' is greater than A). For children earning high scores on the readiness measure, however, subsequent school achievement is better when their school entrance occurs immediately (that is, B is greater than B'). This hypothetical outcome would support a policy of delaying school entrance for children with poor readiness and a policy of timely enrollment for students with high levels of readiness.

From the foregoing discussion, it is apparent that the validation of readiness tests is not a simple or quick task. Some validation studies will require a minimum of one year and may take two years. Studies must take place in a variety of schools, and distinctive features of the programs and curricula used in the schools must be carefully noted, because a particular readiness test might predict well who would profit from one type of remedial or compensatory program but be useless for predicting the impacts of other programs.

Although the discussion so far has stressed predictive validity, two additional points must be emphasized. First, reliability should not be overlooked. As you

FIGURE 29.1   **Possible Interactions Between Readiness and Delayed School Entry**

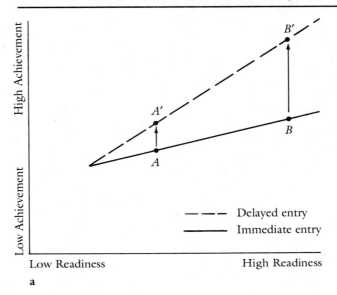

a

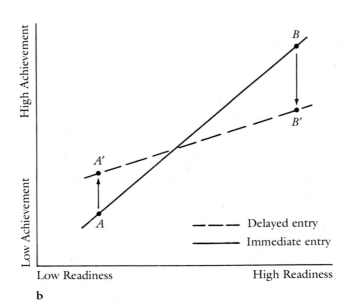

b

may recall from Chapter 7, reliability has a definite effect on validity; an unreliable test must have poor predictive validity. Because readiness tests are routinely used to make important educational decisions about individual children, such tests must meet the highest technical standards. Second, there is little correlation between measures of infant abilities and measures of preschool abilities in children within the normal range of intelligence. This finding has led to much debate about whether the lack of a relationship reflects defects in the instruments at this level or the nature of infant development and the difference between behavioral repertoires of infants and preschoolers.

TESTS USED WITH PRESCHOOLERS, TODDLERS, AND INFANTS

Bayley Scales of Infant Development, Second Edition

*T*he second edition of the Bayley Scales of Infant Development (BSID-II) (Bayley, 1993) shares the format and rationale of the earlier edition. The BSID-II remains a norm-referenced, individually administered test intended to assess developmental functioning of children. However, the norms have been updated, and the age range has been extended through 42 months. In addition, sixty-three new items were added to the Mental Scale and twenty-nine old items were deleted; forty-four new items were added to the Motor Scale and eight old items were deleted. The Behavior Rating Scale was completely revised.

The BSID-II has three subscales. The Mental Scale assesses memory, problem solving, conceptualization, language, and social skills. The Motor Scale assesses fine and gross motor skills. Items assessing mental and motor ability are mixed together; this format requires examiners to identify which items go on each scale and tally them separately. General basal and ceiling rules apply to all items together not individually to the Mental or Motor Scales. The Behavior Rating Scale is separate and assesses "qualitative aspects of the child's test-taking behavior" (p. 1) and allows an examiner to rate arousal/attention, orientation/engagement, emotional regulation, and quality of movement. This scale is completed after the Mental and Motor scales have been administered.

NORMS

The BSID-II was standardized on 1,700 children, fifty boys and fifty girls in each of seventeen age groups. Children between 1 and 6 months are grouped in one-month intervals; children between 6 and 12 months are grouped into three two-month intervals; children between the ages of 12 and 30 months are grouped in six three-month intervals; and children between 30 and 42 months are grouped in two six-month intervals. Each age group closely approximates the U.S. 1988 census update in terms of race/ethnicity, geographic region, parental education, and sex.

SCORES

Each item on the Mental and Motor Scales is scored as C (credit), NC (no credit, incorrect), RF (refused, no credit awarded), O (omit, no credit awarded), RPT (child is reported to have the skill, no credit awarded). Raw score totals for Mental and Motor are obtained by adding the credited items between the basal and ceiling to the basal. Each of these totals can be converted to a normalized standard score with a mean of 100 and a standard deviation of 15. The Mental Scale standard scores are called the Mental Development Index, and Motor Scale standard scores are called the Psychomotor Development Index. The authors also provide confidence intervals (90 percent and 95 percent) in the conversion tables for these indexes. Items can also be combined into facets, or subareas, of cognitive, language, social, and motor functioning. These scores may be of some clinical value to highly experienced examiners.

Items on the Behavior Rating Scale are scored on a five-point scale. Composites can be converted to percentile ranks for Motor Quality, Attention/Arousal, Orientation/Engagement, Emotional Regulation, and the total score. Classifications of behavior (within normal limits, questionable, and non-optimal) are also available from the conversion tables.

RELIABILITY

Alphas were used to estimate the internal consistency of the Mental Scale and the Motor Scale at each age. For the Mental Scale, alpha ranged from .78 to .93; nine of the seventeen coefficients equaled or exceeded .90. For the Motor Scale, alpha ranged from .75 to .91; one coefficient exceeded .90. Alphas associated with the total score from the Behavior Rating Scale ranged from .82 to .92; six of the seventeen coefficients equaled or exceeded .90. Alphas for subscales of the Behavior Rating Scale ranged from .64 with only two coefficients reaching .90. Information about the BSID-II's stability is presented for three age ranges. Thus, the reliability of the Mental Scale and Behavior Rating Scale (total) is sufficient for making important decisions about children in about a third to half of the age ranges; the reliability of the Motor scale is usually inadequate for making important decisions.

Test-retest correlations for the Mental scale were .83, .91, and .87; correlations for the Motor Scale were .77, .79, and .78; correlations for the total Behavior Rating Scale were .55, .90, and .60. The evidence presented in the BSID-II manual indicates limited stability. However, given the rapid development of young children, this finding should be expected.

Interscorer agreement (between the examiner and an observer of the examination) for fifty-one children varied. For the Mental Scale, the correlation between scorers was .96; for the Motor Scale, .75. For the total Behavior Rating Scale, correlations (for two age groups) were .70 and .88. Thus, interscorer agreement appears adequate only for the Mental Scale.

VALIDITY

Several pages of the BSID-II manual review research conducted on the previous edition. However, to the extent that items have been changed, these studies do not establish the BSID-II's validity but rather set the stage for new research. Project staff and subject matter experts as well as users of the scale reviewed the content of the BSID in preparing new items. Particular attention was paid to assessing potential racial or sex bias.

Empirical evidence of the validity of the BSID-II is very limited. Some evidence that the Mental and Motor Scales measure different abilities comes from the procedure for placing the items on each scale. Initially items were placed on the basis of experts' judgments; during field testing, item-total correlations were examined to ascertain if a particular item did indeed relate more closely with the Mental or the Motor Scale. The same procedures were followed for the facets. However, factor analytic techniques were not used to establish the independence of the two scales or the facets.

More empirical evidence was gathered for the Behavior Rating Scale. Factor analyses established that there were two factors (that is, Attention/Arousal and Motor Quality) for children from 1 to 5 months old and three factors (that is, Orientation/Engagement, Motor Quality, and Emotional Regulation) for older children. The authors also compared the performance of children on the Mental and Motor Scales of the BSID-II with their ratings on the BRS. The pattern of correlations was as would be expected: Items requiring orientation or engagement correlated more highly with the BRS Orientation/

Engagement factor than with other factors; items requiring motor responses correlated more highly with the BRS Motor Quality factor than with other factors; and items that have an emotional component correlate more highly with the BRS Emotional Regulation factor than with the other factors. Finally, BRS ratings were modestly correlated with classifications based on the Mental and Motor Scales (hardly surprising, since the items from the scales correlate with the BRS factors).

SUMMARY

The BSID-II is a norm-referenced, individually administered test intended to assess developmental functioning of children between 1 and 42 months of age. The BSID-II has three subscales: the Mental Scale, the Motor Scale, and the Behavior Rating Scale. The scales' norms appear representative in terms of race/ethnicity, geographic region, parental education, and sex. Raw scores for the Mental and Motor Scales are converted to a normalized standard score with a mean of 100 and a standard deviation of 15. Scores from the Behavior Rating Scale can be converted to percentile ranks for Motor Quality, Attention/Arousal, Orientation/Engagement, Emotional Regulation, and the total score. Internal consistency of the Mental Scale is adequate for making important decisions for children at about half of the ages; the consistency of the Motor Scale and the total Behavior Rating Scale is adequate for about one-third of the ages. As should be expected for scales intended for use with this population, scores are moderately stable. Interscorer agreement is adequate only for the Mental Scale. Although the content of the BSID-II appears comprehensive and appropriate, only limited evidence for criterion-related and construct validity is reported.

Infant Mullen Scales of Early Learning

*T*he Infant Mullen Scales of Early Learning (IMSEL) (Mullen, 1989) is an individually administered, norm-referenced test intended to assess mental and motor ability in infants from birth to 36 months of age. Basal and ceiling rules are used. The thirty-seven items in the IMSEL are arranged in the following five scales.

Gross Motor Base Scale (GMB) Items in this test require muscle control, balance, and coordination of large muscle activities. Examples of items (at the oldest age in the level where the item is placed) include lifting and rotating head (4 months), standing unassisted (14 months), and hopping on either foot (39 months).

Visual Receptive Organization Abilities Scale (VRO) Items in this test require visual localization, tracking, and scanning. Examples of items include inspecting own hand (7 months), finding a partially hidden ring (11 months), and nesting cups (27 months).

Visual Expressive Organization Abilities Scale (VEO) Items in this test require fine motor skill (primarily manipulation), hand patterns, and prewriting readiness. Examples of items include reaching and holding with palmar grasp (7 months), taking a Cheerio with a refined pincer grasp (15 months), and stringing three or more beads (39 months).

Language Receptive Organization Abilities Scale (LRO) Items in this test require auditory discrimination and auditory/oculomotor ability. Examples of items include looking at a person who is speaking (4 months), following simple commands (20 months), and comprehending action words (39 months).

Language Expressive Organization Abilities Scale (LEO) Items in this test assess overall verbal expressive abilities. Some examples are smiling and making happy sounds (4 months), using one word (15 months), and repeating numbers (33 months).

SCORES

Clear and specific scoring criteria are provided for each of the thirty-seven items. Suggested starting points are also given in the manual. Because rules for establishing ceilings and basals are used, children are not required to complete all items. Each scale receives a score (age scores, developmental stages, and normalized *T*-scores). Test ages are calculated by adding the number of passed items above the basal to the number of items below the basal and finding, on the test protocol, the number of months that correspond to this sum.[2] Developmental stages are determined by locating the developmental stage (one through eight) in which the test age is located.[3] The number correct can also be converted to *T*-scores by using tables based on the child's age. *T*-scores of 35 or less, in the author's judgment, indicate significant delay and warrant early intervention.

NORMS

No sampling plan was described in the IMSEL manual. The norms, which required eight years to develop, consist of 1,231 children from one hundred different sites. Norm tables are available for the following sixteen age groups:

- 1 month
- 2 months
- 3 months (children 3 and 4 months old)
- 4 months (children 4 and 5 months old)
- 6 months (children 6 and 7 months old)
- 8 months (children 8 and 9 months old)

2. No data are presented in the test manual to indicate how ages were assigned to specific items. Working backward from *T*-scores to test ages indicates that ages are only approximately correct.
3. The basis and meaning of *developmental stage* is unclear, and no references are provided in the manual to suggest the theory underlying these stages.

- 10 months (children 10 and 11 months old)
- 12 months (children 12 and 13 months old)
- 14 months (children 14 and 15 months old)
- 16 months (children 16 to 18 months old)
- 19 months (children 19 to 21 months old)
- 22 months (children 22 to 24 months old)
- 25 months (children 25 to 27 months old)
- 28 months (children 28 to 30 months old)
- 31 months (children 31 to 33 months old)
- 36 months (children 34 to 39 months old)

However, sampling was based on only eleven groups. Because only the number of children in each sampling group is reported, it is not possible to determine the number of children in several norm groups. However, it appears that as many as nine of the eleven norm groups are based on fewer than one hundred children, an inadequate number. For geographic region, the representativeness of the normative samples varies by age; at some ages the norms closely approximate the U.S. population; at other ages they do not. The norms appear representative for sex, race (white, African American, and Asian), and parent occupation.

RELIABILITY

Three types of reliability information is presented in the IMSEL manual. Internal consistency of each subtest was estimated by coefficient alpha for three age groups: at 1–12 months, alpha ranged from .90 to .91; at 14–25 months, alpha ranged from .89 to .91; and at 28–36 months, alpha ranged from .83 to .89. Because alphas are calculated over a large range of ages, they are likely inflated by the correlation of age and item and are likely to overestimate the reliability of the subscales. Thus, the internal consistency of the subtests is sufficiently high to use the IMSEL for screening purposes but insufficiently reliable to make important educational decisions about children.

Stability was assessed by retesting sixty-eight children; average test-retest interval was two weeks. Stabilities are reported for most subtests at four age ranges: 10 to 12 months ($N = 24$, $r_{xx} = .70$–.99); 14

months (N = 15, r_{xx} = .93–.98); 16–25 months (N = 16, r_{xx} = .77–.94); and 28–36 months (N = 13, r_{xx} = .80–.98). Thus, the stability of the IMSEL varies considerably. Before making important decisions about children, examiners should make sure that IMSEL is stable for the ages of the children being assessed.

Interscorer reliability was estimated for each subtest for ten age groups. Except for GMB at 1–2 months (where r_{xx} = .78), all subtests had interscorer agreement exceeding .90. Thus, IMSEL appears to have excellent interscorer reliability.

VALIDITY

Although test items seem to represent the target domains, the author presents no specific information about how specific test items were selected. Therefore, test users must judge the IMSEL's content for themselves. Information about the criterion-related validity of the IMSEL is incompletely reported. The VRO, VEO, LRO, and LEO subscales correlate moderately (r_{xy} = .5–.6) with the total score on the Bayley Scales of Infant Development, and the GMB correlates almost perfectly (r_{xy} = .95) with the Bayley Motor Scale. Some evidence is also presented to suggest that the IMSEL is useful in discriminating children with normal development from children with developmental delays and in discriminating subgroups of children with developmental delays.

Because the IMSEL consists of five independent subtests and because no total score is used, one would expect some evidence of factor independence of the subtests. No factor analyses were conducted; rather, subtest intercorrelations were examined. However, in our opinion the correlations do not suggest subtest independence.

SUMMARY

The IMSEL is an individually administered, norm-referenced test intended for use with children from birth to 36 months of age. The test has five subtests: Gross Motor Base, Visual Receptive Organization, Visual Expressive Organization, Language Receptive Organization, and Language Expressive Organization. The IMSEL is constructed as an age test, but test ages can be converted to normalized T-scores. The technical information that appears in the test manual is very incomplete. With that caveat, the IMSEL's norms appear to be generally representative. Interscorer reliability is excellent, but stability varies by age. Internal consistency is generally only suitable for screening purposes. The information on content validity presented in the IMSEL manual is inadequate, although our inspection of the items suggests content very similar to other developmental measures. The IMSEL appears to discriminate youngsters who are developmentally delayed from those who are not.

Mullen Scales of Early Learning

*T*he Mullen Scales of Early Learning (MSEL) (Mullen, 1992) is an individually administered, norm-referenced test intended to assess modality performance and identify learning ability, learning disability, and mental retardation in children between 21 and 63 months of age. The MSEL differs from the IMSEL in that MSEL does not have a scale for gross motor ability. The 144 items in the MSEL are equally distributed among the test's four subtests. Each subtest is subdivided into nine half-year age intervals, and basal and ceiling rules are used in each subtest. The subtests are as follows.

Visual Receptive Organization Scale (VRO)
Items in this test require visual localization, tracking, and scanning. Examples of items (at specific age levels) include discriminating forms (24 months), matching letters (48 months), and demonstrating memory for form (66 months).

Visual Expressive Organization Scale (VEO)
Items in this test require fine motor skill, eye-hand coordination, and motor planning and control. Examples of items (at specific age levels) include copying a vertical line (24 months), stringing beads (36 months), and copying a square (60 months).

Language Receptive Organization Scale (LRO)
Items in this test require auditory discrimination and auditory/motor ability. Examples of items include comprehending action words (30 months), following three unrelated commands (54 months), and knowing left and right (60 months).

Language Expressive Organization Scale (LEO)
Items in this test assess overall verbal expressive abilities. Some examples are using two-word phrases (24 months), comprehending questions (36 months), and repeating sentences (60 months).

SCORES

Clear and specific scoring criteria are provided for each of the 144 items. Suggested starting points are also given in the manual. Because rules for establishing ceilings and basals are used, children are not required to complete all items. Test ages are computed for each subtest by adding 1.5 months for each item passed above the basal age.[4] Test ages can be converted to normalized *T*-scores by using tables based on the child's age. Thus, test ages correspond to different *T*-scores at different ages, and *T*-scores have the same meaning regardless of a child's age.

NORMS

No sampling plan is described in the MSEL manual. The norms, which required eight years to develop, consist of 1,016 children from one hundred different sites. Norm tables are available for the following ten age groups:

- 22 months (children 22 through 23 months old)
- 25 months (children 24 through 26 months old)
- 28 months (children from 27 to 29 months old)
- 31 months (children 30 through 32 months old)
- 36 months (children 33 through 38 months old)
- 42 months (children 39 through 44 months old)
- 48 months (children 45 through 50 months old)
- 54 months (children 51 through 56 months old)
- 60 months (children 57 through 62 months old)
- 66 months (children 63 through 68 months old)

However, sampling was based on eight groups. (The 21 to 23 month and the 24 to 26 month groups were collapsed into one group, and the 27 to 29 month and 30 to 32 month groups were collapsed into one group.)[5] Except for the collapsed age groups, the number of children in each age group is adequate (that is, between 108 and 140). For geographic region, the representativeness of the normative samples varies by age; at some ages the norms closely approximate the U.S. population while at other ages they do not. The norms appear representative for sex, race (white, African American, and Asian), and parent occupation.

RELIABILITY

Three types of reliability information are presented in the MSEL manual. Internal consistency of each subtest was estimated by coefficient alpha for four age groups: at 24–30 months, alpha ranged from .82 to .88; at 36–42 months, alpha ranged from .87 to .90; at 48–54 months, alpha ranged from .84 to .89; and at 60–66 months, alpha ranged from .74 to .83. Thus, the internal consistency of the subtests is generally insufficiently reliable for making important educational decisions about children.

Stability was assessed by retesting fifty-nine children; the average test-retest interval was two weeks). Stabilities are reported for each subtest at three age

---

4. No data are presented in the test manual that indicate how ages were assigned to specific items. Working backward from *T*-scores to test ages suggests that ages are overestimates of the age group's mean.

5. Thus, the number of children sampled does not correspond to the number of children at four ages (21–23 months, 24–26 months, 27–29 months, and 30–32 months) on whom norm conversions are based.

groups: 24 months ($N = 12$, $r_{xx} = .98–.99$); 30–42 months ($N = 16$, $r_{xx} = .86–.98$); and 48–66 months ($N = 31$, $r_{xx} = .83–.94$). Thus, the MSEL is generally stable enough to use in making important educational decisions about children.

Interscorer reliability was estimated for each subtest for three age groups: 24 months ($N = 12$), 30 months ($N = 14$), and 36–48 months. ($N = 18$). All coefficients equaled or exceeded .98. Thus, MSEL appears to have excellent interscorer reliability.

VALIDITY

Although test items seem to represent the target domains, the author presents no specific information about how specific test items were selected. Therefore, test users must judge the MSEL's content for themselves. Information about the criterion-related validity of the MSEL is incomplete. However, it appears that LRO and LEO subtests correlated highly with the auditory Comprehension and Verbal Ability subtests of the Preschool Language Assessment (r_{xx} from .78 to .95 for two age groups of children). The VEO subtest correlates highly ($r_{xy} = .94$) with the Fine Motor subtest of the Brigance Inventory of Early Development with one group of children and with the Developmental Test of Visual-Motor Integration ($r_{xy} = .81$) with a different group of children. Finally, there is some evidence that the MSEL predicts subsequent performance on the Metropolitan Readiness Tests after a one-year interval.

Because the MSEL consists of four independent subtests and because no total score is used, one would expect some evidence of factor independence of the subtests. No factor analyses were conducted; rather, subtest intercorrelations were examined. However, in our opinion the correlations do not suggest subtest independence. Strikingly absent from the manual is any indication that the MSEL is capable of identifying learning disability and mental retardation in children between 21 and 63 months of age.

SUMMARY

The MSEL is an individually administered, norm-referenced test intended for use with children between the ages of 21 and 63 months of age. The test has four subtests: Visual Receptive Organization, Visual Expressive Organization, Language Receptive Organization, and Language Expressive Organization. The MSEL is constructed as an age test, but test ages can be converted to normalized T-scores. The technical information that appears in the test manual is very incomplete. With that caveat, the MSEL's norms appears to be generally representative. Interscorer reliability is excellent, and stability is generally good. However, internal consistency is generally only suitable for screening purposes. The information related to content validity presented in the MSEL manual is inadequate although our inspection of the items suggests content very similar to other developmental measures. This similarity is borne out by extremely high concurrent validity coefficients with measures such as the Preschool Language Assessment and the Brigance Inventory of Early Development. Other validity coefficients are more modest. No evidence of MSEL's ability to identify children with learning disabilities or mental retardation is presented in the test manual.

Battelle Developmental Inventory

*T*he Battelle Developmental Inventory (BDI) (Newborg, Stock, & Wnek, 1984) is a norm-referenced, individually administered assessment battery designed to test key developmental skills in children from birth to 8 years of age. It is intended to be administered by and used by those who teach infants, toddlers, and preschool children. The BDI was initially developed by a team of investigators who were charged by the federal government with the task of evaluating the impact of the Handicapped Children's Early Education Program. The test was developed by selecting items from existing tests and organizing them into five domains: Personal-Social, Adaptive, Motor, Communication, and Cognitive. Items selected were those thought to measure developmental milestones, and gaps were filled by creating a few additional items. The Inventory was pilot tested in 1980 on about five hundred children from birth to age 8 who were living in Ohio. In 1982–1983 the test was standardized on a national sample, and the norms were recalibrated in 1987.

The BDI is used to gather data on functioning in five domains.

Personal-Social This domain assesses abilities and characteristics that enable a child to engage in meaningful social interaction. Included are measures of the frequency and quality of interactions with adults, the child's ability to express feelings and emotions, development of self-awareness and self-worth, coping, and social development.

Adaptive Domain This domain assesses the extent of a child's independent functioning and attention. Included in this domain are measures of visual and auditory attention, eating-related behaviors, dressing skills, ability to assume responsibility, and toileting.

Motor Domain This domain assesses muscle control, body coordination, locomotion, fine-muscle coordination, and perceptual-motor functioning.

Communication Domain This domain assesses the development of receptive skills and the expression of information, thoughts, and ideas.

Cognitive Domain The cognitive domain assesses ability to discriminate objects, memory, reasoning and judgment, and concept development.

Each domain has a number of subdomains, shown in Table 29.3. There are 341 items on the BDI. Each domain is published in a separate test booklet. This separation facilitates use of the test by more than one person at the same time. Data to be used in completing the response protocols are collected by (1) giving standardized test items, (2) holding interviews with the parents, and (3) making observations of the child in natural settings. There is a screening version of the BDI, which consists of 96 of the 341 items. Details on how to modify specific items for children who show specific kinds of handicaps are described in the manual.

It takes approximately 10 to 30 minutes to administer the screening version of the BDI: 10 to 15 minutes to give the scale to children who are younger than age 3 or older than age 5 and about 20 to 30 minutes to administer the screening version to those who are between 3 and 5. It takes approximately an hour to give the total BDI to children under age 3 or older than 5, and 1.5 to 2 hours to give it to children between ages 3 and 5. The authors recommend that the scale be used for the following purposes: identification of developmental strengths and weaknesses, assessment of children considered "at risk," general preschool and kindergarten screening, IEP development and instructional planning, and monitoring of pupil progress.

SCORES

Individual items on the BDI are scored using a three-point scoring system. Children receive 2 points when they respond according to a specified criterion. They earn 1 point when they attempt a response but do not meet the criterion. They earn 0 points when they cannot or will not attempt an item or when the response is an extremely poor approximation of the desired response.

As noted above, the BDI is arranged into domains and subdomains, or components. Those who use this scale can derive domain scores, component scores, or cluster scores. Scores may be obtained for the following ten major components: Personal-Social, Adaptive, Gross Motor, Fine Motor, total Motor, Receptive, Expressive, total Communication, Cognitive, and total BDI.

The BDI is scored by comparing earned scores to cutoff scores. Cutoff scores and age equivalent scores may be computed for each of the ten major scores.

TABLE 29.3   **Subdomains of the Battelle Developmental Inventory**

Domains and Subdomains	BDI Number of Items	Screening Test Number of Items
Personal-social domain	85	20
Adult interaction	18	
Expression of feelings/affect	12	
Self-concept	14	
Peer-interaction	17	
Coping	10	
Social role	14	
Adaptive domain	59	20
Attention	10	
Eating	14	
Dressing	10	
Personal responsibility	19	
Toileting	6	
Motor domain	62	20
Muscle control	6	
Body coordination	25	
Locomotion	13	
Fine muscle	18	
Perceptual motor	20	
Communication domain	39	18
Receptive	27	
Expressive	32	
Cognitive domain	56	18
Perceptual discrimination	10	
Memory	10	
Reasoning and academic skills	16	
Conceptual development	20	
Total	341	96

Three levels of cutoff are provided in the manual: 1.00, 1.50, and 2.00 standard deviations below the mean. The authors provide three cutoff levels because criteria for program eligibility differ among states. Percentile ranks are provided for each of thirty component scores that may be derived for the BDI.

NORMS

The BDI was standardized during 1982–1983 on a national sample stratified on the basis of geographic region, race, and sex within each age level. The test was given by forty-two examiners at twenty-eight sites in twenty-four states. A total of 800 children participated in standardization of the BDI. The norms for this test were recalibrated in 1987 when some inconsistencies in the norms tables were discovered.

RELIABILITY

Test-retest reliability is provided for an unspecified sample of 183 children drawn from the standardization group and given the test twice four weeks apart. Nearly all reliabilities exceed .90.

VALIDITY

The authors of the BDI address three forms of validity: content, construct, and criterion. Content validity is based on expert opinion. Items for this scale were selected from other measures, and experts placed the items at specified levels and in specified domains. Construct validity was examined by looking at subtest intercorrelations. Evidence for concurrent validity is based on correlations with other measures. The BDI component scores were highly correlated with scores on the Vineland Adaptive Behavior Scale and moderately correlated with performance on other scales. The test was developed by selecting items from other scales; the authors do not indicate the other scales on which BDI items were based.

SUMMARY

The BDI is an individually administered norm-referenced measure of the development of the young child in five major domains. Standardization procedures look reasonable, reliability data are given for an unspecified sample, and evidence for validity is limited.

Boehm Test of Basic Concepts–Revised

*T*he Boehm Test of Basic Concepts–Revised (BTBC-R) (Boehm, 1986) differs somewhat in content from the original version. There are seven new items, one item was divided into two items, two items were deleted, and four items were moved to a downward extension of the test. Like the earlier edition, the BTBC-R is a group-administered, norm-referenced device that assesses knowledge of fifty abstract, relational concepts that occur frequently in preschool and primary curricula. The concepts are "both fundamental to understanding verbal instruction and essential for early school achievement" (Boehm, 1986, p. 1). The BTBC-R is intended primarily for use in identifying children who have not mastered the concepts and in identifying those concepts that a teacher should systematically teach. In addition, Boehm states that the test may be used as part of a battery to identify children who are at risk for learning problems and to evaluate the effectiveness of instruction in the concepts assessed. The test is available in two forms, C and D.

The fifty concepts are arranged in order of increasing difficulty in two booklets. Each booklet takes about 15 to 20 minutes to administer and includes three practice items. The testing format requires children to mark the picture that best answers the question read by the teacher (for example, "Mark the one where the boy is next to the horse"). The items can be categorized as spatial (requiring understanding of the concept of *next to*, for example), quantitative (for example, *few*), temporal (for example, *after*), and miscellaneous (for example, *other*).

SCORES

Two types of scores are provided: pass or fail on each item and a percentile rank for the total score. In addition, tables give the percentage of children passing each item. The interpretive materials for the two types of scores are similar in several respects: Both provide normative data for kindergarten, grade 1, and grade 2; both provide separate norms for the beginning of the year and the end of the year; and both provide a means of comparing a student's performance with that of the total sample and that of other students at the same socioeconomic level.

Forms C and D have separate sets of norms for the percentage of students passing each item. The percentile norms, however, are for Forms C and D combined. This is troublesome, because Forms C and D were standardized separately and were not equated for variations in the samples. Although Boehm claims that the two samples were selected to be comparable in ability, no specifics are given.

NORMS

The standardization sample was intended to be broadly representative of the U.S. population, although it appears that only children from public school who attended regular classes were included. School district size and geographic area were the bases of stratification. The obtained data were statistically weighted to make the sample conform to the national population with respect to the stratification variables.

Boehm claims that her sample is also representative of the socioeconomic levels of schools in the United States. "Participating districts were asked to select groups of school buildings that, together, would provide a sample representative of the range of schools within the districts" (p. 45). Her data are not convincing, however.[6]

RELIABILITY

Although not presented as reliability data in the test manual, information on alternate-form reliability, based on the performances of 625 children, indicates poor reliability: .82 at kindergarten, .77 at first grade, and .65 at second grade. Twenty-four split-half reliability estimates (one for each form, grade/socioeconomic class, and total sample) are also presented. These range from .55 to .87; only ten coefficients exceed .80. Stability estimates (with an interval of one school year) are also given for

6. To estimate the SES of her sample, Boehm used the percentage of children in each school who received subsidized lunches. Schools were classified as high SES if no more than 10 percent of the students were eligible for subsidized lunches and middle class if 11 to 50 percent of the students were eligible.

each form at each grade. The six coefficients range from .55 to .88, with only two of the six exceeding .80.

VALIDITY

Because the BTBC-R is essentially a specialized achievement test, its content validity is of primary concern. Substantial evidence is presented that the words in the test are commonly used, and some evidence is presented that they are important. Some evidence of predictive validity is also presented. The BTBC-R correlates modestly with achievement, assessed after one year. Boehm presents seventeen coefficients of correlation with achievement tests that range from .38 to .64 (median .4). No evidence is presented, however, to show that the BTBC-R can identify children who are at risk for learning problems.

Seven pages of the BTBC-R manual are devoted to a review of validity studies conducted with the BTBC. Because the content of the two devices is so similar—there is about 80 percent overlap between the two devices—many of these studies are applicable to the BTBC-R. Studies reported indicate that the BTBC had some criterion-related validity for achievement, readiness, and language and was sensitive to instruction in the concepts tested; the same studies found no sex differences but did find differences among socioeconomic classes and among ethnic groups.

SUMMARY

The Boehm Test of Basic Concepts–Revised is a group-administered test that assesses knowledge of fifty relational words. Although there is some evidence for the importance of the words (and hence for use of the test as a criterion-referenced device), the device has inadequate reliability and norms for purposes other than screening.

Denver Developmental Screening Test

he Denver Developmental Screening Test (DDST) (Frankenburg, Dodds, Fandal, Kazuk, & Cohrs, 1975) is an individually administered, norm-referenced, multiple-skill device designed for the early identification of children with developmental and behavioral problems. It is intended for use with children from birth to 6 years of age. No special training is needed to administer the screening test, which requires approximately 20 minutes to give, score, and interpret. Test forms and the test manual are available in Spanish.

One hundred and five skills are clustered into four general developmental areas that must be administered in the order in which they are discussed here. The first area is Personal-Social Development. It contains twenty-three items. These can be clustered into three subareas: responding to another person (for example, smiling), playing (playing pat-a-cake, joining in interactive games), and self-care (dressing, washing, feeding). The second area, Fine Motor Development, contains thirty items. These assess grasping and manipulation, building towers of various heights with blocks, drawing, and copying increasingly diffi-

cult geometric designs. The third area is Language Development. The twenty-one items in this area assess the ability of younger children to produce and imitate sounds and require older children to demonstrate factual knowledge (for example, parts of the body and composition of familiar objects) as well as command of more traditional measures of language development such as vocabulary and syntax. The thirty-one items in the fourth area, Gross Motor Development, assess body control (for example, lifting the head, rolling over), mobility (walking, jumping in place), coordination (kicking a ball, riding a tricycle), and balance (balancing on one foot).

SCORES

All items are presented on the scoring sheet in the format shown in Figure 29.2. Across the top and bottom of the scoring sheet are age lines. The child's chronological age (CA) is computed, and a line indicating this chronological age is drawn at the appropriate point on the chart between the top and bot-

FIGURE 29.2   **Sample Scoring Sheet for the DDST**

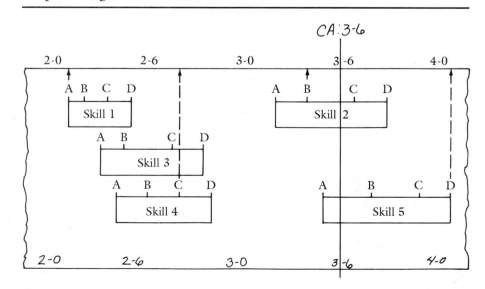

tom age lines. As shown in Figure 29.2, the line for a child who is 3-6 runs through rectangles representing skills 2 and 5. Each skill is represented by a rectangle with four lettered tick marks along one of the horizontal sides. The four tick marks can be extended to intercept the age lines. For skill 1 in Figure 29.2, the tick mark at point A extends to intercept the age line at about 2-1. This indicates that 25 percent of the children in the norm sample could perform skill 1 by the time they were about 2 years, 1 month old. The tick mark labeled B on each skill box extends to indicate the age at which 50 percent of the norm group could perform a skill. As shown in Figure 29.2, 50 percent of the children could perform skill 2 by age 3-4. Tick mark C extends to show the age at which 75 percent of the norm group performed a given skill; 75 percent of the children could perform skill 4 by age 2-8. Tick mark D is the age at which 90 percent of the norm group successfully performed a given skill. In Figure 29.2, 90 percent of the children in the norm group could perform skill 5 by age 4-1.

There is no formal basal rule for the scoring of the DDST.[7] Ceilings are not important since the purpose of the test is to determine developmental lags, not level of functioning. The examiner should administer all test items through which the child's age line passes, and testing in each area should not be terminated until the child passes three items and fails three items.

Each item may be scored pass, fail, passed by report, refusal, or no opportunity. Passed and failed items are observed directly by the examiner. Items passed by report (skills such as washing and drying the hands) are items that are difficult or time-consuming to administer but that can be observed reliably by the child's parents. If a parent reports that the child performs the particular task, the item is scored as a pass. Refusals are items to which the child will not respond whether the items are administered by the examiner or by the parents. If the examiner feels that the child cannot perform the task, the item is scored as failed. No-opportunity scores indicate that the child has not had the chance to learn the skill; such items are not included in the interpretation of the results.

Two types of scores are used. The first score is called a delay. A delay is scored if the child fails an item that is passed by 90 percent of the children who are younger; thus, a delay is an item that the child fails and that lies to the left of the age-line vertical. The second score is the interpretation of the overall results as abnormal, questionable, untestable, and normal. An abnormal is scored when the child has either two delays in each of two developmental areas or one developmental area with two delays and one developmental area with one delay and "no passes intersecting the age line" (Frankenburg et al., 1975, p. 12). A questionable is scored if the child has two or more delays in one developmental area or if the child has one delay and has not passed any items in the section through which the age line passes. An untestable is scored "when refusals occur in numbers large enough to cause the test result to be questionable or abnormal if they were scored as failures" (Frankenburg et al., 1975, p. 12). Outcomes other than the above are scored as normal. If a child earns a score other than normal, the authors recommend that the child be retested in two to three weeks. If the retest result is other than normal and if the parents say the behavior is typical, the children should be referred for further assessment.

NORMS

The DDST was standardized on 543 boys and 493 girls from 2 weeks old through 6-4 years of age who presumably (although the test is not clear on this point) lived in Denver, Colorado. Children with serious, known handicaps or who had experienced difficult births were excluded. The standardization sample approximated the 1960 census in terms of racial-ethnic composition and occupations of the children's fathers.

The number of children in the sample at various ages is limited and is not evenly distributed. The

7. A basal age is the age at which a child performs all tasks correctly and below which the tester can assume that all items will be passed. A basal rule states the number of items a child must pass before a basal age can be assumed.

number of children (in one-month intervals) from 1 month old to 14 months old ranges from thirty-six to forty-three; the total number of children between 5 and 6 years of age is forty-seven. The norms are now twenty years old.

RELIABILITY

The authors report stability data (one-week interval) for the performance of twenty children who ranged in age from 2 months to 5 years, 6 months and who were tested by the same examiner. For each of the twenty children, there was at least 90 percent agreement on the pass-fail decisions on the items administered[8]. The specimen kit also contains a reprint of an article by Frankenburg, Goldstein, and Camp (1971). There the test-retest reliability (percentage-agreement method) of abnormal, questionable, and normal classifications for 186 children was reported to be .97.

Interrater agreement was also evaluated during the standardization of DDST, since it was important to know if two different examiners would elicit the same performances and score them in the same way. Calculated by the percentage-agreement method, interrater reliability ranged from 80 to 95 percent agreement.

VALIDITY

The authors can claim content validity based on their method of selecting items. They surveyed several intelligence and developmental tests and selected items from them. The authors also present data from a paper by Frankenburg, Goldstein, and Camp (1971) to demonstrate a strong relationship between classifications on the DDST (that is, abnormal, questionable, and normal) and scores on the Stanford-Binet Intelligence Scale and the previous edition of the Bayley Infant Scales. This study also indicates low proportions of false positives and false negatives.[9]

SUMMARY

The Denver Developmental Screening Test is a quickly administered and scored device that assesses a child's development in four general areas: Personal-Social Development, Fine-Motor Development, Language Development, and Gross-Motor Development. The device is intended to provide a gross estimate of delayed development and must be followed by a more intensive evaluation. The test's reliability and validity are adequate for a screening device, although the norms are both questionable and very dated.

Developmental Indicators for the Assessment of Learning–Revised

*T*he Developmental Indicators for the Assessment of Learning–Revised (DIAL-R) (Mardell-Czudnowski & Goldenberg, 1990) is an individually administered screening test intended to assess motor, conceptual, and language skills of children from 2 to 6 years of age. Although individual children are screened, the testing procedures are designed to handle large numbers of children; different examiners administer different portions of the test to children who go from one testing area to another. DIAL-R is administered by a four-person screening team that includes one coordinator and three operators, one to administer each of the three DIAL-R screening areas. There are no special qualifications for the operators other than familiarity with the testing materials and procedures and limited special training.

The three subtests of the DIAL-R each consist of eight items. The test manual suggests that some individual items may be plotted as a profile.

---

8. Percentage agreement is the number of agreements divided by the number of agreements plus disagreements.

9. A *false positive* occurs when a child who is diagnosed as abnormal on subsequent evaluation is determined to be normal. A *false negative* occurs when a child who is diagnosed as normal on subsequent evaluation is determined to be abnormal.

Motor In this subtest, the eight items are (1) catching a beanbag; (2) jumping, hopping, and skipping; (3) building with blocks; (4) touching the fingers of each hand to the thumb on that hand; (5) cutting with scissors; (6) matching to sample (choosing a sample from an array to match a sample presented by the tester); (7) copying letters and shapes; and (8) writing first name.

Concepts In this subtest, the eight items are (1) naming nine colors; (2) pointing to various body parts; (3) rote counting; (4) one-to-one correspondence; (5) comprehending positions (for example, "put the block on the box"); (6) identifying fourteen concepts (for example, biggest, night, cold, least); (7) letter naming; and (8) sorting after observing the tester's sorting.

Language In this subtest, the eight items are (1) articulating fifteen words; (2) giving personal data (for example, identifying one's own photograph, giving one's telephone number); (3) remembering a sequence of hand claps, repeating digits, and repeating sentences; (4) naming nine pictured nouns (for example, TV, phone, ambulance); (5) naming pictured verbs (for example, sleep, talk, comb); (6) naming foods eaten; (7) problem solving (that is, social comprehension questions); and (8) sentence length of the child's longest response.

SCORES

Scaled scores are computed for each item. However, these scores are not really scaled scores in the sense that they have the same means and standard deviations. Rather, they are age scores, given in one-year age ranges. These scores are summed for each subtest and converted to another scale: potential problem, OK or potential advanced. Children earning scores of potential problem or potential advanced are to be followed up.

NORMS

DIAL-R was standardized in 1981–1983 on 2,447 children living in six states. The primary goal was to produce norms that would be representative of the U.S. population of children 2 years through 6 years of age and to stratify the sample on the basis of "age, sex, geographic region, size of community, and race" (p. 49). No 6-year-old children were included in the sample. Also noticeably missing is stratification on the basis of socioeconomic class, a variable that has been repeatedly shown to affect the development of children significantly. There are serious shortcomings in the variables that were actually used in stratification. For example, geographic region is sampled by two cities in each of four regions, and the cities are located in only six states. The cities were classified as large (over 50,000) and small (less than 50,000); the large cities are Freeport, New York; Joliet, Illinois; Jacksonville, Florida; and Honolulu, Hawaii. Separate norms for whites and non-whites are available.

The DIAL-R standardized data were reanalyzed in 1990 to provide norms for what is called the AGS version of the test. These are the norms to be used in interpreting pupil performance.

RELIABILITY

Test-retest reliabilities are not readily interpretable since they are computed across age groups. These coefficients range from .76 (Motor) to .90 (Concepts); the reliability of the total score is .87. No stability data are presented on the categorization of scores as potential problem, OK, and potential advanced.

Coefficient alpha was also computed for each subtest for each three-month age group. Thus, there were forty-eight coefficients that ranged from .45 (Language at age 5-6) to .87 (Language at age 2-3); thirty-eight of the coefficients fall below .80, including Motor at all ages. For the total score, reliabilities range from .80 (age 5-3) to .92 (age 2-2); none of the sixteen coefficients fall below .80. Thus, low reliability makes about three-fourths of the subtest scores unsuitable for screening purposes, but the total scores are suitable.

VALIDITY

Twenty-one of the twenty-four items on the DIAL-R were taken from the first edition of the DIAL. In selecting these twenty-one items, the test authors interviewed early childhood and kindergarten teachers to identify behaviors believed necessary for school success. The resulting list of behaviors was reviewed by a group of consultants. The bases for deleting DIAL items and adding DIAL-R items are not specified in the manual. Inspection of the individual items raises some questions. For example, many of the items on the Motor subtest make heavy intellectual demands. Indeed, one factor analytic study reported by Mardell-Czudnowski and Goldenberg indicates that the items on the DIAL-R actually cluster into only two factors: (1) Motor and Concepts and (2) Language.

Construct validity of the DIAL-R was established by showing that parts of the scale correlated with like-named parts of other scales and did not correlate highly with other-named scales. Evidence for criterion-related validity is mixed. The authors reanalyzed the standardization data in 1990, developing new norms. Many of the validity studies were completed using the norms for prior editions of the scale. Data in the manual support the criterion-related validity of the scale.

SUMMARY

DIAL-R is an individually administered screening device assessing development in domains of motor, conceptual, and language behavior. The norms are adequate, reliability is reasonable for the total scale but limited for subtests, and validity is clearly established. The DIAL-R is a useful and technically adequate screening device. Users are advised to use the total score rather than subtest scores in decision making.

Developmental Profile II

T he Developmental Profile II (DP-II) (Alpern, Boll, & Shearer, 1986) is an age scale designed to assess children's development from birth to age 9-6. The first and second editions of the scales differ slightly. Thirty-one of the items from the DP were not included in the DP-II—items above the 9-6 level and sexist items. The manual was also rewritten, but no new norms or items were developed. The DP-II can be administered as a parent interview in about 20 to 40 minutes by anyone who has been trained to use it, or it can be used as a "self-interview" that is completed by a teacher.

The DP-II contains 186 items arranged in five subscales, with usually three items per age level per subscale. The subscales are as follows:

The Physical Scale contains thirty-nine items that assess both gross and fine motor skills.

The Self-Help Scale consists of thirty-nine items that assess both survival and self-care.

The Social Scale contains thirty-six items that assess "expression of needs and feelings, interactions with others, sense of identity, and adherence to rules and regulations."

The Academic Scale consists of thirty-four items that assess cognitive functioning (for example, perception, memory, and categorization).

The Communication Scale contains thirty-eight items that assess verbal and nonverbal expression and language comprehension.

The DP-II is intended for several uses: screening, determining eligibility for special education and related services, planning individual educational programs, evaluating pupil progress, and evaluating educational programs for groups of children. However, its authors recommend that the DP-II be used only for screening unless it is used in conjunction with other assessment procedures.

SCORES

The DP-II is one of the few tests that rely on age scores. Age scores have been widely rejected as inadequate for the reasons discussed in Chapter 5.

Individual items are scored as pass, fail, or no opportunity" (which is counted as fail). Individual items are combined to form an age score for each subscale. These subscale age scores are interpreted as either advanced or delayed. If the developmental age is greater than the chronological age, performance on the subscale is interpreted as advanced; if the developmental age is less than the chronological age, performance on the subscale is interpreted as delayed. Tables are also provided to interpret the magnitude of delays. One table shows the age at which 95 percent of the children in the standardization sample passed the items on each scale. Another table classifies delays as delayed, borderline, and normal. These classifications are not, however, empirical; they are based on the clinical judgments of unspecified individuals.

NORMS

A total of 2,354 normal children ranging in age from 0 to 9-6 make up the normative sample for the DP-II. No sampling plan is discussed, but the few statistics that are presented indicate that the sample is not representative of the U.S. population. It is overwhelmingly middle class (80 percent), with only 9 percent lower-class and 11 percent upper-class children. The sample is also restricted geographically: 91 percent of the children are from Indiana and 9 percent are from Washington state.

RELIABILITY

The discussion of reliability offered in the technical manual of the DP-II does not conform to either psychometric or behavioral models of reliability. The authors present unorthodox estimates of reliability to demonstrate interscorer reliability, stability, and internal consistency. We are unable to evaluate these data in the form presented and must conclude that usable evidence of reliability is absent from the manual.

VALIDITY

No claim of content validity may be made because of the way in which the items were selected for inclusion. The test includes (1) items from existing scales of intelligence, language, social abilities, and physical abilities; (2) items derived from normative data from the research literature in child development; and (3) newly developed items. The factors considered in selecting items included age and sex bias and the performance of children of different ages on an item. No detailed descriptions are given of the domains sampled (and their parameters), however. Thus at other than the most general level, it is unclear what domains the content of the DP-II is intended to represent.

Evidence for other types of validity is also not convincing. Mothers and teachers have a high rate of agreement on children's performances, and there are modest correlations with the Stanford-Binet (Form L-M). The studies cited tend to be flawed methodically, however.

SUMMARY

The Developmental Profile II is an individually administered screening device intended for use with children ranging in age from newborn to 9-6. The norms are unrepresentative, the degree of reliability is unknown, and evidence for validity is scant.

Metropolitan Readiness Tests

*T*he Metropolitan Readiness Tests (MRT) (Nurss & McGauvran, 1986) is the fifth edition of this group-administered test designed to assess a "diverse range of prereading skills" (p. 7) for children in preschool through the middle of kindergarten (Level 1) and "more advanced skills that are important in beginning reading and mathematics" (p. 7) for children in the middle of kindergarten through the fall of first grade (Level 2). As might be expected, the two levels have different behaviors. The five Level 1 subtests are described in general terms below.

Auditory Memory assesses immediate recall of words read by the tester.

Beginning Consonants assesses the discrimination of initial sounds.

Letter Recognition assesses both upper- and lowercase letters.

Visual Matching assesses a child's ability to match a series of letters, words, numbers, or other symbols.

School Language and Listening assesses "basic cognitive concepts, as well as complex grammatical structures"; "the questions require children to integrate and reorganize information, to draw inferences, and to analyze and evaluate" oral material (p. 8).

Following are brief descriptions of the ten Level 2 subtests.

Quantitative Language assesses various mathematical concepts (for example, one-to-one correspondence).

Beginning Consonants assesses discrimination of beginning consonants.

Sound-Letter Correspondence requires a child "to identify letters that correspond to specific sounds in words" (p. 8).

Visual Matching requires the matching of various arithmetic, English, and nonsense symbols.

Finding Patterns requires the child to find various arithmetic, English, and nonsense symbols embedded in larger groupings of symbols.

School Language is essentially the same as the School Language subtest in Level 1.

Listening is about the same as the Listening subtest in Level 1.

Quantitative Concepts assesses various mathematical concepts (for example, conservation and part-whole relationships).

Quantitative Operations assesses "counting and simple mathematical operations" (p. 8).

Copying is an optional subtest that requires the child to copy a printed sentence.

SCORES

Two types of scores are offered: content-referenced and norm-referenced. Content-referenced scores consist of raw scores (+ indicating that the student has learned the skills to proficiency, / that the student is in the process of learning the skills, – that the student needs instruction) and performance ratings. Tables are used to obtain the performance ratings; however, no bases are provided to explain why a particular raw score should be considered to represent proficiency.

Norm-referenced scores combine subtests into four composites at Level 1 (Auditory Skill Area, Visual Skill Area, Language Skill Area, and Pre-Reading Composite) and five composites at Level 2 (the four composites at Level 1 plus a Quantitative Skill Area). Percentile ranks, stanines, scaled scores, and normal curve equivalents are provided for the composites. Neither means nor standard deviations of the standard scores are provided in the technical manual.

Norms

For Level 1, separate norms are available for spring prekindergarten, fall kindergarten, and midyear kindergarten. For Level 2, norms are available for midyear kindergarten, spring kindergarten, and fall grade 1.

A stratified sample of school districts was selected to represent the 1980 U.S. population for fall ($N = 180$ districts), midyear ($N = 140$), and spring ($N = 290$) standardizations. Whether the same school districts participated in more than one norming program is not reported. Stratification variables were size of school district, geographic region, socioeconomic status, and private or public school status. The sample varied by more than 10 percent from the U.S. population; however, the sample data were statistically adjusted so that the data used for the norm tables did approximate the census data.

Reliability

KR-20 coefficients of internal consistency are provided for subtests and composites for fall, midyear, and spring norms. For the Pre-Reading Composite, coefficients exceed .90 for all norms. For the other composites, however, only two coefficients exceed .89 (Visual Skill Area, Level 2, midyear and spring kindergarten), and some are as low as .70 (Language Skill Area, Level 2, spring kindergarten). Stability coefficients (two-week interval) are presented for only two norm groups (Level 1, fall kindergarten and Level 2, spring kindergarten). Only the stability of the Pre-Reading Composite for level 1 exceeded .89; the stabilities of the remaining composites ranged from .74 (Language Skill Area, Level 2) to .88 (Auditory Skill Area, Level 1).

Validity

The most important type of validity for a readiness test is predictive validity; educators want to use a readiness test to learn how students will fare in their various curricula. The results of two predictive-validity studies are presented in the technical manual. Level 2 was administered in the fall to first graders, and either the Metropolitan Achievement Tests or the Stanford Achievement Test Series was administered in the spring. For the Metropolitan, correlations ranged from .34 (Language Skill Area with total reading) to .65 (Pre-Reading with total achievement composite). The MRT was much more predictive of scores on the Stanford: Coefficients ranged from .48 (Language Skill Area) to .83 (Pre-Reading Composite with the total basic battery and the total complete battery). However, for neither study were the curricula in which the students were enrolled described. The information presented is inadequate to establish either content or construct validity.

Summary

The Metropolitan Readiness Tests is a group-administered device best suited for norm-referenced interpretation. Only the Pre-Reading Composite is sufficiently reliable for use in making important educational decisions. The test appears to be an unusually good predictor of achievement on the Stanford Achievement Test Series but only a modest predictor of achievement on the Metropolitan Achievement Tests. The MRT's predictive ability for particular curricula or other achievement tests is unknown, and therefore the test should not be used as a predictive device.

Tests of Basic Experiences 2

*T*he Tests of Basic Experiences 2 (TOBE-2) (Moss, 1979) is a set of group-administered tests designed to assess important concepts that contribute to a child's preparedness for school and learning. The directions for testers are comprehensive and clear; best results are said to occur when group size is five or six. TOBE-2 has two levels, neither of which requires reading: level K (preschool and kindergarten) and level L (kindergarten and first grade). The battery consists of four tests of twenty-six items each: Mathematics, Language, Science, and Social Studies. A practice examination is provided, and there are two demonstration items at the beginning of each test. Administration time is about 20 minutes for the practice test and about 45 minutes for TOBE-2.

The Mathematics test assesses quantitative vocabulary and concepts, geometric shapes, and money. The Language test assesses letter recognition, same-different, prepositions, letter-sound associations, and other vocabulary. The Science test assesses basic facts of botany (for example, plants that grow in dry places), physics (for example, falling objects, buoyancy), and zoology (for example, animal tracks). The Social Studies test assesses social interactions, knowledge of occupations, and knowledge of tools, among other things.

SCORES

Scoring can be done by hand or by machine. Raw scores are summed for each subtest and the total; sums can be converted to percentile ranks, normal curve equivalents (mean = 50, standard deviation ≈ 21), and stanines. A Class Evaluation Record is used to show concepts correctly identified as well as derived scores for each child. The teacher can sum the columns for each concept to find the number of children in the class who correctly identify the concept.

NORMS

The standardization sample consisted of approximately 14,000 children. Since fall and spring testings were conducted in the same schools, the norms to some extent are longitudinal. Midyear norms are interpolated.

The children were intended to represent public school districts in 1970 and Catholic schools in 1975. Public school districts were stratified by geographic region, elementary school population, and relevant (but unspecified) demographic characteristics. Schools within districts were somehow selected, and all children in the target schools who were enrolled in kindergarten and first grade were tested. Catholic schools were stratified by geographic region and enrollment. Selection procedures for preschoolers were not discussed. Although voluminous data are presented, one cannot ascertain the extent to which the sample is representative. The general procedures followed should result in an adequate normative sample, however.

RELIABILITY

Internal-consistency estimates of reliability for each subtest and the total for each form are presented for both fall and spring scores. Reliability estimates range from .76 to .85 for subtests; estimates for total scores all exceed .90. Test-retest correlations for subtests range from .64 to .78 from fall to spring; for the total scores the range is from .84 to .87. Thus, the reliability of the subtests appears adequate for screening purposes.

VALIDITY

Moss (1979) enumerates the components of each subtest and gives the number of items in each component. She also discusses the criteria used for including and excluding individual test items. She included items that were effectively used in the first edition of TOBE, traditionally assessed on similar subtests, relevant, easily illustrated, and free from ethnic-racial-sex bias; she also looked for high item-total correlations (which are necessary for developing a reliable test), and considered item difficulty. Evidence for concurrent or predictive validity was not reported.

SUMMARY

The Tests of Basic Experiences 2 is a series of group-administered devices designed to assess pupil skill development in several areas. There are two levels of the test, with separate tests assessing development in Mathematics, Language, Science, and Social Studies.

Although TOBE-2 was standardized on many children, it is difficult to ascertain from the data in the test manual how representative the sample was. Reliability data are adequate for screening. Users of the tests should be able to evaluate the content validity, since the necessary information is so clearly presented.

Preschool Evaluation Scale

*T*he Preschool Evaluation Scale (PES) (McCarney, 1992) is an individually administered, norm-referenced rating scale intended "to contribute to the early identification of students with developmental delays" (McCarney, 1992, p. 4). Different forms are used for children from birth through 35 months and for children between 36 and 72 months. Designed to assess the domains enumerated in Public Law 99-457, PES assesses performance in the six domains that are briefly described below.

Large Muscle This subscale assesses large muscle movements as well as reflexes, muscle tone, positioning, and use of adaptive equipment. Examples of required movements include waving arms and seating oneself.

Small Muscle This subscale assesses small muscle movements as well as reflexes, muscle tone, positioning, and use of adaptive equipment. Examples of required movements include building a tower of three to four blocks or holding a pencil with three- to four- finger grasp.

Cognitive Thinking This subscale assesses mental concepts such as object permanence, causality, means-end behavior, and spatial relationships, as well as pre-academic skills, including concept development prereading skills and premath skills. Examples of items include recognizing parent visually, enjoying repetitive sound-producing actions, and matching colors.

Expressive Language This subscale measures aspects of communication through verbal expression. Examples of items on this subscale include calling parents "mama" and "dada," naming objects and pictures, and rhyming words.

Social/Emotional This subscale contains test items that sample knowledge of social rules, appropriate play behavior, and demonstration and awareness of feelings and emotions. Examples include smiling in response to adult attention, choosing friends, and initiating play.

Self-help Skills This subscale assesses the child's ability to care for herself or himself. Items assess dressing, toileting, feeding, and self-help.

Although the subtests names are the same, the specific items and the number of items differ on each form. Table 29.4 contains the number of items for each subtest on each form.

SCORES

For each item the child is rated (usually by the child's teacher or aide) on a three-point scale: 0 (cannot perform the behavior), 1 (performs successfully but inconsistently), and 2 (performs successfully and independently). Raw scores on subscales are converted to scaled scores (mean = 10, standard deviation = 3). Subscales are summed to provide percentiles for total scores.

NORMS

No sampling plan is described in the manual, but the norms are based on the ratings of 472 educators from 24 states who rated 2,893 children. The author provides separate norms (combining boys and girls) for different age groups in four-month intervals from birth through 28 months; the number of children in each norm group is clearly presented and adequate. After 28 months, however, the norms become less clear. For example, norm tables are avail-

TABLE 29.4   **Subtests and Number of Items on the PES**

Subtest	Number of Items	
	Birth –35 Months	36–72 Months
Large Muscle	18	11
Small Muscle	16	13
Cognitive Thinking	17	13
Expressive Language	15	15
Social/Emotional	13	17
Self-Help Skills	15	16
Total	94 items	85 items

able for boys from 36 to 47 months, boys from 48 to 59 months, boys from 60 to 72 months, and girls from 36 to 72 months. No rationale is given for the asymmetry of the norms, nor is it possible to ascertain the actual number of children in norm groups after 28 months.

Overall, the norms appear representative of the U.S. in 1980 in terms of sex, race, residence, and geographic area for children between birth and 35 months of age. For children between 36 and 72 months, the norms appear representative in terms of sex and race; urban children and children from the Northcentral region are overrepresented. Although the author notes that children with disabilities were included in the normative sample, no data are provided.

RELIABILITY

The author presents data on the PES's internal consistency, stability, and interrater agreement. The data, however, are incompletely reported.

Alphas are reported for each subscale for two age groups, birth through 35 months and 36 months through 72 months; alphas are not reported for total score. With the exception of the Large Muscle subscale for the older group, all alphas exceeded .90. However, because alphas were calculated across age groups, they are likely to be inflated.

Stability (test-retest reliability) over a thirty-day interval was estimated for each subscale and for the total score on the performance of 391 children of unknown characteristics. Three of the six coefficients equaled or exceeded .90. It is unclear from the author's discussion of the procedures used to estimate stability if the resulting coefficients are contaminated by the effects of age or if the results apply to children of all ages.

To estimate interrater reliability, 142 pairs of educators rated 428 children. A total of ten correlations are presented that correspond to age ranges of the children. Thus, it appears that only total score agreement was estimated. The obtained coefficients ranged from .80 to .89. Agreement for subscale scores is not reported.

VALIDITY

Content Validity Some claim for content validity can be made by the way items were developed. Appropriate literature was reviewed, items were developed, and early childhood professionals reviewed the items. However, there are certain notable omissions. For example, PES ignores receptive language.

Criterion-Related Validity Criterion-related validity was evaluated in two incompletely reported studies. In the first study, sixty children between birth and 35 months of age were assessed with the PES and the Early Learning Accomplishment Profile (ELAP). Correlations between PES subtests and ELAP ranged from .58 (Cognitive Thinking) to .71 (Large Muscle). However, it is unclear what PES scores (that is, raw scores or standard scores) and what ELAP scores were correlated. In the second study, fifty-eight children between 36 and 72 months of age were assessed with the PES and the Learning Accomplishment Profile (LAP). Correlations between the PES subtests and LAP ranged from .61 (Cognitive Thinking) to .80 (Large Muscle). Again, it is unclear what PES scores (that is, raw scores or standard scores) and what LAP scores were correlated. Nonetheless, correlations of the magnitude obtained in the two studies strongly suggests that the PES is measuring constructs similar to those measured by ELAP and LAP.

Construct Validity The author presents three types of information about construct validity: diagnostic, subscale interrelationships, and item validity. Diagnostic validity was investigated by examining 121 children between the ages of 24 and 60 months with the PES. The profiles of these children were compared to the PES profiles of "a corresponding group" of children who were identified as having developmental delays. The developmentally delayed children obtained significantly lower scores than the randomly selected children.

The author also presents subscale intercorrelations to establish that all subscales assess development. Indeed, the subscales are highly intercorrelated for children between birth and 35 months; correlations range from .83 to .92. For older students (between the ages of 36 and 72 months), the correlations are substantially lower, ranging from .60 to .83. These correlations suggest that a single factor underlies the scale, and this finding casts doubt on the differential meaning of the subscales.

The author also presents data on item-total correlations. We believe these data are redundant, given the reliability information provided.

SUMMARY

PES is an individually administered, norm-referenced rating scale intended to facilitate the identification of young children with developmental disabilities. Different forms are available for two different age groups: birth through 35 months and 36 through 72 months. Both forms assess children on six subscales (Large Muscle, Small Muscle, Cognitive Thinking, Expressive Language, Social/ Emotional, and Self-Help Skills). Subscale raw scores are converted to scaled scores, and subscale totals are converted to percentiles. PES norms are generally representative. Reliability information is incompletely reported for internal consistency and stability, although the information that is presented suggests adequate reliability. Nonetheless, users should interpret PES results cautiously. Interrater agreement for total score is marginal (that is, .80 to .89, depending of the age of the children); no interrater agreement is presented for subscales. Content validity is generally adequate, but users should be cautious about generalizing the Expressive Language subscale to receptive language functioning. Criterion-related validity, although incompletely reported, appears adequate. Construct validity is limited, but the PES does appear to discriminate between children with and children without developmental disabilities.

System to Plan Early Childhood Services

*T*he System to Plan Early Childhood Services (Bagnato and Neisworth, 1990) (SPECS) is not a test or scale. It is a rating system to be used by early childhood service teams to reach a consensus about the development, intervention, and evaluation of programs for children between the ages of 2 and 6. SPECS consists of three types of forms: Developmental Specifications, Team Specifications, and Program Specifications.

- *Developmental Specifications* (called Developmental Specs) is used to judge the child's development on six domains that represent the nineteen dimensions shown in Table 29.5. Ratings may be transferred to an Individual Rater Profile to present the ratings graphically.
- *Team Specifications* (called Team Specs) has three parts. The Team Summary is a form on which are recorded the ratings of individual team members. From these ratings, a consensus rating is developed and plotted on the Team Consensus Profile. The Team Consensus Profile is used to complete the Service Matrix.
- *Program Specifications* (called Program Specs) has three purposes: (1) to plan a child's program, (2) to document the child's progress, and (3) to evaluate that program's effectiveness. Program Specs contains ten questionnaires intended to elicit information in five areas: Background Information (assessing family needs, preschool history, and prior assessments); Program Options (assessing a child's service needs in early education and related services); Transition Services, including program options for kindergarten; Service Intensity (assessing the degree and scope of services as required by Public Law 99-457); and a Progress Summary.

SCORES

Ratings on Developmental Specs are made using a five-point scale that ranges from severe difficulty (1

TABLE 29.5   Domains and Developmental Dimensions of SPECS

Domain	Dimensions
Communication	Receptive Language
	Expressive Language
Sensorimotor	Hearing
	Vision
	Gross Motor
	Fine Motor
Physical	Health
	Growth
	Normalcy
Cognition	Basic Concepts
	Problem Solving
Self-Regulation	Temperament
	Play
	Attention
	Self-Control
Self/Social	Self-Esteem
	Motivation
	Social Competence
	Self-Care

point) to typical functioning (5 points). These ratings are to be taken at face value, and neither standard scores or percentiles are used to interpret individual ratings. Differences among raters are resolved through team discussion and negotiation, and a consensus team rating is obtained. Need for service is judged on a four-point scale (no service needed, consultation recommended, direct services recommended, and direct services needed) that is based on the truncated numerical values from the consensus (Average) rating (that is, decimal numbers are rounded down to the next whole number).

RELIABILITY

Stability of Developmental Specs ratings was estimated for two groups; mean interval between ratings was 16.12 days. For early childhood educators, stability coefficients ranged from .62 (Self-Esteem) to .87 (Expressive Language, Hearing, and Problem Solving). For paraprofessional aides, stability coefficients ranged from .60 (Vision) to .88 (Gross Motor). Although these values would normally be considered adequate only for screening purposes and insufficient using SPECS to make important educational decisions for individual children, the typical guidelines for interpreting stability probably should not be applied to SPECS because consensus ratings, not individual ratings, are used in decision making. Thus, the stability of individual ratings is only tenuously related to the stability of the group decision, for which data are not presented in the administration manual.[10]

VALIDITY

SPECS has excellent validity on the surface. It requires the kinds of judgments made every day by individual and family service teams. Aside from this face validity, some claim to the content validity of Developmental Specs can be made from its development. Domains and descriptors were derived from child development literature and the authors' extensive experience; domains and descriptors were then field tested over a period of about fifteen years. The authors also attempt to establish criterion-related validity for Developmental Specs using a variety of norm-referenced tests with children between the ages of 4-0 and 6-5. Although the results are incompletely reported in the administration manual (more information is promised in a still forthcoming technical supplement), SPECS generally shows excellent agreement with these measures.[11] Finally, Developmental Specs ratings accurately identify children already classified as disabled and accurately identify their disability. Thus, one can cautiously conclude there is some evidence for the validity of Developmental Specs.

Of key importance is the validity of SPECS-based decisions about services to be provided to children and their families. One study that addresses this issue is provided in the examiner's manual. In this study, twenty-nine children with special needs were followed for one year. These children were divided into two groups: Children in one group ($N = 7$) were declassified during the year; children in the second group maintained their classification throughout the year. SPECS ratings were consistent with the classification and service needs of both groups. However, the key issue, does SPECS result in better team decision making?, is not addressed empirically in the manual. Thus, users will have to decide for themselves if SPECS fills this need.

SUMMARY

The System to Plan Early Childhood Services is a rating system for use by early childhood service teams to reach a consensus about the development, intervention, and evaluation of programs for children between the ages of 2 and 6. Rating forms are used to evaluate a child's development, plan a child's program, and evaluate that child's progress and his or her program's effectiveness. The technical characteristics of the Developmental Specs are incompletely reported. With this caveat, Developmental Specs probably has adequate stability. Validity information suggests SPECS is sufficiently valid to be used to facilitate decision making.

---

10. Although the SPECS manual states that a technical supplement is available through American Guidance Service, the manual was still not available at the time this review was prepared—four years after the publication of SPECS.

11. Such findings should be expected *if* judgments were based on the results of these tests.

COPING WITH DILEMMAS IN CURRENT PRACTICE

There are three major dilemmas in assessing infants, toddlers, and preschoolers. The first is that the performances of children who are very young are so variable that long-term prediction (for example, one year) is not feasible. This inability to predict precisely is particularly pronounced with shorter, quickly administered (and less reliable) measures. Since there is relatively poor predictive validity, most inferences must be drawn with great care. If individuals wish to use these measures to predict school success, they should recognize that the closer the predicted measure (that is, the criterion) is to the predictor measure (that is, the test), the greater the accuracy of the prediction. For example, language tests predict later language skills better than perceptual-motor tests do.

The second problem occurs when one uses tests of readiness and development as measures of current functioning and current attainment. It tests are to be used in this way, they must be scrutinized. This is especially true when using developmental measures to document pupil progress at the preschool level. To use developmental measures in this way, one must make sure that there is appropriate linkage between the curriculum and the content of the test.

The third dilemma is the fact that students must be labeled to be eligible for preschool programs, but the act of labeling may set up expectations for limited pupil performance.

Those who assess infants, toddlers, and preschool children need to assess within a context of situational specificity. There is much situational variability in performance, and this must be taken into account when making predictions or planning interventions.

SUMMARY

Tests are used with preschoolers, infants, and toddlers for the purpose of screening. Focus generally is on identification of those children who would profit from early intervention. Assessment is based on the notions of prevention and developmental plasticity. It is assumed that it is a good idea to identify students early, intervene, change them, and prevent later problems. The impetus for preschool assessment is largely a legal one. The most recent major federal legislation to affect early assessment is Public Law 99-457.

There have been major advances in early assessment since the law was enacted in 1986. Educators now assess newborn infants, and that assessment typically involves neurobiological appraisal, consisting of assessment of neurological integrity, behavioral organization, needs, temperament, and state of consciousness. Increasingly, early childhood educators are engaged in planning interventions for medically high-risk infants and special needs infants and toddlers. They develop Individual Family Service Plans.

Readiness measures are a special form of preschool assessment. They are administered for the purposes of predicting who is not ready for formal school entry and who will profit from remedial or compensatory intervention. Specific measures of school readiness were reviewed in the chapter.

There are three major dilemmas in early assessment. First, tests are administered for the purpose of predicting later performance, but at these young ages performance is so highly variable that prediction is very difficult. Second, it is dangerous to use preschool measures as indexes of current standing. Third, provision of services is dependent on labeling children, but labeling may set up expectations for limited pupil performance.

STUDY QUESTIONS

1. Differentiate between a *process orientation* and a *skill orientation* toward readiness.
2. Chapter 2 stated that a fundamental assumption in assessment is that only present behavior can be observed; any statement about future performance is an inference. Discuss the use of readiness measures in light of this assumption.
3. In assessing the validity of readiness tests, what considerations are important?
4. What are the four major areas assessed in neurobiological assessment?

ADDITIONAL READING

Bagnato, S., & Neisworth, J. (1979). Between assessment and intervention: Forging an assessment/curriculum linkage for the handicapped preschooler. *Child Care Quarterly, 8*(3), 179–195.

Bagnato, S. J., Neisworth, J. T., & Munson, S. M. (1989). *Linking developmental assessment and early intervention: Curriculum-based prescriptions.* Rockville, MD: Aspen.

Bailey, D. B., & Simeonsson, R. J. (1988). *Family assessment in early intervention.* Columbus, OH: Merrill.

Bailey, D. B., & Wolery, M. (Eds.). (1989). *Assessing infants and preschoolers with handicaps.* Columbus, OH: Merrill.

Bracken, B. A. (1988). Limitations of preschool instruments and standards for minimal levels of technical adequacy. *Journal of Psychoeducational Assessment, 5,* 313–326.

Conoley, J., & Kramer, J. J. (1989). *Buros tenth mental measurements yearbook.* Lincoln, NE: University of Nebraska Press.

Lewis, M., & Sullivan, M. W. (1985). Infant intelligence and its assessment. In B. B. Wolman (Ed.), *Handbook of intelligence: Theories, measurements, and applications.* New York: Wiley.

O'Donnell, K. J., & Oehler, J. M. (1989). Neurobehavioral assessment of the newborn infant. In D. Bailey & M. Wolery (Eds.), *Assessing infants and preschoolers with handicaps.* Columbus, OH: Merrill.

Paget, K., & Bracken, B. (1983). *The psychoeducational assessment of preschool children.* New York: Grune & Stratton.

Paget, K. D., & Barnett, D. W. (1990). Assessment of infants, toddlers, preschool children, and their families: Emergent trends. In T. B. Gutkin & C. R. Reynolds (Eds.), *The handbook of school psychology* pp. 458–486. New York: Wiley.

Paget, K. D., & Nagle, R. J. (1986). A conceptual model of preschool assessment. *School Psychology Review, 15,* 154–165.

Chapter 30

Outcomes-Based
Accountability Assessment

*A*re our schools producing the results we want? This is the question of the decade. If, in 1980, you had asked a Director of Special Education to tell you about special education services in his or her district, the response would probably have been something like the following:

> We serve 427 special education students—212 are students with learning disabilities, 72 are students with mental retardation, and 99 have speech and language disorders. There are 31 students with severe emotional disturbance, and the remainder have a variety of low-incidence conditions. The students are taught by fifty-one special education teachers. Thirty-two hold a license in the area of learning disabilities, whereas eleven are teachers of the mentally retarded. Our district employs two speech and hearing teachers and three school psychologists.[1] Of the 427 students with disabilities, 91 spend most of the day in regular education classes, with occasional pull-out for services in a resource room. We have six self-contained classes and ten resource rooms. Some students receive occupational therapy, physical therapy, and counseling.

Until very recently, the focus in special education was on counting numbers of students served and on provision of services. Administrators could tell you how many students of what types had been tested and were being served in what kinds of settings by whom. What few administrators could do was provide evidence for the results or outcomes of the services provided.

Things have changed dramatically. Over the past ten years, there has been a dramatic shift from a focus on the process of serving students with disabilities to a focus on the outcomes or results of the services provided. Parents, government agencies, business personnel, and the general public want to know about more than just the number of students in school, the number of teachers and

---

1. The numbers here do not add up to the total number of teachers mentioned. As this is only an example, we have not carried it out entirely. We are assuming that there would also be teachers of the gifted, behaviorally disordered, the blind, etc.

their degrees, the quality of facilities, and the types of books in school libraries. They want to know what impact education is having on students—that is, whether students are leaving school prepared for work, college, or other postschool experiences. And they want to know that their investment in education has been worth it. In other words, they want to know about the *outcomes* of schooling.

Much of the impetus for this shift was the publication of *A Nation at Risk: The Imperative for Educational Reform* (U.S. Department of Education, 1983). In this document, the then-Secretary of Education revealed the low status of America's school children relative to their counterparts in other nations and reported that "the educational foundations of our society are presently being eroded by a rising tide of mediocrity that threatens our very future as a nation and a people" (p. 5). In this report, the Secretary argued that the nation was at risk because mediocrity, not excellence, was the norm in education. Recommendations included more time for learning, better textbooks and other materials, more homework, higher expectations, stricter attendance policies, and improved standards, salaries, rewards, and incentives for teachers. The entire nation began to focus on raising educational standards, measuring performance, and achieving results. Policy makers and bureaucrats, who had been spending a great deal of money to fund special education, began demanding evidence of its effectiveness. In essence, they employed the old saw, "The proof of the pudding is in the eating"—arguing that it matters little what you do if it does not produce what you want.

Recent questions about how educational services are provided to students with disabilities echo the importance of looking at outcomes. For example, a special education study group formed by the National Association of State Boards of Education recommended the integration of students with disabilities into general education programs, based on the belief that all children can learn—not in an attempt to save money (National Association of State Boards of Education, 1992). It also pointed out the need for accountability systems that include students with disabilities and for local efforts to restructure schools to make special education an integral part of schools. But the bottom line in education reform is that it needs to focus on assessment of educational outcomes for students in general and for students in special education programs in particular.

There is little disagreement about the *need* to focus our attention on the results of providing educational services to students with disabilities. Yet, until recently, there was no agreement on the kinds of data that ought to be collected and used to assess the results of educational services and no agreement on a conceptual model to guide the practice of assessing outcomes. A major activity of the National Center on Educational Outcomes (NCEO), located at the University of Minnesota, is developing a conceptual model of outcomes and indicators to guide the outcomes assessment process. NCEO developed a Self-Study Guide for states and school districts to use in the development of systems of outcomes and indicators (Ysseldyke & Thurlow, 1993). In this chapter, we rely on the content of the self-study guide and describe the process that a school or school district would go through in developing a system to assess the extent to which it is achieving desired results. We use the model of outcomes and indicators as an example of an outcomes and indicators system but not as the only example. We talk about how the model can be adopted by or adapted to meet the needs of local communities. We describe ways to accomplish the following:

- Involve stakeholders in the assessment process
- Develop, adopt, or adapt a conceptual model of outcomes and indicators
- Establish a data collection and reporting system
- Install an outcomes-based accountability system.

INVOLVE STAKEHOLDERS UP FRONT

Stakeholders are those individuals in a community who have a personal interest in the measurement of educational outcomes: teachers, supervisors, providers of related services, parents, representatives of community agencies, and students. Involving stakeholders "up front" in the process of developing educational outcomes enhances their feeling of being vested in the assessment process and their desire to participate in it. Involvement up front empowers those individuals or groups to chart their own activities and futures.

Decide Why You Want to Measure Outcomes

There are four major reasons why stakeholders want to measure educational outcomes. First, data on the results of service provision can be useful in *improving instructional programs* for students. In fact, to improve instructional practices, it is imperative that school personnel have data illustrating the extent to which what they are doing is achieving desired results. For example, school personnel might want to know the extent to which the math curriculum they are using is resulting in students earning high scores on math tests. Knowledge of results enables professionals to consider making changes in instructional programs. For instructional improvement, it is important that stakeholders reach agreement on assessment goals.

Second, data on outcomes are important for *accountability:* to document for people in authority that desired goals are being met. Tests are regularly given to students in most states, and data are provided to state agencies and school districts within states indicating how pupils are doing. The test scores can be used by legislators and policy makers to decide whether they are "getting their money's worth" from funds invested in education. Data on educational outcomes are also useful in providing *public information* on the outcomes of schooling. You may have seen reports in newspapers indicating how the nation's youth are doing in math, reading, science, or other forms of literacy.

Fourth, and finally, data on outcomes are useful in *policy formulation*. Those who formulate educational policy repeatedly indicate the need to have information on outcomes of schooling in order to allocate resources and establish instructional processes.

Define Terms

The terms *outcomes* and *indicators* are used in many ways in the professional and popular literature. In fact, the multiple uses of the terms cause confusion. For example, some educators talk of assessing educational outcomes, whereas others talk about outcomes-based education. In this chapter, we talk about outcomes-based accountability. Outcomes-based education and outcomes-based accountability are not the same thing. The NCEO defines *outcomes* as "the results of interactions between individuals and schooling experiences." (National Center on Educational Outcomes, 1992, working paper #2) Outcomes may be direct or indirect, positive or negative, and intended or unintended. Knowledge of the procedures necessary to register and vote may be a direct outcome of schooling. Whether a student votes later in life is an indirect outcome; it is determined by many more factors than what is learned in school. Employment is an indirect outcome of schooling. Schooling enables individuals to be employed, but actual employment is the result of many factors in addition to schooling. Those who measure the outcomes of schooling are concerned about both positive outcomes (e.g., learning to read) and negative outcomes (e.g., dropping out of school). And they are concerned about intended outcomes (e.g., the student's becoming a productive citizen) and unintended outcomes (e.g., the student's getting arrested).

Indicators are defined as symbolic representations of one or more outcomes that can be used in making comparisons. They provide ways of knowing what could or should be considered to find out whether desired results are being reached. They can be numbers or other representations such as test scores, levels of participation in activities, or perceptions of student accomplishments by parents or others. In the NCEO model of outcomes and indicators illustrated later in this chapter, we note that stakeholders have decided that an important outcome of schooling is that students "comply with school and community rules." Indicators of this outcome follow:

- Percentage of students who have been suspended or subjected to other disciplinary action
- Vandalism rate and magnitude
- Crime rate and magnitude

Consider the Assumptions That Underlie a Conceptual Model of Outcomes and Indicators

Any system of outcomes and indicators is based on a number of assumptions. Those who want to assess educational outcomes will have to consider carefully the assumptions that underlie the system they develop. The NCEO and stakeholders engaged in much discussion and debate on assessment of educational outcomes and came to agreement on the following:

- A model of outcomes is needed for *all* students and, at the broadest level, should apply to all students regardless of the characteristics of individuals.
- A model of outcomes should primarily focus on intended outcomes but be sensitive to unintended outcomes of schooling.
- A model of outcomes should include both direct and indirect outcomes.
- Indicators of outcomes for students receiving special education services should be related, conceptually and statistically, to those identified for students without disabilities.
- Indicators should reflect the diversity of gender, culture, race, and other characteristics of the students in today's school population.
- Whereas indicators should meet research standards, those that do not may still be used.
- A comprehensive system of indicators should provide the data needed to make policy decisions at the national, state, and local levels.
- A comprehensive system of indicators should be based on demonstrated functional relationships between outcome indicators and indicators of educational inputs, as well as contextual characteristics and processes; however, valued indicators may be included even if functional relationships have not been established.
- A comprehensive system of indicators should be flexible, dynamic, and responsive to review and criticism. It should also change to meet identified needs and future developments in the measurement of inputs, contexts, processes, and outcomes.

DEVELOP, ADOPT, OR ADAPT A MODEL OF OUTCOMES

The outcomes assessment process should be driven by a conceptual model that shows how the educational system should work. The NCEO developed a conceptual model of the educational process by convening groups of stakeholders to identify what they wanted out of the educational system. These stakeholders did not identify a narrow set of desired outcomes; rather, they indicated that they expect students to complete the educational process with a broad set of skills and behaviors that go beyond literacy and academic content knowledge. Stakeholders identified eight domains: physical health, responsibility and independence, contribution and citizenship, academic and functional literacy, personal and social adjustment, satisfaction, presence and participation, and accommodation and adaptation. The model is shown in Figure 30.1. Underlying the model is the assumption that schools, districts, and states differ in the resources available to educate students and that they provide educational opportunities and put students through an educational process. Figure 30.1 illustrates eight domains of outcomes. Two of the domains are shown above and below "Educational Opportunity and Process" because they are as much part of the educational process as an outcome of it. The model illustrated in the figure is now being used in states and local districts to guide the outcomes assessment process.

The outcome domains shown in Figure 30.1 are defined as follows:

- *Physical Health*: healthy behaviors, attitudes, and knowledge related to physical health
- *Responsibility and Independence*: behavior that reflects the ability to function independently and assume responsibility for self
- *Contribution and Citizenship*: participation as a good citizen in society
- *Academic and Functional Literacy*: use of information obtained in school to function in society, to achieve goals, and to develop knowledge
- *Personal and Social Adjustment*: socially acceptable and healthy behaviors, attitudes, and knowledge regarding mental well-being
- *Satisfaction*: favorable attitude toward education
- *Presence and Participation*: an individual's presence in a particular setting and the extent to which meaningful participation occurs

FIGURE 30.1   **NCEO Conceptual Model of Outcomes**

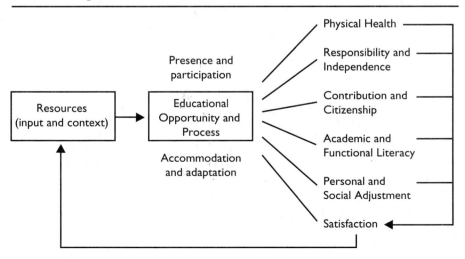

- *Accommodation and Adaptation*: modification made to allow other accomplishments.

Specifying Outcomes and Indicators

Before attempting to develop measures of educational outcomes, of course, the outcomes must be identified. The NCEO model includes a specification of outcomes at six developmental levels: age 3, age 6, grade 4, grade 8, school completion, and post school. The important outcomes were identified through a consensus-building process involving many stakeholder groups. In Figure 30.2, we list the school completion outcomes identified for each of the eight domains in the NCEO model. School personnel will have to engage in a consensus-building process in their own districts to reach agreement about those outcomes that are most important in each of the outcomes domains.

Once outcomes are identified, it is important to work with stakeholders in selecting important indicators of the outcomes. Indicators are symbolic representations of outcomes. NCEO engaged in a process of developing indicators for each of the outcomes specified in their model of outcomes. Figure 30.3 (page 699) shows indicators of citizenship and contribution at school completion.

IDENTIFY SOURCES OF DATA

For an outcomes and indicators system to be put in place, it is necessary to have data on the extent to which the outcomes are being met. Those who engage in outcomes-based accountability will necessarily have to identify sources from which they can get data. In the development of such a system, consider the sources of data shown in Table 30.1 (page 699) as possible places to get information. A fundamental premise to guide the data collection process is that it should rely as much as possible on use of existing information. Developing new data collection instruments and procedures requires a carefully considered process of design, development, field testing, revision, sampling, training, collection, error checking, data entry, and analysis. Outcomes accountability systems that require development of new measures of data collection methodologies probably will not fare well.

INSTALL AN OUTCOMES-BASED ACCOUNTABILITY SYSTEM

A system of outcomes and indicators cannot be installed overnight. Those who use the information on outcomes will need to see personal and programmatic benefits before the system can be considered fully in place. There must be incen-

FIGURE 30.2   **School Completion Outcomes in the NCEO Model**

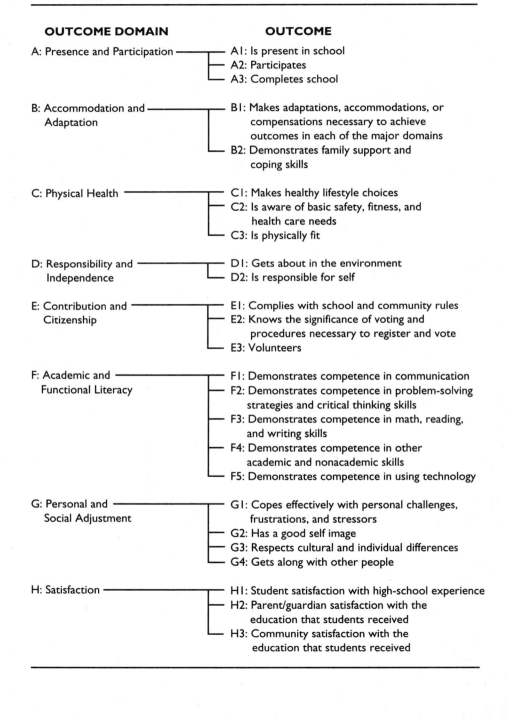

OUTCOME DOMAIN	OUTCOME
A: Presence and Participation	A1: Is present in school
	A2: Participates
	A3: Completes school
B: Accommodation and Adaptation	B1: Makes adaptations, accommodations, or compensations necessary to achieve outcomes in each of the major domains
	B2: Demonstrates family support and coping skills
C: Physical Health	C1: Makes healthy lifestyle choices
	C2: Is aware of basic safety, fitness, and health care needs
	C3: Is physically fit
D: Responsibility and Independence	D1: Gets about in the environment
	D2: Is responsible for self
E: Contribution and Citizenship	E1: Complies with school and community rules
	E2: Knows the significance of voting and procedures necessary to register and vote
	E3: Volunteers
F: Academic and Functional Literacy	F1: Demonstrates competence in communication
	F2: Demonstrates competence in problem-solving strategies and critical thinking skills
	F3: Demonstrates competence in math, reading, and writing skills
	F4: Demonstrates competence in other academic and nonacademic skills
	F5: Demonstrates competence in using technology
G: Personal and Social Adjustment	G1: Copes effectively with personal challenges, frustrations, and stressors
	G2: Has a good self image
	G3: Respects cultural and individual differences
	G4: Gets along with other people
H: Satisfaction	H1: Student satisfaction with high-school experience
	H2: Parent/guardian satisfaction with the education that students received
	H3: Community satisfaction with the education that students received

FIGURE 30.3   **NCEO Indicators: Contribution and Citizenship**

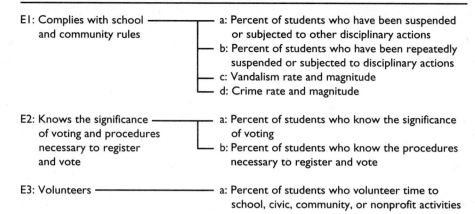

E1: Complies with school
and community rules
— a: Percent of students who have been suspended or subjected to other disciplinary actions
— b: Percent of students who have been repeatedly suspended or subjected to disciplinary actions
— c: Vandalism rate and magnitude
— d: Crime rate and magnitude

E2: Knows the significance
of voting and procedures
necessary to register
and vote
— a: Percent of students who know the significance of voting
— b: Percent of students who know the procedures necessary to register and vote

E3: Volunteers
— a: Percent of students who volunteer time to school, civic, community, or nonprofit activities

TABLE 30.1   **Suggested Sources of Information for One Outcome in the NCEO Model of an Outcomes-Based Accountability System**

Domain	Outcome	Indicators	Sources of Information
Contribution and Citizenship	Complies with school and community rules (School Completion Outcome)	Percent of students who have been suspended or subjected to other disciplinary actions	• School administrative records • Number of discipline contacts between student and principal's office, teacher reports of time-outs, etc. • Teacher questionnaires • State information system
		Percent of students who have been *repeatedly* suspended or subjected to disciplinary actions	• School administrative records • School archival records • Teacher questionnaires • State information system
		Vandalism rate and magnitude	• Parent/student reports • Police and/or school records of vandalism rates, frequency, and severity • *National Longitudinal Transition Study* • Principal's reports • National Education Goals Panel report on safe schools
		Crime rate and magnitude	• Parent/student reports • Police and/or school records of vandalism rates, frequency, and severity • *National Longitudinal Transition Study* • Statewide or local surveys/interviews of juvenile detention and correctional facilities, local jails, and state adult correctional facilities • Principal's reports

tives for teachers, parents, and administrators who will ultimately ensure the success of the system.

Two commonly used incentives are public comparisons and sanctions for failure to meet standards or goals. Public comparisons formally display schools, districts, or states side-by-side. Sanctioning involves negative techniques such as withdrawal of accreditation, takeovers of schools, and reduction of funding based on identification of less-than-adequate outcomes. Both comparisons and sanctions are high-stakes uses of any accountability system. They can lead to overemphasis on appearances, without substantive changes.

The way change in measurement and accountability systems occurs is the way change occurs in any system. State or governmental agencies fund research and demonstration projects, establish networking and recognition systems, and provide resources for use of outcomes-based accountability systems. Personnel in state departments of education provide technical assistance to local school districts that are trying to implement accountability systems.

Once an outcomes-based accountability system is in place and being used, we may be able to identify the extent to which the interventions used with individuals with disabilities are working as we would like them to work. System-wide accountability assessment should enable us to make judgments about the extent of the system's success.

CURRENT STATE PRACTICES IN ASSESSMENT OF EDUCATIONAL OUTCOMES

Since 1991, the National Center on Educational Outcomes has surveyed state assessment personnel to identify state practices and activities in the assessment of educational outcomes for students with disabilities. Some of the major findings of their surveys follow:

- States gather very little data on students with disabilities. They usually gather data only on attendance, participation in programs, and the way in which the student exited the system (e.g., as a graduate or a dropout).
- Few state-level special data collection efforts, other than post-school status studies, yield outcomes data on students with disabilities.
- State-level outcomes information is generated most often from large-scale general education assessments in which students with mild disabilities may participate, but the extent to which they participate is uncertain in most states. In fact, large numbers of students with disabilities are excluded from state assessments (see Chapter 9).
- Several states are exploring ways to collect outcomes data.

In the sections that follow, we describe outcomes assessment practices in four states: Arizona, Kentucky, Michigan, and Utah.

Arizona

Signed into law by the Arizona State Legislature on May 16, 1990, the Arizona Student Assessment Program (ASAP) is a comprehensive program designed to improve teaching, learning, and assessing in the Arizona schools. It consists of six components:

1. Essential skills
2. Performance-based assessment
3. Norm-referenced assessment
4. A district assessment plan
5. Essential skills competency reports
6. District and school report cards

The ASAP initiative emerged from public concern about student achievement, accountability, and assessment. It was developed to create a new approach to curriculum and assessment that would achieve higher standards and more meaningful assessments of students' knowledge and skills. To that end, the key components of ASAP are the essential skills competencies and the performance-based assessments.

Arizona uses two types of assessments to measure student achievement: norm-referenced and performance-based assessment. The Iowa Test of Basic Skills (ITBS) is administered at grades 4, 7, and 11. These assessments provide the state with a way to compare students' achievements.

State personnel are developing a set of performance-based assessments to test students' knowledge and measure those skills that correspond with the essential skills competencies. These competencies form a state curriculum framework and consist of representative skills across five academic domains: reading, writing, mathematics, social studies, and science. The skills require higher-order thinking, stress integrated problem-solving capabilities, and define what students should know and be able to do by the end of third, eighth, and twelfth grades.

Assessments are developed according to Arizona Department of Education specifications and undergo a lengthy review process to detect gender and/or cultural biases. A total of 201 performance-based assessments in the areas of reading, mathematics, and writing have been developed for grades K–12. These assessments serve both accountability and instructional purposes. Each spring, all students in grades 3, 8, and 12 are formally assessed with one form of the performance-based assessment. Two other parallel forms have been developed for teachers to use in each grade for instructional planning, instruction, or assessment.

An Arizona statute requires that all students have the opportunity to master the essential skills and participate in the performance-based assessments. Therefore, students with disabilities who are exempt from norm-referenced testing have the opportunity to be included in performance-based assessments.

Performance-based assessments can be completed by using a mediated assessment for those students with an IEP under the Individuals with Disabilities Education Act (Public Law 101-476) or with an accommodation plan under Section 504 of the Rehabilitation Act of 1973.

Formal guidelines for mediated assessment have been established as part of ASAP. Mediation refers to any assistance related to a student's disability or special circumstances that is given to the student by the test administrator. Examples include flexible time allocation, flexible setting, visual aids, and translations of English text. Students with limited English proficiency who fall within the guidelines may take the assessment with mediation. Spanish versions of the performance-based assessment at all three grade levels are offered to eligible Spanish-speaking children as determined by their teachers.

The performance-based assessments were pilot tested in the spring of 1992 to provide baseline data of student performance and to determine the reliability and validity of measuring the standards. A total of 113,000 students participated, including students with disabilities. Assessment results were published in the summer of 1992, with data reported by district, school, special program, primary language, ethnicity, and gender.

The Arizona Department of Education requires each school district to complete and submit a District Assessment Plan. The purpose of the plan is to report how and when students will be assessed on the essential skills throughout the grades. Districts are required to set mastery levels for the essential skills in reading, writing, and mathematics and to describe how they will report and use the results of assessments.

Starting in the spring of 1993, districts were also required to report the percentage of third-, eighth-, and twelfth-grade students who achieve mastery levels. Districts use a variety of testing options to assess the essential skills and can include their own criterion-referenced tests, their own portfolio assessments, or the state's performance-based assessments. Because all students are expected to learn the essential skills, districts must consider the needs of all students when developing the District Assessment Plan.

Implementation of the ASAP is intended to help promote inclusion in the performance-based assessment program for students with disabilities. The Arizona Department of Education has published the results of sixty-seven ASAP performance assessments at the state, district, and school levels.

Kentucky

The Kentucky Reform Act (KERA) of 1990 formed the basis for massive change in the state's educational system. It is the result of a lawsuit brought against Kentucky by the Coalition for Better Education (CBE), which represented sixty-five school districts. The successful 1988 lawsuit found the state's funding mechanisms inequitable and mandated that the educational system be re-designed.

The cornerstone of this reform effort has been its commitment to a unitary system of education. Special education has been involved from the outset, especially in the mandated reform committees (Curriculum, Governance, and Finance). The Curriculum committee has established six learning goals for all students and built a set of seventy-five valued outcomes related to the six goals. These outcomes have been developed with the input of the business and educational communities (including special education).

To measure progress toward the outcomes, an assessment system called the Kentucky Instructional Results and Information System (KIRIS) was established. Based on the principles of outcomes-based education, KIRIS seeks to include all students in the assessment and accountability processes under KERA. The KIRIS assessments come under the direction of content area advisory committees made up of members from the Department of Education, the University of Kentucky, and a private firm called Advanced Systems for Measurement and Evaluation. There are three parts to KIRIS:

1. Transitional items, which include multiple-choice and open-ended probes for written language, mathematics, science, social studies, and reading
2. Writing portfolios, which include each student's best work from one school year
3. Performance events, which are planned activities that call for students to solve simulated, real-life problems.

Students' results are reported in four performance levels: novice, apprentice, proficient, and distinguished. All students in grades 4, 8, and 12 are assessed. For students with disabilities who become exempt from the KIRIS assessment by the action of an Admissions and Release Committee (ARC), there is an alternative assessment system: the Alternate Portfolio Assessment. This program is for students whose demonstrated cognitive ability and adaptive behavior prevents completion of the regular course of study, even with program modifications. Schools may not place more than 2 percent of their population in the Alternate Portfolio. Schools that do exceed this percentage are monitored by the state education agency. The key concepts of the Alternate Portfolio are as follows:

• The scores of students participating in the assessment are weighted equally with those of students participating in the regular assessment for the school's accountability purposes.
• No preconceived notion exists on what entries to the student's portfolio must look like, as long as each entry is related to the state's valued outcomes.

The unique part of Kentucky's approach under KERA is the expenditure of significant resources to ensure that all students are included in the state assessment system.

Michigan

The Michigan Department of Education collects student achievement data through the Michigan Educational Assessment Program (MEAP). Students are tested on state essential performance objectives for reading, mathematics, and science. Reading and math are assessed in grades 4, 7, and 10; science is tested in grades 5, 8, and 11. MEAP tests are criterion-referenced, standardized achievement batteries. Results are intended to document changes in student achievement relative to the essential skills for each content area.

Data are reported at each level and can be used by individuals, schools, and districts. Students with disabilities are included in MEAP if they receive 51 percent or more of their reading or English instruction in the mainstream setting. Local school personnel may also exclude a student if he or she is "too physically, mentally, or emotionally impaired to manage in a testing situation." Approximately 10 percent of the 1990–1991 MEAP students were students with disabilities. The Department of Education estimates that about 18 percent of students with disabilities who were potential participants were included in the assessment.

Changes in assessment practices for Michigan were made by the State School Aid Act of 1991. It mandates that each student have a portfolio containing records of planning, academic achievements, recognition and accomplishments, and career and job preparation. It also requires the state to develop a new proficiency-testing system in communications, mathematics, and science to determine student eligibility for a state-endorsed diploma. The State Board of Education makes the decision about inclusion or exclusion of students with disabilities in the new testing program.

The Special Education Unit of Michigan has been involved in outcomes planning and evaluation since 1987. It has contracted with a private firm, the Center for Quality Special Education (CQSE), to develop comprehensive descriptions and evaluations of student outcomes for each disability category. The emphasis of Michigan's outcomes effort has been to guide individual student evaluation and instruction. CQSE delineates broad learner outcomes that are further defined by age-level performance indicators (called On-Target Abilities). It conducts Exit Performance Assessments that evaluate a student's progress toward specific outcomes as well as evaluations that profile a learner's overall performance. Learner profiles show each On-Target Ability scored on a scale from "emerging skill" to "strong skill." These profiles serve as a basis for transforming outcomes into objective statements to be used for IEP planning. Student profiles that show some percentage of objectives met may be aggregated for school district or state reports.

Utah

In 1990, Utah replaced its fifteen-year-old assessment program with the Statewide Testing Program. This program was developed in response to concerns about school accountability for student achievement and an interest in a system that allowed for quantifiable comparisions of student achievement. The state legislature mandated an annual statewide testing program that uses a norm-referenced achievement test. The Stanford Achievement Test was chosen to assess all students in grades 5, 8, and 11.

The Statewide Testing Program uses the exclusion criteria specified for the National Assessment of Educational Progress, making students exempt from testing if (1) they are in the mainstream setting less than 50 percent of the school day, (2) they meet Limited English Proficiency criteria, or (3) they meet emergency exclusion criteria. The Department of Education provides Braille and large print editions of the Stanford Achievement Test as part of the program. It encourages staff to make other accommodations as necessary to obtain information about the student, but results of performances on adapted tests are not included in the school profile. The department does not monitor exclusion per se but publishes both the results of the test and the participation rates. An estimated 97 percent of the student population in grades 5 and 8 and 92 percent in grade 11 participate in the statewide test. The state-mandated testing gives a school-by-school and district-by-district comparison of academic achievement scores of students.

Utah also has a separate assessment program known as the Core Assessment Program (CAP). This voluntary program supports classroom instruction; it is not an accountability system. CAP consists of a series of criterion-referenced tests that are designed to test concepts in Utah's Core Curriculum. Neither CAP nor the Core Curriculum are mandated, but both arise from State Board of Education graduation requirements established in 1984. Those requirements demand mastery of certain elements of the Core Curriculum by all students, including students with disabilities unless they are exempted or the Core Curriculum is modified by an IEP (on a case-by-case basis). Districts must assess student performance on the Core Curriculum through a criterion measure of their choice; however, most districts use some piece of the Core Assessment Program. Information about student performance is provided at the individual, school, district, and state levels. Data are not disaggregated for special education populations. Schools are not required, but are strongly encouraged, to share CAP information with parents.

Additionally, Utah has been developing performance assessments with a model that uses eight evaluative criteria and considers the needs of districts and teachers. The first phase of assessments, which were implemented in 1993, included math, science, and social studies. It consisted of four exercises per grade level for teachers to use and one cumulative exercise per grade level for districts to use in conducting a district-level assessment. Possible expansion of the model into other curriculum areas depends on how well it works in the first phase.

SUMMARY

Today, much activity is directed toward demonstrating the extent to which education is working for students with disabilities. This has been part of a larger focus on the results of education. One way to demonstrate results is to systematically evaluate the extent to which desired results or outcomes are being achieved. This, of course, involves specifying the desired outcomes and then measuring or assessing the extent to which they are being met.

As school districts and states establish outcomes-based accountability systems, it is important that they go through a number of steps. Stakeholders must be involved in all phases of the accountability assessment process—especially in the beginning phase. Those who assess the outcomes of schooling must decide specifically why they want to measure results and then carefully define their terms. The process of deciding what outcomes and indicators are to be measured should be a shared process involving representatives of all relevant stakeholder groups.

STUDY QUESTIONS

1. In this chapter you have read about a major shift in education from a focus on the process of educating students to a focus on educational outcomes. What factors have contributed to this shift in focus?
2. Why is it important that stakeholders be involved before, during, and after the development of an outcomes assessment system?
3. What fundamental assumptions underly the process of collecting outcomes assessment information?
4. What do we know about current state practices in assessment of educational outcomes?
5. What steps should state and school district personnel go through as they develop outcomes accountability systems?

ADDITIONAL READING

Ysseldyke, J. E., & Thurlow, M. L. (in press). Outcomes: Watch your language! *Special Services in the Schools*.

Ysseldyke, J. E., & Thurlow, M. L. (in press). What outcomes should be assessed in outcomes-based assessment? *Special Services in the Schools*.

Appendixes

Appendix 1

Areas of the Normal Curve

Area equals the proportion of cases between the z-score and the mean; extreme area equals .5000 less the proportion of cases between the z-score and the mean.

z	.00	.01	.02	.03	.04	.05	.06	.07	.08	.09
0.0	.0000	.0040	.0080	.0120	.0160	.0199	.0239	.0279	.0319	.0359
0.1	.0398	.0438	.0478	.0517	.0557	.0596	.0636	.0675	.0714	.0753
0.2	.0793	.0832	.0871	.0910	.0948	.0987	.1026	.1064	.1103	.1141
0.3	.1179	.1217	.1255	.1293	.1331	.1368	.1406	.1443	.1480	.1517
0.4	.1554	.1591	.1628	.1664	.1700	.1736	.1772	.1808	.1844	.1879
0.5	.1915	.1950	.1985	.2019	.2054	.2088	.2123	.2157	.2190	.2224
0.6	.2257	.2291	.2324	.2357	.2389	.2422	.2454	.2486	.2517	.2549
0.7	.2580	.2611	.2642	.2673	.2704	.2734	.2764	.2794	.2823	.2852
0.8	.2881	.2910	.2939	.2967	.2995	.3023	.3051	.3078	.3106	.3133
0.9	.3159	.3186	.3212	.3238	.3264	.3289	.3315	.3340	.3365	.3389
1.0	.3413	.3438	.3461	.3485	.3508	.3531	.3554	.3577	.3599	.3621
1.1	.3643	.3665	.3686	.3708	.3729	.3749	.3770	.3790	.3810	.3830
1.2	.3849	.3869	.3888	.3907	.3925	.3944	.3962	.3980	.3997	.4015
1.3	.4032	.4049	.4066	.4082	.4099	.4115	.4131	.4147	.4162	.4177
1.4	.4192	.4207	.4222	.4236	.4251	.4265	.4279	.4292	.4306	.4319
1.5	.4332	.4345	.4357	.4370	.4382	.4394	.4406	.4418	.4429	.4441
1.6	.4452	.4463	.4474	.4484	.4495	.4505	.4515	.4525	.4535	.4545
1.7	.4554	.4564	.4573	.4582	.4591	.4599	.4608	.4616	.4625	.4633
1.8	.4641	.4649	.4656	.4664	.4671	.4678	.4686	.4693	.4699	.4706
1.9	.4713	.4719	.4726	.4732	.4738	.4744	.4750	.4756	.4761	.4767
2.0	.4772	.4778	.4783	.4788	.4793	.4798	.4803	.4808	.4812	.4817
2.1	.4821	.4826	.4830	.4834	.4838	.4842	.4846	.4850	.4854	.4857
2.2	.4861	.4864	.4868	.4871	.4875	.4878	.4881	.4884	.4887	.4890
2.3	.4893	.4896	.4898	.4901	.4904	.4906	.4909	.4911	.4913	.4916
2.4	.4918	.4920	.4922	.4925	.4927	.4929	.4931	.4932	.4934	.4936
2.5	.4938	.4940	.4941	.4943	.4945	.4946	.4948	.4949	.4951	.4952
2.6	.4953	.4955	.4956	.4957	.4959	.4960	.4961	.4962	.4963	.4964
2.7	.4965	.4966	.4967	.4968	.4969	.4970	.4971	.4972	.4973	.4974
2.8	.4974	.4975	.4976	.4977	.4977	.4978	.4979	.4979	.4980	.4981
2.9	.4981	.4982	.4982	.4983	.4984	.4984	.4985	.4985	.4986	.4986
3.0	.4987	.4987	.4987	.4988	.4988	.4989	.4989	.4989	.4990	.4990

SOURCE: Presentation of data used in the present volume is from *Statistics: An Intuitive Approach*, Third Edition, by G. H. Weinberg and J. A. Schumaker. Copyright © 1962, 1969, 1974 by Wadsworth Publishing Company, Inc. Reprinted by permission of the publisher, Brooks/Cole Publishing Company, Pacific Grove, California 93950.

Appendix 2

Percentile Ranks for z-Scores of Normal Curves

z	Area[a]	z	Area[a]	z	Area[a]
−4.0	.000	−1.0	.159	2.0	.977
−3.9	.000	−0.9	.184	2.1	.982
−3.8	.000	−0.8	.212	2.2	.986
−3.7	.000	−0.7	.242	2.3	.989
−3.6	.000	−0.6	.274	2.4	.992
−3.5	.000	−0.5	.308	2.5	.994
−3.4	.000	−0.4	.345	2.6	.995
−3.3	.001	−0.3	.382	2.7	.996
−3.2	.001	−0.2	.421	2.8	.997
−3.1	.001	−0.1	.460	2.9	.998
−3.0	.001	0.0	.500	3.0	.999
−2.9	.002	0.1	.540	3.1	.999
−2.8	.003	0.2	.579	3.2	.999
−2.7	.004	0.3	.618	3.3	.999
−2.6	.005	0.4	.655	3.4	1.000
−2.5	.006	0.5	.692	3.5	1.000
−2.4	.008	0.6	.726	3.6	1.000
−2.3	.011	0.7	.758	3.7	1.000
−2.2	.014	0.8	.788	3.8	1.000
−2.1	.018	0.9	.816	3.9	1.000
				4.0	1.000
−2.0	.023	1.0	.841		
−1.9	.029	1.1	.864		
−1.8	.036	1.2	.885		
−1.7	.045	1.3	.903		
−1.6	.055	1.4	.919		
−1.5	.067	1.5	.933		
−1.4	.081	1.6	.945		
−1.3	.097	1.7	.955		
−1.2	.115	1.8	.964		
−1.1	.136	1.9	.971		

[a]Move decimal two places to the right for the percentile rank. Values are rounded to three places.

SOURCE: Presentation of data used in the present volume is from *Statistics: An Intuitive Approach*, Third Edition, by G. H. Weinberg and J. A. Schumaker. Copyright © 1962, 1969, 1974 by Wadsworth Publishing Company, Inc. Reprinted by permission of the publisher, Brooks/Cole Publishing Company, Pacific Grove, California 93950.

Appendix 3

List of Equations Used in the Text

Location in Text	Term Defined	Equation
Chapter 4, p. 91	Mean	$\overline{X} = \dfrac{\Sigma X}{N}$ (Equation 4.1)
Chapter 4, p. 93	Variance	$S^2 = \dfrac{\Sigma (X - \overline{X})^2}{N}$ (Equation 4.2)
		or
		$S^2 = \dfrac{\Sigma X^2}{N} - \left(\dfrac{\Sigma X}{N}\right)^2$
Chapter 4, p. 97	Pearson product-moment correlation coefficient, where X and Y are scores on two tests	$r = \dfrac{N\Sigma XY - (\Sigma X)(\Sigma Y)}{\sqrt{N\Sigma X^2 - (\Sigma X)^2}\ \sqrt{N\Sigma Y^2 - (\Sigma Y)^2}}$
		or
		$r = \dfrac{\Sigma Z_x Z_y}{n}$
Chapter 5, p. 111	Percentile rank for a particular score	% ile = Percent of people scoring below the score plus one-half the percent of people obtaining the score
Chapter 5, p. 113	z-score	$z = \dfrac{X - \overline{X}}{S}$ (Equation 5.1)
Chapter 5, p. 113	Any standard score	$SS = \overline{X}_{ss} + (S_{ss})(z)$ (Equation 5.2)
Chapter 7, p. 142	Coefficient alpha	$r_{aa} = \dfrac{k}{k-1}\left(1 - \dfrac{\Sigma S^2_{items}}{S^2_{test}}\right)$ (Equation 7.2)
Chapter 7, p. 144	Point-to-point agreement	$\dfrac{(100)\ \text{number of agreements on occurrence and nonocurrence}}{\text{number of observations}}$ (Equation 7.3)

Location in Text	Term Defined	Equation
Chapter 7, p. 144	Percent agreement on occurrence	$$\frac{100 \text{ (number of agreements on occurrence)}}{\text{number of observations} - \text{number of agreements on nonoccurrence}} \quad \text{(Equation 7.4)}$$
Chapter 7, p. 146	Spearman-Brown formula to correct for test length	$$r_{xx} = \frac{2r_{(1/2)(1/2)}}{1 + r_{(1/2)(1/2)}} \quad \text{(Equation 7.6)}$$
Chapter 7, p. 151	Standard error of measurement	$\text{SEM} = S\sqrt{1 - r_{xx}}$ (Equation 7.7)
Chapter 7, p. 153	Estimated true score	$X' = \overline{X} + (r_{xx})(X - \overline{X})$ (Equation 7.8)
Chapter 7, p. 155	Lower and upper limits of a confidence interval, where z-score determines level of confidence	Lower limit $= X' - (z)(\text{SEM})$ Upper limit $= X' + (z)(\text{SEM})$ (Equation 7.9)
Chapter 7, p. 157	Reliability of a predicted difference	$$\hat{D} = \frac{r_{bb} + (r_{aa})(r_{ab}^2) - 2r_{ab}}{1 - r_{ab}^2} \quad \text{(Equation 7.10)}$$
Chapter 7, p. 158	Standard deviation of a predicted difference	$S_{\text{dif}} = S_b\sqrt{1 - r_{ab}^2}$ (Equation 7.11)
Chapter 7, p. 158	Reliability of a difference of obtained scores	$$r_{\text{dif}} = \frac{\frac{1}{2}(r_{aa} + r_{bb}) - r_{ab}}{1 - r_{ab}} \quad \text{(Equation 7.12)}$$
Chapter 7, p. 158	Standard deviation of obtained difference	$S_{\text{dif}} = \sqrt{S_a^2 + S_b^2 - 2r_{ab}S_aS_b}$ (Equation 7.13)
Chapter 7, p. 158	Standard error of measurement of a difference	$\text{SEM}_{\text{dif}} = \sqrt{S_a^2 + S_b^2 - 2r_{ab}S_aS_b} \times$ $$\sqrt{1 - \frac{\frac{1}{2}(r_{aa} + r_{bb}) - r_{ab}}{1 - r_{ab}}} \quad \text{(Equation 7.14)}$$
Chapter 7, p. 158	Estimated true difference	$d' = (\text{obtained difference})(r_{xx\,(\text{dif})})$ (Equation 7.15)

Appendix 4

List of Publishers

Those wishing to purchase test specimen kits or secure additional test materials can write to the test publisher. The following is a list of the publishers whose tests are reviewed in this book.

Thomas M. Achenbach, Department of Psychiatry, University of Vermont, Burlington, VT 05401

American Guidance Service, Inc., 4201 Woodland Rd., Circle Pines, MN 55014

CTB/Macmillan/McGraw-Hill, 20 Ryan Ranch Rd., Monterey, CA 93940-5703

Curriculum Associates., Inc., 5 Esquire Rd., North Billerica, MA 01862

Grune & Stratton, 111 Fifth Ave., New York, NY 10003

Hawthorne Educational Services Inc., 800 Gray Oak Drive, Columbia, MO 65201

Marshall S. Hiskey, 5640 Baldwin, Lincoln, NE 68507

Jastak Associates, P.O. Box 3410, Wilmington, DE 19804-0250

Juniper Gardens Children Center, University of Kansas, Lawrence, KS 67039

Learning Concepts, 2501 North Lamar, Austin, TX 78705

Modern Curriculum Press, 13900 Prospect Rd., Cleveland, OH 44136

Pro-Ed, 8700 Shoal Creek Blvd., Austin, TX 78758-6897

Psychological Corporation, 555 Academic Court, San Antonio, TX 78204-2498

The Riverside Publishing Company, 8420 Bryn Mawr Ave., Chicago, IL 60631

Rum River Special Education Cooperative, 430 N. W. 8th Street, Cambridge, MN 55008

Slosson Educational Publications, 140 Pine St., P.O. Box 280, East Aurora, NY 14052

Sopris West, 1140 Boston Ave., Longmont, CO 80300

Teachers College Press, P.O. Box 2032, Colchester, VT 05449

University of Minnesota, 204 Burton Hall, Minneapolis, MN 55414

Western Psychological Services, 12031 Wilshire Blvd., Los Angeles, CA 90025-1251

Appendix 5

How to Review a Test

We have often been asked how we go about analyzing and reviewing tests—both for this book and in general. So we have decided to include a how-to section. Before starting an analysis of a test, you must first assemble the materials. We find that it is best to order a specimen kit and any supplementary manuals available. Be prepared to experience difficulty obtaining material from some test publishers. When you request a specimen kit and supplementary materials, you will occasionally receive all materials. More often, when you review specimen sets, you'll learn that additional materials must be ordered separately. Sometimes it takes a very long time to figure out just what is published where. It may take up to six months to acquire all the material on a test. Sometimes you just never obtain materials. Patience and perseverance are almost always required.

When materials arrive, prepare yourself properly to begin your review. The right setting is very important. A well-ventilated, well-lit room (preferably a bit on the chilly side) and a hard, straight-backed chair are essential.

Next, and more important, adopt a "show me" attitude. Do not expect test authors to admit in the manuals that the test was poorly normed because there was no money to pay testers or that the test has inadequate reliability because they didn't develop enough test items. Test authors put the best possible face on their tests, as might be expected. You simply cannot accept the claims made by test authors and their colleagues who write the technical manuals. If you accepted them at their word, they would only have to say that they had a "good, reliable, valid, and well-normed test." Test authors must *demonstrate* that their tests are reliable, valid, and well-normed.

After assembling the relevant materials and finding a suitable place in which to ask "Where's the proof?" we usually follow these procedures. First, we skim through the material to get a general idea of what the test is intended to do and what is included in each document that accompanies it. We generally keep notes on several separate sheets of paper—one for each topic that we consider: background and purposes, behavior sampled, scores, norms, reliability, and validity.

Then we reread the manuals. You might expect that test authors would organize test manuals neatly so that you could turn to the table of contents, find the section on, for example, reliability, and turn to the pages indicated. Sometimes, yes—but more often, no. If a manual does not have section headings or chapters, we just begin reading and making notes under our headings. If a manual is divided into sections, we start by reading about the behaviors sampled by the test. (It doesn't matter too much where you start, except that validity is best left until last.) Test manuals frequently contain a useful description of the behaviors sampled, but more often they merely name the domains sampled. For example, the authors of a test may say that it assesses reading, but that does not tell you if it assesses reading recognition, reading comprehension, or oral reading. Look at the test directions (especially directions on how to score student responses) and the protocol (the answer form). These materials generally give you a pretty good idea of what behaviors are actually measured. Then, try to describe the behaviors in straightforward terms—avoiding psychological and educational jargon.

Next, we look at the section on norms. When evaluating a test's norms, first note the ages (or grades in the case of achievement tests) of the students on whom the test was normed. Then look for statements describing the students. Also, anticipate quantification of the norm groups. For example, you should anticipate that the test author will tell you how many boys and how many girls and how many persons from various ethnic or racial groups were tested at each age or grade. You should also look for geographic information. For example, what percentage of the sample lived in big cities or in the Northwest? Finally, expect socioeconomic information about the students: parents' occupations, parents' educational attainment, income of the household. Look for an explicit comparison of the characteristics of the norm group with the national population, as described in the most recent census. (Sometimes test authors include all the data and all the comparisons in neat tabular form.) You may find substantial discrepancies between the norm sample and the population. Generally, we look for correspondence between the sample and the population within about 5 percent. Thus, if 31 percent of the sample lived in the Southwest and only 26 percent of the U.S. population live in the Southwest, we would not be overly concerned about the discrepancy. We realize that this is an arbitrary margin of error. If you prefer a different one, that's fine.

Information on scores is apt to be located in many places: in the section on scoring the test, in the description of the norms, in a separate section on scores, in the section dealing with the interpretation of scores, or in the norm tables themselves. Generally, the best place to find information on the types of scores available is the norm tables. These tables allow the conversion of raw scores to derived scores and subtest scores to total scores. The next best place to look is in the section on scoring the test. There you find the directions for crediting responses and combining raw scores into derived scores. In the norms section, you may find phrases such as "percentile norms" or "grade-equivalent norms," sure tip-offs that percentiles and grade equivalents will be available. In the sections on interpretation, you may find information on the proper interpretation of derived scores. For example, many test authors will tell you the mean and standard deviation of standard scores and how they are to be interpreted. However, it pays to double check against the norm tables themselves because test authors occasionally err in their descriptions.

Finding reliability data may be more difficult. If there is a section on reliability, the task is fairly simple. You want to see if there is evidence of each appropriate type of reliability. Demand numbers—do not settle for statements about the test's reliability. The authors should show statistical proof of reliability. Read the tables. You can anticipate finding estimates of generalization across items (split-half, KR-20, coefficient alpha, alternate-form, and so on) and across time (test-retest reliability). If the scoring is difficult, you should also find a section on interscorer agreement. (Data on the extent to which one can generalize across scores can often be found in the section on scoring.) You should find reliability estimates for each subtest at each grade or age. In addition, tables giving the standard error of measurement for each subtest at each grade or age are occasionally provided.

The next step is very important: You must determine what scores are to be interpreted, because those are the ones you must judge for adequacy. In the sections dealing with score interpretation, you will often find the scores that the test authors think are most important. Many tests have subtests that are combined into a total score. Sometimes the subtest scores are stressed over the total score (for example, in the Illinois Test of Psycholinguistic Abilities), whereas in other tests the total score or part scores are stressed more than subtest scores (for example, in the Wechsler Intelligence Scale for Children–Revised. The scores that are identified as important and that are to be interpreted must meet the minimum desirable standards of reliability. Consequently, different test are held to different standards. For example, the subtests on the ITPA must meet a higher standard of reliability than the subtests of the WISC-R because we are urged by the authors to interpret the ITPA subtests but not the WISC-R sub tests.

If there is no section on reliability, check the table of contents to see if there are tables for standard errors of measurement or reliability coefficients. You can usually find all the information that you need in the tables without reading the test. If there are no tables are no section on reliability, there may be no data on reliability in the manuals; this happens frequently. However, reliability information may be hidden in the section on validity, in the section on scores, or in the section on interpretation. Keep a lookout for it as you skim and read.

The evaluation of a test's validity is the most difficult aspect of reviewing a test. If the norms and the reliability are inadequate, there will be severe problems with validity. Even if they are adequate, the authors must still prove that the test is valid for each recommended use. This means that you must learn how the authors recommended using the test. Do not expect to find this information in a section labeled "validity." More often you will find such statements in the beginning of the test manuals or in the promotional materials.

You will always find a statement to the effect that the test measures some domain. How do the test authors prove this? Data on content validity is often included in a section called "the development of the test" or "selection of items."

In these sections, the authors explain how they chose the items in the test. For other tests, the information will be buried elsewhere in the manual. For still others, there will be no mention of how items were chosen—no proof of content validity.

Depending on the particular type of test, you may also find information on concurrent, predictive, and construct validity. Again, you must remember that the purpose of presenting these data is to demonstrate that the test measures the domain its authors claim it measures. The data should logically bear on the issue of validity.

Beyond claims that the test assesses a particular domain, you may find assertions that the test can be used in particular ways. This is especially true of tests of achievement, which authors often assert can be used in program planning. When we see such assertions, we expect to find a large number of test items appropriate for each grade. We look at the test items and at the norm tables to get an idea of the difference in the number of test items at each grade. All you have to do is find the raw score at the fiftieth percentile at two adjacent grades. For example, suppose 17 points correct was the fiftieth percentile at the second grade and 21 points correct was the fiftieth percentile at the third grade. Then, only 4 raw-score points would separate second- and third-grade work. This is probably too few items on which to base an educational plan, although the test may well discriminate among test takers. Sometimes we are told that scores can be used in particular ways. Such assertions are often found in the interpretation sections of the manuals. For example, you may find information on critical levels of performance; the authors may tell you that scores below a particular value are indicative of potential problems or that students earning such scores require special instructional interventions. Check out each assertion for the use of the test and expect to find proof.

Finally, we tend to be suspicious of strange formulations of reliability, validity, or scores. You should be, too. Remember, the test author should provide all the necessary data in clear and usable form. If it isn't there, it isn't your fault, and you should use the test cautiously—or not at all.

Appendix 6

A Brief Explanation of Item-Response Theory[1]

CONCEPTUAL BACKGROUND

Item-response theory (IRT) offers a different way to construct tests. As its name implies, the characteristics of individual test items are at the heart of the theory. Individual test items are important in both IRT and classical psychometric theory, but IRT and classical theory differ in the way test items are viewed and used. We expect the proportion of individuals passing an item (that is, the p-value) to vary as function of the individuals' ability, although this assumption is seldom explicated in classical psychometric theory. Thus, the proportion of individuals getting a valid item correct is correlated with ability.[2]

p-Values in Classical Psychometric Theory

In classical theory, we think of test items and their aggregates as dependent upon the characteristics of the individuals who respond to them. Thus, easy tests are tests on which most people answer most items correctly; more difficult tests are tests on which few people answer most items correctly. Test items do not posses characteristics independent of test takers. Thus, the various statistics used to describe tests are sample specific, and we depend on the performance of a representative sample of individuals to estimate these statistics (for example, p-values, indexes of reliability) and for score interpretation. As we stressed in Chapter 6 (Norms), a relatively large representative normative sample is necessary to provide test users with accurate information about individual items and

1. Our discussion of item-response theory is derived from *Principles of Test Theories* (1990) by Professor Hoi K. Suen, to whom we are indebted for providing useful suggestions after reading drafts of this appendix.
2. When individual test items are negatively correlated or uncorrelated with the ability assessed by the test (usually estimated by the total score on the test), the items ought to be deleted. Deletion of such items ensures the development of a homogeneous test.

total scores. Clearly, descriptive statistics about a test (mean, standard deviation), transformed scores (IQs, *T*-scores, etc.), estimates of reliability, and estimates of validity are closely tied to the normative sample. For example, if a test were normed on relatively homogeneous groups of students with limited ability, we should expect the following consequences.

1. The raw score mean would be lower than the mean of a representative sample.
2. The raw score standard deviation would be less than the standard deviation of a representative sample (because the sample is homogeneous and the range of scores is restricted).
3. Derived scores based on the unrepresentative sample would yield inflated scores for the general population (because the students being assessed are compared to students of limited ability).
4. Internal consistency and stability would be underestimated for a representative sample (because of the constricted range of the sample).
5. Empirical estimates of validity would be attenuated for a representative sample (because of the constricted range of the sample).

It follows from the above example that various statistics that describe the technical characteristics of a test actually describe the test used with a particular group of test-takers. Nowhere is this conclusion clearer than with regard to a test item's *p*-value. Suppose the *p*-value for a group of five-year olds is .25. Twenty-five percent of the five-year olds answer the item correctly; 75 percent do not. Yet, the same item may have a *p*-value of .50 for six-year olds. The *p*-value of an item is not a function of the item but a function of the item *used with a specific sample*.

Classic psychometric theory assumes that good test items discriminate through a wide range of abilities. In addition, a greater proportion of individuals with high total scores should answer the question correctly when compared to individuals with lower total test scores. Because *p*-values and point-biserial correlations are average statistics, one cannot tell from these values alone if an item acts in this way. Therefore, more sophisticated test developers plot item characteristic curves by graphing the *p*-values of an item for individuals with different total test scores (under the assumption that the total score is a good approximation of the underlying ability).

To illustrate, suppose we were developing a test of intelligence. We could calculate and plot *p*-values for a test item for students who had total scores that were extremely low ($p = .10$), very low ($p = .15$), somewhat below average ($p = .25$), average ($p = .50$), somewhat above average ($p = .75$), very high ($p = .90$), and extremely high ($p = .95$). It is implicit in this example that even some students with extremely low scores pass a given item and even some students with extremely high scores fail the item. Thus, although an item may demonstrate good discrimination throughout the range of ability, it is not perfect. In part a of

Figure A6.1, these hypothetical *p*-values are plotted against hypothetical total scores. In this example, the curve (or ogive) is relatively steep. A test author would prefer an item to have this type of curve rather than a relatively flat curve or one that zigzagged across the range of total scores. An item that discriminates perfectly is shown in part b of Figure A6.1. For this perfect item, all students with low ability fail the item and all students with high ability pass the item; how low (or high) student ability is will depend, of course, on the difficulty of the specific item.

Comparing the two curves, you can see that both curves (parts a and b) have three segments, although these segments can be seen more easily in the graph of the perfect item. There are two tails. For the perfect item, the tails are horizon-

FIGURE A6.1   **Item Characteristic Curves for Items with Imperfect Discrimination (a) and Perfect Discrimination (b)**

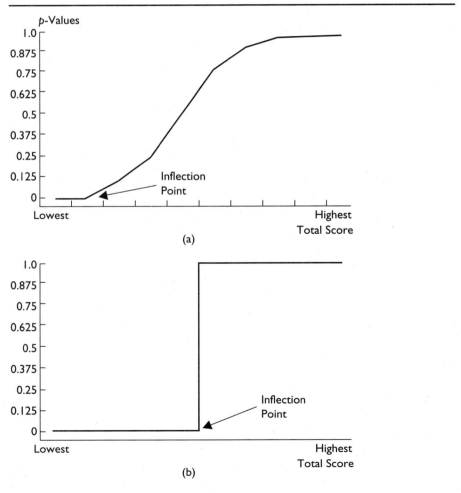

tal; for the imperfect item, the tails flatten as the curve reaches its limits (that is, asymptotes). Both curves have a segment where the curve accelerates (the vertical part of the perfect curve in part b). It is in the accelerating segment of the curve that the test item discriminates most among examinees. The point where the curve begins to accelerate is called the *inflection point*. The left-right placement of the item on the graph is a function of the item mean (*p*-value). Easier items begin to accelerate at the left part of the graph; more difficult items accelerate further to the right.

p-Values in IRT

In IRT, item characteristic curves are generated for the relationship between a person's latent (hidden) ability and the probability of answering an individual item correctly. The mathematics required to estimate these ogives is quite complex, and the actual solution is intractable; however, these ogives can be estimated using logistic models and computers. The relationship between ability and the probability of correctly responding to a test item is a function of three parameters. The discrimination parameter (*a*) is the slope at the inflection point. The difficulty parameter (*b*) is the ability level Θ that corresponds to the inflection point of the ogive. The guessing parameter (*c*) is the lower asymptote of the curve—the point where an examinee has minimal probability of responding correctly.

Because the relationship between the probability of a correct response and ability is effectively represented by a logistic ogival function, their relationship can be determined with the following equations. When all three parameters are used to estimate the relationship between the probability of a correct response to any item (P_i) and ability Θ, the model is called the three-parameter model; this function for the logistic ogive is given in Equation A6.1. However, if we assumed that no guessing occurred, parameter *c* could be eliminated, and the model could be simplified to a two-parameter model; this function for the logistic ogive is given in equation A6.2 below. Similarly, if we assumed that all items have the same discrimination power, *a* could be eliminated, and the model could be simplified to a one-parameter model, often called the Rasch model. This logistic ogive function is given in equation A6.3 below. (In all three equations, *D* is a constant equal to 1.7, and *e* is the base for the natural logarithm.)

$$P_i(0) = c_i + (1 - c_i) \ \frac{1}{1 + e^{-Da_i(\Theta - b_i)}} \tag{A6.1}$$

$$P_i(0) = \frac{1}{1 + e^{-Da_i(\Theta - b_i)}} \tag{A6.2}$$

$$P_i(0) = \frac{1}{1 + e^{-D(\Theta - b_i)}} \tag{A6.3}$$

In practice, it is necessary to estimate the difficulty parameter (b), the discrimination parameter (a), and the guessing parameter (c) on the basis of the performances of a sample of examinees. Because they are characteristics of the item and not of test-takers, these parameters can be estimated (that is, calibrated) independently of the characteristics of any sample of test-takers. Thus, samples used to estimate parameters need not be representative of the population of test-takers at large.

Item parameters are jointly estimated, usually through a logarithmic likelihood function. Basically, we use a mathematical equation to ascertain the probability that a particular pattern of correct and incorrect responses for a group of examinees is associated with specific levels of ability. Accurate estimation of parameters requires that we assume that an examinee's response to one question is not related to the same person's response to another question. This assumption, frequently referred to as local independence, in essence presumes that an item measures only one trait or ability (that is, the item is unidimensional). Once the relationship between each item and the latent trait is estimated, the ability of any other examinee can be estimated from the parameters.

To use item-response theory, test authors must first select the model to be used (three parameters, two parameters, or one parameter) and then estimate parameters. However, an author may not be able to estimate parameters because of the specific characteristics of the sample. Moreover, the obtained data may not fit the model selected.[3] Because the amount of estimation required increases greatly as the number of parameters increases from one to three, the one-parameter Rasch model is more commonly used when constructing tests that are used in applied settings. Estimation is a straightforward operation in the Rasch model because ability and the probability of answering a question correctly are monotonic transformations of the total score and p-values used in classical psychometrics. However, this model is clearly acceptable only in circumstances in which the c parameter (guessing) can be assumed to be zero and the a and the b parameters (difficulty and discrimination) are the same and presumed normal.

INTERPRETING TESTS DEVELOPED USING IRT

In practice, interpreting the results of a test developed using an IRT model is quite similar to interpreting the results of a test developed using classical psychometric theory. There are subtle differences, however, in considering the technical characteristics.

---

3. Several statistical procedures are available to test the goodness of fit of the observed data and the IRT model.

Scores

As is true of tests developed using classical psychometric theory, raw scores from tests developed using IRT have no intrinsic meaning. Indeed, although it is an equal interval scale, the ability scale is indeterminant. Therefore, ability scores are usually transformed to z-scores. After z-scores have been derived for total scores, they can be transformed to any other metric. Under the assumption that ability is normally distributed within age or grade, ability scores can be transformed to derived scores once the means and standard deviations of ages and grades are determined empirically. This determination does require representative norms.

Norms

Because of the assumptions underlying item-response theory, norms play a much smaller role in item selection and estimation of a test's reliability. Norms must be sufficiently large to calibrate the scale (that is, to estimate parameters empirically). The more parameters that must be estimated, the larger the numbers of test items and test-takers that must be employed. Based on the research of several authors, Suen (1990) offered the following recommendations: (1) For the one-parameter model, twenty test items and 200 examinees are required; (2) for the two-parameter model, thirty items and 500 examinees are required; and (3) for the three-parameter model, sixty items and 1,000 examinees are required. As previously mentioned, norms must be representative to estimate derived scores for particular groups (for example, twelve-year olds).

Reliability

Because each ability level has its own unique error variance, no generalized estimates of reliability are provided in IRT. Rather, standard errors of estimation are used for each ability score. This statistic is conceptually equivalent to specific standard errors of measurement for each ability score and will have different values for different ability scores. The actual calculation of this error is determined by the number of parameters used in the IRT model. Therefore, test authors select from the appropriate computational formulas given below to calculate the information function of an item (I). $P_i'\Theta$ is the slope of the curve at Θ. P is the probability of a correct response, and Q is the probability of an incorrect response in equations A6.4 (three-parameter model), A6. 5 (two-parameter model), and A6.6 (one-parameter model). The information function for the total test is the sum of the information functions of all items, as shown in equation A6.7. From the total test information function, the standard error of Θ can be calculated using equation A6.8.

To the extent that the stability of the ability being measured is important, traditional methods (that is, test-retest) are used to estimate this type of reliability. Similarly, to the extent that scoring is a problem, traditional methods of estimating interscorer agreement are used.

$$I(0, \mu_i) = \frac{D^2 a_i^2 Q(\Theta) \left[P_i(\Theta) - c_i \right]^2}{(1 - c_i)^2} \tag{A6.4}$$

$$I(0, \mu_i) = D^2 a_i^2 P_i(\Theta) Q_i(\Theta) \tag{A6.5}$$

$$I(0, \mu_i) = D^2 P_i(\Theta) Q_i(\Theta) \tag{A6.6}$$

$$I(0) = \sum_{i=1}^{k} \frac{P_i'(\Theta)^2}{P_i(\Theta) Q(\Theta)} \tag{A6.7}$$

$$SE(0) = \frac{1}{\sqrt{I(\Theta)}} \tag{A6.8}$$

Validity

The methods used to validate classically developed tests are also used to validate tests developed using IRT. However, tests developed using IRT raise additional validation issues. Test users should expect to see the results of research demonstrating that the items are unidimensional and locally independent; these results frequently come from factor analytic studies. In addition, when a one-parameter (Rasch) model is employed, test users should expect to see evidence that item ogives are normal, such as a likelihood ratio test, a Q_1 statistic, or the like.

References

Achenbach, T. M. (1981). *Child Behavior Checklist for Ages 4–16.* San Antonio, TX: The Psychological Corporation.

Achenbach, T. M. (1986). *The Direct Observation Form (DOF).* Burlington, VT: University of Vermont Department of Psychiatry.

Achenbach, T. M. (1991a). *Integrative guide to the 1991 CBCL, YSR, and TRF profiles.* Burlington, VT: University of Vermont Department of Psychiatry.

Achenbach, T. M. (1991b). *Manual for the Child Behavior Checklist/4–18:* Burlington, VT: University of Vermont Department of Psychiatry.

Achenbach, T. M. (1991c). *Teacher's Report Form (TRF).* Burlington, VT: University of Vermont Department of Psychiatry.

Achenbach, T. M. (1991d). *Youth Self-Report (YSR).* Burlington, VT: University of Vermont Department of Psychiatry.

Achenbach, T. M. (1992). *Child Behavior Checklist/2–3 Years (CBCL/2–3).* Burlington, VT: University of Vermont Department of Psychiatry.

Achenbach, T. M., & Brown, J. S. (1991). *Bibliography of published studies using the Child Behavior Checklist and related materials: 1991 edition.* Burlington, VT: University of Vermont Department of Psychiatry.

Achenbach, T. M., & Edelbrock, C. (1983). *Manual for the Child Behavior Checklist and Revised Child Behavior Profile.* Burlington, VT: University of Vermont Department of Psychiatry.

Achenbach, T. M., & Edelbrock, C. (1987). *Manual for the Youth Self-Report and Profile.* Burlington, VT: University of Vermont Department of Psychiatry.

Achenbach, T. M., & McConaughy, S. H. (1987). *Empirically based assessment of child and adolescent psychopathology: Practical applications.* Newbury Park, CA: Sage Publications.

Adam, A., Doran, D., & Modan, R. (1967). Frequencies of protan and duetan alleles in some Israeli communities and a note on the selection of relaxation hypotheses. *American Journal of Physical Anthropology, 26,* 297–306.

Adams, D. (1991). Writing portfolios: A powerful assessment and conversation tool. *Writing Teacher,* 12–15.

Alberto, P., & Troutman, A. (1990). *Applied behavior analysis for teachers* (3rd ed.). Columbus, OH: Merrill.

Algozzine, B. (1993). Including students with disabilities in systemic efforts to measure outcomes: Why ask why? In J. Ysseldyke & M. L. Thurlow (Eds.), *Views on Inclusion and Testing Accommodations for Students with Disabilities.* Minneapolis: National Center on Educational Outcomes, University of Minnesota.

Algozzine, B., Christenson, S., & Ysseldyke, J. E. (1982). Probabilities associated with the referral to placement process. *Teacher Education and Special Education, 5,* 19–23.

Algozzine, B., & Ysseldyke, J. (1992). *Strategies and tactics for effective instruction.* Longmont, CO: Sopris West.

Alpern, G. D., Boll, T. J., & Shearer, M. (1986). *The Developmental Profile–II (DP-II).* Los Angeles: Western Psychological Services.

American Educational Research Association (AERA), American Psychological Association, & National Council on Measurement in Education. (1985). *Standards for educational and psychological testing.* Washington, DC: American Psychological Association.

American Psychological Association, American Educational Research Association, & National Council on Measurement in Education. (1974). *Standards for educational and psychological tests.* Washington, DC: American Psychological Association.

American Speech and Hearing Association. (1974). Guidelines for audiometric symbols. *American Speech and Hearing Association Journal, 16,* 260–263.

American Speech-Language-Hearing Association. (1990). Guidelines for audiometric symbols. *ASHA, 32 (Suppl. 2),* 25–30.

Anastasi, A. (1980). *Psychological testing* (4th ed.). New York: Macmillan.

Anastasi, A. (1988). *Psychological testing* (5th ed.). New York: Macmillan.

Archbald, D., & Newman, F. (1988). *Beyond standardized testing: Assessing authentic academic achievement in the secondary school.* Reston, VA: National Association of Secondary Principals.

Aronson, E., Blaney, N., Stephan, C., Sikes, J., & Snapp, M. (1978). *The jigsaw classroom.* Beverly Hills, CA: Sage Publications.

Arter, J., & Spandel, V. (1992). Using portfolios of student work in instruction and assessment. *Instructional Topics in Educational Measurement* (May), 36–44.

Arthur, G. (1950). *The Arthur Adaptation of the Leiter International Performance Scale.* Chicago: Stoelting.

Bachor, D. (1990). The importance of shifts in language level and extraneous information in determining word-problem difficulty: Steps toward individual assessment. *Diagnostique, 14,* 94–111.

Bachor, D., Stacy N., & Freeze, D. (1986). *A conceptual framework for word problems: Some preliminary results.* Paper presented at the conference of the Canadian Society for Studies in Education, Winnipeg, Manitoba.

Bagnato, S., & Neisworth, J. (1990). *System to Plan Early Childhood Services.* Circle Pines, MN: American Guidance Service.

Bailey, D. B., & Rouse, T. L. (1989). Procedural considerations in assessing infants and preschoolers with handicaps. In D. B. Bailey & M. Wolery (Eds.), *Assessing Infants and Preschoolers with Handicaps.* Columbus, OH: Merrill.

Baker, E., O'Neil, Jr., H., & Linn, R. (1993). Policy and validity prospects for performance-based assessment. *American Psychologist, 48* (12), 1210–1218.

Ballard, J., & Zettel, J. (1977). Public Law 94-142 and Sec. 504: What they say about rights and protections. *Exceptional Children, 44,* 177–185.

Balow, I. H., Farr, R. C., & Hogan, T. P. (1992). *Metropolitan Achievement Test 7.* San Antonio, TX: The Psychological Corporation.

Barraga, N. (1976). *Visual handicaps and learning: A developmental approach.* Belmont, CA: Wadsworth.

Batsche, G. M., & Peterson, D. W. (1983). School psychology and protective assessment: A growing incompatibility. *School Psychology Review, 12,* 440–445.

Baumgardner, J. C. (1993). *An empirical analysis of school psychological assessment: Practice with students who are deaf and bilingual.* Unpublished doctoral dissertation, University of Minnesota, Minneapolis.

Baxter, G., Shavelson, R., Goldman, S., & Pine, J. (1992). Evaluation of procedure-based scoring for hands-on science assessment. *Journal of Educational Measurement, 29* (1), 1–17.

Bayley, N. (1993). *Manual: Bayley Scales of Infant Development, Second Edition.* San Antonio, TX: The Psychological Corporation.

Beatty, L. S., Gardner, E. G., Madden, R., & Karlsen, B. (1985). *The Stanford Diagnostic Mathematics Test* (3rd ed.). San Antonio, TX: The Psychological Corporation.

Beery, K. E. (1982). *Revised Administration, Scoring, and Teaching Manual for the Developmental Test of Visual-Motor Integration.* Cleveland: Modern Curriculum Press.

Beery, K. E. (1989). *The Developmental Test of Visual-Motor Integration.* Cleveland: Modern Curriculum Press.

Bennett, R. (1993). On the meanings of constructed responses. In R. Bennett and W. Ward (Eds.), *Constructive versus Choice in Cognitive Measurement: Issues in Constructed Response, Performance Testing, and Portfolio Assessment.* Hillsdale, NJ: Lawrence Erlbaum.

Bersoff, D. N. (1979). Regarding psychologists testily: Legal regulation of psychological assessment in the public schools. *Maryland Law Review, 39,* 27–120.

Bleckman, E. (1985). *Solving child behavior problems at home and at school.* Champaign, IL: Research Press.

Bloom, B. (1956). *Taxonomy of educational objectives: The classification of educational goals. Handbook 1. Cognitive domain.* New York: McKay.

Bloom, B., Hastings, J., & Madaus, G. (1971). *Handbook of formative and summative evaluation of student learning.* New York: McGraw-Hill.

Bloom, L., & Lahey, M. (1978) *Language development and language disorders.* New York: Wiley.

Bloomfield, L. (1933). *Language.* New York: Holt, Rinehart, and Winston.

Boehm, A. E. (1986). *Boehm Test of Basic Concepts–Revised.* San Antonio: The Psychological Corporation.

Boehm, A. E., & Weinberg, R. A. (1988). *The classroom observer: A guide for developing observation skills* (2nd ed.). New York: Teachers College Press.

Bower, E. M. (1981). *Early identification of emotionally handicapped children in school* (3rd ed.). Springfield, IL: Charles E. Thomas.

Box, G. (1953). Non-normality and tests on variance. *Biometrika, 40,* 318–335.

Bradbury, R. (1953). *Fahrenheit 451.* New York: Ballantine Books.

Breland, H. (1983). *The direct assessment of writing skill: A measurement review.* (College Board Report No. 83-6). New York: College Entrance Examination Board.

Breland, H., Camp, R., Jones, R., Morris, & Rock, D. (1987). *Assessing writing skill.* New York: The College Board.

Brigance, A. (1977). *BRIGANCE® Diagnostic Inventory of Basic Skills.* North Billerica, MA: Curriculum Associates.

Brigance, A. (1991). *BRIGANCE® Diagnostic Inventory of Early Development–Revised.* North Billerica, MA: Curriculum Associates.

Brigance, A. (1980). *BRIGANCE® Diagnostic Inventory of Essential Skills.* North Billerica, MA: Curriculum Associates.

Broderick, C. B. (1993). *Understanding family process: Basics of family systems theory.* Newbury Park, CA: Sage.

Bronfenbrenner, U. (1979). *The ecology of human development.* Cambridge, MA: Harvard University Press.

Brown, L., & Hammill, D. (1978). *Behavior Rating Profile.* Austin, TX: Pro-Ed.

Brown, L., & Hammill, D. (1983). *Behavior Rating Profile.* Austin, TX: Pro-Ed.

Brown, L., & Hammill, D. (1990). *Behavior Rating Profile* (2nd ed.). Austin, TX: Pro-Ed.

Brown, L., & Leigh, J. (1986a). *Adaptive Behavior Inventory.* Austin, TX: Pro-Ed.

Brown, L., & Leigh, J. (1986b). *The Adaptive Behavior Inventory manual.* Austin, TX: Pro-Ed.

Brown, L., Sherbenou, R., & Johnson, S. (1990). *Test of Nonverbal Intelligence–2.* Austin, TX: Pro-Ed.

Brown, R. (1973). *A first language: The early stages.* Cambridge, MA: Harvard University Press.

Brown, R., & Bellugi, U. (1964). Three processes in the child's acquisition of syntax. *Harvard Educational Review, 34,* 133–151.

Brown, V. L., Hammill, D. D., & Wiederholt, L. (1986). *Test of Reading Comprehension: Revised Edition.* Austin, TX: Pro-Ed.

Brown, V., & McEntire, E. (1984). *Test of Mathematical Abilities.* Austin, TX: Pro-Ed.

Bruer, J. (1993). *School for thought: A science of learning in the classroom.* Cambridge, MA: Massachusetts Institute of Technology Press.

Bruininks, R., Woodcock, R., Weatherman, R., & Hill, B. (1984). *Scales of Independent Behavior.* Austin, TX: DLM.

Bryant, B. (1991). *DTLA-3 software scoring system.* Austin, TX: Pro-ed.

Burns, M. (1981). Groups of four: Solving the management problem. *Learning,* (September), 46–51.

Burt, C. (1959). Class differences in general intelligence: III. *British Journal of Statistical Psychology, 12,* 15–33.

Byrne, M. C. (1978). Appraisal of child language acquisition. In F. L. Darley & D. C. Spriestersbach. *Diagnostic Methods in Speech Pathology* (2nd ed.). New York: Harper & Row.

Caldwell, J., & Goldin, J. (1979). Variables affecting word problem difficulty in elementary school mathematics. *Journal of Research in Mathematics Education, 10,* 323–335.

Calfee, R., & Perfumo, P. (1993). Student portfolios: Opportunities for a revolution in assessment. *Journal of Reading, 36* (7), 532–537.

Camarata, S. (in press). A rationale for naturalistic speech intelligibility intervention. In M. Fey, J. Warren, and S. Warren (Eds.), *Language intervention: Preschool through the early school years.* Baltimore: Brookes.

Camarata, S., & Gandour, J. (1984). On describing idiosyncratic phonologic systems. *Journal of Speech and Hearing Disorders, 49,* 262–266.

Camarata, S., Hughes, C., & Ruhl, K. (1988). Mild/moderately behaviorally disordered students: A population at risk for language disorders. *Language, Speech, and Hearing Services in Schools, 19,* 191–200.

Camarata, S., Nelson, K. E., & Camarata, M. (in press). Comparison of conversation-based to imitation-based procedures for training grammatical structures in specifically language impaired children. *Journal of Speech and Hearing Research.*

Camp, R. (1993). The place of portfolios in our changing views of writing assessment. In R. Bennett and W. Ward (Eds.), *Constructive versus Choice in Cognitive Measurement: Issues in Constructed Response, Performance Testing, and Portfolio Assessment.* Hillsdale, NJ: Lawrence Erlbaum.

Campbell, D., & Fiske, D. (1959). Convergent and discriminate validation by the multi-trait-multi-method matrix. *Psychological Bulletin, 56,* 81–105.

Carroll, J. (1963). A model of school learning. *Teachers College Record, 64,* 723–733.

Carroll, J. B. (1985). The model of school learning: Progress of an idea. In L. W. Anderson (Ed.), *Perspectives on School Learning: Selected Writings of John*

B. Carroll (pp. 82–102). Hillsdale, NJ: Lawrence Erlbaum.

Carrow, E. (1974). *Carrow Elicited Language Inventory,* Austin, TX: Learning Concepts.

Carrow-Wolfolk, E. (1985). *Test for Auditory Comprehension of Language, examiner's manual* (rev. ed.). Allen, TX: Developmental Learning Materials.

Carter, J., & Sugai, G. (1989). Survey on prereferral practices: Responses from state departments of education. *Exceptional Children, 55,* 298–302.

Center, D. B. (1989). *Curriculum and teaching strategies for students with behavioral disorders.* Englewood Cliffs, NJ: Prentice Hall.

Chalfant, J., Pysh, M. V., & Moultrie, R. (1979). Teacher assistance teams: A model for within-building problem solving. *Learning Disability Quarterly, 2,* 85–96.

Chomsky, N. (1957). *Syntactic structures.* The Hague: Mouton.

Cohen, G. (1972). Hemispheric differences in a letter classification task. *Perception and Psychophysics, 11,* 139–142.

Cohen, J. (1960). A coefficient of agreement for nominal scales. *Educational and Psychological Measurement, 20,* 37–46.

Coleman, J., Campbell, E., Hobson, C., McPartland, J., Mood, A., Weinfeld, F., & York, R. (1966). *Equality of educational opportunity.* Washington, DC: National Center for Education Statistics (F. S. 5.238: 380001).

Collins, A. (1993). Alternative assessment in undergraduate science education, with emphasis on portfolios. *Proceedings of the National Science Foundation Workshop on the Role of Faculty from the Scientific Disciplines in the Undergraduate Education of Future Science and Mathematics Teachers.* Washington, D. C.: National Science Foundation.

Conners, C. K. (1989a). *Conners Parent Rating Scales.* North Tonawanda, NY: Multi-Health Systems.

Conners, C. K. (1989b). *Conners Teacher Rating Scales.* North Tonawanda, NY: Multi-Health Systems.

Connolly, A. (1988). *KeyMath–Revised: A Diagnostic Inventory of Essential Mathematics.* Circle Pines, MN: American Guidance Service.

Connolly, A., Nachtman, W., & Pritchett, E. (1976). *Manual for the KeyMath Diagnostic Arithmetic Test.* Circle Pines, MN: American Guidance Service.

Cooper, C. (1977). Holistic evaluation of writing. In C. Cooper & L. Odell (Eds.), *Evaluating Writing: De-scribing, Measuring, Judging.* Buffalo, NY: National Council of Teachers of English.

Corn, A. (1983). Visual function: A theoretical model for individuals with low vision. *Journal of Visual Impairment and Blindness, 77,* 373–377.

Cronbach, L. (1951). Coefficient alpha and the internal structure of tests. *Psychometrika, 16,* 297–334.

Cronbach, L., & Snow, R. (1977). *Aptitudes and instructional methods: A handbook for research on interactions.* New York: Irvington.

CTB/Macmillan/McGraw-Hill. (1992). *California Achievement Tests/5: Technical bulletin 1.* Monterey, CA: Author.

CTB/Macmillan/McGraw-Hill. (1993). *California Achievement Tests/5.* Monterey, CA: Author.

CTB/McGraw-Hill. (1980). *Prescriptive Reading Inventory/Reading System.* Monterey, CA: Author.

Das, J., Kirby, J., & Jarman, R. (1975). Simultaneous and successive syntheses: An alternative model for cognitive abilities. *Psychological Bulletin, 82,* 87–103.

Davilla, R. R. (1989). Letter to Mr. Robert Dawson, November 17, signed by Michael Vader, Acting Assistant Secretary of the U.S. Department of Education.

Davis, A., & Felknor, C. (1994). The demise of performance-based graduation in Littleton. *Educational Leadership, 51* (6), 64–65.

Deno, S. L. (1985). Curriculum-based assessment: The emerging alternative. *Exceptional Children, 52,* 219–232.

Deno, S. L. (1986). Formative evaluation of individual student programs: A new role for school psychologists. *School Psychology Review, 15,* 358–374.

Deno, S., & Mirkin, P. (1977). *Data-based program modification: A manual.* Reston, VA: Council for Exceptional Children.

Dingman, H., & Tarjan, G. (1960). Mental retardation and the normal distribution curve. *American Journal of Mental Deficiency, 64,* 991–994.

Dorans, N., & Schmitt, A. (1993). Constructed response and differential item functioning: A pragmatic approach. In R. Bennett and W. Ward (Eds.), *Constructive versus Choice in Cognitive Measurement: Issues in Constructed Response, Performance Testing, and Portfolio Assessment.* Hillsdale, NJ: Lawrence Erlbaum.

Down, A. L. (1866/1969). Observations on an ethnic classification of idiots. In R. Vollman (Ed.), *Down's*

Syndrome (Mongolism), a Reference Bibliography. Washington, DC: United States Department of Health, Education, and Welfare.

Dunn, L., & Dunn, L. (1981). *Peabody Picture Vocabulary Test–Revised.* Circle Pines, MN: American Guidance Service.

Dunn, L. M., & Markwardt, F. C. (1970). *Peabody Individual Achievement Test.* Circle Pines, MN: American Guidance Service.

Durrell, D., & Catterson, J. (1980). *Durrell Analysis of Reading Difficulty.* San Antonio, TX: The Psychological Corporation.

Dvorine, I. (1953). *Dvorine Pseudoisochromatic Plates* (2nd ed.). Baltimore: Waverly Press.

Dwyer, C. (1993). Innovation and reform: Examples from teacher assessment. In R. Bennett and W. Ward (Eds.), *Constructive versus Choice in Cognitive Measurement: Issues in Constructed Response, Performance Testing, and Portfolio Assessment.* Hillsdale, NJ: Lawrence Erlbaum.

Educational Testing Service. (1990). *Exploring new methods for collecting students' school-based writing: NAEP's 1990 portfolio study.* Washington, DC: U. S. Department of Education. ED 343154.

Ekwall, E. E. (1970). *Locating and correcting reading difficulties.* Columbus, OH: Merrill.

Elliott, C. (1990). *Differential Ability Scales.* San Antonio, TX: Psychological Corporation.

Englemann, S., Granzin, A., & Severson, H. (1979). Diagnosing instruction. *Journal of Special Education, 13,* 355–365.

Englert, C., Cullata, B., & Horn, D. (1987). Influence of irrelevant information in addition word problems on problem solving. *Learning Disabilities Quarterly, 10,* 29–36.

Ervin, S. M. (1964). Imitation and structural change in children's language. In E. H. Lenneberg (Ed.), *New Directions in the Study of Language.* Cambridge, MA: M.I.T. Press.

Farber, B. (1968). *Mental retardation: Its social context and social consequences.* Boston: Houghton Mifflin.

Farnsworth, D. (1947). *The Farnsworth Dichotomous Test for Color Blindness.* San Antonio, TX: The Psychological Corporation.

Feagans, L., Sanyal, M., Henderson, F., Collier, A., & Appelbaum, M. I. (1986). The relationship of middle ear disease in early childhood to later narrative and attention skills. *Journal of Pediatric Psychology, 12,* 581–594.

Fillmore, C. (1968). The case for case. In E. Bach & R. Harms (Eds.), *Universals in Linguistic Theory.* New York: Holt, Rinehart, and Winston.

Fodness, R. (1987). *Test-retest reliability of the Test of Language Development–Intermediate.* Unpublished master's thesis, Central Michigan University, Mt. Pleasant, MI.

Frankenburg, W., Dodds, J., Fandal, A., Kazuk, E., & Cohrs, M. (1975). *Denver Developmental Screening Test, reference manual, revised 1975 edition.* Denver, CO: LA-DOCA Project and Publishing Foundation.

Frankenburg, W., Goldstein, A., & Camp, B. (1971). The revised Denver Developmental Screening Test: Its accuracy as a screening instrument. *Pediatrics, 79,* 988–995.

Frazier, D., & Paulson, F. (1992). How portfolios motivate reluctant writers. *Educational Leadership,* 62–65.

Fredricksen, J., & Collins, A. (1989). A systems approach to educational testing. *Educational Researcher, 18,* 27–32.

Friel-Patti, S., & Finitzo, T. (1990). Language learning in a prospective study of otitis media with effusion in the first two years of life. *Journal of Speech and Hearing Research, 33,* 188–194.

Fromkin, V., & Rodman, R. (1978). *An introduction to language.* New York: Holt, Rinehart, and Winston.

Frostig, M., Lefever, W., & Whittlesey, J. (1966). *Administration and scoring manual: Marianne Frostig Developmental Test of Visual Perception.* Palo Alto, CA: Consulting Psychologists Press.

Frostig, M., Maslow, P., Lefever, D. W., & Whittlesey, J. R. (1964). *The Marianne Frostig Developmental Test of Visual Perception: 1963 standardization.* Palo Alto, CA: Consulting Psychologists Press.

Fuchs, L. (1986). Monitoring progress among mildly handicapped pupils: Review of current practice and research. *Remedial and Special Education 7,* 5–12.

Fuchs, L., & Fuchs, D., (Eds.). (1986). Linking assessment to instructional intervention: An overview. *School Psychology Review, 15* (3), whole issue.

Fuchs, L., Fuchs, D., & Maxwell, L. (1988). The validity of informal reading comprehension measures. *Remedial and Special Education,* 20–28.

Fudala, J. (1970). *Arizona Articulation Proficiency Scale.* Los Angeles: Western Psychological Services.

Fudala, J., & Reynolds, W. (1991). *Arizona Articulation Proficiency Scale.* Los Angeles, CA: Western Psychological Services.

Gardner, E. F., Rudman, H. C., Karlsen, B., & Merwin, J. C. (1982). *Stanford Achievement Test* (7th ed.). San Antonio, TX: The Psychological Corporation.

Gardner, M. (1990). *Expressive One-Word Picture Vocabulary Test.* Novato, CA: Academic Therapy Publications.

Garrett, J. E., & Brazil, N. (1979). Categories used for identification and education of exceptional children. *Exceptional Children, 45,* 291–292.

Gates, A. I., & McKillop, A. S., (1962). *Gates-McKillop Reading Diagnostic Tests.* New York: Teachers College Press.

Gates, A. I., McKillop, A. S., & Horowitz, R. (1981). *Gates-McKillop-Horowitz Reading Diagnostic Tests.* New York: Teachers College Press.

Gearhart, M., Herman, J., Baker, E., & Whittaker, A. (1992). *Writing portfolios at the elementary level: A study of methods for writing assessment.* (CSE Technical Report No. 337). Los Angeles: Center for the Study of Evaluation (UCLA).

Gearhart, M., Herman, J., Baker, E., & Whittaker, A. (1993). *"Whose work is it?" A question for the validity of large-scale portfolio assessment.* (CRESST/CSE Technical Report No. 363). Los Angeles: Center for the Study of Evaluation (UCLA).

Gessell, J. K. (1983). *Diagnostic Mathematics Inventory/Mathematics System.* Monterey, CA: CTB/Mc-Graw- Hill.

Gierut, J. (1989). Maximal opposition approach to phonological treatment. *Journal of Speech and Hearing Disorders, 54,* 9–19.

Ginzberg, E., & Bray, D. W. (1953). *The uneducated.* New York: Columbia University Press.

Gitomer, D. (1993). Performance assessment and educational measurement. In R. Bennett and W. Ward (Eds.), *Constructive versus Choice in Cognitive Measurement: Issues in Constructed Response, Performance Testing, and Portfolio Assessment.* Hillsdale, NJ: Lawrence Erlbaum.

Goldman, R., & Fristoe, M. (1986). *Goldman-Fristoe Test of Articulation.* Circle Pines, MN: American Guidance Service.

Good, R., & Salvia, J. (1989). Curriculum bias in published norm-referenced reading tests: Demonstrable effects. *School Psychology Review, 17*(1), 51–60.

Goodman, A. C., & Chasin, W. D. (1976). Hearing problems. In S. S. Gellis and B. M. Kagan (Eds.), *Current Pediatric Therapy 6.* Philadelphia: W. B. Saunders.

Gordon, C. (1990). Students' and teachers' criteria for quality writing: Never the twain shall meet? *Reflections on Canadian Literacy, 8,* 74–81.

Goslin, D. A. (1969). *Guidelines for the collection, maintenance and dissemination of pupil records.* Troy, NY: Russell Sage Foundation.

Gottesman, I. (1968). Biogenics of race and class. In M. Deutsch, I. Katz, & A. Jensen (Eds.), *Social Class, Race, and Psychological Development.* New York: Holt, Rinehart and Winston.

Goyette, C. H., Conners, C. K., & Ulrich, R. F. (1978). Normative data on the revised Conners Parent and Teacher Rating Scales. *Journal of Abnormal Child Psychology, 6,* 221–236.

Grace, C., & Shores, E. (1992). *The portfolio and its use: Developmentally appropriate assessment of young children.* Little Rock, AR: Southern Association of Children Under Six.

Graden, J., Casey, A., & Bonstrom, O. (1983). *Prereferral interventions: Effects on referral rates and teacher attitudes.* (Research Report No. 140). Minneapolis: Minnesota Institute for Research on Learning Disabilities.

Greenwood, C. R., Carta, J. J. (1994). *Ecobehavioral Assessment Systems Software.* Kansas City, KS: Juniper Gardens Children's Center.

Greenwood, C. R., Carta, J. J., & Atwater, J. (1991). Ecobehavioral analysis in the classroom: Review and implications. *Journal of Behavioral Education, 1,* 59–77.

Greenwood, C. R., Carta, J. J., Kamps, D., & Arreaga-Mayer, C. (1990). Ecobehavioral analysis of classroom instruction. In S. R. Schroeder (Ed.), *Ecobehavioral Analysis and Developmental Disabilities: The Twenty-First Century* (pp. 33–63). New York: Springer-Verlag.

Greenwood, C. R., Delquadri, J., & Hall, V. (1978). *The code for instructional structure and student academic response.* Kansas City, KS: Juniper Gardens Children's Center.

Greenwood, C. R., Delquadri, J., & Hall, R. V. (1989). Longitudinal effects of classwide peer tutoring. *Journal of Educational Psychology, 81,* 371–383.

Gresham, F., & Elliott, S. N. (1990). *Social Skills Rating System.* Circle Pines, MN: American Guidance Service.

Gronlund, N. (1985). *Measurement and evaluation in teaching* (5th ed.). New York: Macmillan.

Gronlund, N. E. (1976). *Measurement and evaluation in teaching* (3rd ed.). New York: Macmillan.

Gronlund, N. E. (1982). *Constructing acheivement tests.* Englewood Cliffs, NJ: Prentice-Hall

Grossman, H. (1983). *Manual of terminology and classification in mental retardation.* Washington, DC: American Association on Mental Deficiency.

Guarmaccia, V. (1976). Factor structure and correlates of adaptive behavior in noninstitutionalized retarded adults. *American Journal of Mental Deficiency, 80,* 543–547.

Guetzloe, E. (1993). The special education initiative: Responding to changing problems, populations, and paradigms. *Behavioral Disorders, 18,* 303–307.

Guilford, J. (1954). *Psychometric methods.* New York: McGraw-Hill.

Guilford, J. P. (1967). *The nature of human intelligence.* New York: McGraw-Hill.

Hacker, J., & Hathaway, W. (1991). *Toward extended assessment: The big picture.* Paper presented at the annual conference of the American Educational Research Association, Chicago, April 3–7.

Hallahan, D., & Cruickshank, W. (1973). *Psychoeducational foundations of learning disabilities.* Englewood Cliffs, NJ: Prentice-Hall.

Hammill, D. D. (1991). *Detroit Tests of Learning Aptitude, 3rd edition.* Austin, TX: Pro-Ed.

Hammill, D., Brown, L., & Bryant, B. (1992). *A consumer's guide to tests in print (2nd ed.).* Austin, TX: Pro-Ed.

Hammill, D., Brown, V., Larsen, S., & Wiederholt, J. (1994). *Test of Adolescent and Adult Language* (3rd ed.). Austin, TX: Pro-Ed.

Hammill, D. D., & Bryant, B. (1986). *Detroit Tests of Learning Aptitude–Primary.* Austin, TX: Pro-Ed.

Hammill, D. D., & Bryant, F. (1991). *Detroit Tests of Learning Aptitude–Primary 2.* Austin, TX: Pro-Ed.

Hammill, D., & Larsen, S. (1988). *Test of Written Language.* Austin, TX: Pro-Ed.

Hammill, D., and Newcomer, P. (1991). *Test of Language Development, Primary 2.* Austin, TX: Pro-Ed.

Hammill, D., Pearson, N., & Voress, J. (1993). *Examiner's manual: Developmental Test of Visual Perception (2nd ed.).* Austin, TX: Pro-Ed.

Hammill, D., & Wiederholt, J. L. (1973). Review of the Frostig Visual Perception Test and the related training

program. In L. Mann and C. Sabatino (Eds.), *The First Review of Special Education* (pp. 33–48). Philadelphia: Buttonwood Farms.

Hansen, J. (1992). Literacy portfolios emerge. *The Reading Teacher, 45*(8), 604–607.

Hardy, L. H., Rand, G., & Rittler, M. C. (1957). *AO H-R-R Pseudoisochromatic Plates.* Buffalo, NY: American Optical Company, Instrument Division.

Haring, N., Liberty, K., & White, O. (1980). Rules for data-based strategy decisions in instructional programs. In W. Sailor, B. Wilcox, & L. Brown (Eds.), *Methods of Instruction for Severely Handicapped Students.* (pp. 159–192). Baltimore: Brooks.

Harrison, P. (1985). *Vineland Adaptive Behavior Scales: Classroom Edition manual.* Circle Pines, MN: American Guidance Service.

Hathaway, S., & McKinley, J. (1970). *Minnesota Multiphasic Personality Inventory.* Minneapolis: University of Minnesota Press.

Hebert, E. (1992). Portfolios invite reflection from students and staff. *Educational Leadership,* (May), 58–61.

Hieronymus, A. N., Hoover, H. D., & Lindquist, E. F. (1986). *Iowa Tests of Basic Skills.* Chicago: The Riverside Publishing Company.

Hisky, M. (1966). *Hiskey-Nebraska Test of Learning Aptitude.* Lincoln, NE: Marshall S. Hiskey.

Hodson, B., & Paden, E. (1983). *Targeting intelligible speech.* San Diego: College-Hill.

Hofmeister, A. (1975). Integrating criterion-referenced testing and instruction. In W. Hively and M. Reynolds (Eds.), *Domain-Referenced Testing in Special Education* (pp. 77–88). Minneapolis: University of Minnesota, Leadership Training Institute/Special Education.

Hoover, H. D., Hieronymus, A. N., Frisbie, D. A., & Dunbar, S. B. (1993). *Iowa Tests of Basic Skills.* Chicago: The Riverside Publishing Company.

Horn, E. (1967). *What research says to the teacher: Teaching spelling.* Washington, DC: National Education Association.

Howell, K. W. (1986). Direct assessment of academic performance. *School Psychology Review, 15,* 324–335.

Hresko, W., & Brown, L. (1984). *Test of Early Socioemotional Development.* Austin, TX: Pro-Ed.

Hull, F., Meilke, P., Timmons, R., & Willeford, J. (1971). The national speech and hearing survey: Preliminary results. *ASHA, 13,* 501–509.

Hurlin, R. G. (1962). Estimated prevalence of blindness in the U.S.—1960. *Sight Saving Review, 32,* 4–12.

Ingram, D. (1976). *Phonological disability in children.* New York: American Elsevier.

Ingram, D. (1981). *Procedures for the phonological analysis of children's language.* Baltimore: University Park Press.

Ireton, H., & Thwing, E. J. (1974). *Minnesota Child Development Inventory.* Minneapolis: Behavior Science Systems.

Isaacson, S. (1988). Assessing the writing product: Qualitative and quantitative measures. *Exceptional children, 54,* 528–534.

Ishihara, S. (1970). *The Ishihara Color Blind Test book (children): 12 plates.* Tokyo: Kanehara Shuppan.

Jenkins, J., & Pany, D. (1978). Standardized achievement tests: How useful for special education? *Exceptional Children, 44,* 448–453.

Jensen, A. (1974). Interaction of Level I and Level II abilities with race and socioeconomic status. *Journal of Educational Psychology, 66,* 99–111.

Johnson, D., & Johnson, R. (1986). *Learning together and alone* (2nd ed.). Englewood Cliffs, NJ: Prentice Hall.

Jose, R. T., Smith, A. J., & Shane, K. G. (1988). Evaluating and stimulating vision in multiply impaired children. In J. Erin (Ed.), *Dimensions: Selected Papers from the Journal of Visual Impairment and Blindness.*

Kappauf, W. E. (1973). Studying the relationship of task performance to the variables of chronological age, mental age, and IQ. In N. Ellis (Ed.), *International Review of Research in Mental Retardation* (Vol. 6). New York: Academic Press.

Karlsen, B., & Gardner, E. (1985). *Stanford Diagnostic Reading Test* (3rd ed.) San Antonio, TX: The Psychological Corporation.

Kaufman, A., & Kaufman, N. (1983). *Kaufman Assessment Battery for Children, interpretive manual.* Circle Pines, MN: American Guidance Service.

Kaufman, A., & Kaufman, N. (1985a). *Kaufman Test of Educational Achievement.* Circle Pines, MN: American Guidance Service.

Kaufman, A., & Kaufman, N. (1985b). *Kaufman Test of Educational Achievement, Brief Form manual.* Circle Pines, MN: American Guidance Service.

Kaufman, A., & Kaufman, N. (1985c). *Kaufman Test of Educational Achievement, Comprehensive Form manual.* Circle Pines, MN: American Guidance Service.

Kazdin, A. E. (1973). The effects of vicarious reinforcement in the classroom. *Journal of Applied Behavior Analysis, 6,* 71–78.

Kelley, M. F., & Surbeck, E. (1985). History of pre-school assessment. In K. D. Paget & B. Bracken (Eds.), *The Psychoeducational Assessment of Pre-School Children.* New York: Grune & Stratton.

Kentucky Systems Change Project for Students with Severe Disabilities. (undated). *The Kentucky Alternative Portfolio Project.* Frankfort, KY: Kentucky Department of Education.

King, R., Jones, C., & Lasky, E. (1982). In retrospect: A fifteen year follow-up report of speech-language disordered children. *Language, Speech, and Hearing Services in Schools, 13,* 24–33.

Kirk, S. A., & Kirk, W. D. (1971). *Psycholinguistic learning disabilities: Diagnosis and remediation.* Champaign: University of Illinois Press.

Kirk, S., McCarthy, J., & Kirk, W. (1968). *Illinois Test of Psycholinguistic Abilities.* Champaign: University of Illinois Press.

Knowlton, M. (1988). *Minnesota Functional Vision Assessment.* Minneapolis: University of Minnesota. Mimeo.

Koehler, P. (1993). Inclusion and adaptation in assessment of special needs students in Arizona. In J. Ysseldyke & M. L. Thurlow (Eds.), *Views on Inclusion and Testing Accommodations for Students with Disabilities.* Minneapolis: National Center on Educational Outcomes, University of Minnesota.

Koening, A. J., & Holbrook, M. C. (1993). *Learning media assessment.* Austin, TX: Texas School for the Blind and Visually Impaired.

Koppitz, E.M. (1963). *The Bender Gestalt Test for Young Children.* New York: Grune & Stratton.

Koppitz, E. M. (1975). *The Bender Gestalt Test for Young Children: Volume II: Research and application, 1963–1973.* New York: Grune & Stratton.

Koretz, D. (1993). New report on Vermont Portfolio Project documents challenges. *National Council on Measurement in Education Quarterly Newsletter, 1* (4), 1–2.

Koretz, D., Klein, S., McCaffrey, D., & Stecher, B. (1993). *Interim report: The reliability of Vermont Portfolio scores in the 1992–93 school year.* (CRESST/CSE Technical Report No. 370). Los Angeles: Center for the Study of Evaluation (UCLA).

Koretz, D., Lewis, E., Skewes-Cox, T., & Burstein, L.

(1992). *Omitted and not-reached items in mathematics in the 1990 National Assessment of Educational Progress (CSE Tech. Rep. 357).* Los Angeles: University of California, National Center for Research on Evaluation, Standards, and Student Testing.

Krug, D. A., Arick, J. R., & Almond, P. A. (1993). *Autism Screening Instrument for Educational Planning* (2nd ed.), Austin, TX: Pro-Ed.

Kubiszyn, T., & Borich, G. (1984). *Educational testing and measurement: Classroom application and practice.* Glenview, IL: Scott, Foresman and Company.

Lachar, D. (1982). *Personality Inventory for Children–Revised.* Los Angeles: Western Psychological Services.

Lahey, M., (1988). *Language disorders and language development.* New York: Macmillan.

Langley, B., & DuBose, R. F. (1989). Functional vision screening for severely handicapped children. In J. Erin (Ed.), *Dimensions: Selected papers from the Journal of Visual Impairment and Blindness.*

Larsen, S., & Hammill, D. (1986). *Test of Written Spelling–2.* Austin, TX: Pro-Ed.

Lashly, K. (1951). The problem of serial order in behavior. In L. Jeffress (Ed.), *Cerebral mechanisms in behavior:* New York: Wiley.

Lee, L. (1974). *Developmental sentence analysis.* Evanston, IL: Northwestern University Press.

Lee, L., & Canter, S. (1971). Developmental sentence scoring: A clinical procedure for estimating syntactic development in children's spontaneous speech. *Journal of Speech and Hearing Disorders, 36,* 315–340.

LeMahieu, P., Eresh, J., & Wallace, Jr., R. (1992). Using student portfolios for public accounting. *The School Administrator, 49* (11), 8–15.

Lentz, F. E., & Shapiro, E. S. (1986). Functional assessment of the academic environment. *School Psychology Review, 15,* 346–358.

Levine, E. (1974). Psychological tests and practices with the deaf: A survey of the state of the art. *Volta Review, 76,* 298–319.

Lidz, C. (1991). *Practitioner's guide to dynamic assessment.* New York: Guilford.

Lindsley, O. R. (1964). Direct measurement and prosthesis of retarded behavior. *Journal of Education, 147,* 68–81.

Linn, R., & Baker, E. (Fall, 1993). Portfolios and accountability. *The CRESST Line: Newsletter of the National Center for Research on Evaluation, Standards, and Student Testing.* Los Angeles: NCRESST, 1, 8.

Loeding, B. L., & Crittenden, J. B. (1993). Inclusion of children and youth who are hearing impaired and deaf in outcomes assessment. In J. Ysseldyke & M. L. Thurlow (Eds.), *Views on Inclusion and Testing Accommodations for Students with Disabilities.* Minneapolis: National Center on Educational Outcomes, University of Minnesota.

Luria, A. (1966). *Higher cortical functions in man.* New York: Basic Books.

MacGinitie & MacGinitie. (1989). *The Gates-MacGinitie Reading Tests.* Chicago: The Riverside Publishing Company.

Madaus, G. (1993). A national testing system: Manna from above? A historical/technological perspective. *Educational Assessment, 1,* 9–26.

Maeroff, G. (1991). Assessing alternative assessment. *Phi Delta Kappan* (December), 272–281.

Mangold, S. S. (Ed.). (1982). *A teacher's guide to the special educational needs of blind and visually handicapped children.* New York: American Foundation for the Blind.

Mann, L. (1971). Psychometric phrenology and the new faculty psychology: The case against ability assessment and training. *Journal of Special Education, 5,* 3–14.

Mann, V. (1993). Phoneme awareness and future reading ability. *Journal of Learning Disabilities, 26,* 259–269.

Mardell-Czudnowski, C., & Goldenberg, D. S. (1990). *Developmental Indicators for the Assessment of Learning–Revised.* Circle Pines, MN: American Guidance Service.

Markwardt, F. (1989). *Peabody Individual Achievement Test–Revised.* Circle Pines, MN: American Guidance Service.

Marston, D., & Magnusson, D. (1985). Implementing curriculum-based measurement in special and regular education settings. *Exceptional Children, 52,* 266–276.

Martin, R. P. (1988). *Assessment of personality and behavior problems: Infancy through adolescence.* New York: Guilford Press.

Maynard, F., & Strickland, J. (1969). *A comparison of three methods of teaching selected mathematical content in eighth and ninth grade general mathematics courses.* Athens, GA: University of Georgia. ED 041763.

McCarney, S. B. (1989a). *Attention Deficit Disorder Evaluation Scale–School Version.* Columbia, MO: Hawthorne Educational Services.

McCarney, S. B. (1989b). *Attention Deficit Disorder Evaluation Scale–Home Version.* Columbia, MO: Hawthorne Educational Services.

McCarney, S. (1992). *Preschool Evaluation Scale.* Columbia, MO: Hawthorne.

McCarney, S. B. (1992). *Early Childhood Behavior Scale: Technical manual.* Columbia, MO: Hawthorne Educational Services.

McCarney, S. B., & Leigh, J. E. (1990) *Behavior evaluation scale–2.* Columbia, MO: Educational Services.

McCauley, R., & Swisher, L. (1984). A psychometric review of language and articulation tests for preschool children. *Journal of Speech and Hearing Disorders, 49,* 34–42.

McConaughy, S. H. (1993a). Advances in the empirically based assessment of children's behavioral and emotional problems. *School Psychology Review, 22,* 285–307.

McConaughy, S. H. (1993b). Evaluating behavioral and emotional disorders with the CBCL, TRF, and YSR cross-informant scales. *Journal of Emotional and Behavioral Disorders, 1,* 40–52.

McConaughy, S. H., Achenbach, T. M., & Gent, C. L., (1988). Multiaxial empirically based assessment: Parent, teacher, observational, cognitive, and personality correlates of Child Behavior Profiles for 6–11-year-old boys. *Journal of Abnormal Child Psychology, 16,* 485–509.

McGhee, R. (1991). A comparison between the DTLA-3 and the WJ-R: A validity study. Unpublished manuscript.

McGrew, K., Thurlow, M. L., Shriner, J., & Spiegel, A. N. (1992). *Inclusion of students with disabilities in national and state data collection programs.* (Technical Report 2). Minneapolis: National Center on Educational Outcomes, University of Minnesota.

McReynolds, L., & Elbert, M. (1981). Criteria for phonological process analysis. *Journal of Speech and Hearing Disorders, 46,* 197–204.

Mercer, C., & Mercer, A. (1985). *Teaching students with learning problems* (2nd ed.). Columbus, OH: Merrill.

Mercer, C., Mercer, A., & Evans, S. (1982). The use of frequency in establishing instructional aims. *Journal of Precision Teaching, 3,* 57–63.

Merrell, K. W. (1994). *Assessment of behavioral, social, and emotional problems.* New York: Longman.

Messick, S. (1989). Validity. In R. L. Linn (Ed.), *Educational Measurement* (3rd ed.) (pp. 13–103). New York: ACE/Macmillan.

Meyer, C. (1992). What's the difference between *authentic* and *performance* assessment? *Educational Leadership, 49*(8), 39–40.

Meisels, S., & Steele, D. (1991). *The early childhood portfolio collection process.* Ann Arbor, MI: Center for Human Growth and Development, University of Michigan.

Miller, G. (1951). *Language and communication.* New York: McGraw-Hill.

Miller, J. (1981). *Assessing language production in children.* Austin, TX: Pro-Ed.

Mills, R. (1989). Portfolios capture rich array of student performance. *The School Administrator, 46* (11), 8–11.

Mischel, W. (1970). Sex typing and socialization. In J. M. Tanner (Ed.)., *Carmichael's Manual of Child Psychology.* New York: Wiley.

Morgan, D. P., & Jenson, W. R. (1988). *Teaching behaviorally disordered students: Preferred practices.* Columbus, OH: Merrill.

Moss, M. (1979). *Tests of Basic Experiences 2: Norms and technical data book.* Monterey, CA: CTB/McGraw-Hill.

Mueller, M. (1965). *A comparison of the empirical validity of the six tests of ability with young educable retardates* (IMRID Behavioral Science Monograph No. 1). Nashville: Institute on Mental Retardation and Intellectual Development.

Mullen, E. (1989). *Infant Mullen Scales of Early Learning, manual.* Circle Pines, MN: American Guidance Service.

Mullen, E. (1992). *Mullen Scales of Early Learning, manual.* Circle Pines, MN: American Guidance Service.

National Association of State Boards of Education. (1992). *Winners all: A call for inclusive schools.* Washington, DC: Author.

National Center on Educational Outcomes. (1992). *An evolving conceptual model of educational outcomes for children and youth with disabilities.* (Working Paper #2). Minneapolis: Author.

National Council of Teachers of Mathematics. (1993). *Assessment standards for school mathematics, working draft.* Reston, VA: Author.

National Mental Health Association. (1993). *All systems failure: An examination of the results of neglecting the needs of children with serious emotional disturbance.* Alexandria, VA: Author.

National Society for the Prevention of Blindness. (1961). *Vision screening in the schools.* New York: Author.

National Society for the Prevention of Blindness. (1966). *Estimated statistics on blindness and vision problems.* New York: Author.

Newborg, J., Stock, J. R., & Wnek, L. (1984). *Battelle Developmental Inventory Screening Test.* Allen, TX: LINC Associates.

Newcomer, P. (1983). *Diagnostic Achievement Battery.* Austin, TX: Pro-Ed.

Newcomer, P. (1986). *Standardized Reading Inventory.* Austin, TX: Pro-Ed.

Newcomer, P. (1990). *Diagnostic Achievement Battery–2.* Austin, TX: Pro-Ed.

Newcomer, P., & Hammill, D. (1988). *Test of Language Development–Primary* (2nd ed.). Austin, TX: Pro-Ed.

Newland, T. E. (1973). Assumptions underlying psychological testing. *Journal of School Psychology, 11,* 316–322.

Nicholson, C. L., & Hibpshman, T. H. (1990). *Slosson Intelligence Test–Revised.* East Aurora, NY: Slosson Educational Publications.

Nihira, K. (1969a). Factorial dimensions of adaptive behavior in adult retardates. *American Journal of Mental Deficiency, 73,* 868–878.

Nihira, K. (1969b). Factorial dimensions of adaptive behavior in mentally retarded children and adolescents. *American Journal of Mental Deficiency, 74,* 130–141.

Nihira, K., Foster, R., Shellhaas, M., & Leland, H. (1975). *AAMD Adaptive Behavior Scale for Children and Adults, 1974 Revision.* Washington, DC: American Association on Mental Deficiency.

Nihira, K., Leland, H., & Lambert, N. (1993). *AAMR Adaptive Behavior Scale–School* (2nd ed.). Austin, TX: Pro-Ed.

Nihira, K., Leland, H., & Lambert, N. (1993). *Examiner's manual, AAMR Adaptive Behavior Scale–Residential and Community,* (2nd ed.). Austin, TX: Pro-Ed.

Nunnally, J. (1967). *Psychometric theory.* New York: McGraw-Hill.

Nunnally, J. (1978). *Psychometric theory.* New York: McGraw-Hill.

Nurss, J. R., & McGauvran, M. E. (1986). *Metropolitan readiness tests.* San Antonio, TX: The Psychological Corporation.

Nuttall, D. (1992). Performance assessment: The message from England. *Educational Leadership, 49* (8), 54–57.

O'Leary, K., & O'Leary, S. (1972). *Classroom management: The successful use of behavior modification.* New York: Pergamon.

Osgood, C. (1957). *Motivational dynamics of language behavior. Nebraska symposium on motivation.* Lincoln, NE: University of Nebraska Press.

Osgood, C. (1963). On understanding and creating sentences. *American Psychologist, 18,* 735–751.

Osgood, C. E. (1957a). A behavioristic analysis of perception and language as cognitive phenomena. In *Contemporary Approaches to Cognition* (pp. 75–118). Cambridge, MA: Harvard University Press. (Cited by Paraskevopoulos & Kirk, 1969).

Osgood, C. E. (1957b). Motivational dynamics of language behavior. In M. R. Jones (Ed.), *Nebraska Symposium on Motivation* (pp. 348–424). Lincoln, NE: University of Nebraska Press. (Cited by Paraskevopoulos & Kirk, 1969.)

Otis, A. S., & Lennon, R. T. (1989). *Otis-Lennon School Ability test.* San Antonio, TX: The Psychological Corporation.

Pandey, T., & Smith, R. (Eds.) (1991). *A sampler of mathematics assessment.* ED 341553.

Paraskevopoulos, J. N., & Kirk, S. A. (1969). *The development and psychometric characteristics of the Revised Illinois Test of Psycholinguistic Abilities.* Champaign, IL: University of Illinois Press.

Paul, D., Nibbelink, W., & Hoover, H. (1986). The effects of adjusting readability on the difficulty of mathematics story problems. *Journal of Research in Mathematics Education, 17,* 163–171.

Paulson, F., Paulson, P., & Meyer, C. (1991). What makes a portfolio a portfolio? *Educational Leadership, 48* (5), 60–64.

Phillips, K. (1990). *Factors that affect the feasibility of interventions.* Workshop presented at Mounds View Schools, unpublished.

Phillips, S. (1992). *Testing condition accommodations for handicapped students.* Paper presented at the annual meeting of the American Educational Research Association, San Francisco, CA.

Piaget, J. (1955). *The language and thought of the child.* Cleveland, OH: World.

Polin, L. (1991). Writing technology, teacher education: K–12 and college portfolio assessment. *The Writing Notebook* (Jan./Feb.), 25–28.

Poole, I. (1934). Genetic development of articulation of consonant sounds in speech. *Elementary English Review, 11,* 159–161.

Porter, R. B., & Cattell, R. (1975). *Children's Personality Questionnaire.* Champaign, IL: Institute for Personality and Ability Testing.

Prechtl, H. F. (1974). The behavioral states of the newborn. *Brain Research, 6,* 185–212.

Prutting, C., & Kirshner, D. (1987). A clinical appraisal of the pragmatic aspects of language. *Journal of Speech and Hearing Disorders, 52,* 105–119.

Psychological Corporation. (1990). *Stanford Achievement Test series, eighth edition: Measuring progress toward America's educational goals.* San Antonio, TX: Harcourt Brace Jovanovich.

Psychological Corporation. (1992a). *Stanford Achievement Test* (8th ed). San Antonio, TX: Harcourt Brace Jovanovich.

Psychological Corporation. (1992b). *Stanford Early School Achievement Test* (3rd ed). San Antonio, TX: Harcourt Brace Jovanovich.

Psychological Corporation. (1992c). *Test of Academic Skills* (3rd ed.) San Antonio, TX: Harcourt Brace Jovanovich.

Psychological Corporation. (1992d). *Wechsler Individual Achievement Test.* San Antonio, TX: Harcourt Brace Jovanovich.

Quay, H., & Peterson, D. (1987). *Revised Behavior Problem Checklist.* Coral Gables, FL: University of Miami.

Quick, A., Little, T., & Campbell, A. (1974). *Project MEMPHIS: Enhancing developmental progress in preschool exceptional children.* Belmont, CA: Fearon.

Reed, M. L., & Edelbrock, C. (1983). Reliability and validity of the Direct Observation Form of the Child Behavior Checklist. *Journal of Abnormal Child Psychology, 11,* 521–530.

Rees, N. S. (1973). Auditory processing factors in language disorders: The view from Procrustes' bed. *Journal of Speech and Hearing Disorders, 38,* 304–315.

Reich, P. (1986). *Language development.* Englewood Cliffs, NJ: Prentice-Hall.

Reschly, D. (1993). Consequences and incentives: Implications for inclusion/exclusion decisions regarding students with disabilities in state and national assessment programs. In J. Ysseldyke & M. L. Thurlow (Eds.), *Views on Inclusion and Testing Accommodations for Students with Disabilities.* Minneapolis: National Center on Educational Outcomes, University of Minnesota.

Resnick, L. (1987). *Education and learning to think.* Washington, DC: National Academy Press.

Reynolds. C., & Kamphaus, R. (1992). *Behavior Assessment System for Children.* Circle Pines, MN: American Guidance Service.

Reynolds, M. (1975). Trends in special education: Implications for measurement. In W. Hively and M. Reynolds (Eds.), *Domain-Referenced Testing in Special Education.* Minneapolis: University of Minnesota, Leadership Training Institute/Special Education.

Reynolds, M. (1993). Inclusion and accommodation in assessment at the margins. In J. Ysseldyke & M. L. Thurlow (Eds.), *Views on Inclusion and Testing Accommodations for Students with Disabilities.* Minneapolis: National Center on Educational Outcomes, University of Minnesota.

Richman, N., Stevenson J., & Graham, P. J. (1982). *Preschool-to-school: A behavioural study.* London and New York: Academic Press.

Riverside Publishing Company. (1994). *Technical Summary I: Riverside 2000.* Chicago: Author.

Roach, E. F., & Kephart, N. C. (1966). *The Purdue Perceptual-Motor Survey.* Columbus, OH: Merrill.

Roberts, J. (1971). *Intellectual development of children by demographic and socioeconomic factors.* (DHEW Publication No. HSM 72-1012). Washington, DC: U.S. Government Printing Office.

Robinson, N., & Robinson, H. (1976). *The mentally retarded child.* New York: McGraw-Hill.

Rubin, R. A., & Balow, B. (1978). Prevalence of teacher-identified behavior problems: A longitudinal study. *Exceptional Children, 45,* 102–111.

Rubin, S. (1969). A re-evaluation of figure-ground pathology in brain-damaged children. *American Journal of Mental Deficiency, 74,* 111–115.

Sabers, D., Feldt, L., & Reschly, D. (1988). Appropriate and inappropriate use of estimated true scores for normative comparisons. *Journal of Special Education, 22* (3), 355–358.

Salvia, J., Algozzine, R., & Sheare, J. (1977). Attractiveness and school achievement. *Journal of School Psychology, (15)*(1), 60–67.

Salvia, J. & Good, R. (1982). Significant discrepancies in the classification of pupils: Differentiating the concept. In J. T. Neisworth (Ed.), *Assessment in Special Education,* Rockville, MD: Aspen Systems.

Salvia, J. & Hughes, C. (1990). *Curriculum-based assessment: Testing what is taught.* New York: Macmillan.

Salvia, J., & Hunt, F. (1984). Measurement considerations in program evaluation. In B. Keogh (Ed.), *Advances in Special Education, Vol. IV.* New York: JAI Press.

Salvia, J., & Meisel, J. (1980). Observer bias: A methodological consideration in special education research. *Journal of Special Education, 14*(2), 261–270.

Salvia, J., Neisworth, J., & Schmidt, M. (1990). *Examiner's manual: Responsibility and Independence Scale for Adolescents.* Allen, TX: DLM.

Salvia, J., Sheare, J., & Algozzine, R. (1975). Facial attractiveness and personal-social development. *Journal of Abnormal Child Psychology, 3*(7), 171–178.

Salvia, J., & Ysseldyke, J. E. (1972). Criterion validity of four tests for red-green color blindness. *American Journal of Mental Deficiency, 76,* 418–422.

Salvia, J., & Ysseldyke, J. E. (1978). *Assessment in special and remedial education.* Boston: Houghton Mifflin.

Scannell, D. P., Haugh, O. M., Lloyd, B. H., & Risinger, C. F. (1993). *Tests of Achievement and Proficiency.* Chicago: The Riverside Publishing Company

Schaie, K. W., & Roberts, J. (1971). School achievement of children by demographic and socioeconomic factors. Washington, DC: DHEW (HSM) No. 72-1011.

Schmidt, M., & Salvia, J. (1984). Adaptive behavior: A conceptual analysis. *Diagnostique, 9*(2), 117–125.

Sharan, S. & Sharan, Y. (1976). *Small group teaching.* Englewood Cliffs, NJ: Prentice-Hall.

Sharp, L., McNear, D., & Bosma, J. (1993). *Braille Assessment Inventory: Parent summary.* Cambridge, MN: Rum River Special Education Cooperative.

Shavelson, R., Baxter, G., & Pine, J. (1991). Performance assessment in science. *Applied Measurement in Education, 4*(4), 347–362.

Shavelson, R., Gao, X., & Baxter, G. (1991). *Design theory and psychometrics for complex performance assessment: Transfer and generalizability.* (Interim Report.) Los Angeles: University of California, Center for Research on Evaluation, Standards, and Student Testing.

Shinn, M. R. (Ed.). (1989). *Curriculum-based measurement: Assessing special children.* New York: Guilford.

Shinn, M., Tindall, G., & Stein, S. (1988). Curriculum-based measurement and the identification of mildly handicapped students: A review of research. *Professional School Psychology, 3,* 69–85.

Shriberg, L., & Kwiatkowski, J. (1980). *Natural process analysis.* New York: John Wiley and Sons.

Shriner, J., & Salvia, J. (1988). Content validity of two tests with two math curricula over three years: Another instance of chronic noncorrespondence. *Exceptional Children, 55,* 240–248.

Shub, A. N., Carlin, J. A., Friedman, R. L., Kaplan, J. M., & Katien, J. C. (1973). *Diagnosis: An instructional aid (reading).* Chicago: Science Research Associates.

Siegler, R. (1989). Strategy diversity and cognitive assessment. *Educational Researcher, 18*(9), 15–20.

Slavin, R. (1983). *Cooperative learning.* New York: Longman.

Slavin, R. (1990). *Cooperative learning: Theory, research, and practice.* Englewood Cliffs, NJ: Prentice-Hall.

Slobin, D. I., & Welsh, C. A. (1973). Elicited imitation as a research tool in developmental psycholinguistics. In C. Ferguson and D. Slobin (Eds.)., *Studies of Child Language Development.* New York: Holt, Rinehart and Winston.

Slosson, R. L. (1971). *Slosson Intelligence Test.* East Aurora, NY: Slosson Educational Publications.

Snow, R. (1993). Construct validity and constructed response tests. In R. Bennett and W. Ward (Eds.), *Constructive versus Choice in Cognitive Measurement: Issues in Constructed Response, Performance Testing, and Portfolio Assessment.* Hillsdale, NJ: Lawrence Erlbaum.

Sonnenschein, J. L. (1983). *Basic Achievement Skills Individual Screener.* Cleveland, OH: The Psychological Corporation.

Spache, G. D. (1981). *Diagnostic Reading Scales.* Monterey, CA: CTB/McGraw-Hill.

Sparrow, S., Balla, D., & Cicchetti, D. (1984a). *Interview edition, expanded form manual, Vineland Adaptive Behavior Scales.* Circle Pines, MN: American Guidance Service.

Sparrow, S., Balla, D., & Cicchetti, D. (1984b). *Interview edition, survey form manual, Vineland Adaptive Behavior Scales.* Circle Pines, MN: American Guidance Service.

Stahl, S., & Miller, P. (1989). Whole language and language experience approaches for beginning reading: A quantitative research synthesis. *Review of Educational Research, 59*(1), 87–116.

Stake, R., & Wardrop, J. (1971). Gain score errors in performance contracting. *Research in the Teaching of English, 5,* 226–229.

Stevens, R., & Rosenshine, B. (1981). Advances in research on teaching. *Exceptional Education Quarterly, 2*(1), 1–9.

Stevens, S.S. (1951). Mathematics, measurement, and psychophysics. In S. S. Stevens (Ed.), *Handbook* of *Experimental Psychology* (p.23). New York: Wiley.

Stokes, S. (1982). *School-based staff support teams: A blueprint for action.* Reston, VA: Council for Exceptional Children.

Suen, H. K. (1990). *Principles of test theories.* Hillsdale, NJ: Lawrence Erlbaum Associates.

Suen, H., & Ary, D. (1989). *Analyzing quantitative behavioral observation data.* Hillsdale, NJ: Lawrence Erlbaum.

Sweetland, R., & Keyser, D. (1991). *Tests: A comprehensive reference for assessments in psychology, education, and business.* Austin, TX: Pro-Ed.

Tanner, J. M. (1970). Biological bases of development. In J. M. Tanner (Ed.), *Carmichael's Manual of Child Psychology.* New York: Wiley.

Terman, L., & Merrill, M. (1916). *Stanford-Binet Intelligence Scale.* Boston: Houghton Mifflin.

Terman, L., & Merrill, M. (1937). *Stanford-Binet Intelligence Scale.* Boston: Houghton Mifflin.

Terman, L., & Merrill, M. (1973). *Stanford-Binet Intelligence Scale.* Chicago: The Riverside Publishing Company.

Thorndike, R. (1963). *The concepts of over- and underachievement.* New York: Columbia University Press.

Thorndike, R. L. (1982). *Applied psychometrics.* Boston: Houghton Mifflin.

Thorndike, R., & Hagen, E. (1978). *Measurement and evaluation in psychology and education.* New York: Wiley.

Thorndike, R., & Hagen, E. (1986). *Cognitive Abilities Test.* Chicago: The Riverside Publishing Company.

Thorndike, R. L., & Hagen, E. (1994). *Cognitive Abilities Test* (2nd ed.). Chicago: Riverside Publishing Company.

Thorndike, R. L., Hagen, E., & Sattler, J. (1985). *Stanford-Binet Intelligence Scale.* Chicago: The Riverside Publishing Company.

Thorndike, R. L., Hagen, E., & Sattler, J. (1986). *Technical manual, The Stanford-Binet Intelligence Scale: Fourth edition.* Chicago: The Riverside Publishing Co.

Thurlow, M. L., Ysseldyke, J. E., & Silverstein, B. (1993). *Testing accommodations for students with disabilities: A review of the literature* (Synthesis Report 4). Minneapolis: National Center on Educational Outcomes, University of Minnesota.

Thurstone, L. L. (1944). *A factorial study of perception.* Chicago: University of Chicago Press.

Tierney, R., Carter, M., & Desai, L. (1991). *Portfolio assessment in the reading and writing classrooms.* New York: Christopher-Gorelon.

Tucker, J. (1985). Curriculum-based assessment: An introduction. *Exceptional Children, 52,* 199–204.

Tyack, D., & Gottsleben, M. (1974). *Language sampling, analysis and training: A handbook for teachers and clinicians.* Palo Alto, CA: Consulting Psychologists Press.

Tyler, R. (1987). Marginality in schools. In R. L. Sinclair & W. J. Ghory (Eds.), *Reaching Marginal Students: A Primary Concern for School Renewal.* Chicago: McCutchan.

U.S. Department of Education. (1983). *A nation at risk: The imperative for school reform.* Washington, DC: Author.

U.S. Department of Education. (1993). *Fifteenth annual report to Congress on the implementation of the Individuals with Disabilities Education Act.* Washington, DC: Author.

U.S. Office of Education. (1977). Assistance to states for education of handicapped children: Procedures for evaluating specific learning disabilities. *Federal Register, 42,* December 29.

U.S. Public Health Service. (1971). *Vision screening of children* (PHS Document No. 2042). Washington, DC: Author.

Valencia, S., McGinley, W., & Pearson, D. (1990). *Assessing reading and writing: Building a more complete picture for middle school assessment.* ED 320121

Van Riper, C. (1939). *Speech correction.* Englewood Cliffs, NJ: Prentice-Hall.

Van Riper, C. (1963). *Speech correction: Principles and methods* (4th ed.). Englewood Cliffs, NJ: Prentice-Hall.

Vygotsky, L. (1962). *Thought and language.* New York: John Wiley and Sons.

Walberg, H. J. (1984). Families as partners in educational productivity. *Phi Delta Kappan, 65,* 397–400.

Walker, D. K. (1973). *Socioemotional measures for preschool and kindergarten children.* San Francisco: Jossey-Bass.

Walker, H. (1983). *Walker Problem Behavior Identification Checklist.* Los Angeles: Western Psychological Services.

Walker, H. M. (1983). Assessment of behavior disorders in school settings: Issues, problems, and strategies. In

M. Noel & N. Haring (Eds.), *Progress or Change? Issues in Educating the Mildly Emotionally Disturbed.* Washington, DC: U.S. Department of Education, USOSE Monograph Series.

Walker, H. M., Hops, H., & Greenwood, C. R. (1984). The CORBEH research and development model: Programmatic issues and strategies. In S. Paine, G. Bellamy, & B. Wilcox (Eds.), *Human Services that Work* (pp. 57–78). Baltimore: Brookes.

Walker, H. M., & McConnell, S. R. (1988). *Walker-McConnell Scale of Social Competence.* Austin, TX: Pro-Ed.

Walker, H. M., & Severson, H. H. (1992). *Systematic Screening for Behavior Disorders* (2nd edition). Longmont, CO: Sopris West.

Walker, H. M., Severson, H., Stiller, B., Williams, G., Haring, N., Shinn, M., & Todis, B. (1988). Systematic screening of pupils in the elementary age range for behavior disorders: Development and trial testing of a multiple-gating model. *Remedial and Special Education, 9*(3), 8–14.

Wallace, G., & Hammill, D. (1994). *Comprehensive Receptive and Expressive Vocabulary Test.* Austin, TX: Pro-Ed.

Wechsler, D. (1967). *Manual for the Wechsler Preschool and Primary Scale of Intelligence.* Cleveland, OH: The Psychological Corporation.

Wechsler, D. (1974). *Manual for the Wechsler Intelligence Scale for Children–Revised.* Cleveland, OH: The Psychological Corporation.

Wechsler, D. (1981). *Manual for the Wechsler Adult Intelligence Scale–Revised.* New York: The Psychological Corporation.

Wechsler, D. (1991). *Wechsler Intelligence Scale for Children–III.* San Antonio, TX: Psychological Corporation.

Wehby, J. H., Dodge, K. A., & Valente, E. (in press). School behavior of first grade children identified as at risk for the development of conduct disorders. *Behavioral disorders.*

Weinberg, R., & Wood, R. (1975). *Observation of pupils and teachers in mainstream and special education settings: Alternative strategies.* Minneapolis: University of Minnesota, Leadership Training Institute/Special Education.

Weiner, F. (1979). *Phonological process analysis.* Baltimore: University Park Press.

Wellman, B. L., Case, I. M., Mengert, I. G., & Bradbury, D. E. (1931). *Speech sounds of young children* (University of Iowa Studies in Child Welfare). Iowa City: University of Iowa Press.

Wepman, J. M. (1973). *Auditory Discrimination Test (rev. ed.).* Chicago: Language Research Associates.

Werner, H., & Strauss, A. A. (1941). Pathology of figure-background relation in the child. *Journal of Abnormal and Social Psychology, 36,* 236–248.

White, O., & Liberty, K. (1980). Behavioral assessment and precise educational measurement. In N. Haring & R. Schiefelbusch (Eds.), *Teaching Special Children* (pp. 31–71). New York: McGraw-Hill.

Whitehurst, G., Fischel, J., Arnold, D., & Lonigan, C. (1992). Evaluating outcomes with children with expressive language delay. In S. Warren & J. Reichle (Eds.), *Causes and Effects in Communication and Language Intervention* (pp. 277–314). Baltimore: Brookes.

Wiederholt, L. (1986). *Formal Reading Inventory.* Austin, TX: Pro-Ed.

Wiederholt, L. & Bryant, B. (1992). *Examiner's manual: Gray Oral Reading Tests–3.* Austin, TX: Pro-Ed.

Wiley, J. (1971). A psychology of auditory impairment. In W. Cruickshank (Ed.), *Psychology of Exceptional Children and Youth.* Englewood Cliffs, NJ: Prentice-Hall.

Wilkinson, G. (1993). *Wide Range Achievement Test–3.* Wilmington, DE: Jastak Associates.

Williams, G. C., & McReynolds, L. V. (1975). The relationship between discrimination and articulation training in children with misarticulations. *Journal of Speech and Hearing Research, 18,* 401–412.

Winitz, H. (1975). *From syllable to conversation.* Baltimore: University Park Press.

Winograd, P., & Gaskins, R. (1992). Improving the assessment of literacy: The power of portfolios. *Pennsylvania Reporter, 23*(2), 1–6.

Witt, J. C., Heffer, R. W., & Pfeiffer, J. (1990). Structured rating scales: A review of self-report and informant rating processes, procedures, and issues. In C. R. Reynolds & R. W. Kamphaus (Eds.), *Handbook of Psychological and Educational Assessment of Children* (pp. 364–394). New York: Guilford.

Wolf, D. (1989). Portfolio assessment: Sampling student work. *Educational Leadership, 46*(7), 35–39.

Wolery, M. (1989). Using direct observation in assessment. In D. B. Bailey & M. Wolery (Eds.), *Assessing Infants and Preschoolers with Handicaps.* Columbus, OH: Merrill.

Wolfram, W. A. (1971). Social dialects from a linguistic perspective: Assumptions, current research and future directions. In R. Shuy (comp.), *Social Dialects and Interdisciplinary Perspectives.* Washington, DC: Center for Applied Linguistics.

Wood, F. H. (1987). Issues in the education of behaviorally disordered students. In R. B. Rutherford, C. M. Nelson, & S. R. Forness (Eds.), *Severe Behavior Disorders of Children and Youth.* Boston: College Hill.

Woodcock, R. (1987). *Woodcock Reading Mastery Tests–Revised.* Circle Pines, MN: American Guidance Service.

Woodcock, R. W., & Johnson, M. B. (1989). *Woodcock-Johnson Psychoeducational Battery–Revised.* Allen, TX: DLM.

Woodcock, R., & Mather, N. (1989a). *Woodcock-Johnson Tests of Cognitive Ability, Standard and Supplemental Batteries, examiner's manual.* Allen, TX: DLM.

Woodcock, R., & Mather, N. (1989b). *Woodcock-Johnson Tests of Achievement Standard and Supplemental Batteries, examiner's manual.* Allen, TX: DLM.

Ysseldyke, J. E. (1973). Diagnostic-prescriptive teaching: The search for aptitude-treatment interactions. In L. Mann and D. A. Sabatino (Eds.), *The First Review of Special Education.* New York: Grune and Stratton.

Ysseldyke, J. E., & Christenson, S. L. (1987a). Evaluating students' instructional environments. *Remedial and Special Education, 8,* 17–24.

Ysseldyke, J. E., & Christenson, S. L. (1987b). *The Instructional Environment Scale.* Austin, TX: Pro-Ed.

Ysseldyke, J. E., & Christenson, S. L. (1993). *The Instructional Environment System–II.* Longmont, CO: Sopris West.

Ysseldyke, J. E., Christenson, S. L., & Kovaleski, J. F. (1994). Identifying students' instructional needs in the context of classroom and home environments. *Teaching Exceptional Children, 26,* (3), 37–41.

Ysseldyke, J. E., & Marston, D. (1982). Gathering decision-making information through the use of non-test-based methods. *Measurement and Evaluation in Guidance, 15,* 58–69.

Ysseldyke, J. E., & Salvia, J. (1974). Diagnostic-prescriptive teaching: Two models. *Exceptional Children, 41,* 181–186.

Ysseldyke, J. E. & Thurlow, M. L. (1993a). *Self-study guide to the development of educational outcomes and indicators.* Minneapolis: National Center on Educational Outcomes, University of Minnesota.

Ysseldyke, J. E., & Thurlow, M. L. (1993b). *Views on inclusion and testing accommodations for students with disabilities.* Minneapolis: National Center on Educational Outcomes, University of Minnesota.

Ysseldyke, J. E., & Thurlow, M. L. (1994). *Participation of students with disabilities in statewide assessment programs.* Minneapolis: National Center on Educational Outcomes, University of Minnesota.

Ysseldyke, J. E., Thurlow, M. L., McGrew, K. S., & Shriner, J. G. (1994). *Recommendations for making decisions about the participation of students with disabilities in statewide assessment programs* (Synthesis Report 15). Minneapolis: National Center on Educational Outcomes, University of Minnesota.

Ysseldyke, J. E., Thurlow, M. L., McGrew, K., & Vanderwood, M. (1994). *Making decisions about the inclusion of students with disabilities in large-scale assessments* (Synthesis Report 13). Minneapolis: National Center on Educational Outcomes, University of Minnesota.

Glossary

Abscissa   The horizontal axis of a graph, representing the continuum on which individuals are measured

Accommodative ability   The automatic adjustment of the eyes for seeing at different distances

Acculturation   A child's particular set of background experiences and opportunities to learn in both formal and informal educational settings

Achievement   What has been learned as a result of instruction

Adaptive behavior   Behavior that allows individuals adapt themselves to the expectations of nature and society

Age equivalent   A derived score that expresses a person's performance as the average (the median or mean) performance for that age group. Age equivalents are expressed in years and months; a hyphen is used in age scores (for example, 7-1). An age-equivalent score is interpreted to mean that the test taker's performance is equal to the average performance of an X-year old.

Aid   An error in oral reading, recorded when a student hesitates for more than 10 seconds and the word or words are supplied by the teacher

Algorithms   The steps, processes, or procedures one goes through to solve a problem or reach a goal

Alternate forms   Two tests that measure the same trait or skill to the same extent and are standardized on the same population. Alternate forms offer essentially equivalent tests; sometimes, in fact, they're called equivalent forms.

Amplitude   The intensity of a behavior

Assessment   The process of collecting data for the purpose of (1) specifying and verifying problems and (2) making decisions about students

Attainment   What an individual has learned, regardless of where it has been learned

Audiogram   A graph of the results of the pure-tone threshold test

Behavioral observation   Observation of behavior other than behavior that has been elicited by a predetermined and standardized set of stimuli (that is, test behavior)

Bimodal distributions   Distributions that have two modes

Biserial correlation coefficient   An index of association between two variables, one of which has been forced into an arbitrary dichotomy (for example, smart/dull) and one of which is equal-interval (for example, grade-point average)

Cash validity   The notion that frequently used tests are valid tests

Category A data   The basic, minimum information schools need in order to operate an educational program, including identifying information as well as information about a student's educational progress

Category B data   Test results and other verified information useful to the schools in planning a student's educational program or maintaining a student "safely" in school

Category C data Information that may be potentially useful to schools. This includes any unverified information, scores on personality tests, and so forth

Classification A type of decision that concerns a pupil's eligibility for special services, special education services, remedial education services, speech services, and so forth

Coefficient alpha The average split-half correlation based on all possible divisions of a test into two parts. Coefficient alpha can be computed directly from the variances of individual test items and the variance of the total test score.

Concurrent criterion-related validity A measure of how accurately a person's current test score can be used to estimate a score on a criterion measure

Conductive hearing loss Abnormal hearing associated with poor air-conduction sensitivity but normal bone-conduction sensitivity

Confidence interval The range of scores within which a person's true score will fall with a given probability

Construct validity A measure of the extent to which a test measures a theoretical trait or characteristic

Consultation A meeting between a resource teacher or other specialist and a classroom teacher to verify the existence of a problem, specify the nature of a problem, and develop strategies that might relieve the problem

Content validity A measure of the extent to which a test is an adequate measure of the [...] Content validity is established by examining three fac- [...] cluded, the completeness of the item [...] content.

[...] ship between two or more variables. [...] two variables go together—that is, [...] reflected by changes in the second

[...] he relationship between two or more

[...] a person's skills in terms of absolute lev-

[...] extent to which a person's score on a [...] at person's score on a test of unknown

[...] sment materials and procedures that mir- [...] her specific instructional objectives have

been accompl[...] s directly in the curriculum being taught

Deciles Bands of percentiles that are [...] centile ranks in width; each decile contains 10 percent of the norm group.

Derived scores A general term for raw scores that are transformed to developmental scores or scores of relative standing

Descriptive statistics Numerical values, such as mean, standard deviation, or correlation, that describe a data set

Developmental scores Raw scores that have been transformed into age equivalents (mental ages, for example), grade equivalents, or developmental quotients using the following formula: $100 \cdot AE/CA$

Deviation IQs Standard scores with a mean of 100 and a standard deviation of 15 or 16 (depending on the test)

Deviation score The distance between an individual's score and the average score for the group, such as z-scores, *T*-scores, etc.

Discriminative stimuli Stimuli that are consistently present when a behavior is reinforced and elicit the behavior even in the absence of the original reinforcer

Disregard of punctuation An error in oral reading in which a student fails to give appropriate inflection in response to punctuation. For example, a student may not pause for a comma, stop for a period, or indicate voice inflection at a question mark or exclamation point.

Distractors Incorrect options contained in a response set

Distributions The way in which scores in a set array themselves. Distributions may be graphed to demonstrate visually the relations among the scores in the group or set.

Duration The length of time a behavior lasts

Ecobehavioral observation Observation targeting the interaction among student behavior, teacher behavior, time allocated to instruction, physical grouping structures, the types of tasks being used, and instructional content. Ecobehavioral assessment enables educators to identify natural instructional conditions that are associated with academic success, behavioral competence, or problem behaviors.

Entitlement In special education, the right to a free and appropriate education, related services, and due process

Equal-interval scales Scales on which the differences between adjacent values are equal but on which there is no absolute or logical zero

Error Misrepresentation of a person's score as a result of failure to obtain a representative sample of times, items, or scorers

Ethnographic observation Observation in which the observer does not participate in what is occurring

Etiology Cause of a disorder

Expressive language The production of language

Free operant A test situation that presents more problems than a student can answer in the given time period

Frequency The tabulation of the number of behaviors with discrete beginnings and endings that occur in a predetermined time frame. When the time periods in which the behavior is counted vary, frequencies are usually converted to rates.

Grade equivalent A derived score that expresses a student's performance as the average (the median or mean) performance for a particular grade. Grade equivalents are expressed in grades and tenths of grades; a decimal point is used in grade scores (for example, 7.1).

Gross mispronunciation An error in oral reading in which a student's pronunciation of a word is in no way similar to the word in the text

Hesitation An error in oral reading in which a student pauses for 2 or more seconds before pronouncing a word

Historical information Information that describes how a person has functioned in the past

Individual consent   Consent by parent (or pupil) required for the collection of family information (religion, income, occupation, and so on), personality data, and other noneducational information

Individualized education plan (IEP)   A document that specifies the long-term and short-term goals of an instructional program, where the program will be delivered, who will deliver the program, and how progress will be evaluated

Informal assessment   Any assessment that involves collection of data by anything other than a norm-referenced (standardized) test

Informed consent   Consent given by a parent or a student to the collection or dissemination of information not directly relevant and essential to the child's education. The assumption underlying the notion of informed consent is that the parent (or pupil) is "reasonably competent to understand the nature and consequences of his decision" (Goslin, 1969, p. 17).

Insertion   An error in oral reading in which a student adds one or more words to the sentence being read

Intelligence   An inferred ability; a term or construct used to explain differences in present behavior and to predict differences in future behavior

Internal consistency   A measure of the extent to which items in a test correlate with one another

Interscorer reliability   An estimate of the degree of agreement between two or more scores on the same test

Inversion   An error in oral reading in which a student says the words in an order different from the order in which they are written

Keyed response   Correct answer in a response set

Kurtosis   The "peakedness" of a curve, or the rate at which a curve rises

Language   A code for conveying ideas (see Bloom & Lahey, 1978; Fromkin & Rodman, 1978). Although there is some variation, language theorists propose five basic components to describe the code: phonology, semantics, morphology, syntax, and pragmatics.

Leptokurtic curves   Fast-rising curves; tests that do not "spread out" (or discriminate among) those taking the test are typically leptokurtic

Mean   The arithmetic average of scores in a distribution

Median   A score that divides the top 50 percent of test takers from the bottom 50 percent. The point on a scale above which 50 percent of the cases (not the scores) occur and below which 50 percent of the cases occur

Metalinguistic   Relating to the direct examination of the structural aspects of language

Mixed hearing loss   Abnormal hearing attributed to abnormal bone conduction and even more abnormal air conduction

Mode   The most frequently obtained score in a distribution

Momentary time sampling   A procedure used in systematic observation to determine when observations will occur. A behavior is scored as an occurrence if it is present at the last moment of an observation interval; if the behavior is not occurring at the last moment of the interval, a nonoccurrence is recorded.

Multiple-skill batteries   Tests that measure skill development in several achievement areas

Negatively skewed distribution An asymmetric distribution in which scores "tail off" to the low end; a distribution in which there are more scores above the mean than below

Nominal scales A scale of measurement in which there is no inherent relationship among adjacent values

Nonsystematic observation Observations in which the observer notes behaviors, characteristics, and personal interactions that seem of significance.

Normal curve equivalents Standard scores with a mean equal to 100 and a standard deviation equal to 21.06

Normative sample, or norm group A group of subjects of known demographic characteristics (age, sex, grade in school, and so on) to whom a person's performance may be compared.

Norm-referenced devices Tests that compare an individual's performance to the performance of his or her peers

Objective-referenced assessment Tests referenced to specific instructional objectives rather than to the performance of a peer group or norm group

Observation The process of gaining information through one's senses—visual, auditory, and so forth. Observation can be used to assess behavior, states, physical characteristics, and permanent products of behavior (e.g., a child's poem).

Omission An error in oral reading in which a student skips a word or group of words

Operationalize To define a behavior or event in terms of the operations used to measure it. For example, an operational definition of intelligence would be a score on a specific intelligence test.

Ordinal scales Scales on which values of measurement are ordered from best to worst or from worst to best. On ordinal scales, the differences between adjacent values are unknown.

Ordinate The vertical axis of a graph of a distribution, showing the frequency (or the number) of individuals earning any given score

Partial-interval recording A procedure used in systematic observation in which an occurrence is scored if the behavior occurs during any part of the interval

Partial mispronunciation One of several kinds of errors in oral reading, including partial pronunciation, phonetic mispronunciation of part of the word, omission of part of the word, or inserting elements of words

Participant-observer approach Observation in which the observer joins the target social group and participates in its activities

Pearson product-moment correlation coefficient (r) An index of the straight-line (linear) relationship between two or more variables measured on an equal-interval scale

Percentile ranks (%iles) Derived scores that indicate the percentage of people whose scores are at or below a given raw score. Percentiles are useful for both ordinal and equal-interval scales.

Phi coefficient An index of linear correlation between two sets of naturally dichotomous variables (for example, male/female, dead/alive)

Phonology Speech sounds

Platykurtic curves Curves that are flat and slow rising

Point biserial correlation   An index of linear correlation between one naturally occurring dichotomous variable (such as sex) and a continuous, equal-interval variable (such as height measured in inches)

Portfolio   A collection of products that provide a basis for judging student accomplishment. In school settings, portfolios typically contain extended projects and may also contain drafts, teacher comments and evaluations, and self-evaluations.

Positively skewed distribution   An asymmetrical distribution in which scores "tail of" to the higher end of the continuum; a distribution in which there are more scores below the mean than above it

Power tests   Untimed tests

Pragmatics   The social context in which language occurs

Predictive validity   A measure of the extent to which a person's current test scores can be used to estimate accurately what that person's criterion scores will be at a later time

Pre-referral assessment   Activities that occur prior to formal referral, assessment, and consideration for placement. The goal of pre-referral assessment and intervention is twofold: (1) verification and specification of the nature of a student's difficulties and (2) provision of services in the least restrictive environment.

Probe   A special testing format that is well suited to the assessment of direct performances. Probes are brief (usually 3 minutes or less), timed, frequently administered assessments that can be used for any purpose.

Prognosis   A prediction of future performance

Qualitative data   Information consisting of nonsystematic and unquantified observations

Qualitative observation   A description of behavior, its function, and context. The observer begins without preconceived ideas about what will be observed and describes behavior that seems important.

Quantitative data   Observations that have been tabulated or otherwise given numerical values

Quartiles   Bands of percentiles that are twenty-five percentile ranks in width; each quartile contains 25 percent of the norm group.

Random error   In measurement, sources of variation in scores that make it impossible to generalize from an observation of a specific behavior observed at a specific time by a specific person to observations conducted on similar behavior, at different times, or by different observers

Range   The distance between the extremes in a set of scores, including those extremes; the highest score less the lowest score plus one

Ratio IQ   A derived score based on mental age in which IQ equals

$$\frac{\text{MA (in months)}}{\text{CA (in months)}} \times 100$$

Ratio scales   Scales of measurement in which the difference between adjacent values is equal and in which there is a logical and absolute zero

Readiness   Extent of preparation to participate in an activity. The term most often refers to readiness to enter school but applies at all levels.

Receptive language   The comprehension of language

Referral A request for help from a specialist. For example, a teacher or parent may refer a student to a specialist who can provide the student with an appropriate educational program.

Reliability In measurement, the extent to which it is possible to generalize from an observation of a specific behavior observed at a specific time by a specific person to observations conducted on similar behavior, at different times, or by different observers

Reliability coefficient An index of the extent to which observations can be generalized. The square of the correlation between obtained scores and true scores on a measure r_{xt}^2

Repetition An error in oral reading in which a student repeats words or groups of words

Representational consent Consent to collect data given by appropriately elected officials, such as members of a state legislature

Sample The representative subset of the population

Scotoma A spot in the eye without vision

Screening An initial stage of assessment in which those who *may* evidence a particular problem, disorder, disability, or disease are discriminated from the general population

Select formats A method of presenting test questions in which students indicate their choice from an array of the possible test answers (usually called response options). True-false, multiple-choice, and matching are the three most common select formats.

Semantics The study of word meanings. Although the scope of the term *semantics* can extend beyond individual words to include sentence meaning, the term generally applies to words.

Sensorineural hearing loss Abnormal hearing associated with both poor bone-conduction sensitivity and poor air-conduction sensitivity

Setting events Environmental events that set the occasion for the performance of an action

Single-skill tests Tests that are designed to measure skill development in one specific content area (for example, reading)

Skew Asymmetry in a distribution; the distribution of scores below the mean is not a mirror image of the distribution above the mean.

Social comparison Observing a peer whose behavior is considered to be appropriate and using the peer's rate of behavior as the standard against which to evaluate the target student's rate of behavior

Social tolerance The threshold above which behaviors are viewed as undesirable by others

Social validity A consumer's reaction to an intervention or assessment

Spearman rho An index of correlation between two variables measured on an ordinal scale

Speed tests Timed tests

Split-half reliability estimate An estimate of internal consistency reliability derived by correlating people's scores on two halves of a test

Standard deviation A measure of the degree of dispersion in a distribution; the square root of the variance

Standard error of measurement (SEM)   The standard deviation of error around a person's true score

Standard scores   The general name for derived scores that have been transformed to produce a distribution with a predetermined mean and standard deviation

Stanines   Standard-score bands that divide a distribution into nine parts; the middle seven stanines are each 0.50 standard deviation wide and the fifth stanine is centered on the mean.

Stem   In select formats, the part of a problem that contains the question

Substitution   An error in oral reading in which a student replaces one or more words in the passage with one or more meaningful words (synonyms)

Supply format   A method of presenting test questions in which a student is required to produce a written or oral response. This response can be as restricted as a number or a word or can be as extensive as a sentence, a paragraph, or several pages of written response.

Syntax   Word order of sentences; syntax includes a description of the rules for arranging the words into a sentence.

Systematic error   Consistent error that can be predicted; bias

Systematic observations   Observations in which an observer specifies or defines the behaviors to be observed and then counts or otherwise measures the frequency, duration, magnitude, or latency of the behaviors

Test   A predetermined set of questions or tasks to which predetermined types of behavioral responses are sought

Testing   Exposing a person to a particular set of questions in order to obtain a score

Test-retest reliability   An index of stability over time

Tetrachoric correlation coefficient   An index of correlation between two arbitrarily dichotomized variables (for example, tall/short, smart/dull)

True score   The score that a student would earn if the entire domain of items were assessed

_T_-score   A standard score with a mean of 50 and a standard deviation of 10

Tunnel vision   Normal central visual acuity with a restricted peripheral field

Validity   The extent to which a test measures what its authors or users claim it measures. Specifically, test validity concerns the appropriateness of the inferences that can be made on the basis of test results.

Validity coefficient   A coefficient that measures the correlation between a test of unknown validity and an established criterion measure

Variance   A numerical index describing the dispersion of a set of scores around the mean of the distribution. Specifically, the variance is the average squared distance of the scores from the mean.

Visual acuity   The clarity or sharpness with which a person sees

Whole-interval recording   A procedure used in systematic observation in which an occurrence is scored if the behavior is present throughout the entire observation interval

_z_-scores   Standard scores with a mean of 0 and a standard deviation of 1

Index

An Invitation to Respond

We would like to find out a little about your background and about your reactions to the sixth edition of *Assessment*. Your evaluation of the book will help us to meet the interests and needs of students in future editions. We invite you to share your reactions by completing the questionnaire below and returning it to College Marketing, Houghton Mifflin Company, 222 Berkeley Street, Boston, MA, 02116.

1. How do you rate this textbook in the following areas?

	Excellent	Good	Adequate	Poor
a. Understandable style of writing	_____	_____	_____	_____
b. Physical appearance/readability	_____	_____	_____	_____
c. Fair coverage of topics	_____	_____	_____	_____
d. Comprehensiveness (covered issues and topics)	_____	_____	_____	_____
e. Examples and case studies	_____	_____	_____	_____
f. Appendixes	_____	_____	_____	_____
g. Organization of chapters	_____	_____	_____	_____

2. Can you comment on or illustrate your above ratings? _____

_____

3. What chapters or features did you particularly like? _____

_____

4. What chapters or features did you dislike or think should be changed? _____

_____

5. What material would you suggest adding or deleting? _____

_____

6. What was the title of the course in which you used this book?_____

_____

7. What was your class standing at the time you took the course in assessment?

Junior _____ Senior _____ Graduate _____ Other _____ (please explain)

_____

8. Have you ever taught before? _____ If so, what courses have you taught?

_____

9. What other courses in assessment or measurement and evaluation have you

taken? _____

_____

10. Will you be teaching in a regular classroom or in a special classroom?_____

_____

11. Do you intend to keep this book for use during your teaching career? _____

_____

12. We would appreciate any other comments or reactions you are willing to

share. _____

_____

_____

_____

_____

_____

_____

"*A* joint committee of the American Educational Research Association, the American Psychological Association, and the National Council on Measurement in Education publishes a document entitled *Standards for Educational and Psychological Testing.* These standards specify a set of requirements for test development and use. It is imperative that those who develop tests behave in accord with the standards and that those who assess students use instruments and techniques that meet the standards. In Parts 3 and 4 of this text we review commonly used tests and talk about the extent to which those tests meet the standards. We provide information to help test users make informed judgments about the technical adequacy of specific tests. " (p. 67)

called the Mental Devel
Scale standard scores are
velopment Index. The a
dence intervals (90 perce
conversion tables for these
combined into facets, or s
guage, social, and motor
may be of some clinical v
examiners.

Items on the Behavior I
five-point scale. Composit
centile ranks for Motor C
Orientation/Engagement
and the total score. C
(within normal limits,
optimal) are also available

RELIABILITY

Alphas were used to estim
of the Mental Scale and th
For the Mental Scale, alph
nine of the seventeen ce
the Moto
coefficien
he total sco
d from .82
aled or exc
chavior Rat
coefficients
D-II's stabi
us, the reli
Rating Sca
ant decision
of the age r
usually inad

orrelations
87; correla
and .78; co
cale were .
d in the BSI
owever, giv
en, this find

Bayley Scales of Infant Development, Second Edition

*T*he second edition of the Bayley Scales of Infant Development (BSID-II) (Bayley, 1993) shares the format and rationale of the earlier edition. The BSID-II remains a norm-referenced, individually administered test intended to assess developmental functioning of children. However, the norms have been updated, and the age range has been extended through 42 months. In addition, sixty-three new items were added to the Mental Scale and twenty-nine old items were deleted; forty-four new items were added to the Motor Scale and eight old items were deleted. The Behavior Rating Scale was completely revised.

The BSID-II has three subscales. The Mental Scale assesses memory, problem solving, conceptualization, language, and social skills. The Motor Scale assesses fine and gross motor skills. Items assessing mental and motor ability are mixed together; this format requires examiners to identify which items go on each scale and tally them separately. General basal and ceiling rules apply to all items together not individually to the Mental or Motor Scales. The Behavior Rating Scale is separate and assesses "qualitative aspects of the child's test-taking behavior" (p. 1) and allows an examiner to rate arousal/attention, orientation/engagement, emotional regulation, and quality of movement. This scale is completed after the Mental and Motor scales have been administered.

NORMS

The BSID-II was standardized on 1,700 children, fifty boys and fifty girls in each of seventeen age groups. Children between 1 and 6 months are grouped in one-month intervals; children between 6 and 12 months are grouped into three two-month intervals; children between the ages of 12 and 30 months are grouped in six three-month intervals; and children between 30 and 42 months are grouped in two six-month intervals. Each age group closely approximates the U.S. 1988 census update in terms of race/ethnicity, geographic region, parental education, and sex.

SCORES

Each item on the Mental and Motor Scales is scored as C (credit), NC (no credit, incorrect), RF (refused, no credit awarded), O (omit, no credit awarded), RPT (child is reported to have the skill, no credit awarded). Raw score totals for Mental and Motor are obtained by adding the credited items between the basal and ceiling to the basal. Each of these totals can be converted to a normalized standard score with a mean of 100 and a standard deviation of 15. The Mental Scale standard scores are